A BIBLIOGRAPHY OF JURISPRUDENCE

BY

R. W. M. DIAS, M.A., LL.B. (Cantab.)
of the Inner Temple, Barrister-at-Law
Fellow of Magdalene College and Lecturer in Law
in the University of Cambridge

THIRD EDITION

LONDON
BUTTERWORTHS
1979

England London	Butterworth & Co (Publishers) Ltd 88 Kingsway, WC2b 6AB
Australia Sydney	Butterworths Pty Ltd 586 Pacific Highway, Chatswood, NSW 2067 Also at Melbourne, Brisbane, Adelaide and Perth
Canada Toronto	Butterworth & Co (Canada) Ltd 2265 Midland Avenue, Scarborough M1P 4S1
New Zealand Wellington	Butterworths of New Zealand Ltd 77–85 Customhouse Quay
South Africa Durban	Butterworth & Co (South Africa) (Pty) Ltd 152/154 Gale Street
USA Boston	Butterworth (Publishers) Inc 19 Cummings Park, Woburn, Mass 01801

©
R.W.M. Dias, 1979

ISBN 0 406 57428 6

Typeset by Scribe Design, Medway, Kent
Printed in Great Britain by Billing & Sons Ltd.,
Guildford, London & Worcester

Preface

The experiment of publishing a *Bibliography* as a companion volume to my textbook on *Jurisprudence* has been reasonably encouraging. In this edition there are, of course, many new references to literature which has appeared since the last publication, but it has also been necessary to eliminate other references which have been superseded or have become obsolete.

This book is capable of standing on its own; but its main object is to lead on from the textbook, which is intended to provide a guiding-thread to the extensive material elsewhere. Jurisprudence is a subject which embraces a diversity of opinions. It is therefore important that scholars should be put on the track of material with which to inform themselves, and this compilation offers the reader an opportunity of steeping himself in different aspects of various topics. The references given here are not exhaustive, but they do include a good deal of the relevant material published in the English language and such as will furnish pointers to other important sources of information, especially Continental. Within these limits an effort has been made to present as many different points of view and shades of opinion as possible and the policy, in cases of doubt, has been to include rather than to exclude.

With a bibliography of this size a breakdown of the references into appropriate topics and sub-topics is preferable to straightforward alphabetical lists. From my point of view the obvious arrangement is to follow the order of the textbook; but there is no magic in arrangement as such, and the various headings and sub-headings set out here should be, in any case, self-explanatory.

Mere lists of references, however arranged and divided, tend to be somewhat daunting. Accordingly, an indication of the substance of each reference has been given to inform the reader what to expect so as to facilitate the selection of his reading. This, it is hoped, will prevent waste of time and might also assist in the planning of work programs. The last consideration is particularly important in the case of undergraduates, who have all too little time at their disposal, and it is hoped that some of them, at any rate, might be helped and encouraged to read more widely than they would otherwise have done.

Finally, I must record heartfelt thanks to my wife and daughter, Julia, for the prolonged sacrifice of their own concerns in order to help with the indices. In this exacting task their patience and devotion to the job often outlasted my own.

July, 1978   R.W.M. Dias

Contents

Abbreviations

The following is a table of the abbreviations used for legal and other periodicals referred to in this Bibliography.

A.J.C.L.	American Journal of Comparative Law
A.J.I.L.	American Journal of International Law
A.J.J.	American Journal of Jurisprudence
A.J.S.	American Journal of Sociology
Am. B.A.J.	American Bar Association Journal
Am. J.L.H.	American Journal of Legal History
Am. L.R.	American Law Review
Am. Phil. Q.	American Philosophical Quarterly
Am. Pol. Sc. R.	American Political Science Review
Ann. L.R.	Annual Law Review
Ann. Sur. Am. L.	Annual Survey of American Law
Aust. L.J.	Australian Law Journal
B.L.R.	Boston Law Review
Br. J.C.	British Journal of Criminology
Br. J. Soc.	British Journal of Sociology
Br. Tax. R.	British Tax Review
Brook. L.R.	Brooklyn Law Review
B.S.A.L.R.	Butterworths South African Law Review
B.Y.I.L.	British Yearbook of International Law
Calif. L.J.	California Law Journal
Calif. L.R.	Californian Law Review
Can. B.J.	Canadian Bar Journal
Can. B.R.	Canadian Bar Review
Cape L.J.	Cape Law Journal
C.I.L.S.A.	Comparative and International Journal of Southern Africa
C.L.J.	Cambridge Law Journal
C.L.P.	Current Legal Problems
C.M.L.R.	Common Market Law Review
Col. L.R.	Columbia Law Review
Corn. L.Q.	Cornell Law Quarterly
Crim. L.R.	Criminal Law Review
Dal. L.J.	Dalhousie Law Journal
D.L.J.	Duke Law Journal
F.L.R.	Fordham Law Review
Geo. L.J.	Georgetown Law Journal
Geo. Wash. L.R.	George Washington Law Review
Harv. L.R.	Harvard Law Review
Hastings Const. L.Q.	Hastings Constitutional Law Quarterly
How. L.J.	Howard Law Journal
I.C.L.Q.	International and Comparative Law Quarterly
I.J.E.	International Journal of Ethics
I.L.Q.	International Law Quarterly

Abbreviations

Ill. L.Q.	Illinois Law Quarterly
Ill. L.R.	Illinois Law Review
I.L.T.	Irish Law Times
Int. Lawyer	International Lawyer
Iowa L.R.	Iowa Law Review
Ir. Jur.	Irish Jurist
Ir. Jur. (N.S.)	Irish Jurist (New Series)
Israel L.R.	Israel Law Review
J.A.L.	Journal of African Law
J.A.L.T.	Journal of the Association of Law Teachers
J.B.L.	Journal of Business Law
J.C.L.	Journal of Comparative Legislation
J. Comm. P.S.	Journal of Commonwealth Political Studies
J. Cr. L.	Journal of Criminal Law
J.L.E.	Journal of Legal Education
J.L. Pol. S.	Journal of Legal and Political Sociology
J.P.J.	Justices of the Peace Journal
J.P.L.	Journal of Public Law
J.S.P.T.L. (N.S.)	Journal of the Society of Public Teachers of Law (New Series)
Jur. R.	The Juridical Review (including New Series)
Kansas L.R.	University of Kansas Law Review
Ken. L.J.	Kentucky Law Journal
L.C.P.	Law and Contemporary Problems
Legal Exec.	Legal Executive
L.G.R.	Local Government Review
L.J.	Law Journal
Lloyd's M.C.L.Q.	Lloyd's Maritime and Commercial Law Quarterly
L.Q.R.	Law Quarterly Review
L.S. Gaz.	Law Society Gazette
L.T.	Law Times
Malaya L.R.	Malaya Law Review
Malayan L.J.	Malayan Law Journal
McGill L.J.	McGill Law Journal
Med. Sci. & L.	Medicine, Science and the Law
Melb. U.L.R.	Melbourne University Law Review
Mich. L.R.	Michigan Law Review
Minn. L.R.	Minnesota Law Review
Miss. L.R.	Missouri Law Review
M.L.R.	Modern Law Review
Nat. L.F.	Natural Law Forum
N.D.L.	Notre Dame Lawyer
New L.J.	New Law Journal
N.I.L.Q.	Northern Ireland Law Quarterly
N.L.J.	Nigerian Law Journal
N.Y.U.L.R. (N.Y.U.L.Q.R.)	New York University Law Review (continuation of New York University Law Quarterly Review)
N.Z.L.J.	New Zealand Law Journal
N.Z.U.L.R.	New Zealand Universities Law Review

Abbreviations

Ont. L.R.	Ontario Law Journal
Os. H.L.J.	Osgoode Hall Law Journal
Ottawa L.R.	Ottawa Law Review
P.A.	Public Administration
P.A.S.	Proceedings of the Aristotelian Society
P.L.	Public Law
Pol. S.	Political Studies
Pol. Sc. Q.	Political Science Quarterly
Rhod. L.J.	Rhodesian Law Journal
Rutgers L.R.	Rutgers Law Review
S.A.L.J.	South African Law Review
Scand. S.L.	Scandinavian Studies in Law
S.L.T.	Scottish Law Times
S.J.	Solicitors' Journal
Sol. Q.	The Solicitor Quarterly
Southern Calif. L.R.	Southern California Law Review
Stan. L.R.	Stanford Law Review
St. Louis U.L.J.	St. Louis University Law Journal
Syd. L.R.	Sydney Law Review
Tasm. L.R.	Tasmanian Law Review
Trans. Gro. S.	Transactions of the Grotius Society
Trans. Jur. S.	Transactions of the Juridical Society
Tul. L.R.	Tulane Law Review
U. Br. Col. L.R.	University of British Columbia Law Review
U.C.L.A.L.R.	University of California Los Angeles Law Review
U.C.L.R.	University of Chicago Law Review
U.G.L.J.	University of Ghana Law Journal
U. Pa. L.R.	University of Pennsylvania Law Review
U.T.L.J.	University of Toronto Law Journal
U. Wes. Aus. A.L.R.	University of Western Australia Annual Law Review
Vand. L.R.	Vanderbilt Law Review
Vir. L.R.	Virginia Law Review
Wash. L.R.	Washington Law Review
W. Ont. L.R.	Western Ontario Law Review
W. Vir. L.Q.	West Virginia Law Quarterly
Yale L.J.	Yale Law Journal
Z.L.J.	Zambian Law Journal

1. General

The Scope of Jurisprudence

1. STONE, J. *Legal System and Lawyers' Reasonings*, (Stevens & Sons, Ltd, 1964), Introduction and chaps. 1 and 5, pp. 162–185: the broad scope of jurisprudence requires that theorising about law should be conducted with the aid of the wisdom of predecessors. The subject cannot be brought within any one philosophy. In chapter 1 the function of language and logic is explained. Words have many meanings and there is no one proper meaning for all people and all purposes. Law is an instrument for achieving certain social purposes. But before its teleology and sociology can be discussed, the nature of the instrument needs to be elucidated. This involves analysis for which logic is employed. The analytical method of approach, its uses and limits are explained. Definition is considered in chapter 5. No definition is likely to prove acceptable, nor will it be adequate for all purposes. A definition is only a mnemonic: what is important is the exposition which it calls to mind. The purpose and function of a definition of "law" are discussed, and the matters, which jurists have thought to require clarification, are indicated.

2. COWEN, D.V. "An Agenda for Jurisprudence" (1964), 49 Corn LQ 609: the questions are posed: are there any significant questions of a jurisprudential character? in what sense are they "significant"? which of them are most urgent? and how may these be effectively taught? In the light of these questions a six-point scheme of study is outlined and discussed.

3. PATTERSON, E.W. *Jurisprudence*, (The Foundation Press, Inc, 1953), Part I: the three chapters comprising this part are important in that they address themselves to various questions relating to the scope of modern jurisprudence, to problems of meaning and of approach. Chapter 2, which includes a discussion of semantics, is especially noteworthy.

4. KANTOROWICZ, H.U. and PATTERSON, E.W. "Legal Science – a Summary of its Methodology" (1928), 28 Col LR 679: the nature of scientific study in general is examined in detail. With reference to legal science, the authors point out its wide coverage. A good many of the technical matters dealt with anticipate what is to be found in this and its companion textbook, but may be read here as indicating the scope of modern jurisprudence.

5. ISAACS, N. "The Schools of Jurisprudence" (1917–18), 31 Harv LR, 373: this is a good and profiting account of the various "schools" of jurisprudence and what each is aiming to do. Each has a valuable part to play.

6. BRYCE, J. *Studies in History and Jurisprudence*, (Oxford, 1901), chap. 12: the metaphysical, analytical, historical and comparative methods of approach are examined. Of these the historical is said to be the most profitable. The parts played by all four methods are considered and it is contended that the historical method should be used in presenting the other three.

7. ALLEN, C.K. *Legal Duties*, (Oxford, Clarendon Press, 1931), chap. 1: various matters concerning the nature and purpose of jurisprudential study are discussed. It is made clear that the author favours general jurisprudence and regards jurisprudence as an inductive discipline.

1

1. POUND, R. *Jurisprudence*, (West Publishing Co, 1959), 1, chap. 1: the different
   senses in which the word "jurisprudence" has been used are explained. The
   divisions into analytical, historical, philosophical and sociological jurisprudence
   are examined in so far as these constitute different methods of approach.

2. MONTROSE, J.L. "The Scope of Jurisprudence" in *Precedent in English Law and
   Other Essays*, (ed. H.G. Hanbury, Irish UP Shannon, 1968), chap. 8: there is
   now a consensus of opinion as to what this subject should and should not cover.
   Austin and Maine are among its founders, but Pound is regarded as the founder
   of the modern subject. The different "schools" are related to the ambiguity of
   the word "law". The relevance of analysis, sociology and philosophy is outlined.
   "Broom v Morgan [1953] 1 QB 597, [1953] 1 All ER 849) and the Nature of
   Juristic Discourse", chap. 19: the first part of this paper discusses the nature of
   juristic discourse. This is discourse about laws as opposed to laws themselves.
   The scope of jurisprudence is considered on this basis. The rest of the paper
   considers two articles on *Broom v Morgan* and the judgments themselves, and
   considers the types of discourses to be found in them, and then the appeals
   made by the authors and the judges to logic, social welfare and justice.

3. BENTHAM, J. *An Introduction to the Principles of Morals and Legislation*, (edd.
   J.H. Burns and H.L.A. Hart, The Athlone Press, 1970, chap. 17, Sect. 2:
   Bentham originates the well-known division into "expositorial jurisprudence",
   explaining what the law is, and "censorial jurisprudence", the critical
   examination of the law in the light of what it ought to be.

4. AUSTIN, J. *Lectures on Jurisprudence*, (5th ed., R. Campbell, John Murray, 1885),
   II, pp. 1071–91: the general basis of approach is advocated. Austin lists the
   topics common to what he calls "the ampler and maturer systems." The study
   of jurisprudence brings in the study of legislation. The value of studying
   jurisprudence and Roman law is also considered. See also W.J. BROWN: *The
   Austinian Theory of Law*, (John Murray, 1906), chap. 7; and J. AUSTIN: *The
   Province of Jurisprudence Determined and the Uses of the Study of Jurisprudence*,
   (ed. H.L.A. Hart, Weidenfeld & Nicholson, 1954), and see also Hart's Introduction.

5. EASTWOOD, R.A. and KEETON, G.W. *The Austinian Theories of Law and
   Sovereignty*, (Methuen & Co, Ltd, 1929), pp. 1–6: this gives a brief account of
   the nature of jurisprudential study and its different varieties. It is a simplified
   introduction to the principal doctrines of Austin.

6. THORNE, C. "Concerning the Scope of Jurisprudence" (1901), 35 Am LR 546:
   this is a protest against the adoption in America of the analytical positivism of
   Austin, which, it is urged, though valuable, should only provide an introduction.

7. DOWDALL, H.C. "The Present State of Analytical Jurisprudence" (1926), 42 LQR
   451: analytical jurisprudence, it is said, satisfies few. The reasons for this, and
   the best way of reorganising the study of legal philosophy and analytical
   jurisprudence are considered.

8. LIGHTWOOD, J.M. *The Nature of Positive Law*, (Macmillan & Co, 1883), chap. 1:
   it is open to each writer to treat law from different points of view and to select
   his own department in it. Jurisprudence includes ideas and principles of the law
   and their improvement. After a discussion of general and particular jurisprudence,
   the author considers the claims of what he calls "applied jurisprudence".

1. CLARK, E.C. *History of Roman Private Law*, (Cambridge University Press, 1914), II, chap. 1: the nature of jurisprudence is discussed generally in relation to its use in legislation and legal education. Towards the end there is also a discussion of its relation to the study of Roman Law.

2. JENKS, E. *The New Jurisprudence*, (John Murray, 1933), chaps. 2–3: this discussion, along traditional lines, deals with the analytical, historical, comparative and critical methods. Chapter 1 gives the author's views on the material covered by jurisprudential study.

3. HOLLAND, T.E. *The Elements of Jurisprudence*, (13th ed., Oxford, Clarendon Press, 1924), chap. 1: jurisprudence is defined as "the formal science of positive law." Various applications of the term are considered and rejected as "improper". Holland himself recognises only general jurisprudence.

4. POLLOCK, F. *Essays in Jurisprudence and Ethics*, (Macmillan & Co., 1882), chap. 1: this is partly a comment on Holland's *Elements of Jurisprudence*, supra, whose views are considered and criticised. Pollock's own views about the scope of the subject appear only indirectly.

5. BUCKLAND, W.W. *Some Reflections on Jurisprudence*, (Cambridge University Press, 1945), chaps. 1 and 6: the first chapter deals primarily with what Austin meant by jurisprudence as being "the philosophy of positive law". It is pointed out that his theories about the nature of law and sovereignty are only a prologue to a study of jurisprudence. In chapter 6 particular and general jurisprudence are considered. It is pointed out that advocates of the general approach do not adhere to it in their treatment.

6. BUCKLAND, W.W. "Difficulties of Abstract Jurisprudence" (1890), 6 LQR 436: this is a critical discussion of the claim of certain English writers on jurisprudence to construct a universal philosophy of law. Holland's position, in particular, is subjected to attack.

7. BROWN, W.J. *The Austinian Theory of Law*, (John Murray, 1906), Excursus F: this is a lengthy and interesting inquiry into the methods of pursuing jurisprudential study. The relation between them is set out in a table (p. 369). Brown's own preference is discussed towards the end, namely, particular or "national" jurisprudence.

8. HALL, J. *Studies in Jurisprudence and Criminal Theory*, (Oceana Publications, Inc, 1958), chaps. 1–2, 6 and 8: the dichotomy between particular and general jurisprudence and between nominalists and realists is considered with reference to jurisprudence and criminal law. Chapter 2 is perhaps the most important, for it contains a plea for what is called "integrative jurisprudence" i.e., one which would combine facts, ideas and evaluations. See also J. HALL: "Integrative Jurisprudence" in *Interpretations of Modern Legal Philosophies*, (ed. P. Sayre, Oxford University Press, New York, 1947), chap. 14. Chapters 6 and 8 are of general interest.

9. HALL, J. "Concerning the Nature of Positive Law" (1948–49), 58 Yale LJ, 545: a purely formal study of positive law is inadequate. The author pleads that the study should widen its scope so as to include past and present experience and standards.

1. HALL, J. *Foundations of Jurisprudence*, (The Bobbs–Merrill Co, Inc, 1973),
   chaps. 1 and 6: an adequate philosophy of law has to integrate structure, fact
   and value. The appropriate concept for such a philosophy is the action of
   certain officials, which would include ideas of rules, certain facts (including
   official behaviour) and the values of achieving certain goals – "law-as-action"
   rather than as behaviour. In Chapter 6 the effectiveness of law, and the
   correctness (rather than validity) of law-as-action is said to rest on sound values.

2. HALL, J. "Integrative Jurisprudence" (1976), 27 Hastings LJ 779: the author
   reflects on and further defends the integrative philosophy, which he set out
   in his book. He also outlines the main differences between this and other
   similar philosophies. At the outset he offers five tests of the adequacy of any
   legal philosophy.

3. BRETT, P. *An Essay on a Contemporary Jurisprudence*, (Butterworths, 1975):
   after surveying the main schools of traditional jurisprudence and "realist"
   methodology, the author finds them wanting because they rely on the
   philosophies and sciences of the past. What is needed is a jurisprudence based
   on contemporary science. Legal systems should be viewed as open hierarchical
   systems in an environment of interaction with other normative systems. It thus
   interrelates with morality and the cultural milieu.

4. SALMOND, J.W. *Jurisprudence*, (7th ed. by J.W. Salmond; 12th ed. by P.J. Fitzgerald, Sweet & Maxwell, Ltd, 1966), chap. 1: this should be taken as a standard
   discussion of the nature of jurisprudence. For comment, see Chapter 1 of R.W.M.
   Dias, *Jurisprudence*, (4th ed., 1976), pp. 21–23.

5. JOLOWICZ, H.F. *Lectures on Jurisprudence*, (ed. J.A. Jolowicz, The Athlone
   Press, 1963), Introduction: the difficulties in the way of giving an explanation
   of what "jurisprudence" means are indicated. As between particular and general
   jurisprudence, the author's own preference for the latter is indicated. He also
   discusses and rejects any attempt to divide the study into analytical, historical
   etc.

6. GRAY, J.C. *The Nature and Sources of the Law*, (2nd ed., R. Gray, The Macmillan
   Co., New York, 1921) , chap. 7: the traditional approaches to jurisprudential
   study are explained and the views of certain writers are criticised. The discussion
   is still a useful one.

7. DEL VECCHIO, G. *Philosophy of Law*, (trans. T.O. Martin, The Catholic University
   of America Press, 1953), chap. 1: a distinction is drawn between the "science of
   law", which is particular, and the "philosophy of law", which is universal. The
   latter comprises logical, phenomenological and deontological aspects. The relation
   between the philosophy of law and other disciplines and the use of the deductive
   and inductive methods are explained.

8. SNYDER, O.C. *Preface to Jurisprudence*, (The Bobbs-Merrill Co, Inc, 1954), I,
   chaps. 1–2: various aspects of jurisprudential study are considered, as well as the
   kind of art and proficiency that constitute skill in the law. The different
   approaches to the subject of jurisprudence are outlined. Chapter 2 makes it clear
   that only particular jurisprudence is being dealt with and explains why.

9. KEETON, G.W. *The Elementary Principles of Jurisprudence*, (2nd ed., Pitman &
   Sons, Ltd, 1949), chap. 1: the different "types" of jurisprudence are surveyed
   generally and discussed.

1. POLLOCK, F. "The History of Comparative Jurisprudence" (1903), 5 JCL (NS) 74: the inter-relation between the historical and comparative methods of approach is examined. The article traces the evolution of the comparative method from Roman times onwards.

2. VINOGRADOFF, P. *Collected Papers*, (Oxford, 1928), II, chaps. 10–11, 16: the first of these chapters pleads for the historical approach to jurisprudential study. The next chapter points out that the 20th century has witnessed events that have dispelled the complacent sway of analytical positivism. There is now a preoccupation with social problems. In the last chapter it is pointed out that analytical positivism is inadequate. The new sociological approach involves historical study.

3. GUPTA, A.C. "The Method of Jurisprudence" (1917), 33 LQR 154: this is primarily a plea that the study of jurisprudence should include ethical and sociological phenomena. It constitutes an answer to Brown's critique of Duguit.

4. SETHNA, M.J. "The True Nature and Province of Jurisprudence from the Viewpoint of Indian Philosophy" in *Essays in Jurisprudence in Honor of Roscoe Pound*, (ed. R.A. Newman, The Bobbs-Merill Co, Inc, 1962), 99: the study of jurisprudence should combine analytical, historical, philosophical and, above all, sociological and functional study. Sociological jurisprudence and the sociology of law are distinguished and the work of the supporters of each is outlined. Particular attention is devoted to Pound's contribution.

5. WURZEL, K.G. "Methods of Juridical Thinking" in *Science of Legal Method. Select Essays by Various Authors*, (trans. E. Bruncken and L.B. Register, Boston Book Co, 1917), pp. 389–96: law is said to have been the first of the social sciences; and the development of thinking about law is outlined.

6. GOODHART, A.L. "An Apology for Jurisprudence" in *Interpretations of Modern Legal Philosophies*, (ed. P. Sayre, Oxford University Press; New York, 1947), chap. 12: jurisprudence, or legal philosophy, fulfils a useful function by explaining the elements of a concept such as law. The author considers certain ideas that have been put forward about law and also proffers his own.

7. WOLHEIM, R. "The Nature of Law" (1954), 2 Pol S 128: the problems that have been encountered in defining "Law" are considered and the methods of its elucidation are critically appraised. Inquiry into the nature of law includes the question of its validity, development and function.

8. CAIRNS, H. "Philosophy as Jurisprudence" in *Interpretations of Modern Legal Philosophies*, (ed. P. Sayre, Oxford University Press, New York, 1947), chap. 4: there has been, and is, an extensive cross-fertilization between science and philosophy, but only a one-way fertilization between science and the social disciplines. The role of philosophy in jurisprudence is considered at length.

9. RADBRUCH, G. "Anglo-American Jurisprudence through Continental Eyes" (1936), 52 LQR 530: in presenting the development of Anglo-American jurisprudence a constant comparison is made with Continental thought. This article is helpful in obtaining a broad view of jurisprudential thought.

10. JONES, J.W. "Modern Discussions of the Aims and Methods of Legal Science" (1931), 47 LQR 62: this is a general survey of the views of certain modern writers. It is of interest as showing the kind of problems that confront jurists.

1. SUMMERS, R.S. "Legal Philosophy Today – an Introduction", in *Essays in Legal Philosophy*, (ed. R.S. Summers, Basil Blackwell, Oxford, 1968), 1: the scope and methods of modern legal philosophy are outlined. As to scope, it is concerned with conceptual analysis and conceptual revision; as to method, there is now a keener awareness of certain errors. Some of the reasons for the revived mutual interest between lawyers and philosophers in their respective subjects are explained.

2. LEWIS, J.U. "Annual Survey of Canadian Law: Part 2. Jurisprudence" (1976). 8 Ottawa LR 427: jurisprudence is understanding the function of law in society (as opposed to mere knowledge). This requires philosophy. The author reviews the Canadian scene, but in the course of so doing conveys an idea of the concerns of jurisprudence – law and morality, professional ethics, law reform, history and philosophy of law, social sciences, methodology and legal education.

3. HART, H.L.A. "Philosophy of Law and Jurisprudence in Britain (1945–52)" (1953), 2 AJCL, 355: this gives a survey of the trends in Britain and assesses their significance.

4. JØRGENSEN, S. *Law and Society*, (Akademisk Boghandel, 1972), Introduction and chap. 1: Law is many things at the same time. Distinctions are drawn between legal science, natural science and social science, and between the analytical, historical and sociological methods. The general pattern of social science investigation is explained as well as the legal science theory of cognition.

5. MONTROSE, J.L. "Legal Theory for Politicians and Sociologists" (1974), 25 NILQ 321: a comprehensive theory of law is a theory of the state. There is a lack of knowledge of legal theory by political theorists. Legal theory has embraced a philosophy and a sociology of law. Both are required to understand legal institutions, and an understanding of legal institutions is required for a full understanding of man and society.

6. COWAN, T.A. "Legal Pragmatism and Beyond" in *Interpretations of Modern Legal Philosophies*, (ed. P. Sayre, Oxford University Press, New York, 1947), chap. 7: the progress of jurisprudential thought from the Middle Ages to the present is rapidly surveyed. The article concludes with remarks on the future shape of the study.

7. CAMPBELL, A.H. "A Note on the Word 'Jurisprudence'" (1942), 58 LQR 334: there has been a transition from the old-fashioned meaning of "jurisprudence" as practical wisdom to that of the nature of law. The different meanings attached to the word by various authors are set out in order.

8. LEFROY, A.H.F. "Jurisprudence" (1911), 27 LQR 180: the article aims at delimiting the word usefully. In the course of the discussion the views of Austin and Holland as to the meaning of "jurisprudence" are critically considered.

9. SALMOND, J.W. "The Names and Nature of the Law" (1899), 15 LQR 367: this is of general interest. Various meanings and synonyms for the terms "law" and "right" are considered.

10. WIGMORE, J.H. "The Terminology of Legal Science" (1914–15), 28 Harv LR 1: the suggested terminology is of general interest. More important are the different types of study which they are designed to signify. The author particularly advocates the study of what ought to be law.

Aims of Legal Education

1. COOK, W.W. "Scientific Method and the Law" (1927), 13 Am BAJ 303: the case-method has turned out good legal technicians, but are they scientifically trained? Contemporary scientific developments show that too much reliance has been placed on deduction and induction. A new approach to law-teaching is necessary. It should introduce students to the new methods of science, to observing the structure and function of society, analysing existing law, studying the actual operation of law and enlisting the co-operation of other social sciences.

2. BODENHEIMER, E. *Jurisprudence*, (Harvard University Press, 1962), pp. 343–46: the need is stressed for training in social problems. It requires a knowledge of national and world history, political theory, economics and philosophy. A lawyer should be a person of culture and breadth of understanding.

3. COHEN, M.R. *Reason and Law*, (The Free Press, Glencoe, 1950), chap. 5: the point is developed that it is important to have a wide coverage in jurisprudence beyond mere technical proficiency. Reference might also be made to chapter 1 on methods of approach.

4. PECZENIK, A. "Doctrinal Study of Law and Science", Österreichische Zeitschrift für öffentliches Recht, XVII/1–2, 1967, 128: doctrinal study consists of statements formulated by jurists and relating to some definite issues, as well as more general statements contained in, *inter alia*, text-books. Six objections to this type of study are considered and rejected.

5. POUND, R. "Do We Need a Philosophy of Law?", (1905), 5 Col LR 339; *Jurisprudence in Action*, (Baker, Voorhis & Co, Inc, 1953), 389: the plea is that law students should be trained in the social, political and legal philosophy of the time. In the past the common law used to be looked to as the bulwark of the individual. Now it tends to be frowned upon because it champions individual rights at the expense of society.

6. BRIDGE, J.W. "The Academic Lawyer: mere working Mason or Architect?" (1975), 91 LQR 488: the function of the academic lawyer is research and instruction. In order to achieve the creative touch of the architect, legal subjects should be considered in their relationship to other disciplines.

7. TUR, R.H.S. "Jurisprudence and Practice" (1976), 14 JSPTL (NS) 38: jurisprudence is a way of doing things, the transmission of a set of skills, techniques, etc. It is a development out of other courses on law; it concerns problems of method and it fosters critical, self-reliant thought. There should be grounding in logic, argumentation and thinking.

8. CROSS, G. "The Lawyer and Justice" (1973, *Presidential Address to the Holdsworth Club*): the concern of lawyers with justice is considered with reference to advising clients, judging disputes, reforming and teaching law. On the whole practitioners are said to be only indirectly concerned with ethical merit, but lawyers as reformers (even of "lawyers' law") and law teachers are very much concerned with it.

9. WILBERFORCE, R.O. "Educating the Judges" (1969), 10 JSPTL (NS) 254: sociological research should be directed to judges in lower courts far more than at present. The development of administrative and arbitral tribunals is not due

to bad education of judges, but necessity. Universities cannot teach law-students everything. There is need for self-education for judges and a kind of sabbatical leave for this purpose.

1. GARDINER, G. and MARTIN, A. "Legal Education" in *Law Reform* Now, (edd. G. Gardiner and A. Martin, Victor Gollancz, 1963), chap. 11: this paper is to some extent now outdated. It begins by reviewing the education of solicitors and barristers as at that date. However, the part dealing with the need for academic training of practitioners is useful.

2. COOK, W.W. "The Utility of Jurisprudence in the Solution of Legal Problems" in *Lectures on Legal Topics*, (The Macmillan Co, New York, 1928), p. 338: conceptual tools need to be analysed in order that their adequacy may be tested. This paper contains an examination of the concept of "right", which will be dealt with in a later chapter.

3. LLOYD, D. *The Idea of Law*, (Penguin Books Ltd, A 688, 1964), chap. 12: concepts exist as ideas and not as concrete entities. This appears to make law a kind of game. Although there are resemblances between law and games, there are important and significant differences. Although concepts are creations of law, they have a vitality and a creative element of their own. A rigid conceptualism has its dangers, but concepts are useful in many ways.

4. RHEINSTEIN, M. "Education for Legal Craftsmanship" (1944–45), 30 Iowa LR 408: the mere mechanical manipulation of legal concepts is rightly deplored. But concepts are very important.

5. HOHFELD, W.N. *Fundamental Legal Conceptions as Applied in Judicial Reasoning*, (ed. W.W. Cook, Yale University Press; London: Humphrey Milford, 1923), chap. 8: this address was delivered in 1914. It constitutes a plea to law schools to train students, not merely to be practitioners, but to play a full part in a developing society.

6. SAMEK, R.A. "The Dynamic Model of the Judicial Process and the *Ratio Decidendi* of a case" (1964), 42 Can BR 433: towards the end of the article the point is made that legal concepts are not fixed, but "open-ended". The analysis of concepts should take this into account.

7. SIMPSON, A.W.B. "The Analysis of Legal Concepts" (1964) 80 LQR 535: the analysis of concepts on the basis simply of the logical function of words or sentences is said to be unfruitful. Instead it is suggested that there should be an investigation into the way in which the meaning of legal terms both diverges from and is related to their non-legal meaning. Attention should be paid to explaining how, when, why and with what consequences this comes about.

8. KELLY, D.St.L. "Legal Concepts, Logical Functions and Statements of Facts" (1968), 3 Tasm LR 43: the author defends Professors Hart and Ross against A.W.B. Simpson's criticisms. It is alleged that the latter misunderstands what they said. In the course of the demonstration there is a discussion of the function of words.

9. MacCORMICK, D.N. "Law as Institutional Fact" (1974), 90 LQR 102: after drawing a distinction between "institutional fact" and "institution", the author deals with "institutions of the law", which include, *inter alia*, contract, ownership

and other legal concepts. Such concepts are essential to analysing legal systems into coherent sets of interrelated rules. His thesis is that the rules regulating institutions should combine precision with flexibility so that values can play their part. Thus jurisprudence becomes a joint legal, philosophical and sociological enterprise.

1. FITZGERALD, P.J. "Are Statutes Fit for Academic Treatment?" (1971), 11 JSPTL (NS) 142: the question concerns statutes as well as academic treatment. In Britain there is little study of statutes in the abstract. This may be because cases are more interesting. But statutes, too, can be seen to have a similar interest if their study is approached in different ways. Since statutes comprise the bulk of the law now, they are particularly fit for academic treatment, and if this were done it will be better for legislation, drafting and interpretation.

For discussions on the place and uses of jurisprudence in legal education, see the following three contributions to (1948–49), 1 JLE:

2. HALL, J. "Introductory Remarks", p. 475: the reasons why jurisprudence has won popularity for itself are considered, and various suggestions are made as to its teaching.

3. NORTHROP, F.S.C. "Jurisprudence in the Law School Curriculum", p. 482: teaching in jurisprudence is considered in the light of the legal needs of contemporary society and the ability of the subject to train people to cope with them. This theme is developed in the light of the factors which make contemporary society unique. The solution is said to lie in a jurisprudence rooted in a natural law philosophy.

4. FULLER, L.L. "The Place and Uses of Jurisprudence in the Law School Curriculum", p. 495: this considers what should be taught, how, at what point in the law school course, and why teach jurisprudence at all. See also L.L. FULLER: "What the Law School can Contribute to the Making of Lawyers", p. 189.

5. GOODHART, A.L. "The Vocational Teaching of Law" (1950), 1 JSPTL (NS), 333: the remarks towards the end of the address are of especial interest. The vocational importance of jurisprudential study is pointed out.

6. BROWNE, D. "Reflections on the Teaching of Jurisprudence" (1953), 2 JSPTL (NS), 79: this is an interesting address on the best way in which jurisprudential teaching might be revised. What it aims at accomplishing and the best methods of achieving its ends are dealt with.

7. HARVEY, C.P. "A Job for Jurisprudence" (1944), 7 MLR 42; W.B. KENNEDY: "Another Job for Jurisprudence" (1945), 8 MLR 18; C.P. HARVEY: ibid., 236: this is a hard-hitting disputation. Harvey complains of the fruitlessly academic approach of traditional law-teaching and advocates a more realistic approach to social problems. The other references are to Kennedy's reply and Harvey's rejoinder.

8. STREET, H. "Law and Administration: Implications for University Legal Education" (1953), 1 Pol S 97: although this is not concerned specifically with jurisprudential teaching, the purpose of the address is to demonstrate the importance of teaching law in relation to finance, psychology, economics, history, politics, sociology, etc.

1. CLARK, E.C. "Jurisprudence: its Uses and its Place in Legal Education" (1885),
   1 LQR 201: this is of interest as indicating the old fashioned approach and how
   much wider the subject is today. Only general and comparative jurisprudence
   are thought to be worth considering.

2. BROWN, W.J. "The Purpose and Method of a Law School" (1902), 18 LQR 78,
   192: the discussion concerns legal education in general. The point is made that
   lawyers need to be educated in the widest sense, and the value of legal history
   and philosophy towards this end is touched on.

3. BROWN, W.J. "Jurisprudence and Legal Education" (1909), 9 Col LR, 238:
   although this article was written at a time when the state of jurisprudence was
   different from what it is now, it is still useful in suggesting some of the points
   that jurisprudential study should cover and what instruction in it should seek to
   achieve.

4. REICH, C.A. "Towards a Humanistic Study of Law" (1964–65), 74 Yale LJ 1402:
   stress is laid on the need for relating the teaching of law to life in its varied
   aspects.

5. SUMMERS, R.S. "Notes on Criticism in Legal Philosophy" in *More Essays in Legal
   Philosophy. General Assessments of Legal Philosophies* , (ed. R.S. Summers,
   Basil Blackwell, Oxford, 1971), 1: criticism is an avenue to progress. It takes
   various forms, whether it is levelled at the problem being considered, or the
   theory representing the result of philosophising. Attention is also paid to
   critical standards and points of view, and lastly to criticism of criticism.

6. HARRIS, P.J. and BUCKLE, J.D. "Philosophies of Law and the Law Teacher"
   (1976), 10 JALT 1: a law teacher always has a philosophy of his own about his
   subject, the purpose of education, definitions, general terms, objectives and his
   role as teacher. Arguments about teaching methods are often at bottom disagree-
   ments about philosophies. Problems arising out of law courses are approached
   on this basis.

7. COTTERRELL, R.B.M. and WOODLIFFE, J.C. "The Teaching of Jurisprudence
   in British Universities" (1974), 13 JSPTL (NS) 73: this sets out the results of an
   extensive survey throughout British Universities. It provides a convenient picture
   of the kind of topics covered in the various courses.

8. SHELDRAKE, P. "Jurisprudence in the Law Course" (1975), 13 JSPTL (NS) 343:
   this gives an analysis of student reactions before and after the course on
   jurisprudence at one university. Statistical lists are given of their opinions as to
   the value and interest of the topics taught. For a comment, see D.N.
   MacCORMICK, "Jurisprudence in the Law Course. A Footnote", ibid. p. 359.

Problems of Language and Definition

9. WILSON, J. *Language and the Pursuit of Truth*, (Cambridge University Press, 1956):
   this is a simplified, short and highly rewarding introduction to semantics. The
   section on "verification" deserves special attention (pp. 51–55).

10. WILLIAMS, G.L. "Language and the Law" (1945), 61 LQR 71, 179, 293, 384;
    (1946), 62 LQR 387: the meaning of words is examined and the lessons to be
    drawn from the analysis are applied iconoclastically to various legal doctrines.

(See, however, for corrective, J. WISDOM: *Philosophy and Psycho-Analysis*, (Basil Blackwell, Oxford, 1957), pp. 249–54).

1. WILLIAMS, G.L. "International Law and the Controversy Concerning the Word 'Law'" in *Philosophy, Politics and Society*, (ed. P. Laslett, Basil Blackwell, Oxford, 1956), chap. 9: the author pursues his analysis of meaning by examining the famous dispute between the followers of Austin and the international lawyers as to the "proper" meaning of the word "law".

2. FARNSWORTH, E.A. "'Meaning' in the Law of Contracts" (1966–67) 76 Yale LJ 939: this article discusses semantic problems of interpretation. The distinction between "interpretation" and "construction" is considered in relation to meaning in general and contracts in particular.

3. STOLJAR, S.J. "The Logical Status of a Legal Principle" (1952–53), 20 UCLR, 181: certain fallacies in legal thinking are exposed. In the course of the discussion (pp. 197–211) different types of definition are explained. This is a useful article both as to the nature of legal conceptions and the judicial process.

4. DEWEY, J. *How We Think*, (D.C. Heath & Co, 1909), chaps. 8–11: chapters 9–11 deal generally with meaning, understanding, concrete and abstract thinking and comparisons between empirical and scientific thinking. Chapter 8 is particularly important for lawyers, dealing as it does with the decisional process.

5. SMITH, J.C. "The Unique Nature of the Concepts of Western Law" (1968) 46 Can BR 191: legal concepts are linguistic constructs. Language forms the ideas with which one approaches problems. Primitive systems evolve concepts which are more factual than Western concepts. The latter were evolved in Classical Roman Law and adopted into the common law.

6. SMITH, J.C. "Law, Language, and Philosophy" (1968), 3 U Br Col LR 59: this gives a review of the different attitudes towards language function that underlie the works of well-known legal philosophers from ancient times to the present. Much of this material is also relevant in later contexts.

7. MacCORMICK, D.N. "Law as Institutional Fact" (1974), 90 LQR 102: the proposition "a contract exists" asserts an institutional fact. This is one the truth of which depends on the occurrence of acts and events and the application of rules to them. Behind the institutional fact lies the institution itself. Institutions of law include concepts, e.g., ownership. An outline of an analysis of law is developed from this basis.

8. COOK, W.W. "'Facts' and 'Statements of Fact'" (1936–37), 4 UCLR, 233: this is a most interesting analysis of the difficulties surrounding the conception of a "fact" for legal purposes. It is also indirectly relevant to the question of the approach to study. For further discussions, see W.W. COOK: "Statements of Fact in Pleading under the Codes" (1921), 21 Col LR 416; N. ISAACS: "Judicial Review of Administrative Findings" (1921), 30 Yale LJ 781; "The Law and the Facts" (1922), 22 Col LR 1; H.C. Dowdall: "Pleading 'Material Facts'" (1929), 77 U Pa LR 945; C. MORRIS: "Law and Fact" (1941–42), 55 Harv LR 1303; J.B. THAYER: *Preliminary Treatise on the Law of Evidence*, (Sweet & Maxwell Ltd., 1898), chap. 5.

9. LAMONT, W.D. *The Principles of Moral Judgment*, (Oxford, 1946), pp. 15–20:

this might be of some indirect relevance. "Observable facts" in ethics differ
from those of physical sciences. An explanation is given of what is meant by the
application of the "scientific method" in ethics.

1. ROBINSON, R. *Definition*, (Oxford, Clarendon Press, 1954): this is a good and
   succinct account of definition. The various types and their functions are
   examined in detail.

2. KANTOROWICZ, H.U. *The Definition of Law*, (ed. A.H. Campbell, Cambridge
   University Press, 1958), especially chaps. 1–2: this short work was to have been
   the prologue to a larger project which never materialised owing to the author's
   death. The process of constructing the most useful definition of law for the
   purpose of the projected work is demonstrated stage by stage.

3. BENTHAM, J. *Theory of Fictions*, (2nd ed., C.K. Ogden, Routledge & Kegan Paul
   Ltd, 1951), Introduction and pp. 75–104: Bentham's account of the function
   of definition is remarkable for its modernity and insight into linguistic problems.
   As Ogden observes in his detailed introduction, Bentham is entitled to rank
   among the foremost linguistic philosophers.

4. HART, H.L.A. "Definition and Theory in Jurisprudence" (1954), 70 LQR 37: the
   technique of definition here advocated is that of explaining the term in
   question in the context of a characteristic proposition rather than in isolation,
   and to explain the conditions under which the proposition is true.

5. HART, H.L.A. *The Concept of Law*, (Oxford, Clarendon Press, 1961, reprinted
   1975), pp. 13–17: this gives a brief account of the difficulties and the part
   played by definition in elucidating the meaning of the word "law".

6. AUERBACH, C.A. "On Professor Hart's Definition and Theory in Jurisprudence"
   (1956), 9 JLE 39: Hart's suggested method of elucidating legal terms is criticised
   in detail. It is alleged that a definition which ignores the purpose or justification
   or origin of a legal or political institution cannot illumine the meaning of that
   institution.

7. HALL, J. *Studies in Jurisprudence and Criminal Theory*, (Oceana Publications, Inc,
   1958), pp. 113 *et seq.*; 125–30: various weaknesses in Hart's method of
   elucidating legal terms are pointed out. The difficulties and problems
   encountered in defining the word "law" are also examined. In another paper
   the author surveys the developments that have taken place in American legal
   thought and proceeds to consider three different functions which definition
   performs in jurisprudential thought.

8. HALL, J. "Analytic Philosophy and Jurisprudence" (1966), 77 Ethics, 14: to
   elucidate terms by seeing how they are used is inadequate, because there are
   different levels of discourse, which have different significance and functions.
   One should elucidate the word "punishment" not by asking how it is used, but
   by relating it to voluntary conduct, social harm, causation; and also by bringing
   that set of interrelations into the larger pattern of the interrelation of principles,
   doctrines and rules.

9. HALL, J. *Foundations of Jurisprudence* (The Bobbs-Merrill Co Inc, 1973), chap. 4:
   "Law" and other legal concepts have distinctive meanings, and a philosophy of
   language should not ignore this. Nominalist jurisprudence and other examples of
   linguistic jurisprudence are considered and criticised.

1. LUMB, R.D. "On a Modern Approach to Jurisprudence" (1960), 5 Jur R 143: Hart's technique of definition is explained and examined, and is alleged to be inadequate.

2. BODENHEIMER, E. "Modern Analytical Jurisprudence and the Limits of its Usefulness" (1955–56), 104 U Pa LR, 1080: this takes issue with Hart's technique. It is alleged that Hart's technique would mean the abandonment of analytical jurisprudence.

3. SIMPSON, A.W.B. "The Analysis of Legal Concepts" (1964), 80 LQR 535, 541 *et seq.*, 553 *et seq.*: Hart's distinction between statements of fact and statements of conclusions is investigated and criticised.

4. HART, H.L.A. "Analytical Jurisprudence in Mid-twentieth Century: a Reply to Professor Bodenheimer" (1957), 105 U Pa LR 953: in this the objections raised by Bodenheimer are dealt with.

5. DICKERSON, F.R. "Statutory interpretation: Core Meaning and Marginal Uncertainty" (1964) 29 Miss LR 1: there is no irreconcilable antinomy between the "core and penumbra" theory of meaning and the "context and purpose" theory. The usage of each speech community determines the core and penumbral meanings with varying degrees of definiteness even when words are taken in isolation. Context and purpose help to select the meaning in the instant case out of the range of potential meanings. This important study has repercussions in statutory interpretation and the Positivist-Naturalist controversy.

6. DICKERSON, F.R. *The Fundamentals of Legal Drafting* (Little, Brown & Co, 1965): the whole of this book, especially chapters 3 and 7, is important to those concerned with the problems of meaning. In Chapter 3 it is pointed out that a legal document is a communication, involving an author, an audience, an utterance and a context. The significance of the last and the principal diseases of language are examined with particular care. Chapter 7 deals with types of definition and the forms they should assume. The part that definition plays in communication should be borne constantly in mind.

7. SAMEK, R.A. *The Legal Point of View* (Philosophical Library, New York, 1974), especially chapters 1–3 and 9: in the opening chapters certain linguistic problems are discussed. The question, "What is X (law)?", initiates the wrong sort of enquiry. Instead, a model of the legal point of view is offered. Definition and conceptual analysis and four different functions of statement are considered. A concept is "bent" by the point of view. The "legal point of view" is compared on this basis with others. In chapter 9 Professor Hart's technique of definition is criticised.

8. WILLIAMS, G.L. "The Definition of Crime" (1955), 8 CLP, 107: the opening part deals generally with definition. The whole article is of interest as bearing on the problem of definition.

9. POUND, R. "Law and the Science of Law in Recent Theories" (1933–34), 43 Yale LJ 525: different persons mean different things when talking of law. This point is developed with reference to five leading jurists of modern times.

10. STONE, J. and TARELLO, G. "Justice, Language and Communication" (1960–61), 14 Vand LR, 331: this is a long and difficult investigation into the function of language in the respective spheres of law and justice.

1. MORRIS, C. *How Lawyers Think*, (Harvard University Press, 1938), chaps. 7–9: definitions depend upon classification. The method of dealing with meaning by "extension" (all instances covered) and "intension" (significance) is also discussed. The latter two chapters deal respectively with a comparison between deductive and inductive logic and with theory and reasoning.

2. MORRIS, C. *Signs, Language and Behaviour* (Prentice-Hall, Inc, 1946): this is of general interest, and might be referred to for an analysis of meaning.

3. PROBERT, W. "Law and Persuasion: the Language Behaviour of Lawyers" (1959–60), 108 U Pa LR 35: language studies should be harnessed in a constructive way to progress in law. This article is concerned with the emotive function of many legal terms.

4. OLIVECRONA, K. "Legal Language and Reality" in *Essays in Jurisprudence in Honor of Roscoe Pound*, (ed. R.A. Newman, The Bobbs-Merrill Co, Inc, 1962), 151, at pp. 169–91: after posing the problem of understanding the concept "right", the question is approached through the function of language. Some words, e.g., "right", do not refer to any thing; they are "hollow" words. They serve as tools of thought and speech.

5. KENDAL, G.H. "The Role of Concepts in the Legal Process" (1962), 1 U Br Col LR 617: the law has to be capable of dealing with the changes that are taking place in the world of ideas. The function of concepts is approached through an examination of meaning.

6. SMITH, G.H. "Of the Nature of Jurisprudence and of the Law" (1904), 38 Am LR 68: accurate definition is said to be of the essence of success in moral and legal sciences. The confused definitions of "law" are examined. A definition of "jurisprudence" is offered and its implication considered.

7. SMITH, G.H. "Logic, Jurisprudence and the Law" (1914), 48 Am LR 801: the first part deals in outline with logic and in this connection the mental processes involved in reasoning are examined. In the second part the author seeks to demonstrate that much of the difficulty concerning "jurisprudence" and "law" is caused by the neglect of logical principles, especially with reference to definition..

8. PATON, G.W. *A Text-Book of Jurisprudence*, (4th ed., G.W. Paton and D.P. Derham, Oxford, Clarendon Press, 1972), chap. 3: the complexities of definition are set out and the different approaches to it are considered.

9. LLOYD, D. *Introduction to Jurisprudence*, (3rd ed., Stevens & Sons, Ltd, 1972), chaps. 1–2, pp. 506–510: the first chapter deals with the scope of jurisprudence. In particular, it concerns the method of science and how far this can be applied to law. Social studies cannot aspire to hypotheses of such uniformity and generality as the physical studies. The second chapter includes a discussion of the problems of meaning and the function and dangers involved in definition. At pp. 506–510 there is a discussion, in the context of Scandinavian Realism, of the parts played by verification and abstract ideas.

10. TAMMELO, I. "Sketch for a Symbolic Juristic Logic" (1955–56), 8 JLE 277: it is alleged that traditional ways of legal thinking are no longer apt. Accordingly, in this article the author attempts to work out a new "symbolic logic".

1. FITZGERALD, P.J. "Law and Logic" (1964), 39 NDL, 570: law and science are not alike in several respects. Law suffers from both semantic and syntactic ambiguities in its language. The question how far the use of logic in laying down and applying law will help is considered.

2. CASTBERG, F. *Problems of Legal Philosophy*, (2nd ed., Oslo University Press; Allen & Unwin, Ltd, 1957), chaps. 1–2: different types of jurisprudential study are listed in the first chapter and explained. The opening of the second chapter is particularly important in that it discusses the approach to the study. The fact that a concept of law is given *a priori* is denied, but it is conceded that the notion of validity has an *a priori* element.

3. COHEN, M.R. "Law and Scientific Method" in *Law and Social Order*, (Harcourt Brace & Co, 1933), 184, 219: the scientific teaching of law is important. By the scientific method is signified the hypothetico-deductive method. The starting point does not consist of certainties, but of guesses which may not be free from error.

4. COHEN, M.R. *Reason and Nature*, (Kegan Paul, Trench, Trubner & Co, Ltd, 1931), chap. 1, sect. 3; Part III: this is of general interest and deals with the part played by reason in the social sciences. Chapter 1 draws attention to the need for hypothesis to guide observation.

5. POPPER, K.R. *Poverty of Historicism*, (Routledge & Kegan Paul, 1957), pp. 139–40: it is argued that the method of science (certainly the most fruitful method for social studies) is that of proceeding by hypothesis and verification. It is stressed that the hypothesis should only be provisional.

6. POPPER, K.R. "Philosophy of Science" in *British Philosophy in Mid-Century*, (ed. C.A. Mace, Allen & Unwin, Ltd, 1957), 135, at pp. 177–79: the author goes on to make the point that falsifiability and refutability are the criteria of the scientific status of a theory. It is also stated that people are born with certain "expectations" or "knowledge" which are prior to all observation.

7. CAIRNS, H. *The Theory of Legal Science*, (The University of North Carolina Press, 1941), especially chaps. 1, 6 and 10: jurisprudence is defined as a function of disorder. It is accepted as axiomatic that all theories of society have to begin with certain unprovable assumptions which cannot be tested conclusively. Hence the method is that of hypothesis and verification. A hypothesis which fails to stand up to verification should be modified or rejected.

8. CAIRNS, H. *Legal Philosophy from Plato to Hegel*, (John Hopkins Press, 1949), chaps. 1 and 15: interest in classical philosophies of the ancient thinkers has revived. The method of study is that of proceeding by hypothesis and verification.

9. COOK, W.W. "The Logical and Legal Bases of the Conflict of Laws" (1923–24), 33 Yale LJ 457: the opening part is of interest for it firmly rejects the *a priori* method in favour of the experimental method of hypothesis and verification.

10. PECZENIK, A. "Empirical Foundations of Legal Dogmatics" (1969), Logique et Analyse (NS) 32: legal dogmatics is the interpretation and systematization of valid legal norms. This is a difficult article for non-philosophers, but it is useful in that it contains models of language learning, followed by an intricate discussion of how far "legal dogmatics is an empirical, although in some respects peculiar, science".

1. PECZENIK, A. "Norms and Reality" (1968), Theoria, 117: this is a continuation of his "Doctrinal Study of Law and Science" (ante, p. 7). The empirical significance of descriptive statements lies in their verifiability, i.e., events by which they are qualified as true or false. Normative statements too can be empirically significant with reference to the events which they qualify as being, e.g., prohibited, permitted.

2. ROSS, A. *On Law and Justice*, (Stevens & Sons, Ltd, 1958), chap. 1: the scope of jurisprudence is dealt with in outline. Doctrinal and sociological studies are regarded as useful, but ethical inquiry is rejected. It is suggested that the nature of law should be approached with the aid of a "tentative orientation of the nature of legal phenomena" to be followed by a more detailed investigation.

3. ROSS, A. *Directives and Norms*, (Routledge & Kegan Paul, Ltd, 1968), chaps. 1–3, 6: the author distinguishes between indicative and directive speech, and classifies the latter into eight types. Fictions and "deontic logic" are also dealt with.

4. KEYSER, C.J. "On the Study of Legal Science" (1928–29), 38 Yale LJ, 413: the function and structure of mathematical and scientific propositions are contrasted. The subject-matter of law, as a branch of science, is human behaviour, i.e., judicial decisions. The possibility of applying the mathematical method to legal science is explored.

5. KORKUNOV, N.M. *General Theory of Law*, (trans. W.G. Hastings, The Boston Book Co., 1909), sects. 3–4: what are called the "encyclopaedic" and "*a priori*" methods are considered and rejected.

6. For general philosophical discussions on the problems of meaning the following might be consulted: C.K. OGDEN and I.A. RICHARDS: *The Meaning of Meaning*, (10th ed., Routledge & Kegan Paul, Ltd, 1949); L. WITTGENSTEIN: *Tractatus Logico-Philosophicus*, (Routledge & Kegan Paul, Ltd, 1922); *The Blue and Brown Books*, (Basil Blackwell, Oxford, 1958); *Philosophical Investigations*, (trans. M. Anscombe, (Basil Blackwell, Oxford, 1953); A. KORZYBSKI: *Science and Sanity*, (2nd ed., The International Non-Aristotelian Library Publishing Co, 1941); M. BLACK: *Language and Philosophy*, (Cornell University Press, 1949), chaps. 3, 5, 6, 8 and 10; S. CHASE: *The Power of Words*, (Phoenix House, Ltd, 1955); *The Tyranny of Words*, (5th ed., Methuen & Co, Ltd, 1943); J. WISDOM: *Philosophy and Psycho-Analysis*, (Basil Blackwell, Oxford, 1957), pp. 36, 149, 248; A.J. AYER: *Language, Truth and Logic*, (Gollancz, Ltd, 1955); *The Problem of Knowledge*, (Pelican Books, A377, 1956); G. RYLE: *The Concept of Mind*, (Hutchinson's University Library, 1949); H.H. PRICE: *Thinking and Experience*, (Hutchinson's University Library, 1953); L.F. VINDING KRUSE: *The Foundations of Human Thought*, (trans. A. Fausbøll and I. Lund, Einar Munksgaard, Copenhagen, 1949); J.O. URMSON: *Philosophical Analysis*, (Oxford, Clarendon Press, 1956); *British Philosophy in Mid-Century*, (ed. C.A. Mace, Allen & Unwin, Ltd, 1957); *The Revolution in Philosophy*, (Macmillan & Co Ltd, 1956); R. Von MISES: *Positivism*, (Harvard University Press, 1951); J.R. WEINBERG: *An Examination of Logical Positivism*, (Routledge and Kegan Paul, Ltd, 1936); *Logic and Language*, (ed. A.G.N. Flew, Basil Blackwell, Oxford, 1955), I and II; C.S. LEWIS: *Studies in Words*, (Cambridge University Press, 1960); W. EMPSON: *The Structure of Complex Words*, (Chatto & Windus, 1952); J. HOSPERS: *An Introduction to Philosophical Analysis*, (Routledge and Kegan Paul, Ltd, 1965); R. CARNAP: *Meaning and Necessity*, (2nd ed.,

University of Chicago Press, 1958); K.R. POPPER: *The Logic of Scientific Discovery*, (Hutchinson & Co Ltd, 1972); N. CHOMSKY: *Problems of Knowledge and Freedom*, (Fontana, William Collins Sons & Co Ltd, 1972); R.H. THOULESS: *Straight and Crooked Thinking*, (Pan Books, London, 1974); A.G.N. FLEW: *Thinking about Thinking*, (Fontana, William Collins, 1975).

Criteria of Identification: Sources

1. SALMOND, J.W. *Jurisprudence*, (12th ed. by P.J. Fitzgerald, Sweet & Maxwell, Ltd, 1966), chap. 3: the important distinction is made between "legal" sources, those which give to a rule the quality of "law", and "historical" sources, those from which the content of a rule may be derived. He also makes the crucial point that the rule that statutes are law is ultimate.

2. AUSTIN, J. *Lectures on Jurisprudence*, (5th ed., R. Campbell, John Murray, 1885), II, pp. 510–550: on his theory of law, the sovereign is the source of a law in the sense that it is his authority which imparts to a rule the quality of being "law". After a lengthy and somewhat confusing discussion of "written" and "unwritten" law, it emerges that in all cases the "source" is the sovereign and the term "a law" is applicable to whatever proceeds from him directly or indirectly. There is also discussion of some of the other meanings of "source".

3. HART, H.L.A. *The Concept of Law*, (Oxford, Clarendon Press, 1961, reprinted 1975), chaps. 5, 6 and pp. 246–247: a "rule of recognition" is required by which to identify "primary" rules. The "rule of recognition" is ultimate because there is no other rule providing a criterion for its validity. It is simply accepted for use in this way. At pp. 246–247 he defends Salmond against Allen's criticism.

4. HART, H.L.A. "Legal and Moral Obligation" in *Essays in Moral Philosophy*, (ed. A.I. Melden, University of Washington Press, 1958), 82: rules are identified as valid by reference to a superior criterion of validity.

5. PATON, G.W. *A Text-book of Jurisprudence*, (4th ed. G.W. Paton and D.P. Derham, Oxford, The Clarendon Press, 1972), chap. 6: this is a brief discussion of "source" of law with reference to the criterion of validity.

6. CROSS, A.R.N. *Precedent in English Law*, (2nd ed. Oxford, Clarendon Press, 1968), chap. 5: this is a discussion of the different meanings of "source" and of the views of Austin, Salmond and Gray. At pp. 207–211 he defends Salmond and points out that the "ultimate rules" are "law" because they are accepted as such.

7. BODENHEIMER, E. *Jurisprudence*, (Harvard University Press, 1962), pp. 269–272: these pages contain a discussion of sources and the adoption of a distinction between "formal" and "non-formal" sources.

8. OLIVECRONA, K. *Law as Fact*, (Einar Munksgaard, Copenhagen; Humphrey Milford, 1939; reprinted by Wildy & Sons, Ltd, 1962), chap. 2 *passim*; second edition (Stevens & Sons, Ltd, 1971), chap. 4: when a rule is promulgated through certain media it acquires a psychological pressure, which is why it is accepted as law.

9. CARDOZO, B.N. *The Growth of the Law*, (Yale University Press, 1924), chap. 2: he makes the point that the term "law" is applicable not only to what has

actually been recognised by courts, but that there is a stage before adjudication when it acquires this character.

1. HOLLAND, T.E. *The Elements Jurisprudence*, (13th ed., Oxford, Clarendon Press, 1924), chap. 5: this gives a general discussion of the various meanings of the term "source".

2. KEETON, G.W. *The Elementary Principles of Jurisprudence*, (2nd ed., Isaac Pitman & Sons, Ltd, 1949), chap. 5: this gives a brief account of the different meanings of "source" and draws attention to the distinction between "binding" and "persuasive" sources.

3. KOCOUREK, A. *An Introduction to the Science of Law*, (Little, Brown & Co, Boston, 1930), pp. 155–158, 185–191: an account is given of the different meanings of "source" with emphasis on "official sources", *i.e.* rule-making by the organs or agencies of the state, as distinguished from "unofficial sources".

4. ALLEN, C.K. *Law in the Making*, (7th ed., Oxford, Clarendon Press, 1964), pp. 268–285: he rejects Salmond's distinction between "legal" and "historical" sources, but he is only using the term source in the sense of the origin of the content of a rule without allowing for the other and, it is submitted, more important formal sense.

5. GRAY, J.C. *The Nature and Sources of the Law*, (2nd ed., R. Gray, The Macmillan Co, New York, 1921), pp. 84, 123–125, 308–309: he distinguishes between "law" and "sources of law" on the basis that "law" is only what the courts propound. Therefore, even a statute is not "law", but only a source of law. Such a view is opposed to that adopted by most lawyers.

6. FRANK, J.N. *Law and the Modern Mind*, (Stevens & Sons, Ltd, 1949), pp. 121–125, 269–271: he pursues the same line as Gray to an even greater extreme.

7. ROSS, A. *On Law and Justice*, (Stevens & Sons, Ltd, 1958), chap. 1, pp. 11–18, chap. 2, chap. 3, pp. 75–78, and pp. 101 *et seq.*: he proceeds on the basis that the test of the validity of law is the likelihood of application by the courts. Sources are thus all the factors which influence the judge's formulation of a rule. Statute is, however, "law" because of the high degree of probability that a court will apply it.

8. HART, H.L.A. "Scandinavian Realism", (1959), CLJ 233, especially pp. 236–240: he criticises Ross. To a judge, law is valid not because of the likelihood that he will apply it; he will apply it because it is law. What judges need is a rule of recognising "law".

9. HUGHES, G.B.J. "The Existence of a Legal System" (1960), 35 NYULR 1001, at pp. 1010–23: certain critical observations are made on the views of Hart and Ross.

10. EKELÖF, P.O. "The Expression 'Valid Rule': a study in Legal Terminology" (1971) Scand. SL 59: if a judge is in doubt whether to apply rule X or rule Y, the question is which of them satisfies the requirements which would make it "valid". Sociological and normative criteria are considered and rejected because both fail to furnish guidance in cases of doubt. If a court resorts to analogy in such cases, some of the criteria of validity are identical with principles for the application of law.

1. PECZENIK, A. "The Concept 'Valid Law'" (1972), Scand. SL 213: the term "valid law" is ambiguous. The descriptive sense in which it is used is analysed into four operations. As to the criteria of validity, the author argues for linguistic rules of recognition, i.e., linguistic custom of speaking of rules as valid. This has both a descriptive and a normative aspect, which is said to reconcile realist and formalist approaches.

2. ANONYMOUS. "How far are Departmental Circulars on Law Binding?" (1970), 134 JPJ 30: the argument is that although these are not binding authorities or binding interpretations of law, they may be the best available authority on questions of fact.

Temporal Approach

3. DIAS, R.W.M. "Legal Politics: Norms behind the *Grundnorm*", (1968), 26 CLJ 233: legal institutions do not exist just for a moment, but endure over periods of time, just as human beings do not exist just for a moment. There are two time-frames, the present time-frame and the continuing time-frame. When considering any phenomenon (legal or otherwise) in the latter all factors involved in the idea of endurance become a part of the concept of it as an enduring thing.

4. DIAS, R.W.M. "Temporal Approach Towards a New Natural Law" (1970), 28 CLJ 75: the implications of the distinction between the present time-frame and the continuum are developed. It is submitted that on the basis of it some controversies can be settled and others seen in a fresh light. Above all, the continuum provides a unifying framework within which to conduct an integrative study of jurisprudence.

5. HURST, J.W. *Justice Holmes on Legal History*, (The Macmillan Co, New York; Macmillan, Ltd, London, 1964): every legal order has a dimension in time, which determines its character, impact and direction. Historical perspective brings out aspects not revealed by mere logical analysis, the dimensions being "sequence" and "context". The approach is similar to the one outlined above, but does not develop in the same direction.

6. TAYLOR, R. "Law and Morality" (1968), 43 NYULR 611: towards the end of the article the author comes close to a temporal approach. Considerations of morality, he says, do not come in except in relation to "law" regarded as an activity, in which case the end to be achieved becomes relevant.

7. FINNIS, J.M. "Revolutions and the Continuity of Law" in *Oxford Essays in Jurisprudence (Second Series)*, (ed. A.W.B. Simpson, Oxford, Clarendon Press, 1973), chap. 3: although not specifically on the time factor, the argument of this paper is concerned with it, especially in relation to such questions as the authority of a repealed law to continue to govern situations occurring before repeal, and also the larger question whether there is such a thing as a legal system considered merely as a set of rules, for there is nothing to give it continuity, duration and identity through time.

8. HALL, J. *Foundations of Jurisprudence*, (The Bobbs-Merrill Co, Inc, 1973): although the author does not specifically adopt a temporal perspective in his treatment, it is submitted that such a perspective is implicit in his whole thesis that law should be considered as "law-as-action". Anything that functions ("action") must take time over its functioning.

2. Advantages and Disadvantages

The Hohfeldian Scheme

1. HOHFELD, W.N. *Fundamental Legal Conceptions as Applied in Judicial Reasoning*, (ed. W.W. Cook, Yale University Press; London: Humphrey Milford, 1923), chaps. 1–5: "advantages" might be associated with the idea of "rights". But "right" is a "chameleon" word representing different jural relations. Precise analysis requires that these are distinguished with the aid of other terms. The first chapter contains the scheme of jural relations; some of the remaining chapters consist of analyses of various topics with its aid.

2. COOK, W.W. "Hohfeld's Contributions to the Science of Law", which is the "Introduction" to W.N. Hohfeld's *Fundamental Legal Conceptions as Applied in Judicial Reasoning*, (*supra*): this provides a somewhat simplified explanation of Hohfeld's scheme together with a sympathetic evaluation of his work.

3. STONE, J. *Legal Systems and Lawyers' Reasonings*, (Stevens & Sons, Ltd, 1964), chap. 4: Hohfeld pointed out the danger of chameleon-hued words, clarified confused usage and revealed new aspects of the concepts involved. Various aspects of his contribution, in relation to those of his predecessors and successors, are considered. Despite certain criticisms which might be levelled against Hohfeld, the author's judgment on him is very favourable.

4. BENTHAM, J. *Of Laws in General*, (ed. H.L.A. Hart, The Athlone Press, 1970), chap. 10 and Appendix B: in this posthumous publication it will be seen that Bentham had anticipated to a remarkable degree the analysis of later jurists. The opposition between duty and liberty is as clear as it is convincing. There is also an elaborate examination of powers in the widest sense. (See also the earlier edition *sub nom. The Limits of Jurisprudence Defined*, ed. C.W. Everett, Columbia University Press, 1945, chap. 2).

5. HART, H.L.A. "Bentham on Legal Rights" in *Oxford Essays in Jurisprudence (Second Series)* (ed. A.W.B. Simpson, Oxford University Press, 1973), chap. 7: this is an acute exposition and critique of Bentham's anticipation of the Hohfeldian distinctions between claims, liberty and power. He also developed aspects neglected by Hohfeld. The discussion includes an analysis of absolute and relative duties and whether it is possible to have a general theory for all three types of rights in the form of "legally respected choice".

6. HART, H.L.A. "Bentham on Legal Powers" (1971–72), 81 Yale LJ 799: Bentham's analysis of powers anticipates Hohfeld and goes considerably beyond his. He distinguishes between powers to interfere physically, "powers of contrectation", and powers to procure people to conform to commands and prohibitions, "powers of imperation". He fails, however, to distinguish between validity and invalidity and illegality, and between power to enter into effective transactions and power to issue legal commands and prohibitions.

7. SALMOND, J.W. *Jurisprudence*, (7th ed., Sweet & Maxwell Ltd, 1924, pp. 70–74; 12th ed., P.J. Fitzgerald, Sweet & Maxwell, Ltd, 1966), chap. 7: in the 7th edition will be found Salmond's own breakdown of the concept of "right", to which W.N. Hohfeld paid tribute and acknowledged indebtedness. In the 12th edition the current editor has incorporated Hohfeld's scheme and eliminated Salmond's.

1. TERRY, H.T. *Some Leading Principles of Anglo-American Law Expounded with a View to its Arrangement and Codification*, (T. & J.W. Johnson, Philadelphia, 1884), chap. 6, SS. 113–127: this analysis is an important forerunner of W.N. Hohfeld's. Four meanings of the term "right" are distinguished, three of which correspond to Hohfeld's distinctions, namely, claim, permissive rights (privileges) and facultative rights, (powers).

2. HEARN, W.E. *The Theory of Legal Duties and Rights*, (Melbourne: John Ferres; London: Trübner & Co, 1883), chap. 8: distinctions are drawn between right (*stricto sensu*), liberty and power.

3. CORBIN, A.L. "Legal Analysis and Terminology", (1919–20), 29 Yale LJ 163: this contains an explanation of certain legal terms and is particularly important for its helpful and simplified exposition of Hohfeld's scheme.

4. RADIN, M. "A Restatement of Hohfeld", (1937–38), 51 Harv LR 1141: this is a critical appraisal of the Hohfeldian scheme which seeks to correct some of the points in the analysis.

5. GOBLE, G.W. "A Redefinition of Basic Legal Terms", (1935), 35 Col LR 535: this is an elaboration of W.N. Hohfeld's work and contains a fresh examination of legal relationships.

6. DICKEY, A. "A Fresh Approach to the Analysis of Legal Relations", (1974), 20 McGill LJ 260: the author begins with the concept of duty, which concerns some action coupled with a requirement of compliance by the actor. Round this he evolves liberty, power and liability. His treatment is to a degree critical of Hohfeld's analysis.

7. PATON, G.W. *A Text-Book of Jurisprudence*, (4th ed. G.W. Paton and D.P. Derham, Oxford, Clarendon Press, 1972), chap. 12: the concept of "right" is considered generally and its various meanings examined. W.N. Hohfeld's scheme is explained in brief.

8. KEETON, G.W. *The Elementary Principles of Jurisprudence*, (2nd ed., Isaac Pitman & Sons, Ltd, 1949), chaps. 11 and 12: the first of these chapters contains a brief account of W.N. Hohfeld together with a more general discussion of rights. The second deals with classification of rights.

9. KOCOUREK, A. "The Century of Analytic Jurisprudence since John Austin", in *Law: A Century of Progress*, (New York University Press; London: Humphrey Milford, 1937), II, p. 194, especially pp. 205–210: this is a historical account of the writers who have followed in the Austinian tradition. At the pages mentioned are to be found J.W. Salmond's and W.N. Hohfeld's analyses with certain critical comments on the latter.

10. KOCOUREK, A. "Plurality of Advantage and Disadvantage in Jural Relations", (1920), 19 Mich LR, 47: analysis on Hohfeldian lines is carried far beyond Hohfeld. Jural relations are sub-divided into 8 "nexal relations", 8 "simple" or "quasi-jural relations" and 8 "naked relations".

11. KOCOUREK, A. "The Alphabet of Legal Relations", (1923), 9 Am BAJ, 237: W.N. Hohfeld's terms are differently presented, the four principal terms following Hohfeld's scheme but with the addition of "common denominators" and "negative terms". (Cf. Chapter 2 of *Jural Relations, infra*).

1. KOCOUREK, A. *Jural Relations*, (2nd ed., The Bobbs-Merrill Co, 1928), chaps. 1–12: jural relations are examined in minute detail. W.N. Hohfeld's scheme of eight terms is elaborated into twenty-four. The whole book is written with the aid of a technical vocabulary covering seventeen pages. This is a most advanced work. An important feature is that Kocourek dispenses with correlatives and opposites by distinguishing between Advantages (claim, immunity, privilege, power) and Disadvantages (duty, disability, inability, liability).

2. PECZENIK, A. "The Concept of Rights" (1969), 11 Archivum Juridicum Cracoviense, 47: "right" should not be identified with factual phenomena, and is ambiguous. The opposition between permissive right and duty is discussed in the light of "weak" and "strong" permissions. The correlation between right to another's behaviour and duty is discussed in the light of Petrazycki's and Hohfeld's analyses and a comparison and evaluation of the two.

3. LLEWELLYN, K.N. *The Bramble Bush*, (New York, 1930), pp. 83–89: W.N. Hohfeld's scheme is considered from the American Realist point of view. The reaction of a court is made the determining factor.

4. SNYDER, O.C. *Preface to Jurisprudence*, (The Bobbs-Merrill Co, Inc, 1954), part V, chap. 1, pp. 707–716: this contains a general examination of W.N. Hohfeld's scheme.

5. WILLIAMS, G.L. "The Concept of Legal Liberty", in *Essays in Legal Philosophy*, (ed. R.S. Summers, Basil Blackwell, Oxford, 1968), 121: this is a specialised treatment of privilege or liberty. Certain modifications of W.N. Hohfeld's scheme are suggested.

6. SMITH, J.C. "Liberties and Choice" (1974), 19 AJJ 87: permission to do something and permission not to do it are not mutually exclusive, since there is here a choice to act either way. The author criticises Williams's suggestion that duty and liberty can co-exist where their content is the same. In such a situation there is no choice, hence no liberty.

7. CAMERON, J.T. "Two Jurisprudential Case Notes", [1964], Jur. R., 155–58: the first part is devoted to an examination of *Musgrove* v. *Chung Teeong Toy*, [1891] AC 272, with reference to W.N. Hohfeld's "liberty". It is stated that there is difficulty in ascribing a no-right to the state correlative to an alien's common law liberty to enter British territory. It is thought that *Musgrove's* case is not a good illustration of liberty; and further that the Hohfeldian scheme is probably not applicable to public law.

8. FARMER, J.A. "Natural Justice and Licensing Applications: Hohfeld and the Writ of Certiorari" [1967], 2 NZULR, 282: the distinction between right, liberty and privilege has acquired significance as a result of developments in administrative law. There is in particular a growing distinction between liberty, as connoting freedom enjoyed by all, and privilege, as connoting a special dispensation from a particular law.

9. HARRIS, J.W. "Trust, Power and Duty" (1971), 87 LQR 31: the author analyses certain doctrines in equity, as applied in recent cases, with the aid of the Hohfeldian analysis. In the course of it he points out certain weaknesses and incompleteness in the scheme. It is very helpful in seeing the practical use to be made of it.

1. SHATTUCK, C.E. "The True Meaning of the Term 'Liberty' in those Clauses in the Federal and State Constitutions which Protect 'Life, Liberty, and Property'", (1890–91), 4 Harv LR, 365: this is earlier than W.N. Hohfeld and is of general interest. The conclusion is reached that liberty connotes absence of restraint.

2. BIGELOW, M.M. *The Law of Torts*, (3rd ed., Cambridge University Press, 1908), pp. 13–16: privileges in tort are discussed. It is pointed out that privilege is the converse of duty.

3. BOHLEN, F.H. "Incomplete Privilege to Inflict Intentional Invasions of Interests of Property and Personality", (1925–26), 39 Harv LR, 307: the occasions when the duty not to do certain things becomes a privilege to do them are discussed.

4. DWORKIN, R.M. *Taking Rights Seriously*, (Duckworth, 1977), chaps. 7 *et seq.*: although Hohfeld is not mentioned, nor his terminology adopted, the analysis of "fundamental rights" can be translated into Hohfeldian terms, especially the distinction between a "right to do a thing coupled with a right not to be prevented" and a "right to do it without a right not to be prevented". (See also "Taking Rights Seriously" in *Oxford Essays in Jurisprudence (Second Series)*, (ed. A.W.B. Simpson, Oxford University Press, 1973, chap. 8).

5. COHEN, L.J. Review of H.L.A. Hart's *The Concept of Law*, (1962), 71 Mind, 395: a good deal of space is given to a critique of Hart's use of the term "power". What is said here may usefully be considered along with Hohfeldian powers.

6. TAPPER, C.F.H. "Powers and Secondary Rules of Change" in *Oxford Essays in Jurisprudence (Second Series)*, (ed. A.W.B. Simpson, Oxford, Clarendon Press, 1973), chap. 10: this is a comparison of the Hohfeldian analysis and Hart's use of it. In particular, the concept of power is examined in detail, especially in relation to the changing of remedial jural relations as distinct from primary relations, and changing relations within the duty-liberty group and/or in the power-disability group.

7. CAMPBELL, A.H. "Some Footnotes to Salmond's Jurisprudence", (1939–40), 7 CLJ, 206–209: certain points connected with W.N. Hohfeld's scheme are amplified.

8. LLOYD, D. *The Idea of Law*, (Penguin Books, Ltd, A 688, 1964), pp. 309–18: the link between legal and moral duties is underlined by the use of "right", which carries a sense of justification. After a discussion of absolute duties and primary and remedial rights, W.N. Hohfeld's scheme is explained in broad terms with illustrative examples.

9. WORTLEY, B.A. *Jurisprudence*, (Manchester University Press, Oceana Publications, Inc, New York, 1967), chap. 16: this gives a general account of rights and duties. Contariety and contradiction are explained in Hohfeldian terms. There are also illustrations of some of the Hohfeldian distinctions.

Evaluation of W.N. Hohfeld's Contribution

10. RANDALL, H.J. "Hohfeld on Jurisprudence" (1925), 41 LQR, 86: this is one of the first English appreciations of W.N. Hohfeld's work. It is a critical appraisal which proceeds on the basis of two main questions: whether Hohfeld's scheme

covers the whole field of legal relations, and whether the scheme does more than is necessary.

1. COOK, W.W. "The Utility of Jurisprudence in the Solution of Legal Problems", in *Lectures on Legal Topics*, (The Macmillan Co, New York, 1928), p. 338: conceptual tools need to be analysed to find out whether they are adequate. The term "right" is examined on this basis and the different meanings that have been attached to it in cases. The value of W.N. Hohfeld's scheme for this purpose is discussed.

2. COOK, W.W. "Privileges of Labor Unions in the Struggle for Life", (1917–18), 27 Yale LJ, 779: the value of W.N. Hohfeld's analysis is demonstrated by its application to the decisions in two important trade union cases. The judicial use of the term "right" confuses different meanings of the term.

3. COOK, W.W. "Note on the Associated Press Case", (1918–19), 28 Yale LJ, 387, 391: this shows that a novel rule of law can be said to have been created in the given case by examining the reasoning in it with the aid of W.N. Hohfeld's scheme.

4. COOK, W.W. "The Alienability of Choses in Action", (1916), 29 Harv LR, 816; "The Alienability of Choses in Action: a Reply to Professor Williston", (1917), 30 Harv LR, 449: the value of W.N. Hohfeld's scheme when expounding the complex relationships involved in this branch of the law is demonstrated.

5. CORBIN, A.L. "Rights and Duties", (1923–24), 33 Yale LJ, 501: rights are analysed generally with the aid of W.N. Hohfeld's scheme.

6. CORBIN, A.L. "Offer and Acceptance, and Some of the Resulting Legal Relations", (1916–17), 26 Yale LJ, 169: the significance of the Hohfeldian power concept is demonstrated by an examination of the changing relationships involved in the formation of contracts.

7. COMMONS, J.R. *Legal Foundations of Capitalism*, (The Macmillan Co, of New York, 1932), pp. 83–134: the economic transactions of people are analysed with the aid of the Hohfeldian table. Criticisms of it, principally by Kocourek, are considered and on the whole rejected. On the other hand, certain improvements in terminology, notably "exposure" in place of "no-right", are suggested. The chief interest of this closely reasoned section lies, not so much in its clarification of the Hohfeldian scheme, but in its detailed application of the scheme to the examination of economic transactions.

8. FLATHMAN, R.E. *The Practice of Rights*, (Cambridge University Press, 1977): in Chapter 2 the Hohfeldian analysis is made the foundation of a liberal theory of rights. The presentation of the analysis is questionable in some respects, and insufficient use is made of the Hohfeldian breakdown of rights in the rest of the book.

9. LLEWELLYN, K.N. *Cases and Materials on the Law of Sales*, (Chicago: Callaghan & Co, 1930), chap. 6: the commentaries interspersed between the cases on Title are written in Hohfeldian language and provide an example of the practicalities of the Hohfeldian scheme. At p. 572 attention is specifically drawn to the immense clarification that would ensue from its use in sorting out problems of Title in sale.

1. HAMSON, C.J. "Moot Case on Defamation", (1948), 10 CLJ, 46: the opposition between W.N. Hohfeld's concepts of privilege and duty is utilised in deciding a hypothetical dispute.

2. SOLOMON, E. "Lease or License", (1959–61), 3 Syd LR, 136: the Hohfeldian analysis is applied to the distinction between lease and license. Since 1952 the grant of a privilege to occupy is a lease. In this light the effect of *Addiscombe Garden Estates, Ltd.* v. *Crabbe*, [1958] 1 QB, 513, is assessed.

3. GOBLE, G.W. "The Sanction of a Duty", (1927–28), 37 Yale LJ, 426: Hohfeld's scheme is utilised to examine the different kinds of sanction.

4. HUSIK, l. "Hohfeld's Jurisprudence", (1924), 72 U Pa LR, 263: this is an unfavourable evaluation of W.N. Hohfeld's work on the basis of three questions: (1) has he shown the traditional usage of "right" to be inadequate? (2) If so, has he succeeded in providing a more acceptable analysis? (3) Is his scheme of practical value?

5. KOCOUREK, A. "The Hohfeld System of Fundamental Legal Concepts", (1920), 15 Ill LQ, 23: this is a critique of W.N. Hohfeld's scheme, objecting in particular to the concept of jural opposite.

6. CORBIN, A.L. "Jural Relations and their Classification", (1920–21), 30 Yale LJ, 226: Corbin defends W.N. Hohfeld against A. Kocourek's criticisms, and in turn considers critically the utility of Kocourek's own more elaborate scheme: (see *Jural Relations, supra*).

7. POUND, R. "Fifty Years of Jurisprudence", (1936–37), 50 Harv LR 557, especially at pp. 571–576: this is a critical appraisal of W.N. Hohfeld's work. Not all Pound's objections have proved acceptable to other writers. He points out, *inter alia*, that some of Hohfeld's opposites are "contrasts"; that there can be more than one correlative and opposite to a term; that "no-right" is meaningless; that "privilege" might have been broken down still more; and that Hohfeld's scheme suffers from Hegelian weaknesses.

8. POUND, R. "Legal Rights", (1915–16), 26 IJE, 92: this article, which is a general discussion of the term "right", contains an incidental criticism of W.N. Hohfeld's scheme. Disability and liability are said to be devoid of any independent jural significance: (on this see W.W. Cook in his "Introduction" to W.N. Hohfeld, *Fundamental Legal Conceptions as Applied in Judicial Reasoning*, (ed. W.W. Cook, Yale University Press; London: Humphrey Milford, 1923), pp. 9–10).

9. POUND, R. *Jurisprudence*, (West Publishing Co, 1959), IV, chaps. 21–24: in these chapters there is a full and critical discussion of rights generally and of W.N. Hohfeld's work in particular. In the main they unify and repeat Pound's earlier criticisms.

10. HONORÉ, A.M. "Rights of Exclusion and Immunities against Divesting", (1959–60), 34 Tul LR, 453, especially 456–458: W.N. Hohfeld is criticised on the ground that rights and duties are not always correlative; and that there is need of an omnibus concept of "right" in addition to specific terms like claims, privileges, etc. It is alleged that he failed to distinguish between a right and the claim by which it is presently enforced, the privilege to which it presently gives rise and the

power which it presently conveys. Rights protected by claims against all are *in rem*, rights not so protected are *in personam*.

1. COWAN, T.A. *The American Jurisprudence Reader*, (Oceana Publications, Docket Series, Vol. 8, 1956), pp. 110–124: this gives reprints of W.W. Cook's "Introduction" to W.N. Hohfeld and R. Pound's "Fifty years of Jurisprudence" (*supra*).

2. BUCKLAND, W.W. *Some Reflections on Jurisprudence*, (Cambridge University Press, 1945), pp. 92–96: the distinctions between rights, liberties, powers and immunities are discussed and W.N. Hohfeld's work is criticised as being needlessly acute.

3. REUSCHLEIN, H.G. *Jurisprudence – its American Prophets*, (The Bobbs-Merrill Co, Inc, 1951), pp. 88–91, 167–179: Hohfeld's work is briefly summed up. It has done much to induce clear thinking, but it has not proved to be juristic salvation.

4. SIMPSON, A.W.B. "The Analysis of Legal Concepts", (1964), 80 LQR, 535, 549–51: W.N. Hohfeld, among others, is in error of trying to link an explanation of legal concepts to a theory of the logical functions of words or sentences. In this way he is forced into introducing metaphysical ideas.

5. MAHER, F.K.H. "The Kinds of Legal Rights", (1965), 5 Melb ULR, 47: we should use legal terms in the sense in which lawyers use them. Hohfeld wavered between such meanings and those which he thought lawyers should use. Hohfeld's scheme is criticised as being an unnecessarily complicated way of solving issues. Various shades of meaning of the term "right" are distinguished.

6. KAMBA, W.J. "Legal Theory and Hohfeld's Analysis of a Legal Right", (1974), 19 Jur R, 249: Hohfeld's scheme is set out and each item in it is explained. (Liberty is said to be non-jural, but privilege and licence are). The main criticism is that Hohfeld lacks a fundamental legal philosophy on which his analysis should be based. Various possibilities are considered: choice (Hart), collectivism (Duguit), authorities and responsibilities (Kocourek), power (Goble), benefit (Bentham).

7. STONE, R.L. "An Analysis of Hohfeld", (1963), 48 Minn LR, 313: the value of W.N. Hohfeld's analysis is appraised from a philosophical point of view. It is asserted that there are certain philosophically invalid assumptions underlying his scheme which prevents its success as a weapon of legal thought.

8. RAZ, J. *The Concept of a Legal System. An Introduction to the Theory of Legal System*, (Oxford, Clarendon Press, 1970), pp. 179–181: Hohfeld, it is said, advanced understanding of rights in one direction, but impeded it in others. Four basic errors which underlie his thinking are set out and explained.

9. SMITH, J.C. "Law, Language, and Philosophy", (1968), 3 U Br Col LR, 59: in the course of reviewing the attitude to language of various legal philosophers, the work of Hohfeld is considered in this light. The conclusion is on the whole critical, but it is useful as a background to an appraisal of Hohfeld's contribution.

10. LLEWELLYN, K.N. *Jurisprudence, Realism in Theory and Practice*, (University of Chicago Press, 1962), chap. 26: this gives a pen-picture of W.N. Hohfeld as a man and as a teacher.

General Analysis of "Rights"

1. OLIVECRONA, K. "Legal Language and Reality" in *Essays in Jurisprudence in Honor of Roscoe Pound*, (ed. R.A. Newman, The Bobbs-Merrill Co, Inc, 1962), p. 151: the function of the word "right" is examined with the utmost clarity. Legal language shapes reality rather than reflects it. All talk of rights is founded on inference, and the word "right" serves as a sign.

2. OLIVECRONA, K. *Law as Fact*, (Einar Munksgaard, Copenhagen; Humphrey Milford, 1939; reprinted by Wildy & Sons, Ltd, 1962), chap. 3: the difficulties of finding a factual basis for rights are examined. Rights "exist" only as conceptions in the mind and are used to awaken patterns of conduct in the minds of people. See also *Law as Fact* (2nd ed., Stevens & Sons Ltd, 1971), chaps. 6 and 7.

3. OLIVECRONA, K. "Law as Fact" in *Interpretations of Modern Legal Philosophies*, (ed. P. Sayre, Oxford University Press, New York, 1947), pp. 542, 549–557: the term "right" in the sense of claim is examined. It is a sign that another person shall conform to a pattern of behaviour.

4. ARNHOLM, C.J. "Olivecrona on Legal Rights. Reflections on the Concept of Rights", (1962), 6 Scand SL, 11: K. Olivecrona's ideas are set out and explained. Towards the end there is a brief comparison of his views with those of certain sociologists.

5. ROSS, A. *On Law and Justice*, (Stevens & Sons, Ltd, 1958), chaps. 5 and 6: in the first of these chapters the ambiguities of terminology and W.N. Hohfeld's scheme are examined. Terms are but tools of language. In the following chapter "right" is considered as a technique of presentation.

6. HÄGERSTRÖM, A. *Inquiries into the Nature of Law and Morals*, (ed. K. Olivecrona, trans. C.D. Broad, Almqvist & Wiksell, Stockholm, 1953), *passim*, especially, chap. 5: Hägerström's views are to be gathered from various portions of his work. "Right" is a "hollow" word, i.e., one can appreciate the object of it, namely, the advantage, but not a right itself. Psychological and historical explanations are given for the continued talk of rights.

7. ALLEN, C.K. "Legal Duties" in *Legal Duties*, (Oxford, 1931), pp. 156, 196–220: the relationship between morality and law is considered, primarily from the angle of duties, but the discussion is relevant also to the question of rights.

8. RATTIGAN, W.H. *The Science of Jurisprudence*, (3rd ed., Wildy & Sons, 1909), pp. 26–37: moral and legal rights are contrasted. Violation of the latter is visited by state action. There is also a general discussion of rights and of kinds of rights.

9. von IHERING, R. *Geist des römischen Rechts*, (Leipzig, 1888), S. 60: this is the *locus classicus* of the "interest" theory of rights.

10. SALMOND, J.W. *Jurisprudence*, (7th ed., Sweet & Maxwell, Ltd, 1924), pp. 237–240; 12th ed., P.J. Fitzgerald, Sweet & Maxwell, Ltd, 1966), pp. 217–221: rights are interests recognised and protected by law. This is a repetition of R. von Ihering's thesis.

11. WIGMORE, J.H. *Select Cases on the Law of Torts*, (Little, Brown & Co, 1912),

11, Appendix A, ss 4–8: this gives an analysis of a legal relation on the basis of interest as an element of a legal *nexus.*

1. VINOGRADOFF, P. "The Foundation of a Theory of Rights", in *Collected Papers*, (Oxford, 1928), II, chap. 20: in order that a right should exist it has to be claimed, declared as a right and enforceable. Historically rights have developed out of the recognition of claims.

2. VINOGRADOFF, P. *Common-Sense in Law*, (3rd ed., H.G. Hanbury, Oxford University Press, 1959), pp. 45–52: right is the range of action assigned to a particular will within the social order established by law. It is founded on claim. Different types of claims are discussed.

3. BROWN, W.J. "Re-analysis of a Theory of Rights", (1924–25), 34 Yale LJ, 765: this is a critical comment on P. Vinogradoff's thesis, considering point by point the arguments advanced.

4. LUNDSTEDT, A.V. *Superstition or Rationality in Action for Peace?* (Longmans, Green & Co, 1925), pp. 110–119: R. von Ihering's doctrine of interest is criticised. "Right" is purely an abstract expression for an actual situation in which, by virtue of certain rules maintained by force, certain actions have certain effects.

5. LUNDSTEDT, A.V. *Legal Thinking Revised*, (Almqvist & Wiksell, Stockholm, 1956), pp. 77–122: the absurdity of talking of rights is emphasised. The phrase "legal right" refers to actual situations. (For a comment on Lundstedt's views generally, see C.K. Allen, *Legal Duties, supra*).

6. OLIVECRONA, K. "The Legal Theories of Axel Hägerström and Vilhelm Lundstedt" (1959), 3 Scand SL, 125: the views of these two writers are explained more simply and clearly than in their originals.

7. WILLIAMS, G.L. "Language and the Law", (1946), 62 LQR, pp. 387, 398–399: this is a brief but illuminating analysis of the term "right" with comments on the views of P. Vinogradoff, A.V. Lundstedt, R. von Ihering and J.W. Salmond.

8. OLIVECRONA, K. "The Concept of a Right according to Grotius and Pufendorff" in *Festschrift für Oscar Adolf Germann*, (Verlag Stämpfli & Cie, Bern, 1969), 175: both Grotius and Pufendorff maintained that a right implied a moral power. After examining this thesis, it is contended that there is a confusion between the primary and secondary rights. The latter is not a *facultas moralis*, but implies that the use of force to enforce one's primary right meets with no moral obstacle.

9. HOLLAND, T.E. *The Elements of Jurisprudence*, (13th ed., Oxford, 1924), chaps. 7 and 8: in the first of these chapters a legal right is said to be the capacity of controlling, with the assent and assistance of the state, the acts of another. The correlation between right and duty and various other ideas are considered. In the following chapter right is analysed into various "elements".

10. GRAY, J.C. *The Nature and Sources of the Law*, (2nd ed., R. Gray, The Macmillan Co, of New York, 1921), chap. 1: this is a general discussion of rights and draws attention to the ambiguity of the term. Right consists of the ability to enforce the correlative duty. Absolute duties, legal and moral rights and rights as interests are also considered.

1. AUSTIN, J. *Lectures on Jurisprudence*, (5th ed., R. Campbell, John Murray, 1885), pp. 281–290 and Lectures 12, 16 and 17: the possibility of there being rights in and against the sovereign is considered. The discussion in Lecture 12 is of particular interest because of the distinction there drawn between "right" and "liberty", i.e., exemption from obligation. Lecture 16 makes the important point that duty is the basis of right. Lecture 17 considers absolute and relative duties and concludes that absolute duties are possible in certain cases.

2. MARKBY, W. *Elements of Law*, (6th ed., Oxford, 1905), chap. 4, SS 140–160: rights and duties are correlative, but not every duty need have a correlative right (absolute duty). The sovereign has neither rights nor duties.

3. BROWN, W.J. *The Austinian Theory of Law*, (John Murray, 1906), pp. 180–181, 192–194: J. Austin's distinction of between "right" and "liberty" is approved. He disagrees with Austin on the point that the sovereign may have rights and duties.

4. POLLOCK, F. *A First Book of Jurisprudence*, (6th ed., Macmillan Co, Ltd, 1929), pp. 61–77: right implies a correlative duty. There are also other applications of right in the sense of freedom and power. The question of rights in and against the state is considered.

5. ALLEN, C.K. "Legal Duties" in *Legal Duties*, (Oxford, 1931), pp. 156, 181–193: both "power" and "interest" are combined in the idea that a right is a legally guaranteed power to realise an interest. Austin's thesis concerning absolute duties is on the whole supported.

6. CAMPBELL, A.H. "Some Footnotes to Salmond's Jurisprudence", (1939–40), 7 CLJ, 206, at pp. 209–211: the question of rights in and against the sovereign is considered. (The commentary is on the 9th ed.).

7. JENKS, E. *The New Jurisprudence*, (John Murray, 1933), chap. 8, pp. 174–188: the conception of absolute duties is rejected. There is in addition a general discussion of rights.

8. BUCKLAND, W.W. *Some Reflections on Jurisprudence*, (Cambridge University Press, 1945), pp. 107–110: the question of rights and duties in the sovereign is considered with reference to the views of J. Austin and others.

9. HART, H.L.A. "Definition and Theory in Jurisprudence", (1954), 70 LQR, 37, at pp. 42–49: the various characteristics of the proposition "A has a right" are discussed. The explanation of the word "right" should take the form of an explanation of the statement in which the word plays a part, the conditions under which the whole statement would be true and how it is used in drawing conclusions.

10. AUERBACH, C.A. "On Professor Hart's Definition and Theory in Jurisprudence" (1956), 9 JLE, 39, especially pp. 40–44: H.L.A. Hart's method of elucidating "right" is criticised on the ground that truth and falsity are inappropriate, and that it does not aid in solving new cases.

11. HALL, J. "Analytic Philosophy and Jurisprudence" (1966), 77 Ethics, 14, especially at pp. 24–26: Professor Hart's method of elucidation is criticised. Legal terms are not so different from non-legal terms, nor is the specification of

conditions necessary to the truth of statements peculiar to legal terms. It is
pointed out that Professor Hart elucidates one "anomalous" term in terms of six
others; and that his demonstration is entirely hypothetical: if the specified
conditions are present then it is true only to *say* that "X has a right".

1. SIMPSON, A.W.B. "The Analysis of Legal Concepts" (1964), 80 LQR, 535:
   Professor Hart's elucidation of "right" is considered in the context of a general
   discussion of elucidation. It is pointed out (p. 557) that his demonstration is no
   more than a truism.

2. MacCORMICK, D.N. "Rights in Legislation" in *Law, Morality, and Society. Essays
   in Honour of H.L.A. Hart* (edd. P.M.S. Hacker and J. Raz, Clarendon Press,
   Oxford, 1977), chap. 11: Hart's treatment of "right" is criticised as being a
   statement about law and about an individual's position in law. This is not so;
   rights are used in the law itself. On the whole, the author prefers the "interest"
   theory and rejects the "will" theory. Rights may be more or less complex; the
   more complex they are, the more institutional in character they are.

3. POUND, R. "Legal Rights", (1915–16), 26 IJE, 92: five senses of the term "right"
   are distinguished:– interest, claim, capacity, liberty and that which is just.
   Consideration is given to how the term "right" came to be so overworked.

4. POUND, R. *Jurisprudence*, (West Publishing Co, 1959), IV, chap. 21: legal concepts
   are discussed generally and the need for an improved terminology is stressed.
   The various meanings of the word "right" and the history of these usages are
   explained.

5. HEARN, W.E. *The Theory of Legal Duties and Rights*, (Melbourne: John Ferres;
   London: Trübner & Co, 1883), chap. 8: the origin of the term "right" is
   examined. Following J. Austin, a right is said to be a consequence of command
   for the benefit of one person and imposing a duty on another. Absolute duties
   are also considered.

6. BENTHAM, J. *Works*, (ed. J. Bowring, William Tait, Edinburgh, 1843), I,
   pp. 301–302: rights are advantages. Rights and duties are inseparable, the latter
   being restraints on liberty.

7. BEALE, J.H. *A Treatise on the Conflict of Laws*, (Baker, Voorhis & Co. 1935), I,
   pp. 58–86: rights are legalised interests in, to, or against a person or thing.
   Various interests and kinds of rights are considered.

8. KORKUNOV, N.M. *General Theory of Law*, (trans. W.G. Hastings, The Boston Book
   Co, 1909), SS. 22, 27, 29: the right-duty obligation is explained. A claim implies
   a duty, If there is no obligation, there is permission, not a right.

9. POUND, R. *Readings on the History and System of the Common Law*, (2nd ed.,
   The Chipman Law Publishing Co, Boston, 1921), chap. 8: this is a compilation
   of various writings. Private interests are maintained by rights, powers and
   privileges. Various spheres of interest are considered.

10. POUND, R. "The Progress of the Law", (1927–28), 41 Harv LR, 175: this is of
    general interest. It consists of an account of Analytical Jurisprudence in the
    course of which he shows how various jurists have dealt with the ambiguity of
    terms that refer both to "law" and "right".

1. MARSHALL, G. "Rights, Options and Entitlements" in *Oxford Essays in Jurisprudence (Second Series)* (ed. A.W.B. Simpson, Oxford University Press, 1973), chap. 9: a "right" is a form of entitlement arising out of moral, social, political or legal rules. The various terms of this formula are examined as well as the relation between rights and obligations.

2. FLATHMAN, R.E. *The Practice of Rights*, (Cambridge University Press, 1977): the practice of rights brings in a sociological dimension. A right is a warrant for acting in pursuit of one's interest often at the expense of another's interest, and such a practice requires justification. A liberal outlook on rights finds the justification in the need to preserve certain types of society and their ethos.

3. SMITH, G.H. "Of the Nature of Jurisprudence and of the Law", (1904), 38 Am LR, 68, at pp. 79–83: this is a shrewd analysis of language forms in legal speech in the course of which the various meanings of "right" are examined. It is an interesting general study.

4. The above does not include the Continental literature on the subject. Reference might be made to B. Windscheid, *Lehrbuch des Pandektenrechts*, I, ii, pp. 155 *et seq.*, which contains eight pages of note references to treatises and monographs.

3. Justice, Perspectives of Power and Liberty

1. ARISTOTLE. *Nichomachean Ethics*, (trans. H. Rackham, The Loeb Classical Library, William Heinemann, Ltd, 1938), V: this famous discussion of justice proceeds by dividing it into distributive and corrective justice and then describes the way each operates. The relation of equity to justice is also considered. (See H. KELSEN, *What is Justice?* (University of California Press, 1957), 110, for a critical study of Aristotle's doctrine).

2. CAHN, E.N. *The Sense of Injustice*, (New York University Press, 1949): justice is what is needed to put right that which would arouse a sense of injustice. Justice in law is discussed with reference to power, freedom and order, security and change.

3. HONORÉ, A.M. "Social Justice" in *Essays in Legal Philosophy*, (ed. R.S. Summers, Basil Blackwell, Oxford, 1968), 61: justice should be considered from the point of view of the citizen to whom just treatment is due. A more finely graded analysis of justice than Aristotle's is given and also of permissible departures from it.

4. JØRGENSEN, S. *Law and Society*, (Akademisk Boghandel, 1972), chaps. 3 and 4: the formal aspect of justice is that equals should be treated equally; the material aspect is reciprocity and retribution. Every decision settles the instant dispute and lays a foundation for settling future disputes. The reality behind distributive justice is bound up with economic and political development. A legal decision has to be a choice of interests; it is the result, not of free, but of limited evaluation.

5. GINSBERG, M. *On Justice in Society*, (William Heinemann, Ltd, 1965): Aristotle's formula of equal treatment of equals, differential treatment of unequals, is worked out in the light of modern social conditions. The main problem is to relate formal justice, which enjoins the exclusion of arbitrariness and justification for differential treatment, and substantive justice, namely the corpus of rights and duties. This is a most important and instructive work.

6. POTTER, H. *The Quest of Justice*, (Sweet & Maxwell, Ltd, 1951): justice, its relation to law, and the means by which it can be achieved, are discussed historically and philosophically.

7. POLLOCK, F. *A First Book of Jurisprudence*, (6th ed., Macmillan & Co, Ltd, 1929), chap. 2: the law presupposes ideals of justice. The relation of law to certain ideals, namely morality, certainty and equality, is outlined.

8. DEL VECCHIO, G. *Justice*, (trans. Lady Guthrie, ed. A.H. Campbell, Edinburgh University Press, 1952): the formal notion of justice is distinct from its content, the former can be universal, while the latter is derived from empirical data of social existence.

9. RAWLS, J. *A Theory of Justice*, (Oxford: Clarendon Press, 1972): a liberal theory of justice, based on a new version of the social contract, is propounded by a philosopher. After rejecting intuitionism and utilitarianism, he argues that a just society is one that is founded on certain "basic principles" that hypothetical rational people would choose in a hypothetical "original position", and in making their choice they are draped with a highly selective "veil of ignorance". The basic principles will furnish criteria not only for a just distribution of goods, but also for choosing all subsequent social institutions.

1. BARRY, B. *The Liberal Theory of Justice*, (Oxford: Clarendon Press, 1973): Rawls's theory of justice is considered step by step with great lucidity. The premises of his argumentation, the assumptions behind them and the reasoning itself are held up and given a vigorous shake. In the result, the whole structure is seen to be self-contradictory, confused and illogical. The book is written, not from a legal point of view, but from that of philosophy, economics and political theory.

2. *Reading Rawls. Critical Studies on Rawls' A Theory of Justice*, (ed. N. Daniels, Basil Blackwell, Oxford, 1975): N. DANIELS: "Introduction": this gives a clear marshalling of some of the principal themes of Rawls's book and co-ordinates the various critiques collected in this volume. 1. T. NAGEL: "Rawls on Justice", p. 1: why should people, who are not in the "original position", be affected by the choice of those who are supposed to be in that position? Some bias is built into the concept of the "original position" and underlies the principles of justice. 2. R.M. DWORKIN: "The Original Position", p. 16: if the social contract is hypothetical, it cannot be binding; the basic principles are acceptable because they are fair independently of the contract. If so, the concept of the "original position" is unnecessary. Rawls's theory is a right-based theory, and the "original position" is tailored so as to yield the rights that are wanted. 3. M. FISK: "History and Reason in Rawls' Moral Theory", p. 53: this considers Rawls's theory from a Marxist point of view. Some form of bias is built into the "original position" in the attempt to reduce the people in it to certain features and not others. "Equality" lies in membership of classes, not of society. 4. R.M. HARE: "Rawls' Theory of Justice", p. 81: Rawls's contract theory is equivalent to other approaches justifying moral theory. Where it differs, there is no reason for preferring Rawls. There is no more justification for the principles of justice than there is in intuitionism. Hare challenges the arguments against utilitarianism. 5. J. FEINBERG: "Rawls on Intuitionism", p. 108: Rawls's attack fails to establish the uniform priority of justice over other considerations. Even Rawls himself does not avoid intuition at times. 6. G. DWORKIN: "Non-Neutral Principles", p. 124: non-neutral principles cannot be ruled out purely by formal arguments. Rawls makes certain questionable assumptions in selecting his neutral principles. 7. D. LYONS: "Nature and Soundness of the Contract and Coherence Arguments", p. 141: he questions the basis of justice in choice and the justification of the choice itself. Rawls's principles of justice are not so different from utilitarianism in their results. 8. T.M. SCANLON: "Rawls' Theory of Justice", p. 169: he suggests that Rawls's reason for advocating choice made behind the "veil of ignorance" lies in a special view of what is good for the individual. He also suggests that Rawls's difference principle should be seen as social co-operation between equals, rather than as a covert manifestation of bias. He also questions Rawl's priority of liberty and its working. 9. R. MILLER: "Rawls and Marxism", p. 206: he points out that Rawls presupposes a society with no sharp class divisions or class desires, and that he therefore tacitly rejects the class-struggle concept. 10. H.L.A. HART: "Rawls on Liberty and its Priority", p. 230: there has been a shift in Rawls's thought from equal liberty to basic liberties. The thesis that liberty should only be limited for the sake of liberty is taken to task. Some criterion of value has to be introduced in choosing between liberties other than that of liberty itself. Whatever advantage may induce an individual to choose a liberty to be exercised by himself may be outweighed by the disadvantage to him through a general exercise of that liberty.
11. N. DANIELS: "Equal Liberty and Unequal Worth of Liberty", p. 253: Rawls omits economic factors from his constraints on basic liberties; and he does not distinguish between different types of liberty in assigning priority to liberty. There may be conflict between the First and Second Principles of Justice because

he underestimates the effect of economic inequalities on political liberties.
12. A.K. SEN: "Rawls versus Bentham: an Axiomatic Examination of the Pure
Distribution Problem", p. 283: comparing Bentham's and Rawls's solutions to
the problem he points out that there are weaknesses in both and that neither
provides a sufficient basis. 13. B. BARBER: "Justifying Justice: Problems of
Psychology, Politics and Measurement in Rawls", p. 292: according to Marxist
theory, departures from equal liberty would be justifiable. Rawls's whole
approach does not relate to historical or political realities. 14. F. MICHELMAN:
"Constitutional Welfare Rights and *A Theory of Justice*", p. 319: he considers
to what extent Rawls's theory of justice as fairness can provide a foundation
for welfare rights.

1. WOLFF, R.P. *Understanding Rawls. A Reconstruction and Critique of* A Theory of
   Justice (Princeton University Press, 1977): Rawls's theory is designed to solve
   the Kantian problem of how to evolve moral and political principles from reason.
   It fails to do so. The author subjects Rawls's theory to philosophical, sociological,
   psychological and economic analysis and concludes that it is fundamentally
   unsound. He also suggests an alternative basis that might be more helpful.

2. MacCORMICK, D.N. "Justice according to Rawls" (1973), 89 LQR, 393: this gives
   a sympathetic account of Rawls's theory of justice. It is contended that his
   argumentative procedure is an acceptable way of arguing out the principles of
   justice. Rawls's version of the social contract, the "veil of ignorance" and
   principles of justice themselves are considered in turn.

3. RAPHAEL, D.D. Review of *A Theory of Justice* by J. Rawls, (1974), 83 Mind,
   118: the book is criticised for its lack of clarity and rigour. Rawls's attempt to
   meet the difficulties of intuitionism by offering the hypothetical contract and
   the priority principle fails. The latter is contradictory of Rawls's own thesis.
   Rawls seeks to offer a substitute for intuition, but his hypothesis is so manipulated
   as to yield a preconceived moral intuition; nor does the hypothesis lead to the
   conclusions, which also are intuitive.

4. BOYNTON, P.A. "The Season of Fiction is Over: a Study of the 'Original Position'
   in John Rawls' *A Theory of Justice*" (1977), 15 Os HLJ, 215: the analytical role
   of the "original position" is considered first with reference to the concept of
   personality and human nature. Next, its justificatory role is considered with
   mention of the bias inherent in it. The conclusion is that Rawls's social contract
   is unworkable in analysis or as justification. He fails to establish an objective
   moral theory. A moral order is no doubt essential, but it is a social expedient,
   which Rawls's theory conceals.

5. BARRY, B. "Justice between Generations" in *Law, Morality, and Society. Essays in
   Honour of H.L.A. Hart* (edd. P.M.S. Hacker and J. Raz, Clarendon Press, Oxford,
   1977), chap. 15: in the course of his theory Rawls propounded the "just savings
   principle" to secure justice between generations by preserving the gains of culture
   and civilisation and the maintenance of just institutions and putting by a suitable
   amount of real capital accumulation. From pp. 276 onwards the author
   criticises Rawls's "justice between generations". He draws attention to the
   asymmetry of power between the present and future generations, and argues
   that those alive today are custodians of the planet and should pass it on no worse
   than when they took over.

6. FRIED, C. *An Anatomy of Values: Problems of Personal and Social Choice*, (Oxford

University Press, 1970): a basic moral principle has to be accepted as universal if people are to live according to a rational life-plan. Human ends are rational if they are governed by principles which are logically consistent with this basic principle. The principle of morality is that all persons are to be treated equally as ends in themselves, while unequal treatment should improve the lot of the least preferred. Unless we accept this principle, we shall be unable to attain those ends which are commonly considered worthwhile. A principle of justice on this basis is of greater value than utilitarian calculations of risk to society.

1. PERELMAN, Ch. *The Idea of Justice and the Problem of Argument*, (trans. J. Petrie, Routledge & Kegan Paul, Ltd, 1963): justice is a complex structure, which has a formal constant element (definition) and a changing substantive element (criteria of application). The formal element is: like persons to be treated alike. The variable substantive criteria for determining similarities and differences are based on essential characteristics. The choice of these is not entirely arbitrary, since there can be reasoning about values.

2. MORRIS, C. *The Justification of the Law*, (University of Pennsylvania Press, 1971): a theory of justice with reference to law is set out. The thesis is that the more law implements the public's genuine and important aspirations, the more just a legal system becomes. The justification of law has a three-fold aspect – justice, reason and conformity with culture. In the light of this, judicial and legislative methods and the relevance of sociology are discussed.

3. VINOGRADOFF, P. "Legal Standards and Ideals" in *Collected Papers,* (Oxford, 1928), II, chap. 18: the criteria discussed in this paper are equality before law, equality of opportunity, due proportion, equity and social movements.

4. *Interpretation of Modern Legal Philosophies*, (ed. P. Sayre, Oxford University Press, New York, 1947): C.K. ALLEN: "Justice and Expediency", chap. 1: this considers how individual liberties are being threatened by executive action. J. HALL: "Integrative Jurisprudence", chap. 14: a philosophy of law should combine axiology, formal analysis and sociology. (See also his *Foundations of Jurisprudence*, (The Bobbs-Merrill Co, Inc, 1973), and "Integrative Jurisprudence" (1976), 27 Hastings LJ, 779). W.E. HOCKING: "Justice, Law and the Cases", chap. 15: the function of justice is dealt with. H. KELSEN: "The Metamorphosis of the Idea of Justice", chap. 18: the changes in meaning of the term "justice" since the time of the Greeks are considered. A.V. LUNDSTEDT: "Law and Justice: a Criticism of the Method of Justice", chap. 21: judgments of value differ from scientific judgments, since they depend on feelings.

5. BODENHEIMER, E. *Jurisprudence*, (Harvard University Press, 1962), chaps. 11–13, 17: the aim of justice is to co-ordinate the diversified efforts of members of the community in a way that will satisfy the reasonable needs and aspirations of individuals. The meaning of justice and the harmony of order and justice are discussed in a highly interesting way. In S. 76 in the last-mentioned chapter value-judgments are explained.

6. BODENHEIMER, E. "Law as Order and Justice" (1957), 6 JPL, 194: the striving of the law towards order and justice is founded upon ideals.

7. LAMONT, W.D. *The Principles of Moral Judgment*, (Oxford, 1946), chap. 5: justice in the sense of distributive justice is examined. It is broken down into equality, liberty and merit. Chap. 6: the relation between morals and social

justice is examined. There is a close connection between an ideal morality and justice, the difference being a matter of emphasis.

1. OFSTAD, H. "Impartiality" in *Legal Essays. A Tribute to Frede Castberg,* (Universitetsforlaget, 1963), 135: impartiality is subjected to detailed investigation. It does lead to the question of justice and the distinction between "correct" and "incorrect" ethical systems.

2. ALLEN, C.K. *Aspects of Justice,* (Stevens & Sons, Ltd, 1958), chaps. 1–5: the first chapter is a general account of the various meanings of justice. Justice is also considered with reference to mercy, expediency and liberty.

3. HOLLAND, D.C. "Equality Before the Law" (1955), 8 CLP, 74: equality before the law does not exist in a number of territories for which the United Kingdom government is responsible.

4. ECKHOFF, T. "Justice and Social Utility" in *Legal Essays. A Tribute to Frede Castberg,* (Universitetsforlaget, 1963). 74: principles of justice and social utility are two of the most important ideas that have impact upon law. These two are compared and contrasted. Both share a place in legal reasoning.

5. KELSEN, H. *What is Justice?,* (University of California Press, 1957), pp. 1, 209: justice is a shifting idea. It is the foundation of contentment and, as such, is purely subjective. Value-judgments are of two sorts. One sort qualifies conduct as legal or illegal (values of the law); the other qualifies the law as just or unjust (values of justice).

6. LLOYD, D. *The Idea of Law,* (Penguin Books, Ltd, A 688, 1964), chap. 6: justice is one of the aims which Man sets himself in order to achieve the good life. It is said that whereas the Greek idea embodied inequality, the modern idea is essentially one of equality. The manner in which the formal principle of equality needs to be filled out is explained at some length. The divergence between ethical and legal justice, and also the manner in which the latter can approximate to the former are discussed.

7. TAYLOR, A. "Functional Aspects of the Lawyer's Concept of Justice", [1966], Jur R, 13: the relation between law and justice has posed problems which have been variously answered. The lawyer's concept of justice is one for judges. "Equality in the law" is a directive to law-makers; "equality before the law" is the specific legal contribution to the concept of justice.

8. STONE, J. and TARELLO, G. "Justice, Language and Communication" (1960–61), 14 Vand LR, 331: this is a lengthy and difficult investigation into the function of legal language and the relation between law and justice. The functions of language in the fields of law and justice differ and should not be merged.

9. BODENHEIMER, E. "The Province of Jurisprudence", (1960–61), 46 Corn LQ, 1: the view that all valuations are matters of personal opinion cannot be accepted. There are areas of uniform, or near uniform, valuation among different men or groups of men. These provide the bottom layer of human normative ordering. Jurisprudence should concern itself with schemes for improving social life.

10. HALL, J. *Living Law of Democratic Society,* (The Bobbs-Merrill Co, Inc, 1949),

Part II: justice is an essential attribute of positive law. Value-judgments can be true in an important sense. They are not nonsense because they cannot be proved. Many people act against their own desires because they want to do the right thing. Scientific perception is not the only source of knowledge.

1. HALL, J. "Justice in the 20th Century" (1971), 59 Calif LR, 752: there is now a heightened interest in law in action and the differences between this and law in books. Even the best systems fall short of their goals, and there is an awareness that legal justice needs to be supplemented by individual efforts, awareness of the values of desert, fairness, freedom and order, value of responsibility in relation to psychological, social and economic facts, and an awareness of the need for a consensus on basic values. The bonds between corrective and distributive justice are discussed with reference to criminal punishment and human rights respectively.

2. MILLER, D. *Social Justice*, (Clarendon Press, Oxford, 1976): the formulae "To each according to his rights", or "To each according to his deserts", or "To each according to his needs" are respectively subjected to examination and criticism. The views of Hume, Spencer and Kropotkin are considered, and each of them is said to presuppose a particular view of society. With regard to notions of social justice found in various types of societies, it is said that a society's concept of justice is an intelligible response to the types of social relations in which individuals in that society find themselves.

3. SCHMIDT, F. "The Four Elements of Law" (1974), 33 CLJ, 246: to regard law as an expression of ruling class interests is too simple. This is only one of four "elements" or purposes: the law of survival, the law of toleration, laws of ruling classes and laws based on agreements. Illustrations are provided from English and Swedish law.

4. HAYEK, F.A. *Law, Legislation and Liberty*, (Routledge & Kegan Paul, Ltd, 1973): Law is spontaneous and unplanned; it evolves rules of just conduct, which are closely linked to individual liberty. Legislation should confine itself to ensuring the conditions within which this development can take place.

5. BIENENFELD, F.R. *Rediscovery of Justice*, (Allen & Unwin, Ltd, 1947): this is of general interest. It seeks to achieve international justice by examining the development of nations. The parallels drawn from individuals are somewhat dubious. In conclusion, a set of absolute values is propounded.

6. BAKER, E.C. "Utility and Rights: Two Justifications for State Action Increasing Equality" (1974–75), 84 Yale LJ, 39: the problem is how total wealth is to be limited so as to increase equality. Utilitarianism is the guaranteed minimum approach, which justifies some degree of state intervention to increase equality. Professor Dworkin's approach is a guaranteed fulfilment approach: one cannot expect people to consent to be bound unless their rights are granted. It is contended that a combination of the two approaches might provide a workable basis.

7. RICHARDS, D.A.J. "Equal Opportunity and School Financing: Towards a Moral Theory of Constitutional Adjudication" (1973–74) 41, UCLR, 32: this is a criticism of the Supreme Court's decision in *San Antonio Independent School District v. Rodriguez*, 411 US, 1 (1973). Law and philosophy are interrelated. Moral analysis in this case would have clarified the equal opportunity ideal;

which is important as constitutional and legal questions depend on it. Pp. 41–52: particular interest attaches to the analysis of principles of distributive justice and the appropriate judicial standards that should be applied.

1. The case of *DeFunis* v. *Odegaard*, 194 Sup Ct, 1704 (1974), raises an interesting and important question of distributive justice. The following critiques of it are examinations of its manifold implications. M.G. PAULSEN: *"DeFunis*: the Road not Taken" (1974), 60 Vir LR, 917; R.M. O'NEIL: "Racial Preference and Higher Education: the Larger Context" (*ibid*), 925; K.L. KARST and H.W. HOROWITZ: "Affirmative Action and Equal Protection" (*ibid*), 955; E. GELHORN and D.B. HORNBY: "Constitutional Limitations on Admissions Procedure and Standards – beyond Affirmative Action" (*ibid*), 975; R.M. DWORKIN: *Taking Rights Seriously*, (G. Duckworth & Co., Ltd., 1977), chap. 9.

Perspectives of Power and Liberty in the Quest for Justice

2. SILVING, H. "The Jurisprudence of the Old Testament" (1953), 28 NYULR, 1129: the main features of the original Jewish state are explained with reference to some modern legal and political problems.

3. SILVING, H. *Sources of Law*, (Wm. S. Hein & Co, Inc, New York, 1968), "The Origins of the 'Rule of Law'" p.233: the doctrines enunciated in the English *Magna Carta* and the earlier Spanish *Charta Magna Leonesa* are traceable to the Bible.

4. ISAACS, N. "The Influence of Judaism on Western Law" in *The Legacy of Israel*, (edd. E.R. Bevan and C. Singer, Oxford, 1927), pp. 377–406: the example of Jewish law is said to have predisposed western Europe towards the "better rule". How this is so is explained in detail.

5. COHN, H. "Praelegomena to the Theory and History of Jewish Law" in *Essays in Jurisprudence in Honor of Roscoe Pound*, (ed. R.A. Newman, The Bobbs-Merrill Co, Inc, 1962), 44: this explains the theoretical basis of Jewish law and the rules that are followed in interpretation.

6. KAGAN, K.K. *Three Great Systems of Jurisprudence*, (Stevens & Sons, Ltd, 1955), especially chap. 4: Jewish, Roman and English law are compared, and the superiority of Jewish law is asserted. Chapter 4 is of interest since it deals at length with the Jewish version of the social contract.

7. EPSTEIN, I. *Judaism. A Historical Presentation*, (Pelican Books, 1959): the story of Israel is presented historically from the earliest times down to the present. The early chapters are especially useful in providing a background for the juristic theory. The rest of the book is of general interest.

8. STONE, J. *Human Law and Human Justice*, (Stevens & Sons, Ltd, 1965), pp. 18–30: this is a convenient account of the Jewish contribution to ideas of justice. The concept of equality of men derives from the fact of being God's children. It is pointed out that the *lex talionis* operated as a limitation on self-help. Explanation is also given as to why Jewish law never evolved a doctrine of natural law or equity superior to positive law.

9. LLOYD, D. *The Idea of Law*, (Penguin Books, Ltd, A 688, 1964), pp. 48–51: the attitude of the Hebrew prophets towards God's law and human law is outlined and is followed by an account of the Greek philosophers.

1. PLATO. *The Republic*, (trans. P. Shorey, The Loeb Classical Library, William Heinemann, Ltd, 1937), I and II: restraint on freedom is an essential condition of virtue. It is the function of the state to educate its citizens in virtue. He surveys the degeneracy of society (especially in Book 8) into various forms of abuse. The only hope for Man lies in a state governed by philosophical wisdom.

2. PLATO. *The Laws*, (trans. R.G. Bury, The Loeb Classical Library, William Heinemann, Ltd, 1926), I and II: the main point is that in default of philosopher kings, a state ruled by law is second best.

3. POPPER, K.R. *The Open Society and its Enemies*, (5th ed., Routledge & Kegan Paul, Ltd, 1966), I and II: the "open society" has set free the critical powers of Man. Both parts constitute a powerful argument against inevitability in evolution. Volume I provides a searching and stimulating examination of Plato's doctrine. It is one of the best critiques.

4. WILD, J.D. *Plato's Modern Enemies and the Theory of Natural Law*, (The University of Chicago Press, 1953): Plato is defended against the attacks of subsequent writers who, it is alleged, have misread his dialogues. A theory of natural law can be found in his works with which to appraise modern naturalist doctrine.

5. HALL, J. *Studies in Jurisprudence and Criminal Theory*, (Oceana Publications Inc, 1958), chap. 3: this gives an interesting account of Plato's attitude to law as evidenced by his works.

6. KELSEN, H. "Plato and the Doctrine of Natural Law" (1960–61), 14 Vand LR, 23: observations of what "is" cannot be causally lined with what "ought to be". Plato's views are considered with reference to two recent expositions of them. See also H. KELSEN: *What is Justice?* (University of California Press, 1957), 82.

7. ARISTOTLE. *Politics*, (trans. H. Rackham, The Loeb Classical Library, William Heinemann, Ltd, 1938): this contains Aristotle's views on the function of the state and the position of slaves. He did not advocate complete freedom. It is of interest to note that under good forms of government he lists monarchy, aristocracy and polity (constitutional government) in that order; while under bad forms of government he lists tyranny, oligarchy and democracy. For further views on natural law, see *Magna Moralia*, (trans. G.C. Armstrong, The Loeb Classical Library, William Heinemann, Ltd, 1936); and The *"Art" of Rhetoric*, (trans. J.H. Freese, The Loeb Classical Library, William Heinemann, Ltd, 1926).

8. SHELLENS, M.S. "Aristotle on Natural Law" (1959), 4 Nat LF, 72: the accounts of natural law in the *Rhetoric*, *Magna Moralia* and *Nichomachean Ethics* are examined and their significance assessed.

9. KELSEN, H. *What is Justice?* (University of California Press, 1957), 110: this is a study in Aristotle's doctrine of Justice.

10. HAMBURGER, M. *The Awakening of Western Legal Thought*, (trans. B. Miall, Allen & Unwin, Ltd, 1942): this small and worth while book summarises the contribution of the Greeks to modern ideas of law. Part I deals with various writers, poets, dramatists and philosophers; Part II assesses what they can teach the world.

11. VINOGRADOFF, P. *Outlines of Historical Jurisprudence*, (Oxford University Press, 1910), II: this contains a very good account of the Greek city-states.

1. STONE, J. *Human Law and Human Justice*, (Stevens & Sons, Ltd, 1965), pp. 9–18: an account is given of the lines of thought underlying early Greek philosophy, the relativism of the Sophists, the absolute idea of Plato and the interpretation of Aristotle. Natural law thinking is entangled with ideas of justice.

2. CICERO, M.T. *De Re Publica*, 111; *De Legibus*, 1–111, (trans. C.W. Keyes, The Loeb Classical Library, William Heinemann, Ltd, 1928): Cicero is the best exponent of natural law doctrines among the Roman writers. These passages contain the substance of his views.

3. JOLOWICZ, H.F. *Historical Introduction to Roman Law*, (3rd ed., Cambridge University Press, 1952), chap. 6: the origin of the Roman *jus gentium* and its connection with the *jus naturale* is explained.

4. BRYCE, J. *Studies in History and Jurisprudence*, (Oxford, 1901), II, pp. 112–71: the way in which the Greeks developed the ideas that underlie natural law are first examined. The emphasis is on the influence of natural law on Roman law and, through it, on international law.

5. CLARK, E.C. *Practical Jurisprudence*, (Cambridge University Press, 1883), I, chap. 10; II, chap. 13: natural law as a motive for obedience is first considered, and then the *jus gentium* of Roman law.

6. EMERTON, W. "Stoic Terminology in Roman Law" (1887), 3 LQR, 64: this might be referred to for general information. See further P. von SOKOLOWSKI: *Die Philosophie im Privatrecht* (1902).

7. AQUINAS, St. T. *Summa Theologica*, (trans. Fathers of the English Dominican Province, R. & T. Washbourne, Ltd, 1915), I, 2, Qq. 90–97: St. Thomas argued in support of stability, even in the face of an occasional injustice. He wove his great scheme out of Greek, Roman and religious philosophy.

8. GROTIUS, H. *De Jure Belli ac Pacis*, (trans. F.W. Kelsey, Oxford, 1925), I, chap. 1, SS 10–17: Grotius set out his views on the law of nature with the utmost clarity and vigour. This is the only guarantee against an abuse of governmental power. Such power originated in a social contract. He proceeded to urge the same pattern of development for nations, basing restraint on freedom of action on consent of nations and so giving rise to international law.

9. RUTHERFORD, T. *Institutions of Natural Law*, (2nd ed., Cambridge, 1779), chap. 1: the book represents a course of lectures on Grotius's masterpiece. Chapter 1 gives a general account of the nature of laws, divine, natural and positive.

10. RATTIGAN, W.H. "Hugo Grotius" in *Great Jurists of the World*, (edd. J. MacDonnell and E. Manson, John Murray, 1913), 169: an account of Grotius's life and career is given. The principal contentions of *De Jure Belli ac Pacis* are explained as part of his contribution to juristic thinking.

11. HOBBES, T. *Leviathan*, (ed. M. Oakeshott, Basil Blackwell, Oxford, 1960): the text provides the uncompromising Hobbesian version of the social contract. The editor in his introduction analyses Hobbes's thesis and relates it to philosophical and political thought. He believes, incidentally, that Hegel achieved harmony of reason and will.

1. BROWN, J.M. "A Note on Professor Oakeshott's Introduction to the Leviathan" (1953), 1 Pol S, 53: Oakeshott's analysis of Hobbes is criticised on a number of important points and should be read as a corrective to Oakeshott's Introduction.

2. BALOGH, E. "Note on Thomas Hobbes" in *Interpretations of Modern Legal Philosophies*, (ed. P. Sayre, Oxford University Press, New York, 1947), chap. 2: Hobbes's work is considered in relation to psychology and legal theory. He is said to represent a reaction against both the Reformation and Renaissance. Freedom of conscience had brought men to anarchy.

3. de MONTMORENCY, J.E.G. "Thomas Hobbes" in *Great Jurists of the World*, (edd. J. MacDonnell and E. Manson, John Murray, 1913), 195: the line of argument of the *Leviathan* is explained. This is followed by an assessment of Hobbes as a lawyer and jurist.

4. CAMPBELL, E. "Thomas Hobbes and the Common Law", (1958), 1 Tasm LR, 20: the views of Hobbes, not on political theory, but on the common law are explained, in particular his equation of "civil law" with natural law. From his basic norm of the need for self-preservation, he was led to the need for civil society, a determinate superior therein and for civil law to be the command of this superior. He has to translate natural law into positive law. The judges, who are the agents of the superior, should therefore apply natural law where necessary.

5. LOCKE, J. *Two Treatises of Government*, (ed. P. Laslett, Cambridge University Press, 1964): Book I is a refutation of Filmer's view of sovereign power. Book II contains Locke's theory of state and government. The editor's Introduction is important as providing a background to Locke's work and explaining its relation to that of Hobbes.

6. HAMILTON, W.H. "Property – According to Locke" (1931–32), 41 Yale LJ, 864: the connection between Locke's view of "property" and the decision of the United States Supreme Court in *Adkins v. Childrens' Hospital* (1923), 261 US, 525, is considered. The use that has been made of Locke's doctrine in America is explained.

7. POLLOCK, F. *Essays in the Law*, (Macmillan & Co, Ltd, 1922), chap. 3: the background to Locke's *Civil Government* is examined and the views of Locke and Hobbes on the social contract are compared.

8. *Southern Methodist University Studies in Jurisprudence*, (ed. A.L. Harding, SMU Press), II, (1955), chap. 2: the theory of Locke is outlined.

9. ROUSSEAU, J-J. *Contrat Social*, (Garnier Freres, Paris): the well-known theory is set out, in French, from p. 239 onwards.

10. GOUGH, J.W. *The Social Contract*, (2nd ed. Oxford, 1957): the origins and various interpretations of the social contract are examined. As a historical explanation of government, the theory has been irretrievably discredited; as an explanation of political obligation it imports a relationship analogous to contract.

11. FRIEDMANN, W. *Legal Theory*, (5th ed. Stevens & Sons, Ltd, 1967), chaps. 7–14: the first of these chapters deals generally with the functions which natural law theory has fulfilled. It is followed by a discussion of the various stages and forms of natural law thought.

1. JONES, J.W. *Historical Introduction to the Theory of Law*, (Oxford, Clarendon Press, 1940), chap. 4: the idea of a law of nature is ascribed to the belief that there are certain principles inherent in the scheme of things. The survey includes a fairly lengthy discussion of the work of Cicero, the Roman period, the Middle Ages and modern natural law thought.

2. BODENHEIMER, E. *Jurisprudence*, (Harvard University Press, 1962), chaps. 1–4, 9–14: in the first four chapters and chapter 9 there are accounts of the theories of philosophers and writers from Greek times down to the present. The other chapters deal more generally with the need for order and justice and with law as the means of achieving these. In chapter 12 there is a discussion of the validity of the unjust law.

3. VINOGRADOFF, P. *Common-sense in Law*, (3rd ed. H.G. Hanbury, Oxford University Press, 1959), chap. 9: rules have a two-fold justification – as authoritative commands and as reasonable propositions. There is an account of the work of the Greeks, Romans and early Churchmen. The influence of naturalist thought on English case-law is dealt with at some length.

4. POUND, R. *An Introduction to the Philosophy of Law*, (Yale University Press, 1922), chaps. 1–2: this is a highly readable account of the various functions which legal philosophy has fulfilled through the ages, natural law in particular. The swing of the paramount social need from power to freedom is brought out.

5. FRIEDRICH, C.J. *The Philosophy of Law in Historical Perspective*, (The University of Chicago Press, 1958), chaps. 1–10, 12–13, 19: various theories of law are explained from the time of the Old Testament and the Greeks down to the present. Throughout the book the underlying theme is that an unjust law is not "law".

6. RUSSELL, B. *History of Western Philosophy*, (Allen & Unwin, Ltd, 1946): although this is not written from a juristic point of view, it is most useful for reference, for it gives a good picture of the movements in philosophical thought.

7. BOWLE, J. *Western Political Thought*, (Oxford University Press, New York, 1948): this provides a careful examination of philosophic thought from the earliest times down to Rousseau.

8. SABINE, G.H. *A History of Political Theory*, (3rd ed., Harrap & Co, Ltd, 1963), Parts I–II: Part I deals with the views of Plato, Aristotle and the Stoics and their influence on Christian theory; Part II deals with the Christian concepts of church and state.

9. CARLYLE, R.W. and CARLYLE, A.J. *A History of Medieval Political Theory in the West*, (3rd ed., Blackwood & Sons, Ltd, 1930–36), I, chaps. 3 and 9; II, Part I, chap. 3, Part II, chap. 3; III, Part II, chap. 1; V, Part I, chaps. 2 and 4: this monumental work need only be used for general reference.

10. CAIRNS, H. *Legal Philosophy from Plato to Hegel*, (John Hopkins Press, 1949): convenient accounts are given of the juristic contributions of some of the great thinkers of history.

11. HERON, D.C. *An Introduction to the History of Jurisprudence*, (J.W. Parker & Son, 1860), Parts II–V: accounts are given of a large number of writers from Greek and Roman times down to the 19th century German philosophers.

1. MILLER, W.M. *The Data of Jurisprudence*, (Green & Sons, 1903), chap. 6: the aim of law is considered with reference to justice, equity, reason, morality, etc. These ideas are correlated with reference to the works of writers throughout the ages.

2. LLOYD, D. *The Idea of Law*, (Penguin Books, Ltd, A 688, 1964), chaps. 1 and 4: the first chapter considers generally views about the part played by Law, which derive from assumptions about the nature of Man – that Man is evil and Law is a means of curbing his passions; that Man is good but became spoiled through sin, so Law is an instrument for realising the goal of his good impulses; that Man is good, but his social environment is responsible for his condition, so Law as an institution of society is a bad thing. Chapter 4 reviews ideas about natural law from the Greek philosophers down to modern versions.

3. OLIVECRONA, K. *Law as Fact*, (2nd ed. Stevens & Sons, Ltd, 1971), chap. 1: Natural law and positivism are compared. From pp. 8–50 naturalist thinking from Grotius to the present day is reviewed.

4. FINCH, J.D. *Introduction to Legal Theory*, (2nd ed. Sweet & Maxwell, Ltd, 1974), pp. 21–45: the law of nature amounts to asserting that what naturally is, ought to be, and also that it ought morally to be so. A very brief account is given of the views of the Greeks, Cicero, Aquinas, Grotius, Hobbes and Blackstone. It also includes reference to the 18th century positivist assault on natural law theory.

5. DIETZE, G. *Two Concepts of the Rule of Law*, (Liberty Fund Inc, 1973): the back and forth swing of the pendulum throughout history, at one period towards a power structure and then towards freedom from power, is illustrated with reference to the movements in 19th and 20th century Germany.

6. VEITCH, E. "Justice at the End of its Tether" [1973], PL, 45: this gives a detailed account of an Ugandan Inquiry into the disappearance of two men and of the way in which governmental power was exercised to thwart a proper finding.

7. MORRIS, C. *The Great Legal Philosophers*, (University of Pennsylvania Press, 1959), chaps. 1–10, 19: extracts are given from the works of Aristotle, Cicero, Aquinas, Grotius, Hobbes, Locke, Montesquieu, Hume, Rousseau, Kant and Dabin.

8. HALL, J. *Readings in Jurisprudence*, (The Bobbs-Merrill Co, 1938), chaps. 1 and 3: the extracts include some from Aristotle, Cicero, Aquinas, Maine, St. German and Stammler. Chapter 3 deals with transcendental idealism.

9. LLOYD, D. *Introduction to Jurisprudence*, (3rd ed., Stevens & Sons, Ltd, 1972), chap. 3: natural law theory has served to preserve the status quo as well as inspire revolution. A brief survey of its history is given. In addition to selected extracts from various writers there are portions of the United States Constitution and of judgments in decided cases.

10. COHEN, M.R. and COHEN, F.S. *Readings in Jurisprudence and Legal Philosophy*, (Prentice-Hall Inc, 1951), chaps. 5, 9 and 10: not all the extracts in chapter 5 are concerned with natural law, but there are portions of Aristotle, Cicero, Aquinas, St. German, Coke, Hobbes and Blackstone. Chapter 9 includes, *inter alia*, passages from Kant and Stammler. Chapter 10 deals with law and metaphysics.

4. Power

Development and Nature of Sovereignty

1. MAITLAND, F.W. *The Constitutional History of England*, (Cambridge University Press, 1908), pp. 251–275, 281–288, 297–301, 330–336, 381–382: this is quite the best account of the historical struggle between Parliament and the prerogative for supreme legislative power.

2. DICEY, A.V. *The Law of the Constitution*, (10th ed., by E.C.S. Wade; London, Macmillan & Co, Ltd, 1961), chaps. 1 and 13: the classic exposition of Parliamentary supremacy is to be found in these chapters, including the contention that Parliamentary sovereignty favours the rule of law and *vice versa*.

3. WADE, E.C.S. Introduction to A.V. Dicey, *The Law of the Constitution*, (*supra*), pp. xxxiv–xcvi: this is an essential corrective to and a modernisation of Dicey's views. There is a full discussion of the relationship between Parliament and the courts with the conclusion that the courts cannot control legislative procedure. There is also a discussion of the position in Commonwealth countries.

4. ALLEN, C.K. *Law in the Making*, (7th ed., Oxford, 1964), pp. 426–469: this is a general account, including a discussion of possible limitations on the power of Parliament, the scope and duration of legislation, and an explanation of "codifying" and "consolidating" statutes.

5. McILWAIN, C.H. *The High Court of Parliament and its Supremacy*, (Yale University Press, 1910), chaps. 2, 3 and 5: the part played by the idea of a "fundamental law" in early times is recounted, and how Parliamentary sovereignty developed. He stresses that originally the legislative functions of the "High Court of Parliament" were not distinct from its judicial functions, and demonstrates that the evolution of the current doctrine of Parliamentary sovereignty was the unhistorical result of strife, not of growth.

6. BARRACLOUGH, G. "Law and Legislation in Medieval England", (1940), 56 LQR, 75: this points out that the developments between the 13th and 15th centuries ultimately determined the issue in the struggle for legislative power. It is when certain processes came to be reserved for different types of royal activities that it became possible to distinguish between the legislative, judicial and executive functions.

7. WINFIELD, P.H. *The Chief Sources of English Legal History*, (Harvard University Press, 1925), pp. 71–74, 84 *et seq.*: this account of ancient statutes shows how judges as well as the Council and Parliament occasionally had a hand in their making.

8. LUCAS, W.W. "The Co-operative Nature of English Sovereignty", (1910), 26 LQR, 54, 247, 349: this detailed inquiry, beginning with Teutonic and Anglo-Saxon times, shows that the king never had ruled entirely on his own.

9. HOLDSWORTH, W.S. *A History of English Law*, (Methuen & Co, Ltd), II, pp. 435–446: this gives an account of how the idea developed that the king should consult others when legislating, and the results of this development are considered.

44

1. HOLDSWORTH, W.S. *Sources and Literature of English Law*, (Oxford, 1925), chap. 2: he makes the important point that although in medieval times the law was regarded as being fundamental, there was never a doctrine that Parliament could not alter the law; the most that lawyers might do was to disregard an Act which violated fundamental law. He also shows how originally the manner and form of legislating was uncertain, and how in the 14th and 15th centuries these began to be clarified; and the effect of this development is considered.

2. MARSHALL, G. *Parliamentary Sovereignty and the Commonwealth*, (Oxford, 1957), chap. 5: this gives a detailed historical review of the doctrine of Parliamentary sovereignty and limitations thereon.

3. WINTERTON, G. "The British *Grundnorm*: Parliamentary Supremacy Re-examined", (1976), 92 LQR, 591: this is an interesting and useful review of the history of Parliamentary supremacy, the abdication of sovereignty by Parliament and judicial review of legislation. Of especial interest are the three interpretations of Parliamentary supremacy at p. 597.

4. DIKE, C. "The Case against Parliamentary Sovereignty", (1976), PL, 283: the author challenges Dicey's classic view and contends that the authorities on which he relied do not support his thesis. It is further contended that a doctrine of absolute sovereignty has not yet been conclusively established in Britain.

5. QUEKETT, A.S. "The Action of Parliamentary Sovereignty upon Local Government", (1919), 35 LQR, 163: this is only of general interest as showing how Parliament has recast executive action in this sphere.

6. McILWAIN, C.H. *Constitutionalism and the Changing World*, (Cambridge University Press, 1939), chaps. 2–3: sovereignty is a juristic concept and has no application outside law. This is a general discussion, which includes the views of a wide range of writers.

7. COHEN, H.E. *Recent Theories of Sovereignty*, (University of Chicago Press, 1937): the views of various modern writers are considered. At the end of the book the contradictory tendencies today and the future of theories on sovereignty are touched on.

8. GIERKE, O. *Political Theories of the Middle Age*, (trans. F.W. Maitland, Cambridge University Press, 1900), chaps. 5, 6 and pp. 92–93: the germ of sovereignty arose in the 12th century. The idea of popular sovereignty in State and Church is traced, and beginnings of modern sovereignty are touched on at the end.

9. MERRIAM, C.E. *History of the Theory of Sovereignty since Rousseau*, (The Columbia University Press, 1900): this is a useful reference work. The theories of various writers are considered, and the general development of ideas on sovereignty is considered at the end.

10. POLLOCK, F. *An Introduction to the History of the Science of Politics*, (Macmillan & Co, 1895), chap. 4: doctrines of sovereignty are considered in the course of a discussion of political theory.

11. BRYCE, J. *Studies in History and Jurisprudence*, (Oxford, 1901), I, pp. 206–207: this argues that even an Act of Parliament which embodies the constitution in a fundamental statute can itself be repealed.

1. HICKS, J.C. "The Liar Paradox in Legal Reasoning", (1971), 29 CLJ, 275: the statement, "All Cretans are liars", propounded by a Cretan, has similarities in the doctrine of precedent and Parliamentary sovereignty. The problem of how far Parliament can bind itself is considered against this background.

2. POLLOCK, F. *A First Book of Jurisprudence*, (6th ed., Macmillan & Co, Ltd, 1929), Part II, chap. 3: this is an orthodox exposition of Parliamentary sovereignty, including a distinction between legal sovereignty and political power.

3. SALMOND, J.W. *Jurisprudence*, (12th ed., P.J. Fitzgerald, Sweet & Maxwell, Ltd, 1966), pp. 115–130: a general account is given of legislation.

Control of Power

4. BLACKSTONE, W. *Commentaries on the Laws of England*, (16th ed., J.T. ... ... Coleridge, T. Cadell and J. Butterworth & Son, 1825), I, pp. 90–91, 160–161: although he talks of statute being void if it is impossible, absurd or contrary to reason, he adds that he knows of no power to control it. He also makes the point that the consent of the King, Lords and Commons are all necessary to constitute a valid statute.

5. STEPHEN, J.F. *Commentaries on the Laws of England*, (21st ed., L.C. Warmington, Butterworth & Co, Ltd, 1950), III, pp. 288–291: this is a brief discussion of what the sovereignty of Parliament means and how it might become a danger to the supremacy of law.

6. MacDERMOTT, J.C. *Protection from Power under English Law*, (Hamlyn Lectures, Stevens & Sons, Ltd, 1957), chap. 3: there is no fundamental rule to which the British Parliament has to conform. There is a discussion of how the dangers consequent upon this might be controlled.

7. BARTLETT, C.A.H. "The Sovereignty of the People", (1921), 37 LQR, 497: this is a general discussion of the influence of the people on the origin of sovereignty: (cf. the doctrine of mandate).

8. MARSHALL, G. *Parliamentary Sovereignty and the Commonwealth*, (Oxford, 1957), chaps. 2–4: these chapters contain a discussion of the Austinian idea of sovereignty, with special reference to illimitability of sovereign power, and the power of judicial review, including the rule as to manner and form of legislating and the enrolled bill rule.

9. BENTHAM, J. *A Fragment on Government*, in *Works*, (ed. J. Bowring, William Tait, Edinburgh, 1843), I, p. 283 *et seq*: this is a comment on Blackstone; but he makes the important point that the supreme governor's authority is indefinite unless limited by express convention. Any excess of it would not then be acceptable. He also makes the point that to say that legislation could be held void is to give a controlling power to the judiciary.

10. JENNINGS, W.I. *Parliament*, (2nd ed., Cambridge University Press, 1957), chap. 1: this gives a general introduction to the authority of a statute and of the influence of public opinion on Parliament.

11. HOOD PHILLIPS, O. *Constitutional and Administrative Law*, (4th ed., Sweet & Maxwell, Ltd, 1967), chap. 3: a brief history of the doctrine of Parliamentary

supremacy is provided, and the point is made that it is based on recognition by the people and the courts. There is also a discussion of the limitations on Parliament's power, both from a practical point of view and also with regard to subject-matter and the manner and form of legislating.

1. SIDGWICK, H. *Elements of Politics*, (2nd ed., Macmillan & Co, Ltd, 1897), p. 627: sovereign power may be unlimited in the sense that there is no law which it cannot alter. But the very structure of a supreme legislature may limit its competence, and it may also be so limited by conditions determining its procedure.

2. LASKI, H.J. *A Grammar of Politics*, (4th ed., Allen & Unwin, Ltd, 1938), chap. 2: the evolution of the modern state is analysed historically and there is a discussion of the limitations that exist on sovereignty and need for these.

3. MIDDLETON, K.W.B. "Sovereignty in Theory and Practice", (1952), 64 Jur R, 135: the question what is meant by sovereignty is discussed and the conclusion is reached that sovereignty is not inconsistent with control by law. It is inconsistent with legal subordination to someone else.

4. KEIR, D.L. and LAWSON, F.H. *Cases in Constitutional Law*, (4th ed., Oxford, 1954), pp. 1–8: this is a general account. Elsewhere in the book are extracts from the *Bilston Corporation* case, *Bradlaugh* v. *Gossett*, *Harris* v. *Minister of the Interior* and from the *Statute of Westminster*.

Judicial Control

5. PLUCKNETT, T.F.T. *Statutes and their Interpretation in the First Half of the 14th Century*, (Cambridge University Press, 1922), chaps. 4 and 6: in the first of these chapters there is an inquiry how far the common law was regarded as fundamental law; in the second there is an account of how courts might ignore statutes, but not hold them void.

6. PLUCKNETT, T.F.T. "Bonham's Case and Judicial Review", (1926–27), 40 Harv LR, 30: this demonstrates how Coke, C.J. in *Bonham's* case misrepresented the authorities. These show that statutes had been ignored rather than held void. There is also a detailed account of the extent to which later judges claimed the power of review.

7. PLUCKNETT, T.F.T. *A Concise History of the Common Law*, (5th ed., Butterworth & Co, Ltd, 1956), pp. 318–325, 330–333: these pages provide a valuable general account of the position of legislation from the earliest times, and of the judicial attitude towards it.

8. LEWIS, J.U. "Sir Edward Coke (1552–1633): His Theory of 'Artificial Reason' as a Context for Modern Basic Legal Theory", (1968), 84 LQR, 330: law enjoins obedience by virtue of being reasonable. It was on this basis that he argued in *Bonham's Case* that even Acts of Parliament, which offend common right and reason, could be avoided. Reason is not "natural reason", but "artificial perfection of reason, gotten by long study". Coke's views, it is said, enabled English Law to modernise itself for the future.

9. BERGER, R. "*Doctor Bonham's Case*: Statutory Construction or Constitutional Theory?" (1969), 117 U Pa LR, 521: what did Coke mean when he showed a

readiness to avoid a statute which was "against reason"? Was he simply interpreting a statute, or propounding a doctrine of judicial review? The author considers the use that has been made of Coke's utterance, and he himself believes that by this phrase Coke meant "against natural law".

1. THORNE, S.E. "Dr. Bonham's Case", (1938), 54 LQR, 543: this is a detailed discussion of the case to show that Coke, C.J. was perhaps only refusing to follow a statute which was absurd on the face of it on the ground of repugnancy. His authorities certainly supported no doctrine of a higher law by virtue of which statutes could be held void.

2. THORNE, S.E. Introduction to *A Discourse upon the Exposicion & Understandinge of Statutes, with Sir T. Egerton's Additions*, (Huntington Lib., 1942), pp. 85–92: *Bonham's* case is further discussed and the disappearance of the medieval idea is outlined.

3. GOUGH, J.W. *Fundamental Law in English Constitutional History*, (Oxford, 1955), chaps. 3 and 6: this discussion of *Bonham's* case seeks to show that to "adjudge a statute void" meant only to interpret it strictly so that the case falls outside it. In the second chapter there is an account of the development of Parliamentary sovereignty in the 17th century.

4. HAVIGHURST, A.F. "The Judiciary and Politics in the Reign of Charles II", (1950), 66 LQR, 62, 229; "James II and the Twelve Men in Scarlet", (1953), 69 LQR, 522: both these discuss the attitude of the judges during the Restoration period.

5. KEETON, G.W. "The Judiciary and the Constitutional Struggle, 1660–1688", (1962), 7 JSPTL (NS), 56: the judges, though not subservient, upheld the prerogative, but even they were not prepared to support all James II's claims. (See also G.W. KEETON, "Judge Jeffreys as Chief Justice of Chester, 1680–83", (1961), 77 LQR, 36).

6. LEDERMAN, W.R. "The Independence of Judiciary", (1956), 34 Can BR, 769, 1139: the first part traces the relation between the Crown and the judges from early times down to the present. The second part deals with the position in Canada.

7. BRAZIER, M. "Judicial immunity and the Independence of the Judiciary", (1976), PL, 397: the extent of the immunities of different kinds of judges is examined at length, and also the power of removal. It is argued that if High Court judges enjoy wide immunity while acting within their jurisdiction, then checks on them need to be strengthened. But there is danger in giving politicians uncontrolled power of removal.

8. HEWART, G. *The New Despotism*, (Ernest Benn, Ltd, 1929): in this well-known book the Lord Chief Justice of England protested against the increasing powers of the executive and the consequent danger to the liberties of the individual and the "rule of law".

1. JOWELL, J. "The Legal Control of Administrative Discretion", (1973), PL, 178: this is a careful inquiry into the pros and cons of using law. There are some kinds of problems which are not susceptible to legal control, but on the other hand the use of law has benefit which should be considered. The question whether administrative processes might be "judicialised" is also examined.

2. GALLIGAN, D.J. "The Nature and Function of Policies within Discretionary Power", (1976), PL, 332: discretion entails power to make policy choices. A coherent and consistent set of guidelines to achieve ends in view can be evolved. The crucial conflict is between the interest of the policy decision-maker and that of the individual in obtaining discretionary recognition of his claim. The way in which there may be legal restraints on the content of policies is also considered.

3. FERNANDO, T.S. "Are the Maintenance of the Rule of Law and the Ensuring of Human Rights possible in a Developing Society?", (1968), 2 Malayan LJ, iii: a former Chief Justice of Ceylon and President of the International Commission of Jurists points out that the Rule of Law establishes a certain relation between the state and the individual. Colonies used to regard self-government as preferable even to good government; but once they attained independence it was realised that the best government is government under the law. Developing countries encounter many threats: non-democratic political parties, distrust of law, nationalism, etc. The problem is to preserve the independence of the judiciary and respect for human rights.

4. RAJAH, A.P. "The Role of Law and Lawyers in a Developing Society", (1975), 1 Malayan LJ, xxi: law not only defines the structure and nature of government, but it is also the instrument of government. Lawyers have not concerned themselves sufficiently with the problems of developing countries. It is important that the Rule of Law should keep pace with change. The extent of power and duty must be determined by law, i.e., the courts; the defence of state necessity should be abolished; the absolute power to change law should lie with Parliament. The lawyers' function is to preserve the Rule of Law. It is important that the working of the law should be explained to the public.

5. RAZ, J. "The Rule of Law and its Virtue", (1977), 93 LQR, 195: government is at bottom composed of people. All people should be ruled by law and obey it, and they should be able to be guided by it. Eight principles are offered as controlling the use of law; these will not prevent some bad uses of law, but will minimise them. Rule of law is a negative virtue. It is to be contrasted with arbitrary power, and it should protect individual freedom and respect for human dignity.

6. SCHREINER, O.D. *The Contribution of English Law to South African Law; and the Rule of Law in South Africa*, (Hamlyn Lectures, Stevens & Sons, Ltd, 1967): in the second part it is contended that South Africa is under the rule of law in the sense that no one is made to suffer in body or goods except for a breach of law established in the ordinary courts (Dicey). The argument fails to distinguish between "rule *by* law", where law is used as an instrument of power, and "rule *of* law", where law is used to check power.

7. DODD, W.F. "Political Safeguards and Judicial Guarantees", (1915), 15 Col LR, 293: the various ways in which the judiciary controls legislation in the United States are discussed.

8. McWHINNEY, E. *Judicial Review in the English-speaking World*, (2nd ed., University of Toronto Press, 1960), chaps. 2, 6 and 10: this general account

begins with Dicey's view of the limits on Parliamentary power; and there is also a discussion of Parliamentary sovereignty and the role of the judiciary.

1. ROSTOW, E.V. "The Democratic Character of Judicial Review", (1952–53), 66 Harv LR, 193: the power of judicial review is essential. He examines the matter primarily from the American angle.

2. DIETZE, G. "America and Europe – Decline and Emergence of Judicial Review", (1958), 44 Vir LR, 1233: reprinted in (1959), 76 SALJ, 398: this historical account shows how the power of judicial review is essential to the freedom of the individual.

Manner and Form

3. JENNINGS, W.I. *The Law and the Constitution*, (5th ed., University of London Press, Ltd, 1959), chap. 4: this includes a discussion of the conclusiveness of the Parliamentary roll and the argument that the legislature can bind itself to observe a particular manner and form for legislating.

4. WADE, H.W.R. "The Basis of Legal Sovereignty", (1955), CLJ, 172: this develops the argument that Parliament cannot bind itself to observe a particular manner and form for legislating because of the unalterable rule that the courts will always apply the latest statute.

5. LLOYD, W.H. "Pylkington's Case and its Successors", (1921), 69 U Pa LR, 20: this discusses how far the observance of the requirements of a statute may be insisted upon by the courts and how far the enrolment of a statute is conclusive.

6. HEUSTON, R.F.V. "Sovereignty" in *Oxford Essays in Jurisprudence*, (ed. A.G. Guest, Oxford University Press, 1961), chap. 7: the rules regulating the composition and functioning of the sovereign are anterior to it. The courts may question the validity of a statute on grounds of composition or procedure, but not on the area of statutory power.

7. HART, H.L.A. *The Concept of Law*, (Oxford, 1961, reprinted, 1975), chaps. 4, 6 and pp. 144–150: this book should be read as a whole; but relevant to the present topic the point is made that legislative authority rests on the acceptance of a rule giving the sovereign the right to give orders and that this is an ultimate rule. Requirements as to manner and form are not limitations on sovereign power. There is also some discussion of Commonwealth problems and how far Parliament can be bound.

8. SWINTON, K. "Challenging the Validity of an Act of Parliament: the Effect of Enrollment and Parliamentary Privilege" (1976), 14 Os HLJ, 345: the judicial power to challenge Acts of Parliament is considered in detail in relation to the enrollment rule and Parliamentary privilege. Enrollment protects some Acts, but not those showing error on their face. This rule is only evidentiary and hence unrelated to Parliamentary sovereignty, which concerns substance. Privilege entitles Parliament to control its own internal proceedings, but courts may still decide whether a matter is within privilege.

9. FULLER, L.L. *The Morality of Law*, (Revised ed., Yale University Press, 1969), pp. 113–17: parliamentary supremacy is considered with special reference to Dicey's classic discussion of it. The point is also made that Parliament only attains its superior position by subjecting itself to the law of its own internal procedure.

1. GRAY, J.C. *The Nature and Sources of the Law*, (2nd ed., R. Gray, The Macmillan Co. of New York, 1921), pp. 74 *et seq*, 152–158, 161–170, 189–197: where sovereignty is vested in a collection of people, such persons are combined for action according to rules and will be obeyed only while they act in accordance with them. There is also a general discussion of the nature of statute and whether publication is a constitutive fact. The last section deals with desuetude and unrepealability.

2. DODD, W.F. "Judicially Non-enforceable Provisions of Constitutions", (1932), 80 U Pa LR, 54: this contains a discussion of the limitations relating to manner and form and those embodied in the text of a constitution as applied in the United States.

3. ROSS, A. *On Law and Justice*, (Stevens & Sons, Ltd, 1958), pp. 78–84: an enactment has force of law only if it has been made in conformity with the proper procedure and within its sphere of competence. A change in the ultimate authority is a purely social-psychological fact lying outside the province of the law.

4. GRANT, J.A.C. "Judicial Control of Legislative Procedure in California", (1948–49), 1 Stan LR, 428: this is of general interest. It deals with the situation that arose in California in 1925 when the courts declined to challenge a statute on the ground that it was for the legislature to determine whether a bill had been properly passed or not.

On the points raised in the Prince of Hanover's *case, the following might be consulted:*

5. PARRY, C. Note on the Decision at First Instance in [1955] CLJ, 142: attention is drawn to the possible effect of the Royal Marriages Act, 1772.

6. NOTE in (1956), 72 LQR, 5: this comments on the Court of Appeal's decision.

7. FARRAN, C.D'O. "An Unusual Claim to British Nationality", (1956), 19 MLR, 289: the Court of Appeal's decision is approved.

8. PARRY, C. "Further Considerations upon the Prince of Hanover's Case", (1956), 5 ICLQ, 61: the questions involved in the Court of Appeal's decision are examined in detail.

9. SMITH, T.B. "British Nationality and the Union of 1707", (1956), SLT, 89: this note on the Court of Appeal's decision, draws attention to the possible effect on the Act of Anne of the Act of Union, 1707.

10. SMITH, T.B. *Studies Critical and Comparative*, (W. Green & Son, Ltd, 1962), pp. 24–27: this is a brief discussion of the question in the light of the decision in the House of Lords.

11. MITCHELL, J.D.B. "The Unimportance of the Case of Prince Ernest", (1957), 20 MLR, 270: this note on the decision of the House of Lords discusses principally what influence the Act of Union, 1707, would have had on the case, and the effect of disregarding the question.

12. PARRY, C. Note on the Decision of the House of Lords in [1957], CLJ, 1.

Written Constitutions

1. CORWIN, E.S. "The 'Higher Law' Background of American Constitutional Law", (1928–29), 42 Harv LR, 149, 365: higher law from an American point of view is discussed.

2. ABRAHAM, H.J. *The Judicial Process*, (3rd ed., New York and Oxford University Press, 1976), chaps. 7–9: the power of the Supreme Court of the United States to declare Acts void is explained, the arguments for and against it are set out, and the part which such a power should play is considered. This account is useful in providing a contrast with the position in Great Britain.

3. LOVELL, C.R. "The Growth of Judicial Review in the United States", (1955), BSALR, 107: it is maintained that the power of review in America had no constitutional basis and developed apart from the Constitution because it was inherent in the form of government.

4. BUCHANAN, G.S. "Judicial Supremacy Re-examined: a Proposed Alternative" (1971–72), 70 Mich LR, 1279: judicial control is ineffective if it is unenforceable. The question is whether decisions of the American Supreme Court should be regarded as obligatory *per se*, or only if supported by another branch of the federal system. Four matters should be considered: fidelity to the wording of the Constitution, predictability of reaction to the Court's construction, generous opportunity for political endeavour and an approximation of legal obligation to the realities of political power. To satisfy these, some compromise is needed.

5. HAINES, C.G. "Judicial Review of Legislation in Canada", (1914–15), 28 Harv LR, 565: judicial review in Canada and America is considered historically. This comparative examination is especially interesting on the view taken of the function of the Judicial Committee of the Privy Council.

6. CAHILL, F.V. *Judicial Legislation*, (The Ronald Press Co, New York, 1952), chap. 3: the power of judicial review in America is explained in detail.

7. BARNETT, J.D. "External Evidence of the Constitutionality of Statutes", (1924), 58 Am LR, 88: this considers, with reference to America, how the courts inform themselves as to the facts behind the law.

8. HIEMSTRA, V.C. "Constitutions of Liberty" (1971), 88 SALJ, 45: this is a comparison of the American and German constitutions on the entrenchment of liberty.

9. DAHRENDORF, R. "A Confusion of Powers: Politics and the Rule of Law" (1977), 40 MLR, 1: in Germany where there are legal institutions explicitly charged with guarding the borderline between basic certainties and political variables, problems arise which concern law and politics – confusion of powers. In Britain where politics are unfettered by codified rules, the separation of powers leaves a gap which has to be filled by judicial rather than by political institutions. The desirability of constitutional limitations, or otherwise, needs to be considered against this background.

10. DICKINSON, J. *Administrative Justice and the Supremacy of Law in the United States*, (Harvard University Press, 1927), especially chaps. 2, 4 and 5: this is of general interest as showing the position in America.

1. FINKELSTEIN, M. "Judicial Self-limitation", (1923–24), 37 Harv LR, 338: "Further Notes on Judicial Self-limitation", (1925–26), 39 Harv LR, 221: the reluctance of judges themselves to interfere in "political questions" is investigated.

2. KAGZI, M.C.J. "Unamendability of a Bill of Rights. A Norm of the Indian Constitutional Jurisprudence", (1971), PL, 205: this article is devoted mainly to a consideration of the implications of *Golak Nath* v. *State of Punjab*, [1967] 2 SCR, 762, in which it was held that the part of the Indian Constitution dealing with a Bill of Rights was unamendable by statute.

3. JACONELLI, J. "The European Convention on Human Rights – the Text of a British Bill of Rights?" (1976), PL, 226: this considers whether the Convention might provide a basis for an United Kingdom Bill of Rights. The various implications of such a step are dealt with.

4. LLOYD, D. "Do we Need a Bill of Rights?", (1976), 39 MLR, 1: a Bill of Rights would have overriding authority over other laws with power in the judiciary to invalidate legislation repugnant to it. This will mean placing judges in a political arena, and many of them would not welcome it. The democratic process of Parliament is better suited to deciding questions of values and conscience than the judicial process, which is geared to fact-finding and deciding rights and wrongs.

5. MILNE, A.J.M. "'Should we have a Bill of Rights?'", (1977), 40 MLR, 389: the basis of human rights is that if we acknowledge fellow human beings, the idea of "fellowship" implies certain universal moral obligations. But as long as the present doctrine of Parliamentary sovereignty exists, there would be no point in having a Bill of Rights, since Parliament could always suspend the Bill when it would be most needed. The article begins with a detailed reply to the arguments against a Bill of Rights advanced by Lloyd.

6. SILKIN, S.C. "The Rights of Man and the Rule of Law", (1977), 28 NILQ, 3: the European Convention for the Protection of Human Rights and Fundamental Freedoms 1950 is a limitation on national sovereignty in that it gives other states a chance to scrutinise how any signatory state safeguards the rights of its citizens. The author considers whether machinery under it could be improved by a reinforcing domestic Bill of Rights; and the effect that domestic devolution might have on Britain's responsibility under the Convention.

7. PESCATORE, P. "The Protection of Human Rights in the European Communities", (1972), 9 CMLR, 73: it is possible to ensure protection of human rights by judicial means even without a declaration of rights. It depends on their being a system of legal redress and a suitably minded judiciary.

8. ZANDER, M. *A Bill of Rights?* (Barry Rose (Publishers), Ltd, 1975): the author gives twelve arguments in favour and fifteen against a Bill of Rights. He considers the setting up of a Human Rights Commission to receive petitions and a Citizen's Rights Commission to investigate and litigate if necessary. He also considers the feasibility of incorporating the European Convention or enacting a new Bill of Rights. The question of entrenchment is avoided. Instead, he thinks a Bill of Rights would act as a brake on legislation, create a presumption that statutes are not intended to contravene its provisions, there should be power to declare void legislation prior to the Bill, and there should be appropriate judicial remedies.

Problems Involving the Union with Scotland and Ireland

1. MARSHALL, G. "What is Parliament? The Changing Concept of Parliamentary Sovereignty", (1954), 2 Pol S, 193: *MacCormick's* case is considered in the light of the position as regards the Commonwealth. The Parliament which can legislate for the United Kingdom is not the Parliament which, after the Statute of Westminster, can legislate for the Dominions. Similarly, the United Kingdom Parliament is not the body that can alter the Treaty of Union.

2. MARSHALL, G. "Parliamentary Supremacy and the Language of Constitutional Limitation", [1955], 67 Jur R, 62: Parliamentary supremacy is discussed with reference to the composition of legislative bodies and methods of functioning.

3. MIDDLETON, K.W.B. "New Thoughts on the Union between England and Scotland", [1954], 66 Jur R, 37: Lord Cooper's dicta in *MacCormick's* case are considered in detail, together with the hypothesis on which the Treaty of Union is to be regarded as a fundamental law.

4. SMITH, T.B. "Two Scots Cases", (1953), 69 LQR, pp. 512–516: this section deals with *MacCormick's* case and considers whether Parliament is competent to alter the Treaty of Union.

5. SMITH, T.B. *British Justice: the Scottish Contribution*, (Stevens & Sons, Ltd, 1961), pp. 201–213: this considers possible fallacies underlying both the Scots and English attitudes towards the Treaty of Union. The Union is more than a treaty and more than ordinary legislation.

6. SMITH, T.B. "The Union of 1707 as Fundamental Law", (1951), PL, 99; *Studies Critical and Comparative*, (W. Green & Son, Ltd, Edinburgh, 1962), chap. 1: this considers the unique nature of the Treaty and the power of the courts when a statute violates its terms.

7. SMITH, T.B. *The United Kingdom*, (Stevens & Sons, Ltd, 1955), pp. 641–650: these pages give a brief account of the significance and implications of the Union and a short discussion of *MacCormick's* case.

8. DICEY, A.V. and RAIT, R.S. *Thoughts on the Scottish Union*, (Macmillan & Co, Ltd, 1920), pp. 19–23, 242–243: Dicey here modifies to some extent the extreme position which he had adopted previously on the sovereignty of Parliament.

9. ANSON, W.R. "The Government of Ireland Bill and the Sovereignty of Parliament", (1886), 2 LQR, 427: it is argued that the Bill amounted to an impairment of the sovereignty of Parliament.

10. JOHNSTON, W.J. "The English Legislature and the Irish Courts", (1924), 40 LQR, 91: this is of general interest. It consists of a historical account of the relations between the two bodies.

Problems Involving the Commonwealth

11. MARSHALL, G. *Parliamentary Sovereignty and the Commonwealth*, (Oxford, 1957), chaps. 6–11: these deal with the history of the Statute of Westminster, and are

followed by detailed discussions of the position with reference to each of the Dominions. The final chapter contains a fully documented account of the South African crisis.

1. JENNINGS, W.I. *Constitutional Laws of the Commonwealth*, (3rd ed., Oxford, 1957), extracts from the relevant cases are set out, including *Trethowan's* case, *Krause* v. *Commissioners for Inland Revenue, Moore* v. *Att.-Gen. for the Irish Free State, British Coal Corp.* v. *R., Ndlwana* v. *Hofmeyer N.O.*, and some of the South African "crisis" cases (*infra*, pp. 57–60); the effect of the Statute of Westminster is also discussed.

2. LATHAM, R.T.E. "The Law and the Commonwealth", in W.K. HANCOCK: *Survey of British Commonwealth Affairs*, (Oxford University Press, 1937), pp. 522–95, (reproduced in facsimile in 1949): where the sovereign is any but a single person, the designation of the sovereign must include a statement of the rules for the ascertainment of its will and these are logically prior to it. There is a discussion of the position obtaining within each Commonwealth country as at 1937. Of especial interest is the analysis of the position in South Africa and the Irish Free State, Latham was probably the first person to suggest a "local root" for their separate legal systems.

3. KEITH, A.B. *The Government of the British Empire*, (Macmillan & Co, Ltd, 1935), pp. 30–48: these pages contain a general account of the developments leading to the Statute of Westminster.

4. ver LOREN van THEMAAT, H. "The Equality of Status of the Dominions and the Sovereignty of the British Parliament", (1933), 15 JCL, (3rd ser.), 47: the question is discussed what the sovereignty of the British Parliament means, and the conclusion is reached that it is not possible to maintain unlimited sovereignty as well as the equality of the Dominions with Great Britain.

5. DIXON, O. "The Law and the Constitution", (1935), 51 LQR, 590: this discusses the working arrangement that was effected between the supremacy of the Crown, of the Law and of Parliament, and how this has been transplanted overseas. The law prescribes the conditions which have to be fulfilled in making statutes, but on the question what may be accomplished by a statute Parliament is supreme over the law. With regard to the Statute of Westminster he concludes that it has restricted the power of the British Parliament to legislate for the Commonwealth.

6. JENNINGS, W.I. "The Statute of Westminster and Appeals to the Privy Council", (1936), 52 LQR, 173: *British Coal Corp.* v. *R.*, and *Moore* v. *Att.-Gen. for the Irish Free State* are discussed in the light of the Statute of Westminster.

7. McWHINNEY, E. "'Sovereignty' in the United Kingdom and the Commonwealth Countries at the Present Day", (1953), 68 Pol Sc Q, 511: did the Statute of Westminster create Dominion status, or was it only declaratory of a fundamental change that had taken place? The gap between these views is brought out in the South African crisis.

8. OYLER, P.A., KENNEDY, W.P.M. and MacDONALD, V.C. "*British Coal Corporation and Others* v. *The King*: Three Comments", (1935), 13 Can BR, 615: these are three different commentaries on this case.

9. FRIEDMANN, W. "*Trethowan's* Case, Parliamentary Sovereignty, and the Limits

of Legal Change", (1950–51), 24 Aust LJ, 103: the case is examined in detail
and the conclusion is that limitations as to manner and form apply to sovereign
Parliaments as well as to non-sovereign Parliaments. There is also an inquiry into
the extent to which courts will interfere.

1. SAWER, G. "Injunction, Parliamentary Process, and the Restriction of Parliamentary
   Competence", (1944), 60 LQR, 83: the *Bilston Corporation* and *Trethowan*
   cases are compared with reference to the manner and form rule.

2. SAWER, G. in *The Commonwealth of Australia*, (ed. G.W. Paton, Stevens & Sons,
   Ltd, 1952), pp. 38–45: this deals with the constitutional structure and of the
   Colonial Laws Validity Act and of *Trethowan's* case.

3. SAWER, G. "Referendum to Abolish the Upper House in New South Wales", (1961),
   PL, 131: the doctrine that courts do not interfere in the legislative processes has
   a limited operation in the case of controlled constitutions. *Trethowan's* case and
   Clayton v. *Heffron* are compared.

4. GRAY, H. "The Sovereignty of Parliament Today", (1953–54), 10 UTLJ, 54:
   the juridical basis of Parliamentary sovereignty is examined. "Parliament" cannot
   be defined without reference to procedure. Parliament can, therefore, bind itself
   as regards both. The Statute of Westminster cannot be repealed without the
   consent of the Dominions.

5. GRAY, H. "The Sovereignty of the Imperial Parliament", (1960), 23 MLR, 647:
   the manner and form requirement in Section 4 of the Statute of Westminster
   must be complied with before legislation will form part of the law of the
   Dominions. There is a discussion of the *Copyright Owners Reproduction Society*
   case and the conclusion is that English courts should also declare that the
   British Parliament is incompetent to legislate for the Dominions without
   complying with Section 4.

6. BENNION, F.A.R. "Copyright and the Statute of Westminster",(1961), 24 MLR,
   355: this is a reply to H. Gray's article (*supra*) to the extent of pointing out that
   the question whether Section 4 imposes a limitation on the British Parliament
   does not arise in connection with the *Copyright Owners Reproduction Society*
   case.

7. DIXON, O. "The Common Law as an Ultimate Constitutional Foundation",
   (1957–58), 31 Aust. LJ, 240: not only did the common law pre-exist the
   Australian system of government, but it is the source of the doctrine of
   supremacy of the British Parliament. Hence, constitutional issues involving
   Parliamentary supremacy should be resolved in the context of the whole law of
   which the common law forms a part. See also the discussion following the
   paper, at pp. 246–54.

8. HANKS, P.J. "Re-defining the Sovereign: Current Attitudes to Section 4 of the
   Statute of Westminster", (1968), 42 Aust. LJ, 286: the Statute of Westminster
   lays down an essential ingredient for the validity of United Kingdom legislation
   for dominions. Unless its provision are complied with, an enactment is not a
   statute. The dispute between Sir Ivor Jennings and Professor H.W.R. Wade is
   reviewed.

9. MITCHELL, J.D.B. "Sovereignty of Parliament – Yet Again", (1963), 79 LQR, 196

the traditional puzzles concerning the implications of Parliamentary sovereignty are re-examined in the light of Scottish, Irish and Commonwealth experience. The old view of sovereignty is too simple and failed to allow for distinctions which are now needed.

1. KENNEDY, W.P.M. "The Imperial Conferences, 1926–30. The Statute of Westminster" (1932), 48 LQR, 191; *Essays in Constitutional Law*, (Oxford, 1934), chaps. 6 and 7: this gives the background of the Statute of Westminster from a Canadian point of view. The interpretation of the Statute is also discussed, but before any case-law had arisen.

2. LLOYD, D. *Introduction to Jurisprudence*, (3rd ed., Stevens & Sons, Ltd, 1972), chap. 4: the text concerns mainly the Benthamite and Austinian theories. There are extracts from Bentham and Austin and some of the Commonwealth case-law.

On the competence of Dominion and Colonial legislatures to legislate extra-territorially even before the Statute of Westminster, see:

3. SALMOND, J.W. "The Limits of Colonial Legislative Power" (1917), 33 LQR, 117;

4. SMITH, H.A. "Extra-territorial Legislation" (1923), 1 Can BR, 338: and "The Legislative Competence of the Dominions" (1927), 43 LQR, 378;

5. KEITH, A.B. "Notes on Imperial Constitutional Law" (1923), 5 JCL, (3rd ser.), 274–275.

The South African Crisis

6. COWEN, D.V. *Parliamentary Sovereignty and the Entrenched Sections of the South Africa Act*, (Juta & Co, Ltd, 1951); the "entrenched sections" did not depend upon the Colonial Laws Validity Act, 1865, and their continued existence does not impair the sovereignty of the Union Parliament; a detailed discussion of the *Trethowan, Moore* and *Ndlwana* cases is included.

7. COWEN, D.V. "Legislature and Judiciary: I", (1952), 15 MLR, 282: this is a full discussion of the "*Votes*" case and the issues involved. The Statute of Westminster has not impaired the "entrenched sections". "Legislature and Judiciary: II", (1953), 16 MLR, 273: this provides a careful examination of the various issues and arguments that were involved in the conflict.

8. COWEN, D.V. "The Entrenched Sections of the South Africa Act", (1953), 70 SALJ, 243: this explains the origin of the "entrenched clauses", together with a discussion of the cases of *Ndobe* and *Ndlwana*.

9. COWEN, D.V. *The Foundations of Freedom*, (Cape Town and Oxford University Press, 1961), chaps. 6 and 7: this gives a general discussion of constitutional safeguards and the role of the courts, and the pros and cons of the power of judicial review.

10. BEINART, B. "The South African Senate", (1957), 20 MLR, 549: the Senate as originally constituted in the South Africa Act, 1909, and its history down to the Senate Act, 1955, are recounted in detail.

11. BEINART, B. "The South African Appeal Court and Judicial Review", (1958),

21 MLR, 587: there is a similar account of the Appeal Court since 1910 and of the power of review.

1. BEINART, B. "Sovereignty and the Law", (1952), 15 Tydskrif vir Hedensdaagse Romeins-Hollandse Reg, 101: certain rules are logically anterior to legislation and a legislature must comply with them in order to be able to legislate.

2. BEINART, B. "Parliament and the Courts", (1954), BSALR, 134: it is for the courts to ensure that the legislature observes the rules with which it should comply in enacting law. Where there is a specific provision governing the manner and form of legislation, Parliamentary privilege does not exclude the courts when such a provision is designed to protect the interests of the outside community. The whole matter is examined with reference to British Parliamentary development.

3. COWEN, Z. "Parliamentary Sovereignty and the Limits of Legal Change", (1952–53), 26 Aust LJ, 236: this is primarily a discussion of the "*Votes*" case.

4. KEETON, G.W. "The Constitutional Crisis in South Africa", (1953), 6 CLP, 22: the political background is reviewed historically, including a discussion of the cases of *Ndlwana* and *Trethowan* and *Doyle* v. *Att.-Gen. for New South Wales.*

5. GRISWOLD, E.N. "The 'Coloured Vote Case' in South Africa", (1951–52), 65 Harv LR, 1361: this case is discussed in relation to the effect of the Statute of Westminster upon the "entrenched sections".

6. GRISWOLD, E.N. "The Demise of the High Court of Parliament in South Africa", (1952–53), 66 Harv LR, 864: the individual judgments in the Appellate Division, which declared invalid the Act setting up the "High Court of Parliament", are analysed.

7. HOOD PHILLIPS, O. *Constitutional and Administrative Law*, (4th ed., Sweet & Maxwell, Ltd, 1967), Appendix, pp. 830–835: the "crisis" cases are discussed.

8. POLLACK, W. "The Legislative Competence of the Union Parliament", (1931), 48 SALJ, 269: this was written before the Statute of Westminster and argues that the Colonial Laws Validity Act alone gives efficacy to the "entrenched" provisions and that with the repeal of that Act, the entrenchment disappears.

9. KEITH, A.B. *The Dominions as Sovereign States*, (Macmillan & Co, Ltd, 1938), pp. 167–183: this is a general discussion with reference to all the Dominions, and stresses the point that the Union of South Africa was a compact between representatives of the separate colonies.

10. McWHINNEY, E. "The Union Parliament, the Supreme Court and the 'Entrenched Clauses' of the South Africa Act", (1952), 30 Can BR, 692: this gives a historical survey down to the "*Votes*" case. The author criticises the purely positivist approach of the Appellate Division and thinks that the court should instead have approached the question in the light of policy considerations, based on a fundamental compact between the four original colonies. The safeguard against any repeal of the 'entrenched' provisions could be found as an integral part of this original agreement.

11. McWHINNEY, E. "Court versus Legislature in the Union of South Africa: the Assertion of a Right of Judicial Review", (1953), 31 Can BR, 52: the "*High Court*" case is examined, as well as the basis of a judicial power of review.

1. McWHINNEY, E. Note on the *"High Court Case"*, (1952), 30 Can BR, 734.

2. McWHINNEY, E. Note on *Collins* v. *Minister of the Interior*, (1957), 35 Can BR, 1203: this comments critically on the positivist approach adopted by the judges.

3. McWHINNEY, E. *Judicial Review in the English-speaking World*, (2nd ed., University of Toronto Press, 1960), chap. 6: the author re-considers the South African crisis and criticises the positivist approach of the judges. He repeats the thesis that something in the nature of a fundamental law is traceable in the country itself as a local root, namely, the original agreement between the two rival European peoples.

4. McWHINNEY, E. "La Crise Constitutionnelle de l'Union Sud-Africaine", (1953), Revue Internationale de Droit Comparé, 542: a detailed treatment is provided of the historical background to South Africa's position within the Commonwealth and a discussion of the "crisis" cases: the positivist approach of the judges to a political issue is criticised.

5. WADE, H.W.R. "The Senate Act Case and the Entrenched Sections of the South Africa Act", (1957), 74 SALJ, 160: the *"High Court Case"* and the *"Senate Case"* are discussed.

6. HAHLO, H.R. and KAHN, E. *The Union of South Africa. The Development of its Laws and Constitution*, (Stevens & Sons, Ltd, 1960), pp. 146–163: this is a general review of the sovereignty of Parliament in South Africa.

7. KAHN, E. in *Annual Survey of South African Law, 1951*, (Juta & Co, Ltd), pp. 1–7: the background to the conflict is surveyed historically. *Ibid., 1952*, pp. 1–28: the *"Votes"* and *"High Court"* cases are summarised with a discussion of their implications. *Ibid., 1953*, pp. 1–4: this gives a brief account of the South Africa Act Amendment Bill, which was dropped, and the Appellate Division Bill. *Ibid., 1955*, pp. 1–13: this gives an account of the Appellate Division Quorum Act, 1955, and the Senate Act, 1955. *Ibid., 1956*, pp. 1–18: the whole of the conflict is summarised.

8. HARRIS, D.R. "The Constitutional Crisis in South Africa", (1959), 103 SJ, 995: this is a general review, recalling the attitude of the Nationalist Government in the 1930's.

9. Le MAY, G.H.L. "Parliament, the Constitution and the 'Doctrine of the Mandate'", (1957), 74 SALJ, 33: the argument is that the idea of a mandate is incompatible with the sovereignty of Parliament.

10. MAY, H.J. *The South African Constitution*, (3rd ed., Allen & Unwin Ltd, 1955), chaps. 2 and 3: a detailed and vivid historical account is given of the events in South Africa down to 1955, especially the history of entrenchment.

11. KENNEDY, W.P.M. and SCHLOSBERG, H.J. *The Law and Custom of the South African Constitution*, (Oxford University Press, 1935, being the first edition of H.J. May, *The South African Constitution, supra*), chaps. 1–3: the background to the South Africa Act and the general nature of the constitution, especially the powers of the legislature, are examined.

12. ANONYMOUS. "The State and the Judiciary", (1897), 14 Cape LJ, 94: this is an account of the constitutional crisis which was precipitated in the Transvaal by

the decision in *Brown* v. *Leyds N.O.* and of the consequent attempt by the Boer government to curb the judiciary.

1. GORDON, J.W. "The Judicial Crisis in the Transvaal", (1898), 14 LQR, 343: the crisis referred to above is discussed with reference to the testing power of the judiciary.

2. The following cases may be consulted on the question whether a sovereign legislature can bind itself: *The Bribery Commissioner* v. *Ranasinghe*, [1965] AC, 172; [1964] 2 All ER, 785; *Ellen Street Estates, Ltd.* v. *Minister of Health*, [1934] 1 KB, 590; *Pylkington's Case*, YB, 33 Hen VI, 17, pl. 8; *Moore* v. *Att.-Gen. for the Irish Free State*, [1935] AC, 484; *McCawley* v. *R.*, [1920] AC, 691; *Att.-Gen. for New South Wales* v. *Trethowan*, [1932] AC, 526; *R.* v. *Ndobe*, [1930] App D, 484; *MacCormick* v. *Lord Advocate*, [1953] SC, 396; *British Coal Corporation* v. *R.*, [1935] AC, 500; *Ndlwana* v. *Hofmeyr N.O.*, [1937] App D, 229; *Copyright Owners Reproduction Society* v. *E.M.I. (Australia) Pty, Ltd*, (1958), 32 ALJR, 306; *Ex p. Bennett; Re Cunningham*, [1967] 86 WN (Pt. 2), (NSW), 323; *Duffy* v. *Ministry of Labour and National Insurance*, [1962] NI, 6; *Krause* v. *Commissioners for Inland Revenue*, [1929] App D, 286; *Harris* v. *Minister of the Interior*, 1952 (2) SA, 428 (AD); *Minister of the Interior* v. *Harris*, 1952 (4) SA, 769 (AD); *Collins* v. *Minister of the Interior*, 1957 (1) SA, 552 (AD).

The Rhodesian Crisis

3. PALLEY, C. *The Constitutional History and Law of Southern Rhodesia 1888-1965* (Oxford: Clarendon Press, 1966): this is a considerable work and is valuable in providing a general background to the UDI crisis. It gives a detailed and revealing analysis of the relations between the United Kingdom and Southern Rhodesia.

4. LEIGH, L.H. "Rhodesia after UDI: Some Aspects of a Peaceful Rebellion", (1966), PL, 148: this was written shortly after UDI. It reviews the constitutional development in Rhodesia and the legal possibilities that arise after UDI.

5. WELSH, R.S. "The Constitutional Case in Southern Rhodesia", (1967), 83 LQR, 64: the judgment of the Court of first instance is analysed and criticised in detail. If, as the Court held, the 1965 Constitution is invalid and the Court continued to recognise the 1961 Constitution, there was no ground for the compromise which it adopted.

6. EEKELAAR, J.M. "Splitting the *Grundnorm*", (1967), 30 MLR, 156: this article outlines the Rhodesian constitutional development down to UDI and summarises the judgment in the UDI Case. In its concluding comment the implication of the judgment on the acceptance of the criterion of validity is dealt with.

7. DIAS, R.W.M. "The UDI Case: the *Grundnorm* in Travail", (1967), CLJ, 5: in this Note the principal points of the judgment are outlined, and there is particular reference to the weakness of Kelsen's concept of the *Grundnorm* and how the criterion of validity might be regarded.

8. LANG, A.J.G. "Madzimbamuto and Baron's Case at First Instance", (1965), Rhod LJ, 65: the main grounds of the judgment are examined. In particular, the court's rejection of the British Secretary of State's statement, its acceptance of the doctrine of necessity and its conclusion on the onus of proof are criticised.

1. PALLEY, C. "The Judicial Process: UDI and the Southern Rhodesian Judiciary", (1967), 30 MLR, 263: judges are influenced by their values. Biographical sketches of the judges concerned in the UDI Case are followed by a critical analysis of the decision.

2. HEPPLE, B.A., O'HIGGINS, P. and TURPIN, C.C. "Rhodesian Crisis: Criminal Liabilities", [1966], Crim LR, 5: the criminal aspects of UDI, especially with regard to treason, are discussed. See also O. HOOD PHILLIPS: "Rhodesian Crisis: Criminal Liabilities. A Short Reply", *ibid.*, at p. 68.

3. WHARAM, A. "Treason in Rhodesia", (1967), CLJ, 189: this article is of general interest. It considers UDI from the angle of the offence of treason in English Law.

4. HONORÉ, A.M. "Allegiance and the Usurper", (1967), CLJ, 213: the Treason Act 1495 provides that service under a *de facto* sovereign is not treason against the *de jure* sovereign. Various interpretations of this provision are considered, followed by the author's own interpretation.

5. HONORÉ, A.M. "Reflections on Revolutions", (1967), 2 Ir Jur (NS), 268: when there is little chance of the old regime being restored after a revolution, are judges authorised to lessen that chance still further by recognising the new regime? Possible bases of such authority in an implied provision in old constitution itself, in natural law, or in a social or moral duty towards the populace are considered.

6. DIAS, R.W.M. "Legal Politics: Norms behind the *Grundnorm*", (1968), 26 CLJ, 233: the judges have contrived to assert their independence of the Smith regime while the regime was asserting its independence of Great Britain. The judgments of the Appellate Division and of the Privy Council are examined and their implications on Kelsen's doctrines considered.

7. EEKELAAR, J.M. "Rhodesia: the Abdication of Constitutionalism", (1969), 32 MLR, 19: this article explains the course of the litigation that has arisen in connection with UDI, with particular reference to the judgments in the Appellate Division and in the Privy Council.

8. BARRIE, G.N. "Rhodesian UDI – an Unruly Horse", (1968), 1 CILSA, 110: the judgments in the *Grundnorm* case are reviewed so as to show the problem confronting the courts.

9. MACFARLANE, L.J. "Pronouncing on Rebellion: the Rhodesian Courts and UDI", (1968), PL, 325: all the different aspects of the *Grundnorm* case are reviewed and examined. The views of the judges on each of them are criticised and the weaknesses and inconsistencies in them exposed. The judges are condemned for failing to measure up to their responsibilities.

10. MACFARLANE, L.J. "Justifying Rebellion: Black and White Nationalism in Rhodesia", (1968), 6 J Comm PS, 54: this may be read for general interest. It deals with the political background to the Rhodesian crisis. Two nationalisms, white and black, were at work demanding rebellion in different ways. See also R. BROWN: "A Comment on L.J. Macfarlane's 'Justifying Rebellion: Black and White Nationalism in Rhodesia'", *ibid.* 155: Macfarlane's article is criticised on the ground that it does not do full justice to African nationalism.

1. MARSHALL, H.H. "The Legal Effects of UDI", (1968), 17 ICLQ, 1022: this gives a brief account of the position in Rhodesia before UDI and the events leading up to the *Grundnorm* Case. The holdings by the Appellate Division and the Privy Council are summarised.

2. CHRISTIE, R.H. "Practical Jurisprudence in Rhodesia", (1968), 1 CILSA, 390: (1969), 2 *ibid*. 3, 206: the first paper considers the effect of the Governor's instruction on the declaration of UDI on the judiciary, and submits that the judges were right not to resign. The second paper contrasts a naturalistic approach, which relates the activities of a revolutionary regime to an objective definition of law, with an approach founded on allegiance. The various judgments in the Appellate Division are examined on this basis. The final paper stresses the importance of the realities of a situation and the inter-relation between the courts and power.

3. BROOKFIELD, F.M. "The Courts, Kelsen and the Rhodesian Revolution", (1969), 19 UTLJ, 326: this is an important article. The judgments of the Rhodesian courts and of the Privy Council in the various cases concerning the legality of the Smith regime are scrutinised critically with reference to Kelsen's doctrine.

4. JAFFEY, A.J.E. "The Rhodesian Constitutional Cases", (1968), Rhod LJ, 138: the case-law, chiefly *Madzimbamuto's* case, is examined in the light of Kelsen's theory. The author contends that the validity of the *Grundnorm* is assumed. Therefore, courts established under the 1961 Constitution could not inquire into the validity of any enactment not made under it. The eventual recognition of the 1965 Constitution was wrong.

5. HAHLO, H.R. "The Privy Council and the 'Gentle Revolution'", (1969), 86 SALJ, 419: the author points to the gap between theory and fact and on that basis defends the Rhodesian judges who accepted the Smith regime.

6. WELSH, R.S. "The Function of the Judiciary in a Coup d'Etat", (1970), 87 SALJ, 168: this criticises Professor Hahlo's contentions. It gives a detailed account of developments down to the acceptance of the Smith regime by the Appellate Division. It is argued that judges who did so should first have resigned their commissions under the 1961 Constitution and accepted new ones from Mr Smith.

7. ZIMMERLI, C.H. "Human Rights and the Rule of Law in Southern Rhodesia", (1971), 20 ICLQ, 239: "Rule of law" involves generality, limitation of the powers of government and of the judiciary by law and an independent judiciary. After a review of events and developments since 1965, it is concluded that Rhodesia violates both the rule of law and fundamental rights.

8. HARRIS, J.W. "When and Why does the *Grundnorm* Change?", (1971), 29 CLJ, 103: after an acute analysis of the meaning of *Grundnorm* and validity, the author applies his analyses to the Rhodesian situation. Criticisms of Kelsen in the light of this are rejected. As legal scientists the judges were bound to accept the change as a matter of reality and fact.

9. EEKELAAR, J.M. "Principles of Revolutionary Legality" in *Oxford Essays in Jurisprudence* (*Second Series*), (ed. A.W.B. Simpson, Oxford University Press, 1973), chap. 2: positivist theory requires that a usurper is to be regarded either as illegal or legal. This is because positivist theory only recognises rules as "law".

But "law" consists also of "principles", which are different from rules only in degree and sometimes not at all. A list of nine such principles are set out which could govern the legalising of a usurper. (See also J.M. FINNIS, "Revolutions and the Continuity of Law", *ibid*., chap. 3).

1. WHARAM, A. "Rhodesia: Ten Years On", (1975), 125 New LJ, 1047: the author defends the thesis that there was no rebellion and considers the implication of calling UDI "rebellion".

2. HOPKINS, J.A. "International Law – Southern Rhodesia – United Nations – Security Council", (1967), CLJ, 1: in this Note the author considers the various resolutions passed by the General Assembly and Security Council and questions their validity.

3. HALDERMAN, J.W. "Some Legal Aspects of Sanctions in the Rhodesian Case", (1968), 17 ICLQ, 672: this is of indirect interest. It deals with the implications of the various actions taken by the United Nations.

4. McDOUGAL, M.S. and REISMAN, W.M. "Rhodesia and the UN: the Lawfulness of International Concern", (1968), 62 AJIL, 1: the actions of the United Nations are justified. The various objections to United Nations action put forward on the Rhodesian side are considered *seriatim* and shown to be unfounded. See also FENWICK, C.G.: "When is there a Threat to Peace? – Rhodesia" (1967), 61 AJIL, 753.

5. HOWELL, J.M. "A Matter of International Concern", (1969), 63 AJIL, 771: this is a critical commentary on the theses of McDougal and Reisman and Fenwick.

6. The following cases may be consulted on the legality of a revolution: *The State* v. *Dosso* (1958), 2 Pak SCR, 180; *Uganda* v. *Commissioner of Prisons, ex p. Matovu* (1966), Eastern Africa LR, 514; *Madzimbamuto* v. *Lardner-Burke* 1968(2) SA, 284; [1969] 1 AC, 645; *Adams* v. *Adams (Attorney-General Intervening)*, [1971] P, 188; [1970] 3 All ER, 572; *Jilani* v. *Government of Punjab* (1972), PLD SC, 139.

Supra-national Control

7. GILMOUR, D.R. "The Sovereignty of Parliament and the European Commission of Human Rights", (1968), PL, 62: the European Convention on Human Rights has the effect of subordinating Acts of Parliament to judicial review according to a set of international norms. The working of this is considered in relation to a set of decisions concerning the Iron and Steel Act 1967.

8. BROTHWOOD, M. "Parliamentary Sovereignty and U.K. Entry", (1968), 118 New LJ, 415: membership of the Common Market will involve modification of present ideas of Parliamentary supremacy. The nearest parallel is said to be the position of Parliament with regard to the Dominions after the Statute of Westminster 1931.

9. *Legal and Constitutional Implications of United Kingdom Membership of the European Communities*, (H.M. Stationary Office, 1967, Cmnd. 3301): the various institutions of the European Community and the differences between regulations, directives, recommendations and opinions are explained. Importance attaches to paras. 22–23, which discuss the implications of Community law

which has direct internal effect. It is said that such law will have internal effect by virtue of an enabling Act of Parliament.

1. BEBR, G. "Directly Applicable Provisions of Community Law: the Development of a Community Concept", (1970), 19 ICLQ, 257: the concept of self-executing treaties is inapplicable; a concept to be determined according to national law by national courts is unacceptable. What is needed is a community concept. The argument of the whole article is detailed and technical.

2. BEBR, G. "Law of the European Communities and Municipal Law", (1971), 34 MLR, 481: this is a detailed and authoritative article on the problems of the relationship between Community and municipal law. The most important cases decided by the European Court and municipal courts are reviewed.

3. DATOGLOU, P.D. "European Communities and Constitutional Law", (1973), 32 CLJ, 256: Community Law is neither International Law nor Constitutional Law; it is *sui generis*. But the development of Community Law depends on the solution of constitutional problems. Also, the Community cannot develop without further limitation of national political autonomy.

4. MARTIN, A. "The Accession of the United Kingdom to the European Communities: Jurisdictional Problems", (1968–69), 6 CMLR, 7: this is a general analysis of the position with regard to Great Britain's entry into the Common Market with particular comment on the Government White Paper.

5. HUNNINGS, N.M. "Constitutional Implications of Joining the Common Market", (1968–69), 6 CMLR, 50: the implications on municipal constitutional law are examined in the light of the Rome Treaty.

6. MITCHELL, J.D.B. "'What do you want to be inscrutable *for*, Marcia?' or the White Paper on the Legal and Constitutional Implications of United Kingdom Membership of the European Communities", (1967), 5 CMLR, 112: this is a critical comment on the Government White Paper and dealing incidentally with the problem of sovereignty.

7. STEIN, E. "Towards Supremacy of Treaty Constitution by Judicial Fiat: on the Margin of the *Costa* Case", (1964–65), 63 Mich LR, 491: this is a general review of the whole problem of the supremacy of Community Law.

8. WILSON, E-F. "United Kingdom Sovereignty and Law vis-a-vis Britain's Entry into the Common Market", (1967), 1 JALT, 41: with regard to the national law of Britain, it is pointed out that it combines five systems: English, Scots, Channel Islands, Northern Irish and Manx law. This is followed by an explanation of the main features of EEC law.

9. de SMITH, S.A. "The Constitution and the Common Market: a Tentative Appraisal", (1971), 34 MLR, 597: there is as yet no sure method of predicting the constitutional impact of membership of the Common Market. There will be many problems. The present paper considers the extent to which the sovereignty of Parliament is likely to be affected.

10. DIPLOCK, K. "The Common Market and the Common Law", (1972), 6 JALT, 3: accession will have little direct effect on English law, but the indirect effects may be considerable. The important point is made that a unilateral contravention by

the British Parliament will be effective in Britain, though it would be in breach of EEC law. He considers also the effect of other aspects of EEC law, and the insularity of English law.

1. WADE, H.W.R. "Sovereignty and the European Communities", (1972), 88 LQR, 1: in this Note the author considers the implication of Britain's entry into the EEC on the sovereignty of Parliament. While observing that everything will depend on the attitude of the judges, it is thought unlikely that they will abandon their traditional allegiance to the ruling Parliament of the day. He suggests either annual legislation asserting the supremacy of Community Law, or a form of words in each statute making it subject to Community Law.

2. TRINDADE, F.A. "Parliamentary Sovereignty and the Primacy of European Community Law", (1972), 35 MLR, 375: Professor Wade's suggestions are rejected in the course of this detailed review of the position. The author suggests the setting up of a Parliamentary Standing Committee for the Scrutiny of Legislation concerning European Community Law. This would ensure that no future statutes conflict with Community Law, and also that existing statutes are repealed or amended before Community Regulations come into force.

3. MITCHELL, J.D.B., KUIPERS, S.A. and GALL, B. "Constitutional Aspects of the Treaty and Legislation relating to British Membership", (1972), 9 CMLR, 134: the authors consider the British Bill before this became the European Communities Act 1972. The discussion includes the problems of direct applicability and the supremacy of Community Law and the sovereignty of Parliament.

4. STEPHENSON, I.S. "Some Legal Consequences of United Kingdom Entry into the European Communities", (1973), 70 LS Gaz, 1837: Parliamentary sovereignty is divided into "theoretical" and "practical" sovereignty. With regard to the former, the question is whether Parliament can repeal the 1972 Act; with regard to the latter, the sovereignty of Parliament has been diminished. The prospects for a European Parliament are also touched on.

5. DREWRY, G.R. "Parliament and the European Communities", (1973), 123 New LJ, 607: this deals with the ways in which Parliament has had to re-adjust to EEC membership. There is need for scrutiny of European legislation and for information.

6. KUTSCHER, H. "Community Law and the National Judge", (1973), 89 LQR, 487: national judges have to accept the idea that Community Law has direct effect within states and takes precedence over the domestic law. States have irrevocably surrendered part of their sovereign powers. The Community is an independent legal order establishing a common law of member states.

7. SCARMAN, L.G. "The Law of Establishment in the European Economic Communities", (1973), 24 NILQ, 61: Britain's accession began a quiet revolution the nature of which is illustrated by the "right of establishment" (Arts. 52–58) abolishing restrictions on the freedom of nationals of one member country to set up in business or a profession in another country. The implementation of this involves social and legal questions. With regard to the sovereignty of Parliament, the author maintains that an Act which is inconsistent with EEC law prevails over the latter. A written constitution might be the only safeguard against this.

8. WYATT, D. "Directly Applicable Provisions of EEC Law", (1975), 125 New LJ, 458,

575, 669, 793: the criteria for direct applicability are reviewed with extensive examination of the case-law. The duty to safeguard individual rights could provide defences as well as actions; directives and decisions can create rights. Community law could serve as an aid in interpreting and implementing national legislation.

1. PHILLIPS, O. HOOD. "Self-limitation by the United Kingdom Parliament" (1975), 2 Hastings Const LQ, 443: the author considers the nature of "Parliament", "legislative supremacy" and "self-limitation". The last implies some "higher law", and he considers the possibility of such a thing with reference to a constitution, international law, natural law, and the EEC. He rejects each and thinks that Parliament can go against or repeal the Act of Accession. The only solution would be a wholly new written constitution, creating a new kind of legislature, which would contain entrenchments concerning the EEC and a Bill of Rights.

2. O'DONOVAN, V. "How Supreme is European Law?", (1976), 126 New LJ, 40, 161: an important decision of the German Federal Constitutional Court is that Community law and national law exist side by side and that fundamental rights of German citizens guaranteed in the *Grundgesetz* cannot be infringed by Community law. This may be justified because Germany has a written constitution, Britain which lacks one is in a weaker position, having to rely on "fundamental principle".

3. O'DONOVAN, V. "National Sovereignty and the European Court", (1976), 73 LS Gaz, 381: civil and common law approaches are contrasted; there is a move in British courts towards the Continental attitude to interpretation. The article examines the binding effect of rulings of the European Court and the significance of overriding national law.

4. THOMPSON, J.M. "The Supremacy of European Community Law?", (1976), SLT, 273: with regard to Community law and future legislation, how far is there a limit on Parliament's power? The wording of Section 2(4) of the European Communities Act 1972 is analysed in detail.

5. WINTERTON, G. "The British *Grundnorm*: Parliamentary Supremacy Re-examined", (1976), 92 LQR, 591, 613–617: membership of the EEC in relation to Parliamentary supremacy is considered. The problems of inconsistent enactments and repeal of the European Communities Act 1972 are considered in the light of the interpretation of supremacy given earlier.

6. HARDING, C.S.P. "European Community Law in the United Kingdom", (1976), 140 JPJ, 456, 470: the application of directly applicable provisions of Community Law in British courts is discussed with reference to cases. A further question is how far aspects of Community Law can affect national law when they are strictly not economic in character.

7. MACKENZIE-STUART, A.J. *The European Communities and the Rule of Law*, (The Hamlyn Lectures, Stevens & Sons, Ltd, 1976): the Communities are based on a system that subjects those administering it to the limitations of law, and which assures individuals of certain rights which would otherwise be neglected by their states and which protect him against arbitrary misuse of power by the Community. The primacy of Community law means that if discrepancy between it and national law is unavoidable, it must prevail. In these lectures a Judge of the European Court reviews the Court of Justice and the judicial process therein,

justiciable issues in Community law, its philosophy, politics and economics and future trends.

8. KANYEIHAMBA, G.W. and KANTENDE, J.W. "The Supranational Adjudicatory Bodies and the Municipal Governments, Legislatures and Courts: a Confrontation", (1972), PL, 107: a supranational court is sufficiently detached to be able to consider sensitive issues dispassionately; on the other hand, it has to tread warily in case its jurisdiction might be barred. The article considers the work of the Court of Appeal for East Africa and shows how it has safeguarded individual liberty against governmental power.

5. Liberty

1. MILL, J.S. *On Liberty and Considerations on Representative Government*, (ed., R.B. McCallum, Blackwell, 1946): each individual should be given freedom to pursue his own happiness so as to contribute to the sum-total of human well-being, i.e., so long as he does not harm others. The enemies of liberty are two — the state and general opinion. Mill's disquisition is essentially an analysis of the values involved in freedom.

2. HART, H.L.A. *Law, Liberty and Morality*, (Oxford University Press, 1963): in the main Mill's thesis is adopted, namely, that the law should not interfere with the freedom of the individual except where it harms others. However, an important qualification is added that the law may interfere on grounds of paternalism to prevent people harming themselves.

3. DEVLIN, P. "Mill on Liberty in Morals" in *The Enforcement of Morals*, (Oxford University Press, 1965), chap. 6: Lord Devlin considers Mill's thesis particularly in relation to homosexuality. The fallacy in the thesis that one should tolerate even that which no one regards as "good" because it is possible that everyone may be mistaken lies in the failure to distinguish between freedom of thought and of action. When it comes to action people have to act according to what they believe to be good and right, even while they may acknowledge that they *may* be wrong.

4. FULLER, L.L. "Freedom — a Suggested Analysis", (1954–55), 68 Harv LR, 1305: a distinction is drawn between freedom to" and "freedom from". The whole question of freedom involves purposive action of the person whose freedom is in question, equal freedom of others with regard to him and a measure of immunity from the actions of others. Freedom and order are not antithetical; but a single planned order is not essential.

5. BERLIN, I. *Two Concepts of Liberty*, (Pamphlet, Oxford, 1958): in this lecture the distinction is drawn between "freedom from" and "freedom to".

6. GOODHART, A.L. "Freedom under the Law", (1960), 1 Tasm LR, 375: in the 19th century liberty and law were opposed to each other, but in the latter part of the 19th century different views began to develop. The interplay of people demanded more control by law, and hence legal control was thought of as necessary to freedom. Political, economic and societal liberty are reviewed in turn on this basis.

7. CARRITT, E.F. "Liberty and Equality", (1940), 56 LQR, 61: consideration is given to the question how far the two are compatible with each other in social existence.

8. PARKER, H.L. "The Role of the Judge in the Preservation of Liberty", (1961), 35 Aust LJ, 63: judges have played an important part in preserving liberty by possessing personal beliefs in the value of individual freedom. In protecting the individual against administrative action, the supervisory jurisdiction of courts should remain elastic.

9. SALMON, C.B. "The Bench. The Last Bulwark of Individual Liberty", (1967). 117 New LJ, 749: the courts have always been, and still are, vigilant in safe-guarding the individual in many different ways. Some recent judicial

developments are considered in this light. It is pointed out, though, that in time of war this vigilance is relaxed.

1. McCRUDDEN, J.C. "Judicial Discretion and Civil Liberties", (1974), 25 NILQ, 119: this is a comparison of the approaches of British and American judges to cases on civil liberties. It is contended that British judges proceed on the basis of order as a requirement of democracy, whereas American judges proceed on an open demonstration view of democracy. British judges tend to confine themselves to the facts of each case, whereas American judges are more conscious of general principles in their Constitution.

2. POLLACK, L.H. "Securing Liberty through Litigation – the Proper Role of the United States Supreme Court", (1973), 36 MLR, 113: this article reviews the major American decisions as illustrating the attitude of the Supreme Court.

3. DUGARD, J. "The Judicial Process, Positivism and Civil Liberty", (1971), 88 SALJ, 181: positivism is the explanation of the attitude that in interpreting statutes judges adhere to the "phonographic" theory, especially in separating law and morals. Positivism is a cloak of concealment of the part values play. Judges do make law, since values are inevitable.

4. *Public Order*, (Conservative Political Centre, 1970): this deals with the increase of violence and disorder. The problem is "to achieve a synthesis of freedom and order". It recommends that to help with this problem the law needs to be simplified. G.R. DREWRY: "Freedom and Order", (1970), 120 New LJ, 1142: this is an outcry against the Conservative Party's *Public Order* to the effect that there should be prior "agreement about basic definitions" before meaningful discussion of these important issues can take place.

5. HUMPHREY, J. "Human Rights and Authority", (1970), 20 UTLJ, 412: human rights are now threatened by an ideology which is opposed to the very concept of authority. We need therefore to defend authority in the name of human rights. The questioning of authority should go with a sense of social responsibility.

6. O'SULLIVAN, R. "The Bond of Freedom", (1943), 6 MLR, 177: justice is the binding principle of states. The great creation of the common law was the free individual.

7. HALE, R.L. *Freedom Through Law*, (Columbia University Press, 1952): this is of general interest. It deals with problems created by freedom over a wide area of law. Much of the book is also concerned with justice. (See L.L. FULLER: "Some Reflections on Legal and Economic Freedoms – a Review of Robert L. Hale's 'Freedom Through Law'", (1954), 54 Col LR, 70).

8. LLOYD, D. *The Idea of Law*, (Penguin Books, Ltd, A 688, 1964), chap. 7: the "open society", i.e., one in which there is scope for the individual, is contrasted with the "closed society", i.e., one in which the community is dominant and the individual counts for nothing. Basic human rights and the principal values are set out and discussed. The chapter concludes with the international protection of human rights.

9. MacDERMOTT, J.C. "The Decline of the Rule of Law", (1972), 23 NILQ, 475: "rule of law" means law and order and also that which makes for a free and ordered society, viz., antithesis of arbitrariness and equality before the law. He

considers the worth of the "rule of law" and the decline of it, e.g., in the increase in crime and trade union defiance of law. The paper concludes with suggestions for improving the position.

1. HAYEK, F.A. *Law, Legislation and Liberty*, (Routledge & Kegan Paul, Ltd, 1973): individual liberty is treated as central to the concept of law, which is viewed as a spontaneous and unplanned growth, which evolves rules of just conduct. Legislation should be confined to providing the conditions for such development.

Law and Morality

2. GOODHART, A.L. *English Law and the Moral Law*, (Stevens & Sons, Ltd, 1955): the link between law and morals is indissoluble. The influence of morals in various branches of the law is considered.

3. WINFIELD, P.H. "Ethics in English Case Law", (1931–32), 45 Harv. LR, 112: morality rests in a consciousness of the difference between good and evil. There is a close connection between morals and law, but there is always an area of morals which is outside the law. The points of contact between morals and law are considered.

4. O'MEARA, J. "Natural Law and Everyday Law", (1960), 5 Nat LF, 83: the judicial process leaves a great deal of discretion to the judge. In applying this he should be guided by natural law, i.e., ethical principles. There are certain basic things which remain good or evil everywhere always.

5. JONES, H.W. "Law and Morality in the Perspective of Legal Realism", (1961), 61 Col LR, 799: the syllogistic form obscures the large element of discretion that there is in the judicial process. The law has a moral dimension. The American Realists, by showing that rules do not control judicial decisions, have shown that this moral dimension is not to be found in rules either.

6. "Round Table Discussion: 'What should be the Relation of Morals to Law?'", (1952), 1 JPL, 259: law, philosophy, theology and psychology are represented in this symposium. It is an interesting collection of views.

7. MERRILLS, J.G. "Law, Morals and the Psychological Nexus", (1969), 19 UTLJ, 46: law influences morals by providing a setting. It ensures security; it is itself a system of norms to which there is a general moral duty to obey; and it provides a standard of comparison when moral decisions have to be made. On the other hand, morality exercises a considerable influence on law.

8. GREEN, L.C. "Law and Morality in a Changing Society", (1970), 20 UTLJ, 422: this is a detailed review of the ways in which changing moral ideas have influence in different branches of the law.

9. HOCKING, W.E. "Ways of Thinking about Rights; a New Theory of the Relation between Law and Morals" in *Law: A Century of Progress*, (New York University Press; London: Humphrey Milford, 1937), II, 242: in the emergence of a right two factors are at work – the pressure of all the interests that form its content and the ethical sense of the group or community that give it its form.

10. COHEN, F.S. "The Ethical Basis of Legal Criticism", (1931–32), 41 Yale LJ, 201: ethical criteria of what ought to be the law cannot be dismissed. The valuation

of law is dependent upon the concept of the good life. The judge's choice is frequently governed by ethics, not logic.

1. FOOT, P.R. "Approval and Disapproval" in *Law, Morality, and Society. Essays in Honour of H.L.A. Hart*, (edd. P.M.S. Hacker and J. Raz, Clarendon Press, Oxford, 1977), chap. 13: morality is a social phenomenon. Many of its concepts cannot be analysed without mention of social facts. An individual cannot approve or disapprove without a special social setting. Approval and disapproval can only exist against a background of agreement about the point that other people's views shall be available in decision making.

2. BARRY, J.V. "Morality and the Coercive Process", (1962), 4 Syd LR, 28: the prohibitions of the law are one of many devices for influencing and controlling society. Justice in the law is only intelligible with reference to ethical standards.

3. COHEN, M.R. *Reason and Law*, (The Free Press, Glencoe, Illinois, 1950), chaps. 2–3: the moral element in criminal law is considered. Chapter 3 considers the standards of moral judgment.

4. MORRIS, H. "Punishment for Thoughts" in *Essays in Legal Philosophy*, (ed. R.S. SUMMERS, Basil Blackwell, Oxford, 1968), 95: it is not enough to say that law is concerned with external conduct, morals with internal conduct. The statement is conceptual in that it says something about the nature of law. The relationship between law (mainly criminal law) and morals is considered from this angle.

5. KOCOUREK, A. *An Introduction to the Science of Law*, (Little, Brown & Co, 1930), pp. 121–36: law and morals may be compared from various points of view, the field of conduct that is governed, method of controlling conduct, attitude regarding conduct, object sought in controlling conduct. Law and morals mutually influence each other.

6. BRINTON, H. "Morals and Law", (1972), 136 JPJ, 251: law and morals are distinct disciplines. There is danger in using words in legislation which are moral concepts. It has to be realised that the problem is a social one.

7. DEVLIN, P. "The Enforcement of Morals", *Maccabaean Lecture in Jurisprudence of the British Academy*, (Oxford University Press, 1959): to what extent should criminal law concern itself with morals and sin? A complete separation of the concept of crime from sin would be disastrous for the criminal law. This theme is developed in a stimulating and original manner.

8. DEVLIN, P. "Law and Morals" *Presidential Address to the Holdsworth Club* (1961): the moral basis of law is investigated further with reference to "real" and "quasi-criminal" law. (See further P. DEVLIN: "Law, Democracy and Morals", (1962), 110 U Pa LR, 635, 640).

9. DEVLIN, P. *The Enforcement of Morals*, (Oxford University Press, 1965): in this series of essays Lord Devlin considers the part played by morality in various branches of law, criminal and civil. It includes the three mentioned above. In the last three essays he carries the discussion on to a different plane. Much of the criticism of the original lectures is answered in the course of the book.

10. GINSBERG, M. *On Justice in Society*, (Heinemann, London, 1965), chap. 12:

neither morality nor law are closed systems. Their separation cannot be defended either as an account of how law works or ought to work. The distinction in the Wolfenden Report between "public" and "private" morality is criticised. Lord Devlin is also criticised for not taking sufficient account of the part law may play in shaping moral sense. There is a careful discussion of what the relation between law and morals should be in the general context of justice.

1. WOLHEIM, R. "Crime, Sin and Mr. Justice Devlin", (1959). Encounter 34: this takes issue with Lord Devlin's "The Enforcement of Morals".

2. HART, H.L.A. *Law, Liberty and Morality*, (Oxford University Press, 1963): the issue discussed is whether the fact that certain conduct is by common standards considered immoral constitutes a justification for making it punishable. This is a detailed answer to Lord Devlin. See also H.L.A. HART: "Immorality and Treason", (1959), The Listener, 162; H.L.A. HART: "The Use and Abuse of the Criminal Law", (1961), 4 Oxford Lawyer, 7; G.B.J. HUGHES: "Morals and the Criminal Law", (1962), 71 Yale LJ, 662; R.S. SUMMERS: Review of H.L.A. HART'S *Law, Liberty and Morality*, (1963), 38 NYULR, 1201.

3. ROSTOW, E.V. "The Enforcement of Morals", (1960), CLJ, 174: Lord Devlin's thesis is, on the whole, defended against the attacks by H.L.A. Hart and R. Wolheim. A society does have a common morality which it is entitled to enforce.

4. WALKER, N. "Morality and the Criminal Law", (1964), How J, 209: according to the "declaratory" theory, the function of criminal law is to indicate current moral opinion and it has been suggested that people's moral standards are affected by what they believe to be current opinion. Hence, according to this theory, prohibition by criminal law is necessary to preserve moral standards, irrespective of whether such prohibition is effective or not. The author concludes that the evidence is against the declaratory theory. He therefore advocates reform of the law relating to abortion, homosexuality, etc. unless a positive justification is proffered for using criminal law for preserving standards in these matters.

5. WALKER, N. and ARGYLE, M. "Does the Law affect Moral Judgments?", (1964), 4 Br JC, 570: the empirical test alluded to above is set out in detail and its results analysed. The conclusion is drawn that the evidence is against the "declaratory" theory of the function of criminal law.

6. DWORKIN, R. "Lord Devlin and the Enforcement of Morals", (1965–66), 75 Yale LJ, 986: the author considers Lord Devlin's argument in support of the proposition that society has a right to protect itself, and how far the social environment should be protected from change. The weakness of Lord Devlin's position is not the assertion that a community's morality counts, but what counts as the community's morality. See also R. DWORKIN, *Taking Rights Seriously*, (Duckworth, 1977), chap. 10.

7. WILLCOCK, I.D. "Crying Wolfenden too Often", (1965), SLT, 113: Lord Devlin's argumentation is criticised. But the author concludes nonetheless that a common morality is desirable and that the state should seek to uphold it. The determination of what conduct should be punished ought to be left to elected and informed representatives, and that in a case of doubt personal liberty ought to prevail.

1. WILLIAMS, G.L. "Authoritarian Morals and the Criminal Law", (1966), Crim LR, 132: Lord Devlin's thesis is answered point by point. In the course of the argument certain aspects of the utilitarian point of view are also clarified.

2. ISON, P.G. "The Enforcement of Morals", (1967), 3 U Br Col LR, 263: the author takes issue with Lord Devlin's thesis point by point. The article is purely destructive, but does not consider possible criticisms of Professor Hart's thesis.

3. HENKIN, L. "Morals and the Constitution: the Sin of Obscenity", (1963), 63 Col LR, 393: the basis of the article is an important contribution. Obscenity is forbidden, not because it excites people, but because it is offensive to that which has become part of the fabric of the society. The government has a responsibility for maintaining communal and individual decency.

4. MITCHELL, B.G. *Law, Morality, and Religion in a Secular Society*, (Oxford University Press, 1967): this is an acute and penetrating analysis of the positions taken up by Lord Devlin and Professor Hart. By clarifying the obscurities and ambiguities in both theses the author shows precisely where they differ. The main trend of the argument overwhelmingly supports Lord Devlin.

5. TEN, C.L. "Crime and Immorality", (1969), 32 MLR, 648: this article begins with a fairly detailed review of the positions taken up by Locke and Mill, and follows this up with a detailed criticism of Lord Devlin's position.

6. CARON, Y. "The Legal Enforcement of Morals and the So-called Hart-Devlin Controversy", (1969), 15 McGill LJ, 9: it may be necessary to enforce legally some aspects of morality, but it is better to avoid using law rather than adopt unworkable rules. The author begins by reviewing some well-known recent decisions involving morality and then turns to the Hart–Devlin controversy. His analysis is designed to show that the two sides are arguing about two different aspects of the problem.

7. SAMEK, R.A. "The Enforcement of Morals. A Basic Re-examination of its Historical Setting", (1971), 49 Can BR, 188: law and morals are separate, though overlapping systems. The author distinguishes between four meanings of "enforcing" morals, and in the light of this analysis considers in detail the positions of Mill, Stephen, The Wolfenden Report, Devlin and Hart. He ultimately supports the view that the immorality of an act should be a relevant factor in deciding whether to make it illegal or not.

8. LLOYD, D. *Introduction to Jurisprudence* (3rd ed., Stevens & Sons, Ltd, 1972), pp. 47–55: the relationship between law and morals and the controversy between Devlin and Hart are outlined. The author is clearly in sympathy with the latter, and argues in favour of moral pluralism, i.e., co-existence of divergent moralities.

9. BRAY, J.J. "Law, Liberty and Morality", (1971), 45 Aust LJ, 452: "law", "morals" and "liberty" are defined at the outset, and attention is drawn to the factors that are common to law and morals. The views of Lord Devlin and Professor Hart are set out and criticised. It is pointed out that there is a distinction between physical and moral harm.

10. BRAY, J.J. "The Juristic Basis of the Law Relating to Offences against Public Morality and Decency", (1972), 46 Aust LJ, 100: after a review of the history of the common law, the exposition of contemporary law is confined to

Australia. The author believes that the law is likely to abandon trying to enforce morality, but to try instead to protect decency. There should be no absolute condemnation of any conduct or matter in the abstract, but each question should be considered in its circumstances and setting. We need to define the bounds of the right not to be shocked.

1. HEUSTON, R.F.V. "Morality and the Criminal Law", (1972), 23 NILQ, 274: this paper sums up the Devlin–Hart debate. Three questions are considered: is there a public morality? – on which Lord Devlin is said to have the better of the argument; may society use the criminal law?; and how are moral judgments ascertained? Both sides in the debate are open to criticism.

2. SARTORIUS, R.E. "The Enforcement of Morality", (1972), 81 Yale LJ, 891: the author considers the Devlin–Hart debate and thinks that the latter's amended version of Mill's thesis is disappointing. Three features of a utilitarian defence of libertarianism are: a conception of value closely tied to the interests of individuals as they themselves perceive these; an especially strong conception of the value of individual freedom of choice; and principled objection to interference with self-regarding conduct.

3. GOODHART, A.L. "The *Shaw* Case: the Law and Public Morals", (1961), 77 LQR, 560: this gives consideration to an important decision which upheld punishment for an act which was obviously wrong morally.

4. SAMUELS, A. "Obscenity and the Law", (1964), 61 LS Gaz, 729: the article shows the difficulty of deciding when a publication should be suppressed on grounds of obscenity. The opposing considerations of freedom to publish and protection of the public are perhaps not investigated as fully as they might have been.

5. MEWETT, A.W. "Morality and the Criminal Law", (1962), 14 UTLJ, 213: this discussion is mainly inspired by the *Shaw* case.

6. STONE, J. *Social Dimensions of Law and Justice*, (Stevens & Sons, Ltd, 1966), pp. 368–81: the social interest in morals is considered and the foregoing controversy is examined. It is pointed out in particular that the distinction between private and public spheres of action is not as clear-cut as might appear.

7. WILLIAMS, D.G.T. "Sex and Morals in the Criminal Law, 1954–1963", (1964), Crim LR, 253: this is a review of the manner in which the courts have used the criminal law to give effect to moral values. The *Shaw* case is criticised for infringing the maxim *nulla poena sine lege*.

8. ANONYMOUS. "Obscenity, Public Opinion and the Law", (1972), 122 New LJ, 3: this is a brief note examining critically *The Pollution of the Mind*, published by a sub-committee of the Society of Conservative Lawyers. The real problem, it is said, is not *how* to define obscenity, but *what* to define.

9. FLETCHER, A.K. "The Legal Regulation of Morality", (1975), 125 New LJ, 1027: this is a comment on the Law Commission's Working Paper (No. 57). If the suggestions were implemented, there would be gaps which will have to be filled in with legislation. Forty cases since 1962 fall into four groups, of which only one would not fall under the proposed legislation. It is pointed out that the ultimate issue of principle is that debated by Lord Devlin and Professor Hart.

1. HARPER, T. "Indecency and Other Things", (1975), 125 New LJ, 71: this considers a proposal by a Home Office working party about indecent exposure and other street offences.

2. ALLEN, C.K. *Legal Duties*, (Oxford, 1931), pp. 196–220: the relation between morality and legal duties is investigated, and their close connection pointed out.

3. LLOYD, D. *The Idea of Law*, (Penguin Books, Ltd, A 688, 1964), chap. 3: laws were originally ascribed to a divine law-giver. The views of the Hebrew prophets and Greek philosophers on the part played by morality are explained. Law and morality share much common ground because both seek to impose certain standards. The reasons why law and morality may diverge and the different attitudes that might be adopted in such cases are also discussed.

4. AMES, J.B. "Law and Morals", in *Lectures on Legal History* and *Miscellaneous Legal Essays*, (Harvard University Press, 1913), 435: early law is alleged to have been unmoral since it attached responsibility to the act. It was the growing morality of the law that led to the supersession of this principle by the fault principle. There has been a corresponding development in contract.

5. POUND, R. *Jurisprudence*, (West Publishing Co, 1959), II, chap. 11: the relationship between law and morals is surveyed.

6. KANTOROWICZ, H.U. *The Definition of Law*, (ed. A.H. Campbell, Cambridge University Press, 1958), chap. 4: the relation between law and morals is considered with a view to a definition of law. The former, it is said, regulates external conduct, while the latter regulates internal conduct.

7. WHITELEY, C.H. & W.M. *The Permissive Morality*, (Methuen & Co, Ltd, 1964): the changes that have taken place in moral attitudes since 1900 are vividly and brilliantly analysed. Though not a treatise on law, this will serve as an important study of the moral climate of contemporary society.

8. COADY, J.M. "Morality and the Law", (1961), 1 U Br Col LR, 442: by moral precepts in law is meant that moral concepts are accepted as governing human conduct, and these are based on principles inherent in human nature itself. Christian moral law has its foundation in natural law. In the earliest days of the common law there was little, if any, conflict between Christian morality and the law because the judges were clerics. The relationship between the two should be preserved.

9. WESTEN, P.K. "Introduction" to "Symposium: Drugs and the Law", (1968), 56 Calif LR, 1: several contrary aspects of a vast problem in the United States are outlined. The difficulty of deciding what attitude to adopt towards a changing, many-sided phenomenon and of making that attitude effective form the background to the discussions that follow. Note: there is a useful bibliography at pp. 162–166.

10. FORT, J. "Social Problems of Drug Use and Drug Policies", (1968), 56 Calif LR, 17: there is a good deal of looseness in the use of the words "drug", "use", "abuse", and "problem". The social and legal policies that have been adopted to deal with drugs are alleged to be the cause of the main social problems because they are irrational and ineffective.

1. GUSFIELD, J.R. "On Legislating Morals: the Symbolic Process of Designating Deviance", (1968), 56 Calif LR, 54: "disinterested indignation" is the feeling that impels one to condemn as immoral that which others do but which need not physically harm anyone. This differs from the feeling that condemns murder, theft, etc., as immoral, for these do physical harm. On this basis the article examines the condemnation of drink and drug addiction.

2. ABRAHAMS, G. *Morality and the Law*, (Calder & Boyars, Ltd, 1971): this book is intended for laymen. It reviews the various ways in which morality has influenced the rules and processes of law in various different branches, illustrated by constant allusion to well-known cases and doctrines.

3. STEVENS, E.G. "Christianity and the Law", (1915), 49 Am LR, 1: this surveys the part which Christian ideas have played in shaping the law.

4. DENNING, A.T. *The Changing Law*, (Stevens & Sons, Ltd, 1953), chap. 4: religion has had much influence in shaping the values of the common law.

5. ST. JOHN STEVAS, N. *Laws and Morals*, (Burns & Oates, 1964): the attitudes of English and American law towards some controversial moral issues are considered in the light of Christian doctrine. Though written under the aegis of Catholicism, the book appraises both Catholic and Protestant views. Before a breach of moral law can be the subject of legal regulation it has to injure the common good and has to be a fit subject for legislation. The legal regulation has to be capable of enforcement and equitable in its incidence and should not cause greater evils than it eradicates.

6. BRYCE, J. *Studies in History and Jurisprudence*, (Oxford, 1901), II, chap. 13: this is of general interest. It deals comparatively with the interrelation between legal systems and different kinds of religion.

7. DOWRICK, F.E. "Christian Values in the Legislative Process in Britain in the Sixties", (1971), 16 AJJ, 156: Christian values still play a part in the formulation of modern legislation. This thesis is illustrated with reference to legislation on divorce, abortion and race relations.

8. PEDLEY, D.R. "Jurisprudential Consideration of Drugs", (1974), 138 JPJ, 306: the Roman Catholic view is outlined and contrasted with the approach of the English Churches, which rely more on social policies. The views of Mill, Stephen, Devlin, Hart and the Wootton Report are considered.

9. PEAR, R.H. "The United States Supreme Court and Religious Freedom", (1949), 12 MLR, 167: the task of the Supreme Court in holding the balance is explained and considered.

10. FELLMAN, D. "Religion in American Public Law", (1964), 44 BLR, 287: this is of general interest. It surveys at considerable length the influence of religious attitudes and traces historically the separation of church and state and the problems to which this gives rise.

11. WULFSOHN, J.G. "Separation of Church and State in South African Law", (1964), 81 SALJ, 90, 226: this article may be compared with the previous one on the position in America. Although there is no state religion, yet the Constitution declares that the people acknowledge God.

Liberty of Industrial Action

1. WEDDERBURN, K.W. *The Worker and the Law*, (Penguin Books, Ltd, 2nd ed., 1971): the development of labour law before and since the decision in *Rookes* v. *Barnard* is reviewed. The main object of the book is to display the interrelation of the various parts of the law in relation to industrial problems and developments. Its value would be greater were it not written from an obviously one-sided point of view. Its best feature is the bibliography at the end.

2. THOMPSON, D. "Protection of the Right to Work", (1963), 41 Can BR, 167: this gives detailed consideration to the case-law on the protection of the individual workmen, especially against trade unions.

3. LLOYD, D. "The Right to Work", (1957), 10 CLP, 36: the courts have shown some flexibility in extending legal remedies to protect the right to work. (See also D. LLOYD: "The Disciplinary Powers of Professional Bodies", (1950), 13 MLR, 281; "Judicial Review of Expulsion by a Domestic Tribunal", (1952), 15 MLR, 413; "Damages for Wrongful Expulsion from a Trade Union", (1956), 19 MLR, 121).

4. NASH, G. "Freedom of Contract and the Right to Work", (1969), 43 Aust LJ, 300, 380: the common law gave only a qualified recognition to freedom of contract and the right to work. The article reviews the attitude of the law from early times.

5. THOMAS, T.C. "Trade Unions and the Members", (1956), CLJ, 67: the *Bonsor* case is considered.

6. WEDDERBURN, K.W. "The Right to Threaten Strikes", (1961), 24 MLR, 572; (1962), 25 MLR, 513, (1964), 27 MLR, 257: these articles consider respectively the decisions at first instance, in the Court of Appeal and House of Lords in *Rookes* v. *Barnard*. See also K.W. WEDDERBURN: (1965), 28 MLR, 205, on *Stratford & Son, Ltd.* v. *Lindley*; C.J. HAMSON: (1961), CLJ, 189; (1964), CLJ, 159; J.A. WEIR: "Chaos or Cosmos? *Rookes, Stratford* and the Economic Torts", (1964), CLJ, 225; D. THOMPSON: "Protection of the Right to Work", (1963), 41 Can BR, 167; W.F. FRANK: "The Right to Strike Reconsidered", (1964), JBL, 199; B. GREAVES: "*Rookes* v. *Barnard*: After the General Election", (1964), 128 JPJ, 770; G.F.L. FRIDMAN: "The 'Right' to Strike", (1964), 114 LJ, 647, 667; ANONYMOUS: "A Trade Dispute?", (1964), 235 LT, 563; O. KAHN-FREUND: (1964), 14 Federation News, 30; O.H. PARSONS, "The Meaning of *Rookes* v. *Barnard*", (1964), LRD; I. CHRISTIE: (1964), 42 Can BR, 464; ANONYMOUS: "Strike On", (1964), 98 ILT, 421; ANONYMOUS: "Intimidation and Trade Unions", (1964), 98 ILT, 431, 437; D.W. SMITH: "*Rookes* v. *Barnard*: an Upheaval in the Common Law Relating to Industrial Disputes", (1966), 40 Aust. LJ, 81, 112.

7. HOFFMANN, L.H. "*Rookes* v. *Barnard*", (1965), 81 LQR, 116: the various aspects of this case are fully discussed. What is of special interest is that, in the author's opinion, the decision of the House of Lords accords with the intention of Parliament as revealed by the Parliamentary history of the Trade Disputes Act, 1906.

8. HARRIS, D.R. "The Right to Strike", (1964), 108 SJ, 451, 472, 493: the House of

Lords' decision in *Rookes's* case is considered. The competing issues are set out, including the point that the case is a triumph of the individual against a union. D.R. HARRIS: "Trade Disputes and the Law", (1964), 108 SJ, 795: this is mainly concerned with *Stratford's* case.

1. RIDEOUT, R.W. "Protection of the Right to Work", (1962), 25 MLR, 137: further consideration of the same topic.

2. RIDEOUT, R.W. "*Rookes* v. *Barnard*", (1964), 3 Sol Q, 193: the cases of *Rookes* v. *Barnard* and *Stratford* v. *Lindley* are discussed in detail and their implications considered.

3. GRUNFELD, C. *Trade Unions and the Individual in English Law*, (Institute of Personnel Management, 1964): this is a convenient account of the law concerning the individual in his relationship to his union. His discussion of *Rookes's Case* is pre-House of Lords.

4. LEWIS, N. "Trade Unions and Public Policy", (1965), 4 Sol Q, 12: there is a real danger in the power of trade unions. The question discussed is how far courts should go in checking oppression by unions.

5. KAHN-FREUND, O. "Trade Unions, the Law and Society", (1970), 33 MLR, 241: abuse of power by trade unions is rare, but it is necessary to guard against the odd case. Some legal control is therefore necessary. The various areas in which abuses could occur are investigated with reference to the law elsewhere and here, and it is urged that certain protective measures are in the interest of the unions themselves.

6. DENNING, A.T. *The Road to Justice*, (Stevens & Sons, Ltd, 1955), chap. 5: this deals, *inter alia*, with freedom of contract, freedom of association, the right to work, the right to strike and industrial combinations.

7. WEILER, P.C. "The 'Slippery Slope' of Judicial Intervention. The Supreme Court and Canadian Labour Relations 1950–1970", (1971), 9 Os HLJ, 1: this is a detailed analysis of Canadian case-law on industrial relations. There is no evidence of judicial bias, but the author nevertheless deprecates judicial intervention in this area because judges tend to regard justice to the individual rather than the broad policy. The result is that case-law fails to evolve general doctrines.

6. Precedent

Nature of Precedent

1. CROSS, A.R.N. *Precedent in English Law*, (2nd ed., Oxford, 1968): this is the most convenient general account of this topic, and might be regarded as the most instructive standard work.

2. ALLEN, C.K. *Law in the Making*, (7th ed., Oxford, 1964), chaps. 3–4: this is another standard work which gives the origin and nature of judicial precedent and a general account of precedent in Roman and Continental law.

3. GRAY, J.C. *The Nature and Sources of the Law*, (2nd ed., R. Gray, Macmillan Co, New York, 1921), pp. 200–216: this is a brief account of precedent in Roman, German, French, Scots and English law.

4. SALMOND, J.W. "The Theory of Judicial Precedents", (1900), 16 LQR, 376; *Jurisprudence*, (12th ed., P.J. Fitzgerald, Sweet & Maxwell, Ltd, 1966), chap. 5: these are both general accounts of precedent, its authority and classification.

5. BLACKSTONE, W. *Commentaries on the Laws of England*, (16th ed., J.T. Coleridge, T. Cadell and J. Butterworth & Son, 1825), I, pp. 70 *et seq.*: precedents must be followed unless flatly absurd or unjust or contrary to reason. This statement has to be understood in the light of the fact that at that date there was no rigid doctrine of *stare decisis* and precedents were still persuasive.

6. CROSS, A.R.N. "Blackstone v. Bentham", (1976), 92 LQR, 516: the author defends Blackstonè against Bentham's criticism by pointing out that whereas Blackstone was thinking of *ratio decidendi* as authoritative for another judge in a later case, Bentham's examples seem to show that he is thinking of *res judicata*.

7. HODGINS, F.E. "The Authority of English Decisions", (1923), 1 Can BR, 470, at pp. 475–478: the reasons for the authority of judicial decisions in England are discussed by a Canadian judge.

8. WILLIAMS, E.K. "*Stare Decisis*", (1926), 4 Can BR, 289: this is a general comparison of the position in England and Canada.

9. SNYDER, O.C. *Preface to Jurisprudence*, (Bobbs-Merrill Co, Inc, 1954), Part III, chap. 3, pp. 412–415: this gives a general introduction and a brief discussion of the basis of *stare decisis*.

10. WINDER, W.H.D. "Precedent in Equity", (1941), 57 LQR, 245: the development of equity from broad principles to precedent is outlined.

11. YALE, D.E.C. *Lord Nottingham's Chancery Cases*, (73 *Selden Society*, 1954), I, Introduction, Part II: this is a valuable account of the development of precedent in equity.

12. GARDNER, J.C. *Judicial Precedent in Scots Law*, (W. Green & Sons Ltd, Edinburgh, 1936), chaps. 1–4: the extent to which *stare decisis* operates in England, France and Scotland, and its development are discussed.

13. SMITH, T.B. *The Doctrine of Judicial Precedent in Scots Law*, (W. Green & Sons,

Ltd, 1952): evolution of *stare decisis* in Scots Law and the extent of English influence is dealt with.

1. WALTON, F.P. "The Relationship of the Law of France to the Law of Scotland", (1902), 14 Jur R, 17: the gulf is growing between the two systems since Scots Law is increasingly becoming a case-law system.

2. WALKER, D.M. "A Note on Precedent", (1949), 61 Jur R, 283: it is pointed out that the bulk of citations in Scottish Courts comes from 20th century cases.

3. SAFFORD, A. "The Creation of Case Law under the National Insurance and National Insurance (Industrial Injuries) Acts", (1954), 17 MLR, 197: this is of general interest as showing how a body of case-law grows up.

4. LEWIS, C. "The Truth about Precedent", (1976), 73 LS Gaz, 957: the binding force of *stare decisis* is theoretical only. The House of Lords is no longer bound by its own decisions, and the Court of Appeal is showing similar reluctance. Even courts of first instance have so many devices for getting round precedents that the whole doctrine is reduced to persuasive authority.

Historical Development

5. PLUCKNETT, T.F.T. *A Concise History of the Common Law*, (5th ed. Butterworth & Co, Ltd, 1956), Part III, chap. 5: this is a convenient and highly instructive account.

6. ALLEN, C.K. *Law in the Making*, (7th ed., Oxford, 1964), pp. 187–235: this gives a general and fairly detailed historical account.

7 ELLIS LEWIS, T. "History of Judicial Precedent", (1930), 46 LQR, 207, 341: (1931), 47 LQR, 411; (1932), 48 LQR, 230: a detailed account of the development down to 1765 will be found in these articles.

8. HOLDSWORTH, W.S. *A History of English Law*, (Methuen & Co, Ltd,), II, pp. 188–192 (Glanvil); 235–236 (Bracton); 525–556 (Year Books); V, pp. 355–378; VI, pp. 551–624: this is useful for referring to different aspects of the development.

9. WINFIELD, P.H. *The Chief Sources of English Legal History*, (Harvard University Press, 1925), chap. 7: a good account of the development of reports and reporting.

10. MORAN, C.G. *The Heralds of the Law*, (Stevens & Sons, Ltd, 1948), chaps. 1–4: a historical account of law reporting is provided.

11. POLLOCK, F. *A First Book of Jurisprudence*, (6th ed., Macmillan & Co, Ltd, 1929), chap. 5, Part II: a historical account of law reports is given with hints on how to find authorities; chap. 6, down to p. 331, deals with the evolution of *stare decisis*: (the rest of the chapter is now out of date).

12. DANIEL, W.T.S. *The History and Origin of 'The Law Reports'*, (William Clowes & Sons, Ltd, 1884): a detailed, documented account of the introduction of the Law Reports by one who played a leading part.

1. "ALEPH-ZERO", "The Incorporated Council of Law Reporting – the History and Development of the Law Reports", (1958), 55 LS Gaz, 483: a brief and very general account.

2. WALLACE, J.W. *The Reporters*, (4th ed., F.F. Heard, Boston, 1882): this gives a detailed account of the early reports and it is a very useful source of information as to particular reporters.

3. PLUCKNETT, T.F.T. "The Place of the Legal Profession in the History of English Law", (1932), 48 LQR, 328: this is principally an account of the Year Books.

4. SIMPSON, A.W.B. "The Circulation of Yearbooks in the Fifteenth Century", (1957), 73 LQR, 492: a further study of the Year Books.

5. SIMPSON, A.W.B. "Keilway's Reports, temp. Henry VII and Henry VIII", (1957), 73 LQR, 89: a particular set of reports is discussed.

6. WAMBAUGH, E. *The Study of Cases*, (2nd ed., Boston, 1894), chaps. 10 and 11: these provide a general account of reports and digests.

7. POLLOCK, F. "Judicial Records", in *Essays in the Law*, (Macmillan & Co, Ltd, 1922), chap. 9: the distinction is explained between the record and a report of a case and the importance of the former.

Law Reporting

8. WINFIELD, P.H. "Early Attempts at Reporting Cases", (1924), 40 LQR, 316: this might be consulted for a short account of the reporting methods in some Year Book cases.

9. LINDLEY, N. "The History of the Law Reports", (1885), 1 LQR, 137: W.T.S. Daniel's book (*supra*) is reviewed, and there is also a critical discussion, *inter alia*, of the subject-matter of reports, mode of reporting and time and form of publication.

10. HEMMING, G.W. "The Law Reports", (1885), 1 LQR, 317: some of the difficulties confronting a reporter are explained; (it is in answer to some of Lord Justice Lindley's criticisms, *supra*).

11. MEWS, J. "The Present System of Law Reporting", (1893), 9 LQR, 179: this is a discussion of reportable and unreportable cases, with criticisms of the present system and suggestions for reform.

12. EVANS, F. "Law Reporting: a Reporter's View", (1904), 20 LQR, 88: this was written before some modern series began, but portrays the atmosphere in which reporters work.

13. HOLDSWORTH, W.S. "Law Reporting in the Nineteenth and Twentieth Centuries", in *Essays in Law and History*, (Oxford, 1946), p. 284: this provides a general account of law reporting.

14. POLLOCK, F. "English Law Reporting", in *Essays in the Law*, (Macmillan & Co, Ltd, 1922), chap. 10: an account is given of modern reporting and the function of an editor based on his own experience.

1. DREWRY, G.R. "Reporting the Law", (1969), 119 New LJ, 801: this gives a brief
   survey of law reporting, including a discussion of the function of an editor.

2. POLLOCK, F. "Government by Committees in England", in *Essays in the Law*,
   (Macmillan & Co, Ltd, 1922), chap. 4, pp. 137–139: a brief account of the
   working of the Incorporated Council of Law Reporting will be found in these
   pages.

3. BURROWS, R. "Law Reporting", (1942), 58 LQR, 96: the function of a law
   reporter in modern times is discussed.

4. *REPORT OF THE LORD CHANCELLOR'S COMMITTEE ON LAW REPORTING*:
   (1940): also found in summarised form in D. and G. FORD, *A Breviate of
   Parliamentary Papers, 1940–1954*, p. 451; and in C.G. MORAN, *The Heralds
   of the Law*, (Stevens & Sons, Ltd, 1948), chap. 9: a review of the history and
   nature of law reports. The Committee reject any radical reform.

5. O'SULLIVAN, R. "On Law Reporting", (1940–41), 4 MLR, 104: this is a discussion
   of the Report of the Lord Chancellor's Committee (*supra*).

6. MORAN, C.G. *The Heralds of the Law*, (Stevens & Sons, Ltd, 1948), chaps. 5–10:
   the present system of law reporting is discussed, together with its problems and
   suggestions for improvement.

7. PARKER, C.F. "Law Reporting and the Revision of Judgments", (1955), 18 MLR,
   496: this is a note on the extent to which judges alter their judgments in the
   process of revision.

The Assessment of Reports

8. ROGERS, S. "On the Study of Law Reports", (1897), 13 LQR, 250, 256 *et seq*.:
   this gives hints on how to read reports and a general account of their educational
   value.

9. WAMBAUGH, E. *The Study of Cases*, (2nd ed., Boston, 1894), chap. 5, sect. 1:
   this contains a discussion of factors relevant to assessing the weight of a case.

10. RAM, J. *The Science of Legal Judgment*, (2nd ed., J. Townshend, Baker, Voorhis
    & Co, New York, 1871), chap. 13: this contains a useful assessment of the worth
    of certain old reports.

11. MORAN, C.G. *The Heralds of the Law*, (Stevens & Sons, Ltd, 1948), chap. 8: this
    contains many sidelights on the problems of using cases.

Authority of the Deciding Tribunal

12. Some of the works referred to below include discussions of the Court of Criminal
    Appeal, which was abolished by the Criminal Appeal Act 1966 (c. 31), and of the
    rule that the House of Lords is bound by its own decisions, which was abolished
    by the *Practice Statement (Judicial Precedent)*, [1966] 2 All ER, 77; [1966]
    1 WLR, 1234.

13. ALLEN, C.K. *Law in the Making*, (7th ed., Oxford, 1964), pp. 236–257: this
    provides an account of the different courts with detailed discussion of some of

the questions that have arisen. The parts dealing with the now defunct Court of Criminal Appeal and the House of Lords binding itself are out of date.

1. SALMOND, J.W. *Jurisprudence*: (12th ed., P.J. Fitzgerald, Sweet & Maxwell, Ltd, 1966), pp. 158–174: a detailed account of the hierarchy of courts with especial attention to the rule (now abolished) that the House of Lords binds itself and an examination of the Rule of *Young's* case will be found.

2. CROSS, A.R.N. *Precedent in English Law*, (2nd ed., Oxford, 1968), chap. 3: this account of the hierarchy of courts is not as complete in detail as Salmond or Allen; chap. 4 has a discussion of the exceptions to *stare decisis*; chap. 8 concerns mainly the question of judicial legislation and prospective overruling.

3. WILLIAMS, G.L. *Learning the Law*, (9th ed., Stevens & Sons, Ltd, 1973), pp. 83–86: a brief, general account of the position is provided.

4. HOOD PHILLIPS, O. and HUDSON, A.H. *A First Book of English Law*, (7th ed., Sweet & Maxwell, Ltd, 1977), Part I: this is a very convenient and readable account of all the tribunals.

5. KIRALFY, A.K.R. *The English Legal System*, (4th ed., Sweet & Maxwell, Ltd, 1967), pp. 98–110: the hierarchy of courts is dealt with in outline, and also the evolution of the doctrine of *stare decisis*.

6. PATON, G.W. *A Text Book of Jurisprudence*, (4th ed., G.W. Paton and D.P. Derham, Clarendon Press, Oxford, 1972), chap. 8, sect. 45: a brief account of the hierarchy of courts is given.

7. MIGNAULT, P.B. "The Authority of Decided Cases", (1925), 3 Can BR 1: this includes (at pp. 2–9) a review of the position in England, and a contrast with the position in France and in Quebec.

8. LAIRD, D.H. "The Doctrine of *Stare Decisis*", (1935), 13 Can BR, 1: the working of the doctrine in the courts of England and Canada is described.

9. ABRAHAM, H.J. *The Judicial Process*, (3rd ed., New York and Oxford University Press, 1976), chap. 6: the book as a whole deals with an analysis of the courts of the United States, Britain and France. A section of this chapter is concerned with the organisation of courts in Britain. Some of the points have since been altered by legislation.

Particular Courts

10. ALLEN, C.K. "Road Traffic Precedents", (1956), 72 LQR, 516: this shows the difficulties confronting magistrates when decisions of the Divisional Court conflict.

11. WINDER, W.H.D. "The Rule of Precedents in the Criminal Courts", (1941), 5 J Cr L, 242: the Court of Criminal Appeal, Divisional Court and the High Court are compared with reference to the working precedent. (The Court of Criminal Appeal has since been abolished).

12. WINDER, W.H.D. "Divisional Court Precedents", (1946), 9 MLR, 257: this is a general account.

1. STONE, O.M. *"Stare Decisis* in the Divisional Court", (1951), 14 MLR, 219: a note on the position.

   The work of the Court of Criminal Appeal was transferred to the Criminal Division of the Court of Appeal by statute in 1966. The following discussions are still relevant to the working of that Division.

2. NOTE: "Judicial Precedents in Criminal Law", (1958), 22 JCL, 155: this is a general discussion of the position.

3. SEABORNE-DAVIES, D. "The Court of Criminal Appeal: the First Forty Years", (1951), 1 JSPTL (NS), 425: the working of the Court is surveyed and critically assessed.

4. GODDARD, R. "Working of the Court of Criminal Appeal", (1952), 2 JSPTL (NS), 1: the day to day work of the Court is recounted.

5. WILLIAMS, G.L. "Bigamy and the Third Marriage", (1950), 13 MLR, 417, at pp. 418, 419: a short discussion of the power of the Court of Criminal Appeal to overrule itself will be found at these pages.

6. ANONYMOUS, "Exceptions to the Rule of *Stare Decisis*", (1958), 92 ILT, 131: The Rule in *Taylor's* case is considered together with the earlier position.

7. PARKER, H.L. "The Criminal Division of the Court of Appeal", (1969), 46 Law Guardian 11: The Riddell Lecture to the Institute of Legal Executives by the Lord Chief Justice is published in an abridged form. Lord Parker outlines the origin of the abolition of the Court of Criminal Appeal and the transfer of its work to the Criminal Division of the Court of Appeal, the principal differences between the Civil and Criminal Divisions and the altered powers of the latter. He also considers the present state of criminal appeals.

8. ZELLICK, G. "Precedents in the Court of Appeal, Criminal Division", (1974), Crim LR, 222: in *Taylor's* case a Full Court of Criminal Appeal overruled a previous decision. In *Gould* a three-judge court overruled a previous five-judge decision. The dicta of judges are inconsistent and confusing. The author sorts out the various alternatives with regard to overruling and considers expressions by other writers.

9. EVERSHED, F.R. *The Court of Appeal in England*, (London, 1950): a general account. See also F.R. EVERSHED: "The Work of Appellate Courts", (1962), 36 Aust LJ, 42.

10. COHEN, L.L. "Jurisdiction, Practice and Procedure of the Court of Appeal", (1951), 11 CLJ, 3: this is a general account of the working of the Court, including a discussion of whether it should be a final court of appeal.

11. ASQUITH, C. "Some Aspects of the Work of the Court of Appeal", (1950), 1 JSPTL (NS), 350: the first part deals with the history of the Court and an account of its day to day work. In the latter part there is special reference to the problems raised by the Rule in *Young's* case.

12. GOODHART, A.L. "Precedents in the Court of Appeal", (1947), 9 CLJ, 349: this

contains introductory remarks on the rule in the House of Lords (since bolished), followed by a detailed discussion and criticism of the Rule in *Young's* case.

1. GOODERSON, R.N. *"Young* v. *Bristol Aeroplane Co. Ltd."*, (1950), 10 CLJ, 432: this deals principally with the first two exceptions to the Rule, including a reply to Goodhart.

2. MASON, G.F.P. *"Stare Decisis* in the Court of Appeal", (1956), 19 MLR, 136: the Rule in *Young's* case is examined in the light of subsequent cases.

3. MEGARRY, R.E. "Fair Wear and Tear and the Doctrine of Precedent", (1958), 74 LQR, 33: a short but illuminating discussion of the first exception to the Rule in *Young's* case.

4. MEGARRY, R.E. "Precedent in the Court of Appeal: How Binding is 'Binding'? " (1958), 74 LQR, 350: a further discussion of the first exception.

5. MONTROSE, J.L. Note in (1954), 17 MLR, 462: on the *incuria* exception.

6. E.K. "Judgements *per incuriam* and the Doctrine of Precedent", (1955), 72 SALJ, 404: a short note on this exception.

7. DREWRY, G. "Precedent and *Per Incuriam"*, (1971), 121 New LJ, 277: the decision of the Court of Appeal in *Broome* v. *Cassell & Co. Ltd* [1971] 2QB, 354; [1971] 2 All ER, 187, extends the *incuria* exception in two ways: by applying it not just to a previous decision of the Court of Appeal itself, but to a decision of the House of Lords; and by applying it to a decision which distinguished, as distinct from ignoring, a relevant authority. See also on this case, R.W.M. DIAS: "The House of Lords and *Per Incuriam"*, (1971), 29 CLJ, 187 (The House of Lords, while affirming the decision, repudiated the *per incuriam* interpretation: [1972] AC, 1027; [1972] 1 All ER, 801).

8. ROBSON, P. "Reason and Revolution", (1972), SLT, 137: the judgments of the House of Lords castigating the Court of Appeal for its view on *stare decisis* in *Broome* v. *Cassell & Co. Ltd*, are criticised.

9. BENTIL, J.K. "The Court of Appeal's Adherence to its Jurisprudence", (1974), 124 New LJ, 733: this considers the pros and cons of whether the Court of Appeal should abandon the rule that it is bound by its own decisions, and suggests that Lord Denning's crusade that it should abandon it deserves wider support.

10. NOTE: in (1946), 62 LQR, 110, 210: this illustrates difficulties of the Rule in *Young's* case.

11. CROSS, A.R.N. *"Stare Decisis* in Contemporary England", (1966), 82 LQR, 203: since 1948 there has been a relaxation of the rigidity of *stare decisis*. This has come about because of a more liberal interpretation of the exceptions to *Young's* case and the invention of possible new exceptions, and also to a narrower conception of what precisely is binding in a case.

12. STEVENS, R. "The Final Appeal: Reform of the House of Lords and Privy Council, 1867–1876", (1964), 80 LQR, 343: during these years appeals to the

House of Lords were abolished but restored in three years. The political factors that were involved are traced in detail.

1. BLOM-COOPER, L.J. and DREWRY, G.R. "The House of Lords: Reflections on the Social Utility of Final Appellate Courts", (1969), 32 MLR, 262: the question whether a two-tier appeal system is desirable or not might be approached by looking at the position elsewhere. But hasty inferences should not be drawn from the situations in other countries; a great many social and other factors need to be taken into account. After a brief review of nine Commonwealth and other countries, the conclusion is that House of Lords does a useful function.

2. BLOM-COOPER, L.J. and DREWRY, G.R. *Final Appeal – a Study of the House of Lords in its Judicial Capacity*, (Oxford University Press, 1972): this is an extremely lengthy and detailed inquiry into the House of Lords, which is quasi-legal and quasi-sociological. It deals with the history of the Lords as a judicial body, applauds judicial activism and considers judicial reasoning. In the part dealing with "Law Lords in Action 1952–1968" there are tables, personal histories of individual judges, their backgrounds, etc.; and there is a further part dealing with "Appeals 1952–1968".

3. DREWRY, G.R. "One Appeal too many? Analysis of the Functions of the House of Lords as a Final Court of Appeal", (1968), 19 Br J Soc, 445: after a review of the history of the House of Lords as an appellate body, the author considers its value as a second court of appeal and marshals the pros and cons. He presents a balanced picture without a firm commitment either way.

4. du PARCQ, H. "The Final Court of Appeal", (1949), 2 CLP, 1: a historical account is given of some of the changes in the working of the House of Lords.

5. DIAS, R.W.M. "Precedents in the House of Lords – a Much Needed Reform", (1966), CLJ, 153: the abolition by means of a practice statement of the rule that the House is bound by its own decisions is considered. Attention is drawn to the need to give effect to a doctrine of prospective overruling.

6. LEACH, W.B. "Revisionism in the House of Lords: the Bastion of Rigid *Stare Decisis* Falls", (1967), 80 Harv LR, 797: the origin of the rule that the House should be bound, how far this was approved by the profession and the manner of its overthrow are set out. The possibilities of adopting a doctrine of prospective overruling are touched on.

7. ANONYMOUS, *"Stare Decisis"*, (1967), 101 ILT, 61: this is a note commenting on the House of Lords' *Practice Statement.*

8. ANONYMOUS, "The Force of Precedent", (1966), SLT, 157: the binding character of *stare decisis* is reviewed from a Scottish point of view and winds up with the *Practice Statement* in 1966.

9. St. JOHN, E. "Lords Break from Precedent: an Australian View", (1967), 16 ICLQ, 808: one at least of the factors behind the Lords' pronouncement may have been the progressive revolt of Australian courts against being bound by British decisions. But this, it is suggested, only triggered a gun already loaded.

1. ANONYMOUS, "Precedent", (1967), 131 JPJ, 595: a brief comment on the Lords' *Practice Statement.*

2. JONES, T.C. "The Implications of the New Doctrine of *Stare Decisis* in the Irish Supreme Court", (1967), 101 ILT, 281, 291, 301, 311, 321: consideration is given to the way in which the new flexibility introduced by an Irish decision in 1965 and the *Practice Statement* of the House of Lords in 1966 is likely to affect advocacy, law-teaching and judicial law-making.

3. BIRNBAUM, H.F. "*Stare Decisis* vs. Judicial Activism. Nothing Succeeds like Success", (1968), 54 Am BAJ, 482: this considers the *Practice Statement* of the House of Lords, and reviews the question whether the old rule that the House was bound by its decisions was one of law or practice and what effect the *Practice Statement* has. This leads to a consideration of the legislative function of courts in Britain and America.

4. HICKS, J.C. "The Liar Paradox in Legal Reasoning", (1971), 29 CLJ, 275: the statement "All Cretans are liars", propounded by a Cretan, has been the subject of age-long consideration. One attempt to solve the problem is Bertrand Russell's Theory of Types. The House of Lords *Practice Statement* that it will not be bound by its own decisions presents the same paradox, and is considered against this background.

5. STONE, J. "On the Liberation of Appellate Judges — How not to do it!" (1972), 35 MLR, 449: the *Practice Statement* of 1966 opened the way for a fuller realisation of the creative task of judges. The conflict between the Court of Appeal and the House of Lords in *Broome* v. *Cassell & Co. Ltd.* [1972] AC 1027; [1972] 1 All ER, 801, is reviewed critically and in detail. The question when the House should depart from its own decisions is considered with reference to *Jones* v. *Secretary of State for Social Services* [1972] AC, 944; [1972] 1 All ER, 145. Three "phases" of this task are distinguished.

6. FREEMAN, M.D.A. "Precedent and the House of Lords", (1971), 121 New LJ, 551: in a later Practice Direction the House of Lords required parties to state if they intend inviting the house to depart from a previous decision of itself. In the light of the sparing use which the House has made of its power, this article considers the significance of the direction.

7. KAVANAGH, P.B. "*Stare Decisis* in the House of Lords", (1972–73), 5 NZULR, 323: the change between the old rule of the House of Lords binding itself and the new rule is said to reflect a difference in attitude towards law as a science and one that is socially sensitive. The article contains a very interesting discussion of the cases since 1966.

8. CROSS, A.R.N. "The House of Lords and the Rules of Precedent" in *Law, Morality, and Society. Essays in Honour of H.L.A. Hart*, (edd. P.M.S. Hacker and J. Raz, Clarendon Press, Oxford, 1977), chap. 8: judicial statements concerning rules of precedent are neither *rationes decidendi* nor *obiter dicta.* Failure to appreciate this has given rise to spurious problems. The author reviews also the position in the Court of Appeal, prospective overruling and the *Practice Statement* of the House of Lords in operation.

9. BRAZIER, R. "Overruling House of Lords Criminal Cases", (1973), Crim LR, 98: the attitude of the House of Lords in using its power to overrule is too cautious.

There is danger in sacrificing justice to certainty. Precedents should be over-ruled if they cause injustice or anomaly or are wrong in principle, if they have been misunderstood or misapplied, and when their precise ambit is unclear.

1. HALDANE, R.B. "The Work for the Empire of the Judicial Committee of the Privy Council", (1921), 1 CLJ, 143: this is useful as showing what the position used to be.

2. RANKIN, G. "The Judicial Committee of the Privy Council", (1939–41), 7 CLJ, 2: this carries the review of the Committee's work further than the previous article.

3. NORMAND, W.G. "The Judicial Committee of the Privy Council – Retrospect and Prospect", (1950), 3 CLP, 1: the modern position is discussed.

4. McWHINNEY, E. *Judicial Review in the English-speaking World*, (2nd ed., University of Toronto Press, 1960), chap. 3: this considers the work of the Privy Council, including at p. 55 a discussion of the Council not binding itself.

5. McWHINNEY, E. "Legal Theory and Philosophy of Law in Canada" in *Canadian Jurisprudence. The Civil Law and Common Law in Canada*, (ed. E. McWhinney, The Carswell Co, Ltd, Stevens & Sons, Ltd, 1958), 1: the positivist role played by the Judicial Committee in Canada until 1949 is deplored, especially the attitude that judges do not make law. The problems facing the Canadian Supreme Court in pursuing a creative role in a heterogeneous community are considered.

6. PALLEY, C. "The Judicial Committee of the Privy Council as Appellate Court – the Southern Rhodesian Experience", (1967), PL, 8: the Privy Council, it is alleged, tends to approach written constitutions with British notions of sovereignty. Two of its decisions are analysed and criticised on this basis.

7. MARSHALL, H.H. "The Judicial Committee of the Privy Council: a Waning Jurisdiction", (1964), 13 ICLQ, 697: the growth and decline of Privy Council jurisdiction is recounted at some length. See also N. BENTWICH: "The Jurisdiction of the Privy Council", (1964), 114 LJ, 67.

8. MENZIES, D. "Australia and the Judicial Committee of the Privy Council", (1968), 42 Aust. LJ, 79: the author traces the work of the Privy Council from the background to s. 74 of the Constitution. On the whole, it is said, the Privy Council has served Australia well.

9. MARSHALL, H.H. "The Binding Effect of Decisions of the Judicial Committee of the Privy Council", (1968), 17 ICLQ, 743: decisions of the Privy Council bind the courts of the country from which the appeals are launched. In this paper the author discusses how far they are binding in other countries.

10. JACKSON, D. "The Judicial Commonwealth", (1970), 28 CLJ, 257: there is no one solution to a given problem for different parts of the Commonwealth. The Privy Council has acknowledged this, and so has an opportunity to lay foundations for different common law structures – common law rather than a common law. The interrelation of Australian and English decisions is considered in some detail.

1. L.M.M. "Abolition of Appeals from the Dominions to the Privy Council", (1947), 97 LJ, 601: this is a review of the growth of its jurisdiction and an account of how successive countries in the Commonwealth have abolished appeals to it.

2. CAMPBELL, E.M. "The Decline of the Jurisdiction of the Judicial Committee of the Privy Council", (1959), 33 Aust. LJ, 196: this reviews the history of its jurisdiction, criticisms of it and the progressive severance of ties by various parts of the Commonwealth and the prospects in those countries. (See also N.B. "The Shrinking Jurisdiction of the Privy Council", (1950), 100 LJ, 496, (1951), 101 LJ, 313; M. NASH: "Functions and Future of the Judicial Committee of the Privy Council", (1974), 124 New LJ, 1171).

3. The following cases might be consulted as illustrating the attitude of different tribunals: *Metropolitan Police District Receiver v. Croydon Corporation* [1956] 2 All ER, 785; *Monmouthshire County Council v. Smith* [1956] 2 All ER, 800; on appeal, [1957] 2 QB, 154; [1957] 1 All ER, 78; *Huddersfield Police Authority v. Watson* [1947] KB, 842; [1947] 2 All ER, 193; *R v. Taylor* [1950] 2 KB, 368; [1950] 2 All ER, 170; *Young v. Bristol Aeroplane Co. Ltd.* [1944] KB, 718; [1944] 2 All ER, 293; *Practice Statement (Judicial Precedent)*, [1966] 2 All ER, 77; [1966] 1 WLR, 1234; *Ibbralebbe v. R.* [1964] AC, 900; [1964] 1 All ER, 251.

On the question whether rules of precedent are rules of "law", the following might be referred to:

4. SALMOND, J.W. *Jurisprudence*, (12th ed., P.J. Fitzgerald, Sweet & Maxwell, Ltd, 1966), pp. 159–161.

5. CROSS, A.R.N. *Precedent in English Law*, (2nd ed., Oxford, 1968), chap. 7, especially pp. 209–211.

6. SIMPSON, A.W.B. "The *Ratio Decidendi* of a Case and the Doctrine of Binding Precedent" in *Oxford Essays in Jurisprudence*, (ed. A.G. Guest, Oxford, 1961), pp. 150–155.

7. MEGARRY, R.E. "Decisions by Equally Divided Courts as Precedents", (1954), 70 LQR, 318; G.L. WILLIAMS, "Decisions by Equally Divided Courts", *ibid.* p. 469; R.E. MEGARRY, *ibid.* p. 471.

The Ratio Decidendi (*Terminology*)

8. MONTROSE, J.L. "The Language of, and a Notation for, the Doctrine of Precedent", (1951–53), 2 Ann LR, 301, 504: this suggests a terminology which might help to avoid the prevailing confusion.

9. MONTROSE, J.L. "Judicial Law Making and Law Applying", (1956), BSALR, 187: a further examination of certain phrases.

10. MONTROSE, J.L. "*Ratio Decidendi* and the House of Lords" (1957), 20 MLR, 124–126: this discusses the ambiguity of the expression "*ratio decidendi*".

Determining the Ratio Decidendi

11. WILLIAMS, G.L. *Learning the Law*, (9th ed., Stevens & Sons, Ltd, 1973), pp. 67–82:

a concise account is given of the whole question, emphasising the point that the principle of a case alters with interpretation.

1. STONE, J. "The *Ratio* of the *Ratio Decidendi*", (1959), 22 MLR, 597: a distinction is drawn between the "descriptive" and "prescriptive" *ratio decidendi*. There is no one *ratio* in a case.

2. STONE, J. *Legal System and Lawyers' Reasonings*, (Stevens & Sons, Ltd, 1964), chaps. 7–8: the syllogistic form of a judgment is exposed. Judges nearly always have a choice. The judicial process is "a continuous creative adaptation of the law to changing social conditions".

3. SAMEK, R.A. "The Dynamic Model of the Judicial Process and the *Ratio Decidendi* of a Case", (1964), 42 Can BR, 433: the concept of *ratio decidendi* belongs to a static model of the judicial process, as opposed to a dynamic model. The concept of binding *ratio decidendi* stems from a failure to distinguish between the two models, from the identification of the judicial process with authoritative pronouncements rather than with reason, justice and social policy, and from the ambiguity of the phrase itself. The task of the judge on a dynamic model is to decide disputes by setting standards. On this view authority is not contrasted with justice etc. Authority is itself "open-textured" and is continually expanding, contracting and reforming.

4. LLEWELLYN, K.N. *The Bramble Bush*, (New York, 1930), chaps. 3 and 4: this stresses the point that the *ratio decidendi* depends on subsequent interpretation.

5. FRANK, J.N. "What Courts Do in Fact", (1932), 26 Ill LR, 645: the difficulty of achieving certainty, how facts are viewed by courts and the complications introduced by plural opinions in appellate courts are surveyed at length.

6. GOODHART, A.L. "Determining the *Ratio Decidendi* of a Case" in *Essays in Jurisprudence and the Common Law*, (Cambridge University Press, 1931), chap. 1: this examines how the *ratio decidendi* is to be determined. It consists of the decision based on the material facts as found by the judge.

7. GOODHART, A.L. "The *Ratio Decidendi* of a Case", (1959), 22 MLR, 117: the original thesis is restated.

8. GOODERSON, R.N. "*Ratio Decidendi* and Rules of Law", (1952), 30 Can BR, 892: this replies to Goodhart's thesis and defends the traditional view that *ratio decidendi* is the principle of law necessary for the decision.

9. SIMPSON, A.W.B. "The *Ratio Decidendi* of a Case and the Doctrine of Binding Precedent" in *Oxford Essays in Jurisprudence*, (ed. A.G. Guest, Oxford, 1961), chap. 6: this includes a discussion of the distinction between "defining" and "determining" the *ratio decidendi.*

10. HARARI, A. *The Place of Negligence in the Law of Torts*, (The Law Book Co. of Australia Pty, Ltd, 1962), chap. 1: a single decision cannot make a principle. Material facts are selected on the basis of certain unarticulated principles, which are not in the case itself. Propositions of law are generalisations based on existing decisions when they are co-ordinated (cf. the "character" of a person). Such generalisations need to be tested for their consistency with other decisions. Since future decisions are unknown, the generalisations are provisional.

1. DERHAM, D.P. "Precedent and the Decision of Particular Questions", (1963), 79 LQR, 49: there is a difference between the bindingness of the decision in a case and of the principle behind it.

2. SNYDER, O.C. *Preface to Jurisprudence*, (Bobbs-Merrill Co, Inc, 1954), Part III, chap. 3, pp. 420–426: an explanation of *ratio decidendi* is given and attention is drawn to the court's discretion in selecting material facts.

3. RAM, J. *The Science of Legal Judgment*, (2nd ed. J. Townshend, Baker, Voorhis & Co, New York, 1871), chaps. 3, 5, 14–17: this is of general interest; it deals with principle and dicta, appellate decisions, distinguishing decisions on particular facts and of decisions in new situations.

4. WAMBAUGH, E. *The Study of Cases*, (2nd ed., Boston, 1894), chap. 2: here will be found the famous test of *ratio decidendi*, namely, to reverse the proposition in question and to see whether this would affect the decision: (*note*: this test can only apply to cases with a single principle). Chap. 3: deals with cases involving several questions.

5. OLIPHANT, H. "A Return to *Stare Decisis*", (1928), 14 Am BAJ, 71, 107, 159: the well-known suggestion is made that the *ratio decidendi* may be constructed out of the decision, not necessarily out of what the judge has said.

6. CROSS, A.R.N. *Precedent in English Law*, (2nd ed., Oxford, 1968), pp. 35–80: this examines the question of *ratio decidendi* and summarises the various views.

7. MONTROSE, J.L. "Precedent in English Law" in *Precedent in English Law and Other Essays*, (ed. H.G. Hanbury, Irish U.P., Shannon, 1968), chap. 1: in the course of a review of the first edition of A.R.N. Cross on *Precedent in English Law*, the author points out that there is no one doctrine of precedent, but that cases reveal various patterns. He is also critical of inadequate analysis of phrases such as "applying a decision", "*ratio decidendi*" and "decision".

8. SALMOND, J.W. *Jurisprudence*, (12th ed., P.J. Fitzgerald, Sweet & Maxwell, Ltd, 1966), pp. 174–183: a general account.

9. PATON, G.W. *A Text-book of Jurisprudence*, (4th ed., G.W. Paton and D.P. Derham, Clarendon Press, Oxford, 1972), chap. 8, sect. 45: this gives an account of *ratio decidendi* in the light of recent analyses of the problems.

10. LLOYD, D. *Introduction to Jurisprudence*, (3rd ed., Stevens & Sons, Ltd, 1972), pp. 715–721: there is no one method of ascertaining the *ratio decidendi*. Well-known difficulties and views are discussed briefly.

11. VINOGRADOFF, P. *Common-sense in Law*, (3rd ed., H.G. Hanbury, Oxford University Press, 1959), chap. 7: this general account demonstrates (at pp. 138 *et seq.*) how a series of later cases may expand or modify the original decision.

12. WRIGHT, R.A. "Precedents", (1943), 8 CLJ, 118, 138 *et seq.*: some of the difficulties of finding the *ratio decidendi* are pointed out.

13. FRIEDMANN, W. *Legal Theory*, (5th ed., Stevens & Sons, Ltd, 1967), pp. 468–474: this discusses distinguishing techniques.

1. FRIEDMANN, W. *"Stare Decisis* at Common Law and under the Civil Law of Quebec", (1953), 31 Can BR, 723, 731–740: the difficulties of finding the *ratio decidendi* and the flexibility inherent in the doctrine of *stare decisis* are discussed.

2. SMITH, T.B. *The Doctrine of Judicial Precedent in Scots Law*, (W. Green & Sons, Ltd, 1952), chap. 4: precedent is examined from the Scottish point of view. Scots Law has a broader approach to the question of *ratio decidendi* than English Law.

3. LANG, A.G. "Is there a *Ratio Decidendi?*" (1974), 48 Aust. LJ, 146: this paper considers Goodhart's view and criticisms of it; is a *ratio* binding? and how does it bind? and the ratio of appellate courts. The questions are discussed with reference to Australian courts and suggestions are offered as to how *ratio decidendi* is ascertained.

The following references are to a debate on *ratio decidendi*, which is primarily useful in so far as it clarifies the attitudes of the various participants:

4. MONTROSE, J.L. *"Ratio Decidendi* and the House of Lords", (1957), 20 MLR, 124, 587.

5. SIMPSON, A.W.B. "The *Ratio Decidendi* of a Case", (1957), 20 MLR, 413; (1958), 21 MLR, 155; (1959), 22 MLR, 453.

6. GOODHART, A.L. "The *Ratio Decidendi* of a Case", (1959), 22 MLR, 117.

7. To complete this controversy, reference to the article by J. STONE, "The *Ratio* of the *Ratio Decidendi*", (1959), 22 MLR, 597, is essential.

Problems Connected with Ratio Decidendi

8. CROSS, A.R.N. *Precedent in English Law*, (2nd ed., Oxford, 1968), pp. 86–101: this gives a detailed account of some of the major problems.

9. GOODHART, A.L. "The 'I think' Doctrine of Precedent: Invitors and Licensors", (1950), 66 LQR, 374: the view that where a judge gives two reasons for his decision, both should be regarded as being the *ratio decidendi*, is critically examined.

10. MEGARRY, R.E. "Precedent in the Court of Appeal: How Binding is 'Binding'?" (1958), 74 LQR, 350: this demonstrates that the Court of Appeal rejected one of two grounds which it had previously given for a decision.

11. MONTROSE, J.L. *"Ratio Decidendi* and the House of Lords", (1957), 20 MLR, pp. 126 *et seq.*: the problems arising out of *Walsh v. Curry* are considered.

12. Notes by J.C.H.M., R.E.M. and J.A. COUTTS in (1948), 64 LQR, 28, 29, 193, 454, 463.

13. COUTTS, J.A. Note in (1950), 71 LQR, 24: the difficulty of extracting the *ratio decidendi* when there is more than one issue and the judges differ is considered.

1. PATON, G.W. and SAWER, G. "*Ratio* and *Obiter Dictum* in Appellate Courts", (1947), 63 LQR, 461: this is a penetrating discussion of some of the problems.

2. WRIGHT, R.A. "Precedents", (1943), 8 CLJ, pp. 127–129: some of the major difficulties are reviewed.

3. HONORÉ, A.M. "*Ratio Decidendi*: Judge and Court", (1955), 71 LQR, 196: this is a discussion of *Fellner* v. *Minister of the Interior*, 1954 (4), SA 523 (AD).

4. GOODERSON, R.N. Note in (1955), 33 Can BR, 612: this, too, is a discussion of *Fellner's* case.

5. R.E.M.: Note in (1950), 66 LQR, 298: this discusses the effect of disagreement among judges in appellate courts and briefly compares the English and Scots practice.

6. ASQUITH, C. "Some Aspects of the Work of the Court of Appeal", (1950), 1 JSPTL (NS), 350: in the latter part there is a discussion of the problems of *ratio decidendi* in tribunals with multiple opinions.

7. STONE, O.M. "Appeals and the Doctrine of Precedent", (1951), 14 MLR, 493: this case-note shows the difficulties of determining what is *ratio* and what is *dictum*.

8. A.M.: "*Ratio Decidendi* in Appellate Courts", (1949), 23 Aust LJ, 355: a short note on the difficulty of extracting the *ratio decidendi* when judges give different reasons.

9. BERMAN, H.T. *The Nature and Functions of Law*, (The Foundation Press, Inc, 1958), 282–374: extracts are given from Llewellyn and Levi and, more important, extracts from selected American cases, followed by questions based on each as to the reasoning in it. There are also a brief comparison with Continental doctrines and a history of *stare decisis*.

10. The following cases and judgments are useful examples of judicial technique: Lord ATKIN and Lord MACMILLAN in *Donoghue* v. *Stevenson* [1932] AC, 562; BRAMWELL, L.J., in *Household Fire Insurance Co.* v. *Grant* (1879), 4 Ex D, 216; SCOTT, L.J., in *Haseldine* v. *C.A. Daw & Son, Ltd.* [1941] 2 KB, 343; [1941] 3 All ER, 156; DENNING, J., in *Central London Property Trust, Ltd.* v. *High Trees House, Ltd.* [1947] KB, 130; [1956] 1 All ER, 256; DENNING and ASQUITH, L.JJ., in *Candler* v. *Crane Christmas & Co.* [1951] 2 KB, 164; [1951] 1 All ER, 426; Lord MACDERMOTT in *Walsh* v. *Curry* [1955] NI, 112; *Scruttons Ltd.* v. *Midland Silicones, Ltd.* [1962] AC, 446; [1962] 1 All ER, 1. *Rylands* v. *Fletcher* (1868), LR 3 HL, 330; DENNING, L.J. in *Broom* v. *Morgan* [1953] 1 QB, 597; [1953] 1 All ER, 849; Viscount SIMONDS and Lord REID in *Davie* v. *New Merton Board Mills, Ltd.* [1959] AC, 604; [1959] 1 All ER, 346; *Fellner* v. *Minister of the Interior* (1954), (4) SA, 524 (AD); *Hedley Byrne & Co, Ltd.* v. *Heller & Partners, Ltd.* [1964] AC, 465; [1963] 2 All ER, 575.

Obiter Dicta

11. CROSS, A.R.N. *Precedent in English Law*, (2nd ed., Oxford, 1968), pp. 80–86: a general account is given of the position of dicta.

1. MONTROSE, J.L. "The Language of, and a Notation for, the Doctrine of Precedent", (1951–53), 2 Ann LR, 325 *et seq*.: this gives, *inter alia*, explanation of obiter dicta.

2. RAM, J. *The Science of Legal Judgment*, (2nd ed. J. Townshend, Baker, Voorhis & Co, New York, 1871), chap. 5, especially pp. 102–107: this gives a general account and an estimate of the weight of various types of dicta.

3. SLESSER, H. *The Judicial Office and Other Matters*, (Hutchinson & Co, Ltd, 1942), a general account.

4. See also the discussion of *Bell* v. *Lever Bros*., by P.A. LANDON: (1935), 51 LQR, 650; T.H. TYLOR: (1936), 52 LQR, 27; C.J. HAMSON: (1937), 53 LQR, 118.

5. R.E.M.: Note in (1944), 60 LQR, 222: this draws attention to the suggested distinction between *"obiter dicta"* and *"judicial dicta"*.

Logic in the Judicial Process

6. GUEST, A.G. "Logic in the Law", in *Oxford Essays in Jurisprudence*, (ed. A.G. Guest, Oxford, 1961), chap. 7: the function of logic in law is explained and certain misconceptions are dispelled.

7. TREUSCH, P.E. "The Syllogism", in J. Hall, *Readings in Jurisprudence*, (Bobbs-Merrill Co, Inc, 1938), p. 539: this provides a useful account of the terminology and nature of syllogistic reasoning with reference to case-law, as well as a demonstration of certain fallacies.

8. COHEN, M.R. "The Place of Logic in the Law", (1916–17), 29 Harv LR, 622: logic is valuable in testing conclusions derived from given premises. It is the latter that need to be examined. "Facts" are not as rigid and principles not as flexible as supposed.

9. SMITH, G.H. "Logic, Jurisprudence and the Law", (1914), 48 Am LR, 801, at pp. 802–818: this is a general account of logic and terminology.

10. COFFEY, P. *"The Science of Logic*: II, pp. 153–157" in J. HALL: *Readings in Jurisprudence*, (The Bobbs-Merrill Co, Inc, 1938), p. 561: this discusses analogy and syllogism.

11. LLOYD, D. "Reason and Logic in the Common Law", (1948), 64 LQR, 468: this is a discussion of the uncertainty of the terms used in legal propositions and of the nature of syllogistic reasoning.

12. JENSEN, O.C. *The Nature of Legal Argument*, (Oxford, 1957), Part I: deductive and inductive reasoning in law are considered, and there is a demonstration of certain misconceptions about logic.

13. STOLJAR, S.J. "The Logical Status of a Legal Principle", (1952–53), 20 UCLR, 181: the various logical processes involved in legal reasoning are considered and stress is laid on the function of values, the "logic of attitudes".

14. HART, H.L.A. "Positivism and the Separation of Law and Morals", (1957–58),

71 Harv. LR, 593, 606: logic has its limitations in that it does not prescribe the interpretation of terms.

1. STONE, J. "Reason and Reasoning in Judicial and Juristic Argument", in *Legal Essays. A Tribute to Frede Castberg*, (Universitets-forlaget, 1963), 170: much trouble has been caused by using formal logic to reach conclusions which it cannot yield. The decisional process is subjected to acute analysis.

2. STONE, J. *Legal System and Lawyers' Reasonings*, (Stevens & Sons, Ltd, 1964), pp. 35–41, chaps. 7 and 8: semantically a judgment cannot possess any one meaning, and not even computers will help in finding what is not there. Judges nearly always have a choice as to how they decide because there may be no exclusive premise from which to reason, or the premise itself may be imprecise in a number of ways. These "categories of illusory reference" are explained in detail. A case yields a number of potentially binding *rationes*. Precedents serve to present a review of social contexts comparable to the present, the rules thought suitable and the results that follow the application of one rule or another. Where choice exists judges may or may not be aware of their responsibility in making acceptable decisions. These involve questions of justice and sociology. Arguments about justice and social facts are a basis for justifying and testing decisions. In this way rhetorical reasoning fits the judicial process better than syllogistic reasoning.

3. JONES, T.C. "Stone on Lawyers' Logic: Twenty Years On", (1965), 31 Ir. Jur, 21: this is principally a critique of J. Stone's *Legal System and Lawyers' Reasonings* in the light of developments since his earlier book in 1946.

4. HOERNLÉ, R.F.A. Review of *Science of Legal Method: Select Essays by Various Authors*, (1918), 31 Harv LR, 807: what is often condemned as bad logic is the bad selection of premises.

5. TAMMELO, I. "Sketch for a Symbolic Juristic Logic", (1955–56), 8 JLE, 277, 300: some fallacies in legal reasoning are dealt with, but in the context of a rather special system of symbols.

6. TAMMELO, I. *Outlines of Modern Legal Logic*, (Wiesbaden: Franz Steiner, 1969): this attempts to set out legal logic in symbolic formulae. It is so complicated in presentation that while it will be readily understood by logicians, it is unlikely to prove attractive to lawyers.

7. BLACKSHIELD, A.R. "Five Types of Judicial Decision", (1974), 12 Os HLJ, 539: judicial dogmatism and pragmatism are contrasting styles of judgment; legalism and realism are contrasting attitudes of theorists. By examining these it is possible to attain a more closely empirical and more flexible understanding of the realities underlying them. The five types are the Proverbial (pro-verbal), Prescriptive, Principial, Pragmatic and Pronormless. The common law fits between the second and third, but also reaches towards the first and fourth. Among theorists, the American realists fall into the last type.

Methods of Reasoning

8. MORRIS, C. *How Lawyers Think*, (Harvard, 1938), especially chaps. 3–5, 8: a careful analysis is given of the deductive and inductive processes, showing that their application is attended by special problems.

1. MORRIS, C. *The Justification of the Law*, (University of Pennsylvania Press, 1971), chap. 4: a simplified but full account is given of logical processes as they figure in law. Logic alone is never enough, since it comes into play after the major problem of settling the premises has been resolved. The general thesis of the book is that law is justified when it reflects the public's genuine and important aspirations, and the judicial process is discussed in this light.

2. MacCORMICK, D.N. "Formal Justice and the Form of Legal Arguments", (1976), 6 Etudes de Logique Juridique, 103: the formal principle of treating like cases alike calls for criteria for establishing likeness and difference. The justification for the instant decision lies in a proposed general principle and the reasons for it. But the principle of justice is forward looking as well as backward looking, i.e., it must be chosen as a basis for future decisions. Such choice is made against the background of overall coherence with the rules, principles, standards and values of the system. Formal and procedural justice thus has value independent of the substantive values of the system.

3. DEWEY, J. *How We Think*, (D.C. Heath & Co, 1909), chap. 8: the thought processes behind giving a judicial decision are examined. The selection of facts and relevant principles and the decision based on them is first explained. Then the shaping of the ideas leading to the judgment is investigated. These are tentatively formed with reference to their fitness for resolving the problem. "Meaning" is used as a tool of judgment.

4. DEWEY, J. "Logical Method and Law", (1924), 10 Corn LQ, 17: the logic of the judicial process is that of finding a reason for the decision already reached.

5. POUND, R. "The Theory of Judicial Decision", (1922–23), 36 Harv LR, 640, 802, 940: the last section is particularly important, analysing as it does the various steps in giving a decision.

6. CARDOZO, B.N. *The Nature of the Judicial Process*, (Yale University Press, 1921): this is a classic exposition by a famous American judge of the various factors that are involved, principally analogy, history, custom and sociology.

7. CORBIN, A.L. "The Judicial Process Revisited: Introduction", (1961–62), 71 Yale LJ, 195: this is mainly an appreciation of Judge Cardozo, but there are comments on certain aspects of his thesis.

8. van VOORHIS, J. "Cardozo and the Judicial Process Today", (1961–62), 71 Yale LJ, 203: growth since 1921 has been marked by a greater emphasis on sociological jurisprudence, the expansion of administrative law and vast increase in legislation. Some of the developments are reviewed in the light of Judge Cardozo's work.

9. STEIN, P.G. "Justice Cardozo, Marcus Terentius Varro and the Roman Juristic Process," (1967), 2 Ir Jur (NS), 367: three of Cardozo's four methods of legal development are reflected in the work of the Roman grammarian Varro, viz., analogy, custom and history ("nature"). Analogical reasoning was introduced into law by Labeo.

10. FRIENDLY, H.J. "Reactions of a Lawyer – Newly made Judge", (1961–62), 71 Yale LJ, 218, especially pp. 229 *et seq.*: how do judges in fact judge? Intuition needs to be trained by experience. The judge's personal beliefs as to the

desirability of a certain result are relevant, but they are kept in a subordinate place.

1. LLEWELLYN, K.N. "The Normative, the Legal, and the Law-jobs: the Problem of Juristic Method", (1939–40), 49 Yale LJ, 1355: beneath all doctrines lie problems which are a proper study for social disciplines. The jobs of the law are the disposal of trouble-cases, which is a "garage-repair" type of job; preventive channelling of conduct and expectations so as to avoid trouble; and to legitimise authoritative action.

2. LLEWELLYN, K.N. *The Common Law Tradition. Deciding Appeals*, (Little, Brown & Co, 1960): the author takes issue with those who deny predictability in the judicial process. There is "reckonability", which is based on a judge's selection of the right rule for the case in hand guided by his "situation-sense". This "situation-sense" is the product of the whole inherited culture and craft of the law. Judicial discretion is not exercised at large, but is conditioned in a predictable way.

3. CLARK, C.E. and TRUBEK, D.M. "The Creative Role of the Judge: Restraint and Freedom in the Common Law Tradition", (1961–62), 71 Yale LJ, 255: this article is principally a criticism of K.N. Llewellyn's *Common Law Tradition* and it comes down firmly on the side of Cardozo's thesis, and is in fact one of a series of articles on Cardozo. Llewellyn saw an objective factor in guiding judges so that they are not free to do as they wish. This thesis is criticised on the ground that Llewellyn underplays the subjective element, and that the failure to take account of the subjective element will lead to a failure to achieve what Llewellyn seeks to achieve, namely, predictability.

4. ALLEN, C.K. "Precedent and Logic", (1925), 41 LQR, 329: this discusses the process of deciding a case: (to some extent this account has been superseded by *Law in the Making*, chap. 3).

5. LEVI, E.H. *An Introduction to Legal Reasoning*, (Chicago, 1948): legal reasoning has a logic of its own. He discusses this with reference to case-law and statute-law.

6. POLLOCK, F. "The Science of Case-law" in *Essays in Jurisprudence and Ethics*, (Macmillan & Co, 1882), p. 237: this seeks to show the analogies between the method of natural scientists and common lawyers, and particularly the process employed by the latter in dealing with novel situations.

7. WASSERSTROM, R.A. *The Judicial Decision*, (Stanford University Press, 1961), chaps. 2–3, 7: these discuss criticisms of the deductive theory, showing that many of them stem from misconceptions of the function of logic. The judicial process is a process of justification, not of discovery. This should be a "two-level procedure of justification", i.e., the decision deduced from the most desirable rule.

8. DWORKIN, R.M. "Does Law have a Function? A Comment on the Two-level Theory of Decision", (1964–65), 74 Yale LJ, 640: Professor Wasserstrom's thesis is criticised on the ground that the assumptions underlying it make it valueless. These are said to be that there is some unique goal or function which a legal system should serve, that judicial decision should involve calculation of the sort discussed, and the absence of legislative rules.

1. SHUMAN, S.I. "Justification of Judicial Decisions", (1971), 59 Calif. LR, 715: there is need for rational justification of judicial decisions. It is necessary to distinguish between justifying decisions and justifying the rules, principles and policies relied on to furnish standards. In connection with the latter there is a further distinction between justifying the principles themselves and reliance on them. Justifying actual decisions and reliance on principles pertain to *stare decisis* and are part of the judicial institution; the others are not.

2. MORRIS, C. "Peace Through Law: the Role and Limits of Judicial Adjudication", (1960–61), 109 U Pa LR, 218: a judicial decision is "rational" only when supported by acceptable rational grounds. Judicial rationality is a work of art. It should satisfy those who have to live with it as being the right answer to the problem, but the judge should also keep within his role.

3. JØRGENSEN, S. *Law and Society*, (Akademisk Boghandel, 1972), chap. 4: a judgment is not exclusively a conclusion, but a decision. The judge's argumentation is directed primarily to convincing the parties that the decision is not arbitrary. The problem of decision depends on the state of legal material and on prevailing legal methods or argument.

4. DEUTSCH, J.G. "Precedent and Adjudication", (1973–74), 83 Yale LJ, 1553: with the aid of a case various fact-patterns are presented to "show" rather than "state" rules. No comprehensive normative theory can be formulated which will guide a court. Precedent is a tool by which a court chooses between various alternative grounds of decision. Precedent operates for the future, so a court has to take account of the future of that decision. It is in this sense that a decision is the creation of a precedent.

5. FRANK, J.N. "What Courts Do in Fact", (1932), 26 Ill LR, 645: this points out the difficulty of attaining certainty because of the uncertainty of "facts"; and that the decision often precedes the explanation.

6. FRANK, J.N. *Law and the Modern Mind*, (Stevens & Sons, Ltd, 1949), chaps. 12, 14: the judge begins with a vaguely formed conclusion and then finds premises to support it. The decision is the result of the judge's personal experience during the hearing. See also J.N. FRANK: *Courts on Trial*, (Princeton, 1950), chaps. 19, 20, 23.

7. ADLER, M.J. "Law and the Modern Mind: a Symposium. Legal Certainty", (1931), 31 Col LR, 91: the parties to a dispute so marshal their authorities as to establish the premises from which the desired conclusion will follow logically. The judge has to choose.

8. OLIPHANT, H. and HEWITT, A. "Introduction" to J. RUEFF, *From the Physical to the Social Sciences: Introduction to a Study of Economic and Ethical Theory*, (trans. H. Green) in J. HALL, *Readings in Jurisprudence*, (Bobbs-Merrill Co, Inc, 1938), p. 355: this is a discussion of the deductive and inductive methods, showing that the selection of premises depends on the choice between different interests.

9. AUBERT, V. "Structure of Legal Thinking" in *Legal Essays, A Tribute to Frede Castberg*, (Universitetsforlaget, 1963), 41: there is a difference in the thinking process involved in practical and juristic work. The former, as a decisional process, differs from scientific thought in that it proceeds by comparison.

1. COOK, W.W. "The Logical and Legal Bases of the Conflict of Laws", (1924), 33 Yale LJ, 457: the premises of a syllogism must be constructed before the deduction is performed.

2. GREEN, L. "The Duty Problem in Negligence Cases", (1928), 28 Col LR, 1014, at pp. 1019–1022: he makes the point that a judicial opinion is a justification in words of a judgment already passed.

3. ROBINSON, E.S. *Law and Lawyers*, (The Macmillan Co, New York, 1935), chap. 8: the psychological processes behind the giving of judicial decisions are examined. The expressed reasons serve to persuade the judge himself and others of the correctness of his original conclusion. Although the mental operations of a judge are his own, yet his acceptance or rejection of them is governed by his estimate of the opinions of others.

4. DICKINSON, J. "Legal Rules and their Function in the Process of Decision", (1931). 79 U Pa LR, 833: this stresses the importance of arguing from rules even though discretion may enter into the process. See also "Legal Rules, their Application and Elaboration", *ibid.*, p. 1052: "application" means employing a rule to decide a case; "elaboration" means the creation of a new rule to fill a gap. These processes are examined in detail, with particular attention to the finding of similarities and dissimilarities.

5. SEIDMAN, R.B. "The Judicial Process Reconsidered in the Light of Role-theory", (1969), 32 MLR, 516: there is a difference between "clear" and "trouble" cases. In the former, there is a rule at hand and the facts fall clearly within the inner core of the categories specified by the rule; in the latter one or other of these conditions is lacking. The judge's tasks differ too. In "clear" cases he is applying a pre-existing rule; in "trouble" cases he makes a rule *ex post facto*.

6. LEVY, B.H. *Cardozo and Frontiers of Legal Thinking*, (New York, 1938), pp. 39–63, 86–96: the judicial method is neither exclusively deductive nor inductive. The judge reaches a conclusion and then proceeds to justify it.

7. SINCLAIR, K. "Legal Reasoning: in Search of an Adequate Theory of Argument", (1971), 59 Calif LR, 821: various theories of logic are being evolved as well as decision and games theories, but there is as yet no comprehensive theory of legal reasoning. The reaction against Austinian jurisprudence led to a turn away from deduction towards induction and analogy, both of which the author finds wanting. What is needed is a return to deduction with a theory centred on the weight and content of supporting deductive reasoning.

8. KEETON, G.W. and LLOYD, D. (edd.): in *The British Commonwealth. The Development of its Laws and Constitutions*, (Stevens & Sons, Ltd, 1955), 1, pp. 15–19: a succinct account of the extent of judicial discretion is provided.

9. LLEWELLYN, K.N. *Jurisprudence. Realism in Theory and Practice*, (Chicago, 1962), chap. 6: it is the use that judges make of precedents that is important, and this is guided by outside considerations.

10. VON MEHREN, A.T. *The Civil Law System: Cases and Materials*, (Prentice-Hall, Inc, 1957), chap. 16, especially at pp. 821–822: a decision is the accommodation of two or more interests, and this is not purely mechanical.

1. POWELL, T.R. "The Judiciality of Minimum-wage Legislation", (1923–24), 37 Harv LR, 545: this gives a demonstration of how the personal views of judges dictated their attitude towards a legislative enactment.

2. McMAHON, B.M.E. "Conclusions on Judicial Behaviour from a Comparative Study of Occupiers' Liability", (1975), 38 MLR, 39: the article considers the old common law categories of visitors according to which occupiers' duties were graded. These conceptual categories were unsatisfactory and to overcome these judges used various devices – re-definition, distinguishing, use of alternative and competing categories and fictions. When compared with the manner in which Civil law systems approach the same problems, the common law methods of reasoning leave much to be desired.

3. WISDOM, J. "Gods", in *Philosophy and Psycho-Analysis*, (Oxford: Basil Blackwell, 1957), 149, at pp. 157–158: in some types of cases the reasoning consists of viewing the facts one way and another so as to be able to perceive similarities and dissimilarities to past cases.

4. WISDOM, J. "Philosophy, Metaphysics and Psycho-Analysis" in *Philosophy and Psycho-Analysis*, (Oxford: Blackwell, 1957), pp. 248–254: a still more forceful presentation of the same point as above.

5. LLOYD, D. *Introduction to Jurisprudence*, (3rd ed., Stevens & Sons, Ltd, 1972), pp. 729–733: this stresses the same point as Wisdom (*supra*), and points out that judicial reasoning has a logic of its own.

6. CASTBERG, F. *Problems of Legal Philosophy*, (2nd ed., Oslo University Press; Allen & Unwin, Ltd, 1957), chap. 3, especially sects. 2–3: this draws attention to the insufficiency of logic in legal thinking which involves the subsumption of cases under normative propositions.

7. JØRGENSEN, S. "Argumentation and Decision" in *Liber Amicorum in Honour of Professor Alf Ross*, (Copenhagen, 1969), 261: to Ross the crucial problems are: What is law? and What does it mean to say that law is valid? Only "is" statements can be verified. Valid law is a normative ideology that animates a judge. It is pointed out that Ross does not tackle the question how the judge himself arrives at his ideas of valid law. Various processes of decision-making are then discussed.

8. FRANK, J.N. "Mr. Justice Holmes and Non-Euclidean Thinking", (1932), 17 Corn LQ, 568: premises should be selected according to their correspondence with observable phenomena or utility.

9. AUSTIN, J. *Lectures on Jurisprudence*, (5th ed. R. Campbell, J. Murray, 1885), II, Excursus on Analogy, pp. 1001–1020: analogical reasoning and the use of the syllogism are explained.

10. VINOGRADOFF, P. *Common-Sense in Law*, (3rd ed., H.G. Hanbury, Oxford University Press, 1959), chap. 7, pp. 132 *et seq.*: the syllogistic form of reasoning and the use of analogy are explained.

11. HAMMOND, W.G. "Appendix G to Legal and Political Hermeneutics", pp. 276–280 in J. HALL, *Readings in Jurisprudence*, (Bobbs-Merrill Co, Inc, 1938), 568: the limits of analogical reasoning are examined.

1. FREUND, E. "Interpretation of Statutes", (1917), 65 U Pa LR, 207: use of analogy in the interpretation of statute is considered.

2. ALLEN, C.K. *Law in the Making*, (7th ed. Oxford, 1964), pp. 285–311: this is a general account of the working of legal induction.

3. PATON, G.W. *A Text-Book of Jurisprudence*, (4th ed., G.W. Paton and D.P. Derham, Clarendon Press, Oxford, 1972), chap. 8, sect. 43: the operation of syllogistic and inductive reasoning is discussed.

4. LLEWELLYN, K.N. *The Bramble Bush*, (New York, 1930), chap. 5, pp. 67–73: this gives an account of the inductive process in constructing premises.

5. O'SULLIVAN, R. "On Law Reporting", (1940–41), 4 MLR, 104, pp. 107 *et seq.*: this discusses how cases were decided before the evolution of *stare decisis* and alleges that the inductive method is without foundation in history or authority.

6. MAYO, L.H. and JONES, E.M. "Legal-policy Decision Process: Alternative Thinking and the Predictive Function", (1964–65), 33 Geo Wash LR, 318: lawyers should now learn to think in terms of process rather than formulae, the movement of events as well as the relevance of formulae. In a very long article the structure and working of a Basic Decisional Model are set out and explained.

7. HIGGINS, R. "Policy Considerations and the International Judicial Process", (1968), 17 ICLQ, 58: the distinction, well-known in International Law, between "legal" and "political" disputes is critically examined. The idea that a judge has simply to apply the law as he finds it is not applicable to international adjudication any more than it is to municipal adjudication. A decision at International Law requires concern with the policy alternatives, including the interests of the parties and also of the world community. The judge's task is a choice between alternatives, and the assessment of extra-legal considerations is part of the legal process.

8. MacDERMOTT, J.C. "The Quality of Judgment", (1970), 21 NILQ, 178: the quality of judgment has to be possessed by a good lawyer at whatever level he functions. This is the ability to get to the heart of a problem without losing sight of detail. The main issues should guide the ascertainment of fact. Drafting of statutes, letters and judgments, arguing in court and the "rule of law" are considered in turn.

9. *Law and Philosophy. A Symposium*, (ed. S. Hook, New York, University Press, 1964), Part III: this is of very general interest only. The various contributions touch on some aspects of the judicial process, but none are penetrating.

10. The following may be consulted as illustrating judicial technique: *Armstrong v. Strain* [1951] 1 TLR, 856; affirmed, [1952] 1 KB, 232; [1952] 1 All ER, 139; *Donoghue v. Stevenson*, [1932] AC, 562; *Hedley Byrne & Co., Ltd. v. Heller & Partners, Ltd*, [1964] AC, 465; [1963] 2 All ER, 575; *Haley v. London Electricity Board* [1965] AC, 778; [1964] 3 All ER, 185; *Myers v. Director of Public Prosecutions* [1965] AC, 1001; [1964] 2 All ER, 881; *South Pacific Co. v. Jensen* (1917), 244 US 205; *Morgan v. Fear* [1907] AC, 425; *Fibrosa Spolka Akcyjna v. Fairbairn Lawson Combe Barbour, Ltd.* [1943] AC, 32; [1942] 2 All ER, 122; *Holmes v. Director of Public Prosecutions* [1946] AC, 588; [1946] 2 All ER, 124; *Foakes v. Beer* (1884), 9 App Cas, 605; *Leathley v. J. Fowler & Co., Ltd*, [1946] KB, 579; [1946] 2 All ER, 326; Lord Diplock in

Home Office v. *Dorset Yacht Co., Ltd,* [1970] AC, 1004, 1058; [1970] 2 All ER, 294, 324.

Judges Making Law

1. CARTER, J.C. "The Ideal and the Actual in the Law", (1890), 24 Am LR, 752: the view that law is custom and that the task of the judges is to discover it is supported.

2. CARTER, J.C. *Law: Its Origin, Growth and Function,* (G.P. Putnam's Sons, 1907), pp. 65 *et seq.*: an elaboration of the above.

3. AUSTIN, J. *Lectures on Jurisprudence,* (5th ed. R. Campbell, J. Murray, 1885), II, pp. 628–647: this is a detailed demonstration of how judges make law as contrasted with legislation.

4. FRANK, J.N. *Law and the Modern Mind,* (Stevens & Sons, Ltd, 1949), pp. 32–37, and Appendix I: explanations are offered of the orthodox view that judges do not make law, with especial reference to the desire for a "father-symbol".

5. LEVY, B.H. *Cardozo and Frontiers of Legal Thinking,* (New York, 1938), pp. 39–46: this is a discussion of the law-making function of judges with an investigation into the reasons for the orthodox theory.

6. VON MEHREN, A.T. *The Civil Law System: Cases and Materials,* (Prentice-Hall Inc, 1957), chap. 16, sects. 3–4: this provides an excellent account of four situations in which judges do make law and the factors affecting this function.

7. GRAY, J.C. *The Nature and Sources of the Law,* (2nd ed., R. Gray, Macmillan Co, New York, 1921), chap. 9: this is a critical discussion of the orthodox view. The conclusion is that judges do make law.

8. POUND, R. "The Theory of Judicial Decision", (1922–23), 36 Harv LR, 802: judicial attitudes depend on current philosophies and the orthodox theory was influenced by the analytical and historical theories of law.

9. POUND, R. *An Introduction to the Philosophy of Law,* (Yale University Press, 1922), pp. 100–129: interpretation of law shades into law-making and law-applying.

10. POUND, R. *Jurisprudence,* (West Publishing Co, 1959), IV, chap. 20, especially sect. 115: law-making inevitably enters into the process of law-applying.

11. COHEN, M.R. "The Process of Judicial Legislation", (1914), 48 Am LR, 161: this challenges the Blackstonian theory by showing how judges make law even when purporting to find it.

12. FULLER, L.L. "What Motives give rise to the Historical Legal Fiction?" in *Recueil d'Etudes sur les Sources du Droit en l'Honneur de F. Geny,* (Lib. du Recueil Sirey, 1934), II, 157: why do judges introduce new doctrine under the linguistic cover of the old? Various possible reasons are considered.

13. DICKINSON, J. "Legal Rules and their Function in the Process of Decision", (1931), 79 U Pa LR, 833: a new rule is created when there is a choice and a balance has to be effected between the rules themselves.

1. CARDOZO, B.N. *The Growth of the Law*, (Yale University Press, 1924), chap. 5: this is a demonstration of how essential the creative function is.

2. LEFROY, A.H.F. "Judge-made Law", (1904), 20 LQR, 399: different types of judge-made law are discussed.

3. LEFROY, A.H.F. "The Basis of Case-law", (1906), 22 LQR, 293: the judicial function in cases *primae impressionis* is considered.

4. THAYER, E.R. "Judicial Legislation: its Legitimate Function in the Development of the Common Law", (1891–92), 5 Harv LR, 172: growth of the law, whether common law or statute law, at the hands of the judges is unavoidable. Examples are provided at length. But no precise rules can be laid down to regulate it.

5. CARPENTER, C.E. "Court Decisions and the Common Law", (1917), 17 Col LR, 593: the theory that judges do not make law is inconsistent with the origin and growth of the law, besides operating unjustly.

6. KAVANAGH, P.B. "Judging as an Act of Will", (1970), 120 New LJ, 529: this is a simplified statement of the discretion that inevitably comes in for various reasons. Logic cannot be the determinant. The point is illustrated with reference to certain recent cases.

7. CLARKE, S.B. "What may be Done to Enable the Courts to Allay the Present Discontent with the Administration of Justice", (1916), 50 Am LR, 161: a a general attack is launched on *stare decisis* and on the law-making power of judges.

8. HALL, R.S. "Do Courts make Laws and should Precedents Command the Obedience of Lower Courts?" (1917), 51 Am LR, 833: this is a defence of the present system against S.B. Clarke's attack (*supra*). The law-making power of the courts is important and necessary.

9. WEILER, P.C. "Legal Values and Judicial Decision-making", (1970), 48 Can BR, 1: the part played by judges in deciding cases is reviewed in detail. There are values in a legal order, but the judges' policy-making function is limited. Adjudication according to established rules is prima facie preferable. There should be fidelity to principle, as distinct from rules; the leeways come in here.

10. HALL, E.M. "Law Reform and the Judiciary's Role", (1972), 10 Os HLJ, 399: to say that legislative power is in the legislature and judicial power is in the courts assumes that the two powers are opposed. But they cannot be neatly distinguished. Judges cannot help "making law". To say that judges must not take political and social issues into account is itself a political decision – to introduce yesterday's politics into today's law. Such an attitude is inadequate. Courts and legislature are pursuing the same ends. (See also F. VAUGHAN: "Emmett Matthew Hall: the Activist as Justice", *ibid.*, p. 411: giving a personal background to Justice Hall).

11. LLEWELLYN, K.N. *The Common Law Tradition. Deciding Appeals* (Little, Brown & Co, 1960): the Bar has lost confidence in the Supreme Court because of the lack of "reckonability". This book is a powerful answer to this charge and seeks to show that there is "reckonability" notwithstanding the creative element. It

derives from the judges' "situation-sense" for each dispute, which is a product of calculable factors.

1. JENKS, E. "English Civil Law", (1916–17), 30 Harv LR, 1, at pp. 13–19: the extent of judicial law-making and its significance are reviewed.

2. ALLEN, C.K. *Law in the Making*, (7th ed., Oxford, 1964), pp. 302–311: judges do make law, but in a different sense from the way in which the legislature does so.

3. LAMBERT, E. "Codified Law and Case Law: their Part in Shaping the Policies of Justice" in *Science of Legal Method: Select Essays by Various Authors*, (trans. E. Bruncken and L.B. Register, Boston Book Co., 1917), chap. 9, sects. 6–9: the orthodox doctrine is a fiction, for judges do make law.

4. EVERSHED, F.R. "The Judicial Process in Twentieth Century England", (1961), 61 Col LR, 761: the judicial function of today is contrasted with that in the past, and also compared with the function in America. Law being a social structure it has to be applied to novel social conditions. Thus the creative function of the judges involves what Cardozo calls the Method of Sociology. This point is illustrated with reference to various branches of the law. At the end some relaxation of *stare decisis* in the highest tribunal is urged. (This has since occurred.)

5. DIPLOCK, K. "The Courts as Legislators", *Presidential Address to the Holdsworth Club*, 1965: the courts by the very nature of their functions have to act as legislators. Because of the doctrine of *stare decisis* in every judgment a court speaks to the future as to the past. Creation of new machinery is for Parliament; the regulation of human relations within that framework is for the courts. Three criticisms of judge-made law and desirable changes in judicial attitude are considered.

6. WRIGHT, R.A. *Legal Essays and Addresses*, (Cambridge University Press, 1939), Preface, pp. xvi–xx: change is accomplished by a perpetual erosion of the authorities.

7. SCARMAN, L.G. "The English Judge", (1967), 30 MLR, 1: judges have much freedom of choice in the way in which they give their decisions. This lays a great responsibility upon them. There is an explanation of the appointment and qualification of judges.

8. DEVLIN, P. "Judges and Lawmakers", (1976), 39 MLR, 1: Lord Devlin answers the criticism that judges tend to be torpid by comparing the functions of judging and lawmaking. He distinguishes between "activist lawmaking", which keeps the law abreast of change in the public consensus, and "creative" or "dynamic lawmaking", which seeks to generate change in the consensus itself. Judicial lawmaking should be confined to the former. Judges need to be impartial and to appear to be so; if they indulged in "creative lawmaking" they would be taking sides. He also compares judicial activism in the common law and in statute law.

9. EDMUND-DAVIES, E. "Judicial Activism", (1975), 28 CLP, 1: judges inevitably act as legislators because law has to react to social needs and Parliament is now no more rapid in its working than it was seventy years ago. Hence, judges are

compelled to react in the interim and on innumerable minor matters. A judge may pay lip-service to *stare decisis* but he does not lack courage to condemn and shake off unjust laws in various ways.

1. JAFFE, L. *English and American Judges as Lawmakers*, (Oxford University Press, 1969): courts and administrative agencies are partners in government, just as courts and legislatures are partners in lawmaking. Judges should exercise a limited role in protecting individuals and minorities from exercises of power and in providing leadership in tackling social problems. All this involves lawmaking power. Questions considered are how judicial activism is reconcilable with democracy, what is meant by "making law" and judicial impartiality.

2. SNYDER, O.C. *Preface to Jurisprudence*, (Bobbs-Merrill Co, Inc, 1954), Part III, chap. 3, pp. 415–418: 426–438: this is a discussion of the basis of the orthodox theory and of how the judges do make law.

3. FRIEDMANN, W. *Legal Theory*, (5th ed., Stevens & Sons, Ltd, 1967), chap. 32: this is a general discussion in the context of precedent as a whole.

4. FRIEDMANN, W. "Legal Philosophy and Judicial Lawmaking", (1961), 61 Col LR, 821: the need for judicial creativeness is discussed from various points of view.

5. LLOYD, D. *The Idea of Law*, (Penguin Books, Ltd, A 688, 1964), chap. 11: judicial independence is important. The traditional view that judges do not make law is unreal in view of the part played by value-judgments. Logic alone cannot resolve problems, and there is a limit to the use of analogy. The binding force of precedent is discussed in general terms and contrasted with the position in Civil Law jurisdictions.

6. LLOYD, D. *Introduction to Jurisprudence*, (3rd ed., Stevens & Sons, Ltd, 1972), pp. 721–727: a general account of judges making law is provided. There is also a comparison of the creativity of British and American judges.

7. LLOYD, D. in *The British Commonwealth. The Development of its Laws and Constitutions*, (edd. G.W. Keeton and D. Lloyd, (Stevens & Sons, Ltd, 1955), I, pp. 23–24: a brief summary of judicial law-making.

8. BRETT, P. *An Essay on a Contemporary Jurisprudence*, (Butterworths, 1975), pp. 49–71: the judicial method is a hypothetico-deductive one in which the judicial hypothesis is formed out of a world of statements, theories and arguments and represents the perception of some pattern out of them, which the judge then proceeds to test. The data in which he works "exists" in this frame of reference and in this sense he "finds" his decision. But the decision does not "exist" until he formulates it, and in this sense he "makes" new material for the world of statements etc. It is when a hypothesis does not fit the material of that world that a decision is "felt" to be wrong.

9. VINOGRADOFF, P. *Common-Sense in Law*, (3rd ed., H.G. Hanbury, Oxford University Press, 1959), chap. 7, pp. 147 *et seq.*: the retroactive operation of precedent is discussed.

10. CARDOZO, B.N. *The Nature of the Judicial Process*, (Yale University Press, 1921), chap. 4: the retroactivity of precedent may not be such a hardship in practice as it might appear.

1. WIGMORE, J.H. Editorial Preface: "The Judicial Function", in *Science of Legal Method: Select Essays by Various Authors*, (trans. E. Bruncken and L.B. Register, Boston Book Co., 1917), pp. xxxvii–xxxviii: the suggestion is advanced that overruling should operate for the future.

2. FREEMAN, R.H. "The Protection Afforded against the Retroactive Operation of an Overruling Decision", (1918), 18 Col LR, 230: this is an enquiry into the extent to which American courts seek to minimise the retroactivity of precedent.

3. Von MOSCHZISKER, R. "*Stare Decisis* in the Courts of Last Resort", (1923–24), 37 Harv LR, 409: difficulties of Wigmore's suggestion (*supra*) are considered.

4. KOCOUREK, A. "Retrospective Decisions and *Stare Decisis* and a Proposal", (1931), 17 Am BAJ, 180: the draft is given of a proposed statute to enable a superior court to apply a principle to the instant case and to overrule it for the future.

5. CARDOZO, B.N. "Jurisprudence" in *Selected Writings of B.N. Cardozo*, (ed. M.E. Hall, Fallon Law Book Co., New York, 1947), pp. 35–36: the suggestion that overruling should operate prospectively and not retrospectively is supported.

6. LEVY, B.H. "Realist Jurisprudence and Prospective Overruling", (1960–61), 109 U Pa LR, 1: a readier acceptance of realist jurisprudence would have enabled prospective overruling to be more widely used. The Blackstonian doctrine obscures the distinction between deciding the instant case and laying down a rule for the future. This article contains a full account of the history of prospective overruling in America down to 1961.

7. SNYDER, O.C. *Preface to Jurisprudence*, (Bobbs-Merrill Co, Inc, 1954), Part III, chap. 3, pp. 418–419: prospective overruling is supported.

8. KEETON, R.E. "Creative Continuity in the Law of Torts", (1961–62), 75 Harv LR, 463, at pp. 486 *et seq.*: prospective and retrospective overruling in the law of torts is considered.

9. FRIEDMANN, W. "Limits of Judicial Lawmaking and Prospective Overruling", (1966), 29 MLR, 593: it is indisputable that judges do make law. If so, it is necessary to consider the limits of their lawmaking function. In this connection the operation of prospective overruling, in criminal and civil cases, is considered.

10. LEACH, W.B. "Divorce by Plane-Ticket in the Affluent Society – with a Side-Order of Jurisprudence", (1966), 14 Kansas LR, 549: prospective overruling would remove the vested interest objection to judicial reform. All courts, civil and criminal, should have the option to give "prospective only" application to overruling decisions. This point is considered in connection with a detailed and amusing study of a divorce case. (See also W.B. LEACH, "Revisionism in the House of Lords: the Bastion of Rigid *Stare Decisis* Falla", (1967), 80 Harv LR, 797; R.W.M. DIAS, "Precedents in the House of Lords – a Much Needed Reform", (1966), CLJ, 153).

11. ANONYMOUS. "Prospective Overruling and Retroactive Application in the Federal Courts", (1961–62), 71 Yale LJ, 907: the declaratory theory of precedent is considered in detail with reference to the constitutional doctrines of the United States. The conclusion is that it should be left to a later court

to decide whether or not to give retroactive effect to a new rule enunciated by a previous court. Such a decision should be reached after a consideration of the criteria relevant to the purpose of the new rule and to the effective and equitable operation of the legal system.

1. MISHKIN, P.J. "Foreword: The High Court, the Great Writ, and the Due Process of Time and Law", (1965–66), 79 Harv LR, 56: the rejection of the Blackstonian myth that judges only declare what is law does not dispense with other good reasons for giving judicial decisions retroactive operation. The question is discussed with reference to leading American cases.

2. STONE, J. *Social Dimensions of Law and Justice*, (Stevens & Sons, Ltd, 1966), pp. 658–667: the question of prospectivity and retrospectivity is discussed in relation to judicial institutions as instruments of legal ordering.

3. WEILER, P.C. "Legal Values and Judicial Decision-making", (1970), 48 Can BR, 1, 29–33: prospective overruling is considered in the general context of the decisional process.

4. KOCOUREK, A. and KOVEN, H. "Renovation of the Common Law through *Stare Decisis*", (1934–35), 29 Ill LR, 971: prospective overruling is advocated as providing for stability of concluded transactions on the one hand, and the need for progress and change for the future. Retrospectivity and its relation to the declaratory theory of precedent are considered in detail and that theory is criticised.

5. FRIEDLAND, M.L "Prospective and Retrospective Judicial Lawmaking", (1974), 24 UTLJ, 170: American, Canadian and English practice are contrasted. Possible techniques for limiting the scope of retrospectivity are considered, e.g., preventing "collateral attacks" on judgments, protecting those who relied on the previous law, use of rules of procedure and evidence, constitutional cases.

6. TRAYNOR, R. "*Quo Vadis*, Prospective Overruling: a Question of Judicial Responsibility", (Pamphlet, University of Birmingham, 1975): an American judge looks critically at the retroactive operation of precedent and considers the effect of overruling with reference to American and English cases. Prospective overruling would be a way of rationally developing the law, but there are dangers in its unwise use.

7. NICOL, A.G.L. "Prospective Overruling: a New Device for English Courts?" (1976), 39 MLR, 542: a judicial decision is descriptive of what the law is believed to be and prescriptive of what it should be for the future. The American technique of prospective overruling is considered as well as varieties of different situations. Nine objections are carefully considered and rejected.

Factors Affecting the Weight of Precedents

8. RAM, J. *The Science of Legal Judgment*, (2nd ed., J. Townshend, Baker, Voorhis & Co., New York, 1871), sects. 2–3: this gives an account of the factors which would increase or reduce the value of a precedent.

9. WAMBAUGH, E. *The Study of Cases*, (2nd ed., Boston, 1894), chap. 5: a detailed account is given of the various considerations that affect the assessment of the value of a case.

1. ANONYMOUS. "The Aged Precedent", (1965), SLT, 53: when may a court upset
   a long-established precedent? Nine factors that may prevent overruling are set
   out. There is also a useful review of a considerable number of cases in which the
   question has been considered.

Pros and Cons of Stare Decisis

2. MULLINS, C. *In Quest of Justice*, (John Murray, 1931), chaps. 3–6: these provide
   an excellent discussion of the precedent system and the pros and cons.

3. GOODHART, A.L. "Precedent in English and Continental Law", (1934), 50 LQR,
   40: detailed consideration is given to the various arguments for *stare decisis.*

4. HOLDSWORTH, W.S. "Case Law", (1934), 50 LQR, 180: this is a defence of *stare
   decisis* on the ground that much of the criticism has been exaggerated.

5. GOODHART, A.L. "Case Law – a Short Replication", (1934), 50 LQR, 196:
   a reply to Holdsworth.

6. ALLEN, C.K. "Case Law: an Unwarrantable Intervention", (1935), 51 LQR, 353:
   while in no way minimising the defects of *stare decisis* he comes down in
   support of it.

7. HOLDSWORTH, W.S. "Precedents in the Eighteenth Century", (1935), 51 LQR,
   441: a short reply to Allen.

8. AUSTIN, J. *Lectures on Jurisprudence*, (5th ed., R. Campbell, J. Murray, 1885), II,
   pp. 647–660: seven objections to judge-made law are presented in detail.

9. WASSERSTROM, R.A. *The Judicial Decision*, (Stanford University Press, 1961),
   chap. 4: this contains a detailed discussion of the pros and cons.

10. RADIN, M. "Case Law and *Stare Decisis*: Concerning Präjudizienrecht in Amerika",
    (1933), 33 Col LR, 199: this is a review of a book by Llewellyn. *Stare decisis* is
    the doctrine that a prior decision is followed, not because it is thought to be
    right, but simply because it is a prior decision. Most of the reasons in support are
    either a form of estoppel or based on the need for certainty. As courts actually
    function, it turns out to be an instrument capable of a great many variations.

11. WRIGHT, R.A. "The Common Law in its Old Home", in *Legal Essays and
    Addresses*, (Cambridge University Press, 1939), pp. 341–345: the objections
    that *stare decisis* leads to uncertainty and voluminous law reports are over-
    estimated.

12. OLIPHANT, H. "A Return to *Stare Decisis*", (1928), 14 Am BAJ, 71, 107, 159:
    this advocates a study of social structure, a re-classification of law and a study
    of the non-vocal behaviour of judges.

13. WIGMORE, J.H. Editorial Preface: "The Judicial Function", in *Science of Legal
    Method: Select Essays by Various Authors*, (trans. E. Bruncken and L.B. Register,
    Boston Book Co. 1917), pp. xxxvi–xlii: *stare decisis* is considered with reference
    to equality, stability and certainty.

1. VON MOSCHZISKER, R. *"Stare decisis* in the Courts of Last Resort", (1923–24), 37 Harv LR, 409: the function of *stare decisis* is considered and the conclusion is that, properly used, it is useful.

2. McKEAN, F.G. "The Rule of Precedents", (1928), 76 U Pa LR, 481: in the course of a general account he considers the extent of such flexibility as there is.

3. WADE, H.W.R. "The Concept of Legal Certainty. A Preliminary Skirmish", (1940–41), 4 MLR, 183: certainty in relation to justice is considered.

4. KOCOUREK, A. *An Introduction to the Science of Law*, (Little, Brown & Co, 1930), pp. 165–85: the doctrine of *stare decisis* is discussed in outline but somewhat special attention is paid to the requirement of certainty.

5. FULLER, L.L. "American Legal Realism", (1934), 82 U Pa LR, 429: the traditional exclusion of social and other such considerations promotes uncertainty. A code is more susceptible to extension than case-law.

6. MARSH, N.S. "Principle and Discretion in the Judicial Process", (1952), 68 LQR, 226: this gives consideration to *stare decisis* in relation to certainty and flexibility.

7. CARDOZO, B.N. *The Nature of the Judicial Process*, (Yale University Press, 1921), chap. 4: adherence to precedent should be the rule, but this should be relaxed in the light of experience.

8. CARDOZO, B.N. *The Growth of the Law*, (Yale University Press, 1924), chap. 1: this is a discussion of certainty with the warning that it should not be allowed to prevent growth.

9. POLLOCK, F. "Judicial Caution and Valour", (1929), 45 LQR, 293: the problem of interpretation is to hold a balance between an excess of caution and an excess of valour.

10. SCHMITTHOFF, C.M. "The Growing Ambit of the Common Law", (1952), 30 Can BR, 48: this is indirectly relevant in that it shows how case-law has tended to relax so as to produce just and reasonable decisions.

11. JACKSON, R.H. "Decisional Law and *Stare Decisis*", (1944), 30 Am BAJ, 334: although *stare decisis* is relaxed in America, it is of value because of the certainty that it imparts. Attention is also drawn to the difficulty caused by the growing bulk of case-law.

12. SPRECHER, R.A. "The Development of the Doctrine of *Stare Decisis* and the Extent to which it should be Applied", (1945), 31 Am BAJ, 501: there is a careful evaluation in the second part of the various arguments for and against the doctrine.

13. DOUGLAS, W.O. *"Stare Decisis"*, (1949), 49 Col LR, 735: *stare decisis* represents a desire for security as the world grows more insecure. There is a suggestion that overruling should include overruling of "All the cases in the same genus as the one which is repudiated, even though they are not before the court".

14. GOLDSCHMIDT, H.W. *English Law from a Foreign Standpoint*, (Pitman & Sons,

Ltd, 1937), chap. 2, sects. 3–4: English law is favourably compared with
Continental systems. The English system does achieve certainty and flexibility.

1. GERLAND, H.B. "The Operation of the Judicial Function in English Law" in
   Science of Legal Method: Select Essays by Various Authors, (trans. E. Bruncken
   and L.B. Register, Boston Book Co, 1917), chap. 8, sects. 5–9: this considers the
   advantages and disadvantages of *stare decisis*, the latter outweighing the former.
   (Note: Gerland is said to have moved in favour of precedent later: H.W. GOLD
   GOLDSCHMIDT, *English Law from a Foreign Standpoint*, pp. 38–39.)

2. RANDALL, H.J. "Case-law on the Continent", (1919), 35 LQR, 101: this is a
   critical review of *Science of Legal Method*, especially the criticisms of the
   English system by H.B. Gerland, (*supra*).

3. POLLOCK, F. *A First Book of Jurisprudence*, (6th ed., Macmillan Co, Ltd, 1929),
   pp. 348–349: the need for consistency as the justification for *stare decisis* is
   accepted. On the whole this is achieved.

4. McLOUD, J.W. "The Value of Precedents", (1894), 28 Am LR, 218: this stresses
   the value of precedents as preserving past wisdom.

5. GOODHART, A.L. "Case Law in England and America", in *Essays in Jurisprudence
   and the Common Law*, (Cambridge University Press, 1931), chap. 3: the
   American system is moving away from *stare decisis* and the reasons for this are
   given.

6. COOPER, T.M. "The Common Law and the Civil Law – a Scot's View", (1950),
   63 Harv LR, 468, 472: consistency should not be blind imitation. *Stare decisis*
   cannot keep the law abreast of social needs.

7. CROSS, A.R.N. "Recent Developments in the Practice of Precedent – the Triumph
   of Common Sense", (1969), 43 Aust LJ, 3: the Australian High Court has refused
   to follow rulings of the House of Lords, the House of Lords has refused to be
   bound by its own rulings, and the Privy Council has upheld the view of the
   Australian High Court. While applauding these developments, certain cautions
   need to be observed. Their implications on the status of *stare decisis* are also
   considered.

8. LLOYD, D. in G.W. KEETON and D. LLOYD (edd.) *The British Commonwealth.
   The Development of its Laws and Constitutions*, (Stevens & Sons, 1955), I,
   pp. 24–26: this gives a brief evaluation of the Common Law system.

9. GOODHART, A.L. "Reporting the Law", (1939), 55 LQR, 29: this draws attention
   to the growing volume of case-law and suggestions for dealing with it.

10. STONE, O.M. "Knowing the Law", (1961), 24 MLR, 475: this is a review of the
    difficulties of finding the law.

11. CARDEN, P.T. "Loose Leaf Law Reports", (1910), 26 LQR, 75: this is interesting
    as a suggestion that would reduce bulk, cost and time.

12. SINGLETON, W.E. "Loose Leaf Law Reports", (1910), 26 LQR, 156: the above
    idea is approved with modifications.

1. BORCHARD, E.M. "Some Lessons from the Civil Law", (1916), 64 U Pa LR, 570: this includes a criticism of *stare decisis* as having outlived its usefulness.

2. TRUMBULL, L. "Precedent versus Justice", (1893), 27 Am LR, 321: *stare decisis* trains people to be followers rather than leaders.

3. GARRISON, L.M. "Blind Adherence to Precedent", (1917), 51 Am LR, 251: a former judge is quoted as stressing the danger of losing sight of principle.

4. MacCORMICK, D.N. "Can *Stare Decisis* be Abolished?" (1967), Jur R, 197: the doctrine originated in the idea that precedents were declaratory of the common law. With the collapse of that fiction, the judges were slow to avow that they do legislate. A decision is justified by showing that it is in accordance, or not in conflict, with authority; that it is desirable; or by using analogies. The effect of abolishing *stare decisis* is considered in relation to these. Although it would no longer be necessary to justify a decision with reference to authority, it should remain sufficient to do so.

5. WALKER, D.M. "Reform, Restatement and the Law Commissions", (1965), Jur R, 245, 256–262: reform of *stare decisis* is advocated in connection with the proposed overhaul of Scots law by the Scottish Law Commission.

6. COOPER, H.H.A. "*Ratio Decidendi*", (1968), 118 New LJ, 1180: a short, but incisive plea that the Law Commission should consider the question of *ratio decidendi*. Practitioners have no time to bring their tools up to date, and it is distressing to find academic lawyers professing uncertainty.

Comparison with other Systems

7. LIPSTEIN, K. "The Doctrine of Precedent in Continental Law with Special Reference to French and German Law", (1946), 28 JCL, (3rd Ser. Pt. III), p. 34: the reasons why Continental systems did not develop *stare decisis* are investigated.

8. ENSOR, R.C.K. *Courts and Judges in France, Germany and England*, (Oxford University Press, 1933), chap. 4: this is a general account of the position of the judge, with particular attention to the need for the English judge to be skilled in finding the law in precedent.

9. DAVID, R. and De VRIES, H.P. *The French Legal System*, (New York, 1958), chap. 4: this shows that in practice the French and Common Law systems do not differ very much.

10. SILVING, H. *Sources of Law*, (Wm. S. Hein & Co, Inc, New York, 1968), "'Stare Decisis' in the Civil and in the Common Law", p. 83: in Civil law countries the function of case-law is to demonstrate by means of examples the operation of statute. A combination of code and case-law is desirable, because both have advantages. Statute economises in wording, but is beset by semantic limitations; case-law is wasteful in its volume, but can amplify statutory provisions. The discussion of case-law includes most of its problems, e.g., *ratio decidendi.*

11. GUTTERIDGE, H.C. *Comparative Law*, (Cambridge University Press, 1949), chap. 7: this is a discussion of the main differences between Common Law and Continental systems and how case-law is used on the Continent.

12. ROSS, A. *On Law and Justice*, (Stevens & Sons, Ltd, 1958), pp. 84–91: the

position in Common Law and Continental countries is similar in practice, but there is a difference in approach due principally to the influence respectively of judges and jurists.

1. LAWSON, F.H. *Negligence in the Civil Law*, (Oxford University Press, 1950), pp. 231–235: this is a note on the structure and procedure of the French courts, the form of a French report and the authority of case-law in France.

2. LAMBERT, E. and WASSERMAN, M.J. "The Case Method in Canada and the Possibilities of its Adaptation to the Civil Law", (1929), 39 Yale LJ, 1: in the course of this discussion it is pointed out that case-law is an important part of the practical application of law in civil law systems.

3. ANCEL, M. "Case Law in France", (1934), 16 JCL (3rd Ser.) 1: this examines how case-law has emerged in France and the position which it now occupies.

4. GARDNER, J.C. *Judicial Precedent in Scots Law*, (W. Green & Sons, Ltd, 1936), chap. 5: the position in France and England is considered with reference to Amos, Ancel, Goodhart and Holdsworth.

5. FRIEDMANN, W. *Legal Theory*, (5th ed., Stevens & Sons, Ltd, 1967), chap. 33: the differences between the Common Law and Continental systems have been exaggerated and they have been narrowed. Other differences have now grown up.

6. COHN, E.J. "Precedents in Continental Law", (1935), 5 CLJ, 366: this shows the bad effects until 1935 of the German provision giving binding effect to decisions of the "Plenum", the United Divisions. (See substantially the same provision: Gerichtsverfassungsgesetz, 1950, 136, I–III).

7. DEÁK, F. "The Place of the 'Case' in the Common and Civil Law", (1933–34), 8 Tul LR, 337: case-law in its wider sense (not *stare decisis*) is discussed.

8. HENRY, R.L. "*Jurisprudence Constante* and *Stare Decisis* Contrasted", (1929), 15 Am BAJ, 11: this is an unfavourable comparison of *stare decisis* when contrasted with the doctrine of *Jurisprudence Constante* of Civil Law.

9. MARSH, N.S. "Deduction and Induction in the Law of Torts: a Comparative Approach", (1950–51), 33 JCL, (3rd Ser., Part III), 59: general principles on the Continent require a great deal of elaboration by case-law, while there are general principles to some extent in English law.

10. VON MEHREN, A.T. *The Civil Law System: Cases and Materials*, (Prentice-Hall, Inc, 1957), chap. 16: this is a comparative discussion of the nature of the problems concerning judicial decisions in American, French and German law.

11. SCHLESINGER, R.B. *Comparative Law: Cases, Text, Materials*, (2nd ed., The Foundation Press, Inc, Brooklyn, 1959), pp. 287–322: notes and questions with illustrative material of the operation of precedents are provided.

12. LLOYD, D. *Introduction to Jurisprudence*, (3rd ed., Stevens & Sons, Ltd, 1972), pp. 710–714: this is a general comparison of precedent in the Common Law and on the Continent, and the intermediate position in America.

13. KOTZÉ, J.G. "Judicial Precedent", (1917), 34 SALJ, 280; (1918), 144 LT, 349:

this is a discussion of the authority of precedent in Roman Law and early Roman-Dutch Law. South Africa has adopted *stare decisis* but not quite as rigidly as English law.

1. KAHN, E. "The Rules of Precedent Applied in South African Courts", (1967), 84 SALJ, 43, 175, 308: the evolution and operation of precedent in Southern Africa from the old Dutch authorities down to the present is set out in detail. The doctrine has not been as rigid as in Britain.

2. MIGNAULT, P.B. "The Authority of Decided Cases", (1925), 3 Can BR, 1: comments thereon at pp. 109, 138, 349: a brief review is given of the position in England and France and then a more detailed account of the position in Quebec.

3. FRIEDMANN, W. "Stare Decisis at Common Law and under the Civil Law of Quebec", (1953), 31 Can BR, 723: Canadian courts have adopted the main features of English practice. Even in Quebec there is a closer approach to it than to the French doctrine.

4. MacGUIGAN, M.R. "Precedent and Policy in the Supreme Court", (1967), 45 Can. BR, 627: this article reviews in detail the attitude towards *stare decisis* in Canada since the abolition of appeals to the Privy Council and the likely effect of the overthrow by the House of Lords of the doctrine of bindingness with regard to themselves.

5. DAVIDSON, C.G. "*Stare Decisis* in Louisiana", (1932–33), 7 Tul LR, 100: this shows how *stare decisis* has been adopted.

6. IRELAND, G. "The Use of Decisions by United States Students of Civil Law", (1933–34), 8 Tul LR, 358: this gives an account of how decisions are used in civilian systems.

7. WALTON, F.P. "The Relationship of the Law of France to the Law of Scotland", (1902), 14 Jur R, 17: this draws attention to the growing gulf between the two systems since Scots Law is increasingly becoming a case-law system.

8. GARDNER, J.C. "A Comparison of the Doctrine of Judicial Precedent in American Law and in Scots Law", (1940), 26 Am BAJ, 774: the position in the two countries is summarised and it is shown that the Scots practice is more flexible than the English.

9. SCHMIDT, F. "The Ratio Decidendi. A Comparative Study of a French, a German and an American Supreme Court Decision", (1965), 6 *Acta Instituti Upsaliensis Jurisprudentiae Comparativae*, 1: each of the three cases which is analysed in detail, concerns a problem of causation. The different methods used by the respective courts to reach more or less the same result are revealed and explained.

10. WALKER, D.M. "A Note on Precedent", (1949), 61 Jur R, 283: this gives a demonstration that the bulk of cases quoted in Scots courts come from this century.

11. BROWN, L.N. "The Sources of Spanish Civil Law", (1956), 5 ICLQ, 364: this explains the nature and the position of "legal doctrine".

7. Statutory Interpretation

1. DICKERSON, F.R. *The Interpretation and Application of Statutes*, (Little, Brown & Co, Boston, 1975): although this is written by an American and largely from an American point of view with occasional references to Great Britain, it is the best jurisprudential exposition of statutory interpretation hitherto. The author deals with the assumptions underlying legislation and the semantic problems involved, and proceeds to examine painstakingly the numerous, well-known formulae that are invoked by courts and the situations confronting them.

2. CROSS, A.R.N. *Statutory Interpretation*, (Butterworth & Co, Ltd, 1976): within the compass of a relatively short book, the author endeavours to rationalise the diverse attitudes and dicta of judges. He does not probe deeply into the wider problems involved in the many-sided exercise of statute interpretation. He offers four "basic rules" (p. 43), and the book is mainly devoted to supporting these and showing how they work with the aid of internal and external aids to construction.

3. WILLIS, J. "Statute Interpretation in a Nutshell" (1938), 16 Can BR, 1: there are no "rules" of interpretation, but only approaches. This is an instructive and critical discussion of the "Literal", "Golden" and "Mischief" Rules and of the various presumptions classified according to different methods of approach.

4. CORRY, J.A. "Administrative Law and the Interpretation of Statutes" (1935–36), 1 UTLJ, 286: this contains a convincing demonstration of how the finding of facts and interpretation influence each other. Even though the "intention of the legislature" is a myth, there should be judicial co-operation with the legislature. The "Literal Rule" is examined in detail with reference to its history and its shortcomings.

5. THE LAW COMMISSION AND THE SCOTTISH LAW COMMISSION: *The Interpretation of Statutes*, (H.M. Stationery Office, 1969): this gives a useful, detached analysis of the nature of the problem, the present status of the so-called "rules" of interpretation and presumptions of intent and of the relevance, reliability and availability of information relating to the contexts of statutes. There is a useful bibliography at the end. See also THE LAW COMMISSION AND THE SCOTTISH LAW COMMISSION: *Published Working Paper on the Interpretation of Statutes*, (1967), on which it is based. For a comment on the "Working Paper", see ANONYMOUS: "Statutory Interpretation" (1967), SLT, 243.

6. MARSH, N.S. "The Interpretation of Statutes" (1967), 9 JSPTL (NS), 416: a member of the Law Commission explains the Commission's approach. Inquiry into statutory interpretation is justified merely because judges approach statutes in what they conceive to be the values of society. Just as there are shades of meaning, so there are shades of ambiguity. The object is to provide more help in marginal cases.

7. FARRAR, J.H. *Law Reform and the Law Commission*, (Sweet & Maxwell, Ltd, 1974), chap. 5: the author considers here the reform of the medium for law reform, viz, statute. After rehearsing the linguistic problems, he considers the problem of interpretation in the light of the Law Commissions' Report. He also touches on other forms of legislation than by means of words alone, e.g., formulae, diagrams, flow charts.

1. WALKER, D.M. "Within the Meaning of the Act" (1969), SLT, 161: this gives a fairly detailed account and commentary on the Law Commission's Report.

2. BLOOM, H. "Law Commission: Interpretation of Statutes" (1970), 33 MLR, 197: this contains a short note on the Law Commission's White Paper, reviewing the problems that require to be faced and how far the Law Commission has done so.

3. NEWELL, D. "Statutory Interpretation: Extending the Mischief Rule" (1976), 120 SJ, 375: this is a commentary on the Law Commission's Report and the Renton Report, and is mainly critical of the recommended exclusion of Parliamentary proceedings. Modern judicial elaborations of the Mischief Rule are also considered.

Historical Development

4. CROSS, A.R.N. *Statutory Interpretation*, (Butterworth & Co, Ltd, 1976), chaps. 1–2: these give a brief, historical account of statute interpretation, beginning with a case reported by Plowden on restrictive interpretation and followed by *Heydon's* case on extensive interpretation. The changing attitude of courts thereafter is dealt with rather cursorily and hence very generally. In Chapter 2 the author considers the views of Blackstone, Bentham, Austin and Gray.

5. McILWAIN, C.H. *The High Court of Parliament and its Supremacy*, (Yale University Press, 1910), chap. 4: law-making and law-interpreting were not mutually exclusive. The legislature was a court and its enactments were not regarded as emanating from a foreign body. There is a detailed account of the development.

6. PLUCKNETT, T.F.T. *A Concise History of the Common Law*, (5th ed., Butterworth & Co, Ltd, 1956), pp. 328–336: in the middle ages interpretation was left to those who ordained the law. The courts used to appeal to the legislature. The historical development of the change in attitude is outlined.

7. PLUCKNETT, T.F.T. *Statutes and their Interpretation in the First Half of the Fourteenth Century*, (Cambridge University Press, 1922), Part I, chap. 3, Part II, chaps. 1–7, 9–10, 14 and Conclusion: not only extra-Parliamentary legislation, but interpretation also, was exercised by various bodies other than the judiciary. The evolution of a number of modern canons of interpretation is traced out in detail.

8. THORNE, S.E. *A Discourse upon the Exposicion & Understandinge of Statutes with Sir T. Egerton's Additions*, (Huntington Library, 1942), Introduction, pp. 1–92, and chaps. 3–11: S.E. Thorne in the Introduction suggests that interpretation in the modern sense began in the sixteenth century. He traces the early attitudes towards statutes. The chapters of the text deal with various canons of interpretation and reflect a most modern outlook.

9. PLUCKNETT, T.F.T. "Ellesmere on Statutes" (1944), 60 LQR, 242: a review of S.E. Thorne's edition of the *Discourse*. Plucknett suggests that the authorship of the *Discourse* should be ascribed to Sir T. Egerton himself (Lord Ellesmere). He answers Thorne's view that interpretation did not exist until the sixteenth century by saying that it did exist in the fourteenth century but was not apparent as at that time statute was regarded as an incident of normal development and not as an intrusion.

1. PLUCKNETT, T.F.T. *Legislation of Edward I,* (Oxford, 1949), chap. 1: the nature
   of statute at this date and the place which it occupied in the process of effecting
   changes are discussed. The objection to S.E. Thorne's contention (*supra*) is
   repeated.

2. LANDIS, J.M. "Statutes and Sources of Law" in *Harvard Legal Essays,* (Harvard
   University Press, 1934), p. 213: in early times the courts acknowledged that
   behind the formal document lay an aim which required sympathetic consideration.
   The change came with ideas as to the separation of powers in the eighteenth
   century. The methods of interpretation today are outdated. A decent respect for
   legislation will ensure a better balance between legislative and judicial development
   of the law.

Legislative Function

3. *Science of Legal Method: Select Essays by Various Authors,* (trans. E. Bruncken and
   L.B. Register, Boston Book Co, 1917): J.H. WIGMORE, "Preface", pp. xxvi–
   xxxvi: this is a discussion of the relationship between the judiciary and legislature.
   Since the legislative process cannot work perfectly some judicial legislation is
   necessary. There is also a discussion of how far legislation can control the judges
   in view of the imperfections of language, and of how far *stare decisis* should apply.
   A. KOCOUREK, "Preface", pp. lvii–lxvii: this discusses the defects of present
   legislative methods and how these might be overcome − by the use of statistical
   data as to the problem to be dealt with as well as data as to the effectiveness of
   remedies, the application of historical and comparative methods to interpret the
   data and a philosophy to evaluate them.

4. BRADLEY, F.E. "Modern Legislation in the United Kingdom" (1894), 10 LQR,
   32: strict interpretation is due, not so much to perversity, as to ambiguity.
   Various suggestions (some no longer feasible) are offered as to how the problem
   might be eased.

5. HORACK, F.E. "The Common Law of Legislation" (1937–38), 23 Iowa LR, 41:
   legislation, like judge-made law, follows precedent. If there is a common law of
   cases, why not a common law of legislation? A new legislative provision sets a
   pattern, which is copied and extended analogically. A predictable development
   might be traced.

6. MORRIS, C. *The Justification of the Law,* (University of Pennsylvania Press, 1971):
   the justification of law is to reflect the public's genuine and important aspirations,
   and the function of legislation is dealt with in the light of this. In Chap. 5,
   especially at pp. 121–131, the need for general rules is discussed with reference
   to Hume, Montesquieu, Rousseau, Kant and Bentham.

7. COHEN, J. "On the Teaching of 'Legislation'" (1947), 47 Col LR, 1301: this
   comments on the failure of law schools to train lawyers for the role of "policy
   makers" and to partake in the legislative process and to advise on the achievement
   of legislative ends.

8. DIAMOND, A.L. "Codification of the Law of Contract" (1968), 31 MLR, 361, 380:
   lawyers are said to regard statutes still as interferences with the natural
   development of the law. The problem is to devise a way of distinguishing between
   statutes laying down limited solutions to limited problems and statutes laying
   down wider principles.

1. STATUTE LAW SOCIETY. *Statute Law Deficiencies*, (Sweet & Maxwell, Ltd, 1970): statute law is considered from the point of view of the public on the basis of a questionnaire sent to 5,000 persons representing the legal profession and other bodies.

Intention of the Legislature

2. DICKERSON, F.R. *The Interpretation and Application of Statutes*, (Little, Brown & Co, Boston, 1975), chaps. 7–8: behind every statute there is an intent. This is not wholly determinable, but is best ascertained when the statute is read in its entirety and in context, supplemented by relevant extrinsic evidence. A gap remains, however, to an unknowable extent between manifested intent and actual intent. The chief function of the concept of "legislative intent" is to put courts in an attitude of deference to the legislature. Beyond the immediate objective of a statute, which may be identified with its "intent", is the wider "legislative purpose" (chap. 8), which may be inferred from external manifestations and which are more vague than those of intent. Judicial lawmaking is required when neither intent nor purpose can be readily inferred.

3. CROSS, A.R.N. *Statutory Interpretation*, (Butterworth & Co, Ltd, 1976), pp. 34–41: "intention of Parliament" is only a phrase used analogically with the intention of an individual. The well-known difficulties created by it are rehearsed. The discussion concludes with an examination of "the meaning of interpretation".

4. CURTIS, C.P. "A Better Theory of Legal Interpretation", in *Jurisprudence in Action*, (Baker Voorhis & Co, Inc, 1953), pp. 135–169: words have no fixed meaning, nor has the legislature any "intention". The author of the words has no control over them because others have the task of applying them to future events. The question is whether the choice made by these others out of the range of possible meanings is reasonable, and the criteria by which this is to be judged transcends the search for intention.

5. PAYNE, D.J. "The Intention of the Legislature in the Interpretation of Statutes" (1956), 9 CLP, 96: the search for legislative intent is a hindrance and not a help. A composite body has no single mind, nor can the framers of provisions in general words be said to have intended to provide for a particular event. Interpretation involves a delegation by the legislature of the power to deal with the unprovided case.

6. JONES, H.W. "Statutory Doubts and Legislative Intention" (1940), 40 Col LR, 957: the judicial process is more than discovery and deduction. The judge is inevitably a legislator because of the imperfections inherent in language and the attempt to regulate the future.

7. COHEN, M.R. "The Process of Judicial Legislation" (1914), 48 Am LR, 161, at pp. 178–187: it is impossible to find the intentions of members of the legislature. The question is not what they intended but what the public are expected to act on. The rules of interpretation are guides to the judges in making law out of statutes.

8. RADIN, M. "Statutory Interpretation" (1929–30), 43 Harv LR, 863: in some cases the judge makes up his mind and selects the interpretation which justifies it. The question whether the legislature envisaged the particular situation is absurd because the legislature has no mind. The rule excluding resort to extrinsic material

makes reference to "intent" unnecessary. Even legislative history may not help
to decide what specific events are to be included.

1. LEVI, E.H. *An Introduction to Legal Reasoning*, (University of Chicago Press, 1948),
   pp. 19–40: rules of interpretation appear to be means of finding legislative
   intent. A detailed account of a particular statute is given to show the ambiguity of
   legislative intent.

2. LLEWELLYN, K.N. *Jurisprudence: Realism in Theory and Practice*, (University of
   Chicago Press, 1962), pp. 227–229: few legislators have any "intention". Even
   where there is an intention, it may be the duty of the tribunal to apply the statute
   narrowly.

3. KELSEN, H. *General Theory of Law and State*, (trans. A. Wedberg, Harvard
   University Press, 1949), pp. 33–34: the "will" of a legislature is a fiction; an
   analysis of the problem follows.

4. HÄGERSTRÖM, A. *Inquiries into the Nature of Law and Morals*, (ed. K. Olivecrona, trans. C.D. Broad, Almqvist & Wiksell, Stockholm, 1953), pp. 74–101:
   these contain a detailed examination of the difficulty of saying that the task of a
   judge is to ascertain the will of the legislature, or of saying that the judge's will
   completes the process.

5. LANDIS, J.M. "A Note on 'Statutory Interpretation'" (1929–30), 43 Harv LR,
   886: this is a reply to M. Radin (*supra*). A statute is a means by which the
   legislature makes its desires known. The intention of the legislature is therefore
   important; the difficulty lies in finding it. The use of legislative history and
   extrinsic material has real significance in this connection.

6. MacCALLUM, G.C. "Legislative Intent" in *Essays in Legal Philosophy*, (ed. R.S.
   Summers, Basil Blackwell, Oxford, 1968), 237: the various shades of meaning
   of the phrase "legislative intent" are subjected to lengthy analysis with no clear-
   cut conclusion. The discussion centres on the debate between M. Radin and
   J.M. Landis, and on the value of different models of legislative intent.

7. HORACK, F.E. "In the Name of Legislative Intention" (1932), 38 W Vir LQ, 119:
   what is meant by legislative intent is considered. Although there is no such thing,
   it is useful to interpret statutes as if there were.

8. HOLMES, O.W. "The Theory of Legal Interpretation" (1898–99), 12 Harv LR, 417:
   the question is not what the legislature meant, but what the statute means.

9. STONE, J. *Legal System and Lawyers' Reasonings*, (Stevens & Sons, Ltd, 1964),
   pp. 31–34, 288–292: a legislator cannot fix the meaning of words for all future
   interpreters. The most one can say is that he intended that his language should
   be understood according to the common interpretation for the time being. This
   explains the stress laid on the ordinary meaning of words and the exclusion of
   preparatory material. At pp. 288–92 an explanation is given, illustrated with
   cases, of how discretion, guided by policy, can come into interpretation.

10. COX, A. "Judge Learned Hand and the Interpretation of Statutes" (1946–47),
    60 Harv LR, 370: reference to legislative intent is useful in the sense of the
    purpose to be accomplished, but it is a chimera in the sense of the meaning of the
    words used.

1. MONTROSE, J.L. "The Treatment of Statutes by Lord Denning" in *Precedent in English Law and Other Essays*, (ed. H.G. Hanbury, Irish U.P., Shannon, 1968), Chap. 9: the problems of statute interpretation are approached from an unusual angle. Not only is Lord Denning's attitude explained, but there is also analysis of "intention of Parliament", "ambiguity" and "interpretation". "Interpretation" is related to ambiguity and is a matter of law; "application" is related to vagueness and is a question of fact. On this basis the author provides a new slant to the question of the use of precedent in statute interpretation.

2. LOYD, W.H. "The Equity of a Statute" (1910), 58 U Pa LR, 76: this used to be a phrase employed in elucidating the intention of the legislature. Although the courts do not now use it, they apply it.

(Discussions of legislative intent also appear in a good many of the following references).

General Problems of Interpretation and Judicial Approach

3. POUND, R. "Common Law and Legislation" (1907–8), 21 Harv LR, 383: legislation is part of the law and should be accepted as such. Four possible attitudes, which courts might adopt and their desirability, are discussed.

4. ROSS, A. *On Law and Justice*, (Stevens & Sons, Ltd, 1958), chap. 4: there is a clear demonstration of the semantic problems underlying interpretation, followed by a discussion of "syntactical", "logical" and "semantic" interpretation. A judge does not act automatically. He may adopt various attitudes, particularly important being his attitude towards pragmatic factors.

5. CROSS, A.R.N. *Precedent in English Law*, (2nd ed., Oxford, 1968), pp. 163 *et seq.*: the courts have applied the analogy of interpreting documents. The intention of the legislature is a myth. There is some discussion of the chief canons of interpretation and some presumptions and of the role of *stare decisis*.

6. POUND, R. "Courts and Legislation" (1915), 7 Am Pol Sc R, 361; *Science of Legal Method: Select Essays by Various Authors*, (trans. E. Bruncken and L.B. Register, Boston Book Co, 1917), chap. 7: this gives a detailed discussion of the three steps involved, (*a*) finding the rule, (*b*) interpreting the rule, and (*c*) applying the rule to the case. A sociological method of interpretation should be employed.

7. POUND, R. *Jurisprudence*, (West Publishing Co, 1959), III, pp. 654–671: there are four possible attitudes which courts might adopt towards legislation. The theory that courts should only interpret and apply, and the theory that law-making is doomed since law resides in the *Volksgeist*, are discussed and rejected.

8. FRIEDMANN, W. *Legal Theory*, (5th ed., Stevens & Sons, Ltd, 1967), pp. 451–462: the problem of statutory interpretation is to balance stability with adaptation to changing circumstances. For this purpose distinctions should be drawn between different types of statutes.

9. FRIEDMANN, W. *Law in a Changing Society*, (Stevens & Sons, Ltd, 1959), pp. 34 *et seq.*: this discusses the questions whether distinctions should be drawn between different kinds of statutes, and whether the application of a single set of rules to statutes of all kinds is satisfactory.

10. FRIEDMANN, W. "Judges, Politics and the Law" (1951), 29 Can BR, 811, at pp. 825–834: these provide a further discussion on the same line as above.

1. de SLOOVÈRE, F.J. "The Functions of Judge and Jury in the Interpretation of Statutes" (1932–33), 46 Harv LR, 1086: the questions of fact and of law that arise in interpreting statutes and in applying them are considered.

2. BODENHEIMER, E. *Jurisprudence*, (Harvard University Press, 1962), pp. 272–280; 347–368: the distinction between the judicial and legislative functions is explained. If the legislative purpose is discoverable, the judges should give effect to it. But if this contemplates wholly different circumstances, restrictive interpretation should be adopted. Pp. 347–368: "historical" and "contemporaneous" interpretation of constitutions are explained.

3. GRAY, J.C. *The Nature and Sources of the Law*, (2nd ed., R. Gray, The Macmillan Co, New York, 1921), pp. 170–189: it is with the interpretation of the courts that statutes are imposed upon the community. Difficulties in interpretation arise when the legislature did not have any "intent" with regard to the question before the court. Here the judge has to create law by giving to the words the meaning which he would have given them.

4. PITAMIC, L. "Some Aspects of the Problem of Statutory Interpretation" (1933), 19 Am BAJ, 582: the problem is primarily a linguistic one since language grows and sense changes. The judges' task is to synthesise the thoughts extracted from the text.

5. BLACKSTONE, W. *Commentaries on the Laws of England*, (16th ed., J.T. Coleridge, T. Cadell and J. Butterworth & Son, 1825), I, pp. 86–92: statutes are classified as declaratory of the common law or remedial. As to the latter, ten rules of construction are given, of which the mischief rule comes first. The remainder comprise rules which are still familiar, but some have since been abandoned or modified.

6. BENTHAM, J. *A Comment on the Commentaries*, (ed. C.W. Everett, Oxford, 1928), pp. 107 *et seq.*: the author takes Blackstone to task in his usual fashion, but quite a number of his criticisms are not altogether fair as he fails to appreciate the context of Blackstone's statements. Other criticisms are acute.

7. BENTHAM, J. *Of Laws in General*, (ed. H.L.A. Hart, The Athlone Press, 1970), pp. 162 *et seq.*: interpretation is strict or liberal, depending on the "completeness" of a law. When the will attributed to the legislator is that which he really entertained, interpretation is strict. When the will attributed by a court is that which the legislator failed to entertain, interpretation is liberal. Liberal interpretation may be either extensive or restrictive, depending on whether the provision has to be extended or cut down.

8. CROSS, A.R.N. "Blackstone v. Bentham" (1976), 92 LQR, 516: the author defends Blackstone against Bentham. Blackstone had said, *inter alia*, that a court is entitled to pay heed to the effects and consequences of interpretation. Bentham misinterpreted this as referring to the effects and consequences of the law or the act which is prohibited.

9. AUSTIN, J. *Lectures on Jurisprudence*, (5th ed., R. Campbell, John Murray, 1885), II, pp. 624–630, 989 *et seq.*: the literal meaning is the primary index to legislative intent. This is interpretation proper. With it must be contrasted "spurious interpretation", which occurs when a judge extracts a meaning that is not the literal sense of the words and gives to a statute an extensive or restrictive effect.

Statutory Interpretation 121

1. POUND, R. "Spurious Interpretation" (1907), 7 Col LR, 379: the Austinian distinction is taken up. "Genuine interpretation" is where the judge attempts to ascertain the intention of the law giver; "spurious interpretation" is where he makes, unmakes or remakes the law. In an age of legislation the latter becomes an anachronism. Its good and bad elements are considered.

2. SNYDER, O.C. *Preface to Jurisprudence*, (The Bobbs-Merrill Co, Inc, 1954), Part III, chap. 2, pp. 354–366: statutes do not cater for all contingencies. Genuine interpretation is making an application within the framework of the statute – "interstitial" legislation. Statutes not susceptible to genuine interpretation are those conferring a wide discretion and those which are vague.

3. FREUND, E. "Interpretation of Statutes" (1917), 65 U Pa LR, 207: there is a discussion of the strict and liberal construction of statutes and the use of analogy.

4. FULLER, L.L. *The Morality of Law*, (Revised ed., Yale University Press, 1969), pp. 82–91: the idea that legislative intent is directed to particular situations is rejected. It is directed at some problem. The "mischief" rule is therefore favoured. It is also argued that it is better to speak of the "intent" of the "intent of the statute" rather than of the legislature or legislators. Judicial creativeness, as such, deserves neither praise nor blame; it is called into being in effecting a relation between the mischief aimed at and the remedy provided.

5. LLOYD, D. *Introduction to Jurisprudence*, (3rd ed., Stevens & Sons, Ltd, 1972), pp. 738–743: the old attitude was that the common law is the basis of law and that statutes are woven into it. There is a brief discussion of the narrow and broad approaches. Pp. 435–496: extracts are given from *Heydon's Case, Seaford Court Estates, Ltd v. Asher, Magor & St. Mellons R.D.C. v. Newport Corporation, Assam Railways v. Commissioners of Inland Revenue* (1935), AC, 445. W. FRIEDMANN: *Law and Social Change in Contemporary Britain*; H.C. GUTTERIDGE: *Comparative Law*.

6. WILLIAMS, G.L. "Language and the Law" (1945), 61 LQR, 71, at pp. 179 *et seq.*, 302–303, 392 *et seq*; (1946), 62 LQR, 387, at pp. 402 *et seq.*: the ambiguities of words are discussed and explained. In marginal cases the function of the judge must be legislative. There is also a discussion of the different kinds of meaning.

7. HART, H.L.A. *The Concept of Law*, (Oxford, 1961, reprinted 1975), pp. 123–125: with verbally formulated generalisations uncertainties occur in particular cases. Canons of interpretation may lessen, but cannot remove the uncertainties. It is difficult to regulate unambiguously in advance fact-situations that are not contemplated.

8. HORACK, F.E. "The Disintegration of Statute Construction", in M.R. COHEN and F.S. COHEN: *Readings in Jurisprudence and Legal Philosophy*, (Prentice-Hall, Inc, New York, 1951), pp. 524–526: statute interpretation is simply the expression of judicial practice. The legislature should provide adequate sources of interpretation.

9. EVERSHED, F.R. "The Judicial Process in Twentieth Century England" (1961), 61 Col LR, 761: statutory interpretation is becoming increasingly the task of the judiciary. This reduces itself to battles about words rather than the application and evolution of principles. In the result law tends to lose popular support and respect; it also undermines the spirit of obedience and encourages evasion. A liberal attitude towards interpretation is advocated. It is also suggested that if

parliamentary history were looked at, this might have the effect of forcing still
greater adherence to the literal rule of interpretation.

1. DIPLOCK, K. "The Courts as Legislators", *Presidential Address to the Holdsworth
   Club*, 1965: courts describe what they do as being "interpretation", but they are
   legislating most of the time, since they have to deal with matters which the
   framers of an Act never contemplated. When statutes try to provide in detail for
   every contingency, this drives the courts to adopt a narrow semantic attitude.
   Where the Parliamentary design is clear, the courts should give effect to it. Where
   it is not clear, they are forced back on the literal rule. The danger of this is that
   it becomes a habit and the courts act on it even when the Parliamentary objective
   is clear.

2. REID, J.S.C. "The Judge as Law Maker" (1972), 12 JSPTL (NS), 22, 27–29:
   codifying statutes should be interpreted like principles of common law.
   Difficulties arise over statutes creating new law. Part of the trouble is due to the
   involved style of drafting; shorter sentences might be better. Reference to Hansard
   is not likely to be helpful. For ready-made solutions to problems, which may not
   wear well, statute is the answer. For orderly growth and durability, the common
   law is the answer. It would be undesirable to try to speed up the common law
   process.

3. DEVLIN, P. "Judges and Lawmakers" (1976), 39 MLR, 1: judges should only be
   "activist lawmakers", i.e., keep the law abreast of the public consensus. The
   public is generally not interested in the common law, and therefore there is a
   consensus in favour of activist lawmaking. When the public does become
   interested in a matter, it calls for a statute, and the consensus here only gives
   warrant to interpret the statute. There is a presumption that Parliament has said
   all that it wants to say.

4. MACMILLAN, H.P. *Law and Other Things*, (Cambridge University Press, 1938),
   pp. 147 *et seq.*: the ambiguity of language is discussed with reference to the
   interpretation of certain phrases in decided cases. There is also allusion to a few
   of the canons of interpretation.

5. DICKERSON, F.R. "Statutory Interpretation: Core Meaning and Marginal
   Uncertainty" (1964), 29 Miss LR, 1: this study is more important in connection
   with the general problem of meaning. Its relevance to statutory interpretation
   is that it reveals the parts played respectively by the meaning of words in isolation
   and in the light of context and purpose, and the indispensible relationship between
   them. Thus, it becomes wrong to treat the so-called "literal" and "purpose"
   canons as opposing and alternative approaches.

6. DUGDALE, D.F. "The Statutory Conferment of Judicial Discretion" (1972),
   NZLJ, 556: discretion is inappropriate in matters concerning good manners
   (e.g., indecency), where its exercise may appear to be politically motivated, and
   where it would introduce needless uncertainty into commercial practice. There
   is also a tendency for discretion to harden into rules. It is legitimate to confer
   discretion where change is needed but it is impossible to foresee every likely
   situation; but here there should be clear guidelines.

7. BURROWS, J.E. "Statutes and Judicial Discretion" (1976), 7 NZULR, 1: statutes
   conferring discretion have four drawbacks: they lead to inconsistent decisions;
   they lead to uncertainty which hinders forward planning; appellate courts
   become reluctant to upset discretionary decisions; and people have no means of

knowing the likely decision in advance. As against this, discretion gives flexibility and justice to individuals.

1. FRIENDLY, H.J. "The Gap in Lawmaking – Judges who Can't and Legislators who Won't" (1963), 63 Col LR, 787: the discussion concerns mainly the problems of a federal system like that in America. The author advocates the setting up of an agency drawn from legislators and the judiciary.

2. AMOS, M.S. "The Interpretation of Statutes" (1933–35), 5 CLJ, 163: this is of general interest. It deals with the unsympathetic attitude of the judges and with drafting.

3. HAWKINS, F.V. "On the Principles of Interpretation with Reference especially to the Interpretation of Wills" (1858–63), 2 Trans Jur S, 298; J.B. THAYER, *Preliminary Treatise on the Law of Evidence*, (Sweet & Maxwell, Ltd, 1898), Appendix C: this is of general interest and deals with the problem of giving a meaning to the written word.

The "Purpose" Approach

4. DAVIES, D.J.Ll. "The Interpretation of Statutes in the Light of their Policy by the English Courts" (1935), 35 Col LR, 519: according to *Heydon's Case*, the judge should co-operate with the legislature. The reasons for the present restrictive attitude are discussed. Statutes should be accompanied by explanatory memoranda.

5. RADIN, M. "Statutory Interpretation" (1929–30), 43 Harv LR, 863: interpretation according to purpose is not necessarily what the legislature intended, but the use to which the courts put the statute. The courts should interpret statues by selecting one out of a number of likely consequences which the statute might have.

6. RADIN, M. "A Short Way with Statutes" (1942–43), 56 Harv LR, 388: the main task of the courts should be to implement the purpose of the statute. If the purpose is clear the implemental part should not be made more important. Both the purpose and means are to be found by reading the words of the statute; extrinsic material is relevant, but not controlling. *Heydon's Case* is restated in a modernised form.

7. LASKI, H.J. Note on the Judicial Interpretation of Statutes, in Annexe V to the *Report of the Committee on Ministers' Powers*, (1932, Cmd. 4060), pp. 135–137): an independent assessment of legislative intent is valuable, but the methods employed are defective. Statutes should have attached to them explanatory preambles and memoranda.

8. FRANKFURTER, F. "Some Reflections on the Reading of Statutes" (1947), 47 Col LR, 527: interpretation is neither an opportunity for the judge to make words mean what he wants, nor an unimaginative ritual. The judges should seek to effectuate the aim of the legislature as evinced in the wording. To exclude all extrinsic material overlooks the fact that enactments live in an environment; on the other hand, recourse to legislative history and the like should not outweigh the importance of the statute itself.

9. LLEWELLYN, K.N. *Jurisprudence: Realism in Theory and Practice*, (University of

Chicago Press, 1962), pp. 227–229: legislation is meaningless without reason and purpose. A statute should be implemented according to its purpose so as to keep the law as a working whole.

1. EKELÖF, P.O. "Teleological Construction of Statutes" (1958), 2 Scand SL, 75: if a given situation is so common that the authors of the statute must have contemplated it, the statute applies to it. If this is not clear, the judge should consider the cases to which the statute does apply and consider what purpose it seeks to achieve with regard to these. In uncertain cases the statute should be made to apply so as to fulfil that purpose.

2. COX, A. "Judge Learned Hand and the Interpretation of Statutes" (1946–47), 60 Harv LR, 370: imprecise words should be construed according to the social purpose behind them. Legislative history might help, and so might evidence of specific applications contemplated by legislative committees.

3. FRANK, J.N. "Words and Music: Some Remarks on Statute Interpretation" (1947), 47 Col LR, 1259: a literal interpretation may sometimes be appropriate, sometimes not. A judge should at all times co-operate imaginatively with the legislature. Judicial creativeness is inevitable, but judges should not let their personalities run riot. The importance of finding the facts of each case is stressed.

4. FRANK, J.N. *Courts on Trial, Myth and Reality in American Justice*, (Princeton University Press, 1950), chap. 21: this repeats the point that judicial creativeness should be kept within proper bounds.

5. FRANK, J.N. *Law and the Modern Mind*, (Stevens & Sons, Ltd, 1949), pp. 279–284: this should be read subject to the above two contributions. The personality of the judge is underlined and also the importance of determining the facts.

6. BRUNCKEN, E. "Interpretation of the Written Law" (1915), 25 Yale LJ, 129: in cases of doubt a statute should be construed to mean that which the legislator would have expressed had he been in possession of the facts of the instant case. If there are several possible interpretations that one should be selected which will promote maximum social harmony.

7. WOOD, J.C.E. "Statutory Interpretation: Tupper and the Queen" (1968), 6 Os HLJ, 92: the basis of positivism and the shortcomings of the "plain meaning" rule of interpretation are considered. Law is a purposive enterprise. Therefore, statutes should be construed according to the legislative purpose.

8. SANDS, C.D. "Statute Construction and National Development" (1969), 18 ICLQ, 206: the judicial task with statutes is not to discover what the law is, but how to construe it. This is a matter which vitally affects the future life of a country.

Approach to Particular Types of Statutes

9. JENNINGS, W.I. "Courts and Administrative Law – the Experience of English Housing Legislation" (1935–36), 49 Harv LR, 426: this is a detailed demonstration of the failure of the restrictive approach which, in this sphere, is said to stem from a bias against administrative action.

10. JENNINGS, W.I. "Judicial Process at its Worst" (1937–39), 1 MLR, 111: an

account is given of the failure of judicial interpretation of the Public Health Acts over forty-six years to find a solution to an urgent problem.

1. REYNOLDS, J.I. "Statutory Covenants of Fitness and Repair: Social Legislation and the Judges" (1974), 37 MLR, 377: the article begins with the background of social conditions that led to statutory covenants. It then proceeds to show how courts have frustrated the social policy and purpose behind provisions of the Housing Acts 1957 and 1961 by introducing common law doctrines of contract and tort. See also ROBINSON, M.J. "'Social Legislation and the Judges': a Note by Way of Rejoinder" (1976), 39 MLR, 43: this answers Reynold's criticisms point by point.

2. PORTER, S.L. "Case Law in the Interpretation of Statutes", *Presidential Address to the Holdsworth Club*, 1940: this considers the attempts of case-law to adapt the wording of the Workmen's Compensation Act to the facts of individual situations.

3. DODS, M. "A Chapter of Accidents: an Essay on the History of Disease in Workmen's Compensation" (1932), 39 LQR, 60: this gives a detailed account of the chaos created by the application of the "plain and ordinary" meaning to the words "injury" and "accident".

4. de SMITH, S.A. "The Limits of Judicial Review: Statutory Discretions and the Doctrine of Ultra Vires" (1948), 11 MLR, 306: judges are more sympathetic now than they used to be, but uncertainty is created by the conflicting canons of interpretation of statutes conferring discretion.

5. de SMITH, S.A. "Statutory Restriction of Judicial Review" (1955), 18 MLR, 575: this discusses the different judicial attitudes.

6. de SMITH, S.A. *Judicial Review and Administrative Action*, (Stevens & Sons, Ltd, 1959), chaps. 3, especially pp. 58–60, and chap. 7: statutory interpretation is discussed in relation to the *ultra vires* rule, and conflicting approaches.

7. WILLIS, J. "Three Approaches to Administrative Law: the Judicial, the Conceptual, and the Functional" (1935–36), UTLJ, 53, pp. 59–69: judicial interpretation is coloured by three prejudices – against statute law, against disregard of private rights and against discretionary powers in the executive.

8. WHEATCROFT, G.S.A. "A Six-finger Exercise in Statutory Construction" (1965), Br Tax R, 359: this is a complicated article on a maze of problems of the utmost technicality. It does illustrate the special expertise that is called for in dealing with taxing statutes.

9. BEUTEL, F.K. "The Necessity of a New Technique of Interpreting the N.I.L. (Uniform Negotiable Instruments Law) – the Civil Law Analogy" (1931–32), 6 Tul LR, 1: this is of general interest. It shows the confusion wrought by conflicting judicial attitudes towards interpretation. The transition from precedent to written law calls for a new technique.

Continental and Common Law Methods of Interpretation

10. KOHLER, J. "Judicial Interpretation of Enacted Law" in *Science of Legal Method: Select Essays by Various Authors*, (trans. E. Bruncken and L.B. Register, Boston

Book Co, 1917), chap. 6: interpreting a statute is not merely finding its meaning, but selecting from amongst various meanings the correct one. The criterion by which the selection should be made is that which will prove most beneficial in practice. Regard must be paid, first to the purpose, then to the consistency of the provision, and finally to the social history.

1. GÉNY, F. "Judicial Freedom of Decision: its Necessity and Method" in *Science of Legal Method: Select Essays by Various Authors*, (trans. E. Bruncken and L.B. Register, Boston Book Co, 1917), chap. 1: this is an account of the "free-law" method of interpretation by one of its pioneers.

2. EHRLICH, E. "Judicial Freedom of Decision: its Principles and Objects" in *Science of Legal Method: Select Essays by Various Authors*, (trans. E. Bruncken and L.B. Register, Boston Book Co, 1917), chap. 2: this develops further the "free-law" method of interpretation.

3. GUTTERIDGE, H.C. "A Comparative View of the Interpretation of Statute Law" (1933), 8 Tul LR, 1: interpretation refers not only to the ascertainment of meaning but also to the creative activity in extending and limiting the scope of the language. Continental judges carry the investigation into legislative intent further than English judges. There is a comparison of their respective methods, as well as an evaluation of the "free-law" and "social purpose" methods.

4. GUTTERIDGE, H.C. *Comparative Law*, (Cambridge University Press, 1946), chap. 8: English law is rich in canons of construction, Continental law in theories. There is an account of the "free-law" and "social purpose" approaches and of the difference in approach between English and Continental judges. The difficulties of unifying systems is also discussed.

5. BONNECASE, J. "The Problem of Legal Interpretation in France" (1930), 12 JCL (Ser. 3), 79: after quoting from the works of various writers the view is rejected that the legislature has infinite prevision, that the judge's task is simply to interpret the meaning of words, or that his task is simply to interpret having regard to contemporary social conditions. The judge should pay attention to the literal wording and to the social end in view at the time when the statute was made.

6. SMITH, H.A. "Interpretation in English and Continental Law" (1927), 9 JCL (Ser. 3), 153: interpretation is a study of contexts. There is a needless gulf between English and Continental practice. *Heydon's Case* is consistent with the latter.

7. REGISTER, L.B. "Judicial Powers of Interpretation under Foreign Codes" (1917), 65 U Pa LR, 39: this is of general interest. It considers the function of the judiciary under some Continental codes.

8. KAUFMAN, A. and HASSEMER, W. "Enacted Law and Judicial Decision in German Jurisprudential Thought" (1969), 19 UTLJ, 461: this article may be read for general interest. It provides information as to the wholly different context in which courts have to approach interpretation from courts in common law countries.

Canons of Interpretation

1. DICKERSON, F.R. *The Interpretation and Application of Statutes*, (Little, Brown & Co, Boston, 1975), chaps. 11–13: these chapters examine the strict and liberal interpretations, the reading and application of statutes and legislative attempts to control the activities of courts in this regard. The discussions should help to place the detailed treatment in practitioners' treatises in a jurisprudential setting.

2. CROSS, A.R.N. *Statutory Interpretation*, (Butterworth & Co, Ltd, 1976): the principal thesis of the book is that the three classical canons of interpretation, the "literal", "golden" and "mischief" rules, have now fused into one, namely, a version of the "literal" rule, which takes account of context and purpose. This is analysed into four "basic" rules.

3. ALLEN, C.K. *Law in the Making*, (7th ed., Oxford, 1964), pp. 482–530: this discusses generally the various canons and their shortcomings and suggested improvements.

4. LLEWELLYN, K.N. *The Common Law Tradition. Deciding Appeals*, (Little, Brown & Co, 1960), Appendix C, and pp. 371–382: parallel columns give opposing canons of interpretation on a wide range of points. There are twenty-eight canons of "Thrust and Parry", and nineteen of "Thrust and Counterthrust".

5. SALMOND, J.W. *Jurisprudence*, (12th ed., P.J. Fitzgerald, Sweet & Maxwell, Ltd, 1966), pp. 131–140: this discusses the literal and free methods of interpretation, the canons of interpretation, and their defects.

6. WILLIAMS, G.L. *Learning the Law*, (9th ed., Stevens & Sons, Ltd, 1973), chap. 7: normally the literal meaning is adopted, subject to the context. In cases of doubt the function is legislative rather than interpretative. A brief account is given of the principal canons and presumptions.

7. HOOD PHILLIPS, O. and HUDSON, A.H. *A First Book of English Law*, (7th ed., Sweet & Maxwell, Ltd, 1977), chap. 11: this is a convenient account of the various canons and presumptions with a criticism of the present position.

8. KIRALFY, A.K.R. *The English Legal System*, (4th ed., Sweet & Maxwell, Ltd, 1967), pp. 121–136: this gives a general account of the canons and presumptions and of the internal and external aids to interpretation.

9. PATON, G.W. *A Text-Book of Jurisprudence*, (4th ed., G.W. Paton and D.P. Derham, Clarendon Press, Oxford, 1972), pp. 250–254: the canons of interpretation are wide enough to produce divergent results. There is a general discussion of the present position and of the difficulties that it creates.

10. KEETON, G.W. *The Elementary Principles of Jurisprudence*, (2nd ed., Pitman & Sons, Ltd, 1949), pp. 89–95: this is a general discussion of the principal canons of interpretation.

11. VINOGRADOFF, P. *Common-Sense in Law*, (3rd ed., H.G. Hanbury, Oxford University Press, 1959), pp. 86–106: a court's first duty is to apply the "literal" canon of interpretation. There is also a discussion of the court's power to add to or supply gaps in the wording so as to modernise a provision.

1. DRIEDGER, E.A. "A New Approach to Statutory Interpretation" (1951), 29 Can BR, 838: this regroups the various canons of interpretation under four Rules:-Rule of Language, Rule of Inferred Intent, Rule of Declared Intent, Rule of Presumed Intent.

2. KOCOUREK, A. *An Introduction to the Science of Law*, (Little, Brown & Co, Boston, 1930), pp. 161–165, 191–202: a distinction is drawn between official and unofficial sources of interpretation, and an account is given of "grammatical", "logical", "spurious" and "historical" interpretation.

3. SILVING, H. *Sources of Law* (Wm. S. Hein & Co, Inc, New York, 1968), "Statutes" p. 9: the bindingness of interpretation dispenses with the question whether or not it is right. Therefore, rules of interpretation are of more interest than the interpretation itself, since words mean what the law says they shall mean. The subjective and objective approaches depend upon legal fiat. Rules of interpretation would be useful in establishing a method of arriving at understanding and certainty.

4. CRAIES, W.F. *Statute Law*, (6th ed., S.G.G. Edgar, Sweet & Maxwell, Ltd, 1963): this is a standard work giving a detailed account of the canons and presumptions.

5. ODGERS, C.E. *The Construction of Deeds and Statutes*, (4th ed., Sweet & Maxwell, Ltd, 1956), Part II: this, too, is a standard work. It is to be noted that Part I deals with the interpretation of other documents, which reflects the tendency to assimilate statutes and other documents.

6. MAXWELL, P.B. *The Interpretation of Statutes*, (11th ed., R. Wilson and B. Galpin, Sweet & Maxwell, Ltd, 1962): this is perhaps the best of the standard treatises.

7. DWARRIS, F. *A General Treatise on Statutes*, (2nd ed., Wm. Benning & Co, 1848), chaps. 1, 8–11: this is of general interest only as showing the position in the first half of the nineteenth century. Chap. 11 is of the greatest interest, containing a discussion of the relation between legislation and judicial interpretation and between interpretation and judicial legislation.

Restrictive Approach: Strict Interpretation and Presumptions

8. HOPKINS, E.R. "The Literal Canon and the Golden Rule" (1937), 15 Can BR, 689: the "literal" canon is discussed in relation to the "golden rule" with reference to a particular case.

9. E.J.C. Note in (1947), 63 LQR, 156: this draws attention to the absurd result of refusing to fill in a gap left by a particular statute.

10. KAHN-FREUND, O. Note in (1949), 12 MLR, 97: this discusses the problem created by the repeal of a statutory definition but where the word defined appears also in an unrepealed provision.

11. G.L.W. Note in (1951), 14 MLR, 333: the absurdity resulting from a literal interpretation is pointed out.

12. MITCHELL, J.D.B. Note in (1952), 15 MLR, 219: this deals with the conflict between a strict and liberal approach and the unfortunate results of the former.

1. SNELL, J. "Trouble on Oiled Waters – Statutory Interpretation" (1976), 39 MLR, 402: one canon is that the natural meaning must be followed despite absurdity; another is that if the natural meaning produces absurdity, inconsistency or illogicality, the court may adopt another meaning. But what is "natural meaning" and "ambiguity"? These points are illustrated with reference to a House of Lords decision.

2. A.L.G. Note in (1960), 76 LQR, 215; J.L. MONTROSE, *ibid.*, at p. 359: both comment on the literal interpretation adopted in *Hinchy's* case.

3. de SMITH, S.A. Note in (1956), 19 MLR, 541: this comments on the strict interpretation of an Act by which the House of Lords held that it had no jurisdiction.

4. COUTTS, J.A. Note in (1937–38), 1 MLR, 166: examples are given of the restrictive interpretation of a Northern Ireland statute so as not to infringe private rights. If Parliamentary debates had been resorted to, the result would have been different.

5. ABRAHAMSON, M.W. "Trade Disputes Act – Strict Interpretation in Ireland" (1961), 24 MLR, 596: this is a scathing comment on strict interpretation in the light of two Irish cases and the Parliamentary history of the Act in question.

6. STOUT, R. "Is the Privy Council a Legislative Body?" (1905), 21 LQR, 9: this considers several of the canons of statutory interpretation and the attitude adopted by the Judicial Committee of the Privy Council.

7. BURROWS, J.E. "The Cardinal Rule of Statutory Interpretation in New Zealand" (1968–9), 3 NZULR, 253: this article discusses the effect of the Acts Interpretation Act, 1924, on the previous common law approach to interpretation. Since the approach of British courts has much influence in New Zealand, there is a good deal of discussion of the British rules and presumptions.

8. For a long history of criticism of strict interpretation, see Notes in (1890), 6 LQR, 121; (1893), 9 LQR, 106, 110, 207; (1894), 10 LQR, 9, 109–110, 112, 291; (1897), 13 LQR, 235–236; (1899), 15 LQR, 111; (1900), 16 LQR, 222–223; (1901), 17 LQR, 122; (1904), 20 LQR, 114–115; (1921), 37 LQR, 5; (1943), 59 LQR, 296–297 (comment rather than criticism); (1960), 76 LQR, 30, 211, 380.

9. WILLIAMS, G.L. "The Origin and Logical Implications of the *Ejusdem Generis* Rule" (1943), 7 The Conveyancer (NS), 119: the rule may date from 1729. The maxim may thwart the intention of the legislature. The ways in which the maxim itself may be deprived of effect are considered.

10. de PINNA, L.A. "Marginal Notes and Statutes", (1964), 114 LJ, 3: this is a short survey of the use of marginal notes, preambles, recitals in deeds, and schedules. L.A. de PINNA: "Schedules to Statutes" (1964), 114 LJ, 519: this is a continuation of the discussion.

11. ANONYMOUS. "Headings and Marginal Notes" (1960), 124 JPJ, 247: this considers briefly when these might be used and cases in which they have been used.

1. RADZINOWICZ, L. *A History of English Criminal Law*, (Stevens & Sons, Ltd, 1948), I, pp. 83–106: these pages contain a detailed account of the spirit in which courts used to interpret statutes imposing capital punishment. They tried, on the one hand, to give effect to legislative policy, and on the other hand to interpret doubts in favour of the individual.

2. JACKSON, R.M. "Absolute Prohibition in Statutory Offences", in *Modern Approach to Criminal Law*, (edd. L. Radzinowicz and J.W.C. Turner, Macmillan & Co, Ltd, 1945), p. 262: this discusses the extent to which *mens rea* is interpreted as being necessary to the commission of statutory offences.

3. DEVLIN, P. *Samples of Law Making*, (Oxford University Press, 1962), chap. 4: this shows how the courts are constructing a new body of law.

4. HALL, L. "Strict or Liberal Construction of Penal Statutes" (1934–35), 48 Harv LR, 748: the evolution of the strict construction of penal statutes is outlined. There is a careful discussion of its pros and cons and proposals for reform.

5. POLLOCK, F. "*Abrams v. U.S.*" (1920), 36 LQR, 334: this is a critical discussion of the construction of a penal statute by the American Supreme Court.

6. See also Notes in (1949), 65 LQR, 142; (1951), 67 LQR, 13; C.H. de WAAL: Note in (1959), CLJ, 173; (1960), 76 LQR, 179.

7. GOODHART, A.L. Note in (1950), 66 LQR, 314: retrospective legislation is dealt with. A distinction should be drawn between civil and criminal cases. The primary purpose of civil law is not deterrence but the accomplishment of some purpose, and retrospective legislation may well accomplish this. The primary purpose of criminal law is deterrence, and retrospective legislation will not deter but will operate as revenge.

8. PLUCKNETT, T.F.T. *Statutes and their Interpretation in the First Half of the Fourteenth Century*, (Cambridge University Press, 1922), Part II, chap. 9: this discusses the retrospective effect of statutes.

9. WHEATCROFT, G.S.A. "The Attitude of the Legislature and the Courts to Tax Avoidance" (1955), 18 MLR, 209: a distinction is drawn between tax avoidance and tax evasion. The attitudes of the courts, the revenue department and of the legislature are considered. Strict interpretation should be abolished.

10. FLETCHER, E. "Retrospective Fiscal Legislation" (1959), Br Tax R, 412: after due warning retrospective fiscal legislation is an effective deterrent against tax evasion. The history of such legislation is considered, its benefits and drawbacks.

11. L.C.B.G. Note on Statutes (1950), 13 MLR, 482: this discusses the retrospective effect of s. 26 of the Finance Act, 1950.

12. ANONYMOUS. "Acts of Prerogative: Retrospective Legislation" (1962), 233 LT, 539: this discusses the propriety of the threat of retrospective legislation to reverse the decision in a case.

13. BALLARD, F.A. "Retroactive Federal Taxation" (1934–35), 48 Harv LR, 592: this considers the position in America.

1. MANN, F.A. "The Interpretation of Uniform Statutes" (1946), 62 LQR, 278: when Parliament adopts international treaties, which aim at international uniformity, the courts should adopt the same aim. The attitude of English courts is considered and the suggestion is made that Parliament should here be regarded, not as law-giver, but as law-transformer. Its function is different.

2.. LAUTERPACHT, H. "Some Observations on Preparatory Work in the Interpretation of Treaties" (1934–35), 48 Harv LR, 549: this is of general interest and does not deal with interpretation of statute, but useful none the less.

3. WINDER, W.H.D. "The Interpretation of Statutes Subject to Case Law" (1946), 58 Jur R, 93: the discussion is based on *Barras* v. *Aberdeen Steam Trawling & Fishing Co, Ltd*. Parliament can be presumed to intend that the judicial meaning given to a word should continue to be adopted.

4. GRODECKI, J.K. Note in (1957), 20 MLR, 636: this comments on a case which concerned the interpretation of a statutory provision which was re-enacted in another statute.

5. R.E.M. Note in (1941), 57 LQR, 312: the settled judicial meaning given to a word under one statute should not be departed from when that word is adopted in another statute unless there is clear evidence to the contrary.

6. OWEN, A. "Judicial Interpretation of Statutes" (1955), 105 LJ, 534: the same point is made as above.

7. FOX, H.M. "Judicial Control of the Spending Powers of Local Authorities" (1956), 72 LQR, 237: this contains an account of the judicial interpretation of statutes conferring powers.

8. ALLEN, C.K. *Law and Orders*, (2nd ed., Stevens & Sons, Ltd, 1956), chap. 8: some of the problems of the interpretation of delegated legislation are considered.

9. C.K.A. Note in (1958), 74 LQR, 358: this discusses *Ross-Clunis* v. *Papadopoullos* and the distinction between "no ground" and "no reasonable ground" on which an official could "satisfy himself".

10. DIAMOND, A.L. "Repeal and Desuetude of Statutes" (1975), 28 CLP, 107: the main point is that the fact that obsolete statutes are periodically repealed is no evidence that they were in force before repeal. The author deals in turn with the effect of formal, limited and implied repeals and desuetude.

11. MURRAY, D.B. "When is a Repeal not a Repeal?" (1953), 16 MLR, 50: the repealing technique of draftsmen is considered and the attitude of the courts towards repeal provisions.

Exclusion of Legislative History

12. DICKERSON, F.R. *The Interpretation and Application of Statutes*, (Little, Brown & Co, Boston, 1975), chaps. 9–10: these have to be understood against the American background where there is more widespread use of legislative history than in Britain. The author argues against the use of it for a variety of reasons. They are, he says, virtually useless for interpretation purposes and tend to be unreliable at best even for confirmatory purposes.

1. CROSS, A.R.N. *Statutory Interpretation*, (Butterworth & Co, Ltd, 1976), chap. 6: on the whole the author would support the ban on resort to legislative history and extrinsic material where the meaning of a statute is clear. Where there is doubt, he would allow judges a limited freedom to resort to them.

2. KILGOUR, D.G. "The Rule Against the Use of Legislative History: 'Canon of Construction or Counsel of Caution'?" (1952), 30 Can BR, 769: *prima facie* there is a case for the admission of legislative history. Its exclusion is not as absolute as might be thought. The origin of the rule is considered and the conclusion is that it is a counsel of caution and not a rule.

3. MacQUARRIE, J.T. "The Use of Legislative History" (1952), 30 Can BR, 958: this is a reply to Kilgour (*supra*), arguing that it is more than a counsel of caution.

4. de SLOOVÈRE, F.J. "Extrinsic Aids in the Interpretation of Statutes" (1940), 88 U Pa LR, 527: this gives careful consideration to the possible bases on which such aids might be admitted.

5. EASTWOOD, R.A. "A Plea for the Historical Interpretation of Statute Law" (1935), JSPTL 1: the canons of interpretation give effect to an artificial "intention" which is the creation of the canons themselves. Extrinsic material should be admitted.

6. DAVIS, K.C. "Legislative History and the *Wheat Board* Case" (1953), 31 Can BR, 1: the refusal to consult legislative history violates the intention of the legislature. Legislative history should not be used to contradict the clear wording of the statute, but to elucidate doubtful words. The pros and cons are considered.

7. CORRY, J.A. "The Use of Legislative History in the Interpretation of Statutes" (1954), 32 Can BR, 624: careful consideration is given to what constitutes "legislative history". Most of it is unrecorded. Resort to it will be unhelpful in Great Britain or Canada. It is not possible to conceal the need for judicial legislation.

8. MacDONALD, V.C. "Constitutional Interpretation and Extrinsic Evidence" (1939), 17 Can BR, 77: this is a factual discussion of how far the British North America Act, 1867, has been interpreted in the light of extrinsic aids.

9. MILNER, J.B. Correspondence on the Use of Legislative History, (1953), 31 Can BR, 228–230: the queston is not so much the "will of Parliament" as of the government department concerned. Legislative history may prove to be as ambiguous as the wording.

10. JACKSON, R.M. Note in (1939), 55 LQR, 488: this discusses the use of reports of Royal Commissions.

11. BENAS, B.B. "Problems for the Conveyancer. The Construction of Statutes" (1952), 102 LJ, 269: this comments on a reference to Hansard in a case so as to elucidate the intention of Parliament.

12. JONES, H.W. "Extrinsic Aids in the Federal Courts" (1939–40), 25 Iowa LR, 737: the use of such aids to discover the meaning and purpose of an enactment is carefully discussed. It includes a consideration of discussions in committees, debates, social background and general statistical information.

1. MILLER, C.A. "The Value of Legislative History of Federal Statutes" (1925), 73 U Pa LR, 158: such history may be useful in the form of memoranda and briefs prepared for committees and may lessen judicial legislation.

2. COX, A. "Judge Learned Hand and the Interpretation of Statutes" (1946–47), 60 Harv LR, 370: this includes an account of how Judge Hand resorted to legislative history occasionally when the social purpose could not otherwise be discovered and when the point at issue was small.

3. JACKSON, R.H. "The Meaning of Statutes: what Congress Says or what the Court Says" (1948), 34 Am BAJ, 535: the root trouble is the absence of guidance from an accepted and consistent set of principles. Resort to legislative history is badly overdone. It is of dubious help and poses serious problems; it is not available to the lawyer when advising his client. (These remarks coming from a Judge of the Supreme Court carry a great deal of weight).

4. NOTE in (1936–37), 50 Harv LR on "Legislation", 813, at p. 822: extrinsic material is relevant in so far as it helps to elucidate the factual situation before the court.

5. SCHMIDT, F. "Construction of Statutes" (1957), I Scand SL, 157: legislative material constitutes "secondary directives" in giving guidance to a court. It has not the absolute character of the "primary directives", i.e., the statutory text and precedents. This includes a discussion of what legislative material should consist of and of its value.

Liberal Approach. (See also *supra*, *The "Purpose" Approach*)

6. FULLER, L.L. "Positivism and Fidelity to Law – a Reply to Professor Hart" (1957–58), 71 Harv LR, 630, at pp. 661–669: this is an incisive examination of Hart's distinction between the "core" of agreed application of words and the "penumbra" of unsettled applications showing where it breaks down. All statutory provisions can only be interpreted in the light of purpose and policy.

7. LEVI, E.H. *An Introduction to Legal Reasoning*, (University of Chicago Press, 1948), pp. 19–40: the method of applying statute is only superficially deductive. Reference is made first to the kind of examples which the words do cover from which the court argues by analogy. Judicial interpretation gives a broad direction to the statute.

8. CROSS, A.R.N. *Precedent in English Law*, (2nd ed., Oxford, 1968), pp. 163 *et seq.*: the general account includes a reference to the analogical method, the case in hand being compared with situations which were intended to be covered.

9. EKELÖF, P.O. "Teleological Construction of Statutes" (1958), 2 Scand SL, 75: the analogical method of interpretation is referred to in another context. One should consider the situations to which the statute does apply in order to discover the purpose which it seeks to achieve with regard to them.

10. PECZENIK, A. "*Analogia Legis*: Analogy from Statutes in Continental Law" (1971), Proceedings of the World Congress for Legal and Social Philosophy, 329: a norm has different spheres of application – established by linguistic reading, juristic interpretation of "the proper meaning", extensive application. In this essay a legal philosopher analyses analogy and its operation.

1. FRIEDMANN, W. Note in (1941–43), 6 MLR, 235: this discusses an instance of what is described as a "welcome and timely return to the principles of *Heydon's Case*".

2. GRUNFELD, C. Note in (1950), 13 MLR, 94: this discusses a decision in which the literal and mischief canons of interpretation were applied.

3. The following cases may be consulted as illustrating the attitude of the courts towards statutory interpretation: *Jones* v. *Secretary of State for Social Services* [1972] AC, 944; [1972] 1 All ER, 145; *Maunsell* v. *Olins* [1975] AC, 373; [1975] 1 All ER, 16; *Black-Clawson International, Ltd* v. *Papierwerke Waldhof-Aschaffenburg A.G.* [1975] AC, 591; [1975] 1 All ER, 810; *H.P. Bulmer, Ltd* v. *J. Bollinger S.A.*, [1974] Ch. 401; [1974] 2 All ER, 1226; *Magor and St. Mellons R.D.C.* v. *Newport Corporation* [1950] 2 All ER, 1226; on appeal, [1952] AC, 189; [1951] 2 All ER, 839; *Roberts* v. *Hopwood* [1925] AC, 578; *Liversidge* v. *Anderson* [1942] AC, 206; [1941] 3 All ER, 338; *Prescott* v. *Birmingham Corporation* [1955] Ch. 210; [1954] 3 All ER, 698; *Ross-Clunis* v. *Papadopoullos* [1958] 2 All ER, 23; [1958] 1 WLR, 546; *Cutler* v. *Wandsworth City Stadium* [1949] AC, 398; [1949] 1 All ER, 544; *Att.-Gen.* v. *H.R.H. Prince Ernest Augustus of Hanover* [1957] AC, 436; [1957] 1 All ER, 49; *Inland Revenue Commissioners* v. *Hinchy* [1960] AC, 748; [1960] 1 All ER, 505; *R.* v. *Board of Control, ex parte Winterflood* [1938] 2 KB, 366; [1938] 2 All ER, 463; *London & North Eastern Railway Co.* v. *Berriman* [1946] AC, 278; [1946] 1 All ER, 255; *Hilder* v. *Dexter* [1902] AC, 474; *Ellerman Lines, Ltd.* v. *Murray* [1931] AC, 126; *Corocraft, Ltd.* v. *Pan American Airways, Inc,* [1969] 1 QB, 616; [1969] 1 All ER, 82; *Re Macmanaway* [1951] AC, 161; *Escoign Properties Ltd.* v. *Inland Revenue Commissioners* [1958] AC, 549; [1958] 1 All ER, 406; *Becke* v. *Smith* (1836), 2 M & W, 191; *Heydon's Case* (1584), 3 Co Rep, 7a; *Miller* v. *Oregon* (1907), 208 US, 412; *Brown* v. *Board of Education* (1954), 347 US, 483.

8. Custom

1. ALLEN, C.K. *Law in the Making*, (7th ed., Oxford, 1964), chaps. 1 and 2 and Excursus A: this is the fullest and most convenient account for the student. The various theories about customary law are considered; and in chapter 2, which is more important for present purposes, the conditions under which local custom is accepted as law are examined in detail.

2. BRAYBROOKE, E.K. "Custom as Source of English Law" (1951), 50 Mich LR, 71: the distinction between custom of the people and of the courts is stressed, and the role of the latter is regarded as vital. The point is also made that customary popular action carries with it the reaction of those whose interests are invaded by such action.

3. SALMOND, J.W. *Jurisprudence*, (12th ed., P.J. Fitzgerald, Sweet & Maxwell, Ltd, 1966), chap. 6: the significance of custom and the reasons for its reception are first discussed. After that the various types of customs are dealt with in detail.

4. SALT, H.E. "Local Ambit of a Custom" in *Cambridge Legal Essays*, (edd. P.H. Winfield and A.D. McNair, W. Heffer & Sons, Ltd, 1926), 279: this essay delimits in detail what is meant by saying that a custom is "local". The case-law on various types of claims based on custom and their classifications is considered.

5. PLUCKNETT, T.F.T. *A Concise History of the Common Law*, (5th ed., Butterworth & Co Ltd, 1956), Part III, chap. 3: a feature of early English customary law was its flexibility and adaptability. The modern requirement of antiquity is shown to have been historically non-existent. The growth of new customs and the parts they played in various aspects of early English law are pointed out.

6. PLUCKNETT, T.F.T. *Legislation of Edward I*, (Oxford, 1949), pp. 6—10: the point is repeated that custom at this period was "an instrument for legal change rather than the fossilized remains of a remote past". The requirement of antiquity was not conceived of in the same way as now.

7. VINOGRADOFF, P. "Customary Law" in *The Legacy of the Middle Ages* (edd. C.G. Crump and E.F. Jacob, Oxford, 1926), 287: the operation of custom in the Middle Ages in various countries, principally in the spheres of family law, land law and commercial usages, is described. With regard to land law in England, the influence of the customs of the military class is to be noted.

8. BLACKSTONE, W. *Commentaries on the Laws of England*, (16th ed., J.T. Coleridge, T. Cadell and J. Butterworth & Son, 1825), I, pp. 67—68; 74—79: general custom, or the common law, is first discussed, then local custom. His exposition of the proof and legality of the latter might be regarded as classic. It is note-worthy that Blackstone does not sufficiently distinguish between popular custom and the custom of the courts.

9. STEPHEN, J.F. *Commentaries on the Laws of England*, (21st ed., L.C. Warmington, Butterworth & Co, Ltd, 1950), I, pp. 18—21; 365—366: the requirements of local custom are set out; usages of trade are also considered.

10. BENTHAM, J. *A Comment on the Commentaries*, (ed. C.W. Everett, Oxford, 1928), ss 18—19: this is a point by point (and occasionally captious) commentary on

Blackstone's treatment of the subject. Much attention is devoted to the requisites of local custom, in particular the requirement of reasonableness.

1. BENTHAM, J. *Of Laws in General*, (ed. H.L.A. Hart, The Athlone Press, 1970), chap. 15: to speak of customary law is a fiction, since custom as a source of law is incomplete by itself.

2. AUSTIN, J. *Lectures on Jurisprudence*, (5th ed., R. Campbell, John Murray, 1885), I, pp. 101–103; II, pp. 523, 536–543: a law is what the sovereign commands. Customs become laws when adopted by the courts by virtue of "tacit commands" of the sovereign. Independent of this, custom is only "positive morality".

3. BROWN, W.J. *The Austinian Theory of Law*, (John Murray, 1906), Excursus D: sound theory should be founded on existing facts and not on *a priori* conceptions of law. Custom has been and still is, a source of law. The question when custom becomes "law" is discussed at length, and the conclusion is that it does so when the judges declare it. The fact that judges say that it has previously been law is only a form of "the fiction of judicial incompetence". Judges are bound by their own practice.

4. HART, H.L.A. *The Concept of Law*, (Oxford, 1961, reprinted 1975), pp. 44–47: in the course of an attack on Austin's general thesis the point is made that a coercive order, as Austin viewed it, requires a creative act. If so, custom presents a difficulty. The Austinian solution by way of "tacit command" is shown to be inadequate.

5. LOBINGIER, C.S. "Customary Law" in *Encyclopaedia of the Social Sciences*, (ed. E.R.A. Seligman, Macmillan & Co, Ltd, 1931), IV, 662: repetition may explain the origin of customs, but it fails to indicate the point at which the differentiation between law and non-legal custom occurs. Custom is said to become law when it is recognised in some way as governing a class of relations segregated as jural (*sic*). Some of the factors involved in the transition are indicated.

6. KELSEN, H. *General Theory of Law and State*, (trans. A. Wedberg, Harvard University Press, 1949), pp. 126–128: custom is a law-creating agency only if the "constitution" so permits. He disagrees with Austin on the ground that if custom is not "law" till the judges adopt it, the same should be true of statute. The difference between statute law and custom is that the former is a centralised agency, the latter is not.

7. SILVING, H. *Sources of Law*, (Wm. S. Hein & Co, Inc, New York, 1968), "Customary Law", p. 125: custom is the legal corollary of evolution and is a basic element in all law. When a legal order proclaims to be the same despite change even in fundamental principles, this can only be on the basis that it has changed by customary evolution, customary law being part of the legal order.

8. CARTER, J.C. *Law: Its Origin, Growth and Function*, (G.P. Putnam's Sons, 1907), especially pp. 120–136: all law is said to be custom, though not *vice versa*. Law begins as the product of automatic action of society. Legislation may reinforce custom, but is doomed if it goes against it.

9. CARTER, J.C. "The Ideal and the Actual in the Law" (1890), 24 Am LR, 752, especially at p. 760: this repeats the above thesis, and adds that in doubtful cases the courts have to declare custom. The legislative function is supplementary to the judicial, namely, to catch the new and growing custom which is forming and to give it formal shape.

1. GRAY, J.C. "Some Definitions and Questions in Jurisprudence" (1892–93),
   6 Harv. LR, 21, at pp. 28–33: the idea that custom is law is examined and
   rejected. Custom as such has little influence. An additional factor is judicial
   opinions as to morality.

2. GRAY, J.C. *The Nature and Sources of the Law*, (2nd ed., R. Gray, The Macmillan
   Co, New York, 1921), chap. 12: according to his thesis that law is what the
   judges declare, custom is never "law" by itself, only a source of "law". Judicial
   decisions may also in some cases give rise to custom. J.C. Carter's view (*supra*)
   is subjected to particular criticism.

3. DICKINSON, J. "The Law behind Law" (1929), 29 Col LR, 113, at pp. 125 *et seq.*:
   J.C. Carter's theory (*supra*) is criticised. The conclusion is reached that custom
   may inspire rules of law, but is not law *ex proprio vigore*.

4. HOLLAND, T.E. *The Elements of Jurisprudence*, (13th ed., Oxford, 1924),
   pp. 56–63: custom becomes law when it is enforced by political authority.
   When a court decides that a custom exists, it does so prospectively and
   retrospectively, which explains why a judge declares a custom to have been law
   before.

5. BUCKLAND, W.W. *Some Reflections on Jurisprudence*, (Cambridge University
   Press, 1945), pp. 52–56: the difficulties facing the Austinian view of custom are
   considered. Buckland's own solution is that what is law is not the custom, but
   the statement of the characteristics which customs should possess.

6. ROSS, A. *On Law and Justice*, (Stevens & Sons, Ltd, 1958), pp. 91 *et seq.*: a legal
   custom implies that legal rules, otherwise upheld, are not observed in a certain
   area, but are replaced by the customary rule. Outward behaviour is an indication
   that a feeling of obligation exists. The position in England is briefly reviewed.

7. BODENHEIMER, E. *Jurisprudence*, (Harvard University Press, 1962), pp. 318–324:
   this is a general discussion of the conditions under which custom is transformed
   into law. Austin's views are considered and criticised, but some of the problems
   involved in the alternative view are also considered.

8. PATTERSON, E.W. *Jurisprudence*, (The Foundation Press, Inc, 1953), pp. 223–230:
   a distinction is drawn between the "external" element and the "internal" element
   in custom, the former being the regular behaviour, the latter the conviction. The
   tests of local custom in English law are summarised. American applications of
   custom are chiefly commercial usages. No final conclusion is reached as to
   whether custom is "law".

9. VINOGRADOFF, P. *Common-sense in Law*, (3rd ed., H.G. Hanbury, Oxford
   University Press, 1959), chap. 6: the significance of custom as a source of law is
   discussed as well as the tests that it has to satisfy. The importance of custom in
   various parts of the Commonwealth is also touched on.

10. CROSS, A.R.N. *Precedent in English Law*, (2nd ed., Oxford, 1968), pp. 155–163:
    in the course of discussing the relation of custom to precedent, the question when
    custom becomes law is dealt with. W.W. Buckland's view (*supra*) is rejected, and
    the conclusion is that custom today is law before it is upheld by the courts.

11. COHEN, M.R. *Reason and Law*, (The Free Press, Glencoe, Illinois, 1950), pp. 65–67:
    a definition of "law" which would exclude custom (e.g., Austin's) cannot be

refuted by adducing a different use of the word. Law as custom and law as legislation are both said to be realities. Arbitrary definition cannot disprove the existence of one or the other. The important thing is to examine their interaction.

1. EHRLICH, E. *Fundamental Principles of the Sociology of Law*, (trans. W.L. Moll, Harvard University Press, 1936), chap. 19: in Roman law custom became law by passing through juristic law. At p. 455 the point is made that legal propositions do not arise fully formed, but as the creation of jurists.

2. SADLER, G.T. *The Relation of Custom to Law*, (Sweet & Maxwell, Ltd, 1919), chap. 4: he agrees with the view that custom is law because it will be recognised by the courts. Some customs are recognised, but not others, because the former bear certain marks. Examples of state recognition of custom are drawn from Roman, English, Welsh, Indian and Dutch law.

3. PECZENIK, A. "The Concept 'Valid Law'" (1972), Scand SL, 213, 233–238: the question whether custom is "law" *ex proprio vigore* or not depends on a linguistic rule of recognition. The linguistic rule adopted by a judge-orientated lawyer will see the judicial decision as creating a duty to follow the custom; one adopted by a people-orientated lawyer will see the judge as being under a duty to follow a custom; one adopted by a statute-orientated lawyer will see the statute as creating the duty to follow the custom.

4. KEETON, G.W. *The Elementary Principles of Jurisprudence*, (2nd ed., Isaac Pitman & Sons, Ltd, 1949), chap. 6: this is an account of general and local custom and of the views of the principal writers.

5. PATON, G.W. *A Text-Book of Jurisprudence*, (4th ed., G.W. Paton and D.P. Derham, Clarendon Press, Oxford, 1972), chap. 7: this contains a general discussion of the common law position concerning local and mercantile customs.

6. POUND, R. *Jurisprudence*, (West Publishing Co, 1959), III, pp. 389–409: the basis of customary law is considered with reference to the Austinian and Historical School viewpoints. Custom and law react upon each other. Custom is also considered with reference to ancient and modern Civil law, Continental law and International law.

7. POLLOCK, F. *A First Book of Jurisprudence*, (6th ed., Macmillan & Co, Ltd, 1929), Part II, chap. 4: local custom is an addition or exception to the common law. The various conditions of its validity are discussed, and there is also some mention of conventional custom.

8. LLOYD, D. *Introduction to Jurisprudence*, (3rd ed., Stevens & Sons, Ltd, 1972), pp. 571–576: a very broad account is given of the part played in Roman and English law by general, local and conventional custom.

9. LLOYD, D. *The Idea of Law*, (Penguin Books, Ltd, A688, 1964), chap. 10, especially pp. 228–31, 240–50: law exists on more than one level, and it is necessary to appreciate the underlying social norms which determine much of its functioning. A mere habit lacks the sense of social compulsion. It is this socially obligatory element that is characteristic of custom. The development of law through custom in archaic, feudal and medieval European societies is traced out. The common law is said to be a bridge between customary and codified law. Local customs, constitutional customs and mercantile customs are explained briefly.

1. KOCOUREK, A. *An Introduction to the Science of Law*, (Little, Brown & Co, 1930), pp. 159–161: this is a summarised and elementary account of the different types of custom, together with brief indications of the requirements of each.

2. CLARK, E.C. *Practical Jurisprudence*, (Cambridge University Press, 1883), pp. 316–323: the terminology and classifications in Blackstone, Hale and Austin are considered.

3. KORKUNOV, N.M. *General Theory of Law*, (trans. W.G. Hastings, The Boston Book Co, 1909), pp. 410–419: customary law is built up outside all forms. Custom is said to be law according to the formula "what has been done ought to be done".

4. PAULSON, S.L. "*Jus Non Scriptum* and the Reliance Principle" (1976), 75 Mich LR, 68: in place of the sequence of practice followed by a sense of obligatoriness, the author contends that all unwritten norms originate and derive validity from a principle akin to estoppel. If a party continues to acquiesce in a course of action by another, this could lead to an expectation by the latter that he can rely on non-interference by the former – the "reliance principle". The point is illustrated with reference to international law.

5. RATTIGAN, W.H. *The Science of Jurisprudence*, (3rd ed., Wildy & Sons, 1909), pp. 72–77: the growth of custom in early societies is considered with particular reference to India. On the question when custom becomes law, the view is taken that it is law *ex proprio vigore*.

6. VINOGRADOFF, P. *Custom and Right*, (Oslo, 1925), chap. 2: the growth of customary law in the face of the rivalry between custom and law is traced out in Roman law and medieval canon law and the laws of certain European countries. The idea of long usage is shown to have been developed by the canonists of Europe.

7. VINOGRADOFF, P. *Collected Papers*, (Oxford, 1928), II, chaps. 22 and 23: the procedure for ascertaining custom in northern France is contrasted with that in early English law. In the latter chapter the attitude of the courts towards custom is traced from early times. The beginnings of legal rules are non-litigious.

8. SCHECHTER, F.I. "Popular Law and Common Law in Medieval England" (1928), 28 Col LR, 269: the domain of the common law was scanty, so local law was very important and active. The forces by which it diminished in favour of royal justice are discussed.

9. CARDOZO, B.N. *The Nature of the Judicial Process*, (Yale University Press, 1921), pp. 58–64: this is of general interest. Custom is touched on in the context of the influences at work upon the judicial mind.

10. POLLOCK, F. *Essays in Jurisprudence and Ethics*, (Macmillan & Co, 1882), pp. 54–59: in the context of a general discussion of the nature of man-made law, the imitative force behind custom is emphasised. The requirement of immemorial user in English law is ascribed to the lesson learnt of the danger of relying on solitary or few instances.

11. HALL, J. *Readings in Jurisprudence*, (The Bobbs-Merrill Co, 1938), chap. 20: this might usefully be consulted for extracts from English and American cases as well as for extracts from various writers, whose works are included here. There are also other extracts which are more appropriate to other contexts.

1. The following cases may be consulted: *Simpson* v. *Wells* (1872), LR 7 QB, 214; *Bryant* v. *Foot* (1868), LR 3 QB, 497; *Mercer* v. *Denne* [1904] 2 Ch, 534; *Mills* v. *Colchester Corporation* (1867), LR 2 CP, 476; *Broadbent* v. *Wilkes* (1742), Willes 360; *Wilson* v. *Willes* (1806), 7 East, 121; *Lawrence* v. *Hitch* (1868), LR 3 QB, 521; *The Tanistry Case* (1608), Dav IR, 28; *Johnson* v. *Clarke* [1908], 1 Ch, 303; *Blundell* v. *Catterall* (1821), 5 B & Ald, 268; *Coventry (Earl)* v. *Wills* (1863), 12 WR, 172; *Sowerby* v. *Coleman* (1867), LR 2 Exch, 96; *Goodwin* v. *Robarts* (1875), LR 10 Exch, 337; *Crouch* v. *Crédit Foncier of England* (1873), LR 8 QB, 374; *Iveagh* v. *Martin and Another* [1961], 1 QB, 232; [1960], 2 All ER, 668.

Usage

2. DEVLIN, P. *Samples of Lawmaking*, (Oxford University Press, 1962), chap. 2: this gives an account of how trade customs as a source of commercial law have gradually disappeared in the face of the written contract.

3. CHORLEY, R.S.T. "The Conflict of Law and Commerce" (1932), 48 LQR, 52: the law is in disfavour with business people because it does not adapt itself rapidly enough to new commercial practices.

General Custom

4. GREER, F.A. "Custom in the Common Law" (1893), 9 LQR, 153: the part played by custom is examined. After distinguishing between general, local and conventional customs, the former is considered in detail. General custom of the realm is equivalent to the common law.

5. MARKBY, W. *Elements of Law*, (6th ed., Oxford, 1905), ss 79–91: there is a general account of the part played by custom in various countries. In England, instead of resorting to Roman law, the judges resorted to the custom of the realm, which became the common law.

6. SIMPSON, A.W.B. "The Common Law and Legal Theory" in *Oxford Essays in Jurisprudence (Second Series)*, (ed. A.W.B. Simpson, Oxford University Press, 1973), chap. 4: just as statements of customs are not to be identified with the practices themselves, so rules of common law are not identical with the common law itself. This consists of the acceptance as more or less accurate by a specialist profession of statements in rule form of received ideas and practices. This is why there is no one authentic statement of a common law rule and why decisions were long treated as illustrations of "the common law". Setting up criteria of identification and use of authority are a symptom of the breakdown of a system of customary law.

Background Reading

7. JOLOWICZ, H.F. *Historical Introduction to Roman Law*, (3rd ed., Cambridge University Press, 1952), pp. 363–365: the part played by custom in Roman law is explained.

8. GUTTERIDGE, H.C. *Comparative Law*, (Cambridge University Press, 1946), pp. 80–81: a very brief account is given of the part played by custom in Continental countries.

1. ROBERTSON, L.J. "The Judicial Recognition of Custom in India" (1922), 4 JCL, (Ser. 3), 218: the attitude of Indian courts is shown to be different from that of English courts, since custom plays a more important part. The rigid tests applied by English courts cannot be applied.

2. ALLOTT, A.N. "The Judicial Ascertainment of Customary Law in British Africa" (1957), 20 MLR, 244: customary law here, as in Britain, is a derogation from the general law, but there are differences in finding it, while the fluid nature of customary law presents new problems.

3. HANNIGAN, A.St.J.J. "Native Custom, its Similarity to English Custom and its Mode of Proof" (1958), 2 JAL, 101: custom is not law till the courts pronounce it to be so. In Ghana custom is akin to English conventional custom rather than local custom.

4. VANDENBOSCH, A. "Customary Law in the Dutch East Indies" (1932), 14 JCL (Ser. 3), 30: the position here might usefully be compared with that in Britain, India and Africa.

9. Values

Importance of Values

1. CARDOZO, B.N. *The Growth of the Law*, (Yale University Press, 1924), chaps. 2–5: analysis of the judicial function should bring in the genesis, operation, growth and ends of the law, for these give direction to legal thinking. This theme is developed by one of the most famous American judges.

2. LLEWELLYN, K.N. *The Common Law Tradition. Deciding Appeals*, (Little, Brown & Co, 1960): the major contribution of this book is to show how the whole ethos, tradition and craftsmanship of the profession shape the judge's "situation-sense" when he decides any particular case. "Situation-sense" is said to provide a basis for a reasonable measure of predictability of judicial decisions.

3. SIMPSON, A.W.B. "The Common Law and Legal Theory" in *Oxford Essays in Jurisprudence (Second Series)*, (ed. A.W.B. Simpson, Oxford University Press, 1973), chap. 4: this considers professional ethos on a grand scale. A common law rule is never stated in the same way by judges or authors, but all the different statements are to the same broad effect. Therefore, rules of common law are not identical with "the common law" itself, which is the acceptance as more or less correct by the profession of formulations of received ideas and practices to be used in the rational decision of disputes.

4. DICKINSON, J. "The Law Behind Law" (1929), 29 Col LR, 285: jural laws are not propositions about factual situations, but value-judgments on social relations. The article inquires into the "higher law" from which courts derive guidance.

5. COHEN, F.S. "Modern Ethics and the Law" (1934), 4 Brook LR, 33: logic can offer its services to desirable or undesirable ends. In deriving a rule from a given case, one has to decide that some facts in it are crucial, others not. This choice is dictated by a sense of values. The function of ethics is considered on this basis.

6. REID, J. "Is and Ought after Darwin" (1977), 40 MLR, 249: as our knowledge of "facts" becomes less objective in that we construct sense out of the world, so does our criticism of "values" as being uncertain decline in importance. Our need for values cannot be denied since many of our actions are the product, not of knowledge, but of an assessment of the desirability of their consequences. Norms are a part of culture.

7. SEARLE, J.R. "How to Derive 'Ought' from 'Is'" in *Theories of Ethics*, (ed. P.R. Foot, Oxford University Press, 1970), chap. 7: the traditional axiom that "ought" cannot be derived from "is" fails to give a coherent explanation of commitment, responsibility and obligation. There is a difference between statements of "brute" fact and "institutional" fact. The latter presuppose some institution ("obligation", "responsibility" etc. are institutionalized). Within these systems the statement of an "is" ("he promised") does give rise to an "ought" ("therefore he ought to carry it out").

8. MacCORMICK, D.N. "Law as Institutional Fact" (1974), 90 LQR, 102: after demonstrating the essential part played by institutions (e.g., contract) and institutional facts (e.g., existence of a particular contract), the author discusses the degree of certainty with which rules regulating institutions should be stated. These should prescribe for the ordinary case, but should leave room for

modifications in particular cases influenced by principles. Principles have no criteria of validity. They influence the purposes of rules and institutions, which brings in values.

1. POUND, R. "Justice According to Law" (1913), 13 Col LR, 696; (1914), 14 Col LR, 1, 103: the administration of law involves a technical (legal) and non-technical (discretionary) element. Justice according to law requires administration of the law according to standards which may be ascertained in advance of dispute. But this is not always possible and a discretionary element has to come in. The pros and cons of various forms of adjudicating disputes are considered. See also R. POUND: *Justice According to Law*, (Yale University Press, 1952) and *Jurisprudence*, (West Publishing Co., 1959), II, chap. 13.

2. POUND, R. *Law and Morals*, (The University of North Carolina Press, 1926): the theme of the book is the need for values in relation to the process of law-making and law-applying. The influence of the ideal element is traced from Greek times and the weakness of the positivist attitude is pointed out.

3. POUND, R. *The Spirit of the Common Law*, (Marshall Jones Co, 1921): this is of general interest, dealing with the various ideals which the common law has striven to achieve.

4. POUND, R. "A Comparison of Ideals of Law" (1933–34), 47 Harv LR, 1; (1933), 7 Tul LR, 475: ideals are part of the law. It is possible to compare the ideals of a particular age.

5. POUND, R. "Mechanical Jurisprudence" (1908), 8 Col LR, 605: the marks of a scientific law are conformity with reason, uniformity and certainty. But this must not be allowed to degenerate into technicality. Institutions should be founded on policy and adapted to human needs.

6. WAITE, J.B. "Judge-made Law and the Education of Lawyers" (1944), 30 Am BAJ, 253: the process of judicial law-making and also the training of judges for that task are considered.

7. RADCLIFFE, C.J. *The Law and its Compass*, (Faber & Faber, 1961): the law requires a compass by which to steer its course, i.e., values. In this connection the influence of Christianity, public policy and natural law is considered.

8. KNAFLA, L.A. "Conscience in the English Tradition" (1976), 26 UTLJ, 1: the author traces the use of conscience in the development of personal action in the 15th–17th centuries. Synderesis is the highest power of the soul to discern goodness and evil and was a collection of universal principles; reason was descended from it and was identified with the mind; conscience was collected habits shaped by reason.

9. WRIGHT, R.A. "Causation and Responsibility in English Law" (1955), CLJ, 163, especially pp. 164 *et seq.*: legal thought has an approach of its own. The "ought" of legal duty and the attribution of responsibility involves a reasoned value-judgment. This must be so since legal decisions give effect to the idea of "ought". Value-judgments are a necessary and integral part of the common law.

10. MORRIS, J.W. "Law and Public Opinion", *Presidential Address to the Holdsworth Club* (1958), the influence of public opinion on certain types of cases is considered.

1. SUMMERS, R.S. "Naive Instrumentalism and the Law" in *Law, Morality, and Society. Essays in Honour of H.L.A. Hart*, (edd. P.M.S. Hacker and J. Raz, Clarendon Press, Oxford, 1977), chap. 6: naive instrumentalism is the belief that laws serve social goals and every law brings about social change. But "legal goals" are complex, and laws are not all directly or indirectly mandatory, for they may cancel or excuse. How laws "serve" goals brings in legal techniques. The author distinguishes five techniques.

2. HARPER, F.V. "The Forces Behind and Beyond Juristic Pragmatism in America" in *Recueil d'Etudes sur les Sources du Droit en l'Honneur de F. Gény*, (Librairie du Recueil, Sirey, 1934), II, 243: philosophy has followed science, but it leads the social sciences. This is because it gives direction and method. Juristic thought relates to the future and is creative, but there are limits to this.

3. FRIEDMANN, W. *Law in a Changing Society*, (Stevens & Sons, Ltd, 1959), chaps. 1–8 and 10: law reacts to social pressures. In these chapters this thesis is demonstrated with reference to different branches of the law in turn.

4. FRIEDMANN, W. *Legal Theory*, (5th ed., Stevens & Sons, Ltd, 1967), chaps. 17, 26–28, 31–33: the last three chapters deal with the values which the law seeks to attain. The earlier chapters deal with certain value philosophies.

5. FRIEDMANN, W. "Legal Theory and the Practical Lawyer" (1941), 5 MLR, 103: it is impossible to avoid having to take values into account in the administration of law. The way in which they operate and the limits of their influence are considered.

6. FRIEDMANN, W. "Legal Philosophy and Judicial Lawmaking" (1961), 61 Col LR, 821: the importance of values and of the need to make a creative choice between competing policies and ideals is illustrated from many points of view. A judge is not absolutely unfettered, but within limits he has considerable latitude.

7. JONES, J.W. "Modern Discussions of the Aims and Methods of Legal Science" (1931), 47 LQR, 62, at pp. 78–84: the creative role of the judge is emphasised and some account is given of leading theories.

8. DENNING, A.T. *The Changing Law*, (Stevens & Sons, Ltd, 1953), especially chaps. 1–2: the spirit of the British constitution is said to rest on the instinct for justice, for liberty and for balancing right with duty, power with safeguard. Various aspects of the law are dealt with in this connection.

9. SCHMITTHOFF, C.M. "The Growing Ambit of the Common Law" (1951), 29 Can BR, 469: (1952), 30 Can BR, 48: the common law has been able to adapt itself to the changes of the post-war world. The discussion concerns mainly administrative law, but there are interesting sidelights on the working of precedent, contract and other branches.

10. *Science of Legal Method: Select Essays by Various Authors*, (trans. E. Bruncken and L.B. Register, The Boston Book Co., 1917): this is a collection of writings of various Continental jurists, but there is one chapter contributed by R. Pound; and there are, in addition, Prefaces by Anglo-American jurists. The discretionary element in the judicial process is considered from several different angles. Of these perhaps the most interesting is that of F. Gény, who advocates the method of "free scientific research".

1. *Recueil d'Etudes sur les Sources du Droit en l'Honneur de F. Gény*, (Librairie du Recueil Sirey, 1934), II, M. FRANKLIN, p. 30: "M. Gény and Juristic Ideals and Methods in the United States": this deals generally with Gény's influence in America. A. KOCOUREK, p. 459: "Libre Recherche in America": the premises on which the "free law" movement is founded are explained and some account is given of the writers whose works constitute the background and foreground. J. DICKINSON, p. 503: "The Problem of the Unprovided Case": the problem is of finding grounds for reaching a decision where the grounds are not supplied by existing rules. J.G. ROGERS, p. 552: "A Scientific Approach to Free Judicial Decision": the norms of social conduct are not rules but examples. The social structure is a major element of the law itself.

2. WORTLEY, B.A. "Francois Gény" in *Modern Theories of Law*, (ed. W.I. Jennings, Oxford University Press, 1933), 139: marginal cases occur and logic alone cannot fill gaps. A legal system should seek to realise an ideal of justice and utility. Judicial discretion is vital — free scientific research according to justice and social utility. (See also B.A. Wortley, *Jurisprudence*, (Manchester U.P., Oceana Publications Inc, NY, 1967, chap. 12).

3. STONE, J. *Legal System and Lawyers' Reasonings*, (Stevens & Sons, Ltd, 1964), pp. 212–223: a legislator cannot express his will on everything. It is in these spheres, according to Gény, that there has to be "free scientific research". Conceptions and deduction from them are important where the legislator intended given concepts to be worked out. Beyond this the logical method is harmful when applied to the changing relations in society.

4. KANTOROWICZ, H.U. and PATTERSON, E.W. "Legal Science — a Summary of its Methodology" (1928), 28 Col LR, 679, at pp. 698–707: the place of values in any treatment of law is considered. The "gap" problem comes into prominence in the application of law. Here the "free law" method is advocated.

5. CAIRNS, H. "The Valuation of Legal Science" (1940), 40 Col LR, 1: observation suggests corrections in theory; corrections in theory prompt refinements in observations. Such a procedure is open to jurisprudence. The vital question is whether a complete descriptive science of law can be constructed without introducing value elements. It is argued that a complete description has to include ethical and behaviour elements.

6. BRETT, P. "The Implications of Science for the Law" (1972), 18 McGill LJ, 170: the author deplores the fact that law has grown out of touch with the scientific outlook, but "science" is any knowledge appropriate to the subject-matter. In relation to law this includes ethics, justice and humanity, which it would be unscientific to exclude. The difficulty is to see how these could be imported "scientifically" without a further re-definition of "scientific method". He condemns as unscientific four major features of the legal system: adversary trial, certain basic rules of evidence, concepts of conduct and *stare decisis*.

7. MILLER, A.S. and HOWELL, R.F. "The Myth of Neutrality in Constitutional Adjudication" (1959–60), 27 UCLR, 661: neutrality is a myth and impossible in constitutional cases. Neutral observation is not possible even in the physical sciences. It is more useful to search for the values that can be furthered by the judicial process. What is needed is a purposive jurisprudence.

8. McDOUGAL, M.S. and LEIGHTON, G.C.K. "The Rights of Man in the World

Community: Constitutional Illusions versus Rational Action" (1949–50), 59 Yale LJ, 60: this is of general interest. It concerns the interdependence of human values in the world community.

1. FREUND, P.A. *On Law and Justice* (The Belknap Press of Harvard University Press, 1968): this is a collection of various papers by the author. Their central theme is the judiciary. He shows how changing values have broadened the problems of constitutional law in America and how the judges (especially the Supreme Court) has had to react to them. In the last part he gathers these threads together by giving accounts of some individual judges and how each of them has viewed the problems. His overall point is that law and the legal process can be a contribution to general education.

2. MARSH, N.S. "Civil Liberties in Europe" (1959), 75 LQR, 530: this is a general discussion of what is implied by "civil liberties" especially with reference to the Convention for the Protection of Human Rights and Fundamental Freedoms 1950.

3. FRIED, C. *An Anatomy of Values: Problems of Personal and Social Choice*, (Oxford University Press, 1970): law partakes of the value of the ends which it serves. The legal structure is part of a relationship (e.g., marriage) and not just a means of protecting it. A good deal of attention is paid to respect for privacy.

4. HARVEY, W.B. "A Value Analysis of Ghanaian Legal Development since Independence" (1964), 1 UGLJ, 4: "law" is said to be value-neutral, being merely a technique of social ordering available for use in support of any value-judgment that the manipulators of the technique entertain. The developments in Ghana are recounted and their significance assessed. The value of nationhood is said to be paramount.

5. LAMONT, W.D. *The Value Judgment*, (Edinburgh University Press, 1955), chaps. 1 and 10: the nature of value-judgments is carefully examined, and the contrast between value-judgment and moral judgment investigated. This is recommended as one of the most useful non-legal discussions of the subject.

6. SHKLAR, J.N. *Legalism*, (Harvard University Press, 1964): this book is an attack on "legalism", which is the attitude of mind that makes a morality of ule following. Justice is an ideal of legalism, but need not be exclusive. Legalism is but one among many moralities in a pluralist society. The morality of rule following is an instrument of politics and it may succeed in some situations and not in others. The whole book is a powerful plea for the widest accommodation of diverse ideologies and ideals.

7. WILLIAMS, G.L. "Language and the Law" (1946), 62 LQR, 387: the place of value-judgments is considered in the context of a general discussion of the function of language in law.

8. KENDAL, G.H. "Value and the Law" (1971), 2 Can BJ (NS) No. 2, p.12: this is a brief Note on the inescapable part which values play in law. The argument is abstract but the points made are telling.

9. LAUN, R. *Stare Decisis. The Fundamentals and the Significance of Anglo-Saxon Case Law*, (Pamphlet, 2nd ed., Otto Meissners, Hamburg, 1947): what is it in prior decisions that is followed and should be followed? The ultimate source of all legal and moral obligations lies within the individual. Case-law is proof that

true law evolves from those required to obey. Precedents derive their authority from value judgments transcending courts and the state.

1. FARRAR, J.H. *Law Reform and the Law Commission*, (Sweet & Maxwell, Ltd, 1974), chap. 6: in this chapter the author examines the part played by public opinion and the values underlying society in the matter of law reform. The problems facing the Law Commission and the manner in which it conducts its task are explained and assessed.

The Judicial Method

2. CARDOZO, B.N. *The Nature of the Judicial Process*, (Yale University Press, 1921): this is a classic exposition of the various factors at work in the judicial application of the law and the factors of which a judge takes account.

3. CARDOZO, B.N. *The Paradoxes of Legal Science*, (Columbia University Press, 1928), especially chaps. 2–3: judges have to balance values and should guard against substituting their own scale of values. Legal concepts are subordinate to expediency and justice.

4. HAND, L. "How Far is a Judge Free in Rendering a Decision?" in *The Spirit of Liberty*, (Hamish Hamilton, 1954), 103: the question is how far a judge should follow the dictates of his conscience or abide by the letter of the law. This is a simple but valuable examination of this matter by a well-known American judge. "The Speech of Justice", p. 13: judges are not passive interpreters of the law. They need to adopt a broader and more comprehensive outlook.

5. SUTHERLAND, A.E. "Judicial Reticence and Public Policy" (1958), 3 Jur R, 1: legislators should lay down broad policy; judges should apply this to specific cases. Even the determination of future policy lies to a large extent in remembrance of things past. But when an unprovided case does arise, it is no use pretending that it is covered by the past; the true basis of the decision should be openly avowed.

6. DENNING, A.T. "The Way of an Iconoclast" (1959), 5 JSPTL (NS), 77: an iconoclast is one who is not content to accept the cherished beliefs simply because they have been long accepted. Lord Denning reviews several areas of the law where cherished doctrines were examined and challenged. This is the only way to preserve the law from stagnation and decay.

7. DENNING, A.T. "Giving Life to the Law" (1976), 1 Malaya LR, ciii: the law must not be allowed to lay a dead hand on society. The judiciary has an important part to play in this respect. Aspects of the judicial role are considered in relation to literal interpretation of statutes, the binding force of precedent, and the increase in crime.

8. WASSERSTROM, R.A. *The Judicial Decision*, (Stanford University Press, 1961): this is a careful investigation into the nature of the judicial process. The author's own preference is for what he calls the "two-level justification", i.e., a rule is a justification for a decision provided the rule itself is justifiable on utilitarian grounds.

9. GOTTLIEB, G. *The Logic of Choice*, (Allen & Unwin, Ltd, 1968): this work is an important analysis of how rules, principles and standards are used in reaching

judicial decisions. He takes pains to point out that facts are not self-evident, but can be stated differently depending upon the context. Moral and policy considerations are incorporated into legal declarations.

1. SLESSER, H. *The Art of Judgment*, (Stevens & Sons, Ltd, 1962): the opening chapter is a demonstration of the judicial method by an English judge. He utters a caution against the tendency to exaggerate the discretionary element. See further H. SLESSER: *The Judicial Office and Other Matters*, (Hutchinson & Co, Ltd, 1942), chap. 3.

2. HODSON, F.L.C. "Judicial Discretion and its Exercise", *Presidential Address to the Holdsworth Club* (1962): too much discretion is bad. The scope of discretion is considered in relation to matrimonial disputes, criminal law, tort and public policy.

3. KILMUIR, The Lord (D. Maxwell-Fyffe). "The State, Citizen and the Law" (1957), 73 LQR, 172: the problem of maintaining a just balance between the State and the individual is considered. Formerly, the State merely "held the ring"; now it enters into the battle. The law remains the right means for resolving conflicts between public and private interests. It should continue to change as social problems change.

4. SCRUTTON, T.E. "The Work of the Commercial Court" (1921–23), 1 CLJ, 6: the attributes of a good legal system are discussed. The portion relating to the need for impartiality is particularly interesting, and there are useful sidelights on the personal influence of particular judges.

5. REID, J.S.C. "The Judge as Law Maker" (1972), 12 JSPTL (NS), 22: the importance of certainty is stressed. But fine distinctions destroy it, so it is necessary to think more widely than the instant case. The guiding lines for the judge should be common sense, legal principle and public policy.

6. HARDING, R.W. "Lord Atkin's Judicial Attitudes and their Illustration in Commercial Law and Contract" (1964), 27 MLR, 434: Lord Atkin's philosophy is revealed as being a wide, all-pervading commonsense, a firm sense of practicality and social responsibility and concern for principle. The influence of these factors is illustrated with reference to three famous cases.

7. POLLOCK, F. "Judicial Caution and Valour" (1929), 45 LQR, 293: the judicial function covers declaration of law and extension of it. In cases of first impression both caution and valour are required. The problem is to hold a balance between these two.

8. BARWICK, G. "Courts, Lawyers, and the Attainment of Justice" (1958), 1 Tasm LR, 1: in the first part of this paper it is pointed out that theoretically the courts neither make law nor do they seek to attain abstract justice. But there is room in applying the law to give effect to current views, although personal idiosyncrasies also have some influence.

9. CATTERALL, R.T. "Judicial Self-restraint: the Obligation of the Judiciary" (1956), 42 Am BAJ, 829: the author cautions against the tendency of judges of the American Supreme Court to substitute their economic, moral and political convictions for the written wording of the Constitution. This could lead to judicial despotism. Developments in this direction since the last century are surveyed.

1. CANTRALL, A.M. "The Judge as a Leader: the Embodiment of the Ideal of Justice" (1959), 45 Am BAJ, 339: by virtue of his office the judge, especially a local judge, is a leader of his community and represents the legal system to them. He accordingly has a responsibility towards them. The author criticises the costs, delays and other anachronisms of the judicial process.

2. STEVENS, R. "The Role of a Final Appeal Court in a Democracy: the House of Lords Today" (1965), 28 MLR, 509: appeal courts are concerned with areas where the law is uncertain and where creative decisions are called for. Historically appeal courts were established for the development of the law. The attitude of the House of Lords is traced down to the present time, and it is pointed out that since the 1950's there has been a departure from its former "mechanistic" thinking.

3. McCRUDDEN, J.C. "Judicial Discretion and Civil Liberties" (1974), 25 NILQ, 119: this is a comparison of the judicial approach to civil liberties in Britain and America. The British premise is law and order as the prime requirement of democracy, whereas the American premise is open demonstration as an important aspect of democracy. In the absence of general principles in a constitution, British courts think in terms of the facts of each case, whereas American courts think more in terms of principle.

4. DICKINSON, J. *Administrative Justice and the Supremacy of Law in the United States*, (Harvard University Press, 1927), pp. 216 *et seq.*: to treat legal concepts as fixed and to apply them mechanically is harmful. The courts have been compelled to formulate principles of valuation.

5. DICKINSON, J. "Legal Rules and their Function in the Process of Decision" (1931), 79 U Pa LR, 833, at pp. 850–55: "Legal Rules, their Application and Elaboration", *ibid.* 1052: law is not a complete and coherent system. Discretion inevitably comes into its application. This depends not only on the nature of the case, but on the definiteness or vagueness of the rule. The application of a rule means the employment of it to decide a case; elaboration of a rule means the creation or extension of a rule to fill a gap. Both involve the use of value-judgments.

6. CONANT, M. "Systems Analysis in the Appellate Decision-making Process" (1970), 24 Rutgers LR, 293: general systems theory is a method of viewing a problem or process in terms of its total relevant environment. There is a complex intertwining of law and policy in legal material and there needs to be an integration of parts of analytical and sociological jurisprudence. Illustrations are drawn from contract, statute-law and constitutional law.

7. SEIDMAN, R.B. "The Judicial Process Reconsidered in the Light of Role-theory" (1969), 32 MLR, 516: the familiar difficulties in deciding the unprovided case are discussed from a sociological angle. There are norms prescribing how a judge is to choose which other norms to apply to the facts. These are "rules of recognition". In "clear" cases the rule is clear and the facts fall within its "core" meaning; in "trouble" cases there is some inadequacy in the "rule of recognition" itself. Here he has a creative task to perform and the problem is one of value.

8. FRIEDMANN, W. "Judges, Politics and the Law" (1951), 29 Can BR, 811: on one view judges should ignore political and social considerations; on another view, political legislation cannot be dealt with otherwise. The common law would not exist if judges had not from time to time laid down new principles to meet new social problems.

1. PALLEY, C. "Rethinking the Judicial Role. The Judiciary and Good Government" (1969), ZLJ, 1: sooner or later political questions resolve themselves into judicial ones. The problems of modern societies, especially developing ones, call for a re-appraisal of governmental institutions, including the judiciary. Courts are a political phenomenon; they should consider the goals of society as well as protect the individual.

2. GROVE, D.L. "The 'Sentinels' of Liberty? The Nigerian Judiciary and Fundamental Rights" (1963), 7 JAL, 152: what use has been made of the fundamental rights provision in the Nigerian Constitution? The cases fall into two groups, one concerning individuals alone, the other concerning the individual in relation to other interests. The latter involves balancing interests. The judicial attitude towards various freedoms is illustrated with the aid of cases.

3. HART, H.L.A. "The Ascription of Responsibility and Rights" in *Logic and Language*, (ed. A.G.N. Flew, Blackwell, 1955), 1, 145: legal concepts are not determinate and judges have often to decide the question of responsibility in order to decide what legal label to apply.

4. LLEWELLYN, K.N. "Impressions of the Conference on Precedent" in *Jurisprudence: Realism in Theory and Practice*, (University of Chicago Press, 1962), 116: precedents control judicial action even against the judges' inclinations, but sometimes when the urge of policy or justice is strong enough judges do find a way round them. Within limits precedents can be manipulated to favour one side or the other, but this is not governed by arbitrary considerations.

5. FULLER, L.L. "Reason and Fiat in Case Law" (1945–46), 59 Harv LR, 376: the judge's freedom of choice is limited, particularly by the consideration that his decision will become a precedent. Hence his choice has to be shorn of personal predilections and it has to conform to sentiments of justice.

6. NELLES, W. "Towards Legal Understanding" (1934), 34 Col LR, 862, 1041: the forces that develop law are examined at length. It is unreal to regard the judicial process as mechanical. There has to be a different conception of it.

7. MENDELSON, W. "The Judge's Art" (1960–61), 109 U Pa LR, 524: this is a sympathetic examination of judicial creativeness.

8. von MEHREN, A.T. *The Civil Law System: Cases and Materials*, (Prentice-Hall, Inc, 1957), chap. 16, pp. 821–23: this is a brief but valuable study of the judicial process. In the pages mentioned its flexibility and its non-mechanical nature are emphasised.

9. COHEN, F.S. "The Problems of a Functional Jurisprudence" (1937), 1 MLR, 5: there is often a "plaintiff principle" and a "defendant principle". The choice between them depends upon unstated considerations.

10. MILLER, A.S. "On the Need for 'Impact Analysis' of Supreme Court Decisions" (1964–65), 53 Geo LJ, 365: judicial decisions should be evaluated according to their social effects. A judge chooses between opposing premises on the basis of what the impact of the decision is thought to be – "jurisprudence of consequences". Courts now have an affirmative function, viz, to co-operate with other branches of government. Evaluation of this function requires more than just explanation of the bases of decision.

1. LERNER, M. "The Supreme Court and American Capitalism" (1932–33), 42 Yale LJ, 668, at pp. 686–701: a course of decisions is examined first and then the nature of the judicial process. The function of the Court is to partake in forming policy. The judge does not fashion new law according to his own views. The various considerations that govern his choice are considered.

2. McWHINNEY, E. "The Supreme Court and the Bill of Rights – the Lessons of Comparative Jurisprudence" (1959), 37 Can BR, 16: there is a need for a value-oriented jurisprudence. The problem is to define the limits of the new absolutes. The judicial function is considered in this light.

3. SCHWARTZ, B. "The Changing Role of the United States Supreme Court" (1950), 28 Can BR, 48: the sense of values of the Supreme Court is discussed in relation to national and individual interests.

4. HAND, L. *The Bill of Rights. The Oliver Wendell Holmes Lectures 1958*, (Harv UP 1958): The Supreme Court's power to review governmental acts is not to be found in, or inferred from, the Constitution. Such power has to be assumed, but it should be used sparingly. It should not be used to question the substance of governmental acts, and in this respect the Court has been exceeding its province.

5. WECHSLER, H. "Toward Neutral Principles of Constitutional Law" (1959–60), 73 Harv LR, 1: the author takes issue with Judge Hand as to when courts may review legislative action. Courts do have to make value-choices, but this should be done according to principles. A principled decision is one which rests on reasons with respect to all the issues in a case and in their generality and neutrality transcend the immediate issues. Certain recent leading cases are criticised on the ground that the courts did not act on such principles.

6. POLLAK, L.H. "Racial Discrimination and Judicial Integrity: A Reply to Professor Wechsler" (1959–60), 108 U Pa LR, 1: it is true that courts should act on the sort of principles advocated by Professor Wechsler, but it is argued that in the cases criticised by him the courts did in fact do so.

7. HART, H.M. "The Time Chart of the Justices" (1959–60), 73 Harv LR, 84: reason is the life of the law, and this means the acceptance of impersonal and durable principles. He, therefore, agrees with Professor Wechsler. The trouble is that the Supreme Court has too much work to get through.

8. HENKIN, L. "Some Reflections on Current Constitutional Controversy" (1960–61), 109 U Pa LR, 637: constitutional issues today are different from those of the past. In dealing with the "Controversy of the Professors" (at pp. 650 *et seq.*) the author agrees with Professor Wechsler, but thinks that the cases he attacked are defensible.

9. MILLER, A.S. and HOWELL, R.F. "The Myth of Neutrality in Constitutional Adjudication" (1959–60), 27 UCLR, 661: application of "neutral" principles without value-choices is impossible. Neutrality is unattainable in social or even in natural sciences. Choices between values are motivated by the entire biography and heredity of the person making the choice. Judges should be guided by a teleological jurisprudence, which makes them participants in government. Decisions should be made with reference to the effects of decisions. (See also A. MUELLER and M.L. SCHWARTZ: "The Principle of Neutral Principles"

(1960), 7 UCLALR, 571: this also questions the possibility of "neutral" principles.

1. GOLDING, M.P. "Principled Decision-making and the Supreme Court" in *Essays in Legal Philosophy*, (ed. R.S. SUMMERS, Basil Blackwell, Oxford, 1968), 208: one cannot apply "neutral" principles in choosing between competing values. One may choose with reference to some other principle, which is more comprehensive or superior, When there is no such principle, a court may still formulate a principle which will serve in other cases of its type. Such a principle is "general" insofar as it transcends the instant case, but it is not "neutral" save as to its future application.

2. WEILER, P.C. "Two Models of Judicial Decision-making" (1968), 46 Can BR, 406: the author examines in detail the adjudicatory model of deciding disputes and the policy making model. In connection with the former he considers, *inter alia*, the fact that only specific disputes come before courts, the adversarial process and the established system of standards used in the process. He deals with the limitations of this model and the degree of creativity which it allows and the parts played by principles and values. In connection with the latter he considers the personal responsibility of judges, their recruitment and accountability, the collegiate character of decision-making and the legitimacy of judicial activism in a democracy. On the whole he is doubtful of entrusting to judges the review of administrative actions and the safeguarding of a bill of rights.

3. WEILER, P.C. "Legal Values and Judicial Decision-making" (1970), 48 Can BR 1: the function of values in the judicial process is examined in detail. Judges should abide by rules preferably, but there are leeways whenever principles, as distinct from rules, are invoked.

4. COVAL, S.C. and SMITH, J.C. "Some Structural Properties of Legal Decisions" (1973), 32 CLJ, 81: when rules, or their application, conflict or lead to undesirable results, "second-order rules" come into play to resolve the conflict or guide application. These derive from the social goals to be served and are found explicitly. They are versions of other implicit "anomaly resolving rules". In this way the choice between values could be made dependent on a hierarchy of rules which are integral to law. This paper is reproduced as Chapter 9 of J.C. SMITH, *Legal Obligation*, (University of London: the Athlone Press, 1976).

5. PECZENIK, A. "Principles of Law" (1971), 2 Rechtstheorie 17: no one can be competent in philosophy, logic, sociology and law at once. A lawyer needs a combination of legal qualifications and a general knowledge of extra-legal principles. These principles and how to choose between them are discussed from a philosophical point of view.

6. STONE, J. " 'Result-orientation' and Appellate Judgment" in *Perspectives of Law. Essays for Austin Wakeman Scott*, (edd. R. POUND, E.N. GRISWOLD, A.E. SUTHERLAND, Little, Brown & Co, 1964), 347: the result of deciding with reference to "result-orientation" would not be different from deciding with reference to "neutral" principles. It is not possible to know what principle is applicable without reference to the facts. Professor Wechsler's thesis is tenable only within very modest limits.

7. BROWN, R.A. "Police Power – Legislation for Health and Personal Safety" (1928–29), 42 Harv LR, 866: a large number of decisions on certain statutes are reviewed. These show that the attitude of the courts is to treat the individual and property, not as ends in themselves, but in conjunction with social needs.

1. SCOTT, W.C. "Judicial Logic as Applied in Delimiting the Concept of Business 'Affected with a Public Interest'" (1930), 19 Ken LJ, 16: this examines the technique used by American courts in giving effect to public interests and public regulation. The "functional" method is contrasted with the "physical analogy" method.

2. NELLES, W. "The First American Labor Case" (1931–32), 41 Yale LJ, 165: this reviews the decision in a criminal prosecution for conspiracy arising out of trade combination. It shows clearly how values played a major part.

3. BINGHAM, J.W. "Some Suggestions Concerning 'Legal Cause' at Common Law" (1909), 9 Col LR, 16, 136: one cannot know how a judge will decide a case, but one can grasp the method, considerations and influences which guide the courts. Judges decide as considerations of justice and policy dictate.

4. ROBSON, W.A. *Justice and Administrative Law*, (3rd ed., Stevens & Sons, Ltd, 1951), chap. 5, especially pp. 409–18: this is an inquiry into the "judicial spirit". The impartiality of the "good judge" is legendary. The administration of justice requires as much prejudice in one sense and absence of prejudice in another, i.e., prejudice as to what is socially desirable.

5. GOODHART, A.L. "The New York Court of Appeals and the House of Lords" in *Essays in Jurisprudence and the Common Law*, (Cambridge University Press, 1937), chap. 13: judges do not reach their conclusions on quite such uncertain bases as "hunches" and their reasons are not merely cloaks. This may be true in doubtful cases, but not in the majority.

6. WADE, H.W.R. "The Concept of Legal Certainty. A Preliminary Skirmish" (1940–41), 4 MLR, 183: the extent of judicial discretion is considered. Judges do contrive to keep individual preferences to a minimum.

7. FRANKFURTER, F. "John Marshall and the Judicial Function" (1955–56), 69 Harv LR, 217: the vision of a single man gave direction to the American Constitution, which was until then largely a paper scheme of government.

8. FRANKFURTER, F. "The Constitutional Opinions of Mr Justice Holmes" (1916), 29 Harv LR, 683: the influence of individual personalities is important. The point is illustrated with reference to Mr Justice Holmes's insight.

9. FRANKFURTER, F. "Twenty Years of Mr Justice Holmes's Constitutional Opinions" (1922–23), 36 Harv LR, 909: judges of the Supreme Court move in a field of statesmanship, which marks the boundaries between state and individual. The interpretation of the Constitution is inspired by considerations outside the law. The work of Mr Justice Holmes is reviewed along these lines.

10. LEVY, B.H. *Cardozo and Frontiers of Legal Thinking*, (New York, 1958), chap. 2: judges do make law. The choice between various considerations is governed by convenience and fitness. The judge has to be a careful student of public opinion.

11. PATTERSON, E.W. "Cardozo's Philosophy of Law", (1940), 88 U Pa LR, 71, especially pp. 165 *et seq.*: Mr Justice Cardozo made explicit the value problems implicit in the judicial process.

12. HAMILTON, W.H. "Preview of a Justice" (1938–39), 48 Yale LJ, 819: this is an appraisal of Mr Justice Frankfurter. It seeks to show how heredity, culture,

impulse and reaction that make up personality pass into legal opinions. Logic alone is sterile; a scheme of values makes an interpreter a creator.

Ideals

1. RAWLS, J. *A Theory of Justice*, (Oxford: Clarendon Press, 1972): a modern, comprehensive theory of justice is set out by a professor of philosophy. The distribution of "primary goods" and all institutions, e.g., constitution, law, etc., are to be evaluated according to two ideal Principles of Justice. (For critiques, see *ante*, pp. 33–34.

2. MORRIS, C. *The Justification of the Law*, (University of Pennsylvania Press, 1971): the ideals of law are the public's genuine and important aspirations. The just quality of a system is measured according to the degree to which it succeeds in implementing these.

3. COHEN, F.S. "Field Theory and Judicial Logic" (1949–50), 59 Yale LJ, 238: a dependable approach to the prediction of judicial decisions might be found by observing the judge's use of precedent, which will reveal his value-patterns. Even though individual judges may vary in their opinions, certain lines of precedents are discoverable.

4. DOWRICK, F.E. "Lawyers' Values for Law-reform" (1963), 79 LQR, 556: this is an interesting approach to the question of values. The work of various bodies that have from time to time been appointed to make recommendations on law reform is reviewed in order to extract the values on which each proceeded.

5. DOWRICK, F.E. "Laymens' Values for Law Reform" (1966), 82 LQR, 497: most of the members of Royal Commissions are laymen. The author reviews the values of these persons since 1945: equal treatment, sanctity and preservation of human life, importance of monogamous marriage (divided opinion on matrimonial offence and breakdown), liberty, fair trial, clarity and simplicity of law, severer punishment for intentional and reckless conduct, and respect for law.

6. POUND, R. "The Ideal Element in American Judicial Decision" (1931–32), 45 Harv LR, 136: judicial ideals as to social order are a decisive factor of legal development. This ideal element should receive the same thorough analysis as the precept element.

7. POUND, R. "Juristic Science and Law" (1917–18), 31 Harv LR, 1047: this challenges the idea that law is something that is always given. Law is not wholly made up of rules. There are rules, standards and principles. The modern functional approach takes account of the social environment of the law.

8. POUND, R. "Do We Need a Philosophy of Law?" (1905), 5 Col LR, 339: *Jurisprudence in Action*, (Baker, Voorhis & Co, Inc, 1953), 389: at the date when this was written the main trouble was alleged to be that the courts paid too much respect for the individual and too little for society. What was needed was philosophy of social values.

9. POUND, R. "A Survey of Social Interests" (1943–44), 57 Harv LR, 1: the three major "planes" on which interests may be considered are individual, public and social. When weighing them, they should be considered on the same plane. A detailed scheme of interests is given. See also R. POUND: *Jurisprudence*, (West Publishing Co, 1959), IV; and for further references, see *post*, Chap. 20.

1. STONE, J. *Social Dimensions of Law and Justice*, (Stevens & Sons, Ltd, 1966), Chaps. 4–8, 12, 14: Pound's scheme of individual and social interests is examined in detail. The main concern is to show how the content of substantive law in various branches is shaped by the interplay of interests. Chapter 12 discusses the way in which people come to hold values. The discussion is tentative since knowledge on the subject is still rudimentary. Chapter 14 ties up the nature of the judicial process with social values.

2. O'SULLIVAN, R. "A Scale of Values in the Common Law" (1937), 1 MLR, 27: freedom of the individual had become accepted by the time of Elizabeth. Free will is said to rank highest at common law. Next comes well-being and integrity, property, conveyance and contract.

3. STEIN, P.G. and SHAND, J. *Legal Values in Western Society*, (Edinburgh University Press, 1974): this book provides a survey of some of the principal values in western democracies since Roman times. The discussion ranges over the function of law in relation to order and justice and individual values relating to personal sanctity, privacy, property and commercial dealings.

4. DIAS, R.W.M. "The Value of a Value-study of Law" (1965), 28 MLR, 397: interests are "measured" with reference to some yardstick, and it is these yardsticks that are of importance, not so much the interests themselves. There is a detectable hierarchy of yardsticks in the form of national and social safety, sanctity of the individual and sanctity of property in that order. Beyond that the pattern of values is a shifting one.

5. ELIAS, T.O. "Law in a Developing Country" (1970), 4 NLJ, 1: after a review of the state of law and legal theory in Nigeria, the tasks ahead are said to be: to promote economic growth and social well-being, to elevate man's moral nature, to unify different ethnic communities, and to evolve a common law out of the existing bodies of law.

Public Policy

6. LLOYD, D. *Public Policy*, (University of London Press, 1953), chaps. 1–4, 7–8: English and French law are compared. Public policy is considered generally and not specifically with reference to particular decisions. Various public and individual values are considered.

7. LLOYD, D. "Law and Public Policy" (1958), 8 CLP, 42: every new decision is a form of legislation, but judicial legislation is not openly avowed. Public policy is discussed in relation to civil law systems.

8. WINFIELD, P.H. "Public Policy in the English Common Law" (1928–29), 42 Harv LR, 76: the influence of public policy on English judges, its nature and limits are investigated historically. The most that judicial interpretation of public policy can do is to keep it abreast of prevailing ethical standards.

9. WRIGHT, R.A. "Public Policy" in *Legal Essays and Addresses*, (Cambridge University Press, 1939), chap. 3: the part played by public policy in the development of English law is carefully considered. It does not enable judges to give free rein to their personal opinions.

10. RADCLIFFE, C.J. *The Law and its Compass*, (Faber & Faber, 1961), chap. 2: public policy and its influence upon the law are considered at some length.

156 Values

1. KNIGHT, W.S.M. "Public Policy in English Law" (1922), 38 LQR, 207: this gives a general account and history of the doctrine.

2. RAM, J. *The Science of Legal Judgment*, (2nd ed., J. Townshend, Baker, Voorhis & Co, New York, 1871), chap. 6, S. 1: public policy, convenience and inconvenience are considered as grounds of decision in doubtful cases.

Values in Relation to Official Actions

3. SUMMERS, R.S. "Evaluating and Improving Legal Processes – a Plea for 'Process Values'" (1974–75), 60 Corn LQ, 1: legal and other processes can be evaluated not only by results but also as processes – "morality of process". Process values include (1) participator governance, (2) process legitimacy (legal, political, moral), (3) process peacefulness, (4) humaneness and respect for human dignity, (5) personal privacy, (6) consensualism, (7) process fairness, (8) procedural rule of law (not too wide discretion, machinery to keep officials within the rules), (9) procedural rationality (ascertainment of evidence, weighing it, calm deliberation, impartiality, reason for decision), (10) timeliness and finality. The values relating to the evaluation of results include (1) liberty, (2) substantial justice, (3) income and wealth, (4) formal and substantial equality of opportunity, (5) personal security, (6) community peace, (7) human dignity.

4. WADE, E.C.S. "The Courts and Administrative Process" (1947), 63 LQR, 164: law is an expression of the prevailing balance between competing interests. The article considers how the courts might be used more effectively in relation to administrative process.

5. ALLEN, C.K. *Law and Orders*, (2nd ed., Stevens & Sons, Ltd, 1956): this is a detailed inquiry into the development of administrative action and a review of judicial action in relation to it.

6. PARKER, H.L. "Recent Developments in the Supervisory Powers of the Courts over Inferior Tribunals", *Lionel Cohen Lectures V*, (Magnes Press, 1959): the function of the courts today is to help, not merely check, governmental action. In the light of this policy, the methods employed by the courts are considered.

7. DEVLIN, P. "The Common Law, Public Policy, and the Executive" in *Samples of Law Making*, (Oxford University Press, 1962), chap. 6: this deals with the way in which judicial policy operated in the past. Today there is less inclination to act as watch-dogs on the executive.

8. LLOYD, D. "Ministers' Powers and the Courts" (1948), 1 CLP, 89: on the one hand, there is the view that the State oppresses the individual and that the function of the courts is to protect him; on the other, there is the view that the courts frustrate the best intentions of government. The question is how far the courts sit in judgment upon acts of the executive.

9. LASKI, H.J. "Judicial Review of Social Policy in England" (1925–26), 39 Harv LR, 832: to apply principle to new facts is to legislate. But a judge should be chary of applying his own beliefs. Nothing is more dangerous than the judicial use of authority to suppress views or experiments which they dislike.

10. McWHINNEY, E. *Judicial Review in the English-speaking World*, (University of

Toronto Press, 1956), pp. 46 *et seq.*: this shows how in time of emergency the courts side with the executive.

1. HAMSON, C.J. *Executive Discretion and Judicial Control*, (Stevens & Sons, Ltd, 1954): this is of general interest. It compares the English and French methods of administrative control.

2. JONES, H.W. "The Rule of Law and the Welfare State" (1958), 58 Col LR, 143: the meanings of "welfare state" and "rule of law" are explained first. The author denies that the welfare state is destructive of a "rule of law". On the contrary, the more practical question is how it can be made to fulfil its task in a welfare state.

3. KALES, A.M. "'Due Process', the Inarticulate Major Premise and the Adamson Act" (1916–17), 26 Yale LJ, 519: a statute depriving a person of his liberty or property will be void if it violates a fundamental condition of the social structure. What is a fundamental condition should be fully argued before the court.

4. CORWIN, E.S. "Judicial Review in Action" (1926), 74 U Pa LR, 639: this deals with the nature and development of the discretionary power of the courts in the United States.

5. HEWART, C. *The New Despotism*, (Ernest Benn, Ltd, 1929): this well-known book is a judicial protest against the increasing powers of the executive.

6. The following collection of papers published in (1960–61), 59 Mich LR, are of interest: W.B. HARVEY: "The Rule of Law in Historical Perspective", p. 487, and "The Challenge of the Rule of Law", p. 603; L.K. COOPERRIDER: "The Rule of Law and the Judicial Process", p. 501; F.E. COOPER: "The Executive Departments of Government and the Rule of Law", p. 515; P.G. KAUPER: "The Supreme Court and the Rule of Law", p. 531; W.W. BISHOP: "The International Rule of Law", p. 553; S.D. ESTEP: "The Legislative Process and the Rule of Law: Attempts to Legislate Taste in Moral and Political Beliefs", p. 575.

Values in Relation to Individual Actions

7. KEETON, R.E. "Creative Continuity in the Law of Torts" (1961–62), 75 Harv LR, 463: the expansion and refusal to expand responsibility are rooted in policy, and policy considerations are inherent in every doctrine. The part that should be played by doctrine is dealt with in detail.

8. LIPSTEIN, K. "Protected Interests in the Law of Torts" (1963), CLJ, 85: this is a comparison of the valuation of interests in tort. But the general point is made that the protection of private interests should vary with the way in which they are evaluated in a changing society and changing economy.

9. BOHLEN, F.H. "Mixed Questions of Law and Fact" (1924), 72 U Pa LR, 111: it is futile to try to fix minute, definite standards. What are needed are broad general standards, which give general directions for the construction of the appropriate standard for each particular case. In negligence, for example, the "reasonable man" is a personification of the court's social judgment.

10. BOHLEN, F.H. "Fifty Years of Torts" (1936–37), 50 Harv LR, 725, 1225: this is

of general interest. It reviews the development of the law of tort and the factors that have influenced it.

1. BOHLEN, F.H. *Studies in the Law of Torts*, (The Bobbs-Merrill Co, 1926), chap. 7: the background to the Rule in *Rylands v.Fletcher* is investigated as well as the corresponding situation in America.

2. MARSH, N.S. "Principle and Discretion in the Judicial Process" (1952), 68 LQR, 226: this deals with the expansion of the law of torts. The determination of a duty of care is an act of judicial discretion.

3. ISAACS, N. "Fault and Liability" (1918), 31 Harv LR, 954: tortious responsibility develops so as to conform to a standard that is constantly approaching the goal of ethics. The views of O.W. Holmes and J.H. Wigmore are considered.

4. DIAS, R.W.M. "Remoteness of Liability and Legal Policy" (1962), CLJ, 178: an attempt is made to show that the change from the principle of strict liability in tort to that of fault was prompted by a shift in fundamental policy, and that this is reflected in the changed attitude of the courts towards remoteness of damage.

5. DENNING, A.T. "Law in a Developing Community" (1955), 33 PA, 1: the operation of the law of negligence is affected by value-judgments. See especially the remarks on hospital cases at pp. 4–6.

6. MONTROSE, J.L. "Is Negligence an Ethical or a Sociological Concept?" (1958), 21 MLR, 259: the question in negligence cases is what ought to be done (ethical) not what is done by everyone else (sociological).

7. LEFLAR, R.A. "Negligence in Name Only" (1952), 27 NYULR, 564: there can be answerability in negligence without fault. Negligence can be redefined in terms of "typicality", i.e., typical activities which carry with them the duty to compensate typical injuries.

8. PATON, G.W. "Negligence" (1949–50), 23 Aust LJ, 158: the law of negligence is discussed generally and the importance of policy is stressed.

9. TERRY, H.T. "Negligence" (1915–16), 29 Harv LR, 40: negligence is conduct which creates an unreasonable risk. The various factors that are considered in determining reasonableness are explained.

10. CLERK, J.F. and LINDSELL, W.H.B. *Torts*, (14th ed., Sweet & Maxwell, Ltd, 1975), chap. 13, ss. 896–910: the various considerations that have to be balanced in deciding whether any given piece of conduct amounts to negligence are considered in detail. Attention is also paid to the effects on law of the social policy of trying to prevent harm and of insurance.

11. MALBURN, W.P. "The Violation of Law Limiting Speed as Negligence" (1911), 45 Am LR, 214: this gives consideration to the social policy behind such laws.

12. SCHULMAN, H. "The Standard of Care Required of Children" (1927–28), 37 Yale LJ, 618: the standard depends upon whether the child is plaintiff or defendant. A subjective standard is applied in the former case, i.e., a more lenient one; an objective standard is applied in the latter.

1. HORNBLOWER, W.B. "Insanity and the Law of Negligence" (1905), 5 Col LR, 278: should a man be held responsible for what he was physically or mentally incapable of controlling? Ultimately the question is one of policy.

2. POWELL, R. "The Unreasonableness of the Reasonable Man" (1957), 10 CLP, 104: the Reasonable Man is a doll. His power of reasoning may be relevant sometimes, but not always. Therefore, "reasonable" is what he does, not what he thinks.

3. FRIEDMANN, W. "Modern Trends in the Law of Torts" (1937), 1 MLR, 39: this is a general discussion showing the relation between the law and social conditions.

4. JAMES, F. "Accident Liability: Some Wartime Developments" (1945–46), 55 Yale LJ, 365: in various branches of the law of tort there is a tendency to modify the fault principle in favour of distributing the loss as equitably as possible. See further, "Accident Liability Reconsidered. The Impact of Liability Insurance" (1947–48), 57 Yale LJ, 549.

5. THAYER, E.R. "Public Wrongs and Private Action" (1913–14), 27 Harv LR, 317: the question when breach of a statute grounds an action in negligence is considered. The statute sets an arbitrary standard, and a reasonable man is not supposed to violate statutes.

6. WILLIAMS, G.L. "The Effect of Penal Legislation in the Law of Tort" (1960), 23 MLR, 233: this considers the effect of the increasing forms of statutory responsibility.

7. STEINER, J.M. "Economics, Morality and the Law of Torts" (1976), 26 UTLJ, 227: the rights to be assigned are a species of wealth. The issue is which interest government will support. The legal system is part of government. Therefore, the question is, who uses government and for what ends, i.e., who decides and on what criteria? Economic theories of the law of "interaction damage" are untenable. The issues are ultimately political.

8. LLEWELLYN, K.N. "What Price Contract? – an Essay in Perspective" (1930–31), 40 Yale LJ, 704: the law of contract is considered from a functional point of view.

9. PATTERSON, E.W. "Judicial Freedom of Implying Conditions in Contract" in *Recueil d'Etudes sur les Sources du Droit en l'Honneur de F. Gény*, (Librairie du Recueil Sirey, 1934), II, 379: the judge has latitude in deciding what words amount to a condition and how it should be interpreted. The question is, why do judges imply terms? The answer is considered in relation to various types of implied conditions.

10. CLARKE, P.H. "Unequal Bargaining Power in the Law of Contract" (1975), 49 Aust LJ, 229: certain recent cases show that there seems to be a new willingness on the part of courts to consider inequality in bargaining and to set aside or refuse to enforce contracts against the weaker party. The distinction between a bad and an oppressive bargain is a real one.

11. GRACE, J. "Inequality of Bargaining Power" (1975), 125 New LJ, 762: this is devoted to a discussion of a decision of the Court of Appeal giving relief to an individual against his bank.

1. EASTWOOD, R.A. "Trade Protection and Monopoly" (1950), 3 CLP, 100: this deals with the changing conception of public policy. The influence of policy considerations is traced out historically.

2. KORAH, V.L. "The Restrictive Practices Court" (1959), 12 CLP, 76: the law of conspiracy and restraint of trade were unequal to deal with restrictive trading agreements. The policy behind the establishment of the new Court is explained.

3. GOODHART, W.H. "The *Yarn Spinners'* Case and the Sherman Anti-Trust Act" (1959), 75 LQR, 253: a useful comparison is made of American judicial interpretation of the anti-trust legislation and the attitude of English judges. In England the Restrictive Practices Court has been able to make a fresh start.

4. STEVENS, R. "Justiciability: The Restrictive Practices Court Re-examined" (1964), PL, 221: the working of the Court over some years and its handling of policy questions is reviewed.

5. WHITEMAN, P.G. "The New Judicial Approach to the Restrictive Trade Practices Act, 1956" (1967), 30 MLR, 398: at first the courts tended to interpret "agreement" in the narrow sense of contracts. A radical departure came in 1963 when they started to interpret it in the light of the underlying purpose.

6. CUNNINGHAM, J.P. "Restrictive Trade Practices. Three Recent Judgments viewed in Perspective" (1971), 87 LQR, 481: this begins with an account of the origin of the Restrictive Practices Court and how it was to work. In view of the changed climate today and the practice under the Treaty of Rome, it is argued that the time is ripe for a revision of its structure so that it may operate in an administrative, rather than a judicial, mould.

7. DONALDSON, J. "Lessons from the Industrial Court" (1975), 91 LQR, 181: the Industrial Court differed from ordinary courts. The court staff prepared the cases. The speed with which it worked minimised disputes as to fact. There was a need for a department which combined the services of an advice bureau and an ombudsman. It might have had a chance of success had the legislation behind it concentrated on the factors giving rise to a dispute rather than on the industrial action resulting from the dispute.

8. O'HIGGINS, P. and PARTINGTON, M. "Industrial Conflict: Judicial Attitudes" (1969), 32 MLR, 53: this is a statistical survey of fifty civil and twenty criminal cases referred to in three leading treatises. Such conclusions as are drawn from this limited material are necessarily tentative.

9. KAHN-FREUND, O. "Spare-time Activities of Employees" (1946), 9 MLR, 145: this considers the important decision in the *Hivac* case.

10. LEWIS, W.A. "Spare-time Activities of Employees (1946), 9 MLR, 280: this gives further consideration to the *Hivac* case and the questions that it raises.

11. LEWIS, W.A. "Monopoly and the Law" (1943), 6 MLR, 97: lawyers have diverged in their attitude from that of economists. By confusing different meanings of freedom lawyers have come in the result to support monopoly. The shortcomings of the law are pointed out. (This was written before the Restrictive Practices Court was established).

1. DENNING, A.T. *The Road to Justice*, (Stevens & Sons, Ltd, 1955), chap. 5: this deals, *inter alia*, with freedom of contract, freedom of association, the right to work, the right to strike and industrial combinations.

2. The following cases may be consulted as illustrating the part played by value-judgments: *Sommersett's Case* (1772), 20 State Tr. 1; *Liversidge v. Anderson* [1942] AC, 206; [1941] 3 All ER, 338; *R. v. Halliday, ex parte Zadig* [1917] AC, 260; *Ross-Clunis* v. *Papadopoullos* [1958] 2 All ER, 23; [1958] 1 WLR, 546; *Reade* v. *Smith* [1959] NZLR, 996; *Horwood* v. *Millar's Timber & Trading Co, Ltd* [1917] 1 KB, 305; *Eastham* v. *Newcastle United Football Club, Ltd* [1964] Ch. 413; [1963] 3 All ER, 139; *Best* v. *Samuel Fox & Co, Ltd* [1952] AC, 716; [1952] 2 All ER, 394; *R* v. *Board of Control, ex parte Rutty* [1956] 2 QB, 109; [1956] 1 All ER, 769; *Richardson* v. *L.C.C.* [1957] 2 All ER, 330; *R. v. Kemp* [1957] 1 QB, 399; [1956] 3 All ER, 249; *Bratty* v. *Att.-Gen. for Northern Ireland* [1963] AC, 386; [1961] 3 All ER, 523.

Entick v. *Carrington* (1765), 19 State Tr. 1029; *Elias* v. *Pasmore* [1934] 2 KB, 164; *Chic Fashions (West Wales), Ltd* v. *Jones* [1968] 2 QB, 299; [1968] 1 All ER, 229; *Att.-Gen.* v. *De Keyser's Royal Hotel, Ltd* [1920] AC, 508; *Burmah Oil Co, (Burma Trading), Ltd* v. *Lord Advocate* [1965] AC, 75; [1964] 2 All ER, 348; Viscount SUMNER in *Levene* v. *I.R.C.* [1928] AC, 217; Lord GREENE in *Howard de Walden* v. *I.R.C.* [1942] 1 KB, 389; [1942] 1 All ER, 287; *Metropolitan Asylum District* v. *Hill* (1881), 6 App Cas, 193; *Edgington, Bishop and Withy* v. *Swindon, B.C.* [1939] 1 KB, 86; [1938] 4 All ER, 57; *Att.-Gen. of New Zealand* v. *Lower Hutt City Corporation* [1964] AC, 1469; [1964] 3 All ER, 179; *Green (H.E.) & Sons* v. *Minister of Health* [1948] 1 KB, 34; [1947], 2 All ER, 469; *R* v. *Electricity Commissioners* [1924] 1 KB, 171; *Franklin* v. *Minister of Town and Country Planning* [1948] AC, 87; [1947] 2 All ER, 289.

Smith v. *Baker & Sons* [1891] AC, 325; *Summers* v. *Salford Corporation* [1943] AC, 283; [1943] 1 All ER, 68; *English Hop Growers, Ltd* v. *Dering* [1928] 2 KB, 174; *Ronbar Enterprises, Ltd* v. *Green* [1954] 2 All ER, 266; *Parisv. Stepney B.C.* [1951] AC, 367; [1951] 1 All ER, 42; *Hivac, Ltd* v. *Park Royal Scientific Instruments, Ltd* [1946] Ch 169; [1946] 1 All ER, 350; *Cranleigh Precision Engineering Ltd* v. *Bryant and Another* [1964] 3 All ER, 289; *Latimer* v. *A.E.C., Ltd* [1953] AC, 643; [1953] 2 All ER, 449; *Davie* v. *New Merton Board Mills, Ltd* [1959] AC, 604; [1959] 1 All ER, 346; *Lister* v. *Romford Ice & Cold Storage Co, Ltd* [1957] AC, 555; [1957] 1 All ER, 125; *I.C.I., Ltd* v. *Shatwell* [1965] AC, 656; [1964] 2 All ER, 999; *Bonsor* v. *Musicians' Union* [1956] AC, 104; [1955] 3 All ER, 518; *Rookes* v. *Barnard* [1964] AC, 1129; [1964] 1 All ER, 367; *Stratford (J.T.), & Son, Ltd* v. *Lindley* [1965] AC, 269; [1964] 3 All ER, 102.

Donoghue v. *Stevenson* [1932] AC, 562; *Rylands* v. *Fletcher* (1868), LR 3 HL, 330; *Hedley Byrne & Co, Ltd* v. *Heller & Partners, Ltd* [1964] AC, 465; [1963] 2 All ER, 575; *Lloyds Bank, Ltd* v. *Savory* [1933] AC, 201; *Ward* v. *L.C.C.* [1938] 2 All ER, 341; *L.P.T.B.* v. *Upson* [1949] AC, 155; [1949] 1 All ER, 60; *Daly* v. *Liverpool Corporation* [1939] 2 All ER, 142; *Daborn* v. *Bath Tramways Motor Co, Ltd, and Trevor Smithey* [1946] 2 All ER, 333; *East Suffolk Rivers Catchment Board* v. *Kent* [1941] AC, 74; [1940] 4 All ER, 527; *Haley* v. *London Electricity Board* [1965] AC, 778; [1964] 3 All ER, 185; *Cassidy* v. *Ministry of Health* [1951] 2 KB, 343; [1951] 1 All ER, 574; *Roe* v. *Ministry of Health* [1954] 2 QB, 66; [1954] 2 All ER, 131.

Egerton v. *Earl Brownlow* (1853), 4 HLC, 1; *Beresford* v. *Royal Insurance Co, Ltd* [1938] AC, 586; [1938] 2 All ER, 602; *Bowman* v. *Secular Society* [1917] AC, 406; *Bourne* v. *Keen* [1919] AC, 815; *R.* v. *Martin Secker & Warburg Ltd* [1954] 2 All ER, 683; *Shaw* v. *D.P.P.* [1962] AC, 220; [1961] 2 All ER, 446

Wilson v. *Glossop* (1888), 20 QBD, 354; *National Bank of Greece & Athens S.A.* v. *Metliss* [1958] AC, 509; [1957] 3 All ER, 608; *Short* v. *Att.-Gen. of Sierra Leone* [1964] 1 All ER, 125; *Roberts* v. *Hopwood* [1925] AC, 578; *Prescott* v. *Birmingham Corporation* [1955] Ch 210; [1954] 3 All ER, 698; *Re Walker's Decision* [1944] KB, 644; [1944] 1 All ER, 614.

U.S. ex rel. Weinberg v. *Schotfeldt* (1938), 26 Federal Reporter Supplement, 283; *Schtraks* v. *Government of Israel* [1964] AC, 556; [1962] 3 All ER, 529; *Aksionairoye Obschestvo A.M. Luther* v. *James Sagor & Co* [1921] 3 KB, 532; *Lorentzen* v. *Lydden & Co* [1942] 2 KB, 202; *Anglo-Iranian Oil Co. Ltd* v. *Jaffrate* [1953] 1 WLR, 246; *Zoernsch* v. *Waldock* [1964] 2 All ER, 256; [1964] 1 WLR, 675.

Some Implications of Value-study

1. DENNING, A.T. "The Independence of the Judges" *Presidential Address to the Holdsworth Club* (1950): in the USSR judges are part of the machinery for effectuating executive policy; in England the judges are not so dependent. In a country like England judicial independence is very important.

2. DENNING, A.T. "The Independence and Impartiality of the Judges" (1954), 71 SALJ, 345: the position of the judiciary in a "free" society is further considered. See also A.T. DENNING: *The Road to Justice*, (Stevens & Sons, Ltd, 1955), chap. 2.

3. WILEY, A. "A Free Judiciary: American System Contrasted with the Soviet" (1948), 34 Am BAJ, 441: an independent judiciary is essential to protect the individual against state power. The article gives a comparison of the training, selection and appointment of American and Soviet judges.

4. BORRIE, G. "Judicial Conflicts of Interest in Britain" (1970), 18 AJCL, 697: the British practice has reduced to a minimum the possibility of conflict between the judicial role and political and financial interests. The various ways in which independence from governmental and political interests, on the one hand, and from business, financial and personal interests, on the other hand, is achieved are explained in turn.

5. ELWYN-JONES, F. "Independence of the Judiciary" (1976), 1 Malaya LR, viii: the Lord Chancellor draws attention to the significance of the judicial oath, and also the extent of the Lord Chancellor's power to dismiss subordinate judges. Even where he has the power, he will not interfere with the exercise of judicial discretion.

6. SIDHU, G.T.S. "Independence of the Judiciary" (1976), 1 Malaya LR, ix: judicial independence may be protected in a constitution. Whether judges retain their independence depends on themselves. They must keep abreast of the progress of a nation.

7. BAMFORD, B.R. "Aspects of Judicial Independence" (1956), 73 SALJ, 380;

various means for securing judicial independence and the attributes of an independent judge are considered.

1. GYANDOH, S.O. "The Role of the Judiciary under the Constitutional Proposals for Ghana" (1968), 5 UGLJ, 133: this is an extremely useful article on the nature of judicial decision-making. The Constitutional proposals of 1968 are surveyed critically with reference to judicial independence and the role of the judiciary in safeguarding the Constitution and fundamental rights. See also S.O. GYANDOH: "Principles of Judicial Interpretation of the Republican Constitution of Ghana" (1966), 3 UGLJ, 37.

2. COOPERRIDER, L.K. "The Rule of Law and the Judicial Process" (1960–61), 59 Mich LR, 501: how far are judges controlled by law? This depends on the extent of the desire on their part to decide as far as possible according to authority. The "rule of law" is not a myth.

3. DIAS, R.W.M. "The Value of a Value-study of Law" (1965), 28 MLR, 397, 410–20: the implications of a value-oriented approach are considered, especially with reference to the study of law, the nature of the judicial process and the concept of law.

4. STEVENS, R. "Justiciability: the Restrictive Practices Court Re-examined" (1964), PL, 221: although the main theme is the work of the court, the point is made that judges are immune from criticism so long as their function is thought to be simply to administer law, good or bad. The wisdom of Parliament in entrusting this Court, which is there to make policy decisions, to the judiciary and thereby laying them open to criticism, is doubted.

5. GARLAN, E.N. *Legal Realism and Justice* (Columbia University Press, 1941): it is pointed out in answer to the American Realists that ideals should be included among the elements of a judgment. Any attempt to determine what the law is involves simultaneously an attempt to determine what is desirable.

6. LAWSON, F.H. "The Creative Use of Legal Concepts" (1957), 32 NYULR, 909: a distinction is drawn between concepts that come into litigation and those which are used as guides to action. The lawyer has to make creative use of concepts.

7. HOGG, J.E. "Legal Conceptions from a Practical Point of View" (1906), 22 LQR, 172: the writer assumes that legal concepts are rigid and argues that they should be adapted to modern conditions. The assumption is questionable, but his thesis is acceptable.

8. MOORE, W.U. and SUSSMAN, G. "The Lawyer's Law" (1931–32), 41 Yale LJ, 566: in advising a client a lawyer has to take account of many factors. One of these is the intuitional judgment. He should accordingly systematise more the bases of intuitional judgments.

9. SCHMIDHAUSER, J.R. "*Stare Decisis*, and the Background of the Justice of the Supreme Court of the United States" (1962), 14 UTLJ, 194: a statistical study is provided of the extent to which personal background factors influence judges to adhere to precedent or to dissent from majority opinions. The general conclusion is to express a very qualified agreement with the proposition that personal background does influence judicial behaviour.

1. WEYRAUCH, W.O. *The Personality of Lawyers*, (Yale University Press, 1964): interviews with a cross-section of German lawyers are analysed and evaluated. They reveal the extent to which personal and professional predilections influence their outlook and thinking.

2. GROSSMAN, J.B. "Social Backgrounds and Judicial Decision-making" (1965–66), 79 Harv LR, 1551: how far is a judge the captive or creature of personal values? Different types of study, which have sought to answer this question, are set out and explained.

3. PALLEY, C. "The Judicial Process: UDI and the Southern Rhodesian Judiciary" (1967), 30 MLR, 263: the decision in the *UDI Case* is approached through the personal histories of the judges involved in it.

4. SHAPIRO, M. "The Supreme Court and Constitutional Adjudication: of Politics and Neutral Principles" (1962–63), 31 Geo Wash LR, 587: the role of the Supreme Court in constitutional cases is appraised in the light of the debate between those who view it as a political instrument and those who see it as applying neutral and impartial principles.

10. Duty

1. GOODHART, A.L. *English Law and the Moral Law*, (Stevens & Sons, Ltd, 1955) especially chaps. 1 and 2: this is an important study of duty conceived as an "ought". The point is made with emphasis that command and sanction are not its distinctive criteria. Law is a prescription for conduct, not a description of it. The feeling of obligation is analysed, and also the distinction between the obligation of law and that of religion, morality, etc.

2. FULLER, L.L. *The Morality of Law*, (revised ed., Yale University Press, 1969), especially chaps. 1 and 2: in Chapter 1 the relation between duty and morality is examined. A distinction is drawn between the "morality of aspiration", which concerns ideals, and the "morality of duty", which is embodied in duties, and parallels are drawn with certain economic principles. Chapter 2 deals mainly with the "inner" morality, without which there can be no valid legal system (as to which, see *post*, Chapter 22); but pp. 65–70 may be consulted on conflicting duties, and pp. 108–10 on the association of law with force.

3. OLIVECRONA, K. "Law as Fact" in *Interpretations of Modern Legal Philosophies*, (ed. P. Sayre, Oxford University Press, New York, 1947), chap. 25: the concepts of "duty" and "rule" are examined. The former is said to involve the idea of action, imperative expression and the feeling of being bound. The function of rules is also dealt with.

4. HART, H.L.A. *The Concept of Law*, (Oxford, Clarendon Press, 1961, reprinted 1975), pp. 33–41, 54–58, 79–88; chap. 6 *passim*: in the course of rejecting the idea of nullity as a sanction, the point is made that law without sanction is perfectly conceivable. The idea of obligation is examined and particular stress is laid on the use of it as a general standard of conduct, the "internal" and "external" aspects of rules. In Chapter 6 stress is laid on "rules of recognition" by which prescriptions of conduct are identifiable as "law".

5. ALLEN, C.K. "Legal Duties" in *Legal Duties*, (Oxford, Clarendon Press, 1931), pp. 156–220: the views of L. Duguit and A.V. Lundstedt are first discussed, and then from p. 196 onward the nature of duty itself. Duty cannot be "enforced" otherwise than by conscience; "legal enforcement" means the operation of a prescribed penalty. There is also a lengthy examination of the relationship between legal and moral duties.

6. CASTBERG, S.F. *Problems of Legal Philosophy*, (2nd ed., Oslo University Press; Allen & Unwin, Ltd, 1957), pp. 23, 24–33: "law" is valid and hence duty is "legal" because of certain accepted postulates of "validity". The idea of duty as an "ought" is defended against the attacks of other Scandinavian Realists.

7. HÄGERSTRÖM, A. *Inquiries into the Nature of Law and Morals*, (ed. K. Olivecrona, trans. C.D. Broad, Almqvist & Wiksell, Stockholm, 1953), chap. 3, especially pp. 116–256: the nature of command and its content are examined as a prelude to an investigation of the nature of duty. A feeling of inner compulsion is bound up with the feeling of duty. This feeling is said to be "external", i.e., not founded on valuations or a desire to avoid unpleasantness. It is an association of ideas with a certain form of expression. Various theories are considered and also the connection between legal and moral duty.

8. OLIVECRONA, K. *Law as Fact*, (Einar Munksgaard, Copenhagen; Humphrey

Milford, 1939; reprinted by Wildy & Sons, Ltd, 1962), especially pp. 42–49: the feeling of being bound is analysed into a psychological association of ideas with the imperative form of expression and certain procedures. Chapter 2 stresses the psychological effect of constitutional forms of law-making; Chapter 4 considers the parts played by force, fear and morality. See further *Law as Fact*, (2nd ed., Stevens & Sons, Ltd, 1971), pp. 120–134.

1. OLIVECRONA, K. "The Imperative Element in Law" (1964), 18 Rutgers LR, 794: the imperative form in which law is expressed is subjected to further examination. Austin's Command theory, and certain other theories, which have been proffered in its place, are criticised. The importance of the imperative element is that it has suggestive influence over people. The Command theory neglects this suggestive force, but it is a mistake, while rejecting the Command theory, to neglect the imperative element altogether.

2. OLIVECRONA, K. "Legal Language and Reality" in *Essays in Jurisprudence in Honor of Roscoe Pound*, (ed. R.A. Newman, The Bobbs-Merrill Co, Inc, 1962), 151: the views of J. Austin, the American Realists, A. Hägerström and A.V. Lundstedt are touched on. "Duty", like the word "right", is said to be a "hollow" word, (cf. "pound" as monetary unit). There is no object corresponding to it.

3. von MISES, R. *Positivism*, (Harvard University Press, 1951), chaps. 25 and 26, especially pp. 320–321: "ought" is examined, and the analysis ties up well with K. Olivecrona's idea of "independent imperative" by furnishing a psychological explanation of how it comes about. In Chapter 26 the importance of regulating conduct is stressed.

4. LUNDSTEDT, A.V. *Legal Thinking Revised*, (Almqvist & Wiksell, Stockholm, 1956), pp. 35–53; 77–122: legal duties are devoid of objectivity. Duty is a feeling which drives people to do or to abstain. The expression "legal duty" labels the effect on a person's behaviour of the maintenance of diverse rules of law.

5. AUSTIN, J. *Lectures on Jurisprudence*, (5th ed., R. Campbell, John Murray, 1885), chaps. 22–24: these give the "command" theory of duty in which command, duty and sanction are interrelated. Sanction is the conditional evil in the event of disobedience, which "enforces compliance" with the command. Various ways in which breaches of duty can be committed are also considered.

6. TAPPER, C.F. "Austin on Sanctions" (1965), CLJ, 271: Austin's requirement of sanction as a test of law and in relation to obligation is subjected to penetrating analysis. His analysis is shown to be so vague as to leave numerous questions unanswered, and it is also inconsistent and self-contradictory.

7. BROWN, W.J. *The Austinian Theory of Law*, (John Murray, 1906), pp. 5–11: this is a restatement of the Austinian position.

8. HART, H.L.A. "Legal and Moral Obligation" in *Essays in Moral Philosophy*, (ed. A.I. Melden, University of Washington Press, 1958), 82: J. Austin's thesis of duty being sanctioned by the chance of evil is criticised. (For the purpose of the argument the necessity for sanctions is conceded though they may not be essential – see p. 99). The main argument shows how the creation of obligations leads to the foundation of a legal system.

9. MacCORMICK, D.N. "Legal Obligation and the Imperative Fallacy" in *Oxford Essays in Jurisprudence (Second Series)*, (ed. A.W.B. Simpson, Oxford University

Press, 1973), chap. 5: the distinction between rules creating obligations and other rules lies in the difference in criticisms levelled at violation. Violation of a duty entails criticism of what a person has done; violation of a "procedural" rule entails criticism of how he has done it. The bindingness of law lies, on the one hand, in duties of citizens, who are under the law and who cannot change it at their wish, and, on the other hand, in the duties of officials in respect of the law, which they must apply fairly and honestly.

1. SMITH, J.C. *Legal Obligation*, (University of London: the Athlone Press, 1976): obligation is a species of "ought"; and the idea of "ought" invites a request for reasons, which are based on a cause-effect relation with a desired end. Obligation thus has a teleological and evaluative aspect; there is a means-end relation between the "institution of ordering" (social practice, rule) and a desired state of affairs. The author proceeds to apply this thesis to generality and equality in law, law and morality, the judicial process, structural properties of rules and fundamental rights.

2. RAZ, J. "Promises and Obligations" in *Law, Morality, and Society. Essays in Honour of H.L.A. Hart*, (edd. P.M.S. Hacker and J. Raz, Clarendon Press, Oxford, 1977), chap. 12: promises may be expressions of an intention to act, or of an intention to undertake obligations. The latter view is preferred. The author investigates the relation between promises and rules and rules and obligations.

3. HEARN, W.E. *The Theory of Legal Duties and Rights*, (Melbourne: John Ferres; London: Trubner & Co, 1883), chaps. 4 and 5: duty is regarded as being more important than right; command, duty and sanction are associated. A clear distinction is drawn between primary and secondary duties. Sanctions are inseparable from duty and various types of sanctions are considered.

4. TERRY, H.T. *Some Leading Principles of Anglo-American Law Expounded with a View to its Arrangement and Codification*, (T. & J.W. Johnson & Co., Philadelphia, 1884), pp. 84–87: duty is described from the point of view of one who is commanded or forbidden to do something. The content of duties is discussed with reference to the consequences, conduct and the state of mind. This idea is further elaborated in "Duties, Rights and Wrongs" (1924), 10 Am BAJ, 123.

5. JENKS, E. *The New Jurisprudence*, (John Murray, 1933), chaps. 6 and 8: a consideration of whether reward can operate as a sanction precedes an account of penal and remedial sanctions. Duty is regarded as being more important than right. The contingent sanction is said to be essential to it.

6. HUMPHREY, J.P. "On the Definition and Nature of Laws" (1945), 8 MLR, 194, at pp. 196–203: the article considers the specific marks of "a law", not of "law". Sanction is declared to be essential, but the different meanings of the term and duty-situations where sanctions are not present are not even mentioned.

7. CORBIN, A.L. "Rights and Duties" (1923–24), 33 Yale LJ, 501, especially at pp. 505–6, 514 *et seq.*: the distinction between legal and moral duties is said to lie in the sanction. The idea of enforcement and the various types of sanctions are considered. Breach of duty is constituted by conduct.

8. GOBLE, G.W. "The Sanction of a Duty" (1927–28), 37 Yale LJ, 426: the author assumes that sanction is the test of a duty and proceeds to consider which of all possible court reactions is the most useful one to regard as sanction.

1. PATTERSON, E.W. *Jurisprudence*, (The Foundation Press, Inc, 1953), pp. 159–170: this is of general interest on the nature of sanctions. Legal sanctions are confined to harmful consequences imposed by officials. The need for sanctions is considered, but not with specific reference to duties.

2. KELSEN, H. "Value Judgments in the Science of Law", in *What is Justice?* (University of California Press, 1957), 209: duties are not dealt with directly, but the article is important in stressing the part played by the "ought" in law.

3. KELSEN, H. *General Theory of Law and State*, (trans. A. Wedberg, Harvard University Press, 1949), pp. 50–64, 71–74: sanctions are provided in order to bring about conformity of behaviour with what the legislator desires. Behaviour is wrongful only when a sanction is attached. To be under a duty means that contrary behaviour will involve a sanction. But Kelsen cannot avoid the "ought" contained in both duty and sanction (pp. 60–1).

4. KELSEN, H. "The Pure Theory of Law" (trans. C.H. Wilson, 1934), 50 LQR, 474, especially at pp. 494–6: this emphasises duty as a "normative obligation" and ties it to sanction.

5. KANTOROWICZ, H.U. *The Definition of Law*, (ed. A.H. Campbell, Cambridge University Press, 1958), pp. 23–25, 37–40: the ideas implicit in "ought" are considered, with special mention of a basic and absolute rule on which the validity of all other rules depends.

6. VINOGRADOFF, P. *Common-sense in Law*, (3rd ed., H.G. Hanbury, Oxford University Press, 1959), chaps. 2 and 3: this discussion of the command theory provides a useful background to the concept of duty by pointing out that enforcement is not sufficient; recognition and purpose are just as important.

7. HEXNER, E. *Studies in Legal Terminology*, (The University of North Carolina Press, 1941), chap. 1: this is of general interest. Law as a system of rules prescribing social conduct is discussed.

8. DAUBE, D. *Forms of Roman Legislation*, (Oxford, 1956), pp. 23–30: it is of interest to note that in Roman Law where a rule was well known the praetors only thought it necessary to specify the sanction for its contravention. When a *new* rule was laid down, the "ought" or "ought not" was first specified and then the sanction was prescribed.

9. DIAS, R.W.M. "The Unenforceable Duty" (1959), 33 Tul LR, 473: the importance of sanctionless duties in Roman and English Law is discussed.

10. HARRIS, J.W. "Trust, Power and Duty" (1971), 87 LQR, 31, at pp. 47 *et seq.*: in discussing certain developments in equity cases, the author contends that the courts have utilised four separate concepts of "duty", which are to be found in legal speech: duty as correlative to claim, sanction concept, rule prescribing what one ought to do, and the expression of someone's will. As he points out, the attachment of sanction is only one aspect.

11. HACKER, P.M.S. "Sanction Theories of Duty" in *Oxford Essays in Jurisprudence* (*Second Series*), (ed. A.W.B. Simpson, Oxford, Clarendon Press, 1973), chap. 6: reasons for action are analysed variously and the views of Bentham, Mill and Hart are considered. The main defect of the sanction theories is said to be that they emphasise too much the sanction and too little the duty-imposing standards of conduct. Duty is a guide to action.

1. HALL, J. *Foundations of Jurisprudence*, (The Bobbs-Merrill Co, Inc, 1973), chap. V: various theories about sanction are considered as well as the "sanctionless duty". The author submits the idea of "privation" and how "sanction by nullity" might be accommodated within this.

2. PAULSON, S.L. "Classical Legal Positivism at Nuremberg" (1975), 4 Philosophy and Public Affairs, 132, 151–157: the author argues that the rejection by the War Crimes Tribunal of the defence that to punish the accused would be tantamount to *ex post facto* legislation is an implicit rejection of the idea that prohibitory duties must always have sanctions. The duties not to commit war crimes had always existed, but the sanction machinery was inadequate. What the Charter of the Tribunal did was not to create offences *ex post facto*, but to provide machinery to deal with them.

3. MUNZER, S. "Validity and Legal Conflict" (1972–73), 82 Yale LJ, 1140: in the course of discussing the wider issue of validity, there is a discussion of the nature and types of conflict in rules imposing duties and rules creating permissions. What does it mean for two rules to conflict? and, what does it mean for two rules to conflict in particular situations only by virtue of some act or omission?

4. SHKLAR, J.N. *Legalism*, (Harvard University Press, 1964), Part II, especially pp. 39–56: the whole book is a sustained attack on Positivist and Naturalist theory and particularly their respective attitudes towards the separation of law and morality. Their controversy is unsatisfying since both sides think in terms of "legalism", i.e., rule following. But this is itself one morality among others, and they should all be accepted as part of a social continuum.

5. HOLMES, O.W. "The Path of the Law", in *Collected Legal Papers*, (Constable & Co, Ltd, 1920), pp. 173–4: this is a pioneer expression of the view that primary rights and duties are meaningless terms and that, subject to allegedly negligible exceptions, only secondary rights and duties matter.

6. LLEWELLYN, K.N. *The Bramble Bush*, (New York, 1930), pp. 82–5: following O.W. Holmes's view, primary rights and duties are rejected; all that matter are secondary duties, or what the courts will do. The judgment of a court is regarded as a certain test of duty.

7. ROSS, A. *On Law and Justice*, (Stevens & Sons, Ltd, 1958), pp. 52–58, 158–64, 364: judges obey norms of decision because they feel bound by them; citizens obey norms of conduct for many reasons. It might be desirable to abandon the notion of duty; but in so far as it is used, it denotes situations in which a person is subjected to a sanction. The ideas of "prescription" and "prohibition" are derivatives of norms addressed to judges.

8. ROSS, A. *Directives and Norms*, (Routledge & Kegan Paul, Ltd, 1968), chaps. 4–5: norms are a species of directive. They need to be general, effective and felt to be binding. There are two sets of norms: those directed to judges, and, from a psychological point of view, those directed to citizens.

9. GOTTLIEB, G. *The Logic of Choice*, (Allen & Unwin, Ltd, 1968): the main concern of this work is with the judicial process, but it contains an important discussion of rules, principles and standards. Rules may be regulatory or constitutive. Following a rule differs from obeying a command in that the former involves more policy considerations than the latter.

10. BUCKLAND, W.W. *Some Reflections on Jurisprudence*, (Cambridge University

Press, 1945), pp. 86–92, 96–106: the idea of sanction is dealt with, and particularly noteworthy is the discussion of sanction by nullity. O.W. Holmes's view that primary rights and duties are unnecessary is answered. (Compare the view on p. 106 that sanction is only a piece of machinery with the view on pp. 111–112 that a duty with no sanction is "meaningless"). See also "The Nature of the Contractual Obligation" (1944), 8 CLJ, 247, which is a more detailed answer to Holmes.

1. LAMONT, W.D. *The Principles of Moral Judgment*, (Oxford, 1946), chap. 3: the arguments proceed on a different line from that adopted in the chapter. Rights are said to refer to interests and duties are consequent on them.

General Treatises

2. SALMOND, W. *Jurisprudence*, (12th ed., P.J. Fitzgerald, Sweet & Maxwell, Ltd, 1966), pp. 100–104, 216–217, 233–234: duty is "legal" because it is "legally recognised, not necessarily because it is legally enforced or sanctioned". The distinction between primary and secondary rights and duties is explained with reference to enforcement. The importance of "imperfect rights" (i.e., sanctionless duty-situations) is also pointed out.

3. POLLOCK, F. *A First Book of Jurisprudence*, (6th ed., Macmillan & Co, Ltd, 1929), pp. 58–61, 69–72: this is a general discussion in the course of which the point is made that while negative duties can be "enforced" by physical constraint, positive duties are "enforceable" only indirectly. Positive duties contemplate performance rather than breach; with negative duties breach is more prominent.

4. GRAY, J.C. *The Nature and Sources of the Law*, (2nd ed., R. Gray, The Macmillan Co, New York, 1921), chap. 1: this is another general discussion of rights and duties and their relation to morality, command and protection.

5. MARKBY, W. *Elements of Law*, (6th ed., Oxford, 1905), ss 181–192: this follows the Austinian association of command, duty and sanction. Primary and secondary duties are explained, and the point is made that duties regulate conduct.

6. HOLLAND, T.E. *The Elements of Jurisprudence*, (13th ed., Oxford, Clarendon Press, 1924), pp. 87, 131–133: legal duties are distinguishable from moral duties in that the former will be enforced by the power of the state.

7. KOCOUREK, A. *An Introduction to the Science of Law*, (Little, Brown & Co, 1930), pp. 240–242, 247–50, 321–23: duty is explained in relation to claim, the latter being regarded as the principal concept. Law not only prescribes conduct, but also on occasions authorises it, and on this basis the relationship between duties and powers is explained.

8. KOCOUREK, A. *Jural Relations*, (2nd ed., The Bobbs-Merrill Co, 1928), pp. 9–10 note; chap. 19: the different meanings of "duty" are briefly indicated. In Chapter 19 sanctions, their origin and function, are examined. The special terminology which Kocourek employs is very prevalent in this chapter and it is, therefore, difficult to read. Its substance is also found in "Sanctions and Remedies" (1924), 72 U Pa LR, 91. See also "Tabulae Minores Jurisprudentiae" (1920–21), 30 Yale LJ, 215, at p. 222, where a distinction is drawn between enforceable and unenforceable jural relations, which are labelled respectively "nexal" and "simple".

1. PATON, G.W. *A Text-Book of Jurisprudence*, (4th ed., G.W. Paton and D.P. Derham, Clarendon Press, Oxford, 1972), pp. 78–81, 297–298: sanction is examined with reference to Austin's general theory of law, but not specifically with reference to duty. It is said that preoccupation with sanction leads to a false view of law. "Antecedent" and "remedial" (i.e., primary and secondary) rights are considered and the view of the American Realists is rejected.

2. KEETON, G.W. *The Elementary Principles of Jurisprudence*, (2nd ed., Isaac Pitman & Sons, Ltd, 1949), chap. 11: the discussion is mainly in terms of rights, but is relevant to duties also. The point is made that enforceability is not essential.

3. SNYDER, O.C. *Preface to Jurisprudence*, (The Bobbs-Merrill Co, Inc, 1954), pp. 223–36: sanction is regarded as essential to the concept of law and hence of duty. It is possible that the writer is using the term "sanction" in a sense wider than in this book, for nullity is included. Laws without sanction are considered and it is argued that these have at least indirect sanctions.

4. KORKUNOV, N.M. *General Theory of Law*, (trans. W.G. Hastings, The Boston Book Co. 1909), ss 27–29: this is a general discussion of legal relationships, and duty is regarded as being of basic importance.

5. POUND, R. *Jurisprudence*, (West Publishing Co, 1959), I, p. 409: IV, chap. 24: in the first volume the origin of the idea of duty is examined briefly. Its history and relation to morals is more fully examined in the fourth volume. The sanctionless duty in English and Roman Law is noted.

Obedience

6. BRYCE, J. *Studies in History and Jurisprudence*, (Oxford, 1901), II, chap. 9: the reasons for obedience are listed in the order of indolence, deference, sympathy, fear and reason.

7. STJERNQUIST, P. "How are Changes in Social Behaviour Developed by Means of Legislation?" in *Legal Essays. A Tribute to Frede Castberg*, (Universitetsforlaget, 1963), 153: the psychological repercussions of law that go towards its acceptance by the community are investigated. The influence of legislation can only be assessed in relation to other social influences. Different types of laws require different conditions for their acceptance by the community.

8. HONORÉ, A.M. "Groups, Laws and Obedience" in *Oxford Essays in Jurisprudence (Second Series)* (ed. A.W.B. Simpson, Oxford University Press, 1973), chap. 1: to say that something is "law" is to strike an attitude towards the question whether it should be obeyed or not and how to deal with disobedience. The idea of obedience is approached through that of a "group" and the connection between the institution of laws and securing obedience. There has to be group understanding about prescriptions curtailing liberty, and these prescriptions must secure substantial compliance. For a short comment, see S.L. PAULSON, Review in (1974), 87 Harv. LR, 898, at pp. 901–908.

9. JENNINGS, W.I. *The Law and the Constitution*, (5th ed., University of London Press, Ltd, 1959), Appendix IV: the argument is directed at showing that fear of sanctions and the enforcement by the state, though important, are not the reason for obedience. Enforcement implies obedience by the instruments of enforcement.

1. DENNING, A.T. *The Road to Justice*, (Stevens & Sons, Ltd, 1955), pp. 2–3: people obey the law because this is a thing which they ought to do, not because law is commanded or because of sanctions. This sense of obligation derives from habit and the morality of the law itself.

2. LEWIS, J.U. "Blackstone's Definition of Law and Doctrine of Legal Obligation as a Link between Early Modern and Contemporary Theories of Law" (1968), 3 Ir Jur (NS), 337: laws are products of a lawmaker's will. Obligations originate in that will or, from the subject's point of view, from fear of punishment. A man may be bound morally and legally, but that is a concurrence of two obligations. In this way Blackstone laid the foundations for the modern separation of law and morals.

3. BENTHAM, J. *Of Laws in General*, (ed. H.L.A. Hart, The Athlone Press, 1970), pp. 68–70, 133–148, 248: law derives its force from the motives on which it relies to produce desired aims. These may be alluring or coercive, threats of punishment and rewards. They include physical, political, religious and moral motivations. They are contained in laws addressed to officials, which in turn derive their force from other laws. See also BENTHAM, J. *The Limits of Jurisprudence Defined*, (ed. C.W. Everett, Columbia University Press, 1945), chap. 13.

4. BENTHAM, J. *Works*, (ed. J. Bowring, Wm. Tait, Edinburgh, 1843), III, pp. 199–200, 230 *et seq.*; VIII, pp. 380–81: reward is considered as an inducement to conform to certain behaviour.

5. SUMMERS, R.S. "The *New* Analytical Jurists" (1966), 41 NYULR, 861: Austin's error is said to be that he translated the conceptual question, "What is an obligation?" into an empirical one, "What is likely to happen if subjects do not comply?" He points out that a person still has an obligation even though there may be no possibility that a sanction will be imposed for non-compliance.

6. LEWIS, J.U. "John Austin's Concept of 'Having a Legal Obligation': a Defence and Reassessment in the Face of Some Recent Analytical Jurisprudence" (1975), 14 W Ont LR, 51: the author defends Austin against Summers's attack. Austin defined a law in psychological terms and located the act of legislating in the lawmaker's will – the wish that another shall do or forbear and an intention to inflict sanction. These are two separate aspects of a psychological process of commanding, not a translation of a conceptual question into an empirical one. Nevertheless, he criticises Austin for saying that what is just is anything which accords with some law. Law is a purposive social institution and, as such, value-laden. Austin's theory thus fails in its intellectual coherence.

7. LLEWELLYN, K.N. *Jurisprudence: Realism in Theory and Practice*, (University of Chicago Press, 1962), chap. 18: this deals with law-observance vs. law-enforcement. Observance is not a matter of rules, but of habit and practice among various social groups. Law-observance requires as a prerequisite that folkways shall first have developed in accordance with the purposes behind the law.

8. FRIED, C. "Moral Causation" (1963–64), 77 Harv LR, 1258: how are people made to comply with actions which they would not do spontaneously? An important method of accomplishing this is by making the actions the right thing to do so that people feel a moral obligation to comply. This is "moral causation" and it is distinguishable from psychological causation and moral persuasion.

1. SCHWARTZ, R.D. and ORLEANS, S. "On Legal Sanctions" (1966–67), 34 UCLR, 274: this reports the results of a field experiment of the effectiveness of sanction and of appeal to conscience in securing compliance with the law. The results differed according to the status of the subjects, but they did show that the threat of sanction does deter violations by inducing a moralistic attitude to the law. At the same time, threat of punishment also produced some resistance to compliance.

2. LEWIS, J.U. "Karl Olivecrona: 'Factual Realism' and Reasons for Obeying a Law" (1970), 5 U Br Col LR, 281: the "binding force" of obligation has no objectivity; it lies in people's feelings of being bound. This feeling is connected with the apparatus of organised force and the maintenance of constant psychological pressure to condition the subjects. Moral ideas are shaped by legal enforcement. The author criticises Olivecrona principally on the ground that his atomistic view of "reality" gave him a false start in his analysis of obligation, and his failure to perceive that laws do have reference to values.

3. The following cases may be consulted in connection with the nature of duty: *Cattle* v. *Stockton Waterworks Co.* (1875), LR 10 QB, 453; *Mogul S.S. Co.* v. *McGregor, Gow & Co.* (1889), 23 QBD, 598; *Corbett* v. *Burge, Warren and Ridgley, Ltd.* (1932), 48 TLR, 626; *Hedley Byrne & Co. Ltd.* v. *Heller & Partners, Ltd* [1964] AC, 465; [1963] 2 All ER, 575; *Commissioner for Railways* v. *Quinlan* [1964] AC, 1054; [1964] 1 All ER, 897; *Best* v. *Samuel Fox & Co. Ltd.* [1952] AC, 716; [1952] 2 All ER, 394; *R.* v. *Dudley and Stephens* (1884), 14 QBD, 273; *Haynes* v. *Harwood* [1935] 1 KB, 146; *Maddison* v. *Alderson* (1883), 8 App Cas, 467; *Curwen* v. *Milburn* (1889), 42 Ch D, 424; *Spencer* v. *Hemmerde* [1922] 2 AC, 507; *Seymour* v. *Pickett* [1905] 1 KB, 715; *Zoernsch* v. *Waldock* [1964] 2 All ER, 256; [1964] 1 WLR, 675; *Broom* v. *Morgan* [1953] 1 QB, 597; [1953] 1 All ER, 849; *Case of the Sheriff of Middlesex* (1840), 11 Ad & El. 273; *R.* v. *Larsonneur* (1933), 97 JP, 206.

11. Conduct

Act

1. FITZGERALD, P.J. "Voluntary and Involuntary Acts" in *Oxford Essays in Jurisprudence*, (ed. A.G. Guest, Oxford University Press, 1961), chap. 1: the use of the term "act" is discussed with reference to criminal and civil law and evidence. Emphasis is laid on controllability as an important feature of an "act" in the law.

2. WILLIAMS, G.L. *Criminal Law: The General Part*, (2nd ed., Stevens & Sons, Ltd, 1961), chap. 1, especially ss. 8–13: although the substance is criminal law, there is a good deal of general discussion of the nature of "act" and its components – movement, circumstances and some, at any rate, of its consequences.

3. O'CONNOR, D. "The Voluntary Act" (1975), 15 Med Sci & L, 31: the idea of voluntary act as determined by controllability by will is no longer adequate. The operation of the will is preceded by perception, cognition and evaluation of data, and aberrations in any of these can affect the act. These new dimensions affect the concepts of insanity and self-induced involuntariness.

4. FLETCHER, G.P. "Prolonging Life" (1967), 42 Wash LR, 999: this is a stimulating discussion of the distinction between "act" and "omission" primarily from the criminal law point of view. In order to deal with the social and moral problems arising out of heart-, lung-, kidney-machines and the like, it is forcefully argued that acts ending terminal diseases should be subsumed under omission.

5. RYLE, G. *The Concept of Mind*, (Hutchinson's University Library, 1949), chap. 3, especially pp. 69–74: this discussion from a non-legal point of view is rewarding for a lawyer. It disposes of the need to talk of willing as a separate operation. At pp. 69–74 the distinction between voluntary and involuntary action is dealt with and the point is made that this distinction comes into prominence when the question of responsibility arises.

6. AUSTIN, J.L. "A Plea for Excuses" (1956–57), 57 PAS, 1: this, too, discusses action in relation to responsibility, but from a different angle. Voluntary and involuntary actions are also dealt with, though not from a legal point of view.

7. HART, H.L.A. "The Ascription of Responsibility and Rights", in *Logic and Language*, (ed. A.G.N. Flew, Blackwell, 1955), I, 145: the language of lawyers refers to human behaviour with a view to ascribing responsibility or exemption therefrom. P. 187 *et seq.*, deal with "action" from this angle. The statement, "He did it", is not descriptive, but an ascription of responsibility for an action. (For modification, see H.L.A. Hart, *Punishment and Responsibility, Essays in the Philosophy of Law*, Clarendon Press, Oxford, 1968, "Preface"). See also H.L.A. Hart, "Negligence *Mens rea* and Criminal Responsibility" in *Oxford Essays in Jurisprudence*, (ed. A.G. Guest, Oxford University Press, 1961), pp. 34–38. This essay is referred to below under "Negligence".

8. MACKIE, J.L. "The Grounds of Responsibility" in *Law, Morality, and Society. Essays in Honour of H.L.A. Hart*, (edd. P.M.S. Hacker and J. Raz, Clarendon Press, Oxford, 1977), chap. 10: acts and results may be intended or not; an action (whole performance) includes some acts that are intended and some that are not. This paper seeks to re-establish the traditional and natural account of

voluntariness and intentionality which would lead to the same results that
Professor Hart advocates.

1. HART, H.L.A. "Varieties of Responsibility" (1967), 83 LQR, 346: four different
   uses of the term "responsibility" are distinguished. Of these the most important
   is "Liability-responsibility". The relationship between legal and moral
   responsibility is touched upon.

2. GLOVER, J. *Responsibility*, (Routledge and Kegan Paul; New York, Humanities
   Press, 1970): this is a philosophical consideration of responsibility and only
   marginally relevant to lawyers. The author himself prefers a modified version of
   determinism, but not so as to exclude moral responsibility of agents. On this
   basis he considers admissible excuses and then turns to the question of punishment.

3. ROSS, A. *On Guilt, Responsibility and Punishment*, (Stevens & Sons, Ltd, 1975):
   the author argues that the statement "A is responsible for B" is either a
   prediction that he will be found guilty, or a directive that he should be found
   guilty. If made outside a court, it is a prediction; if made inside a court it is a
   directive to the judge. This analysis does not take account of the judge himself,
   who is neither predicting nor directing, but ordering punishment.

4. STONE, F.F. "A Problem for Pericles" (1971), 59 Calif LR, 769: the debate
   between Pericles and Protagoras concerned responsibility for the death of a
   person by a javelin thrown during a lawfully organised competition. It involved
   the responsibility of the thrower, the organisers and of the javelin. The issues are
   discussed with reference to modern American cases.

5. KOCOUREK, A. *Jural Relations*, (2nd ed., The Bobbs-Merrill Co, 1928), chap. 16:
   after examining the traditional views of the nature of "act", the submission is
   made that "act" is the legal concept of some result of bodily movement or some
   result attributable to its absence. An act in law creates a jural relationship. Since
   the latter is conceptual, so is the former.

6. KOCOUREK, A. *An Introduction to the Science of Law*, (Little, Brown & Co,
   1930), pp. 266 *et seq.*: this is a further discussion on the same line as above.

7. HALL, J. "Analytic Philosophy and Jurisprudence" (1966), 77 Ethics, 14;
   especially pp. 19–24: this criticises both J.L. Austin and H.L.A. Hart. A
   statement, e.g., "He did it", is not simply an ascription of responsibility. It is to
   some extent descriptive because it presupposes competence and normality in the
   actor and causation. So, too, *mens rea* means not only that excuses are excluded
   but also that the defendant intentionally or recklessly did whatever it is. An
   excuse is itself descriptive of a mental state, which is why it functions as an
   excuse.

8. HALL, J. *General Principles of Criminal Law*, (2nd ed., The Bobbs-Merrill Co, Inc,
   1960), chap. 6: "act" is generally discussed with a view to elucidating what
   constitutes criminal conduct. What is required is a term that will cover voluntary
   actions and inactions, and the term "effort" is suggested.

9. BRANDEN, N. "Free Will, Moral Responsibility and the Law" (1969), 42 Southern
   Calif LR, 264: this argues for a new concept of free will. Traditional approaches
   are rejected as unsound psychologically and in law.

1. BENTHAM, J. *An Introduction to the Principles of Morals and Legislation*, (edd.
   J.H. Burns and H.L.A. Hart, The Athlone Press, 1970), chaps. 7–12; chaps. 7,
   ss. 5 *et seq.*, 8, 9, 10: transactions are resolved into acts, circumstances, intention
   as to the act and as to the consequences, consciousness and consequences. In
   addition there are motive and general disposition. All these are developed in detail.

2. RAZ, J. *The Concept of a Legal System. An Introduction to the Theory of Legal
   System*, (Clarendon Press, Oxford, 1970), pp. 50–57: Bentham's analysis of
   conduct is set out, but the symbolic presentation of the argument makes it
   difficult to read. This analysis is part of an account of the structure of a norm
   according to Bentham's view and, as will be seen later in the book, it is preferred
   to that of Kelsen.

3. AUSTIN, J. *Lectures on Jurisprudence*, (5th ed., R. Campbell, John Murray, 1885),
   I, pp. 365–367, 410–416: acts are said to be movements of the body consequent
   upon determinations of the will, and forbearances are voluntary inactions. Acts
   are distinguished from their consequences.

4. SALMOND, J.W. *Jurisprudence*, (12th ed., P.J. Fitzgerald, Sweet & Maxwell, Ltd,
   1966), pp. 352–367: an "act" has to be subject to the will and includes the
   circumstances and, as it has no natural boundaries, some, but not necessarily all,
   its consequences.

5. PATON, G.W. *A Text-Book of Jurisprudence*, (4th ed., G.W. Paton and D.P. Derham,
   Clarendon Press, Oxford, 1972), chap. 13, s. 68: this gives a general discussion
   of "act" as including volition, motive, intent, circumstances and consequences;
   and of inaction as including intentional inaction (forbearance) and failure to
   comply with a duty (omission).

6. COOK, W.W. "Act, Intention and Motive in the Criminal Law" (1916–17), 26 Yale
   LJ, 645: "act" and "intention" are ambiguous terms. "Act" should be confined
   to willed muscular movement. A consequence is intended when the actor desires
   it to happen as the result of the act, or when he adverts to a result which will
   necessarily follow.

7. PERKINS, R.M. "A Rationale of *Mens Rea*" (1938–39), 52 Harv LR, 905–907;
   912: "act" is discussed with reference to *actus reus* in criminal law. The necessity
   for voluntary conduct is discussed with reference to actions and inactions.

8. BRETT, P. *An Essay on a Contemporary Jurisprudence*, (Butterworths, 1975),
   pp. 71–81: rational action must be understood as action within an unquestioned
   and undetermined frame of cultural knowledge as to the ordinary run of human
   experience. On this basis the author criticises prevailing concepts of act, *mens rea*,
   foresight, and certain rules of evidence and procedure.

9. ARNOLD, C. "Conceptions of Action" (1977), 8 Syd LR, 86: some actions are
   performed by performing other actions, e.g., killing a deer by shooting it.
   "Basic" acts are those which do not include other acts. The difference between
   these and "non-basic" acts lies in different descriptions of some single "basic"
   action in relation to its consequences. The views of Bentham and Hart are critically
   examined; Austin's view is defended. The author's thesis is applied to some cases
   concerning the place and time of commission of crimes.

10. TERRY, H.T. *Some Leading Principles of Anglo-American Law Expounded with a*

View to its Classification, Arrangement and Codification. (T. & J.W. Johnson & Co, Philadelphia, 1884), ss. 77–86: "act" is discussed generally with reference to the will, instinctive movements, omissions and motive. In a wide sense "act" includes some of its consequences.

1. MARKBY, W. *Elements of Law*, (6th ed., Oxford, 1905), ss. 213–216: the analysis follows that of J. Austin.

2. HOLLAND, T.E. *The Elements of Jurisprudence*, (13th ed., Oxford, 1924), pp. 108–125: the account lays some stress on "movements of the will", which should be regarded with some suspicion in the light of later analyses.

3. KEETON, G.W. *The Elementary Principles of Jurisprudence*, (2nd ed., Isaac Pitman & Sons, Ltd, 1949), pp. 198–207: the analysis follows that of J. Bentham with illustrations drawn from modern case-law.

4. HOLMES, O.W. *The Common Law*, (Little, Brown & Co, 1881), pp. 54–57: this short analysis contains Holmes's famous definition of "act" as a "voluntary muscular contraction". Circumstances, on this view, are relevant only to determine the wrongfulness of an act.

Automatism

5. JENNINGS, J. "The Growth and Development of Automatism as a Defence in Criminal Law" (1961–62), 2 Os HLJ, 370: this contains a discussion of the English authorities and the relation between automatism and insanity.

6. McDERMOTT, T.L. "The Path of Automatism" (1962), 1 Tasm LR, 695: this is another review of the law in comparison with insanity.

7. HOWARD, C. "Automatism and Insanity" (1962), 4 Syd LR, 36: the conclusion is reached that automatism will only be accepted as a defence when the action is performed in a state of unconsciousness and in circumstances not amounting to insanity.

8. WILLIAMS, G.L. "Automatism" in *Essays in Criminal Science*, (ed. G.O.W. Mueller, Fred. B. Rothman & Co, New York, Sweet & Maxwell Ltd, London, 1961), chap. 12: this is an investigation of the question whether or not automatism should be treated as insanity.

9. ELLIOTT, I.D. "Responsibility for Involuntary Acts: Ryan v. The Queen" (1967–68), 41 Aust LJ, 497: it is not enough to speak of voluntary act as a "willed movement", for this is as much in need of explanation as voluntary act. Voluntariness is part of *mens rea*, not of *actus reus*. These points arose in *R. v. Ryan* (1967), 40 ALJR, 488.

10. TODD, E.C.E. "Insanity as a Defence in a Civil Action of Assault and Battery" (1952), 15 MLR, 486: this is a discussion of *Morriss v. Marsden* (civil case), which concerned the question of liability for the involuntary conduct of a person who had been found unfit to plead so far as the criminal law was concerned.

11. PREVEZER, S. "Automatism and Involuntary Conduct" (1958), Crim LR, 361, 440: this is a discussion of involuntary conduct with reference principally to

Hill v. *Baxter*, an important case on automatism. It tries to show to what extent the legal treatment of the subject is inadequate.

1. EDWARDS, J.Ll.J. "Automatism and Criminal Responsibility" (1958), 21 MLR, 375: *Hill* v. *Baxter* is discussed further.

2. ORCHARD, G.F. "Drunkenness, Drugs and Manslaughter" (1970), Crim LR, 132, 211: this is a critical discussion of the decision in *R.* v. *Lipman* [1970], 1 QB, 152. In the course of it there is some discussion of automatism.

3. TURNER, J.W.C. "Towards the Deodand" (1960), Crim LR, 89, 168: judicial interpretation of statute can make a person responsible even for involuntary conduct. One such instance, *Kensington Borough Council* v. *Walters*, is fully dealt with.

4. PARSONAGE, M. "Epilepsy and Driving" (1969), 133 JPJ, 290: the law has to provide against disasters and so forbids epileptics from driving. After explaining the nature of epileptiform attacks, a doctor considers whether, subject to safeguards, those who have been free from attacks for a certain number of years should be allowed to drive.

5. ASHWORTH, A.J. "Reason, Logic and Criminal Liability" (1975), 91 LQR, 102: duress, necessity, automatism, insanity and drunkenness are discussed in relation to the requirement of contemporaneousness of *actus reus* and *mens rea*. The requirement of fault in the cause producing involuntariness is a response to social need.

6. CROSS, A.R.N. "Blackstone v. Bentham" (1976), 92 LQR, 516: Blackstone maintained that voluntary drunkenness is no defence to a criminal charge, even though it may produce automatism. Bentham's criticism proceeds on the mistaken ground that the threat of punishment will not be effective on a drunken man at the material time.

Causation

7. GREEN, L. "Are there Dependable Rules of Causation?" (1929), 77 U Pa LR, 601: the question is one of responsibility, and rules cannot be devised to take the place of decision. Formulae about causation are needed in order to present the issue that has to be decided.

8. JAMES, F. and PERRY, R.F. "Legal Cause" (1951), 60 Yale LJ, 761: this is a critical appraisal of the "but for" test and of concurrent cause, one or both of which may involve blameworthiness. On this latter question, the different opinions of various writers are discussed. The varying interpretations of "proximate cause" are also discussed.

9. KELSEN, H. *What is Justice?* (University of California Press, 1957), pp. 303, 325: the idea of causation is traced back to revenge – cause attracts effect just as wrong attracts punishment. Modern scientific ideas of causation separated themselves from revenge when the theological interpretation of nature was abandoned, but they continued to be based on the analogy of revenge – one cause, one effect. In the second essay the above point is developed further. With a normative science like law the connection between wrong and retribution is one of imputation – what ought to happen in certain circumstances.

1. PEASLEE, R.J. "Multiple Causation and Damage" (1933–34), 47 Harv LR, 1127: the main point of interest is the discussion of the concurrence of an innocent and a blameworthy cause. The view is submitted that in this event the party to blame should be absolved on grounds of justice and policy. Other variations are also considered.

2. CARPENTER, C.E. "Concurrent Causation" (1935), 83 U Pa LR, 941: this provides a clear analysis of the difficulties involved, especially in the application of the "but for" test. If of two concurrent causes one is innocent and the other guilty, the latter should not be absolved (C.E. Peaslee, *supra*, criticised).

3. SCHMIDT, F. "The Ratio Decidendi. A Comparative Study of a French, a German and an American Supreme Court Decision" (1965), 6 *Acta Instituti Upsaliensis Iurisprudentiae Comparativae* 1: each of the three cases involved causation of injury by either of two or more potential tortfeasors. In all of them relief was given, for different reasons, regardless of the fact that it was impossible to attribute the injury to any one tortfeasor.

4. HART, H.L.A. and HONORÉ, A.M. *Causation in the Law*, (Oxford, 1959): this monograph deals exhaustively with the subject and also with related topics, such as voluntary and involuntary conduct. It incorporates articles by the authors under the same title in (1956), 72 LQR, 58, 260, 398.

5. WILLIAMS, G.L. "Causation in the Law" (1961), CLJ, 62: this discusses causation in the light of H.L.A. Hart and A.M. Honoré's monograph. The application of the "but for" test and cases of concurrent cause are considered.

6. WILLIAMS, G.L. *Joint Torts and Contributory Negligence*, (Stevens & Sons, Ltd, 1951), pp. 239 *et seq.*: this also explains the "but for" test and the way in which certain problems are dealt with in tort.

7. KEETON, R.E. *Legal Cause in the Law of Torts*, (Ohio State University Press, 1963): the principal thesis is that causation is founded on the "risk" principle, and that this is a rule of causation in a "cause-in-fact" sense. It is conceded that departures and modifications do come in.

8. COLE, R.H. "Windfall and Probability: A Study of 'Cause' in Negligence Law" (1964), 52 Calif LR, 459: the term "cause" is used for different purposes, at times to prevent an unfair pecuniary advantage being derived by the plaintiff, at others to decide whether the defendant was involved at all. This brings in policy decisions and prediction of probabilities. On this basis, various analyses, including that of H.L.A. Hart and A.M. Honoré, are examined.

9. MORRIS, C. "On the Teaching of Legal Cause" (1939), 39 Col LR, 1087: "factual" and "legal" cause are discussed, and there is a demonstration of how most tests of causation that are commonly used beg the question.

10. MUNKMAN, J. "Note on the Causes of an Accidental Occurrence" (1954), 17 MLR, 134: a chance happening is the result of the intersection of several cause sequences at a given place and time. The distinction is made between the "stage setting" and the factors that make the accident happen.

11. WRIGHT, R.A. "Causation and Responsibility in English Law" (1955), CLJ, 163:

causation is an experimental generalisation and lawyers should concentrate on
how it operates. Decisions on causation are value-judgments.

1. BOHLEN, F.H. *Studies in the Law of Torts*, (The Bobbs-Merrill Co, 1926), chap. 9:
   causation is the test by which courts ascertain whether a particular harm is to be
   ascribed to a particular action for the purpose of responsibility.

2. BEALE, J.H. "Recovery for Consequences of an Act" (1895–96), 9 Harv LR, 80:
   "The Proximate Consequences of an Act" (1920), 33 Harv LR, 633: the analysis
   contained in these articles has now become traditional and has come to be known
   as the "insulation" theory. Many modern discussions are evaluations of it.

3. SMITH, J. "Legal Cause in Actions of Tort" (1911–12), 25 Harv LR, 102, 223, 303:
   various tests are considered and the "substantial factor" test is advocated.

4. TERRY, H.T. "Proximate Consequences in the Law of Torts" (1914–15), 28 Harv
   LR, 10: intended and foreseeable consequences are "proximate"; what is meant
   by a "violating cause" that may intervene is discussed.

5. EDGERTON, H.W. "Legal Cause" (1924), 72 U Pa LR, 211, 343: no hard and fast
   rule can be evolved, the solution depends upon the balancing of conflicting
   interests. Legal cause means justly attachable cause, the legal view of causation
   being rooted in a desire to reach a just result.

6. McLAUGHLIN, J.A. "Proximate Cause" (1925–26), 39 Harv LR, 149: this is a
   step-by-step account of the attitude that courts adopt towards various types of
   results; the "active force" theory is put forward.

7. GREGORY, C.O. "Proximate Cause in Negligence – a Retreat from 'Rationalisation'",
   (1938–39), 6 UCLR, 36, especially pp. 58 *et seq.*: the "directness" and
   "foreseeability" tests are thought to reflect differences in policy concerning the
   desirable legal incidence of negligent conduct.

8. CARPENTER, C.E. "Workable Rules for Determining Proximate Cause" (1932),
   20 Calif LR, 229, 396, 471: these represent an attempt to formulate a practical
   approach to the problems.

9. GREEN, L. *Rationale of Proximate Cause*, (Vernon Law Book Co, 1927): the
   decisive question is whether the hazard came within the rule which the actor
   violated. The foreseeability test is discussed and rejected and factual cause is
   treated as being of minor importance.

10. ANONYMOUS. "Proximate and Remote Cause" (1870), 4 Am LR, 201: this
    provides a detailed historical account of the development of the idea of proximate
    cause.

11. BOGGS, A.A. "Proximate Cause in the Law of Tort" (1910), 44 Am LR, 88: the
    author provides a collection of conflicting writings and cases on causation.

12. BINGHAM, J.W. "Some Suggestions Concerning 'Legal Cause' at Common Law"
    (1909), 9 Col LR, 16, 136: the selection of possible cause is always limited
    according to the point of view; for legal purposes this is responsibility. The result
    has to fall within the purpose of the duty that has been infringed.

1. POUND, R. "Causation" (1957–58), 67 Yale LJ, 1: this gives a general discussion of causation in the light of the social problem that is involved, including a discussion of the views of some of the writers mentioned above.

2. WIGMORE, J.H. *Select Cases on the Law of Torts*, (Little, Brown & Co, 1912), II, 865–875: the causation element in tortious liability is discussed, primarily in the light of the "but for" test.

3. HEYTING, W.J. "Proximate Causation in Civil Actions" (1932), 44 Jur R, 239, especially pp. 261–285: this discusses foreseeability as a test of causation.

4. POLLOCK, F. *A First Book of Jurisprudence*, (6th ed., Macmillan & Co, Ltd, 1929), pp. 141–171: proximate consequences are treated as being part of the act, remote consequences as connected with intention.

5. MUELLER, G.O.W. "Causing Criminal Harm" in *Essays in Criminal Science*, (ed., G.O.W. Mueller, Fred B. Rothman & Co, New York, Sweet & Maxwell, Ltd, London, 1961), chap. 7: for purposes of criminal law the "but for" test should be satisfied first. It is also recognised that human conduct is purposive and it is the purpose that establishes the nexus with the outside world.

6. HALL, J. *General Principles of Criminal Law*, (2nd ed., The Bobbs-Merrill Co, Inc, 1960), chap. 8: causation is discussed in factual and legal perspective. Causation is a question largely turning on policy.

7. WILLIAMS, G.L. "Causation in Homicide" (1957), Crim LR, 429: this discussion is based on a case in which it was held that a wound which resulted in death owing to allegedly improper medical treatment did not "cause" the death.

8. CAMPS, F.E. and HAVARD, J.D.J. "Causation in Homicide – a Medical View" (1957), Crim LR, 576: two medical experts criticise the decision, which is the basis of G.L. William's article (*supra*). The question should turn, not on whether the treatment was improper, but whether it was administered in good faith.

9. FLETCHER, G.P. "Prolonging Life" (1967), 42 Wash LR, 999: the distinction between "causing" harm and "permitting" harm to occur is discussed in the context of the criminal liability of a person who switches off a mechanical device for keeping someone alive, and of a person who fails to switch it on.

10. MACINTOSH, J.C. "Concurrent Negligence" (1928), 45 SALJ, 314: the question of *novus actus interveniens* is considered.

11. GOODHART, A.L. "The Third Man or Novus Actus Interveniens" (1951), 4 CLP, 177: the problems raised by *novus actus interveniens* are discussed with a view to subsuming them under the foreseeability principle.

12. BOBERG, P.Q.R. "Reflection on the *Novus Actus Interveniens* Concept" (1959), 76 SALJ, 280: English and South African cases on the subject are reviewed.

13. McGREGOR, H. "Variations on an Enigma: Successive Causes of Personal Injury" (1970), 33 MLR, 378: the case of *Baker* v. *Willoughby* [1970] AC, 467, is discussed in relation to causation and remoteness. The decision is applauded although it runs contrary to a rigid causal approach.

1. STRACHAN, D.M.A. "Variations on an Enigma: the Scope and Application of the 'But For' Causal Test" (1970), 33 MLR, 386: continuing the discussion of *Baker* v. *Willoughby* [1970] AC, 467, the author emphasises the need to modify the 'but for' test.

2. "AQUARIUS". "Causation and Legal Responsibility" (1941), 58 SALJ, 232: considerations of policy and justice ultimately determine the result.

3. "AQUARIUS". "Causation and Legal Responsibility" (1945), 62 SALJ, 126: contributory negligence as a cause of the plaintiff's harm is examined in detail with reference to English and South African authorities to show that relative blameworthiness, and not causation, has been the determining factor.

4. *Pierce* v. *Hau Mon* (1944), Appellate Division, 175 (South Africa): the judgment of Watermeyer, C.J., is a judicial demonstration of quantitative blameworthiness as the basis of contributory negligence.

5. MACINTYRE, M.M. "The Rationale of Last Clear Chance" (1939–40), 53 Harv LR, 1225: this shows that the doctrine of the "last clear chance" was only an escape through the avenue of comparative fault from the old rule of the common law.

6. BOURKE, J.P. "Damages: Culpability and Causation" (1956), 30 Aust LJ, 283: "fault" and "responsibility" under the Law Reform (Contributory Negligence) Act, 1945, are discussed with reference to the case-law.

Omissions

7. KIRCHHEIMER, O. "Criminal Omissions" (1941–42), 55 Harv LR, 615: this is a careful examination of the duty to act, which is the foundation of responsibility for omissions.

8. FLETCHER, G.P. "Prolonging Life" (1967), 42 Wash LR, 999: liability for omissions lets in considerations of policy as to when a duty to act should be recognised. The artificiality of the traditional concepts of "act" and "omission" is mercilessly exposed.

9. HUGHES, G.B.J. "Criminal Omissions" (1957–58), 67 Yale LJ, 590: the duty to act is discussed together with a further analysis of the *mens rea* that is required.

Intention and Recklessness

10. WILLIAMS, G.L. *Criminal Law: The General Part*, (2nd ed., Stevens & Sons, Ltd, 1961), chap. 2: this is a detailed analysis of intention and recklessness. Although it deals primarily with criminal law, it is of general relevance.

11. PASSMORE, J.A. and HEATH, P.L. "Intentions" (1955), Aristotelian Society Supplementary Volume 29, 131: Passmore mainly advocates the "coherence" theory, Heath evaluates both this and the "planning" theory. Both analyses could be of legal importance.

12. TURNER, J.W.C. "Mental Element in Crimes at Common Law" in *The Modern Approach to Criminal Law*, (edd. L. Radzinowicz and J.W.C. Turner, Macmillan & Co, Ltd, 1945), 195, especially pp. 199–211: this analysis is now classic. The

disputed question how far, if at all, negligence grounds responsibility in manslaughter does not affect the analysis of intention and recklessness.

1. ANSCOMBE, M. "Intention" (1956–57), 57 PAS, 321: "reason" and "cause" for acting are distinguished. An intentional action is an action the "why" of which is not a causal "why". Motive may explain actions; it does not determine, i.e., cause, them.

2. GOTLIEB, A.E. "Intention, and Knowing the Nature and Quality of an Act" (1956), 19 MLR, 270: the analysis does not follow the same line as in most books. Intention is also discussed in relation to the M'Naghten Rules of insanity.

3. STRACHEN, B. "The Mystery of a Man's Mind – his Intention" (1966), 130 JP, 447: this short article concerns itself with proof of intention.

4. WATSON, K.T. "The Meaning of Recklessness" (1961), 111 LJ, 166: the meaning of this term is considered in relation to the Prevention of Fraud (Investments), Act, 1958, s. 13 (1).

5. KENNY, A.J.P. "Intention and *Mens Rea* in Murder" in *Law, Morality, and Society. Essays in Honour of H.L.A. Hart* (edd. P.M.S. Hacker and J. Raz, Clarendon Press, Oxford, 1977), chap. 9: there are three parallel theories of intention. Murder requires an intent either to kill or to create a serious risk of death; the intent must be direct, i.e., should include the direct intent to bring about a state of affairs from which one knows that death will certainly follow.

6. KENNY, A.J.P. "Intention and Purpose in Law", in *Essays in Legal Philosophy*, (ed. R.S. Summers, Basil Blackwell, Oxford, 1968), 146: a philosopher examines points raised by the legal bracketing of liability for foreseen consequences and intended consequences. The acute difficulties of defining "intention" are indicated.

7. WHITE, A.R. "Intention, Purpose, Foresight and Desire" (1976), 92 LQR, 569: different meanings of "intention" and juristic analyses are examined. Intention and purpose are different. There are also difficulties in saying that intention implies desire. It only implies foresight when the intention is actually carried out or where the intended results actually occur. Foresight and desire by themselves do not imply intention.

8. For further general analyses of intention reference might be made to the writings of J. Bentham, J. Austin, J.W. Salmond, W.W. Cook, R.M. Perkins, H.T. Terry, W. Markby, T.E. Holland, G.W. Keeton and O.W. Holmes, which are referred to under "Act"; and of J.H. Wigmore and J. Hall, which are referred to under "Causation". For analyses of Intention in relation to matrimonial suits, the following might be consulted:

9. BIGGS, J.M. *The Concept of Matrimonial Cruelty*, (The Athlone Press, 1962), Part II: this provides a very clear account of the law prior to the cases of *Gollins* and *Williams*. Chapter 5 analyses the cases dealing with the mental element.

10. ALLEN, C.K. "Matrimonial Cruelty" (1957), 73 LQR, 316, 512: motive and intention are discussed in the latter part. The analysis of intention differs somewhat from traditional accounts.

1. HALL, J.C. "Matrimonial Cruelty and *Mens Rea*" (1963), CLJ, 104: this is a careful examination of intention in this branch of the law with especial reference to the M'Naghten Rules.

2. GOODHART, A.L. "Cruelty, Desertion and Insanity in Matrimonial Law" (1963), 79 LQR, 98: the nature of the presumption involved in the statement that "a man is presumed to intend the natural and probable consequences of his conduct" is examined. The point is made that the choice between a subjective and an objective view of cruelty depends upon policy.

3. BROWN, L.N. "The Offence of Wilful Neglect to Maintain a Wife" (1960), 23 MLR, 1: this is a discussion of what is meant by "wilful" in this context.

4. BROWN, L.N. "Cruelty without Cupability or Divorce without Fault" (1963), 26 MLR, 625: the cases of *Gollins* and *Williams* are analysed at length and their impact on the law of divorce considered. For other discussions of *Gollins* and *Williams*, see C.T. LATHAM: "Intent and Cruelty" (1963), 127 JPJ, 126, 699; "What is Cruelty?" (1964), 128 JP, 783; R. LOWE: "New Look at Cruelty" (1963), 113 LJ, 668, 683, 731; NOTE in (1964), 235 LT, 339; L. ROSEN: "Legal Cruelty and Cruelty" (1964), 108 SJ, 887.

Inadvertence and Negligence

5. WILLIAMS, G.L. *Criminal Law: The General Part*, (2nd ed., Stevens & Sons, Ltd, 1961), chap. 3: the "mental" and "conduct" theories are set out, together with a discussion of what is meant by "gross negligence".

6. HART, H.L.A. "Negligence, *Mens Rea* and Criminal Responsibility" in *Oxford Essays in Jurisprudence*, (ed. A.G. Guest, Oxford University Press, 1961), chap. 2: if criminal responsibility were to be attached to "gross negligence", this would not be a form of "absolute liability", since what is required is an ability to control actions. Negligence is a failure to exercise the capacities to advert, think about and control behaviour.

7. SALMOND, J.W. *Jurisprudence*, (7th ed., Sweet & Maxwell, Ltd, 1924), 408; and J.W. SALMOND on *Torts*, (17th ed., R.F.V. Heuston, Sweet & Maxwell, Ltd, 1977), p. 193: negligence is a state of mind. It is not a separate tort either. (Note that P.J. Fitzgerald, the editor of *Jurisprudence* and R.F.V. Heuston, the editor of *Torts*, adopt different views from that of the author).

8. BIGELOW, M.M. *The Law of Torts*, (3rd ed., Cambridge University Press, 1908), pp. 18–21, 96–98: negligence is a state of mind, though external standards are applied to the proof of it.

9. STREET, H. *The Foundations of Legal Liability*, (Thompson & Co, New York, 1906), I, pp. 71–123: negligence is not a separate tort. As to whether it is a state of mind or conduct, it is argued that there is truth in both views.

10. POLLOCK, F. *Law of Torts*, (15th ed., P.A. Landon, Stevens & Sons, Ltd, 1951), pp. 336–337: negligence is the contrary of diligence. It is therefore conduct.

11. TERRY, H.T. "Negligence" (1915–16), 29 Harv LR, 40: negligence is conduct, not a state of mind. The question what conduct is to be treated as negligent is investigated.

1. EDGERTON, H.W. "Negligence, Inadvertence, and Indifference; the Relation of Mental States to Negligence" (1925–26), 39 Harv LR, 849: negligence is unreasonably dangerous conduct.

2. SEAVEY, W.A. "Negligence – Subjective or Objective" (1927–28), 41 Harv LR, 1: this analysis is in partial support of the "conduct" theory. The terms "subjective" and "objective" cannot be used in their literal sense. There is no standard "reasonable man", hence the test is only partly objective.

3. PROSSER, W.L. *Handbook of the Law of Torts*, (2nd ed., West Publishing Co, 1955), chap. 5, pp. 119–123, 147–152: negligence is conduct which falls below a certain standard established by law.

4. WHITE, A.R. "Carelessness, Indifference and Recklessness", (1961), 24 MLR, 592; "Carelessness and Recklessness – a Rejoinder" (1962), 25 MLR, 437: carelessness connotes conduct (not taking care), indifference connotes a state of mind (not paying attention to certain risks). On this basis J.W. Salmond, F. Pollock and G.L. Williams are criticised.

5. FITZGERALD, P.J. and WILLIAMS, G.L. "Carelessness, Indifference and Recklessness: Two Replies" (1962), 25 MLR, 49: these are two short replies answering the criticisms made by A.R. White (*supra*).

6. For further general analyses of Negligence reference might be made to the writings of J. Austin, G.W. Keeton, G.W. Paton and T.E. Holland, which are referred to under "Act"; and of J.H. Wigmore and J. Hall, which are referred to under "Causation". For the general nature of Negligence as a tort, in addition to standard works, such as J.F. Clerk & W.H.B. Lindsell on *Torts* (14th ed., Sweet & Maxwell, Ltd, 1975), and J. Charlesworth: *Negligence*, (6th ed., R.A. Percy, Sweet & Maxwell, Ltd, 1977), reference might be made to the following:

7. PROSSER, W.L. *Handbook of the Law of Torts*, (2nd ed., West Publishing Co, (1955), chap. 6.

8. BOHLEN, F.H. *Studies in the Law of Torts*, (The Bobbs-Merrill Co, 1926), chap. 1.

9. GREEN, L. *Judge and Jury* (Vernon Law Book Co, 1930), chaps. 3 and 4.

10. MACHIN, E.A. "Negligence and Interest" (1954), 17 MLR, 405.

11. PAYNE, D.J. "The Tort of Negligence" (1953), 6 CLP, 236.

12. Person

General

1. PATON, G.W. *A Text-Book of Jurisprudence*, (4th ed., G.W. Paton and D.P. Derham, Clarendon Press, Oxford, 1972), chap. 16: this is a convenient general account of "person" as a right and duty bearing unit. Human beings and corporate persons are dealt with as well as practical problems concerning the liability of unincorporated associations.

2. SALMOND, J.W. *Jurisprudence*, (12th ed., P.J. Fitzgerald, Sweet & Maxwell, Ltd, 1966), chap. 10: this is also a general discussion of various aspects of the topic, including the legal position of animals, the dead, unborn children and dual capacity. Legal persons, sole and aggregate, are explained, and the purpose of incorporation.

3. KEETON, G.W. *The Elementary Principles of Jurisprudence*, (2nd ed., Pitman & Sons, Ltd, 1949), chap. 13, especially pp. 162 *et seq.*: this is a fairly good general account of the subject.

4. POUND, R. *Jurisprudence*, (West Publishing Co, 1959), IV, pp. 191–261; 384–405: this is a full and detailed account of natural and legal persons and of the various theories concerning the latter.

5. GRAY, J.C. *The Nature and Sources of the Law*, (2nd ed., R. Gray, The Macmillan Co, New York, 1921), chap. 2: this is another general account of "normal" and "abnormal" persons. The account of juristic persons includes descriptions of Roman and Continental legal institutions.

6. HOLLAND, T.E. *The Elements of Jurisprudence*, (13th ed., Oxford, 1924), pp. 93–100; 339–357: these pages contain another general account of "natural" and "artificial" persons.

7. POLLOCK, F. *A First Book of Jurisprudence*, (6th ed., Macmillan & Co, Ltd, 1929), Part I, chap. 5: natural and artificial persons are considered. Pollock thinks the realist view to be the soundest view, although he points out that the common law has not formally committed itself to any view. Corporate liability for wrongdoing is also touched on.

8. MARKBY, W. *Elements of Law*, (6th ed., Oxford, 1905), ss. 131–145: this is a very general account of natural and juristic persons.

9. JENKS, E. *The New Jurisprudence*, (John Murray, 1933), chap. 7: legal persons are considered with reference to will. Jenks inclines towards the realist theory.

Human Beings

10. BARRY, J.V. "The Child *en ventre sa mere*" (1940–41), 14 Aust LJ, 351: the attitude of the law towards the unborn child is generally discussed.

11. WINFIELD, P.H. "The Unborn Child" (1942), 8 CLJ, 76: the extent to which the unborn child is recognised in the law of property, criminal law, contract and tort is dealt with.

186

1. ATKINSON, S.B. "Life, Birth, and Live-birth" (1904), 20 LQR, 134: this article discusses in detail the question when a child is deemed to be born alive, (based on the state of medical knowledge at that date).

2. WILLIAMS, G.L. *The Sanctity of Life and the Criminal Law*, (Faber & Faber Ltd, 1958), chaps. 1, 5–6, 8: the author deals challengingly with the social, moral, religious, medical, legal and other aspects of abortion and euthanasia. The boundaries of the law are luminously expounded (although some developments since publication call for modification in detail).

3. AUSTIN, J. *Lectures on Jurisprudence*, (5th ed., R. Campbell, John Murray, 1885), I, pp. 347–355: Austin deals with physical or natural persons and legal or fictitious persons. But his treatment of the former is more valuable than the latter, since he was writing before the Companies Act.

4. WHITFELD, L.A. "The Rule as to Posthumous Children – the Decision in *Elliott v. Joicey*" (1935–36), 9 Aust LJ, 294: this is principally a note on the case, which is a decision of the House of Lords as to when a child *en ventre sa mere* is to be regarded as living.

5. WRIGHT, C.A. Note in (1935), 13 Can BR, 594: another note on the case of *Elliott v. Joicey*.

6. SEABORNE-DAVIS, D. "Child-killing in English Law" in *Modern Approach to Criminal Law*, (edd. L. Radzinowicz and J.W.C. Turner, Macmillan & Co, Ltd, 1945), chap. 17: the question when a child becomes a person in the eyes of the law relating to homicide is dealt with in the course of a general discussion.

7. CANNON, R.W. "Born Alive" (1964), Crim LR, 748: an accused stabbed a pregnant woman, who was very near to giving birth. The child was surgically extracted alive, but died three days later of a stab wound that had damaged it *in utero*. The particular discussion of when a child is "born alive" is on p. 754.

8. ANONYMOUS. "Injury to an Unborn Child" (1939), 83 SJ, 185: the matter is considered with reference to the law of tort, crime and property.

9. Congenital Disabilities (Civil Liability) Act, 1976, renders a person liable to a child in respect of a disability caused by a pre-natal occurrence affecting its parent. This Act gives effect to the recommendations contained in the Law Commission's Report No. 60, Cmnd. 5709. See also B. HOGGETT, "Unborn Child and the Law of Tort" (1976), 120 SJ, 807, 829; P.J. PACE, "Civil Liability for Pre-natal Injuries" (1977), 40 MLR, 141.

10. WILLIAMS, G.L. "The Legal Unity of Husband and Wife" (1947), 10 MLR, 16: the origin of the idea and the significance of it in various branches of the law are discussed in detail. (The position dealt with is prior to the Law Reform (Husband and Wife) Act, 1962).

11. KAHN-FREUND, O. "Inconsistencies and Injustices in the Law of Husband and Wife" (1952), 15 MLR, 133; (1953), 16 MLR, 34, 148: these articles are of general interest and a useful discussion of the position prior to the Law Reform (Husband and Wife) Act, 1962.

12. MOSSE, R.L. "Can a Person Sue Himself?" (1944), 94 LJ, 262: dual capacity is

dealt with in connection with a case in which a widow, as administratrix of the estate of her infant son, who had been killed in a collision, sued herself as administratrix of her deceased husband's estate, he having been killed in the same collision.

Miscellaneous

1. DUFF, P.W. "The Personality of an Idol" (1927), 3 CLJ, 42: the interesting decision of the Judicial Committee of the Privy Council recognising the personality of an idol is discussed.

2. VESEY FITZGERALD, S.G. "Idolon Fori" (1925), 41 LQR, 419: this article, too, deals with the personification of a Hindu idol.

Corporation Sole

3. MAITLAND, F.W. "The Corporation Sole" and "The Crown as a Corporation" in *Selected Essays*, (edd. H.D. Hazeltine, G. Lapsley, P.H. Winfield, Cambridge University Press, 1936), chaps. 1 and 2; *Collected Papers*, (ed. H.A.L. Fisher, Cambridge University Press, 1911), pp. 210, 244: in these two classic essays the origin of the corporation sole is investigated and the attribution of the idea to the Crown.

4. KEETON, G.W. *The Elementary Principles of Jurisprudence*, (2nd ed., Pitman & Sons, Ltd, 1949), pp. 152–162: this is one of the best short discussion of the topic.

5. BLACKSTONE, W. *Commentaries on the Laws of England*, (16th ed., J.T. Coleridge, T. Cadell and J. Butterworth & Son, 1825), I, pp. 239–250, 467: the prerogative and its attributes are discussed. In the latter place corporations aggregate and sole are dealt with.

6. CARR, C.T. *The General Principles of the Law of Corporations*, (Cambridge University Press, 1905), chap. 4: this contains a general account of the corporation sole and its early history.

The Crown

7. POLLOCK, F. and MAITLAND, F.W. *The History of English Law before the Time of Edward I*, (2nd ed., with Introduction by S.F.C. Milsom, Cambridge University Press, 1968), I, pp. 511–526: the early history of the position of the Crown is examined in detail. Many features were incompatible with the idea of a corporation sole.

8. HOLDSWORTH, W.S. *A History of English Law*, (5th ed., Methuen & Co, Ltd), III, pp. 480–482; IV, pp. 202–203; IX, pp. 4–7: these pages give brief historical accounts of the Crown as a corporation sole.

9. PATON, G.W. *A Text-Book of Jurisprudence*, (4th ed., G.W. Paton and D.P. Derham, Clarendon Press, Oxford, 1972), pp. 348–353: in the course of a discussion of the state as a legal person it is pointed out that the idea of the Crown as a corporation sole is used instead in English law. The anomalies are also considered, especially in the sphere of commonwealth relations.

1. MOORE, W.H. "The Crown as Corporation" (1904), 20 LQR, 351: the position of the Crown in relation to the British Empire and some of the difficulties that arise are considered. This is of general interest as throwing a light on the position before the Dominions attained their present position.

2. HAGGEN, G.L. "The Function of the Crown" (1925), 41 LQR, 182: this deals with the various respects in which the Crown becomes the means of expressing the corporate capacity of the nation. There is also an account of the growth of the idea.

3. BORCHARD, E.M. "Governmental Responsibility in Tort" (1926–27), 36 Yale LJ at pp. 774–780: the state as a person is dealt with, and English and Continental thought on the matter are contrasted.

4. G.A.H. "The Crown as Protector of Infants" (1961), 105 SJ, 673: this is a brief discussion of a judicial decision on the matter.

5. ANONYMOUS. "Local Authorities and Parental Rights" (1961), 231 LT, 342: this deals with the same point as above.

6. JEWELL, R.E.C. "Education and Deprived Children: Statute and Prerogative" (1962), 125 JPJ, 320, 356: this is a further discussion of the Crown's powers as *parens patriae*.

Corporation aggregate

7. GOWER, L.C.B. *The Principles of Modern Company Law*, (3rd ed., K.W. Wedderburn, O. Weaver, A.E.W. Park, Stevens & Sons, Ltd, 1969), chap. 4: this contains a full discussion of the extent to which a company is distinct from its members and generally the advantages and disadvantages of incorporation.

8. BERLE, A.A. and MEANS, G.C. *The Modern Corporation and Private Property*, (The Macmillan Co, New York, 1933): this contains an important study of the separation of ownership from the power to control, and the consequences of this development. The whole book is a synthesis of a legal and economic approach.

9. BURNHAM, J. *The Managerial Revolution*, (Putnam & Co, Ltd, 1944): the managers will gain control over the instruments of production and gain preference in the distribution of products indirectly through their control of the state. This theme is developed with reference to various countries.

10. CARR, C.T. *The General Principles of the Law of Corporations*, (Cambridge University Press, 1905): this volume contains a general discussion of corporate personality, the attitude of the courts, creation, extinction and some of the theories on the subject.

11. POLLOCK, F. and MAITLAND, F.W. *The History of English Law before the time of Edward I*, (2nd ed., with Introduction by S.F.C. Milsom, Cambridge University Press, 1968), I, pp. 660–667: this contains an account of the early corporate idea in the form of boroughs and guilds.

12. KE CHIN WANG, H. "The Corporate Entity Concept (or Fiction Theory) in the Year Book Period" (1942), 58 LQR, 498: (1943), 59 LQR, 72: the separateness of the corporate entity had not become established at this date, but there were

developments in that direction. If any theory is applicable, it would be the
Realist theory; but the point is made that the matter is simply one of convenience.

1. LUBASZ, H. "The Corporate Borough in the Common Law of the Late Year-Book
   Period" (1964), 80 LQR, 228: this paper is partly in answer to that of Ke Chin
   Wang. The question is not whether the fiction theory had been received into the
   common law, but what the common law theory was. Since ecclesiastical groups
   require license for their establishment, the fiction theory is appropriate for them.
   A township is not so found and often goes back to time immemorial. The
   question is not how it was created, but what it meant to be a borough.

2. HOLDSWORTH, W.S. *A History of English Law*, (5th ed., Methuen & Co, Ltd),
   III, pp. 469–490: a historical account is given of the many groups which existed
   in English law and of their nature. At pp. 482–487 an account is given of the
   development of the separation of the corporation from its members.

3. ULLMANN, W. "The Medieval Theory of Legal and Illegal Organisations" (1944),
   60 LQR, 285: the medieval commentators on Roman law were the first to
   attempt to establish a criterion for distinguishing between legal and illegal
   organisations.

4. RAYMOND, R.L. "The Genesis of the Corporation" (1905–6), 19 Harv LR, 350:
   this considers the origin of the idea, who invented it, the principle on which it
   rests and what the idea is. The idea originates, it is said, in a mode of thought, and
   the extent to which a group is treated as one depends on practical convenience.

5. LASKI, H.J. "The Personality of Associations" (1915–16), 29 Harv LR, 404: no
   lawyer dares to neglect the phenomenon of group life. Some of the ways in
   which this phenomenon shows itself are set out.

6. FIFOOT, C.H.S. *Judge and Jurist in the Reign of Queen Victoria*, (Stevens & Sons,
   Ltd, 1959), chap. 3: this gives an account of how the judges in successive cases
   and step by step accepted the idea of corporate liability into the common law.

7. ARNOLD, T.W. *The Folklore of Capitalism*, (Yale University Press; London: Oxford
   University Press, 1937), chaps. 8–10: human needs are met by institutions which
   are initially founded on some ideology. The business corporation evolved out of
   the small trader with whom was associated the ideology of freedom of the
   individual to acquire wealth. This ideology, when carried over to large
   corporations, results in monopolies.

8. DOUGLAS, W.O. and SHANKS, C.M. "Insulation from Liability through
   Subsidiary Corporations" (1929–30), 39 Yale LJ, 193: this shows, mainly with
   reference to tort and contract, how corporate responsibility has developed
   within business units using corporate form.

9. PICKERING, M.A. "The Company as a Separate Legal Entity" (1968), 31 MLR,
   481: the *persona* of a company is an elusive idea made up of several facets, viz.,
   extent, nature and the manner in which its capacity is to be exercised. Within
   this framework the author considers carefully the legal capacity of companies and
   the *ultra vires* rule, subsidiary companies, procedural capacities and the
   exceptions to the separate entity doctrine.

10. CATALDO, B.F. "Limited Liability with One-man Companies and Subsidiary

Corporations" (1953), 18 LCP, 473: the doctrine of limited liability need not rest on the separateness of the corporate entity. The point is considered with reference to the one-man company and subsidiary companies.

1. FULLER, W. "The Incorporated Individual: a Study of the One-man Company" (1937–38), 51 Harv LR, 1373: this is devoted to a discussion of the various problems that arise with reference to their special judicial results and implications.

2. MANSON, E. "One Man Companies" (1895), 11 LQR, 185: this article is an interesting early comment on actual control being vested in a ruling spirit in most companies and on shareholders being but dividend drawers.

3. MANSON, E. "The Evolution of the Private Company" (1910), 26 LQR, 11: this is a general defence of one-man companies.

4. MASTEN, C.A. "One Man Companies and their Controlling Shareholders" (1936), 14 Can BR, 663: this examines the various situations in which respectively the company is treated as being distinct from its members and when it is not.

5. SILK, J. "One Man Corporations – Scope and Limitations" (1952), 100 U Pa LR, 853: the elucidation of these has been mainly a judicial task. Various questions concerning the capacity of the sole shareholder to bind his company, use its property for his personal benefit and his own personal liability are dealt with.

6. KIRALFY, A.K.R. "Some Unforeseen Consequences of Private Incorporation" (1949), 65 LQR, 231: this draws attention to certain important matters, such as fire insurance, special bank account, identification of the dominant share-holder and so on.

7. WALKER, E.S. "Corporate Personality (or the Metaphysics of a Local Authority)" (1959), 123 JPJ, 89: this is a short note on some early definitions.

8. H.N.B. "Proving a Company's Intention" (1956), 100 SJ, 695, 851: a single individual usually controls the details of a company's property interests, subject to the general direction by the Board. This article deals with the question how this might best be proved in court.

9. FRIDMAN, G.F.L. "A Company's Mind" (1957), 24 Solicitor 149: this is a discussion, with reference to the principal cases, of how a mental state can be imputed to a corporation through an individual who is sufficiently high up in the managerial hierarchy.

10. EDITORIAL: "The Mind of a Company" (1957), 1 JBL, 14: this is a short comment on imputing the mind of managers to a company.

11. ARNOLD, J.C. "The Control of a Company" (1959), 26 Solicitor 167; (1960), 27 Solicitor 13: in these two short discussions what is meant by "control" for specialised purposes is discussed. The principal question is whether, for purposes of the valuation of shares for estate duty, a court is bound by the register of members or may look beyond it.

12. PENNINGTON, R.R. "Control of a Company" (1960), 104 SJ, 1088: this article is of limited interest: it is concerned with a point that arose in a particular dispute.

1. FRANKS, M. "'Control' and 'Controlling Interest'" (1957), 107 LJ, 467: the question what is meant by these terms for special purposes is dealt with.

2. WORMSER, I.M. *Frankenstein Incorporated*, (McGraw-Hill Book Co, Inc, 1931), this is a general account, with a brief historical introduction, of the evils of big business corporations unless those in control heed the public good. Attention is also drawn to the shortcomings of the law.

3. MERVYN JONES, J. "Claims on Behalf of Nationals who are Shareholders in Foreign Companies" (1949), 26 BYIL, 225: this is concerned with corporations at international law. Diplomatic intervention is permissible on behalf of nationals, which include corporations. The problem of intervention on behalf of nationals, who are shareholders in foreign corporations, is also considered.

4. ANONYMOUS: "Residence of Companies" (1959), 26 Solicitor 299, 305: this is a discussion of what "residence" means for tax purposes.

5. D.R.S.: Note on "Residence of a Company" (1960), Br Tax R, 58: a particular decision on the point is discussed.

Lifting the Mask of Personality

6. GOWER, L.C.B. *The Principles of Modern Company Law*, (3rd ed., K.W. Wedderburn, O. Weaver, A.E.W. Park, Stevens & Sons, Ltd, 1969), chap. 10: a detailed discussion of the attitude of the courts in penetrating the corporate mask.

7. WORMSER, I.M. *The Disregard of the Corporate Fiction and Allied Corporate Problems*, (Baker, Voorhis & Co, 1927), chaps. 1–2: this is a further detailed investigation of the judicial attitude, English and American, to penetrating the corporate mask. See also I.M. WORMSER, "Piercing the Veil of Corporate Personality" (1912), 12 Col LR, 496.

8. NOTE: "'Corporate Entity' – its Limitations as a Useful Legal Conception" (1926–27), 36 Yale LJ, 254: this is a discussion of two cases in which the corporate entity was ignored in order to reach a just result. But the "entity idea" is sometimes convenient; no rules can be laid down as to when it will be used and when not.

9. HOGG, J.E. "The Personal Character of a Corporation" (1915), 31 LQR, 170; (1917), 33 LQR, 76: the *Daimler* case is discussed as decided by the Court of Appeal and House of Lords respectively.

10. VAUGHAN WILLIAMS, R.E.L. and CHRUSSACHI, M. "The Nationality of Corporations" (1933), 49 LQR, 334: a detailed examination of the *Daimler* case and of its implications is included in this discussion.

11. McNAIR, A.D. "The National Character and Status of Corporations" (1923–24), 4 BYIL, 44: this article is principally a discussion of the *Daimler* case.

12. NOREM, R.A. "Determination of Enemy Character of Corporations" (1930), 24 AJIL, 310: this is a further critique of the *Daimler* case in the light of the law as it stood up to that date.

1. DOMKE, M. "The Control of Corporations" (1950), 3 ILQ, 52: an account is given of the American law as to the enemy character of corporations.

2. SAMUELS, A. "Lifting the Veil" (1964), JBL, 107: the separate *persona* will be recognised·and acted upon prima facie unless public interest and public policy require otherwise. The circumstances in which the mask will be lifted are briefly reviewed.

3. LLOYD, D. *The Idea of Law*, (Penguin Books, Ltd, A 688, 1964), pp. 300–9: there is a brief discussion of human beings and group persons. The realist theory, in particular, is criticised. The methods of incorporation and consequences are explained with special reference to the separateness of the corporate person.

4. LEWIS, J.R. "Using the Veil for Improper Purposes" (1966), 4 Legal Exec. 72: this is a short summary of the ways in which courts strive to prevent fraud and injustice being perpetrated behind the corporate facade.

5. RUTHVEN, E.K.B. "Lifting the Veil of Incorporation in Scotland" (1969), Jur R 1: Scots law has not really faced this question, so the lead has come from England. Parallels are drawn for Scotland from the examination of English cases. These are grouped under the headings of statutory cases, trade with the enemy and common law instances.

6. KAHN-FREUND, O. "Some Reflections on Company Law Reform" (1944), 7 MLR, 54–59: this article was written before the Companies Act, 1948, but it contains a useful discussion of the abuse of the separateness of the corporate entity.

7. COHN, E.J. and SIMITIS, C. "'Lifting the Veil' in the Company Law of the European Continent" (1963), 12 ICLQ, 189: the positions in West Germany, Switzerland, France and Italy are reviewed in the light of the Anglo-American attitude.

The Ultra Vires Rule

8. GOWER, L.C.B. *The Principles of Modern Company Law*, (3rd ed., K.W. Wedderburn, O. Weaver, A.E.W. Park, Stevens & Sons, Ltd, 1969), chap. 5: this is probably the best and most easily accessible discussion of the problem in the light of modern case-law.

9. STONE, F.F. "*Ultra Vires* and Original Sin" (1939–40), 14 Tul LR, 190: an amusing and instructive discussion. Just as Man was created by God and fell from grace as the result of original sin, so he in turn created corporations, whose sins assume many forms. The wages of corporate sin and the means of punishing and of redressing its evils are also dealt with.

10. HARNO, A.J. "Privileges and Powers of a Corporation and the Doctrine of *Ultra Vires*" (1925–26), 35 Yale LJ, 13: the Hohfeldian analysis is applied to the problem, which is made to appear in a new light. While privileges and immunities can be accorded to individual members, their powers of wrongdoing need not be similarly treated.

11. STREET, J.H.A. *A Treatise on the Doctrine of Ultra Vires*, (Sweet & Maxwell, Ltd,

1930): this is a very detailed technical treatment of the topic and useful for reference.

1. CARDEN, P.T. "Limitations on the Powers of Common Law Corporations" (1910), 26 LQR, 320: the question whether the doctrine of *ultra vires* applies to common law corporations is considered with reference to possible changes in the attitude of the law.

2. HUDSON, A.H. "Common Law Corporations and *Ultra Vires*" (1961), 28 Solicitor 7: it is argued that the *ultra vires* doctrine has no application to these.

3. FURMSTON, M.P. "Common Law Corporations and *Ultra Vires*" (1961), 24 MLR, 518: a further consideration of the question.

4. WARREN, E.H. "Executed *Ultra Vires* Transactions" (1909–10), 23 Harv LR, 496: "Executory *Ultra Vires* Transactions" (1910–11), 24 Harv LR, 534: the discussion of both these topics is conducted in the light of the question how far the personality of a corporation extends.

5. HARRIMAN, E.A. "*Ultra Vires* Corporation Leases" (1900–1), 14 Harv LR, 332: various objections to the validity of such leases are considered.

6. CARPENTER, C.E. "Should the Doctrine of *Ultra Vires* be Discarded?" (1923–24), 33 Yale LJ, 49: after an examination of the present Anglo-American law the conclusion is reached that the doctrine should be abolished.

7. STEVENS, R.S. "A Proposal as to the Codification and Restatement of the *Ultra Vires* Doctrine" (1926–27), 36 Yale LJ, 297: this is of general interest and reveals some of the difficulties.

8. ULLMANN, W. "The Delictual Responsibility of Medieval Corporations" (1948), 64 LQR, 77: the evolution of the medieval doctrine is examined in detail, showing that it cannot be fitted into any modern theory. This article is particularly interesting for the light it sheds on the functional attitude of the medieval lawyers.

9. WELSH, R.S. "The Criminal Liability of Corporations" (1946), 62 LQR, 345: this is perhaps the best discussion of this question.

10. EDGERTON, H.W. "Corporate Criminal Responsibility" (1926–27), 36 Yale LJ, 827: the American point of view is presented, but there is also reference to English cases.

11. CANFIELD, G.F. "Corporate Responsibility for Crime" (1914), 14 Col LR, 469: the corporate entity is not a fiction in the sense of a supposition contrary to fact. It is analogous to implied conditions. The entity theory is then considered with reference to criminal responsibility.

12. LEE, F.P. "Corporate Criminal Liability" (1928), 28 Col LR, 1, 181: this is a detailed discussion of the Anglo-American law as to the criminal responsibility of shareholders, directors, officers, and employees, concluding with a discussion of the relevance of the "entity" theory.

13. WARREN, E.H. "Torts by Corporations in *Ultra Vires* Undertakings" (1925), 2 CLJ, 180: the position in English law is considered by an American lawyer.

1. GOODHART, A.L. "Corporate Liability in Tort and the Doctrine of *Ultra Vires*" in *Essays in Jurisprudence and the Common Law*, (Cambridge University Press, 1937), chap. 5: E.H. Warren's views *(supra)* are considered. The logical conclusion is reached that corporations cannot be responsible for *ultra vires* torts.

2. CLERK, J.F. and LINDSELL, W.H.B. *Torts*, (14th ed., Sweet & Maxwell, Ltd, 1975), ss. 189–195: this sets out the position in the English law of tort.

3. WINFIELD, P.H. and JOLOWICZ, J.A. *A Textbook of the Law of Tort*, (10th ed., W.H.V. Rogers, Sweet & Maxwell, Ltd, 1975), pp. 605–607: it is pointed out, in opposition to A.L. Goodhart *(supra)*, that there is no reason to suppose that the law is logical in its approach to these questions.

4. SALMOND, J.W. *The Law of Torts*, (17th ed., R.F.V. Heuston, Sweet & Maxwell, Ltd, 1977), pp. 428–431): the position in the English law of torts is set out and the views summarised.

5. STREET, H. *The Law of Torts*, (6th ed., Butterworth & Co, Ltd, 1976), pp. 463–465: the tortious responsibility of corporations and of unincorporated bodies is dealt with.

6. ASHTON-CROSS, D.I.C. "Suggestion Regarding the Liability of Corporations for the Torts of their Servants" (1950), 10 CLJ, 419: some illuminating Scottish decisions are referred to in the discussion of the problem generally.

Public Corporations

7. ROBSON, W.A. "The Public Corporation in Britain Today" in *Problems of Nationalised Industry*, (ed. W.A. Robson, George Allen & Unwin, Ltd, 1952), chap. 1: this is an examination of the public corporations set up by the nationalisation legislation and of their structure and control, both Parliamentary and ministerial. (The other chapters are also useful on more detailed aspects. For the pre-nationalisation position, see *Public Enterprise*, ed. W.A. Robson, Allen & Unwin, Ltd, 1937).

8. GRIFFITH, J.A.G. and STREET, H. *Principles of Administrative Law*, (4th ed., Isaac Pitman & Sons, Ltd, 1967), chap. 7: this is another discussion of public corporations and of their control, Parliamentary, ministerial and judicial.

9. *The Public Corporation: A Comparative Symposium*, (ed. W. Friedmann, Stevens & Sons, Ltd, 1954): various authors respectively discuss the working of public corporations in various countries. The editor discusses the position in Britain (pp. 162–189), and sums up at pp. 541–594.

10. WADE, E.C.S. "The Constitutional Aspect of the Public Corporation" (1949), 2 CLP, 172: this is a careful examination of the public corporation, both before and after nationalisation, with reference to the factors that influenced its form and structure. Particular attention is devoted to the problem of control.

11. FRIEDMANN, W. "The New Public Corporations and the Law" (1947), 10 MLR, 233, 377: this is an early appraisal of what was at that date still experimental.

12. FRIEDMANN, W. *Law and Social Change in Contemporary Britain*, (Stevens & Sons, Ltd, 1951), chap. 9: this contains a further analysis of some of the juristic questions that arise.

1. WADE, E.C.S. and PHILLIPS, G.G. *Constitutional Law*, (7th ed., E.C.S. Wade and A.W. Bradley, Longmans, 1967), chap. 21: this is a general account and of their position in the framework of the constitution.

2. WADE, H.W.R. *Administrative Law*, (2nd ed., Oxford, 1967), pp. 33–41: a short and general account.

3. GORDON, L. *The Public Corporation in Great Britain*, (Oxford University Press, 1938): this is a pre-war study, which is of interest in that the problems of control that might be adopted for the semi-independent bodies that then existed are considered and assessed.

4. CHESTER, D.N. "Public Corporations and the Classification of Administrative Bodies" (1953), I Pol S, 34: this investigates the origin and use of the term "public corporation" and inquires into their nature with a view to classifying them.

Unincorporated Associations

5. MAITLAND, F.W. "The Unincorporate Body" in *Selected Essays*, (edd. H.D. Hazeltine, G. Lapsley, P.H. Winfield, Cambridge University Press, 1936), chap. 3: *Collected Papers*, (ed. H.A.L. Fisher, Cambridge University Press, 1911), III, p. 271: the connection between trusts and corporations is considered. The trust is shown to have been "a most powerful instrument of social experimentation"; an important result being that it was a substitute for personified institutions.

6. MAITLAND, F.W. "Trust and Corporation" in *Selected Essays*, (*supra*), chap. 4; *Collected Papers*, (*supra*), p. 321: this comparison of trust and corporate bodies shows how greatly the trust concept fulfilled the function of incorporation from early times. There is also a valuable discussion of unincorporated bodies.

7. FORD, H.A.J. *Unincorporated Non-profit Associations*, (Oxford, Clarendon Press, 1959): this is one of the best and most convenient accounts of unincorporated associations. Is there a theory on which these may be held liable for harm suffered by persons as a result of group activity? This kind of activity has attracted to itself special rules and a legal order cannot remain neutral with regard to them.

8. LLOYD, D. *The Law Relating to Unincorporated Associations*, (Sweet & Maxwell, Ltd, 1938), especially the Introduction and Conclusion: the thesis is that there should be varying degrees of personality which can be accorded to each particular class of association according to the exigencies of the particular case.

9. LASKI, H.J. "The Personality of Associations" (1915–16), 29 Harv LR, 404: associations do have a reality of their own that manifests itself as much in law as in ordinary speech.

10. WARREN, E.H. *Corporate Advantages Without Incorporation*, (Baker, Voorhis & Co, New York, 1929), especially pp. 1–15, 841–846: philosophy has nothing to contribute; it is what the courts do that matters. A legal unit is "whatever has capacity to acquire a legal right and/or incur a legal obligation".

11. FRIEDMANN, W. *Law and Social Change in Contemporary Britain*, (Stevens & Sons, Ltd, 1951), chaps. 7, 9: the trust and corporation are considered.

Developments since F.W. Maitland's day have narrowed the distinction between unincorporate and incorporated bodies.

1. FRIEDMANN, W. *Law in a Changing Society*, (Stevens & Sons Ltd, 1959), chap. 9: this is a general discussion of the role played by corporations in the national and international scene.

2. GOWER, L.C.B. *The Principles of Modern Company Law*, (3rd ed., K.W. Wedderburn, O. Weaver, A.E.W. Park, Stevens & Sons, Ltd, 1969), chap. 11: companies are distinguished from other types of association (including public corporations).

3. WARREN, E.H. "Collateral Attack on Incorporation. A. *De Facto* Corporations" (1906–7), 20 Harv LR, 456; (1907–8), 21 Harv LR, 305: these two articles are also relevant on the *ultra vires* rule and how far the matter depends on the extent of corporate personality. The first article is less relevant than the second, but both should be read together. Where the legislature has not incorporated an association the rights and duties are of individuals.

4. CARPENTER, C.E. "*De Facto* Corporations" (1911–12), 25 Harv LR, 623: this considers the varying degrees to which American courts recognise the corporate nature of unincorporate associations. It is an answer to E.H. Warren's contention (*supra*).

5. DODD, E.M. "Dogma and Practice in the Law of Associations" (1928–29), 42 Harv LR, 977: a concept should be examined with a view to finding out what it means and whether that meaning is in accord with social policy. On this basis the author controverts E.H. Warren's thesis (*supra*) with reference to history and trend of modern decisions.

6. BURDICK, F.M. "Are Defectively Incorporated Associations Partnerships?" (1906), 6 Col LR, 1: after an examination of the authorities the conclusion is in the affirmative.

7. CHAFEE, Z. "Internal Affairs of Associations Not for Profit" (1929–30), 43 Harv LR, 993: the attitude of Anglo-American courts to such bodies is examined as well as the relationship between them and their members and the nature of the remedies available.

8. WEDDERBURN, K.W. "Corporate Personality and Social Policy: the Problem of the Quasi-corporation" (1965), 28 MLR, 62: the modern tendency on the part of the courts is to interpret statutes concerning group activities as granting impliedly either corporate status or at least the ability to sue and defend in the group name. The changed attitude of the courts in this sphere has been governed by considerations of policy.

9. WILLIAMSON, R.M. "The Free Church Case" (1904), 20 LQR, 415: this is of general interest. The background of the case is set out and the implications of the decision are briefly considered.

10. LLOYD, D. "Actions Instituted by or Against Unincorporated Bodies" (1949), 12 MLR, 409: this deals in detail with the problems created by various sorts of unincorporated bodies in the procedural field.

11. LLOYD, D. "The Disciplinary Powers of Professional Bodies" (1950), 13 MLR, 281:

in this the author considers the exercise of powers by unincorporated bodies and the attitude of the courts.

1. ANONYMOUS. "Expulsion of Member of Club" (1926), 70 SJ, 828: in the light of an unreported decision the relationship between members and a club is considered.

2. STURGES, W.A. "Unincorporated Associations as Parties to Actions" (1923–24), 33 Yale LJ, 383: this article should be read as suggesting a reason why such associations used not to be able to sue in their own name.

3. LLOYD, D. Note in (1953), 16 MLR, 359: the law is unsatisfactory with regard to the tortious responsibility of unincorporated associations and the use of a representative action.

4. KEELER, J.F. "Contractual Action for Damages against Unincorporated Bodies" (1971), 34 MLR, 615: this paper considers the possibility of holding that a contract is made with the committee of management whose members have a right to be indemnified out of the funds, and that a creditor may be subrogated to this right of indemnity and so be able to proceed directly against the funds.

5. NOTE: "Unions as Juridical Persons" (1956–57), 66 Yale LJ, 712: this is an inquiry in some detail into the Anglo-American law. The conclusion is reached that unions are juridical persons.

6. NOTE: "Responsibility of Labor Unions for Acts of Members" (1938), 38 Col LR, 454: various aspects of the matter are dealt with.

7. WITMER, T.R. "Trade Union Liability: the Problem of the Unincorporated Corporation" (1941–42), 51 Yale LJ, 40: the British *Taff Vale* case and the American *Coronado* case are discussed. Attention is drawn to the tendency to assimilate these bodies to corporations.

8. DICEY, A.V. "The Combination Laws as Illustrating the Relation Between Law and Opinion in England During the 19th Century" (1903–4), 17 Harv LR, 511: this is a consideration of the body of rules which regulate the freedom of workmen to combine for the purpose of determining by agreement the terms on which they will sell their labour, and the corresponding freedom of employers to combine for determining by agreement the terms on which they will engage labour. (See also *Law and Public Opinion in England during the 19th Century*, (2nd ed., Macmillan & Co, Ltd, 1932), pp. 154, 169).

9. GELDART, W.M. "The Status of Trade Unions in England" (1912), 25 Harv LR, 579: a trade union is shown to constitute an aggregate of phenomena which bears a resemblance to a corporation.

10. KAHN-FREUND, O. "The Illegality of a Trade Union" (1944), 7 MLR, 192: the influence of the old common law attitude towards trade unions in the interpretation of legislation is discussed.

11. SHIRBANIUK, D.J. "Actions By and Against Trade Unions in Contract and Tort" (1957–58), 12 UTLJ, 151: the English and Canadian law is considered at length. In view of the acceptance in practice of unions as entities distinct from their members, the formal recognition of them as "persons" would not be a radical one.

1. GRAVESON, R.H. "The Status of Trade Unions" (1963), 7 JSPTL (NS), 121: this is a very general account of their legal position and touches indirectly on the problem of their *persona*.

2. LLOYD, D. "Damages for Wrongful Expulsion from a Trade Union" (1956), 19 MLR, 121: a full discussion of the *Bonsor* case with particular attention to how far a registered trade union is a legal entity.

3. THOMAS, T.C. "Trade Unions and Their Members" (1956), CLJ, 67: the implications of the *Bonsor* decision are considered.

4. SYKES, E.I. "The Legal Status of Trade Unions" (1957), 2 Syd LR, 271: this is a discussion of the position of registered and unregistered trade unions, mainly with reference to the *Bonsor* case.

5. CAMPBELL, E. "Legal Personality, Trade Unions, and Damages for Unlawful Expulsion" (1954–56), 3 U Wes Aus ALR, 393: although the article is concerned with *Bonsor's* case and the position of trade unions in the light of a detailed survey of English and Australian law, it also discusses the various theories as to legal personality. It is, on the whole, a very good discussion.

6. WEDDERBURN, K.W. "The *Bonsor* Affair: a Post-script" (1957), 20 MLR, 105: a further investigation into the *Bonsor* case with particular reference to the extent to which a trade union is a "legal entity".

7. WEDDERBURN, K.W. "The Right to Threaten Strikes" (1961), 24 MLR, 572; (1962), 25 MLR, 513: these two articles are based respectively on the decision at first instance and on appeal of *Rookes* v. *Barnard*, a conspiracy case. They are of indirect relevance to the question of the nature of trade unions at law. (See further (1964), 27 MLR, 257).

8. WEDDERBURN, K.W. "Corporate Personality and Social Policy: the Problem of the Quasi-corporation" (1965), 28 MLR, 62: the orthodox view that "persons" in law are either human beings or corporations failed to provide solutions for an increasing number of situations which developing society threw up. The courts are now more ready to treat a body or institution as a "legal entity".

9. ANONYMOUS: "Legal Entities" (1964), 235 LT, 578: this is a note on "entities" that are neither human beings nor corporations. Such entities are creatures of statute, and which can sue and be sued.

Theories

10. HALLIS, F. *Corporate Personality*, (Oxford University Press, 1930): this is a detailed study of most of the better known theories on the subject. In the Introduction there are some questionable assertions, especially that English lawyers have adopted the Fiction Theory.

11. DUFF, P.W. *Personality in Roman Private Law*, (Cambridge University Press, 1938), chaps. 1, 9: in the first chapter words such as *"persona"*, *"caput"* and *"universitas"* are examined. The last chapter is a clear, critical account of various modern theories.

12. WOLFF, M. "On the Nature of Legal Persons" (1938), 54 LQR, 494: an incisive

and often amusing discussion of four of the principal theories, with the Fiction Theory preferred.

1. MICHOUD, L. *La Théorie de la Personnalité Morale*, (2nd ed., Librarie Générale de Droit et de Jurisprudence, Paris, 1924), I and II: this work, in French, is one of the outstanding surveys of this subject. Volume I, which deals with the concept of person, is especially relevant.

2. MACHEN, A.W. "Corporate Personality" (1910–11), 24 Harv LR, 253, 347: some of the leading Continental theories are reviewed. The nature of corporate personality is examined in an interesting way. The law recognises the unity of a group as a fact. Hence the important question is not why it does so, but why it refuses to recognise, e.g., partnership unity. A corporation is no fiction, but its personality is, and this is said to be why the distinction between incorporated and unincorporated bodies is so vague.

3. SMITH, B. "Legal Personality" (1927–28), 37 Yale LJ, 283: the fact that courts decide on grounds of utility is emphasised. Much confusion has arisen because of the tendency to read into legal persons the attributes of human beings.

4. COHEN, F.S. "Transcendental Nonsense and the Functional Approach" (1935), 35 Col LR, 809, especially pp. 809–817: the dangers of "thought without roots in reality" are pointed out with reference to corporations. The whole article is a powerful plea for a functional approach to legal problems.

5. VINOGRADOFF, P. "Juridical Persons" in *Collected Papers*, (Oxford, 1928), chap. 17: the life of a group has two sides, the social which is real, and the legal which is artificial. The relative importance of these two varies with the individualist or collectivist values of the system.

6. DEWEY, J. "The Historical Background of Corporate Personality" (1925–26), 35 Yale LJ, 655: the concept of "person" is a purely legal one, but some popular notions have crept in because of the belief that before anything is entitled to be called "person" it should possess certain properties. The article also examines the historical background of some of the theories.

7. DEWEY, J. *Philosophy and Civilisation*, (G.P. Putnam's Sons, 1931), 141: in this essay a modern philosopher examines the conception of "legal person". Many needless difficulties are said to have been caused by the use of the wrong logical method. On this basis the approaches of the various theories are examined.

8. HART, H.L.A. "Definition and Theory in Jurisprudence" (1954), 70 LQR, 37, at pp. 49–59: the theoretical difficulty arises when the question is asked what "it" is that owes money whenever it is said that "Smith & Co. owe White £10". The answer is to be found by elucidating the whole statement and how it is used in drawing conclusions.

9. NÉKAM, A. *The Personality Conception of the Legal Entity*, *(Harvard Studies in the Conflict of Laws*, Harvard University Press, 1938), III: the premise of the argument is that legal ideas are the product of emotion clothed with reason. The tendency in modern times is to regard the individual as the unit, and from this has stemmed the idea that "legal entities" should resemble individuals.

10. POLLOCK, F. "Has the Common Law Received the Fiction Theory of Corporation?"

in *Essays in the Law*, (Macmillan & Co, Ltd, 1922), chap. 6: the answer, according to Pollock, is that English law has not committed itself to any theory. On the whole, he favours the realist theory.

1. DUGUIT, L. *The Progress of Continental Law in the 19th Century*, (John Murray, London, 1918), 87–100: personality exists only where there is will. If a group has a will apart from the wills of its members, it is a "person". But Duguit's main concern is whether the group is pursuing a purpose which conforms with social solidarity. If it is, all actions within that purpose should be recognised and protected. A collective will is unprovable; but there is such a thing as collective purpose.

2. BRODERICK, A. "Hauriou's Institutional Theory: an Invitation to Common Law Jurisprudence" (1965), 4 Sol Q, 281: the state may grant legal "personality" to a group which is not organised or rationalised. When this happens there is talk of the fiction theory. But when an institution is organised, it has a "moral personality", and the state ought then to accord legal personality to it.

3. BERLE, A.A. "The Theory of Enterprise Entity" (1947), 47 Col LR, 343: this article is concerned mainly with the development of the corporation in modern business and the divergence between corporate theory and economic facts. The corporate entity takes its being from the reality of the underlying enterprise. This theory might be said to systematise the law of corporations and is a functional theory. See also W.O. DOUGLAS and C.M. SHANKS, "Insulation from Liability Through Subsidiary Corporations" (1929), 39 Yale LJ, 193; G.D. HORNSTEIN, "Legal Controls for Intra-corporate Abuse" (1941), 41 Col LR, 405; C.L. ISRAELS, "Implications and Limitations of the 'Deep Rock Doctrine'" (1942), 42 Col LR, 376.

4. MOORE, W.U. "Rational Basis of Legal Institutions" (1923), 23 Col LR, 609: to ask what is the rational basis of an institution is to pose a non-existent problem. The question should concern the purpose of institutions. This depends on the end, and the end is chosen before the rational process is directed towards achieving it. But ends are but means to other ends. So the real question is: what are the means to legal institutions, and to what proximate ends are legal institutions means?

5. STONE, J. *Social Dimensions of Law and Justice*, (Stevens & Sons, Ltd, 1966), pp. 367–432: these pages deal with the development of the corporation and the severance of control from ownership. The problems of social responsibility, which this has created, is alluded to.

6. WORTLEY, B.A. *Jurisprudence*, (Manchester University Press; Oceana Publications, Inc, New York, 1967), chap. 18: this chapter on "Personality" gives a very general account. It is chiefly important in stressing that the tendency of legal development has been towards the concept of enterprise unity.

7. KORKUNOV, N.M. *General Theory of Law*, (trans. W.G. Hastings, The Boston Book Co, 1909), s. 28: law presupposes conflicting interests and relations between individuals. Corporations are said to be "moral" persons. The Fiction, Realist and Purpose theories are mentioned. Legal personality is likened to parentheses in algebra.

8. HOHFELD, W.N. *Fundamental Legal Conceptions as Applied in Judicial*

Reasoning, (ed. W.W. Cook, Yale University Press, London: Humphrey Milford, 1923), chaps. 6–7: this theory dissolves a company into a multitude of jural relations between individuals. "Corporate personality" is a procedural device of convenience.

1. KOCOUREK, A. *Jural Relations*, (2nd ed., The Bobbs-Merrill Co, 1928), chap. 17: a distinction is drawn between the idea of "legal person" and "legal personality". The former is a concept to which is attributed a capacity for being in legal relationship; the latter is the sum total of legal relationships.

2. RADIN, M. "The Endless Problem of Corporate Personality" (1932), 32 Col LR, 643: it contains a critical review of the controversies as well as of corporate existence and responsibility. So far as a "person" means that a group constitutes a new item, there is no support in the facts; as facilitating reference to a complex group of facts, the idea of "person" is useful. (See also M. RADIN, "A Restatement of Hohfeld" (1937–38), 51 Harv LR, 1141, at pp. 1160–1162).

3. TIMBERG, S. "Corporate Fictions" (1946), 46 Col LR, 533, especially pp. 540 *et seq.*: corporate autonomy is discussed in various contexts, national and international. The nominalist view, M. Radin's in particular (*supra*), is criticised. The question is when and how far should the state dispel the corporate fiction. There is not just one fiction, there are many.

4. CANFIELD, G.F. "The Scope and Limits of the Corporate Entity Theory" (1917), 17 Col LR, 128: personality is a legal conception, but it is not a fiction because it involves no false deduction or pretence. Canfield opposes the Hohfeldian nominalism and holds to the entity theory.

5. BATY, T. "The Rights of Ideas – and of Corporations" (1919–20), 33 Harv LR, 358: the "real existence" of corporations is a shorthand phrase. But there is something; "person" is an idea, the idea of groupness.

6. PICKERING, M.A. "The Company as a Separate Legal Entity" (1968), 31 MLR, 481: the view that a company is a separate entity is supported. The exceptions are classified as exceptions to the principles delimiting the scope of a company's legal capacity, exceptions to the principle of separate property and contractual rights, and exceptions to the company's independent procedural capacity.

7. SNYDER, O.C. *Preface to Jurisprudence*, (The Bobbs-Merrill Co, Inc, 1954), Part V, chap. 2, pp. 778–786: this is a general discussion of the nature of natural and juristic persons. The Hohfeldian view is supported.

8. KELSEN, H. *General Theory of Law and State*, (trans. A. Wedberg, Harvard University Press, 1949), pp. 93–109: even a physical person is the unification of a complex of legal norms. Therefore, the contrast between physical and juristic persons is mistaken. See also H. KELSEN, *Pure Theory of Law*, (trans. M. Knight, University of California Press, 1967), pp. 168–192.

9. KELSEN, H. "The Pure Theory of Law" (trans. C.H. Wilson), (1934), 50 LQR, 474, at pp. 496–498: this is a simplified version of the same thesis as above.

10. von SAVIGNY, F.C. "Jural Relations" (trans. W.H. Rattigan, *Savigny's System of Modern Roman Law*, Bk. II, Wildy & Sons, 1884), pp. 175 *et seq.*: Savigny is the principal supporter of the Fiction Theory. This gives the original version of his thesis.

1. SALMOND, J.W. *Jurisprudence*, (7th ed., Sweet & Maxwell, Ltd, 1924), chap. 15, pp. 339–342: Salmond was the principal exponent of the Fiction Theory among English writers. The 7th edition is the last by Salmond himself: (but see now 12th edition, P.J. Fitzgerald, pp. 328–330).

2. JONES, J.W. *Historical Introduction to the Theory of Law*, (Oxford, 1940), chap. 6: the Fiction Theory is indirectly discussed in the course of a general account of the use of fictions.

3. SOHM, R. *The Institutes. A Text-Book of the History and System of Roman Private Law*, (trans. J.C. Ledlie, Oxford, 1901), pp. 195–205: the Realist Theory is rejected. Juristic personality is said to be created by law, but is not fictitious.

4. GIERKE, O. *Natural Law and the Theory of Society 1500–1800*, (trans. E. Barker, Cambridge University Press, 1934), Introduction, pp. lvii–lxxxvii: in the Introduction Barker examines the principal theories, especially the Fiction, Bracket and Realist Theories. He propounds his own view of the "personality of purpose". In the main text the Realist Theory of Gierke, its chief supporter, is to be found in detail.

5. GIERKE, O. *Political Theories of the Middle Age*, (trans. F.W. Maitland, Cambridge University Press, 1900), Introduction, pp. xviii–xliiii: in this classic Introduction Maitland made Gierke's work familiar to the English public. He elaborates Gierke's ideas, but considers also the Fiction, Concession and Bracket Theories. Although Maitland is thought to have been a convert to the Realist Theory, he does not commit himself and leaves the question unanswered. Chapters 3, 4 and 8 of the main text contain Gierke's views on the idea of unity in Church and State, organism and personality.

6. MAITLAND, F.W. "Moral Personality and Legal Personality" in *Selected Essays*, (edd. H.D. Hazeltine, G. Lapsley, P.H. Winfield, Cambridge University Press, 1936), chap. 5; *Collected Papers*, (ed. H.A.L. Fisher, Cambridge University Press, 1911), III, p. 304: the nature of natural persons and corporations is discussed. He stresses the fact that a united body differs from its component members by no fiction of law but in the very nature of things.

7. GELDART, W.M. "Legal Personality" (1911), 27 LQR, 90: there is a discussion of the Fiction and Realist Theories and the latter is preferred. Groups other than corporations are recognised in law because they are real and not a pretence.

8. BROWN, W.J. "The Personality of the Corporation and the State" (1905), 21 LQR, 365: corporate personality is not a mere metaphor or fiction. A corporation is real, but in a sense different from human beings. They are psychical realities, having unity of spirit, purpose, interests and organisation.

9. BROWN, W.J. *The Austinian Theory of Law*, (John Murray, 1906), pp. 254–270: in this Excursus the state and corporations are examined. He repeats his view as to the nature of corporations and argues that on this basis the state is a legal person.

10. VINOGRADOFF, P. *Common-sense in Law*, (3rd ed., H.G. Hanbury, Oxford University Press, 1959), pp. 52–61: legal persons are considered in the context of rights and duties. The Realist Theory is favoured.

11. DEISER, G.F. "The Juristic Person" (1919), 57 U Pa LR, 131, 216, 300: "*persona*

ficta" is said to be an inheritance from Roman law. The idea of a corporation rests on the conception of rights and of concerted action. Various ways of looking at the problem are considered, the Realist view being ultimately favoured.

1. McDOUGAL, W. *The Group Mind*, (Cambridge University Press, 1920): this is of general interest. It analyses the group mind from a psychological point of view. The author would support the Realist Theory as against the Fiction Theory.

2. FOLEY, H.E. "Incorporation, Multiple Incorporation, and the Conflict of Laws" (1928–29), 42 Harv LR, 516: the principal theories are discussed. Legal personality is the law-created capacity to enter into relationships at law. An incorporated association is a real entity. When several states incorporate the same association, that body has several personalities.

3. YOUNG, E.H. "The Legal Personality of a Foreign Corporation" (1906), 22 LQR, 178: the practice of courts normally proceeds on something like a Fiction Theory. But the solution of problems involving a corporation which is subject to rights and duties of another system of law proceeds on a Realist conception.

4. YOUNG, E.H. "The Status of a Foreign Corporation and the Legislature" (1907), 23 LQR, 151, 290: the nature of corporate personality is discussed *passim.*

5. FRIEDMANN, W. *Legal Theory*, (5th ed., Stevens & Sons, Ltd, 1967), chap. 34: he points out that the various theories have not sought to solve any problems, but to explain the nature of personality. The principal theories are briefly reviewed.

6. PECZENIK, A. "Norms and Reality" (1968), *Theoria*, 117, 125: after discussing in what sense normative statements can be empirically significant, the conclusion is applied to the empirical significance of "legal person". One can say when such a statement as "a legal person exists" can and cannot be used by relying on knowledge of certain observable events.

13. Possession

1. SHARTEL, B. "Meanings of Possession", (1932), 16 Minn LR, 611: the traditional attempts to define possession have failed because they attempt the impossible. There are many meanings of the term and these can only be understood with reference to the purpose in hand. The elaboration of this theme is one of the best contributions to the subject.

2. BINGHAM, J.W. "The Nature and Importance of Legal Possession" (1915), 13 Mich LR, 534, especially pp. 549–565; 623 *et seq.*: after a survey of related terms, the situations of "being in possession" are considered. What is meant when it is said that legal possession exists is that a person has certain rights called "possessory" rights. The vesting of these rights is determined by practical juridical considerations of justice and policy.

Roman Law

The following is a very brief selection. The Continental literature is enormous.

3. von SAVIGNY, F.C. *Rechts des Besitzes,* (6th ed., trans. as *Possession,* by E. Perry, S. Sweet, 1848): this is the classic exposition of the *animus* and *corpus* theory.

4. von IHERING, R. *Der Besitwille,* (Jena, 1889; trans. by O. de Meulenaere in the Supplement to *L'Esprit du Droit Romain,* A. Maresque, 1891): *Grund des Besitzesschutzes,* (Jena, 1868; trans. as above in the Supplement, A. Maresque, 1882): these deal with possession and with the interdicts. They contain a painstaking demolition of Savigny's theory, as well as his own theory.

5. LIGHTWOOD, J.M. "Possession in Roman Law", (1887), 3 LQR, 32: the author was one of the earliest advocates of Ihering's theory, which is here examined and the reasons why possession was protected considered.

6. BOND, H. "Possession in the Roman Law", (1890), 6 LQR, 259: this draws attention to the failure to distinguish between the questions, Why was possession protected? and, Why should possession be protected? Ihering's theory is considered with approval.

7. BUCKLAND, W.W. *A Text-book of Roman Law from Augustus to Justinian,* (3rd ed., P. Stein, Cambridge University Press, 1963), pp. 196–199: this contains a brief summary of the theories of Savigny and Ihering with some comment on each.

8. RADIN, M. *Handbook of Roman Law,* (West Publishing Co, 1927), pp. 384–392: he shows that the *corpus* and *animus* theory does not fit many cases. Ihering's critique of Savigny is approved, but even with his theory there are difficulties. There is a different group of claims in different situations called possession. There is no essential characteristic.

9. DIAS, R.W.M. "A Reconsideration of *Possessio*", (1956), CLJ 235: *possessio* was a device of legal policy and convenience. This can be illustrated by an examination of the texts.

10. BASNAYAKE, S. "Possession in a Mixed Legal System – the Sri Lanka Experience" (1975) 24 ICLQ 61: this article reviews the evolution of possession through

Roman-Dutch and English Law in Sri Lanka in various branches of law. In the latter part various theories are considered in the light of this development.

English Law

In addition to the articles by B. Shartel and J.W. Bingham (*supra*), the following are relevant to the thesis that possession is a device of convenience.

1. KOCOUREK, A. *Jural Relations*, (2nd ed., Bobbs-Merrill Co, 1928), chap. 20: the law is concerned only with jural relations between parties, which in the case of possession are the right to possess and the right of possessing. The investitive facts are exhausted as soon as the jural relation is created. There is no further need for an additional enduring fact called possession. In ultimate analysis the matter is one of policy.

2. PATON, G.W. "Possession", (1935), 1 *Res Judicata*, 187: the law of possession represents a clash between logic and convenience. Not only does the terminology vary, but many complicating factors enter into the decision in particular circumstances.

3. PATON, G.W. *A Text-book of Jurisprudence*, (4th ed., G.W. Paton and D.P. Derham, Clarendon Press, Oxford, 1972), chap. 22: possession is a fact to which the law attaches certain consequences. For reasons of convenience and policy each system builds differently round the fact of physical control. There is an outline of the theories of Savigny and Ihering and of the clash between convenience and theory.

4. LIGHTWOOD, J.M. *A Treatise on Possession of Land*, (Stevens & Sons, Ltd, 1894), chaps. 1, 2 and 4: there is a comparison of Roman and English law, as well as a critical discussion of Savigny, Holmes and Pollock and Wright. In chapter 4 attention is drawn to some of the artificial doctrines connected with possession.

5. THAYER, A.S. "Possession", (1904–5), 18 Harv LR, 196: attempts to define possession are necessarily futile. The conditions under which legal possession exists are technical and subject to no limit of variation. Holmes's explanation of physical power is criticised.

6. THAYER, A.S. "Possession and Ownership", (1907), 23 LQR, 175, especially pp. 175–187, 314: if possession follows from taking, this implies a rule that taking gives the right of possession. This rule developed from the habitual submission of others. Possession as the continuous dealing with a thing to the exclusion of others is a fiction.

7. HARRIS, D.R. "The Concept of Possession in English Law", in *Oxford Essays in Jurisprudence*, (ed. A.G. Guest, Oxford University Press, 1961), chap. 4: possession is used as a functional and relative concept. In doubtful cases the judges' views as to the merits and policy come in. The factors relevant to possession are considered.

8. BENTHAM, J. *Of Laws in General*, (ed. H.L.A. Hart, The Athlone Press, 1970), pp. 273–276: what is meant by possessing a thing is examined. Physical and legal possession are contrasted. The latter carries title to the thing. See also *The Limits of Jurisprudence Defined*, (ed. C.W. Everett, Columbia University Press, 1945), pp. 78–85.

1. BENTHAM, J. *Works*, (ed. J. Bowring, Wm. Tait, 1843), 1, pp. 221–222, 326–327; III, pp. 188–189: the advantages of possession and reasons for protecting it are considered. He points out that the idea of possession differs according to the nature of the subject-matter and the circumstances.

2. WILLIAMS, G.L. "Language and the Law", (1945), 61 LQR, 384, at pp. 390–391: this exposes the fallacy in Salmond's theory and indicates that there is a complex legal idea which is governed by the purpose of the particular rule.

Adaptations of Savigny's theory to English Law

3. SALMOND, J.W. *Jurisprudence*, (7th ed., 1924, chaps. 13 and 14; 11th ed., G.L. Williams, 1957. chaps. 13 and 14; 12 ed., P.J. Fitzgerald, Sweet & Maxwell, Ltd, 1966), chap. 9: this is a detailed account based on the *corpus* and *animus* theory. The author's own views have been modified considerably by the successive editors.

4. HOLMES, O.W. *The Common Law*, (Little, Brown & Co, Boston, 1881), chap. 6: the author adopts the Savignian thesis of *corpus* and *animus*, laying stress on the latter.

5. HOLMES, O.W. "Possession", (1877–78), 12 Am LR, 688: this is an earlier version of what later appeared in *The Common Law*, but it includes certain matters not discussed therein.

6. POLLOCK, F. and WRIGHT, R.S. *An Essay on Possession in the Common Law*, (Oxford, 1888), Part I: the emphasis is on *corpus* rather than on *animus*.

7. POLLOCK, F. *A First Book of Jurisprudence*, (6th ed., Macmillan & Co, Ltd, 1929), pp. 181–193: a very general discussion of possession and of its legal effects, but proceeding on the "classic" line.

8. POUND, R. *Jurisprudence*, (West Publishing Co, 1959), V, chap. 29: possession is defined as physical control with the will to exercise such control for oneself. There is a discussion of the reasons why possession is protected and of the physical and mental elements.

9. TAY, A.E.S. "The Concept of Possession in the Common Law: Foundations for a New Approach" (1964), 4 Melb ULR, 476: possession "is present control of a thing, on one's own behalf and to the exclusion of all others". This is submitted as the "standard case" in comparison with which divergent uses of the term "possession" can be understood.

10. HARRIS, D.R. "Comment", (1964), 4 Melb ULR, 498: the author takes issue with Miss Tay's contention (*supra*), pointing out not only certain weaknesses in her position but also that basically it is not very dissimilar to his own.

11. TERRY, H.T. *Some Leading Principles of Anglo-American Law Expounded with a View to its Classification, Arrangement and Codification*, (Philadelphia, 1884), chap. 10: this begins by accepting Savigny's theory without question. Although English law is admitted to be different from Roman law, the *corpus* and *animus* theory is applied none the less and various aspects of English law discussed in the light of it.

12. MARKBY, W. *Elements of Law*, (6th ed., Oxford, 1905), chap. 9: this, too, begins with an acceptance of Savigny's theory and an explanation of the physical and

mental elements. Of 25 pages in the chapter, only four and a half (pp. 197–203) are in fact devoted to English law.

1. AUSTIN, J. *Lectures on Jurisprudence*, (5th ed., R. Campbell, John Murray, 1885), I, pp. 51–53: Austin's lectures finished prematurely and he never discussed possession. In these introductory pages he foreshadows a future discussion and draws certain distinctions. It is, perhaps, noteworthy that he alludes to Savigny's treatise as "consummate and masterly; and of all books which I pretend to know accurately, the least alloyed with error and imperfections" (p. 53).

2. HOLLAND, T.E. *The Elements of Jurisprudence*, (13th ed., Oxford, 1924), pp. 194–208: he refers to Savigny's theory as "the accepted view", but Ihering has an honourable mention. The treatment is based largely on Holmes.

3. KEETON, G.W. *The Elementary Principles of Jurisprudence*, (2nd ed., Pitman & Sons, Ltd, 1949), chap. 15: possession depends on the degree of control and anything short of the requisite degree is "custody". Possession is the continuing exercise of a claim to the exclusive control of a thing. This leads to a discussion of *corpus* and *animus*.

4. STEWART, R.D. "The Difference Between Possession of Land and Chattels", (1933), 11 Can BR 651: "actual" possession is a matter of fact, "legal" possession is established by law. The former requires *animus* and *corpus*. The degree of control differs in the case of land and chattels.

5. GOODEVE, L.A. *Modern Law of Personal Property*, (9th ed., R.H. Kersley, Sweet & Maxwell, Ltd, 1949), pp. 32–41: possession requires control, which varies with the nature of the chattel, and the intention to control. Cases which do not fit into these requirements are "exceptions".

6. CROSSLEY VAINES, J. *Personal Property*, (4th ed., Butterworth & Co, Ltd, 1967), pp. 47–55: this account chiefly follows Pollock and Wright, and distinguishes between control or *de facto* possession, legal possession without control and the right to possess.

7. MATTHEWS, A.S. "Mental Element in Possession", (1962), 79 SALJ 179: this argues that convenience and policy are only explanations of the prevailing confusion; the courts do not use them as determinants. The article is limited to interdict possession (*mandament van spolie* of Roman-Dutch law), the treatment of which largely follows Holmes.

8. HALL, J.S. "Possession, Custody, and Ownership: a Philosophical Approach" (1960), 27 The Solicitor, 85: this, too, is influenced by Holmes. The law must be subordinated to instinct and must uphold the desire to retain what is possessed. Possession implies a degree of control, which varies. There is an account of seisin in early land law and of the philosophisings of Kant and Locke.

9. GOODHART, A.L. "Three Cases on Possession", in *Essays in Jurisprudence and the Common Law*, (Cambridge University Press, 1937), chap. 4: a demonstration of the unfortunate results of applying preconceived theories about possession to *Bridges* v. *Hawkesworth, South Staffordshire Water Co* v. *Sharman* and *Elwes* v. *Brigg Gas Co*.

10. FIFOOT, C.H.S. *Judge and Jurist in the Reign of Queen Victoria*, (Stevens & Sons,

Ltd, 1959), chap. 4: this tries to explain the persistence of Savigny's influence notwithstanding Ihering's demolition of his theory. After a discussion of some situations in civil and criminal law the conclusion is reached that possession is a word which has a changing content.

Special aspects of possession

For the history of the subject, especially the connection between possession and seisin, the following might be consulted.

1. POLLOCK, F. and MAITLAND, F.W. *The History of English Law before the time of Edward I*, (2nd ed., with Introduction by S.F.C. Milsom, Cambridge University Press, 1968), pp. 29–46.

2. MAITLAND, F.W. *Collected Papers*, (ed. H.A.L. Fisher, Cambridge University Press, 1911), 1, "Seisin of Chattels", p. 344; "Mystery of Seisin", p. 358; "The Beatitude of Seisin", pp. 406, 432.

3. AMES, J.B. "The Disseisin of Chattels", in *Select Essays in Anglo-American Legal History*, (Cambridge University Press, 1909), III, p. 541.

4. HOLDSWORTH, W.S. *A History of English Law*, (5th ed., Methuen & Co, Ltd), III, pp. 88–101; VII, pp. 23–31, 447–478.

5. BARLOW, A.C.H. "Gift *Inter Vivos* of a Chose in Possession by Delivery of a Key", (1956), 19 MLR 394: this considers some of the cases on the delivery of a key.

6. CLERK, J.F. "Title to Chattels by Possession", (1871), 7 LQR 224: this considers the extent to which a bailee can recover damages against a wrongdoer by virtue of his possession.

7. DICEY, A.V. *A Treatise on the Rules for the Selection of the Parties to an Action*, (Wm. Maxwell & Son, 1870), pp. 333–366: trespass to land can be brought by a possessor. The distinction between occupation and possession is discussed as well as the right to possess as the basis for suing in trespass to goods.

8. RIESMAN, D. "Possession and the Law of Finders", (1939), 52 Harv LR 1105: this is an elaborate discussion of finder cases. It argues that possession is largely irrelevant and shows the contrdictions that result by arguing on the basis of possession. The word possession may have an inner core of fairly settled meaning, but for the lawyer the periphery is more important. Here, certainly in finder cases, varieties of complex social interests come in. The article also contains a comment on Shartel's view.

9. MARSHALL, O.R. "The Problem of Finding", (1949), 2 CLP 68: this begins with an examination of legal policy and proceeds on that basis to consider the position of the finder in relation to various other persons. Possession is necessarily a very flexible concept.

10. TAY, A.E.S. "'Bridges v. Hawkesworth' and the Early History of Finding" (1964), 8 Am JLH 224: the early history of the law relating to finding is set out. This leads the author to the conclusion that *Bridges* v. *Hawkesworth* is not wrongly

decided, but is the last representative of an earlier line of decisions based on the forms of action.

1. TAY, A.E.S. "Possession and the Modern Law of Finding" (1964), 4 Syd LR 383: A piece-meal approach to possession will only hinder the predictable application of the law. The finding cases are reviewed in order to demonstrate that they bring out the fundamental criteria of possession. Each situation should be considered in the light of control as the basis of possession.

2. TAY, A.E.S. "Problems in the Law of Finding: the U.S. Approach" (1964), 37 Aust LJ 350: the American case-law, it is submitted, has developed the distinction between property that has been misplaced (i.e. put down and left) and property that has been lost.

3. TAY, A.E.S. "The Essence of Bailment: Contract, Agreement or Possession?" (1966), 5 Syd LR 239: bailment is analysed as a relation between a person and a thing, requiring neither agreement with, nor knowledge of, a particular bailor.

4. TAY, A.E.S. "Bailment and the Deposit for Safe-keeping" (1964), 6 Malaya LR 229: this continues the previous theme with an examination of a number of authorities.

5. TAY, A.E.S. "Possession, Larceny, and Servants: Towards Tidying up a Historical Muddle" (1965–66), 16 UTLJ 145: possession is not manual detention; it is control. A servant *qua* servant is only a master's instrument, i.e., so long as the servant's actions are part of the master's use or enjoyment.

6. RUSSELL, W.O. *On Crime,* (12th ed., J.W.C. Turner, Stevens & Sons, Ltd, 1964), II, pp. 1027–1156: this is a full historical account of the part played by possession in the law of larceny.

7. TURNER, J.W.C. "Two Cases on Larceny", in *Modern Approach to Criminal Law,* (edd. L. Radzinowicz and J.W.C. Turner, Macmillan & Co, Ltd, 1948), chap. 19: this deals with the artificial reasoning in *R. v. Middleton* and *R. v. Riley.*

8. EDWARDS, J.Ll.J. "Possession and Larceny", (1950), 3 CLP 127: the dichotomy between "physical" and "legal" possession is discussed, followed by a demonstration of the difficulties that have arisen and the distinctions that have been drawn in larceny cases.

9. CROSS, A.R.N. "Larceny and the Formation of a Felonious Intent After Taking Possession", (1949), 12 MLR 228: this is a note on *Ruse v. Read.*

10. CARTER, P.B. "Taking and the Acquisition of Possession in Larceny", (1957), 14 MLR 27: this draws an interesting distinction between obtaining possession and "taking" in the sense of knowing that one has obtained the possession.

11. LOWE, J.T. "Larceny by a Trick and Contract", (1957), Crim LR 28, 96: this shows that the effect of the decisions would seem to be that in criminal law a person may be said to have taken and carried away goods without consent when, on the same facts, in civil law he may be said to be in possession with consent.

12. NOTE in (1930), 46 LQR 135: a critique of *R. v. Harding.*

13. WYLIE, J.C.W. "Adverse Possession: an Ailing Concept?" (1965), 16 NILQ 467: this article may be consulted for a general review of the manner in which possession has been used by courts in connection with this branch of the law.

14. Ownership

1. HONORÉ, A.M. "Ownership" in *Oxford Essays in Jurisprudence*, (ed. A.G. Guest, Oxford University Press, 1961), chap. 5: ownership of a standard type is considered, its incidents, the nature of the thing owned, title and split ownership.

2. TURNER, J.W.C. "Some Reflections on Ownership in English Law" (1941), 19 Can BR, 342: this article begins with a brief examination of the way in which different writers have used the word "ownership" and of its history. The conclusion is that the characteristic feature of ownership is its enduring quality.

3. SALMOND, J.W. *Jurisprudence*, (7th ed., Sweet & Maxwell, Ltd, 1924), chap. 12: this edition contains the classic discussion by Salmond himself. For versions modified by subsequent editors, see 11th. edition, G.L. Williams, chap. 12, especially p. 303, note (c), in which the main criticisms of Salmond's analysis are considered. For G.L. Williams' own criticism see also "Language and the Law" (1945), 61 LQR at p. 386, where the point is made that ownership is used in different senses. 12th edition, P.J. Fitzgerald, (1966), chap. 8: Salmond's original treatment is considerably modified.

4. COOK, W.W. "Hohfeld's Contribution to the Science of Law" in W.N. Hohfeld, *Fundamental Legal Conceptions as Applied in Judicial Reasoning*, (ed. W.W. Cook, Yale University Press, 1923), pp. 11–15: Salmond's analysis is criticised for its failure to distinguish between claims, etc.

5. COOK, W.W. "The Utility of Jurisprudence in the Solution of Legal Problems" in *Lectures on Legal Topics*, (The Macmillan Co, New York, 1928), pp. 338–358: this is an analysis of ownership with the aid of the Hohfeldian table into a multitude of claims, etc.

6. KOCOUREK, A. *Jural Relations*, (2nd ed., The Bobbs-Merrill Co, 1928), chap. 18: the concept of "thing" is analysed in detail. "Ownership" is examined both as a jural relation and as an infra-jural relation. The conclusion is that it is an infra-jural relation between a person and a thing-element.

7. ROSS, A. "Tu-Tu" (1956–57), 70 Harv LR, 812: the lessons to be drawn from the analysis of a taboo word are applied to terms like "ownership". This word, it is said, has no semantic reference and is only a technique of presentation.

8. SIMPSON, A.W.B. "The Analysis of Legal Concepts", (1964), 80 LQR, 535, 551: Ross's thesis is criticised. Concepts are useful. The fact that a word has no semantic reference, i.e.. that the "thing" does not exist, does not imply that the word has no meaning.

9. HARGREAVES, A.D. *An Introduction to the Principles of Land Law*, (4th ed., G.A. Grove and J.F. Garner, Sweet & Maxwell, Ltd, 1963), chap. 6: this is probably the clearest and most convenient historical account. There is a comparison of the English and Roman law as to the concept of absolute ownership. Emphasis is placed on the historical need to conceive of interests in land as "things".

10. POLLOCK, F. and MAITLAND, F.W. *The History of English Law before the Time of Edward I*, (2nd ed., with an introduction by S.F.C. Milsom, Cambridge University Press, 1968), II, chap. 4, ss. 2, 6–7: this is an incomparable survey of

the development of the idea of ownership in land and chattels through the remedies that were available.

1. HOLDSWORTH, W.S. *A History of English Law*, (Methuen & Co, Ltd), III, chap. 1, ss. 5–7; VII, chaps. 1, ss. 1–2; 2, ss. 1–2: this is a detailed historical account of the shaping of the idea of ownership in land and chattels.

2. LIGHTWOOD, J.M. *A Treatise on Possession of Land*, (Stevens & Sons, Ltd, 1894), chaps. 5 and 6: this remains as one of the best accounts of the development in land law. It is enriched by fruitful comparisons with Roman law.

3. HARGREAVES, A.D. "Terminology and Title in Ejectment" (1940), 56 LQR, 376: a careful argument is presented to the effect that English law still knows no absolute ownership, but only relatively of title. (See also A.D. Hargreaves, "Modern Real Property" (1956), 19 MLR, 14, especially, pp. 16 *et seq.*).

4. HOLDSWORTH, W.S. "Terminology and Title in Ejectment – a Reply" (1940), 56 LQR, 479: in reply to A.D. Hargreaves it is argued that English law does recognise an absolute ownership.

5. CHESHIRE, G.C. *The Modern Law of Real Property*, (12th ed., E.H. Burn, Butterworths, 1976), pp. 28–40: this explains the nature of the title in land with reference to the doctrine of estates and the remedies.

6. MEGARRY, R.E. and WADE, H.W.R. *The Law of Real Property*, (4th ed., Stevens & Sons Ltd, 1975), pp. 33–39, 1003–1010: this also is an explanation of the nature of title in land with reference to the effect of limitation.

7. DENMAN, D.R. *Origins of Ownership*, (Allen & Unwin, Ltd, 1958): in this study the evolution of ownership in land is traced in detail. It might be consulted for the background.

8. THAYER, A.S. "Possession and Ownership", (1907), 23 LQR, 175, 314: possession and ownership are investigated with reference to Roman and English law. In the latter part he discusses the relativity of ownership in English law.

9. KIRALFY, A.K.R. "The Problem of a Law of Property in Goods", (1949), 12 MLR, 424: the evolution of ownership in chattels is dealt with. There are signs now of the recognition of an absolute ownership in them.

10. NOYES, C.R. *The Institution of Property*, (Humphrey Milford, 1936): this work may be used for reference. It examines the nature of property and ownership in Roman law and its evolution in English feudal law. The modern structure is analysed.

11. BENTHAM, J. *Works*, (ed. J. Bowring, William Tait, 1843), I, pp. 308–9: property is the creation of law; it is the foundation of the expectation of deriving certain advantages from the thing said to be possessed.

12. AUSTIN, J. *Lectures on Jurisprudence*, (5th ed., R. Campbell, John Murray, 1885), II, pp. 774–783, 789–802: things and ownership are considered in a general way. He also considers what he calls "modes of property", which include life interests.

13. TERRY, H.T. *Some Leading Principles of Anglo-American Law Expounded with a*

View to its Classification, Arrangement and Codification, (T. & J.W. Johnson & Co, Philadelphia, 1884), ss. 45–47: this is chiefly an examination of "thing", drawing attention to some of the analytical difficulties.

1. CROSSLEY VAINES, J. *Personal Property*, (4th ed., Butterworths, 1967), chap. 4: attention is drawn to the distinction between ownership of real and personal property.

2. BATTERSBY, G. and PRESTON, A.D. "The Concepts of 'Property', 'Title' and 'Owner' used in the Sale of Goods Act 1893" (1972) 35 MLR 268: these terms in the Act can only be understood against the background of the general meaning of property in goods. Looked at in this light the Sale of Goods Act has a more coherent structure than is commonly supposed. The idea of relative title is fundamental in the law. The uses of the terms in different sections are explained.

3. KEETON, G.W. *The Elementary Principles of Jurisprudence*, (2nd ed., Sir Isaac Pitman & Sons, Ltd, 1949), chap. 14: this contains a general discussion of co-ownership and of legal and equitable ownership.

4. PATON, G.W. *A Text-Book of Jurisprudence*, (4th ed., G.W. Paton and D.P. Derham, Clarendon Press, Oxford, 1972), chap. 21: there is a useful discussion of the concept of thing and of ownership.

5. POUND, R. *Jursiprudence*, (West Publishing Co, 1959), V, chap. 30: ownership is dealt with in detail. The limitations imposed upon its component liberties and powers have always existed, it is the emphasis that has varied.

6. HOLLAND, T.E. *The Elements of Jurisprudence*, (13th ed., Oxford, 1924), pp. 101–107, 208–216: in the earlier part things are discussed and classified; the latter part is a general discussion of ownership.

7. MARKBY, W. *Elements of Law*, (6th ed., Oxford, 1905), chap. 8: he appears to subscribe to the "residuary right" view of ownership. He does not define ownership, but owner. A discussion of the peculiar English doctrine of estates is included.

8. HEARN, W.E. *The Theory of Legal Duties and Rights*, (John Ferres, Melbourne; Trubner & Co, London, 1883), chap. 10, s. 1: ownership is a collective term for an aggregate of "rights". These are generally described.

9. POLLOCK, F. *A First Book of Jurisprudence*, (6th ed., Macmillan & Co, Ltd), Part I, chaps. 6–7: the first chapter is concerned with "thing", (see also "What is a 'Thing'?" (1894), 10 LQR 318); the latter part of the second chapter deals with ownership. This describes it in terms of the residue of the privileges of use and powers of disposal allowed by law.

10. VINDING KRUSE, L.F. *The Right of Property*, (Oxford University Press, I (trans. P.T, Federspiel, 1939), II (trans. D. Philip, 1953): this is of general interest. The first volume, which deals with types and objects of property is of greater relevance than the second, which is a detailed account of the transfer of property. Of particular interest are the analysis of thing (p. 121), real and personal rights (p. 124) and the limitations of property (p. 165).

11. WILSON, G.P. "Jurisprudence and the Discussion of Ownership" (1957), CLJ 216:

it is suggested that ownership should be considered in the context of the use of things.

1. For some of the difficulties and doubts concerning the concept of thing, the following might be consulted: H.W. ELPHINSTONE: "What is a Chose in Action?" (1893), 9 LQR 311; C. SWEET: "Choses in Action" (1894), 10 LQR 303, (on the whole agreeing with Elphinstone); S. BROADHURST: "Is Copyright a Chose in Action?" (1895), 11 LQR 64; T.C. WILLIAMS: "Property, Things in Action and Copyright", *ibid*, 223 (replying to Broadhurst); C. SWEET: "Choses in Action", *ibid*, 238. (See also F. Pollock, *supra*).

2. CAMPBELL, A.H. "Some Footnotes to Salmond's Jurisprudence" (1940), 7 CLJ 206, at pp. 217–220: there are observations on trust and beneficial ownership and legal and equitable ownership, and also critical comments on Salmond's thesis as to ownership.

3. SCOTT, A.W. *The Law of Trusts*, (3rd ed., Little, Brown & Co, 1967), ss. 1, 130: it is argued that under the guide of enforcing personal rights the Chancellors evolved a new property interest, a form of equitable ownership. The beneficiary's interest is treated as an equitable estate in land.

4. SCOTT, A.W. "The Nature of the Rights of the Cestui Que Trust", (1917), 17 Col LR, 269: the nature of the beneficiary's interest in the trust property is discussed and the views of various writers are considered. The conclusion is that it is an interest in the property, a kind of ownership.

5. WILLIAMS, G.L. "Interests and Clogs" (1952), 30 Can BR 1004: what is meant by an "interest in property" is considered. This does not deal directly with the beneficiary's interest in trust property but the discussion is useful for the light it throws on this matter.

6. LATHAM, V. "The Right of the Beneficiary to Specific Items of the Trust Funds" (1954), 32 Can BR 520: this is an important discussion as to how far the beneficiary "owns" the subject-matter of the trust. Attention is drawn to the demands of justice and convenience in resolving this question in different situations.

7. STONE, H.F. "The Nature of the Rights of the *Cestui Que Trust*" (1917), 17 Col LR 467: this is in reply to A.W. Scott (*supra*). The beneficiary has only personal rights against the trustee and no proprietary rights in the *res*.

8. HART, W.G. "What is a Trust?" (1899), 15 LQR 294: towards the end of this article useful observations are made on the nature of "trust ownership".

9. HART, W.G. "The Place of Trust in Jurisprudence" (1912), 28 LQR 290: after a discussion of the various views as to whether trusts create real or personal rights, the conclusion is drawn that they are personal.

10. MAITLAND, F.W. *Equity*, (ed. J.W. Brunyate, Cambridge University Press, 1936), pp. 17, 29–32, 106–152: he denied that law and equity were in conflict and that the beneficiary was not the owner of the trust property because the trustee was. Equitable rights are *in personam* with a resemblance to rights *in rem*.

11. LANGDELL, C.C. *A Brief Survey of Equity Jurisdiction*, (2nd ed., The Harvard Law Review Association, 1908), chap. 1: equitable rights are *in personam*.

1. WINFIELD, P.H. *The Province of the Law of Tort*, (Cambridge University Press, 1931), pp. 109–112: the beneficiary's right is considered and the views of the chief protagonists are mentioned. He thinks the right is *in rem*.

2. HANBURY, H.G. "The Field of Modern Equity" (1929), 45 LQR 196, 197–199: equitable rights and interests are hybrids standing mid-way between rights *in rem* and *in peronam.* See also *Modern Equity*, (10th ed., R.H. Maudsley, Stevens & Sons Ltd, 1976), pp. 446 *et seq.*

3. SWAN, K.R. "Patent Rights in an Employee's Invention" (1959), 75 LQR 77: this is of general interest. It deals with the ownership of inventions and considers the position as between employer and employee.

4. WIREN, S.A. "The Plea of the *Jus Tertil* in Ejectment" (1925), 41 LQR 139: this contains a full examination of the authorities as at that date.

5. ATIYAH, P.S. "A Re-examination of the *Jus Tertil* in Conversion" (1955), 18 MLR 97: this is a critical account of the generally accepted view. The article is indirectly relevant on the question whether absolute ownership in chattels is recognised or not.

6. JOLLY, A. "The *Jus Tertii* and the Third Man" (1955), 18 MLR 371: a reply to P.S. Atiyah which throws light on the right to obtain possession as constituting ownership.

7. BUCKLAND, W.W. *A Text-Book of Roman Law from Augustus to Justinian*, (3rd ed., P. Stein, Cambridge University Press, 1963), pp. 186–189: this is a brief description of *dominium* in Roman law, which might be contrasted with the idea of ownership in English law.

8. ALLOTT, A.N. "Towards a Definition of 'Absolute Ownership'" (1961), JAL 99: this is of general interest, especially the suggested final definition. The problem is considered mainly with reference to African land law. See also S.R. SIMPSON: "Towards a Definition of 'Absolute Ownership' II", *ibid*, p. 145: this criticises the need for a definition and the definition itself; A.N. Allott's reply, *ibid*, p. 148.

9. VINOGRADOFF, P. *Outlines of Historical Jurisprudence*, (Oxford University Press, 1922), II, chap. 10: this considers the extent to which and the basis on which things are attributed to persons. It varies in different systems according to the social order. This thesis is developed mainly with reference to Greek law.

10. MALINOWSKI, B. *Crime and Custom in Savage Society*, (Kegan Paul, Trench, Trubner & Co, Ltd, 1926), chap. 2: this is of general interest. It deals with ownership among the Tobriand islanders. Ownership carried distinct obligations.

11. LOWIE, R.H. "Incorporeal Property in Primitive Society" (1927–28), 37 Yale LJ 551: this is also of general interest. It deals with the extent to which ownership was recognised in primitive societies. There is a form of communism up to a point (ownership of necessaries), but private ownership of incorporeal property (spells and incantations).

12. LLOYD, D. *The Idea of Law*, (Penguin Books, Ltd, A 688, 1964), pp. 319–25: the difficulties of comprehending the nature of ownership are indicated with reference to the ownership of "property", of "rights" and of "things".

Ownership in relation to society

1. COHEN, M.R. "Property and Sovereignty" in *Law and the Social Order*, (Harcourt, Brace & Co, New York, 1933), 41: property and sovereignty are now distinguished, but early law makes no such distinction. This is because ownership of land meant political power. Property as power, the justifications of property and limitations on property rights are dealt with.

2. PHILBRICK, F.S. "Changing Conceptions of Property in Law" (1938), 86 U Pa LR 691: the distinction is drawn between property for use, which is held for consumption, and property for power, which is available for alienation. These two ideas are developed in some detail.

3. ELY, R.T. *Property and Contract in their Relation to the Distribution of Wealth*, (The Macmillan Co, New York, 1914) I, Book I, chap. 3, 5: property, private property, public property are defined and discussed with reference to their individual and social aspects.

4. HALLOWELL, A.I. "The Nature and Function of Property as a Social Institution", (1943), I JL Pol S, 115: property implies not only rights and duties but also specific social sanctions. The core of property as a social institution lies in a complex system of recognised rights and duties with reference to the control of valuable objects.

5. HARDING, R.W. "The Evolution of Roman Catholic Views of Private Property as a Natural Right" (1963), 2 Sol Q 124: it is alleged that Thomas Aquinas did not regard private property as a natural right, but as a right which natural law permitted and condoned. It derives its strength from convenience, not principle. Common ownership, however, was the natural right. The change in doctrine to the effect that private ownership is a natural right is a subsequent development ascribed to Papal interpretation.

6. BRODERICK, A. "The Radical Middle: The Natural Right of Property in Aquinas and the Popes", (1964), 3 Sol Q 127: R.W. Harding's thesis is refuted. For Aquinas private property is a natural right. When human reason, reflecting upon experience, perceives that general benefit would not best be achieved by common property, then private property comes into being. Hence, in so far as private property rests on a judgment of the consequences by human reason, it is a natural right. On this basis later Papal Encyclicals are examined so as to show that they did not discard Aquinas's doctrine of common property and substitute an absolutist doctrine.

7. BERLE, A.A. and MEANS, G.C. *The Modern Corporation and Private Property*, (The Macmillan Co, New York, 1939), Books I and II: this discusses corporate ownership and how this has brought about the divorce between ownership and control.

8. JONES, J.W. "Forms of Ownership", (1947–48), 22 Tul LR, 82: the most important part of this article for present purposes is the discussion of the "control" theory of ownership and "value" theory which seeks to protect as many interests as possible from expropriation.

9. FRIEDMANN, W. *Law in a Changing Society*, (Stevens & Sons, Ltd, 1959), chap. 3: this discusses the part played by property in society, with mention of the concept

of the trust and estates and shows how a functional and elastic concept has developed. The changes brought about by corporate enterprise are also touched on. (This is a revised version of *Law and Social Change in Contemporary Britain*, (Stevens & Sons, Ltd, 1951), chap. 2.)

1. COHEN, M.R. and COHEN, F.S. *Readings in Jurisprudence and Legal Philosophy*, (Prentice-Hall Inc, New York, 1951), chap. 1: extracts from a number of writers, ancient and modern, are given, including a number already referred to above. This is a most useful compilation.

2. STONE, J. *Social Dimensions of Law and Justice*, (Stevens & Sons, Ltd, 1966), pp. 243–254: ownership is considered with reference to the prevailing social and economic order according to which the law protects interests in property. The sociological implications of philosophic theories of property are also dealt with.

3. RENNER, K. *The Institutions of Private Law and their Social Functions*, (trans. A. Schwarzschild, ed. O. Kahn-Freund, Routledge & Kegan Paul, Ltd, 1949): this classic analysis is mainly concerned with showing how the owner-producer has been replaced by the capitalist employer and labouring employee. The editor's introduction should also be read in which attention is drawn to certain developments which have taken place since Renner wrote. (See W. FRIEDMANN: *Legal Theory*, 5th ed., Stevens & Sons, Ltd, 1967, pp. 368–373, for a summary of Renner's thesis).

4. STEIN, P.G. and SHAND, J. *Legal Values in Western Society*, (Edinburgh University Press, 1974), chap. 9: this chapter discusses in general terms property as a value, its justification, contents and modern developments. There is also a brief section on the Marxist analysis of property.

5. AVINERI, S. *The Social and Political Thought of Karl Marx* (Cambridge University Press, 1970), chap. 6: the author refutes the charge made by J. BURNHAM, *The Managerial Revolution* (Putnam & Co, Ltd, 1944), that Karl Marx had failed to take account of the managerial revolution. Marx did foresee it (*Capital*, Foreign Languages Publishing House, Moscow, 1954, Vol. III, chap. 27), but he treated it as an internal development of capitalism whereby the capitalist becomes alienated from his capital just as the worker becomes alienated from his labour.

6. HAZARD, J.N. *Law and Social Change in the U.S.S.R.*, (Stevens & Sons, Ltd, 1953), chap 1: property is the key to power, and ownership is an instrument of social change. An account of nationalisation in Russia is given.

7. GSOVSKI, V. *Soviet Civil Law*, (Ann Arbor, University of Michigan Law School, 1948), I, chap. 16: the nature of ownership in Russia is explained. Within the limits of the law, the owner has the right to possess, liberty to use and power to dispose. An account is also given of "personal ownership", which is said to differ from private ownership in capitalist countries.

8. *The Law of the Soviet State*, (ed. A.Y. Vyshinski, trans. H.W. Babb, The Macmillan Co, New York, 1948), chap. 3, s. 5: this considers the economic basis of the Soviet order. It explains in an entirely partial manner the progress of the USSR towards nationalising means of production and the two forms of socialist property, state property and property of the co-operative societies, on the one hand, and private property on the other.

1. SCAMMELL, E.H. "Nationalisation in Legal Perspective", (1952), 5 CLP, 30: the
    question of national ownership is considered with reference to commercial
    undertakings and services, the common features of difficult cases and their
    implications.

2. JEWKES, J. "The Nationalisation of Industry", (1953), 20 UCLR, 615: this
    discusses the pros and cons of nationalisation in Britain with reference to its
    efficiency in raising the standard of living. The conclusion is that nationalisation
    has proved barren.

3. HANSON, A.H. *Parliament and Public Ownership*, (Cassell & Co, Ltd, 1961): the
    question of the nature and extent of parliamentary control over nationalised
    industries is considered. It provides useful general reading.

4. *Nationalisation. A Book of Readings*, (ed A.H. Hanson, Allen & Unwin, Ltd, 1963):
    the editor's "Introduction" gives a brief, general idea of the why and the how of
    nationalisation. The extracts give detailed analyses of particular aspects.

15. Legal Change

1. SCARMAN, L.G. *English Law – the New Dimension*, (Hamlyn Lectures, Stevens & Sons, Ltd, 1974): in his Hamlyn Lectures a judge of the Court of Appeal begins by stressing the need for a legal system to adapt to change if it is to survive. He proceeds to consider the challenge from overseas in the form of the need to entrench human rights and for a new attitude towards legislation emanating from the Common Market. The social challenge is most important: the welfare state throws up problems concerning distributive rather than corrective justice, and if the law cannot adapt to this situation, then the system will develop outside legal control. He goes on to consider the problem of environmental integrity and the multitude of problems posed in industrial relations and by devolution. In conclusion he considers the feasibility of a written constitution with a Bill of Rights and curtailment of unlimited legislative power.

2. FRIEDMANN, W. *Law in a Changing Society*, (Stevens & Sons, Ltd, 1959): the book begins with a demonstration of how law has reacted to social change, and also how it can be used to readjust interests and institutions so as to meet change. It then proceeds to deal specifically with developments in different branches of law. See also *Law and Social Change in Contemporary Britain*, (Stevens & Sons, Ltd, 1951), which represents an earlier version of the same theme.

3. WEERAMANTRY, C.G. *The Law in Crisis. Bridges of Understanding*, (Capemoss, London, 1975), especially chap. 5: law must keep pace with society. There is increasing disillusion with law because of a variety of factors amongst which the failure of lawyers to communicate with the public figures prominently. In Chapter 5 particular stress is laid on the need to adapt to movements in philosophy, power, commerce and technology.

4. POUND, R. "The Task of the Law in the Atomic Age" in *Law, State and International Legal Order. Essays in Honor of Hans Kelsen* (edd. S. Engel and R.A. Metall, University of Tennessee Press, 1964), p. 233: Man is surrounded by dangers from the development of technology by unleashing forces which he cannot control. The chief task of law is to uphold security. In the past methods were evolved to achieve this by certain forms of trial procedures, principles of liability and systems of punishment and redress. These methods are inadequate to deal with modern problems. Therefore we must not hesitate to change institutions when they cease to be relevant.

5. SILKIN, S.C. "The Rights of Man and the Rule of Law" (1977) 28 NILQ 3: the "rule of law" is a framework within which can be set man's needs in a changing society. The idea expresses the need for order, but it must also provide machinery for adaptation. Protection of the Rights of Man is considered in this context.

6. *Is Law Dead?* (ed. E.V. Rostow, Simon and Schuster, New York, 1971): D.M. POTTER: "Changing Patterns of Social Cohesion and the Crisis of Law under a System of Government by Consent", chap. 7: this paper traces American development since the Civil War. The idea of consent has changed with the changed character of the society. R.L. HEILBRONER: "The Roots of Social Neglect in the United States", chap. 8: why is America not the most advanced state socially although it is the richest? The negro population has tended to identify need with race, there is little idea of social magnanimity and there is no social-democratic working class party. H. CRUSE: "The Historical Roots of American Social Change and Social Theory", chap. 9: change through law should be possible,

since there is an implied social theory for democratic social change built into the American scheme of society. M. HARRINGTON: "Revolution", chap. 10: the Marxist idea of violent revolution has become outdated. What is needed is a legal revolution. W.H. RIKER: "Public Safety as a Public Good", chap. 11: public peace is something that no one can achieve alone. Everyone should partake in it.

Technological Development: Computers

1. TAPPER, C.F.H. *Computers and the Law*, (Weidenfeld and Nicolson, 1973): this is the first systematic treatise in Britain. It is written in non-technical language. After explaining the working of computers, it goes on to consider their impact on the law of evidence, privacy, legislation, case-law, litigation, international law and land registration. In the course of the whole book there is ample demonstration of how law has had to adapt to the new technique and also of the need to adapt still further.

2. TAPPER, C.F.H. "The Uses of Computers for Lawyers", (1965), 8 JSPTL (NS) 261: the use of computers in law in Great Britain has been backward largely because the profession is unable to cope with the cost involved and because of the special problems involved in law. The possible uses of computerization to lawyers are enumerated. Of these information storage and retrieval are paramount. How this could be made to work is discussed in detail.

3. TAPPER, C.F.H. "The Solicitor and the Computer" (1968) 118 New LJ 55: the solicitor has to provide an essentially human service to clients, which cannot be computerised. It is all the more important, therefore, to relieve him of routine work which can be computerised so that he may devote more time and energy to the human tasks. Suggestions are offered as to recording the legal histories of clients (cf. medical records), registers and police records and how legal information might be classified and stored according to the concepts involved.

4. DICKERSON, F.R. "Some Jurisprudential Implications of Electronic Data Processing", (1963), 28 LCP, 53: computerization is a help, not a substitute for the methods of lawyers. The chief objections to its use are considered in detail and shown to spring from uninformed or unreal fears.

5. DICKERSON, F.R. "Automation and the Lawyer", (1965), *Res Gestae*, 5: the various possible uses of computers to lawyers in their daily work and to legal researchers is outlined. Some indication is also given of the likely impact of such new techniques, principally in the law of evidence.

6. FREED, R.N. "Prepare Now for Machine-assisted Legal Research" (1961) 47 Am BAJ 764: legal research is a two-stage operation, collation of relevant information and analysis of it. Computers can help the former process, but their success will depend on indexing.

7. J.T.E. "Computers and Discovery" (1967) 117 New LJ 917: the existing rules governing judicial orders for discovery will have to be reconsidered in the light of computer techniques of storing and retrieving information.

8. HOWELL, B.R. "Law and the Computer" (1968) 6 Legal Exec 120: this short article reviews the developments that have taken place and the research that is being done in Britain and in America. The uses of computers to lawyers are outlined.

1. HUDSON, C.A. "Some Reflections on Information Retrieval" (1968) 6 Os HLJ 259:
   the article begins with a survey of the methods of information storage that have
   been used since pre-Norman times. Case-law depends not only on how a case
   happens to be reported, but also on what cases the reporter chooses to report.
   If every decision were computerized the conception of case-law will alter. So, too,
   computerization of statute-law could reduce the human element between the
   source of information and its recipients.

2. POPE, K.S. "The Lawyer and the Computer" (1969) 43 Aust LJ 463: the manager
   of a computer manufacturing firm explains the working of computers and the
   ways in which they could assist lawyers. Non-technical people will find an interesting and simple account of how computers work.

3. LEITCH, W.A. "A Canadian Contrast on 'Computers and the Law'" (1969) 20
   NILQ 274: computers can search at great speed and with great accuracy. After an
   account of the uses and working of computers, the author considers the reactions
   of certain lawyers.

4. GOTTSCHALK, K. "The Computer and the Law" (1969) 66 LS Gaz 168: four
   problems are discussed. (1) At what stage should there by copyright protection
   for authors whose materials are computerized – at input or output stage? (2)
   Should there be copyright or patent protection for programs? (3) How may the
   individual's right to privacy be safeguarded when with the aid of computers a
   great deal of information can be collated easily? (4) How far are computer data
   admissible as evidence? Computers, it is said, can aid the law, in three ways,
   namely by facilitating information retrieval, helping in the prevention and detec-
   tion of crime and in performing everyday legal processes.

5. BELLORD, N.J. "Computers and Lawyers – a Personal View" (1974) 124 New LJ
   858: the computer is to intellectual processes what the steam engine was to
   industrial processes. Lawyers will have to master this new technique if they are
   not to be swept aside, and it is easier for them to bridge the gap than for computer experts to master the law. The article provides a very good explanation of
   what computers are and do.

6. STEPHENS, G.E. "The Lawyer and the Computer" (1975) Lloyd's MCLQ 166: the
   knowledge that computers can retrieve should be adapted to the needs of lawyers.
   There must be no loss of justice. There are certain benefits from case retrieval,
   and from the uses of models for teaching and research and to explore new fields.
   Legal classifications for producing computer tables will open up new areas of
   study.

7. RUOFF, T. "Soon every Solicitor will need a Computer" (1976) 120 SJ 363,
   379, 394, 414: the main problem is to overcome prejudice. The articles review the
   value of computers in assessing payments, time recording, accounts and keeping
   trust accounts. Difficulties may arise through use of incompatible systems. The
   best way of utilising the new techniques for storing information in vital books,
   drafting wills and engrossments is also dealt with.

8. WHITE, R.C.A. "Information Storage and Retrieval of Legal Materials" (1972) 69
   LS Gaz 730: the problem as to how a lawyer researches has been insufficiently
   investigated. More progress has been made on the semantic-linguistic problem of
   how to index and analyse material. How are questions to be framed? How are

documents to be labelled? The article reviews in detail the experiments of various pioneers and organisations.

1. CAMPBELL, C.M. "Law and Computers" (1970) SLT 197: this is a report of a conference on the impact of computers concerning privacy, copyright, evidence, aids to legal work, full storage or abstracts of texts, financial problems and production of documents.

2. MELVILLE, L. "Legal Protection of Softwear" (1969) 119 New LJ 1169: programmes require great skill and cost and "softwear houses" have sprung up. Consideration is given to the extension of the law of patents and copyright to novel concepts and of the law of hire and sale. The question of a Softwear Act is also considered.

3. McFARLANE, G. "Legal Protection of Computer Programs" (1970) JBL 204: hardware (machines) are protected by patent law; proprietary rights in softwear (what is fed into machines) poses many difficulties. Copyright law involves the question when softwear is "published" and what constitutes "infringement".

4. MELVILLE, L. "Can Computer Programs be Protected?" (1976) LS Gaz 568: the problems of protecting softwear is further considered. Could they be patented? The differences of opinion and the problems are reviewed in the light of some British and American cases.

5. TAPPER, C.F.H. *Computers and the Law*, (Weidenfeld and Nicolson, 1973), chap. 3: the danger to privacy is investigated at length. It is pointed out that this may not be as great as might appear, but there is real danger nonetheless. Suggested safeguards include the filing of information under topics rather than individuals, the creation of a controlling agency with power to issue binding directives, the regular publication of the purposes for which information is required, constant scrutiny by a review body and the evolution of a code of professional ethics.

6. *Computers and Privacy*, Cmnd. 6353, 6354: the problems are further reviewed in this White Paper, and a number of the suggestions made by Mr Tapper have been adopted and recommended.

7. MICHAEL, D.N. "Speculations on the Relation of the Computer to Individual Freedom and the Right to Privacy" (1964–65) 33 Geo Wash LR 270: the speculations are limited to the next twenty years, since after that people's values will have changed completely. Computers enable the easy and rapid collation of data which at present is scattered and open up possibilities of recording new data, keeping track of individuals, and generally making such data available. The impact of these possibilities on privacy and freedom is considered.

8. MILLER, A.R. "Personal Privacy in the Computer Age: the Challenge of a New Technology in an Information Oriented Society" (1969) 67 Mich LR 1091: computers provide a new form of power. It can be beneficial, but it also has grave dangers to privacy, which is fundamental to democratic traditions of individual autonomy. It is necessary therefore to start now to solve the privacy problems. In this 155-page article the author examines in great detail the practice and use of computer techniques and the dangers which they pose.

9. GOTLIEB, A.E. "Computers and Privacy" (1971) 2 Can BJ (N.S.) No. 4, p. 27: computers have instilled fear in laymen because of their capabilities. The author

considers whether it might be possible to establish a connection between machines and the values of society via the ways in which they are used. The greatest current threat is to privacy and possible safeguards are explored.

1. WHITEAR, G. "Privacy and the Computer" (1972) 122 New LJ 555: computers have proved successful in the actual legal process. But there is danger in the area of individual rights. Should information be centralised? What is needed may be a system of authorisation. Various alternative safeguards are considered.

2. CORBETT, J. "Computers and the Protection of Privacy" (1976) 126 New LJ 556: privacy is not a simple idea; it is related to other values, e.g., freedom of speech. Two kinds of computer systems are the statistical information system and the intelligence system. The latter poses a threat in that more information about a person may be gathered than is necessary. The extent of this problem is considered and the White Paper recommendations.

3. ANONYMOUS. "Computer Privacy" (1972) 136 LGR 631: this deals with the possibility of the misuse of personal records. The notes of guidance issued by the Computer Panel of the Local Authorities Management Services and Computer Committee are considered and the points to watch are outlined.

4. WESTIN, A.F. *Privacy and Freedom* (Atheneum, New York, 1967): this is of general interest, dealing with the history of privacy and the new tools that have been developed for invading privacy. Chapter 7 concerns information collection and data surveillance.

5. WESTIN, A.F. and BAKER, M.A. *Databanks in a Free Society – Computers, Record-keeping and Privacy* (Quadrangle Books, New York, 1972): fourteen uses of computer databanks are examined in order to assess the likely effects of computers and how far it is possible to regulate them through courts, legislation and administrative processes. Computers have increased efficiency, reduced mistakes and provided broader bases for decisions.

6. RULE, J.B. *Private Lives and Public Surveillance* (Allen Lane, 1973): for the purpose of social control there has to be a large-scale system of surveillance, which is not prohibitive in cost, and which shows when rules are broken and obeyed and by whom. The most economic and efficient is when the clientele itself contacts the system and so supplies the necessary information.

Medical Developments

For the impact of medical developments on legal concepts, it will be useful to consult some of the references in Chapter 11 on "Conduct", especially under the headings "Automatism", "Causation", "Omission" and "Negligence".

7. SIMPSON, C.K. "The Moment of Death: a New Medico-legal Problem" (1968) 112 SJ 435: new techniques of keeping people alive pose medical, moral and legal problems. A leading pathologist draws attention to some of these.

8. HILLMAN, H. and ALDRIDGE, T.M. "Towards a Legal Definition of Death" (1972) 116 SJ 323: death is not a single instant; it is a continuous loss of organisation. There is an important distinction between the outlook of a medical practitioner, who waits for a later stage of disorganisation, and that of a surgeon needing tissue for transplantation. Six criteria of death are suggested: (i) deep

unconsciousness with no evident improvement over a period of days; (ii) brain
damage as seen by clinical examination; (iii) X-rays of the skull indicating severe
tissue displacement or disorganisation; (iv) dilated pupils (indicating also severe
brain damage); (v) lack of electrical activity in the brain for several consecutive
hours or days; (vi) frequency of respiration or circulation, or the dependence of
these on artificial aids.

1. SKEGG, P.D.G. "Irreversibly Comatose Individuals: 'Alive' or 'Dead'?" (1974) 33
   CLJ 130: these are people who cannot return to consciousness. For the purpose
   of the argument it makes no difference whether the brain is damaged beyond the
   point that there can be no return to spontaneous respiration, or whether it is not
   damaged to that extent. Courts tend to leave the question of death to the medical
   profession. It is urged that irreversebly comatose individuals should legally be
   treated as dead. The consequences of this view are considered.

2. KENNEDY, I.M. "Alive or Dead. The Lawyer's View" (1969) 22 CLP 102: the
   author discusses the moment of death, the law relating to organ transplants and
   a doctor's duty to his patient. The question, what is death? poses potential
   medico-legal conflict. Alternative approaches are considered.

3. KENNEDY, I.M. "The Legal Effect of Requests by the Terminally Ill and the Aged
   not to Receive Further Treatment from Doctors" (1976) Crim LR 217: the issue
   is self-determination vs. paternalism. Consent is at the root of self-determination,
   but this is already limited within narrow, ill-defined limits, and it can be abused.
   The question is whether consent is appropriate at all in a medico-legal context.

4. KENNEDY, I.M. "Switching off Life Support Machines: the Legal Implications"
   (1977) Crim LR 443: three kinds of case are distinguished: the unconscious dying
   patient, the chronically dependent patient (e.g., in an iron lung) and the tempo-
   rarily dependent emergency patient. With regard to the first the crucial decision is
   not switching *off* the machine, but switching it *on*. If the patient meets the
   criteria of brain death, there is no need to switch it on; if he breathes but has no
   ability to sustain himself but still shows signs of brain function, here the decision
   arises as to whether to switch it on. If he breathes and has ability to sustain himself, there is no need to switch it on. With regard to the second category, a distinction has to be drawn between the patient who requests death, and where there is
   no consent.

5. CASTEL, J-G. "Some Legal Aspects of Human Organ Transplantation in Canada"
   (1968) 46 Can BR 345: this is a long and detailed review, beginning with different kinds of transplants and the problem of death. The legal problems are first
   considered in relation to live donors, recipients, hospitals and surgical teams with
   reference to consent of adults, minors, married women and persons of unsound
   mind. The sale of organs and the use of cadavers are also dealt with.

6. BAYLIS, P. "The Legal Aspects of Organ Transplantation" (1970) 10 Med Sci & L
   259: the author sets out the present law concerning organ donations where the
   deceased expressly consented in his life-time and where he did not. He criticises
   the existing law and suggests modifications. The deceased's wish should prevail
   over his family's veto. If he has expressed no wish, only the consent of the
   immediate family should be required. Death should be certified by one or two
   doctors not concerned with the use of the organ. The coroner's consent should
   only be needed if the removal of the organ might interfere with a post mortem.

1. PACE, P.J. "Defining Human Death" (1976) 126 New LJ 1232: the problem is to protect the medical profession, reassure the public and provide help for patients needing transplants. The article reviews various tests proffered by different medical schools and some statutory attempts at definition and prescription of limits.

2. DWORKIN, G. "The Law Relating to Organ Transplantation in England" (1970) 33 MLR 353: the medical, legal and ethical issues are in ferment. The legal position with regard to the use of the human body, or parts of it, is considered in various aspects. This article is useful as a focus of many of the problems involved.

3. ZELLICK, G. "Organ Transplantation" (1972) 122 New LJ 1078: this paper is based mainly on the report of the Bar Council on the medical and social problems involved. The availability of consent has to have limits. With regard to cadaver donors, consent may be given in advance, or there may be implied consent unless a wish has been indicated during life against the use of organs after death. The consent of relatives is also considered. The paper also considers switching off mechanical systems, and the definition of "death".

4. WALTON, T. "When is a Woman not a Woman?" (1974) 124 New LJ 501: this discusses the problem of determining sex and the consequential legal problems that arise. Various different forms of "sex-change" are distinguished. The article is a plea that the law should adapt itself to the increasing facts of society.

Disobedience

5. SINGER, P. *Democracy and Disobedience* (Oxford: Clarendon Press, 1973): in a model democracy the reasons for obedience are that the system represents a fair compromise and the fact of participation. These reasons hold good more or less theoretically in large societies. But the actual workings of Western democracies do not fulfil the first reason and the second only to a limited degree. No satisfactory basis for obedience in large-scale societies has been forthcoming. The author can only suggest certain minor improvements as going some way towards minimising the objections.

6. KADISH, M.R. and KADISH, S.H. *Discretion to Disobey. A Study of Lawful Departures from Legal Rules* (Stanford University Press, 1973): those who benefit from the law need not always have to obey it, for their disobedience may be "legitimated" by the law itself. This thesis, it is submitted, is unsubstantiated. In support are adduced some loose and unconvincing linguistic usages and some instances (e.g., disobedience of an unconstitutional statute, a policeman who fails to arrest, a proescutor who fails to prosecute).

7. RAWLS, J. *A Theory of Justice* (Oxford: Clarendon Press, 1972), especially pp. 350–391: a "just society" is one which is organised on the basis of two basic principles of justice. In a just (or nearly just) society the occasional unjust law should be obeyed, provided its burden is evenly distributed, it is not too onerous in itself and does not infringe the basic principles. The "principle of fairness" enjoins one to abide by the institutions of a just legal order the benefits of which one accepts, and civil disobedience is justified only when there occurs infringement of the basic principles, all other means of redress fail and no injury is inflicted on the innocent.

1. RAWLS, J. "Legal Obligation and the Duty of Fair Play" in *Law and Philosophy. A Symposium*, (ed. S. Hook, New York University Press, 1964), 3: this is the opening contribution, and its thesis is that obedience is based on fair-play – if one accepts the benefits of a just legal order, then fair-play requires one to obey it. But the author's limitations on the scope of this doctrine deprive it of much of its value; the succeeding contributions indicate its weaknesses. This paper is an early version of his later theory of justice.

2. DWORKIN, R.M. *Taking Rights Seriously*, (Duckworth, 1977), chaps. 7 *et seq*.: there is a distinction between a "right to do a thing coupled with a right not to be prevented" and a "right to do it without a right not to be prevented". Fundamental rights are of the first kind; their recognition in a society is the majority's promise to minorities that their dignity and equality will be respected. It is argued that when a majority disobey a law, then respect for law requires that that law ought to be changed. (The implications of such a doctrine are not faced.) There is a further distinction between what a person feels he has a right to do and whether it is a right thing for him to do. Fundamental rights are of the latter kind; the state may interfere in the first kind of situation, but not in the second. Fundamental rights are "rights against government", and are best entrenched in a constitution. See also R.M. DWORKIN, "Taking Rights Seriously" in *Oxford Essays in Jurisprudence (Second Series)*, (ed. A.W.B. Simpson, Oxford University Press, 1973), chap. 8.

3. LLOYD, D. *The Idea of Law*, (Penguin Books, Ltd, A 688, 1964), chaps. 2–3: "legitimate subordination" means obedience to someone who is entitled to require obedience. Such authority may be derived from morality, personal ascendancy of an individual, tradition, or the ascendancy of institutions. Further, although Law has to depend for its ultimate efficacy on the degree to which it is backed by force, this does not mean that Law is force. But force cannot be dispensed with because of the basic aggressive drives in human nature, which have to be repressed in order to subject people to social discipline. In the course of the discussion in Chapter 3 of Law and Morality, the moral duty to obey the law is touched on.

4. STEIN, P.G. and SHAND, J. *Legal Values in Western Society* (Edinburgh University Press, 1974), pp. 46–52: deference to authority is needed to preserve society. The argument that it is unfair to enjoy the benefits of society without a reciprocal obligation presupposes that laws are directed towards the good of society. The discussion includes violent and non-violent disobedience, disobedience to dramatise a cause or to precipitate change as well the limitations of the law.

5. HUGHES, G.B.J. "Civil Disobedience and the Political Question Doctrine", (1968), 43 NYULR, 1: civil disobedience takes two forms: that of an individual refusing to obey, and organised campaigns to change policy or practice. The moral conviction of a law-breaker may be a ground for imposing a light sentence, but this has its danger. Courts do not rule on issues involving "political question", but they should not shelve their responsibilities.

6. TAYLOR, R. "Law and Morality", (1968), 43 NYULR, 611: enforcement and enforceability are the key to the notion of a "law". Considerations of morality do not come in except in relation to "law" considered as an activity, in which case the end to be achieved becomes relevant.

7. LYNN, C. "We must Disobey!" (1968), 43 NYULR, 649: in a very few pages the

point is made that individuals who disobey and are willing to accept the penalty are in fact submitting to the system. If it is the system that has to be changed there has to be mass disobedience.

1. PUNER, N.W. "Civil Disobedience: an Analysis and Rationale" (1968), 43 NYULR, 651: the characteristics and types of civil disobedience and the different attitudes towards obedience are explained first. On this basis the American case-law is examined at length. The conclusion is that civil disobedience has a part to play in human betterment. Obedience is the norm, so disobedience needs to be justified and, within limits, it could be accommodated.

2. WASSERSTROM, R.W. "The Obligation to Obey the Law", in *Essays in Legal Philosophy*, (ed. R.S. Summers, Basil Blackwell, Oxford, 1968), 274: disobeying law is usually wrong, because "illegal" is usually also "immoral" and morally right conduct is usually not illegal. But it does not follow that disobedience is always immoral. The author distinguishes between the claim that there is an absolute obligation to obey the law, and a prime facie obligation, which casts the onus of justifying disobedience on the violator. The various arguments in support of both these claims are considered in turn and rejected.

3. COLE, W.G. "Private Morality and Public Law", (1968), 54 Am BAJ, 158: student and other protesters do not realise the implications of their demands. They claim adult status but do not accept the responsibilities that go with these. There is also a basic lack of loyalty. Private conscience cannot be set above law, because if this happens those who advocate it will be among the first victims.

4. MORRIS, E.F. "American Society and the Rebirth of Civil Obedience", (1968), 54 Am BAJ, 653: dissent and protest are protected by the American Constitution. Disobedience is not quite the same. If it goes beyond a test case it is to be deplored, for it is self-defeating in that it destroys rights. The law must remain supreme.

5. BRAY, J.J. "Law, Liberty and Morality" (1971) 45 Aust LJ 452, pp. 461 *et seq.*: in the concluding part of this paper the author considers disobedience on grounds of conscience. He distinguishes between "This law commands me to do what I think morally wrong"; "This law forbids me to do what I think morally compulsory"; "This law commands me to do what I think is stupid"; and "This law forbids me to do what I think is harmless".

6. DREWRY, G.R. "The Politics of Disobedience" (1972) 122 New LJ 455: political opposition to legislation is one thing, political disobedience is another. A suggested distinction, proposed by a Member of Parliament, is between the ordinary law, which must be obeyed, and political or ideological law, which has to depend on "elected bodies" (e.g., trade unions or local authorities) for implementation. The author rightly criticises this and the vagueness of the proposed distinction.

7. LEWIS, J.U. "Obligation and the Law" (1971) 5 Ottawa LR 84: the author begins by considering various reasons that have been advanced as to why people ought to obey the law, and also the meaning of "obligation". Laws, he says, are prescriptive of behaviour with a view to achieving ends. In his view, obligation should be viewed as a means to such ends. The content of laws are necessary for the attainment of the public good.

8. PARSONS, O.H. "Should All Laws Always be Obeyed?" (1972) 122 New LJ 908:

the "law and order" approach to "rule of law" requires obedience to the enacted law; the "social contract" approach is based on the governed agreeing to abide by laws which are morally reasonable and socially acceptable. The author considers superior orders to commit crimes; laws which offend the conscience of a substantial minority; and laws which are out of touch with current views, especially those which have been steamrollered through by the legislature.

1. SMITH, M.B.E. "Is there a Prima Facie Obligation to Obey the Law?" (1972–73) 82 Yale LJ 950: what governments enjoy legitimate authority? and, have subjects of any government a prima facie obligation to obey? are separate issues. Most people violate trivial laws for a slight gain. Violation of law becomes a matter of moral concern when it is believed to be wrong apart from its illegality. Subjects do have a prima facie obligation to obey particular laws when disobedience of them has serious consequences or goes against *mala in se*. The author considers and rejects the "benefit" theory where individuals who receive benefits from governments are under a duty to obey; the "implied consent" theory; and the "utility" or general good theory.

2. WALZER, M. *Obligations: Essays on Disobedience, War, and Citizenship* (Oxford University Press, 1970), especially Part I: not all obligations, but those included in the book, are said to be based on consent. Conscription is therefore wrong, except in social emergency when social safety is endangered. The state should rely on volunteers. But it is also contended that members of oppressed minorities owe obligations to the rest of their groups even though they have not consented to identify themselves with them. Group disobedience may sometimes impose duties on members to disobey.

3. *Is Law Dead?* (ed. E.V. Rostow, Simon and Schuster, New York, 1971): P. GAY: "Law, Order and Enlightenment", chap. 1: law and order was crucial for men of enlightenment. Formal law concerns its shape and existence, substantive law concerns its content. It is a mistake not to see conflict in legitimate rights and to abridge freedom in the name of freedom. E.V. ROSTOW: "The Rightful Limits of Freedom in a Liberal Democratic State: of Civil Disobedience", chap. 2: the case for civil disobedience is considered and the obligation to obey valid law in a society of consent. There can be no acknowledgement of a right of civil disobedience. In this detailed inquiry the position of negroes and students under a system of social contract is considered. R.P. WOLFF: "In Defense of Anarchism", chap. 3: a reasoned case is put forward that the theory of democracy is wrong. There are no circumstances in which a state can validly demand obedience. The solution lies in moral autonomy. C. DYKE: "Freedom, Consent, and the Costs of Interaction", chap. 4: the concept of freedom, will, freedom and community and freedom and consent are analysed. Freedom is a political problem. It becomes necessary to act so as to force a mutual adjustment of freedom in a society. H. ARENDT: "Civil Disobedience", chap. 6: civil disobedience is compatible with American laws. It must be given the same niche as other special interests and allow it representation so as to influence Congress.

4. DAUBE, D. *Civil Disobedience in Antiquity* (Edinburgh U.P. 1972): these six lectures are of general interest. In them the author deals with instances of non-violent resistance to authority among the ancient Jews, Greeks and Romans. The underlying message is that practically every form of current protest is matched in history from which lessons may usefully be learned by all sides.

Machinery of Change

1. MAINE, H.J.S. *Ancient Law*, (ed. F. Pollock, John Murray, 1930), chaps. 1–3: in this classic work the author distinguishes between "static" and "progressive" societies. The characteristic feature of the latter is they develop their law beyond the point reached by both through legal fictions, equity and legislation. (Modern anthropologists question whether these stages were as clearly separated as Maine had imagined.) See A.S. DIAMOND, *Primitive Law*, (2nd ed., Longmans, Green & Co, 1971), especially p. 346; O. KAHN-FREUND, "Recent Legislation on Matrimonial Property" (1970), 33 MLR 601, who points out that in matrimonial property the courts appear to have moved from equity to fiction.

2. VAIHINGER, H. *The Philosophy of "As If"*, (trans. C.K. Ogden, Routledge & Kegan Paul, Ltd, 1924): this is of general interest only. The author points out that the use of fictions is indispensable to the working of the human mind.

3. FULLER, L.L. *Legal Fictions*, (Stanford University Press, 1967): this book reproduces three articles in (1930–31) 25 Ill LR. The nature of fictions, their use, the parts they play, and their classification are elaborately set out. In the second chapter the motivations behind the resort to fictions are investigated. The final chapter considers whether fictions are indispensable to human thinking, and in this connection the view of Vaihinger is considered.

4. ARISTOTLE. *Nichomachean Ethics*, (trans. H. Rackham, The Loeb Classical Library, William Heinemann, Ltd, 1938), V: the principle of distributive justice requires equal distribution among equals and that of corrective justice is to redress the balance when this has been disturbed. But over and above this there develops a need for a justice that will correct legal justice. This is equity, the function of which is to mitigate in diverse ways the effects of a strict application of law in particular cases.

5. *Equity in the World's Legal Systems. A Comparative Study* (ed. R.A. Newman, Établissements Émile Bruylant, Brussels, 1973): this collection of 33 essays by scholars from East and West provides one of the best surveys of the role of equity in legal development and reform. It covers equity in ancient Jewish, Roman, Canon, Muslin and medieval common law, as well as modern English, Scots, French, German, Swiss, Belgian, Dutch, Italian, Spanish, Argentinian, Japanese, Greek, Swedish, Hungarian, Russian, Chinese, Polish and International law.

6. BUCKLAND, W.W. *Equity in Roman Law*, (University of London Press, 1911): Roman equity originated not solely through the work of the praetors, but in a large measure through the commentaries of the jurists and, in a lesser degree, through imperial legislation. In this book the author shows how Roman Law had anticipated the English rules of equity.

7. BUCKLAND, W.W. "Praetor and Chancellor" (1939) 13 Tul LR 163: the Roman praetor and the English Chancellor are obvious parallels. The contributions of both are carefully assessed.

8. STEIN, P.G. *Regulae Iuris. From Juristic Rules to Legal Maxims*, (Edinburgh University Press, 1966): *lex* connoted declared law, *jus* connoted law crystallised out of decisions. The idea of "rule", *regula*, was imported into law from the Grammarians for whom it connoted "guide". The way in which the jurists and later the emperors developed and married the threads is traced out in detail.

9. VINOGRADOFF, P. *Common-Sense in Law*, (3rd ed., H.G. Hanbury, Oxford University Press, 1959), chap. 8: this gives consideration to the concept of equity. It deals with the part played by fairness in the interpretative process.

1. HOHFELD, W.N. *Fundamental Legal Conceptions as Applied in Judicial Reasoning*,
   (ed. W.W. Cook, Yale University Press; London: Humphrey Milford, 1923), chap.
   3: the table of jural relations is applied to demonstrating that common law and
   equity did conflict, despite Maitland's dictum to the contrary. This is a technical
   article, but does illustrate indirectly the part played by equity in English law.

2. DENNING, A.T. "The Need for a New Equity" (1952) 5 CLP 1: English equity has
   become too rigid. Legislation is unable to effect remedies because it is slow and
   uncertain. Some put certainty before justice; others put justice before certainty.
   The task is to strike the right balance, but it is very necessary that the due needs
   of justice should be met.

3. DENNING, A.T. "The Way of an Iconoclast" (1959) 5 JSPTL (N.S.) 77: a judge,
   who has modified legal doctrines more often than most in order to keep them
   abreast of modern needs, reviews several areas of the law where long cherished
   doctrines were challenged.

4. KEETON, R.E. *Venturing to do Justice. Reforming Private Law* (Oxford University
   Press, 1969): the conflict between continuity and creativity is constant. The role
   of the judiciary in law reform is considered first in conjunction with the legislature. There should be maximum judicial creativity; illustrations are given in the
   development of American tort law.

Law Reform

5. *Jeremy Bentham and the Law. A Symposium* (edd. G.W. Keeton and G. Schwarzenberger, Stevens & Sons, Ltd, 1948): Bentham still remains as the greatest reformer
   Britain has produced. It is not practicable to itemise his manifold ideas, many of
   which have long since been accepted. This collection of essays, especially Part II,
   gives some idea of his contribution.

6. KIRBY, M.D. "Law Reform, Why?" (1976) 50 Aust LJ 459: there is tension
   between stability and change. Law reform is not simply change, but change for
   the better. Therefore, law reformers should face the values which they use as their
   touchstone. Reform is needed to repair the inadequacy of law when current laws
   are overtaken by technology; to remove outmoded laws which are out of step
   with current morality and values; to remove injustice by righting plain wrongs;
   to simplify the law and make it more accessible.

7. SCARMAN, L.G. "Lawyers and the Welfare State" (1976) 10 JALT 67: changes are
   taking place and lawyers should be able to cope with them. The author demonstrates the problem with reference to social security and legal services offered to
   the public.

8. SHATWELL, K.O. "Some Reflections on the Problems of Law Reform" (1957–58)
   31 Aust LJ 325: the author reviews the 19th and 20th century reforms and
   criticises British law revision committees as at that date. There are two patterns
   for reform: "living law" and "book law". He provides a detailed examination of
   the issues and problems.

9. GOODHART, A.L. "Law Reform in England" (1959–60) 33 Aust LJ 126: this is an
   answer to Professor Shatwell. Law reformers should find out the defects of the
   existing law, what practical steps can be taken and foretell the likely results of
   those steps. The author then deals with the work of two special committees in

England dealing with whole fields of law, two dealing with limited topics, and the Law Reform Committee.

1. BEETZ, J. "Reflections on Continuity and Change in Law Reform" (1972) 22 UTLJ 129: factors favouring stability and change are reviewed. The author questions the assumption that private law is of lesser social importance and does not involve policy, as well as the assumption that lawyers should not be concerned with policy. It is too late to begin large-scale short-term reform of substantive law. In the short-term adjectival law should have priority; in the middle and long-term administrative law.

2. SAWER, G. "The Legal Theory of Law Reform" (1970) 20 UTLJ 183: continuous law reform should be a topic for study and instruction. Reform should aim at intelligibility, saving in cost and time, appropriateness to material needs and morality of the day, compatibility with the contemporary sense of justice, punishment should be justifiable by public good and proportioned to the offence, and there should be opportunity for fair trial. There is a distinction between a rule-bound achievement of social purposes and free achievement.

3. WOODMAN, G. "A Basis for a Theory for Law Reform" (1975) 12 UGLJ 1: what is needed is a set of principles of how existing law can be replaced by a better set. The author rejects the *ad hoc* approach and the arguments against a general theory, and also Bentham's utilitarian theory and Pound's interest theory. Law concerns the use of state power, and the desirability of a law is to be judged by its consequences. It is necessary to study the values of the society and the distribution of influence in relation to law-making power, and also to examine all possible laws and their likely effects.

4. *The Division and Classification of the Law* (ed. J.A. Jolowicz, Butterworths, 1970): the first paper by J.A. JOLOWICZ, "Fact Based Classification of Law" argues that law reform should be on a factual, not a conceptual, basis, i.e., of law as it operates in society, taking the facts of social and economic life as they are rather than the conceptual categories of various branches of law. The remaining papers take issue with this thesis, pointing out difficulties and objections.

5. DOWRICK, F.E. "Lawyers' Values for Law Reform" (1963) 79 LQR 556: the work of various bodies that from time to time have been charged with law reform is examined in order to discern the values on which they proceed.

6. DOWRICK, F.E. "Laymens' Values for Law Reform" (1966) 82 LQR 497: a lawyer's role is thought to be to know and apply the law; legislation is an art practised by laymen in Parliament. Most members of Royal Commissions are non-lawyers. The values on which they appear to proceed are examined.

7. KAHN-FREUND, O. "On Uses and Misuses of Comparative Law" (1974) 37 MLR 1: the use of comparative law as a tool of law reform requires a knowledge of not only other systems, but also of their social and political environments especially. Its use is thus distinctly limited. The point is illustrated with reference to various branches of law.

8. WATSON, A. "Legal Transplants and Law Reform" (1976) 92 LQR 79: law reformers looking to comparative law should seek the ideas, which can be incorporated into their own systems. This can be done without necessarily knowing the political, social or economic conditions of those other systems. These and other

factors obtaining in the reformers' own systems are crucial, but the extent to
which they obtained in the other systems is not. See also A. WATSON; *Legal
Transplants* (Edinburgh: Scottish Academic Press, 1974).

1. FARRAR, J.H. "Law Reform Now — a Comparative View" (1976) 25 ICLQ 214:
   the development of law reforming agencies, with particular reference to the
   English and Scottish Law Commissions and in other countries which have adopted
   the Law Commissions model, is set out. Law reform has problems and limits. Law
   as an instrument has certain limits. There are also difficulties in the concept of
   reform, which is to make the law better. Should Law Commissions dictate the
   criteria of "better"?

2. MUNKMAN, J. "Good and Bad Law Reform" (1974) 124 New LJ 81: bad law
   reform is tinkering without improving. The common law at its best is characterised
   by its lucidity, principle and simplicity. It should be amended in the same spirit,
   or left alone. There is too much adherence to slogans, e.g., "consumer protection",
   "social realities", etc. The author is very critical of the kind of reform currently
   popular.

3. LYON, J.N. "Law Reform Needs Reform" (1974) 12 OsHLJ 421: law reform
   includes the entire legal process, laws, lawyers, institutions. Hitherto reform has
   been only of written laws. It is unfruitful to treat law reform simply as the
   production of quantities of reports. Reform should identify and clarify the
   values and standards of the system, and reform be directed to achieving them.
   First priority should be to make the existing machinery work better; then that
   machinery should be examined so as to improve it. (For comment, see J.W.
   MOHR: "Comment", *ibid.*, p. 437).

4. SHERIDAN, L.A. "Law Teachers and Law Reform" (1976) 10 JALT 89: this article
   considers the possible involvement of the academic lawyer in law reform. It is
   suggested that he has a particularly valuable part to play in the sphere of comparative law.

5. PATON, G.W. *A Text-book of Jurisprudence* (4th ed., G.W. Paton and D.P. Derham,
   Clarendon Press, Oxford, 1972), pp. 259—262: these pages summarise the main
   issues and problems confronting law reformers. The use of special committees,
   Royal Commissions, Law Revision Committee, Law Reform Committee and the
   Law Commissions are outlined.

6. WADE, E.C.S. "The Machinery of Law Reform" (1961) 24 MLR 1: the working of
   various bodies as at that date are set out. The author rejects the distinction
   between lawyers' law and politicians' law, and draws attention to the difficulty of
   getting Parliament to implement proposals and the almost total indifference that
   then existed to the law in other countries.

7. HUTTON, N. "Mechanics of Law Reform" (1961) 24 MLR 18: this is a follow-up of
   Professor Wade's paper to explain how proposals are implemented. Parliamentary
   time is of the essence, and there are problems of drafting. Illustrations are taken
   with reference to actual bills and cases.

8. DEVLIN, P. "The Process of Law Reform" (1966) 63 LS Gaz 453: reform is first
   mooted and discussed and then translated into law. It is at the latter stage that the
   flow gets blocked through lack of Parliamentary time. It would help if wide
   support were secured in advance through public discussion, if law reform bills began

in the House of Lords, if the second reading of such bills were taken in committee and if judges had power to refer uncovered situations to the Law Commission.

1. *The Reform of the Law*, (ed. G.L. Williams, Victor Gollancz, Ltd, 1951): the central proposal is to establish a Ministry of Justice to supervise constantly the substantive and procedural aspects of the law. Various branches of the law are then dealt with in the succeeding contributions.

2. *Law Reform and Law Making. A Reprint of a Series of Broadcast Talks*, (W. Heffer & Sons, Ltd, 1953): judges need to play a more active role in evolving principles. Various sources and hindrances to law reform are analysed. Thereafter distinguished authorities, including a judge, deal with reform of equity, rent law, administrative law, contract, criminal law and law making.

3. *Law Reform* Now, (edd. G. Gardiner and A. Martin, Victor Gollancz, Ltd, 1963): the contributions begin with a review of the then existing machinery for law reform, including government departments, *ad hoc* committees, permanent committees, and considers the feasibility of a Ministry of Justice and a Law Commission. (Lord Gardiner, as Lord Chancellor, was principally responsible for the subsequent establishment of the English and Scottish Law Commissions). The other contributions deal respectively with the administration of justice (and it is noteworthy that the proposal to create a new Family Division of the High Court has since been implemented), constitutional and administrative law, contact and tort, land law, family law, commercial and company law, industrial law, criminal law, revenue law and legal education.

4. GARDINER, G. "The Role of the Lord Chancellor in the Field of Law Reform" (1971) 87 LQR 326: the Lord Chancellor can be very effective, but it rests with the individual Lord Chancellor. The author reviews his own functions in various aspects of improving the law and its administrations: courts, administration, local family courts, legal education, permanent Law Commission, improvement of the statute book and intelligible legislation.

5. CHORLEY, R.S.T. and DWORKIN, G. "The Law Commissions Act, 1965" (1965) 28 MLR 675: this article gives the history of the Act setting up the Law Commission, from the earliest ideas even before Lord Gardiner's introduction of the measure, its progress through Parliament and the comments and fears voiced at the time.

6. SCARMAN, L.G. "Law Reform – the Experience of the Law Commission" (1968) 10 JSPTL (NS) 91: this is a review of the work of the Law Commission to date by its Chairman. He explains the origin, the authority and membership of the Commission. It does not usurp the functions of the courts or of Parliament.

7. FARRAR, J.H. *Law Reform and the Law Commission*, (Sweet & Maxwell, Ltd, 1974): the book begins by reviewing the concept of law reform and the evolution of law reform institutions from early times until the creation of the Law Commissions in 1965. The work, powers and practice of the Law Commissions are then examined in turn. The influence of public opinion and values is also considered, as well as law reform in the international sphere.

8. WALKER, D.M. "Reform, Restatement and the Law Commissions" (1965) Jur R 245: the defective state of English and Scots law is of long development. The

author reviews the opportunities ahead for the Scottish Law Commission and hopes that their work will not be frustrated by the Parliamentary bottleneck.

1. SCARMAN, L.G. *Law Reform. The New Pattern* (Lindsay Memorial Lectures, Routledge & Kegan Paul, Ltd, 1967): law reform is a social and moral problem as well as a legal one. Courts have the technical learning and perhaps the social awareness, but no opportunity nor sufficient power. Therefore, reform has to come from government. The Law Commissions were the government's response. They should not be inhibited from proposing reform in controversial areas, but difficulty arises in translating these into law in Parliament. Parliament must adjust itself to the new machinery which it has created. With the increase in statute law, it is now necessary to look first to statute law, and to case law only if the law is not in a statute. There must also be reform of statute law.

2. SUTTON, R.J. "The English Law Commission: a New Philosophy of Law Reform" (1966–67) 20 Vand LR 1009: the new philosophy is to give the Commission freedom to enable it to stimulate legislation. Flexibility, independence and early consultation with interested parties and the legislature are essential. The structure, work and program of the Commission are discussed.

3. GOWER, L.C.B. "Reflections on Law Reform" (1973) 23 UTLJ 257: it is important that the Law Commission should be free to choose its own programs, but it should also have a close relation with the legislative process. Explanation is given of consultation with the public through working papers, liaison with draftsmen, the problems of harmonising different systems of law (English and Scots), and problems raised by lawyers' law, social issues, procedural law, the need for adequate social research and, above all, how reformers should make value judgments. (See also L.C.B. GOWER: "Law Reform" (1973) 4 Can BJ (NS) No. 3, p. 1).

4. SIMON, J.E.S. and WEBB, J.V.D. "Consolidation and Statute Law Revision" (1975) PL 285: attempts since 1549 are reviewed. The different kinds of consolidation and statute law repeal are examined in turn.

5. DIAMOND, A.L. "The Work of the Law Commission" (1976) 10 JALT 11: the author reviews the terms of reference and limitation on the choice of programs for study by the Law Commission, the working papers and the topics of the law. Three types of codification – creeping, long-term and instant – are also considered.

6. EDMUND-DAVIES, E. "Ferment in the Law" (*Presidential Address to the Holdsworth Club*, 1977): change for the sake of change is self-defeating. It should be demonstrably better and not introduce more inconvenience than it is worth. The work of the Law Revision Committee, of which the author was Chairman, and of the Law Commission are reviewed. A piece-meal approach to codification is favoured.

7. SAMEK, R.A. "Pornography as a Species of Second-order Sexual Behaviour. A Submission for Law Reform" (1973) 1 Dal LJ 265: the author begins by considering the function of law reform, which has a social aspect of evaluating behaviour and of bringing about change in social practice, and a legal aspect of evaluating and reforming existing law. We should know the kind of behaviour to be controlled and whether it is controllable by law. Although law reform has a

semantic aspect, this is inapplicable to, e.g., obscenity, which depends on values. The author proceeds with a submission to the Canadian Law Commission.

Drafting

1. BENTHAM, J. "Nomography, or the Art of Inditing Laws", in *Works*, (ed. J. Bowring, Wm. Tait, Edinburgh, 1843), III, chaps. 3–9: "Nomography" is the form to be given to the matter of which law is composed. With a view to improving draftsmanship, various kinds of imperfections are discussed and suggestions offered as to how legal language might be simplified.

2. DICKERSON, F.R. *The Fundamentals of Legal Drafting*, (Little, Brown & Co, 1965): this is a most readable and informative account of the problems of drafting legal documents, including statutes. It shows the process of preparing a document through various stages and how this process improves and clarifies its substance. As such it contains much that is of value to all persons engaged in legal writings of every sort. See also F.R. DICKERSON, *The Interpretation and Application of Statutes*, (Little, Brown & Co, Boston, 1975).

3. THORNTON, G.C. *Legislative Drafting* (Butterworth & Co, Ltd, 1970): this is written primarily from a British point of view, but bringing to bear the author's experience in drafting gained abroad. It deals with a selection of problems relating to drafting, and is of general interest.

4. *Rules of Drafting*, supplied by L.R. MacTAVISH, K.C., (1948), 26 Can BR 1231: this is a set of detailed precepts which are "designed to ensure certainty and clarity of meaning and conciseness of expression".

5. MacDERMOTT, J.C. "Some Requirements of Justice" (1964) Jur R 103, 104–12: the difficulty is to find unequivocal language in which to convey the intention of Parliament. The "literal" school adheres to the plain meaning of words unless Parliament has authorised the contrary; the "realist" school looks at the policy of the statute and the body of law of which it has become a part. Four suggestions are offered: (a) greater use of preambles; (b) at some stage of the legislative process measures should be scrutinised by special teams of "clause-tasters"; (c) statutes might themselves state "This Act shall be liberally construed" and applied to promote its underlying purposes and policies; (d) courts should have discretionary powers to order costs in cases of interpretation to be paid out of public funds.

6. CONARD, A.F. "New Ways to Write Laws", (1947), 56 Yale LJ 458: laws should be drafted with more emphasis on making the public understand what they command than on controlling judges. The latter are more likely to be influenced by clear statements of purpose. There should be titles, headings and sub-divisions; jargon should be avoided, there should be short sentences, examples and directives rather than propositions in the form "if X then Y".

7. GRAHAM-HARRISON, W.M. "An Examination of the Main Criticisms of the Statute Book and the Possibility of Improvement", (1935), JSPTL 9, especially, pp. 34 *et seq.*: this is a detailed investigation into the charges levelled at statutes, showing that draftsmen are not always to blame. The conflicting approaches and canons of interpretation adopted by the judges also lead to confusion.

1. WILSON, W.A. "The Complexity of Statutes" (1974) 37 MLR 497: this article is a demonstration of different kinds of expressions used in statutes: relational phrases, probative expressions, operative sentences, substitutions, hypothetical provisions, factorial sentences, additional sentences, purpose sentences, identifications, unit facts, and various uses of grammar, tense, and types of fact.

2. RAM, G. "The Improvement of the Statute Book", (1951), 1 JSPTL (N.S.) 442: the process of making an Act is described with special reference to the task of the draftsman. Explanatory memoranda are not thought to be of assistance to the judges because of amendments during the passage through Parliament.

3. BONNER, G.A. "Statute Law – a Proposal for Reform" (1976) 73 LS Gaz 747: reform of the law should not overshadow the importance of format and layout. The present methods of repeals, and amendments result in oddities and complexity. It is suggested that when a statute undergoes several amendments and repeals, what is left and what is new should be collated and re-enacted as a single statute.

4. CARR, C. "The Mechanism of Law-making", (1951), 4 CLP 122: this explains the origin of some modern drafting practices.

5. AMOS, M.S. "The Interpretation of Statutes", (1933–35), 5 CLJ 163: in the course of a discussion on interpretation the point is made that drafting a text into two languages, (e.g., international treaties) induces clarity. (Cf. South African statutes).

6. HIRANANDANI, S.K. "Legislative Drafting: an Indian View", (1964), 27 MLR 1: the problems that confront a draftsman are stated with the utmost clarity. This short account should stand as one of the best and most convenient accounts on the topic.

7. DRIEDGER, E.A. "The Preparation of Legislation", (1953), 31 Can BR 33, especially pp. 36–42: an account is given of the various matters which a draftsman has to consider.

8. DICKERSON, F.R. "Legislative Drafting in London and in Washington", (1959) CLJ 49: the drafting in England by a few and in America by a large group is contrasted. This includes a general discussion of draftsmen and their methods.

9. MONTGOMERIE, J. Note in (1955), 18 MLR 503: this discusses briefly bad draftsmanship of the Rent Acts.

10. TUNNICLIFFE, D. "If, but only if . . . Some thoughts on Parliamentary Drafting" (1970) 67 LS Gaz 395: while some shortcomings of statute are not the fault of the draftsman, he has a real control over the style of drafting. He is answerable only to the Prime Minister and the Attorney-General on legal points. Parliament is concerned only with policy, not with bad drafting. What is needed is overall drafting policy, use of a syntactician, answerability to Parliament through a Minister, and also some subordination to the Law Commission.

Codification

11. STONE, F.F. "A Primer on Codification" (1955) 29 Tul LR 303: codification involves a method. What is the problem for which codification is proposed? What

are the main features of codification as a method? What are its advantages and disadvantages?

1. FIELD, D.D. "Codification" (1886) 20 Am LR 1: the author represented the American counterpart of Thibaut in advocating codification. Judges should not make law and the public are entitled to know the law in advance. No country has gone back on a code.

2. CARTER, J.C. "The Province of the Written and the Unwritten Law" (1890) 24 Am LR 1: this opposes Field's project. See also D.D. FIELD: "Codification – Mr. Field's Answer to Mr. Carter", *ibid.*, p. 255; S. WILLISTON: "Written and Unwritten Law" (1931) 17 Am BAJ 39: this reviews the Field–Carter controversy on the issue of codification.

3. POUND, R. *Jurisprudence*, (West Publishing Co, 1959), III, chap. 19: the question of codification is reviewed fully.

4. AUSTIN, J. *Lectures in Jurisprudence*, (5th ed., R. Campbell, J. Murray, 1885), II, pp. 660–680: Austin supports codification and considers the French and Prussian codes.

5. FRANK, J.N. *Law and the Modern Mind*, (Stevens & Sons, Ltd, 1949), chap. 17: a code cannot dispense with judge-made law.

6. CALVERT, H. "The Vitality of Case-law under a Criminal Code", (1959), 22 MLR, 621: codification does not dispense with case-law or with the necessity for it.

7. LLOYD, D. "Codifying English Law", (1949), 2 CLP, 155: this discusses the possibility of codifying English Law.

8. LLOYD, D. in *The British Commonwealth. The Development of its Laws and Constitutions*, G.W. KEETON and (edd.) (Stevens & Sons, Ltd, 1955), I, pp. 34–35: a summary of the above.

9. WRIGHT, R.A. "The Common Law in its Old Home", in *Legal Essays and Addresses*, (Cambridge University Press, 1939), pp. 338–341: this points out the difficulties that arise even with codified law, and that codification is not a universal panacea.

10. SALMOND, J.W. "The Literature of the Law", (1922), 22 Col LR, 197: this includes a discussion of the possibility of codifying the Common Law.

11. FULLER, L.L. "American Legal Realism", (1934), 82 U Pa LR, 429, at pp. 438–442: the development of the Common Law is inhibited by the absence of "doctrinal bridges"; a code would provide these.

12. BEST, W.M. "Codification of the Laws of England", (1856), Trans Jur S, 209: the principle of codification is unsound, amendment and consolidation is preferable.

13. CHALMERS, M.D. "An Experiment in Codification", (1886), 2 LQR, 125: this considers the arguments against codification in the light of the Bills of Exchange Act, 1882.

14. CHALMERS, M.D. "Codification of Mercantile Law", (1903), 19 LQR, 10: a continuation of the above thesis.

1. DOWDALL, H.C. "Suggestions for the Codification of the Law of General Average", (1895), 11 LQR, 35: a draft of the proposed Code with explanatory notes.

2. STONE, H.F. "Some Aspects of the Problem of Law Simplification", (1923), 23 Col LR, 319: this gives consideration to the question of codification and argues for a restatement of the law.

3. GRUEBER, E. "Holtzendorff's Encyclopädie", (1885), 1 LQR, 62: the possibility of a codification of English Law on the lines of "Holtzendorff" is explored.

4. AMOS, M.S. "The Code Napoleon and the Modern World", (1928), 10 JCL, (3rd Ser.), 222: this is of general interest as providing some account of the operation of the Code in France and elsewhere.

5. PATON, G.W. *A Text-book of Jurisprudence* (4th ed., G.W. Paton and D.P. Derham, Oxford: Clarendon Press, 1972), pp. 254–257: in the main two kinds of countries go in for codification: those with well-developed systems which have little chance of development, and under-developed systems which cannot grapple with new problems. No code can be comprehensive, and the real test is the measure of its flexibility. The exegetical and creative approaches to the French Code are briefly discussed.

6. SCARMAN, L.G. "Codification and Judge-made Law. A Problem of Co-existence", (University of Birmingham, Faculty of Law, 1966): the establishment of the Law Commission is a historic event. The Chairman of the Law Commission considers the task ahead of them and the creative task the judiciary will have to play under a codified system.

7. SMITH, T.B. "Unification of Law in Britain: Problems of Coordination", (1967), Jur R (NS) 97: following the establishment of the Law Commission, the problems of unification are considered at three different levels, national, regional and universal.

8. HAHLO, H.R. "Here Lies the Common Law: Rest in Peace" (1967) 30 MLR 241: the author criticises the codification program of the Law Commission. Codification will not bring law closer to the layman, nor be a cure for uncertainty, nor provide answers to all the questions of detail that will arise. It will involve a long period of uncertainty and a heavy price by way of preparation and re-learning. He also comments on the instalment method of codifying branches of the law adopted by the Law Commission and on the "broad principles" v. "detailed provisions" approach.

9. GOWER, L.C.B. "A Comment" (1967) 30 MLR 259: Professor Gower, a member of the Law Commission, defends the decision to codify Contract against Professor Hahlo's attack. English Law has not shown itself to be as adaptable in this sphere as elsewhere, and it is absurd that there should be fundamental differences between English and Scots Law. It is, moreover, unsatisfactory to impose specialised codes, e.g., Sale of Goods Act, on the corpus of an uncodified general law of contract.

10. TOPPING, M.R. and VANDENLINDEN, J.P.M. *"Ibi Renascit Jus Commune"* (1970) 33 MLR 170: this is an answer to Professor Hahlo on two questions: Why codify? and Is the cost too high? The authors argue that many of Professor Hahlo's points do not touch the real issues or else exaggerate difficulties. The advantages do outweigh the cost.

1. HAHLO, H.R. "Codifying the Common Law: Protracted Gestation" (1975) 38 MLR
   23: this is a reply to M.R. Topping and J.P.M. Vandenlinden. The main area of
   disagreement, it is said, concerns the time and effort required to draft and learn a
   code. That those authors underestimate these is said to be shown by the progress
   over the past ten years.

2. WILSON, J.F. "Evolution or Revolution? – Prospects for Contract Law Reform"
   (University of Southampton Pamphlet, 1969): defects need to be reformed before
   codification, and it will be more helpful to focus attention on particular branches
   of contract before codifying the general law of contract. The author points to
   Continental experience to show that the advantages of codification are largely
   illusory and also in considering the form which codification should assume.

3. DIAMOND, A.L. "Codification of the Law of Contract" (1968) 31 MLR 361: a
   code does make the law more accessible. It also facilitates law reform, both by
   the effort of codifying and later by revising the code. The cases for and against
   codification are carefully argued.

4. CHARTRAND, O.R. "Codification: Equals Simplification: Equals Comprehension"
   (1973) 4 Can BJ (NS) No. 1, p. 25: a French Canadian deplores Napoleon's
   failure to conquer England, for English Law would then have had a code. A code
   saves time, for the spade-work will have been done. Its terse, precise organic
   statement of the law makes law more accessible. The rule of law is jeopardised
   when people are in ignorance of the law.

5. JOINT COMMITTEE OF THE YOUNG BARRISTERS COMMITTEE OF THE BAR
   COUNCIL AND THE YOUNG SOLICITORS GROUP OF THE LAW SOCIETY:
   Memorandum on "Codification of the Law" (1970) 58 Law Guardian 11: codification means a number of things. The Law Commission aims at creating a
   limited number of codes which would contain all the law. If this could be
   achieved, it would be admirable; but it is only a dream. Three things need to be
   done: (1) a restatement of the existing law on any subject; (2) a sifting of evidence
   that it is unjust and needs amendment; (3) a consideration of whether the proposed
   solutions will cure the injustice or produce equal or worse injustices.

6. TWINING, W. *Karl Llewellyn and the Realist Movement* (Weidenfeld and Nicolson,
   1973), chapters 11 and 12 and Appendices E and F: Llewellyn played a leading
   part in the production of the Uniform Commercial Code. The chapters, which
   give an account of this part, are also informative on the problems of a major codification. Appendix E also deals with that project, but Appendix F gives
   Llewellyn's proposed codes for the Pueblos.

7. FARRAR, J.H. *Law Reform and the Law Commission* (Sweet & Maxwell, Ltd,
   1974), pp. 57–62: there are different patterns for codification: broad principles
   as in the French *Code Civil*, or detailed provisions as in the German *BGB*, or
   detailed provisions with examples. The arguments for and against codification are
   set out.

16. Positivism. British Theories

Positivism

1. AGO, R. "Positive Law and International Law", (trans. J.A. Hammond, 1957), 51 AJIL, 691: the development of the idea of positive law from medieval times is traced. Originally it denoted law resulting from some creative act as opposed to natural law; then such law was treated as the only "valid" law; more recently there have been further changes. The value of positivism and its weakness are indicated.

2. HART, H.L.A. "Analytical Jurisprudence in Mid-twentieth Century: a Reply to Professor Bodenheimer" (1956–57), 105 U Pa LR, 953: certain misunderstandings about positivism are corrected. A distinction is drawn between law and legal concepts, on the one hand, and between theories of law and definitions of concepts. It is incorrect to say that analytical jurisprudence needs no assistance from other disciplines.

3. HART, H.L.A. "Positivism and the Separation of Law and Morals" (1957–58), 71 Harv LR, 593: this is a modernistic defence of the separation of the "is" and the "ought". It is also important in clarifying what it is that positivists maintain as distinct from what they have been supposed to maintain. See also L.L. FULLER, "Positivism and Fidelity to Law – A Reply to Professor Hart", *ibid.*, p. 630: which challenges Hart's thesis.

4. DICKERSON, F.R. "Statutory Interpretation: Core Meaning and Marginal Uncertainty", (1964), 29 Miss LR, 1: Hart seeks to find the "is" of law in the inner core of meaning which most words possess. Fuller rejects this, arguing that context purpose (i.e., considerations of "ought") determine meaning in each given instance. In this study the author reconciles this apparent conflict by showing the importance of both and how they are interrelated.

5. MORISON, W.L. "Some Myths about Positivism", (1959–60), 68 Yale LJ, 212: this also dispels some of the misconceptions that have gathered round Austin's contribution to jurisprudence, and presents his work afresh.

6. KOCOUREK, A. "The Century of Analytical Jurisprudence since John Austin" in *Law: A Century of Progress*, (New York University Press, 1937), II, 194: the meaning of "analytical jurisprudence" is first considered; then the work of Austin and others in the analytical field; and finally the contribution as a whole is appraised.

7. KESSLER, F. "Theoretic Bases of Law" (1941–42), 9 UCLR 98, at pp. 105–8: positivism is regarded as being the necessary opponent of natural law. It would be wrong to assume that considerations of justice have no part in it, for justice lies in security and the ending of disorder. The contribution and defects of positivism are briefly reviewed.

8. KESSLER, F. "Natural Law, Justice and Democracy – Some Reflections on Three Types of Thinking about Law and Justice" (1944–45), 19 Tul LR 32, at pp. 39–54: positivism is reviewed and explained. The element of justice in it, namely, the care of security, is further developed. Its weaknesses are also pointed out.

9. FULLER, L.L. *Law in Quest of Itself*, (The Foundation Press, Inc, 1940): the controversy between the naturalists and positivists is critically considered. The

separation of the "is" and the "ought" is subjected to especial condemnation as narrow and misleading. In no legal activity can "ought" be avoided.

1. STUMPF, S.E. "Austin's Theory of the Separation of Law and Morals" (1960–61), 14 Vand LR 117: an explanation is given of the evolution of the separation of law from morals and of Austin's distinction between what the law is and whether it is good or bad. It is said that the very concept of law is meaningless until the nature of Man is brought into consideration; and it is alleged that Austin himself contemplated implicitly the moral characteristics of law and sovereignty.

2. COHEN, M.R. "Positivism and the Limits of Idealism in the Law" (1927), 27 Col LR 236: positivism is itself an ideal. The notion that law is a complete and closed system is false. But, on the other hand, it is necessary to distinguish between the law that is and the law that ought to be. The two are inseparable, but never completely identified.

3. LASERSON, M.M. "'Positive' and 'Natural Law' and their Correlation" in *Interpretation of Modern Legal Philosophies*, (ed. P. Sayre, Oxford University Press, New York, 1947), chap. 20: this is a complicated statement of a simple theme, viz., the lag between positive law and natural law.

4. HALL, J. "Concerning the Nature of Positive Law" (1948–49), 58 Yale LJ 545: a full understanding of positive law depends upon a sound understanding of history. Modern positivism seems to be largely a restatement of ancient viewpoints, including the exclusion of morality as "ideology". But a sharp separation between law and ethics is untrue, inadequate and misleading.

5. BRECHT, A. "The Myth of *Is* and *Ought*" (1940–41), 54 Harv LR 811: the history and the logic behind the separation of the "is" and "ought" is examined. The gulf between them is not unbridgable, for it is said that the feeling that something ought to be is a part of human equipment.

6. REID, J. "Is and Ought after Darwin" (1977) 40 MLR 249: what we "know" about facts and "feel" about values are both determined in important ways by evolution. We are not observers of everything external to us but constructors, who use operations to make sense of the world. Our beliefs are conditioned by needs, which in turn are determined by our nature and environment. As our knowledge of fact becomes less objective, so our criticism of values as uncertain declines in importance. Prescriptive rules have a fundamental part to play in the prediction of conduct in that they have a large descriptive element. In this way there can be a bridge between "is" and "ought".

7. RAZ, J. *Practical Reason and Norms* (Hutchinson, 1975): they key to understanding the normativity of law lies in the way normative language is used to describe law and legal situations. The author seeks an unified logic of all concepts of a normative theory. Such a logic provides reasons for actions. "First order" reasons are reasons for acting; "exclusionary" reasons are reasons to act for a reason or to refrain from acting for a reason. Law is an exclusionary system, which excludes the application of non-legal reasoning. The question of "authority" is also considered.

8. SHKLAR, J.N. *Legalism*, (Harvard University Press, 1964): "legalism" is the attitude of mind that makes a morality out of rule following. Both Positivist and Naturalist legal theorists are of this way of thinking. But rule morality is only one among

many in a pluralist society. To make it exclusive is to constrict one's outlook. The Positivist insistence on a separation between the "is" and the "ought" is an ideology. The book is a sharp attack on Positivism and Naturalism.

1. POUND, R. "The Scope and Purpose of Sociological Jurisprudence" (1910–11), 24 Harv LR 591, at pp. 594–98: the principal features of analytical jurisprudence are set out as well as the objections to it from a sociological point of view.

2. POUND, R. "The Progress of the Law" (1927–28), 41 Harv Lr 175: analytical jurisprudence on the Continent is reviewed during the years 1914–1927. It includes a certain amount of restatement of the original Austinian position.

3. POUND, R. "Fifty Years of Jurisprudence" (1936–37), 50 Harv LR 557, at pp. 564–82: the revival of analytical jurisprudence in the 19th century and the work of Continental and of Anglo-American analytists is reviewed.

4. POUND, R. "Classification of Law" (1923–24), 37 Harv LR 933, at pp. 945–51: the part played by analytical and historical theories in the matter of classification is considered.

5. SUMMERS, R.S. "The *New* Analytical Jurists" (1966) 41 NYULR 861: the "new" analytical jurists are those since World War II. They concern themselves with analysis of the existing conceptual framework of and about law, new conceptual frameworks with accompanying terminologies, rational justifications of institutions and practices, and purposive implication. Their methodologies concern tracing sources of errors, e.g., converting conceptual questions into questions of fact, urge to grind an axe, misleading and irrelevant models, reductionist impulse, essentialism, misuse of definition *per genus et differentiam*. The new jurists are less doctrinaire and less positivist.

6. BRYCE, J. *"Studies in History and Jurisprudence"*, (Oxford, 1901), II, pp. 178–84: this is a critical appraisal of the Bentham-Austin approach.

7. AMOS, M.S. "Some Reflection on the Philosophy of Law" (1927), 3 CLJ 31: on Austin's work it is maintained that the path of advancement is to be found in his tradition. It is useful to be able to regard law as a logical edifice of axioms.

8. BODENHEIMER, E. *Jurisprudence*, (Harvard University Press, 1962), pp. 89–93: the origins of positivism and what it contends are explained. Attention is drawn to the emphasis that was placed on tested or verifiable data.

9. FRIEDMAN, W. *Legal Theory*, (5th ed., Stevens & Sons, Ltd, 1967), chap. 21: this contains a brief explanation of the evolution and chief contentions of positivism.

10. LLOYD, D. *The Idea of Law*, (Penguin Books, Ltd, A. 688, 1964), chap. 5: the impetus for positivism came with the Renaissance. The distinction between the "is" and the "ought", and Bentham's separation of law as it is from law as it ought to be are explained. Austin was concerned with the scientific exposition of the fundamental notions which provide the framework of a system. This gave rise to conceptual analysis, the limitations of which are indicated.

11. OLIVECRONA, K. *Law as Fact* (2nd ed., Stevens & Sons, Ltd, 1971), chaps. 1–2: in the first chapter an outline is given of the history of natural law and positivist thinking with reference to Grotius, Pufendorff, Bentham, Austin and some

modern thinkers, and it ends with a discussion of the meaning of "positivism".
The second chapter deals with the character of positive law.

1. LOCKE, J. *An Essay on Human Understanding*, (33rd ed., William Tegg, 1862): this
   is of general interest; it constitutes one of the principal challenges of the a
   priorism of natural law theories and, as such, might be regarded as providing a
   foundation for positivism.

2. HUME, D. *A Treatise on Human Nature* in *The Philosophical Works of David Hume*,
   (edd. T.H. Green and T.H. Grose, Longmans, Green & Co, 1874), I: this is also of
   general interest; it constitutes the most formidable attack on the prevailing ideas
   and inspired the positivist attitude of mind. A cardinal tenet is that an "ought"
   cannot be derived from an "is". (His *Inquiry Concerning Human Understanding*
   is essentially an abridgement of the present work).

3. STERN, K. "Either-Or or Neither-Nor" in *Law and Philosophy. A Symposium*. (ed.
   S. Hook, New York University Press, 1964), p. 247: on Hume's thesis that an
   "ought" cannot be derived from an "is" the author suggests that there may be
   some types of statements which are neither normative nor descriptive. In these
   cases it might be possible to derive a normative conclusion from non-normative
   premises.

4. COMTE, A. *The Positive Philosophy*, (trans. H. Martineau, Bell & Sons, 1896), I,
   chap. 1: the nature and methods of a positive philosophy are explained. Comte
   regarded positivism as the third stage in the development of thinking, representing the turning away from the resort to ultimate principles.

5. FINCH, J.D. *Introduction to Legal Theory* (2nd ed., Sweet & Maxwell, Ltd, 1974),
   pp. 16–20, 27–36: legal theory is concerned with the nature of law rather than
   with content. It considers the "is" and different senses of the "ought". The
   separation of the "is" and the "ought" is defended.

Imperative Theories

6. LEWIS, J.U. 'Blackstone's Definition of Law and Doctrine of Legal Obligation as a
   Link between Early Modern and Contemporary Theories of Law" (1968) 3 Ir Jur
   (NS) 337: the historical setting is vital in understanding Blackstone's thought. His
   purpose was to meet the need for a methodological foundation for English law.
   His definition of law is imperative: "prescribed by the supreme power in a state,
   commanding what is right and prohibiting what is wrong". Legally speaking, the
   sovereign decides what is right and wrong; but Blackstone was speaking non-
   legally and morally when he spoke of the subject's moral obligation to obey.

7. BENTHAM, J. *Of Laws in General*, (ed. H.L.A. Hart, University of London. The
   Athlone Press, 1970): the source of a law is in the will of a sovereign, which may
   take the form of commands, prohibitions or permissions. Every law needs to be
   considered in respect of eight respects, each of which is elaborated in detail.
   Austin's later work was clearly derived from Bentham and is far less satisfactory
   in many respects. Of especial interest is Bentham's analysis of sovereignty and the
   possibility of legal self-bindingness; while the four "aspects" of a sovereign's will,
   which he worked out with the "logic of imperation", is more incisive than
   Hohfeld's work over a century later. The first publication of this work of
   Bentham was under the title, *The Limits of Jurisprudence Defined*, (ed. C.W.
   Everett, Columbia University Press, 1945).

1. RAZ, J. *The Concept of a Legal System. An Introduction to the Theory of Legal System* (Clarendon Press, Oxford, 1970), chaps. 3–4: these chapters deal, not with Bentham's contribution to sociology, but his analytical contribution to legal theory. He analysed a simple law into "an act and the aspect" and he alone, it is said, appreciated that every law is made up of parts created at different times in other contexts. Bentham postulated a primary law imposing an obligation and a secondary law imposing a sanction. In this respect his analysis is superior to that of Kelsen, who attempted to unify both into a single law.

2. HART, H.L.A. "Bentham's *'Of Laws in General'*" (1971) 2 Rechtstheorie, 55: some of Bentham's principal contributions to jurisprudence are outlined. In particular, attention is drawn to subtle and important differences between his ideas on sovereignty and those of Austin. Other important aspects are his method of "rational reconstruction" (model) and "deontic logic" (logic of the will).

3. HART, H.L.A. "Bentham on Legal Rights" in *Oxford Essays in Jurisprudence (Second Series)* (ed. A.W.B. Simpson, Oxford University Press, 1973), chap. 7: Bentham's interest theory of rights is expounded and commented on acutely. For a brief explanation and review of Hart's exposition, see S.L. PAULSON, Review of *Oxford Essays in Jurisprudence (Second Series)*, (1974) 87 Harv LR 898, at pp. 905–907.

4. HART, H.L.A. "Bentham on Legal Powers" (1971–72) 81 Yale LJ 799: Bentham had anticipated much of the modern analysis. He went further and distinguished between powers to interfere physically, "power of contrectation", and powers to procure people to act according to commands or prohibitions, "power of imperation". The author points out, however, that Bentham failed to distinguish between validity and invalidity from illegality, and between powers to enter into legally effective transactions and powers to issue legal commands and prohibitions.

5. JAMES, M.H. "Bentham on the Individuation of Laws" in *Bentham and Legal Theory* (ed. M.H. James, reprint of articles in (1973) 24 NILQ), 91: Bentham saw "Law" as the sum-total of laws, and wanted to eliminate principles from legal interpretation. To this end each law must possess completeness and unity. This can only be accomplished if laws are "individuated" with reference to classes of acts, each class of acts being the centre of an individual law. The various detailed implications of this as worked out by Bentham are set out.

6. LYSAGHT, L.J. "Bentham on the Aspects of a Law" in *Bentham and Legal Theory* (ed. M.H. James, reprint of articles in (1973) 24 NILQ), 117: assuming that most laws can be stated in an imperative form (as Bentham maintained), a theoretical framework for this has considerable explanatory power. The "logic of imperation", the relation between command, prohibition, non-command and permission, is explained.

7. LYONS, D.B. *In the Interest of the Governed. A Study in Bentham's Philosophy of Utility and Law* (Clarendon Press, Oxford, 1973), chaps. 6–7: this is a discussion of Bentham's deontic logic and imperational theory of law. The second of the chapters concerns motivation and the force of a law, in particular how permissive laws may be said to "bind" or "coerce".

8. HART, H.L.A. "Bentham and the Demystification of the Law" (1973) 36 MLR 2: tearing away the mystiques of the law permeate Bentham's work. The imperative character of law is, in his view, concealed by natural law and the wording of laws

conferring powers, creating title, etc.; prolixity conceals much and emotive
language cloaks misgovernment. The jargon, ceremonial and procedure of the law
is like religion which has not seen a reformation. The author also considers those
aspects of modern law which Bentham would have attacked.

1. PAREKH, Bhikhu. *Bentham's Political Thought* (Croom-Helm, 1973): this is a
   collection of Bentham's legal and political thought. The legal portions consist of
   material already published in separate volumes as well as an unpublished tract,
   "What a Law Is", which deals explicitly with the imperative basis of laws.

2. AUSTIN, J. *Lectures on Jurisprudence*, (5th ed., R. Campbell, John Murray, 1885),
   I, chaps. 1–6: the nature of law and sovereignty need to be clarified before
   embarking upon a study of the leading notions of law, which to Austin was
   jurisprudence. The idea of law, strictly so called, as the command of a sovereign
   supported by sanction is developed in detail.

3. AUSTIN, J. *The Province of Jurisprudence Determined and the Uses of the Study of
   Jurisprudence*, (ed. H.L.A. Hart, Weidenfeld and Nicholson, 1954): this contains
   the first six lectures on law and sovereignty. In the Introduction Hart summarises
   Austin's thesis and the criticisms of Bryce and Maine. He also alludes to Austin's
   failure to take account of the notion of a rule (see further H.L.A. Hart, *The
   Concept of Law, infra*).

4. HOBBES, T. *A Dialogue between a Philosopher and a Student of the Common Laws
   of England* in *The English Works of Thomas Hobbes*, (ed. W. Molesworth, John
   Bohn, 1840), vol. 6: Hobbes refutes Coke's thesis that law is "artificial reason"
   and says it is simple "natural reason", and that it is constituted as "law" by the
   command of the sovereign. A judgment is "law" only between the parties, so he
   would reject the law-constitutive force of precedent. Custom is not "law" of its
   own.

5. HALE, M. "Sir Matthew Hale on Hobbes: an Unpublished Manuscript", first
   published by F. Pollock and W.S. Holdsworth in (1921), 37 LQR 274; also in
   W.S. Holdsworth, *A History of English Law*, (Methuen & Co, Ltd, 1945), V, Appendix III: Hale challenges Hobbes's thesis that the basis of laws is sovereign authority,
   as well as Coke's thesis that it is "artificial reason". Law, says Hale, is a socio-
   historical product. Also, sovereign powers accrue to the sovereign by certain laws
   of the kingdom and, as such, there are certain inherent qualifications of these
   powers.

6. YALE, D.E.C. "Hobbes and Hale on Law, Legislation and the Sovereign" [1972 B]
   31 C LJ 121: Hobbes's views on the origin and nature of the sovereign power in
   Britain and the answer to it advanced by Hale are compared. The latter's position
   was that sovereignty could well be supreme, but it does not have to be unlimited;
   it could be limited by the constitutional framework into which it is born.

7. MILL, J.S. "Austin on Jurisprudence" in *Dissertations and Discussions*, (Longmans,
   Green, Reader and Dyer, 1868), III, p. 206: this is a lengthy review of Austin's
   theory of law and his analysis of legal concepts. It is particularly interesting as
   being the comments of one of Austin's most famous pupils.

8. STEPHEN, L. *The English Utilitarians*, (Duckworth & Co, 1900), III, pp. 317–36:
   the work of Austin as the inheritor of the utilitarian tradition is assessed.

1. SCHWARZ, A.B. "John Austin and the German Jurisprudence of his Time", (1934–35), 1 Politica, 178: the nature and extent of the German influence on Austin is assessed in detail. There is also a brief review of his influence on Continental writers.

2. HOLDSWORTH, W.S. *Some Makers of English Law*, (Cambridge University Press, 1938), pp. 248–64: a useful account is given of Bentham and Austin, which might be read as a general background to their work.

3. DILLON, J.F. *The Laws and Jurisprudence of England and America*, (Macmillan & Co, 1894), chaps. 11 and 12: the work of Bentham is appraised (but this was before the discovery and publication in 1945 of *The Limits of Jurisprudence Defined*). Reference might also be made to chapter 1 where there is a brief consideration of the Austinian definition of law.

4. EASTWOOD, R.A. and KEETON, G.W. *The Austinian Theories of Law and Sovereignty*, (Methuen & Co, Ltd, 1929): this short book is one of the best simplified restatements of the Austinian position. The doctrine of sovereignty, in particular, is dealt with in some detail and is traced out historically.

5. BROWN, W.J. *The Austinian Theory of Law*, (John Murray, 1906), chaps. 1, 2, 3, 5, Excursus B, E: the chapters reproduce the Austinian text in an abridged form with occasional notes. Excursus B deals with sovereignty. The distinction between "legal" and "political" sovereignty is examined. In Excursus E various objections to the conception of positive law as the command of state are considered.

6. HEARNSHAW, F.J.C. *The Social and Political Ideas of some Representative Thinkers of the Age of Reaction and Reconstruction*, (ed., F.J.C. Hearnshaw, Harrap & Co, Ltd, 1932), chap. 9: the life and work of Austin is portrayed against the background of social conditions and ideas. His theories of law and sovereignty are outlined with particularly critical comments on the latter.

7. MANNING, C.A.W. "Austin Today: or 'The Province of Jurisprudence' Re-examined" in *Modern Theories of Law*, (ed. W.I. Jennings, Oxford University Press, 1933), chap. 10: this is a re-interpretation of the Austinian theory so as to make it adaptable to modern society. What it says is therefore not necessarily what Austin himself said.

8. OLIVECRONA, K. *Law as Fact*, (Einar Munksgaard, Copenhagen; Humphrey Milford, 1939; reprinted by Wildy & Sons, 1962), chap. 1: the nature of a rule of law is considered. There is a convincing demolition of the command theory and an explanation of the imperative form in which rules are expressed. In *Law as Fact* (2nd ed., Stevens & Sons, Ltd, 1971), chap. 2, he repeats and amplifies the points made in the first edition.

9. HART, H.L.A. *The Concept of Law*, (Oxford, Clarendon Press, 1961, reprinted 1975), chaps. 2–4 and 10: Austin's concept of law is reconstructed afresh to demonstrate its weaknesses, which are developed at length. In chapter 10 the similarities and differences between municipal and international law are considered.

10. RAZ, J. *The Concept of a Legal System. An Introduction to the Theory of Legal System* (Clarendon Press, Oxford, 1970), chaps. 1–2: the analysis of a legal system does not lie in the analysis of just a law, but in the internal relation between laws. Austin's analysis of a law thus sheds no light, except indirectly, on

the concept of a legal system. In these two chapters Austin's views on sovereignty, command and other key ideas are examined from a legal system orientation and there are new criticisms of everything that has long been criticised.

1. HONORÉ, A.M. "Real Laws" in *Law, Morality and Society. Essays in Honour of H.L.A. Hart* (edd. P.M.S. Hacker and J. Raz, Clarendon Press, Oxford, 1977), chap. 5: there is no way of settling the form of individuality of laws other than by seeing them as they appear in professional discourse. There are metaphysical laws, act-situation laws, professional laws and rules, individual rules of law. Six types of laws are distinguished: existence laws, rules of inference, categorising rules, rules of scope, position-specifying rules, directly normative rules.

2. KELSEN, H. *General Theory of Law and State*, (trans. A. Wedberg, Harvard University Press, 1949), pp. 30–37: in the general context of developing a "pure" theory of law, the command theory is rejected as introducing an "impure" (psychological) element. The "will" of a legislator breaks down on analysis.

3. MacCORMICK, D.N. "Legal Obligation and the Imperative Fallacy" in *Oxford Essays in Jurisprudence (Second Series)* (ed. A.W.B. Simpson, Oxford University Press, 1973), chap. 5: the notion of command is subjected to searching analysis. The use of imperative language is not essential to it, and it is appropriate only in a context of superiority. An "ought" cannot be derived from command, but from the premise that what a given authority orders ought to be obeyed. Legislation is not commanding; it lays down rules while commands direct acts and forbearances.

4. CLARK, E.C. *Practical Jurisprudence*, (Cambridge University Press, 1883), Part 1: this is an interesting and wide-ranging discussion of the notion of law centred on Austin. The derivation of the word and its synonyms in other languages are considered and it is shown to connote that which is fitting or proper, not what is commanded.

5. WILLIAMS, G.L. "International Law and the Controversy Concerning the Word 'Law'" in *Philosophy, Politics and Society*, (ed. P. Laslett, Blackwell, Oxford, 1956), chap. 9: much of the dispute between the Austinians and the International lawyers as to whether International Law is "properly" called "law" is exposed as verbal.

6. PAULSON, S.L. "Classical Legal Positivism at Nuremberg" (1975) 4 Philosophy and Public Affairs, 132: the defence of "act of state" presupposes the Austinian thesis that a sovereign state cannot be subject to a duty imposed by any superior authority. The defence of "superior orders" presupposes the Austinian thesis that the validity of a sovereign's command cannot be impugned by appeal to moral grounds. The defence of "*ex post facto* legislation" presupposes the Austinian association of duty with sanction. The Tribunal's rejection of all three defences amounted to a rejection of Austinian positivism.

7. HARRISON, F. *On Jurisprudence and the Conflict of Law*, (Oxford, 1919), chap. 2 and Annotations by A.H.F. Lefroy, II–III: Austin's view is said to be appropriate only to lawyers. It concentrated on force, not on regularity which is also implied in the word "law". The nature of enabling laws and laws relating to construction and procedure as well as rules are considered.

8. CROSS, A.R.N. *Precedent in English Law*, (2nd ed., Oxford, 1968), pp. 199–201: Austin's theory is considered with reference to judicial precedent. His idea of "tacit command" is examined and rejected.

1. GRAY, J.C. *The Nature and Sources of the Law*, (2nd ed., R. Gray, The Macmillan Co, New York, 1921), pp. 85–89: the command theory is critically reviewed. In particular, the weakness is indicated of saying that one commands things to be done when one has power (which is not exercised) of forbidding them to be done.

2. GRAY, J.C. "Some Definitions and Questions in Jurisprudence" (1892–93), 6 Harv LR 21, at pp. 25–27: the law does not comprise all the sovereign's commands, for there are commands, which are not law. On the other hand, law includes much that are not sovereign commands.

3. VINOGRADOFF, P. *Common-sense in Law*, (3rd ed., H.G. Hanbury, Oxford University Press, 1959), chap. 2: the command theory is rejected as being inadequate from a historical point of view. Law depends, not on enforcement, but ultimately on recognition.

4. VINOGRADOFF, P. *Outlines of Historical Jurisprudence*, (Oxford University Press, 1920), I, pp. 115–123: Austin's contribution is critically examined. The separation between law and positive morality is condemned, and the emphasis on sanction is regarded as misleading. The difficulties of Austin's theory of sovereignty with reference to the United States of America are pointed out.

5. POUND, R. *Jurisprudence*, (West Publishing Co, 1959), II, pp. 68–79, 132–163: in the first section the progress of the analytical movement in England is recounted. In the second section the doctrines are considered, beginning with the views of Austin and then of his successors.

6. STONE, J. *Legal System and Lawyers' Reasonings* (Stevens & Sons, Ltd, 1964), chap. 2: Austin's system is not a literal representation of any particular legal order; it gives a hypothetical order. It is an apparatus for seeing the degree of logical consistency within a given order and not a representation of the law itself. There is, therefore, a gap between his hypothetical system and an actual system. Austin underestimated this gap. Consistently with this, it is said that Austin's use of "sovereignty", "command" etc. is not descriptive, as with Hobbes and Bodin. Logical coherence is best seen if a legal order is arranged as if its propositions were commands of a sovereign.

7. JONES, J.W. *Historical Introduction to the Theory of Law*, (Oxford, 1940), chap. 3: the notion of sovereignty and its relation to law is traced historically from Bodin to Austin.

8. BODENHEIMER, E. *Jurisprudence*, (Harvard University Press, 1962), pp. 93–98: this contains a brief review of the work of Austin and of the Austinians.

9. FRIEDMANN, W. *Legal Theory*, (5th ed., Stevens & Sons, Ltd, 1967), chaps. 22–23: in the first of these chapters the work of Austin and the modifications of his successors are dealt with. There is mention also of the counterparts of the imperative theory in Germany and France. The second chapter appraises analytical study.

10. LIGHTWOOD, J.M. *The Nature of Positive Law*, (Macmillan & Co, 1883), chap. 13: Austin's views are set out and explained at length.

11. MARKBY, W. *Elements of Law*, (6th ed., Oxford, 1905), chap. 1: Markby was one of Austin's earliest followers. His views are adopted as the basis of the book. Austin's position is defended against certain criticisms of it.

1. HOLLAND, T.E. *The Elements of Jurisprudence*, (13th ed., Oxford, 1924), chap. 4:
   Austin's theory is modified to the extent of saying that positive law is enforced
   by sovereign political authority, not so much commanded.

2. HEARN, W.E. *The Theory of Legal Duties and Rights*, (Melbourne: John Ferres;
   London: Trubner & Co, 1883), chap. 1: the command theory is adopted and
   explained and certain objections to it are considered.

3. SALMOND, J.W. *Jurisprudence*, (7th ed., Sweet & Maxwell, Ltd, 1924), chap. 2:
   the author states that law consists of rules that are recognized and acted on by
   courts. This chapter gives his famous analysis of "civil law", including a discussion
   of the imperative theory. In the 11th ed. (G.L. Williams, 1957), pp. 53–58, the
   command theory is considered in general terms, and some objections to it are
   contained in Note (b) on p. 55. In Appendix I sovereignty is treated, and, although
   Austin is not specifically mentioned, some implications of his theory come into it.
   In the 12th ed. (P.J. Fitzgerald, 1966), pp. 25–35, the editor deals more fully
   with the command theory and outlines the principal objections that various
   writers have made.

4. KEETON, G.W. *The Elementary Principles of Jurisprudence*, (2nd ed., Isaac Pitman
   & Sons, Ltd, 1949), chaps. 3 and 4: after a brief historical introduction Austin's
   theory of sovereignty is explained. The discussion of the nature of law is substantially concerned with the imperative theory.

5. PATON, G.W. *A Text-Book of Jurisprudence*, (4th ed., G.W. Paton and D.P. Derham,
   Clarendon Press, Oxford, 1972), pp. 4–14, 74–82, 339–343: these pages contain
   brief accounts of Bentham and Austin, and the latter's theory is outlined, both as
   to the nature of law, sovereignty, and international law.

6. PATTERSON, E.W. *Jurisprudence*, (The Foundation Press, Inc, 1953), pp. 82–91:
   the requirements of the imperative theory of law are considered. The separation
   of the law that is from what ought to be law as well as an excessive reliance on
   logic are condemned. There are further allusions at pp. 107–8, 123–24 and 127.

7. JENKS, E. *The New Jurisprudence*, (John Murray, 1933), pp. 36–41: the idea of
   law as a command is considered and rejected. The need for generality in law is
   also dealt with.

8. LLOYD, D. *Introduction to Jurisprudence*, (3rd ed., Stevens & Sons, Ltd, 1972),
   chap. 4: sovereignty, the imperative theory and the principal objections to them
   are set out. Bentham's views are discussed first and then Austin's with a comparison of the two to bring out the flexibility and superiority of the former. The
   extracts from various writers include those from Bodin, Hobbes, Rousseau,
   Bentham, Austin, Bryce, de Jouvenal, Rees, Hart, Fuller and Hohfeld. The case-law
   is taken from cases mentioned in Chapter 3 of this book.

9. JOLOWICZ, H.F. *Lectures on Jurisprudence*, (ed. J.A. Jolowicz, The Athlone
   Press, 1963), chap. 1 and pp. 106–18: the first chapter gives an easy introduction
   to Austin's theory of law and sovereignty. Pp. 106–18 contain criticisms of
   Austin's idea of sovereignty and of law as command.

10. SAMEK, R.A. *The Legal Point of View* (Philosophical Library, New York, 1974)
    chap. 6: the views of Hobbes, Blackstone, Bentham and Austin are considered.
    They are alleged to be "essence of law" models. Hobbes's model is primarily

political and not confined to any particular point of view. The views of Bentham and Austin are considered in detail. The former, it is said, constricted his very flexible view by forcing it into a command model. The latter superimposed his own model concepts on ordinary concepts and then sought to justify them on the basis of factual criteria.

1. HALL, J. *Foundations of Jurisprudence* (The Bobbs-Merrill Co Inc, 1973), pp. 28–35: the contempt of Bentham and Austin was for those earlier moralists who made intuition and common sense the method of discovering one's duties. There is important common ground between utilitarianism and classical natural law theory.

2. BUCKLAND, W.W. *Some Reflections on Jurisprudence*, (Cambridge University Press, 1945), chaps. 1, 5, 9 and pp. 107–10: Austin's views as to law and sovereignty are presuppositions in his study of jurisprudence. In the main, Austin is defended against some of his critics but his confusion of the legal and political sovereign is pointed out. The question of rights and duties in the sovereign is considered at the end.

3. TAYLOR, R. "Law and Morality" (1968) 43 NYULR 611: laws are described as particular commands addressed by particular men to others. Their authority is the power of the commander to secure obedience. On this basis the separation of law and morals, enforceability, enforcement and the "perfect law" are explained.

4. FULLER, L.L. "American Legal Philosophy at Mid-century" (1953–54), 6 JLE 457, at pp. 459–67: in the course of a review of E.W. Patterson's *Jurisprudence (supra)*, the Austinian theory is considered as well as the implications of a concept of law supported by force.

5. CAMPBELL, A.H. "Some Footnotes to Salmond's Jurisprudence" (1940) 7 CLJ 206, at pp. 209–11: the problems connected with rights and duties in the sovereign are considered. These do not arise if law is not conceived of as emanating from the will of the sovereign.

6. HASTIE, W. "Introduction" to G.F. Puchta and Others: *Outlines of the Science of Jurisprudence*, (trans. W. Hastie, T. & T. Clark, Edinburgh, 1887): this is a general appraisal of the contribution of the analytical school and pointing out its limitations. A more historical approach is advocated.

7. TAPPER, C.F. "Austin on Sanctions" [1965] CLJ 271: the view that Austin, though he may have been wrong, was at least clear and consistent is challenged. By examining his views on sanctions it is shown that he was muddled, inconsistent and ambiguous. But it is also pointed out that it is in these very inconsistencies that one finds the real value of Austin, namely, the germs of so many subsequent theses.

8. MONTROSE, J.L. "Return to Austin's College" in *Precedent in English Law and Other Essays*, (ed. H.G. Hanbury, Irish U.P., Shannon, 1968), chap. 4: this gives a useful general account of Austin's thought and the place of jurisprudence in legal education.

9. SMITH, J.C. "Law, Language, and Philosophy" (1968) 3 U Br Col LR 59: in the course of reviewing the attitude to language of various legal philosophers, Austin's technique is explained and considered.

1. RADBRUCH, G. "Anglo-American Jurisprudence through Continental Eyes", (1936), 52 LQR 530: the greater part of this article is devoted to an appraisal of the work of Austin and his successors, which is compared with contemporary developments in Continental juristic thought.

H.L.A. Hart

2. HART, H.L.A. *The Concept of Law*, (Oxford, Clarendon Press, 1961, reprinted 1975): after demolishing Austin in the first four chapters, he proceeds to formulate his own concept of law as the union of primary rules (creating duties) and secondary rules (creating powers and the "rule of recognition"). On this basis he considers various well-known questions concerning law, and in chap. 10 deals with the similarities and differences between municipal and international law.

3. HART, H.L.A. "Positivism and the Separation of Law and Morals" (1957–58) 71 Harv LR 593: positivism has many meanings, but the bone of contention between positivists and naturalists lies in the insistence of the former on separating the "is" and the "ought".

4. SMITH, J.C. "Law, Language, and Philosophy" (1968) 3 U Br Col LR 59: in the course of reviewing the attitude to language of various legal philosophers, Professor Hart's technique is explained and considered.

5. FULLER, L.L. "Positivism and Fidelity to Law – a Reply to Professor Hart" (1957– 58) 71 Harv LR 630: is the positivist separation of the "is" and the "ought" a distinction that is, or ought to be? For the distinction just cannot be preserved in practice. Professor Hart's contentions are considered point by point.

6. FULLER, L.L. *The Morality of Law*, (Yale University Press, revised ed., 1969), pp. 133– 145, 153–157, 184–186: Hart's basic distinction between rules conferring powers and rules imposing duties is criticised as being too unsure. Hart's contention that power conferred by his "rule of recognition" is inextinguishable is also controverted as being unfounded; and his distinction between "pre-legal" and "legal" societies is rejected as bearing no correlation to anthropological data: pp. 133– 145. Hart's views as to the relation between law and morality are criticised at pp. 153–157 and 184–186.

7. COHEN, L.J. Review of H.L.A. Hart, *The Concept of Law* (1962) 71 Mind, 395: Hart's key distinction between "primary" and "secondary" rules is examined, and the idea that the clue to law lies in their union is rejected as being unhelpful. In particular, the different sorts of powers contained in the "secondary rules" category are critically examined and it is alleged that Hart tends to overload the power concept.

8. SUMMERS, R.S. "Professor H.L.A. Hart's Concept of Law" (1963) DLJ 629: this analysis is recommended as being one of the best critiques of Hart's book. The article begins by explaining the theory and then points out certain objections to it. The concluding section is especially valuable for it sets out Hart's analytical methods.

9. RAZ, J. *The Concept of a Legal System. An Introduction to the Theory of Legal System* (Clarendon Press, Oxford, 1970), pp. 197–200: the "rule of recognition" is examined and criticised. This, it is alleged, is not a "secondary rule" in the category of powers, where Hart placed it, but a "primary rule" imposing an

obligation on officials. It is their behaviour which determines the rule of recognition.

1. HILL, R.E. "Legal Validity and Legal Obligation" (1970) 80 Yale LJ 47: a close examination of Hart's "internal point of view" and his idea of "obligation" shows that there is a value element. Validity can be established by value-free criteria, but obligation cannot be, it requires that valid law conforms to justice and morality.

2. SARTORIUS, R.E. "Hart's Concept of Law" in *More Essays in Legal Philosophy. General Assessments of Legal Philosophies* (ed. R.S. Summers, Oxford, 1971; reprinted from (1966) 52 Archiv fur Rechts und Sozialphilosophie, 161) 131: this penetrating critique points out that the distinctions between "primary" and "secondary" rules are manifold and there is no such thing as *the* distinction. The valuable distinction between the "internal" and "external" aspects of rules is independent of the distinction between primary and secondary rules. The "rule of recognition" is not an all-sufficient test of validity. Indeed, the concept of "valid law" is itself a "cluster concept"; there is no "essence" of validity.

3. SAMEK, R.A. *The Legal Point of View* (Philosophical Library, New York, 1974), chapters 8–9: Professor Hart's views are subjected to searching criticism. It is said that he misrepresents Austin's position by comparing it to the "gunman" situation writ large. Hart fails to justify his own model for elucidating law on the ground that it is fruitful for the purpose for which he constructed it. The views of Dworkin, Summers and Pound are also considered at length.

4. MacCORMICK, D.N. "Law as Institutional Fact" (1974) 90 LQR 102: in the latter part it is pointed out that there are rules which are both power-conferring and duty-imposing, while other rules provide for the alteration of a legal position on the occurrence of events (e.g., contract discharged by frustration) and these are not powers. Hence a legal system cannot be explained simply on the basis of rules conferring powers and imposing duties.

5. SIMPSON, A.W.B. "The Common Law and Legal Theory" in *Oxford Essays in Jurisprudence (Second Series)* (ed. A.W.B. Simpson, Oxford University Press, 1973), chap. 4: the drift of this paper is to show that the common law cannot be conceived as a set of rules. It consists of the acceptance as more or less accurate of statements of received ideas and practices.

6. TAPPER, C.F.H. "Powers and Secondary Rules of Change" in *Oxford Essays in Jurisprudence (Second Series)* (ed. A.W.B. Simpson, Oxford University Press, 1973), chap. 10: Hart's use of the Hohfeldian concepts of duty and power and the differences between his use of them and Hohfeld's are examined. Eight differences between primary and secondary rules are set out and eight characteristics of power are explained.

7. RUBEN, D-H. "Positive and Natural Law Revisited" (1972) 49 The Modern Schoolman 295: the crucial point in this paper is a distinction between "reason" and "motive" for obeying, and Hart's analysis of "obligation" is critically examined in the light of it. The differences between Blackstone and Austin and between Hart and Fuller are reviewed.

8. FINCH, J.D. *Introduction to Legal Theory* (2nd ed., Sweet & Maxwell, Ltd, 1974), chaps. 4–5: in the first of these chapters the theories of Bentham and Austin are

outlined and compared, the second chapter contains a highly sympathetic account of Hart's view.

1. HUGHES, G.B.J. "Rules, Policy and Decision Making" (1967–68) 77 Yale LJ 411: the author criticises Hart, pointing out that the "games" analogy has limits when applied to the legal process. Further, courts do resort to policy notions. The question is: are these "legal"? Hart's dichotomy between "rules" and "discretion" (policy) is too simple. A concept of law requires the inclusion of all the elements of decision making, including policies and principles.

2. TAYLOR, E.H. "H.L.A. Hart's Concept of Law in the Perspective of American Legal Realism" (1972) 35 MLR 606: the author criticises Hart's critique of realism. Since realists have not formulated a theory of law a close comparison is not possible. Realists allow more scope for morality than Hart; they do not deny rules but only deny that certainty can be achieved through them; Holmes's prediction idea was not a definition, but only a matter of focus.

3. RAZ, J. "The Identity of Legal Systems" (1971) 59 Calif LR 795: laws are part of a legal system. The identity of a legal system depends on the criterion or criteria which determine whether any set of normative statements is a complete description of a legal system. Identity has two aspects, scope and continuity. Three issues are discussed in relation to them. The relation between existence and efficacy makes the institutionalised character of law indispensable to identity. The distinction between making a new law and applying an existing one brings Hart's rule of recognition under review. This is criticised, but said to be acceptable on the whole. The relation between law and state makes the continuity of a political system connected to identity. In this connection the interaction of legal and non-legal norms becomes relevant, and constitutional and administrative legal norms are more important than others.

4. MAHER, G. "The Identity of the Scottish Legal System" (1977) Jur R 21: two different notions of legal system should be kept distinct: the conditions necessary for a society to have a legal system, e.g., a division of labour so that different legal tasks are performed by different institutions; and the juristic method by which the corpus of norms is ordered, understood and interpreted. The problem of the identity of a Scottish legal system is considered in the light of this.

5. *Law, Morality, and Society. Essays in Honour of H.L.A. Hart* (edd. P.M.S. Hacker and J. Raz, Clarendon Press, Oxford, 1977): P.M.S. HACKER, "Hart's Philosophy of Law", chap. 1: this paper reviews Hart's contributions: use of linguistic analysis to clarify important distinctions, function of definition (which had a good and bad influence on Hart), open-texture concepts, sociological dimension (which led him to reject Kelsen), the vital distinction between the internal and external points of view and the concept of social obligation, law as the union of primary and secondary rules (which is unclear), rule of recognition and the problem of unity. G.P. BAKER: "Defeasibility and Meaning", chap. 2: the purpose of jurisprudence is to increase understanding. Much of Hart's work sought the equilibrium between the possibility of giving genuine explanations of legal concepts and statements, and the *sui generis* character of legal concepts and statements. It is said that there is an inconsistency in maintaining that meaning is connected to speech-acts and that the internal point of view is a matter of people's attitude to rules. Notwithstanding inadequacies in his analysis, it is possible to construct a theory of meaning to accord with his analysis of defeasible concepts. J.R. LUCAS: "The Phenomenon of Law", chap. 4: law is intelligible only in a social context. Hart's

"rule" is ambiguous; the distinction between primary and secondary rules is unclear and softens on examination; and he is unhappiest dealing with the unjust law. The centre of gravity of a legal system lies in the primary rules of pre-legal systems and the *mores* they embody. J.M. FINNIS: "Scepticism, Self-refutation, and the Good of Truth", chap. 14: the author disputes Hart's view that knowledge is more disputable an aspect of the good for Man than survival. Truth and knowledge of it is a "good" worthy of human pursuit. One cannot coherently deny that truth is a "good".

1. DWORKIN, R.M. "The Model of Rules I" in *Taking Rights Seriously* (Duckworth, 1977), chap. 2: the author points to the part played by doctrines, principles, standards and policies, as distinct from rules of law. They originate independently of a "rule of recognition" and they work differently from rules. The latter apply in an all-or-nothing fashion, whereas doctrines, etc. have a dimension of weight. Rules cannot be contradictory, doctrines etc. can be. Resort to them is more than just a matter of discretion. If they are part of "law", then Hart's positivist concept ceases to be adequate. (This chapter is a reprint of "Is Law a System of Rules" in *Essays in Legal Philosophy* (ed. R.S. Summers, Basil Blackwell, Oxford, 1968, p. 25).

2. DWORKIN, R.M. "Hard Cases" in *Taking Rights Seriously* (Duckworth, 1977), chap. 4: a proposition of law is true if the best justification that can be provided for propositions of law already shown to be true furnish a better case for that proposition than for the contrary proposition. It is false if that justification furnishes a better case for the contrary proposition than for it.

3. DWORKIN, R.M. "No Right Answer" in *Law, Morality, and Society. Essays in Honour of H.L.A. Hart* (edd. P.M.S. Hacker and J. Raz, Clarendon Press, Oxford, 1977), chap. 3: concepts describing occasions of official duty do not have the same structure as duty. Propositions of law are not equivalent in meaning to propositions about official duties. Vagueness does not suggest that there is no right answer. For all practical purposes there will always be a right answer.

4. CHRISTIE, G.C. "The Model of Principles" (1968) DLJ 649: Dworkin's thesis is faulty in its basis. Hart's "open-textured" nature of rules allows for discretion. The author disagrees with Dworkin's all-or-nothing nature of rules. If rules are more fluid than this, then rules too can have "weight". Dworkin gives no example of a complete statement of a rule incorporating all its exceptions.

5. GROSS, H. "Standards as Law" (1968–69) Ann Sur Am L 575: Hart fails to explain how an item is not law in spite of authority; Dworkin fails to give examples of how what is law is determined otherwise than by rules. Both reason and authority are bases of ascribing the quality of "law" to a proposition. A criterion for "law" should include both. When there is no authority, there are standards by which to choose between competing arguments.

6. TAPPER, C.F.H. "A Note on Principles" (1971) 34 MLR 628: this is a comment on Dworkin's thesis. Principles may be regarded as standards to which judges may have recourse in their application and adaptation of rules to specific, but as yet unsettled, fact-situations. Discretion comes in when rules are treated as susceptible to modification in marginal cases.

7. SARTORIUS, R.E. "Social Policy and Judicial Legislation" (1971) 8 Am Phil Q 151: if Dworkin contends that judges have a duty to use some principles but not

others, then there must be some fundamental test for distinguishing one set from the other. The author accepts a distinction between rules and principles, but argues that a "master rule" is required to distinguish both from what is not law.

1. RAZ, J. "Legal Principles and the Limits of Law" (1971–72) 81 Yale LJ 823: this paper takes issue with Dworkin. A principle alludes to a number of rules. Rules, like principles may conflict, so Dworkin's contention that rules cannot conflict, but principles can, disappears. Further, rules too may have "weights". The nature, role and source of principles are reviewed. The paper concludes by discussing the possibility of a criterion of identity.

2. SHUMAN, S.I. "Justification of Judicial Decisions" (1971) 59 Calif LJ 715, 723 *et seq*: to say that rules dictate results only indicates what it is to be a rule; it says nothing about decision-making. In the course of a general discussion of the judicial process, Dworkin's thesis is examined and criticised in certain respects.

3. EEKELAAR, J.M. "Principles of Revolutionary Legality" in *Oxford Essays in Jurisprudence (Second Series)* (ed. A.W.B. Simpson, Oxford University Press, 1973), chap. 2: in the course of a discussion of the legality of revolutionary regimes, the author discusses Dworkin's distinction between "rules" and "principles". It is contended, however, that the difference is not in kind but in the degree of generality, and also that the difference in their sources becomes unimportant in practice, especially in systems which do not have a doctrine of *stare decisis*.

4. DWORKIN, R.M. "The Model of Rules II" in *Taking Rights Seriously* (Duckworth, 1977), chap. 3: the author answers his critics. Sociology describes behaviour. Professor Hart's "rule of recognition" as observable in the behaviour of officials is similar. The question is what it is that makes it normative. A social practice justifies a normative rules, but cannot constitute it. He criticises Hart, Sartorius and Raz.

5. BELL, R.S. "Understanding the Model of Rules: Towards a Reconciliation of Dworkin and Positivism" (1971–72) 81 Yale LJ 912: Dworkin is said to fail in his attack on positivism. The author defends the rule model. He draws a distinction between "rulings", "rules of law" and "legal rules". Rules of law are about legal rules. He considers "hard" cases and doubts whether they call for discretion. Principles do not frame obligations, hence they cannot be the basis for decisions.

6. COVAL, S.C. and SMITH, J.C. "Some Structural Properties of Legal Decisions" (1973) 32 CLJ 81: it is argued that Dworkin's "principles" are "second-order" rules, which come into play when first-order rules conflict. They are just as precise as first-order rules and function along with them. Hence, Dworkin's "principles" can be fitted into a rule model of law. (This paper is reprinted in J.C. SMITH, *Legal Obligation* (London: Athlone Press, 1976), chap. 9).

7. STEINER, J.M. "Judicial Discretion and the Concept of Law" (1976) 35 CLJ 135: after a comparison of the models offered respectively by Professors Hart and Dworkin, the author considers two critiques of Dworkin neither of which is said to be satisfactory. On the other hand, Dworkin fails to displace Hart's rule model in favour of a principle model.

8. MARSHALL, G. "Positivism, Adjudication, and Democracy" in *Law, Morality, and Society. Essays in Honour of H.L.A. Hart* (edd. P.M.S. Hacker and J. Raz,

Clarendon Press, Oxford, 1977), chap. 7: Dworkin's criticisms of law as a system of rules uses arguments about the judicial process. Is there a connection between positivism and the nature of adjudication? The argument is an examination of the positivist and Dworkinian theses on the basis of the attitudes of two imaginary judges representing each side. There is a basis for agreement between them. Positivists can find room for legal principles as well as rules and also to weigh and balance them.

Sovereignty

1. LEWIS, J.U. "Jean Bodin's 'Logic of Sovereignty'" (1968) 16 Pol S 206: Bodin defined law in terms of source (sovereign will) as well as content (God's will and law of nature as limitations on sovereign power). In this way his work pointed forwards in two directions: unlimited sovereign power (Hobbes) and an ethical foundation for sovereign power. Bodin sensed that a value-free definition of sovereignty was inadequate.

2. REES, W.J. "The Theory of Sovereignty Restated" in *Philosophy, Politics and Society*, (ed. P. Laslett, Blackwell, Oxford, 1956), chap. 4: the different senses in which the word "sovereignty" can be used are distinguished and analysed in order to discover what would be a useful approach today. The Austinian conception figures prominently in the discussion, as well as the traditional objections to it.

3. MAINE, H.J.S. *Lectures on the Early History of Institutions*, (John Murray, 1875), chaps. 12 and 13: here Maine formulates his famous historical criticism of the Austinian theory of sovereignty, especially in the second of the two chapters.

4. BRYCE, J. *Studies in History and Jurisprudence*, (Oxford, 1901), II, chap. 10: a distinction is drawn between the *de jure* and *de facto* sovereign. Austin's commander is the former, but he is shown to have attributed to it features appropriate to the latter. The views of Bentham and Austin are subjected to detailed criticism.

5. DEWEY, J. "Austin's Theory of Sovereignty" (1894), 9 Pol Sc Q 31: it is alleged that some, Maine in particular, misconceived Austin's theory, which is re-examined chiefly with reference to the United States. When ascribing sovereignty to part of the body politic, important questions and difficulties arise.

6. MATTERN, J. *Concepts of State, Sovereignty and International Law*, (John Hopkins Press, Baltimore; Humphrey Milford, 1928), chap. 5: the Austinian theory of sovereignty and its modifications by Dicey and Brown are set out. The whole book is of general interest as providing an account of theories of sovereignty since Bodin.

7. SIDGWICK, H. *Elements of Politics*, (2nd ed., Macmillan & Co, 1897), pp. 23–29, chap. 31 and Appendix A: some of the limitations on sovereign power are considered as well as the difficulties which Austin's view encounters with reference to the American Constitution. In chapter 31 the whereabouts of sovereignty are shown to be a more complex matter than was assumed by Austin. Appendix A is a critique of Austin's doctrine. The ideas of the illimitability of sovereignty and "tacit command", in particular, are rejected.

8. DICEY, A.V. *The Law of the Constitution*, (10th ed., E.C.S. Wade, Macmillan & Co, Ltd, 1961), pp. 71–85: in the course of his classic exposition of the doctrine of

the sovereignty of Parliament, Dicey considers the difficulties of Austin's concept of sovereignty and the limitations that do exist on Parliamentary sovereignty.

1. MERRIAM, C.E. *History of the Theory of Sovereignty since Rousseau*, (The Columbia University Press, 1900), chap. 8: the origins of the Austinian theory and the views of Bentham are explained. There is also an account of the theory itself and of the principal criticisms of it.

2. LASKI, H.J. *A Grammar of Politics*, (4th ed., Allen & Unwin, Ltd, 1938), chap. 2: sovereignty is considered historically as a theory of law and as a theory of political organisation. In the historical context, the views of Bodin and Hobbes, *inter alia*, are mentioned. As a theory of law, the Austinian view is examined (pp. 50–55). The assumptions that underlie it make it useless as an explanation of the modern state for political purposes.

3. LINDSAY, A.D. *The Modern Democratic State*, (Oxford University Press, 1947), chap. 9: the origins of the doctrine of sovereignty are traced out and the Austinian version of it, its merits and weaknesses are examined. Sovereignty is claimed for the constitution, and the argument follows H. Kelsen's analysis, though Kelsen is not mentioned (as to Kelsen, see next chapter).

4. HARRISON, F. *On Jurisprudence and the Conflict of Laws*, (Oxford, 1919), chap. 1 and Annotation by A.H.F. Lefroy, 1: Austin's view on sovereignty is, within limits, appropriate only to a lawyer. From a historical point of view it is open to objection, and in this connection Maine's criticisms are considered.

5. HEARN, W.E. *The Theory of Legal Duties and Rights*, (Melbourne: John Ferres; London: Trubner & Co., 1883), chap. 2: the Austinian theory of sovereignty is adopted and explained.

6. JENKS, E. *The New Jurisprudence*, (John Murray, 1933), pp. 73–84: the main criticism is directed at Austin's idea of "political society" and the requirement that there has to be a sovereign in every such society. The attributes which Austin claimed for his sovereign are also considered and rejected.

7. McILWAIN, C.H. *Constitutionalism and the Changing World*, (Cambridge University Press, 1939), chap 4: sovereign power is a purely juristic term and has no application outside law. The discussion is in general terms, but the theories of Bodin, Hobbes and Austin are alluded to in the course of it, especially the influences on Austin.

8. DICKINSON, J. "A Working Theory of Sovereignty" (1927), Pol Sc Q, 524: three types of sovereignty are distinguished, legal sovereignty, sovereignty in international law and popular (political) sovereignty. Although this is not based on Austinian premises, it could usefully be read alongside that theory.

9. MITCHELL, J.D.B. "A General Theory of Public Contracts" (1951) 63 Jur R, 60: the conflict between the sanctity of contracts and sovereignty is considered. In the course of it there is a critical appraisal of the conceptions of sovereignty of Bodin, Hobbes and Austin.

10. POUND, R. "Law and State – Jurisprudence and Politics" (1943–44) 57 Harv LR, 1193, at pp. 1211–21: sovereignty rose into prominence with the rise of centralised governments after the Middle Ages. It is a juristic conception and the part which it plays is considered.

1. van KLEFFENS, E.N. "Sovereignty in International Law", (1953) 1 Hague Receuil, 1: this is of general interest only. It is a long and detailed account of the origins of the word "sovereignty" and of the development of the idea from antiquity, Greek, Roman and medieval times down to the present. It deals entirely with the part played by the doctrine in international law.

2. FRIEDRICH, C.J. *The Philosophy of Law in Historical Perspective*, (University of Chicago Press, 1958), chaps. 8 and 11: in the first of these chapters the work and influence of Bodin is dealt with. In the latter that of Hobbes, Bentham and Austin is considered in relation to each other.

3. SNYDER, O.C. *Preface to Jurisprudence*, (The Bobbs-Merrill Co Inc, 1954), Part II, chaps. 2 and 3: this is of general interest. Some of the traditional questions that have arisen in connection with sovereignty, both nationally and internationally, are posed. The discussion proceeds from an American point of view.

4. SCHWARZENBERGER, G. "The Forms of Sovereignty", (1957), 10 CLP, 264: this article might usefully be referred to on Austin's requirement that the sovereign should not be dependent upon some other sovereign.

5. LLOYD, D. *The Idea of Law*, (Penguin Books, Ltd, A 688, 1964), chap. 8: the origins of the modern idea of sovereignty and Austin's idea of law as the command of a Sovereign are outlined. (In this connection reference might also be made to Chapter 2 on Law and Force). It is said that a legal theory is required to accomodate limitations on a sovereign legislature and judicial review, while a power theory is required in revolutionary situations. The chapter also deals with state sovereignty in relation to international law.

6. FINCH, J.D. *Introduction to Legal Theory* (2nd ed., Sweet & Maxwell, Ltd, 1974), pp. 146–151: the "legal character" of international and municipal law is discussed with allusions to Austin, Kelsen and Hart.

7. Reference might also be made to the following:– O. GIERKE, *Political Theories of the Middle Age*, (trans. F.W. Maitland, Cambridge University Press, 1900), chaps. 5, 6 and pp. 92–93; H.E. COHEN, *Recent Theories of Sovereignty*, (University of Chicago Press, 1937); F. POLLOCK, *An Introduction to the History of the Science of Politics*, (Macmillan & Co, 1895), chap. 4. See also the bibliography in Chapter 4, section entitled *Development and Nature of Sovereignty*.

17. The Pure Theory

1. KELSEN, H. *Pure Theory of Law*, (trans. M. Knight, University of California Press, 1967): this is an English translation of the second German edition of *Reine Rechtslehre*, (1960). It makes accessible to English readers the principal exposition of Kelsen's theory. Modifications in his thought are indicated in notes.

2. KELSEN, H. *General Theory of Law and State*, (trans. A. Wedberg, Harvard University Press, 1949): in this austerely reasoned book the Pure Theory is set out in full. Of all Kelsen's many works this also is easily accessible and might be regarded as representing his mature views, modified in some respects so as to meet earlier criticisms.

3. KELSEN, H. *What is Justice?* (University of California Press, 1957): of this collection of essays the following are the most relevant:— "Value Judgments in the Science of Law" (p. 209): this contains an outline of the pure theory and shows his views on the relation between values and the law. "The Law as a Specific Social Technique" (p. 231): in which law as a coercive order monopolising the use of force is developed, as well as the relation between wrongdoing and sanction. "Why Should the Law be Obeyed?" (p. 257): this considers various possibilities and rejects them all in favour of the position occupied by the *Grundnorm*. "The Pure Theory of Law and Analytical Jurisprudence" (p. 266): which considers the relationship of justice to the maintenance of a positive legal order and of sociological to normative jurisprudence. "Law, State and Justice in the Pure Theory of Law" (p. 288): which stresses the need to free the science of law from animism and how and why considerations of justice should be kept apart.

4. KELSEN, H. "The Pure Theory of Law" (trans. C.H. Wilson), (1934), 50 LQR, 474; (1935), 51 LQR, 517: the aims and contentions of the pure theory are set out. Some of the forms of expression used in these articles have been altered in the *General Theory of Law and State (supra)*.

5. KELSEN, H. "The Function of the Pure Theory of Law", in *Law: A Century of Progress*, (New York University Press, 1937), 231: the Pure Theory is general jurisprudence. The distinction between the science of law and sociology, morals and politics needs to be maintained.

6. KELSEN, H. "The Pure Theory of Law and Analytical Jurisprudence" (1941–42) 55 Harv LR 44: the Pure Theory is a science which seeks the fundamental principles of any order. It expels value judgments. Natural law is not concerned with legal reality, but with its defence or attack. A norm "exists" when it is valid. Validity is distinct from efficacy. Science deals with the "is"; and sociology is a branch of the "is". Jurisprudence deals with validity, sociology with efficacy. Also dealt with are the concept of "norm", coercion, duty and right, the hierarchy of norms, law and state and international law.

7. KELSEN, H. "On the Basic Norm" (1959), 47 Calif LR, 107: a norm means that something ought to be done. The "existence" of a norm is its validity, which derives ultimately from the Basic Norm. Kelsen is at pains to refute the suspicion that the Pure Theory is "a kind of natural law doctrine".

8. KELSEN, H. "What is the Pure Theory of Law?" (1959–60), 34 Tul LR, 269: law is not a fact; one cannot infer an "ought" from an "is". As a prescription, a norm

is neither true nor false; it is valid or invalid. Effectiveness is a condition of validity, but not identical with it. There is an explanation of "purity" and of the basic norm.

1. POLLOCK, F. "Laws of Nature and Laws of Man" in *Essays in Jurisprudence and Ethics*, (Macmillan & Co, 1882), 42: this was not written with reference to Kelsen, but the substance is relevant. Natural laws do not involve disobedience and punishment. On the other hand, human laws are not just statements of what will happen on disobedience, for they are needed to guide people who do not wish to disobey and, moreover, the "happening" of the penalty is dependent on many factors.

2. KELSEN, H. "Centralisation and Decentralisation" in *Authority and the Individual*, (Harvard Tercentenary Publications, Harvard University Press, 1937), p. 210: the Pure Theory is given practical application to a modern problem. Since, according to the theory, "state" and "legal order" are identical, centralisation and decentralisation are particula. forms of the legal order; they are shown to be problems concerning validity relating to jurisdiction and the creation of legal norms.

3. KELSEN, H. "Derogation" in *Essays in Jurisprudence in Honor of Roscoe Pound*, (ed. R.A. Newman, The Bobbs-Merrill Co, Inc, 1962), 339: a norm may lose its validity in various ways. Derogation means repeal. Repeal relates to the norm repealed, therefore it is a dependent norm and it cannot be violated.

4. KELSEN, H. "Professor Stone and the Pure Theory of Law" (1964–65) 17 Stan LR 1128: Kelsen joins issue with Professor Stone's criticisms in the course of which he clarifies his basic positions. Even without a knowledge of Stone's critique, this paper is very helpful in understanding Kelsen.

5. KELSEN, H. "On the Pure Theory of Law" (1966) 1 Isreal LR 1: this reviews the main points of his theory: the pure theory is a general theory, law is a type of norm, it is a coercive order ("norm", "obligation", "responsibility" are essential), positivism, purity, identity of law and state, and the basic norm.

Commentaries and Critiques

6. EBENSTEIN, W. *The Pure Theory of Law*, (University of Wisconsin Press, 1945): this sets out in a somewhat uncritical fashion the general Kelsen doctrine. It also endeavours to show that the doctrine is not without practical importance (chap. 5).

7. EBENSTEIN, W. "The Pure Theory of Law: Demythologizing Legal Thought" (1971) 59 Calif LR 617: this is a straightforward explanation of Kelsen's doctrine, from its Kantian origin, the quest for scientific universality, causality and normativity, imputation, the basic norm, tension between norms and efficiacy, theory of concretization and the implications of the theory for political theory.

8. LAUTERPACHT, H. "Kelsen's Pure Science of Law" in *Modern Theories of Law*, (ed. W.I. Jennings, Oxford University Press, 1933), chap. 7: a general account is given of Kelsen's doctrine. The criticism is made of the wholesale rejection of natural law and also that there might be an element of natural law in the doctrine.

9. LATHAM, R.T.E. "The Law and the Commonwealth" in W.K. HANCOCK: *Survey of British Commonwealth Affairs*, (Oxford University Press, 1937), pp. 522–95, (reproduced in facsimile in 1949): the structure of the Commonwealth is examined

in the light of what is meant by formal unity, based on Kelsen's analysis. The nature of the *Grundnorm* is considered in detail with reference to constitutional law; it can be indeterminate and shifting. The discoverability of a *Grundnorm* in the Commonwealth is even more difficult.

1. VOEGELIN, E. "Kelsen's Pure Theory of Law" (1927), 42 Pol Sc Q 268: this is a review of Kelsen's *Allgemeine Staatslehre*, 1925. Explanation is given of the separation of the "ought" from the "is" and the centre of gravity of Kelsen's doctrine as resting on enforcement. A demonstration is given of how Hohfeld's distinctions of "right" might be deduced from enforcement (*quaere* whether this would correspond with practice in view of sanctioness duty-situations).

2. PARKER, R. "The Pure Theory of Law" (1960–61) 14 Vand LR 211: this is a simplified re-statement of Kelsen's doctrine. Its weakness in relation to inter-national law is pointed out.

3. de BUSTAMANTE y MONTORO, A.S. "Kelsenism" in *Interpretations of Modern Legal Philosophies*, (ed. P. Sayre, Oxford University Press, New York, 1947), chap. 3: certain developments and re-interpretations of Kelsen's doctrines, neo-Kelsenism, so as to meet the needs of the day are explained. Value-judgments, it is argued, should be placed above the law.

4. PATTERSON, E.W. "Hans Kelsen and his Pure Theory of Law" (1952–53) 40 Calif LR 5: a short biography of Kelsen is followed by an account of his chief contri-butions to legal theory.

5. WILK, K. "Law and the State as Pure Ideas: Critical Notes on the Basic Concepts of Kelsen's Legal Philosophy" (1940–41) 51 Ethics 158: this contains an acute analysis of the correspondence between the normative world of law and social reality. Kelsen, it is alleged, fails to draw an adequate distinction between norma-tive and other types of hypothetical judgments. The further criticisms are both penetrating and shrewd.

6. HÄGERSTRÖM, A. *Inquiries into the Nature of Law and Morals*, (ed. K. Olivecrona, trans. C.D. Broad, Almqvist & Wiksell, Stockholm, 1953), pp. 51–55, 257–98: the earlier passage is a criticism of an early and misleading statement by Kelsen as to the nature of the "ought". The latter chapter is a detailed review of Kelsen's thesis. The practical emptiness of his theory is pointed out and there are some damaging criticisms of his views on international law. (Note that these comments were made on Kelsen's publications in 1911 and 1925).

7. ROSS, A. Review of Kelsen's *What is Justice?* (1957) 45 Calif LR 564: this is a short but penetrating commentary on the essays contained in the book. The observations on Kelsen's basic conceptions should be particularly noted.

8. ROSS, A. *On Law and Justice*, (Stevens & Sons, Ltd, 1958), pp. 66–67, 80–84: the treatment of "validity" might usefully be contrasted with Kelsen's treatment of it. This, to Ross, is the basis of a prediction that a judge will act in a certain way.

9. HART, H.L.A. "Kelsen Visited" (1962–63) 10 UCLALR 709: this reviews a debate between the author and Kelsen with reference to three puzzles. Although norms are prescriptive, legal rules formulated by the science of law are descriptive – this means that the descriptive element in rules is a rational reconstruction of norms. Delict is behaviour upon which a sanction becomes applicable – why does

Kelsen say that this is all a definition of delict can be, but add that it is correct only when the condition of the socially detrimental character of the conduct is satisfied? The relation between law and morality – there cannot be a relation between law and morality so that a valid rule of law is contradicted by a valid rule of morality – the topic of "collision of duties".

1. RAZ, J. *The Concept of a Legal System. An Introduction to the Theory of Legal System* (Clarendon Press, Oxford, 1970), chaps. 3–9: the greater part of this book consists of an acute critique of Kelsen's doctrines and is by far the best aspect of it. The aim is to work out the structure of a legal system and Kelsen's contribution to this end are closely examined. His criteria of *Grundnorm*, chains of validity, his failure to allow for powers as well as shifts in his position are mercilessly attacked. By comparison, Bentham's contribution is preferred.

2. CHRISTIE, G.C. "The Notion of Validity in Modern Jurisprudence" (1963–64) 48 Minn LR 1049: legal norms, as prescriptions of conduct, cannot be true or false; but assertions of validity can be true or false with reference to their validity. The views of validity of Kelsen and Ross are considered and compared with reference to concrete situations. Kelsen's analysis is preferred.

3. MUNZER, S. "Validity and Legal Conflict" (1972–73) 82 Yale LJ 1140: the denial of conflict stems from the hypothesis of some single co-ordinating criterion of validity. Valid rules can conflict. Law is not neat and tidy because the criterion for distinguishing what is law and what is not law rests on a plurality of rules. Nor is there any necessary consistency in the various prohibitions and permissions of the law, since laws are produced by fallible human beings.

4. LUNDSTEDT, A.V. *Legal Thinking Revised*, (Almqvist & Wiksell, Stockholm, 1956), pp. 402–6: Kelsen's doctrine is sharply criticised. The attempt to free a theory of law from the world of fact is rejected as absurd. The whole doctrine is criticised for failing to take account of actual activities and the influence of the maintenance of law on the feelings of people.

5. STONE, J. *Legal System and Lawyers' Reasonings* (Stevens & Sons, Ltd, 1964), chap. 3: Kelsen's theory of law is critically reviewed and its limitations pointed out. The assertion that what *is* cannot justify what *ought to be* is criticised on the ground that, on Kelsen's own showing, the validity of every norm does depend in part at least on the efficacy of the system. Further, the difficulties and ambiguities inherent in the "basic norm" concept are exposed, and various other aspects of his doctrine, especially with regard to international law, are also dealt with.

6. STONE, J. "Mystery and Mystique of the Basic Norm", (1963), 26 MLR 34: this is an acute inquiry into the obscurity that still surrounds Kelsen's idea of the *Grundnorm*. His various statements about it are collated from different writings to show that Kelsen may not be clear in his own mind. Its range of possible meanings and their implications are considered.

7. KELSEN, H. "Professor Stone and the Pure Theory of Law" (1964–65) 17 Stan LR 1128: in reply to Professor Stone's criticisms, contained principally in his *Legal System and Lawyers' Reasonings*, Kelsen points out that Stone has misunderstood and misrepresented much of what he has written. This must be read alongside Stone's critique.

1. GOLDING, M.P. "Kelsen and the Concept of 'Legal System' " in *More Essays in Legal Philosophy. General Assessments of Legal Philosophies*, (ed. R.S. Summers, Oxford, 1971), 69: Kelsen aims at a rational reconstruction of a legal system. This involves the way in which legal norms are stated as representing the structural relations between them. Kelsen's theory is explained on this basis and criticised. The notions of "validity", "existence" and "structure" are considered and certain criticisms made of Kelsen's treatment of them.

2. SAMEK, R.A. *The Legal Point of View*, (Philosophical Library, New York, 1974), chapter 7: this is a long and detailed criticism of the many aspects of Kelsen's doctrine. Throughout there is a comparison with the author's own "legal point of view".

3. MacCORMICK, D.N. "Legal Obligation and the Imperative Fallacy" in *Oxford Essays in Jurisprudence (Second Series)* (ed. A.W.B. Simpson, Oxford University Press, 1973), chap. 5: it is wrong to confuse the imperative with the normative. A recent example of the "imperative fallacy" is said to be Kelsen's insistence that "acts of will" are "oughts".

4. HARRIS, J.W. "Kelsen's Concept of Authority" (1977) 36 CLJ 353: Kelsen's normative schema is subjected to acute scrutiny, in particular the thesis that a particular norm is "authorised" if it can be subsumed under a more general norm. The author is only in partial agreement and points out that subsumption is a sufficient, but not a necessary condition of normative authority, and that authorising is not the function of a distinct kind of norm.

5. HARRIS, J.W. "When and Why does the *Grundnorm* Change?" (1971) 29 CLJ 103: the nature and function of the *Grundnorm* are carefully analysed, with the position in Britain used as illustration. Four senses of "validity" are distinguished. The problem of the change of a *Grundnorm* in relation to efficacy is considered in the light of these analyses and applied to the Rhodesian situation. Criticisms of Kelsen drawn from that situation are rejected.

6. PAULSON, S.L. "Constraints on Legal Norms: Kelsen's View in the *Essays*" (1975) 42 UCLR 768: in this review of Kelsen's *Essays in Legal and Moral Philosophy* (trans. P. Heath, ed. O. Weinberger, Reidel Publishing Co, Mass, 1973) the author examines Kelsen's views on the limitations imposed on the substance of laws and by form. In the course of it he deals with the concept of validity in relation to authorisation and the basic norm.

7. HUGHES, G.B.J. "Validity and the Basic Norm" (1971) 59 Calif LR 695: the author attacks the *Grundnorm*, but says that its rejection need not impair Kelsen's theory. He distinguishes between weak and strong senses of the *Grundnorm* and indicates the difficulties in both. He also considers in what sense the *Grundnorm* is an "ought", law and morals and international law.

8. SUMMERS, R.S. "The Technique Element in Law" (1971) 59 Calif LR 733: the techniques of the law do not explain what social functions law performs, but how law helps in their performance. He amplifies Kelsen's statement of techniques into five: grievance-remedial, penal, administrative-regulatory, public benefit-conferring and private arranging. Such an analysis can have descriptive, normative and pedagogic value.

9. MAHER, G. "The Identity of the Scottish Legal System" (1977) Jur R 21: Kelsen's

theory is inapplicable to a peaceful merger of two states, each passing its own statute of merger. Since there is here no break in the legality of either, the two systems must remain, e.g., England and Scotland in 1707. What, then, is the British *Grundnorm*? Is there any British law? To argue that 1707 amounted to a revolution presents difficulties on historical facts and also because there was no break in legality.

1. WILSON, C.H. "The Basis of Kelsen's Pure Theory of Law" (1934–35) 1 Politica 54: there is first an explanation of the main ideas in Kelsen's doctrine. Criticisms are then levelled at the necessity for a fundamental norm, the distinction between a theory of law and ethics, the notion of validity, and finally the whole theory is alleged to suffer from contradictions.

2. STARKE, J.G. "Fundamental Views and Ideas of Hans Kelsen (1881–1973)" (1974) 48 Aust LJ 388: this is a useful review of the salient points of Kelsen's teachings: the concept of a "pure" theory, "norm", "legal order", "validity", the distinction between validity and efficacy, criteria of legal norms, concept of "delict", conduct and liability and its imputation to organs of the state, identity of law and state, absence of any distinction between law-creation and law-application, discounting legal metaphors, international and municipal law.

3. *Law, State and International Legal Order. Essays in Honor of Hans Kelsen* (edd. S. Engel and R.A. Métall, University of Tennessee Press, 1964): E. AZKIN: "Analysis of State and Law Structure", p. 1: the Pure Theory presents an incomplete picture, and the question is whether coherence and consistency may be too high a price for incompleteness. The author submits that Kelsen's scheme offers the best method for a systematic study of normative relations within the state. He sets out two models, one of the abstract Kelsen scheme and the other of the corresponding state institutions. H. AUFRICHT: "The Theory of Pure Law in Historical Perspective", p. 29: the unending enthusiasm for Kelsen's theory is due to new insights into special fields of law, into the relation between international and domestic law and the organisation of the whole of a legal order. Kelsen was an advisor to the government and the architect of the Austrian Federal Constitution, 1920, and he did much work on features of the Austrian system. O. BONDY: "Hans Kelsen's Relativistic Approach to Ethics", p. 51: both law and ethics are normative orders, but law is distinguished by coercion. Morality includes all other social norms. The ethical theory emerging from Kelsen's work is considered in relation to typical problems of morality. Moral values are established by the individual as his own moral law and, therefore, create relative values. H. SILVING: "The Lasting Value of Kelsenism", p. 297: the lasting value of Kelsen's work lies in its legal methodology than in its theory of law. It is pointed out that the dichotomy between "is" and "ought" are historical incidents of particular linguistic structures. R.J. VERNENGO: "About Some Formative Rules for Legal Languages", p. 339: Kelsen chose propositions of legal science as his starting point. There are four kinds of validity spheres, but these are only partial sets of the formation rules that regulate the use of meaningful sentences by legal science.

4. PATTERSON, E.W. *Jurisprudence*, (The Foundation Press, Inc, 1953), pp. 259–65: Kelsen's doctrine is outlined with illustrative references to America. Certain general criticisms are made of it.

5. LLOYD, D. *Introduction to Jurisprudence*, (3rd ed., Stevens & Sons, Ltd, 1972), chap. 5: the influence of Kant and Hume on Kelsen is mentioned and the

differences between Austin and Kelsen are summarised. Allusion is made to the ambiguities of the *Grundnorm* and to the difficulties of trying to unify municipal and international law.

1. FRIEDMANN, W. *Legal Theory*, (5th ed., Stevens & Sons, Ltd, 1967), chap. 24: a summary of Kelsen's doctrine is followed by a careful evaluation of it.

2. JONES, J.W. *Historical Introduction to the Theory of Law*, (Oxford, 1940), chap. 9: while Austin has been criticised as being too abstract, Kelsen would say that a theory of law cannot be too abstract. The essence of a rule is found in the possibility of disobedience, not obedience. An account of the theory then follows.

3. ALLEN, C.K. *Law in the Making* (7th ed., Oxford, 1964), pp. 52–64: a general account of the doctrine is followed by a criticism of its sterility. The *Grundnorm* is likened to Austin's sovereign in a new guise. The considerable difficulties of ascertaining it in international law are pointed out.

4. BODENHEIMER, E. *Jurisprudence*, (Harvard University Press, 1962), pp. 98–102: this gives a brief general account of the doctrine and the "theory of concretization".

5. BODENHEIMER, E. 'Power and Law: a Study of the Concept of Law" (1939–40) 50 Ethics, 127, at pp. 130–33: this, too, gives a brief account of the doctrine.

6. COWAN, T.A. "Law Without Force" (1971) 59 Calid LR 683: for Kelsen the essence of law is force. The opposite of war is law, but force is the partner of law. Would peace means world law, which means world force, which is world war. Natural law provides no answer, since it is the ally of revolution and also requires force. Law without force is control, e.g. contract. When force is used, e.g., criminal law, this is not "law".

7. JOLOWICZ, H.F. *Lectures on Jurisprudence*, (ed. J.A. Jolowicz, The Athlone Press, 1963), chap. 11: the principal points in Kelsen's theory are simply and attractively stated.

8. CASTBERG, F. *Problems of Legal Philosophy*, (2nd ed., Oslo University Press; London: Allen & Unwin, Ltd, 1957), pp. 44–47: Kelsen's doctrine is outlined in the course of a general discussion of validity. The question as to which postulate of validity should be adopted has to be answered with reference to social reality. The validity of customary law is said to pose some difficulty.

9. BUCKLAND, W.W. *Some Reflections on Jurisprudence*, (Cambridge University Press, 1945), pp. 18–24: Kelsen's views as to the identity of state and law and the nature of law are considered critically. The difficulties surrounding the notion of the *Grundnorm*, especially in international law, are pointed out.

10. CROSS, A.R.N. *Precedent in English Law*, (2nd ed., Oxford, 1968), pp. 204–207: comment is made on the *Grundnorm* being "presupposed" and that a change in it amounts to a "revolution". It is said that the abandonment of the doctrine of *stare decisis* would be a "revolution" only in a strained sense of the term.

11. PATON, G.W. *A Text-Book of Jurisprudence*, (4th ed., G.W. Paton and D.P. Derham, Clarendon Press, Oxford, 1972), pp. 14–19, 86–87, 347–348: these three passages deal respectively with a simplified general account of the theory, the position of international law and the identity of state and law.

1. GINSBERG, M. *Reason and Unreason in Society*, (Longmans, Green & Co, Ltd, 1947), pp. 234–39: the sense in which Kelsen is to be described as a positivist is examined. The *Grundnorm* may be grounded in "impure" factors, but if it is based on morals the separation between law and morality cannot be maintained. The question is raised whether such a separation itself is moral.

2. DIAS, R.W.M. "Legal Politics: Norms behind the *Grundnorm*" (1968) 26 CLJ 233: the Rhodesian UDI Case shows the working in practice of a revolutionary situation. Kelsen's doctrines do not apply here and some of its limitations are exposed.

3. BROOKFIELD, F.M. "The Courts, Kelsen and the Rhodesian Revolution" (1969) 19 UTLJ 326: a good deal of light is shed on Kelsen's doctrines in the course of this exhaustive review of the various judgments in the Rhodesian crisis cases.

4. OJO, A. "The Search for a *Grundnorm* in Nigeria – the Lakanmi Case" (1971) 20 ICLQ 117: the legality of certain laws of the Federal Military Government depended on whether there had been a revolution or just a "constitutional emerency". The decision in the case alluded to is criticised on the ground that the fact of a revolution having being laid down by decree, legality followed.

5. DATE-BAH, S.K. "Jurisprudence's Day in Court in Ghana" (1971) 20 ICLQ 315: this is an interesting account of a Ghanaian case in which the court rejected Kelsen and preferred to abide by the letter of the law. The views of the judges are criticised in that no good reasons were given why Kelsen's thesis was to be treated as irrelevant.

6. EEKELAAR, J.M. "Principles of Revolutionary Legality" in *Oxford Essays in Jurisprudence (Second Series)* (ed. A.W.B. Simpson, Oxford University Press, 1973) chap. 2: it is a mistake to suppose that "legal" rules can only exist within the framework of an operatuve system and that once the system collapses decisions about its successor cannot be "legal". Such decisions are made according to "principles". Rules and "principles" are both normative and decisions based on the latter are not necessarily different from those based on the former. (Kelsen did recognise the "principle of effectiveness". The present author's arguments repeats much of what Kelsen would have said, but he seeks to add further limiting principles).

7. FINNIS, J.M. "Revolutions and the Continuity of Law" in *Oxford Essays in Jurisprudence (Second Series)* (ed. A.W.B. Simpson, Oxford University Press, 1973), chap. 3: there are three sorts of rules distributing authority – rules of succession to office, rules of competence, and rules of the succession of rules. There cannot be a violation of the first sort without also a violation of the third; but the first can be violated without violating the second. Different kinds of revolutions, when rules cease to exist, and devolution are considered against the background of Kelsen.

8. IYER, T.K.K. "Constitutional Law in Pakistan: Kelsen in the Courts" (1973) 21 AJCL 759: this reviews the important decisions, *State* v. *Dosso*, (1958) 2 Pak. SCR 180; *Madzimbamuto* v. *Lardner-Burke*, 1968 (2) SA 284; and *Jilani* v. *Government of Punjab*, (1972) PLD (SC) 139. Kelsen's thesis is examined in the light of them. *Jilani*, which repudiated Kelsen *in toto*, is commended.

9. KAUFMAN, A. and HASSEMER, W: "Enacted Law and Judicial Decision in German Jurisprudential Thought" (1969) 19 UTLJ 461, 469–476: this gives a brief, but clear, account of the main points of Kelsen's doctrine and of the task of the judge as seen in the light of it.

1. SILVING, H. "Analytical Limits of the Pure Theory of Law", (1942–43), 28 Iowa
    LR, 1: the claims of a "pure science" of law and attacks against it are considered
    with reference to what such a science purports to do and how far it can be "pure".
    The relation between jurisprudence and natural sciences and ethics is critically
    reviewed.

2. SILVING, H. "Law and Fact in the Light of the Pure Theory of Law" in *Interpre-
    tation of Modern Legal Philosophies*, (ed. P. Sayre, Oxford University Press, New
    York, 1947), chap. 31: the relationships between law and fact, substantive law
    and procedure, law and justice are explained. The finding of fact in a case is part
    of the concretizing process.

3. JONES, J.W. "Modern Discussions of the Aims and Methods of Legal Science",
    (1931), 47 LQR 62, at pp. 78–84: Kelsen's Pure Theory is outlined, and its
    principal weaknesses and implications are indicated.

4. FRIEDRICH, C.J. *The Philosophy of Law in Historical Perspective*, (University of
    Chicago Press, 1958), pp. 171–77: the place of Kelsen's theory in the evolution
    of legal theory is examined. The *Grundnorm* should be considered in relation to
    historical, political and other realities.

5. HALL, J. *Foundations of Jurisprudence* (The Bobbs-Merrill Co Inc, 1973), pp.
    35–39, 62–72: there are important differences between Kelsen and Austin on
    the one hand, and Kelsen and the Scandinavian Realists on the other. The
    Kelsenian notion of validity is considered and attacked.

6. GOLUNSKII, S.A. and STROGOVICH, M.S. "The Theory of the State and Law" in
    Soviet Legal Philosophy, (trans. H.W. Babb, Harvard University Press, 1951),
    pp. 419–22: Kelsen's doctrine is criticised from a Marxist point of view. The
    abstract nature of his thought is said to mark the decline of bourgeois legal thought.

7. HART, H.L.A. *The Concept of Law*, (Oxford, Clarendon Press, 1961, reprinted 1975),
    chap. 6: the criterion of validity depends upon the acceptance of a "rule of
    recognition" with which to identify rules of law. This must in turn rest on extra-legal
    considerations. It should be noted that this is not a restatement of Kelsen's *Grund-
    norm*, but something similar to it.

8. STONE, J. *Legal System and Lawyers' Reasonings*, (Stevens & Sons, Ltd, 1964),
    pp. 131–34: Professor Hart's "rule of recognition" is considered in the context
    of a discussion of Kelsen's doctrines. Certain objections are made as to what is
    implied by "recognition".

9. PECZENIK, A. Review of *Die Wiener rechtstheoretische Schule. Schriften von Hans
    Kelsen, Adolf Merkl, Alfred Verdross*, 1968. (1970) 1 Rechtstheorie, 206: the
    review is used as an opportunity to discuss the salient points of the Pure Theory,
    drawing attention to the contributions of Merkl and Verdross (note especially the
    latter's criticism of Kelsen from a naturalist angle). The author also relates some of
    these difficulties to his own thesis that the *Grundnorm* is best understood as a
    linguistic rule informing us in descriptive terms what phenomena should be called
    "law".

10. FINCH, J.D. *Introduction to Legal Theory* (2nd ed., Sweet & Maxwell, Ltd, 1974)
    pp. 111–130: this consists of a rather general review of Kelsen's doctrine and
    some criticisms of it are refuted. The account will not be readily followed unless
    the reader has knowledge of Kelsen's doctrine beforehand.

The Pure Theory and International Law

1. KELSEN, H. "The Pure Theory of Law and Analytical Jurisprudence" (1941–42) 55 Harv LR 44, 68: after a survey of the analytical aspects of his theory, the author turns to his monist view of international and municipal law. The existence and acknowledgement of international law by states is explicable only on the hypothesis of the primacy of international law.

2. JONES, J.W. "The 'Pure' Theory of International Law" (1935), 16 BYIL 5: the main points in a dualist conception of the relationship between municipal and international law and its implications are first considered. This leads on to a consideration of the advantages of a monist conception. But there are difficulties here too, of which the chief is the selection of a *Grundnorm*. It is alleged that Kelsen has given his hypothesis a "political core".

3. KUNZ, J.L. "On the Theoretical Basis of the Law of Nations", (1925), 10 Trans Gro S, 115: an avowed Kelsenite puts forward the case for the primacy of international law. The fact that Kelsen could see no theoretical reason for preferring the primacy of international law is alleged to be the weak point in his theory. See further J.L. KUNZ, "The Vienna School of Law and International Law" (1936), 11 NYULQR, 370.

4. COHEN, H.E. *Recent Theories of Sovereignty*, (University of Chicago Press, 1937), chap. 5: this considers Kelsen's attitude towards the question of sovereignty in international law. There has to be a choice between the primacy of municipal law and of international law. In choosing the latter Kelsen abandons juristic purity and makes an ethical choice.

5. MATTERN, J. *Concepts of State, Sovereignty and International Law*, (John Hopkins Press, Baltimore: Humphrey Milford, 1928) chap. 10: this gives an account of the views of Kelsen and Verdross of the state and international law.

6. STERN, W.B. Note on "Kelsen's Theory of International Law", (1936), 30 Am Pol Sc R, 736: the basis of customary international law is said to be *pacta sunt servanda*, but the international legal order is analogous to primitive law. This state of affairs is gradually being overcome.

7. JANZEN, H. "Kelsen's Pure Science of Law", (1937), 31 Am Pol Sc R, 205: there is a general explanation of the Pure Theory, both as to its municipal and international aspects. The doctrine of the unity and primacy of the latter is developed in some detail and in the course of it the criticisms of J.W. Jones and W.B. Stern (*supra*) are considered.

8. LLOYD, D. *The Idea of Law*, (Penguin Books, Ltd, A 688, 1964), pp. 193–98: these pages provide a brief explanation of Kelsen's hierarchy of norms. The *Grundnorm* is considered with reference to municipal and international law.

9. *Law, State and International Legal Order. Essays in Honor of Hans Kelsen* (edd. S. Engel and R.A. Métall, University of Tennessee Press, 1964): E. HAMBRO: "The Theory of the Transformation of International Law into National Law in Norwegian Law", p. 97: Kelsen maintained that international law is directly binding on states and other organs, and if this happens not to be the case, this is because of the positive law of the given state. The author considers this in relation to Norwegian law and shows that the latter has primacy over international law, but

that the two systems will be interpreted harmoniously where necessary and possible. J.H. HERZ: "The Pure Theory of Law Revisited: Hans Kelsen's Doctrine of International Law in the Nuclear Age", p. 107: Kelsen's Theory of international law is said to be a sophisticated natural law theory in that the nature of law cannot be conceived otherwise than as a coherent system of sanctioned norms. Its chief weakness lies in "sanctioned norms" by way of war and reprisals and the procedure of concretization. H.J. MORGENTHAU: "The Impartiality of the International Police", p. 209: Kelsen showed the unity between the legal and political orders, international and municipal. In the national sphere, when dealing with piecemeal violations of the law the police are impartial; but in dealing with organised challenge to the legal order itself, it has to be partial in support of the *status quo*, which is connected with the degree of popular support. This analysis is applied to an international police force. O. SCHACHTER: "Interpretation of the Charter in the Political Organs of the United Nations", p. 269: Kelsen presented a juristic, not a political, approach to the problems of the United Nations by offering all the possible interpretations and leaving it to the authorities to choose which they preferred. The author considers the criteria of choice. J.G. STARKE, "The Primacy of International Law", p. 307: there are three senses in which the term "primacy of international law" is used. While Kelsen's analysis fails to fit all the facts, the author thinks the analogy of federal law may support Kelsen's monism.

1. *Law and Politics in the World Community*, (ed. G.A. Lipsky, University of California Press, 1953): this collection of essays deals severally with specific problems and they all bear some relation to Kelsen's teachings. The volume is of general interest only, but the editor's Introduction is useful as an assessment of Kelsen's work in the international sphere.

18. Historical and Anthropological Approaches

The Historical School

1. von SAVIGNY, F.C. *On the Vocation of Our Age for Legislation and Jurisprudence,* (2nd ed., trans. A. Hayward, Littlewood & Co, 1831): Savigny constantly likens the national character of law to that of language. Law, like language, grows, strengthens and dies with the development of the nation. This theme and the function of jurists are outlined.

2. von SAVIGNY, F.C. *System of the Modern Roman Law,* (trans. W.H. Rattigan, Wildy & Sons, 1884), ss. 7–16: the positive law lives in the general consciousness of the people. The idea of what constitutes a "people" is elaborated so as to allow for local variations. The role of jurists and of legislation is explained.

3. PUCHTA, G.F. in *Outlines of the Science of Jurisprudence,* (trans. W. Hastie, T. & T. Clark, Edinburgh, 1887), especially pp. 37–63: peoples have different individualities, natures and tendencies. These constitute the national character, which is reflected in the particular system. The common consciousness constitutes the national mind and spirit.

4. KANTOROWICZ, H.U. "Savigny and the Historical School of Law" (1937), 53 LQR, 326: details of Savigny's academic career are given and also an explanation of the rise in prestige of the academic profession. There is an important difference between Austin and Savigny, the former's work being rationalisation and the latter's sociological description. Savigny's advocacy of Roman Law as the "national" law of Germany is closely examined.

5. BRYCE, J. "The Interpretation of National Character and Historical Environment on the Development of the Common Law" (1908), 24 LQR, 9: this is a most interesting inquiry into the causes of the differences between the legal ideas and methods of the Common Law and other systems.

6. DICKINSON, J. "Social Order and Political Authority" (1929), 23 Am Pol Sc R, 293, at pp. 301–12, 593: custom is said to be an agency of social control. The interests of individuals are largely produced by it. Custom also helps to adjust competing interests.

7. EHRLICH, E. *Fundamental Principles of the Sociology of Law,* (trans. W.L. Moll, Harvard University Press, 1936), chap. 19, especially pp. 443–61: there is a damaging criticism of the views of Savigny and Puchta. These are said to refer to two different things, namely, customary law which is a norm of conduct, and juristic law which is a norm for decision. Legal propositions do not emerge ready made; they are always the creation of jurists.

8. WEYRAUCH, W.O. *The Personality of Lawyers,* (Yale University Press, 1964): though not devoted to Savigny's doctrines, the whole of the investigation analysed in this book discredits Savigny's idea that lawyers reflect a specialised manifestation of the *Volksgeist*. On the contrary, it reveals the peculiar and unrepresentative character of the prejudices and predilections of the legal profession.

9. STAMMLER, R. "Fundamental Tendencies in Modern Jurisprudence" (1923), 21 Mich LR, 623: the events of 1814 which led to the publication of Savigny's

On the Vocation are reviewed in detail. The three main contentions of the Historical School are considered and it is concluded that the contribution of the School has been to show that legal development is dependent upon historical limitations to some extent.

1. POPPER, K.R. *The Open Society and its Enemies*, (5th ed., Routledge & Kegan Paul, Ltd, 1966): this edition combines both volumes. They constitute a closely reasoned argument against the inevitability of historical development. There is an important distinction between scientific prediction and historical prophecy, which has been overlooked all too often. Volume II begins with a critical examination of Hegel's doctrine. See also K.R. POPPER: *Poverty of Historicism*, (Routledge & Kegan Paul, Ltd, 1957).

2. AUSTIN, J. *Lectures on Jurisprudence*, (5th ed., R. Campbell, John Murray, 1885), II, pp. 675–81: Savigny's views are considered in the general context of the desirability of codification. Savigny's objections to codification are considered and rejected. It is noteworthy that J. Bentham is said to belong to the Historical School (p. 679).

3. KORKUNOV, N.M. *General Theory of Law*, (trans. W.G. Hastings, The Boston Book Co, 1909), pp. 116–22: the Historical School opposed the hypotheses of Natural law with that of evolution, but it does not explain how the spirit of the people is formed. The theory was thus incomplete and this enabled Natural law to reappear in the ideas of Hegel.

4. LEONHARD, R. "Methods Followed in Germany by the Historical School of Law" (1907), 7 Col LR, 573: although one cannot judge a law without knowledge of its special history, yet uncongenial laws do exist. The principal objections to the Historical School are formulated.

5. SUMNER, W.G. *Folkways. A Study of the Sociological Importance of Usages, Manners, Customs, Mores and Morals*, (Ginn & Co, Publishers, The Athenaeum Press, Boston, U.S.A., 1907), especially chaps. 1 and 2: the theme of this work is closely akin to that of Savigny and is essentially a parallel development. Folkways is a societal force and grows unconsciously. Folkways give rise to laws; they are not themselves law.

6. SAWER, G. *Law in Society*, (Oxford, 1965), pp. 171–4: this is a brief commentary on the work of W.G. Sumner and a comparison of his work with that of Savigny.

7. POUND, R. *Interpretation of Legal History*, (Cambridge University Press, 1923), chap. 6: while refraining from evolving a theory of law from the work of great lawyers, attention is forcefully drawn to the significant contributions made by such people to the development of law.

8. ROSS, A. *On Law and Justice*, (Stevens & Sons, Ltd, 1958), pp. 344–47: the Historical School is criticised as being a Natural Law philosophy which conceals a political attitude.

9. CARTER, J.C. *Law: Its Origin, Growth and Function*, (G.P. Putnam's Sons, New York, 1907): he begins by arguing for a philosophy of law in interpreting the progress of law. After considering and rejecting competing philosophies, he finds the explanation in custom, of which law is a specialised agency. Judges are the mouthpiece of custom; legislation has a part to play, but its role is secondary.

1. CARTER, J.C. "The Ideal and the Actual in the Law" (1890), 24 Am LR, 752: justice is the aim of all law. Legislation does not always achieve it. This is because the just rule has to be found, not made. Law is the unconscious product of the society.

2. ARONSON, M.J. "The Juridical Evolutionism of James Coolidge Carter" (1953–54), 10 UTLJ, 1: this gives a detailed account of Carter's evolutionary interpretation of law.

3. GRAY, J.C. *The Nature and Sources of the Law*, (2nd ed., R. Gray, The Macmillan Co, New York, 1921), pp. 89–93; 233–39; 283–91: Savigny's views are outlined and the principal difficulties considered. In the latter passage Mr. Carter's views are explained and subjected to careful criticism.

4. BRYCE, J. *Studies in History and Jurisprudence*, (Oxford, 1901), II, pp. 184–86: this is of general interest. The advantages and weaknesses of the historical method are dealt with.

5. WALTON, F.P. "The Historical School of Jurisprudence and Transplantation of Law" (1927), 9 JCL (3rd ser.), 183: Savigny's theory and the way in which he sought to justify his advocacy of Roman law are explained. The criticism is developed that his theory fails to account for the successful exportation of legal systems to other countries.

6. LIPSTEIN, K. "The Reception of Western Law in Turkey" (1956), 6 Annales de la Faculte de Droit d'Instanbul, 10, 225: the reception of Swiss law in Turkey in 1926 is examined in various aspects. There is a difference between the reception of Roman law in Europe and receptions of modern law, the latter being determined by codification and colonial policies. This and the next article contain important and interesting demonstrations that the *Volksgeist* is strongest, or even only extant in family law.

7. LIPSTEIN, K. "The Reception of Western Law in a Country of a Different Social and Economic Background: India" (1957–58), 8–9 Revista del Instituto de Derecho Comparado, 69, 213: the reception of English law in India is examined on lines similar to the above.

8. SMITH, T.B. "Legal Imperialism and Legal Parochialism" (1965), 10 Jur R (NS), 39: "legal imperialism" is the spread of law as an aspect of an expanding culture. In this connection the spread of the Code Napoleon, Roman-Dutch Law and English Law provide outstanding examples. "Legal parochialism" is the viability of one's own system as a cultural phenomenon. Law is an expression of culture. In a declining culture law will not be a creative development. On this basis the position in Scotland is discussed.

9. WATSON, A. *Legal Transplants*, (Edinburgh: Scottish Academic Press, 1974): this is a work on comparative legal history and legal development. The author provides wide-ranging examples of the transplantation of legal techniques and doctrines, and his thesis is that the success of transplantation does not necessarily depend on the political, social or economic conditions of the parent system.

10. KAHN-FREUND, O. "On the Uses and Misuse of Comparative Law" (1974), 37 MLR, 1: the author agrees largely with Montesquieu that law is very much bound up with its local cultural and physical environment, particularly the social and

political. The thesis is illustrated with reference to certain branches of law, commercial law, family law and industrial law.

1. WATSON, A. "Legal Transplants and Law Reform" (1976), 92 LQR, 79: this is a brief reply to Kahn-Freund's contention that for comparative law purposes, an understanding of the social, political and economic background of a system are essential. The author gives numerous examples, both in Montesquieu's day and later, in refutation of the contention.

2. HARDY, M.J.L. *Blood Feuds and the Payment of Blood Money in the Middle East*, (Beirut, 1963): this little book is of interest as showing the resilience of ancient custom in the face of the introduction of Western ideas. It also shows the difficulties with which one legal system adjusts itself to procedures taken from some other cultural background.

3. POUND, R. "Comparative Law and History as Bases for Chinese Law" (1947–48), 61 Harv LR, 749: the problem in China at that date was whether to adopt the latest legal institutions of Western societies or to adapt traditional Chinese institutions. The practicability of each is illuminatingly considered.

4. CLARK, E.C. *Practical Jurisprudence*, (Cambridge University Press, 1883), Part I, chaps. 7, 11–16: this is a historical and philological investigation into the meanings of the word "law". Law used to connote that which was considered to be fitting, the sanction being general displeasure. See also E.C. CLARK: *History of Roman Private Law. Part II. Jurisprudence*, (Cambridge University Press, 1914), I, s. 5.

5. BARKER, E. Introduction to O. GIERKE: *Natural Law and the Theory of Society, 1500–1800*, (trans. E. Barker, Cambridge University Press, 1950), s. 4: the factors against which the Historical School reacted are set out and there is an attempt to enter into what it is that is signified by *Volksgeist*. The part played by Gierke on the side of the "Germanists" as against the "Romanists", such as Savigny, is also explained. See also E. TROELTSCH, Appendix I, in which he traces the divergence between Germanic and West European thought. The former embraced the ideal of a historically-creative group-mind.

6. GIERKE, O. *Natural Law and the Theory of Society, 1500–1800, (supra)*: in this is set out the group-theory of legal evolution.

7. HEGEL, G.W.F. *Philosophy of Right*, (trans. T.M. Knox, Oxford, 1967): this most difficult work might be used for reference.

8. STACE, W.T. *The Philosophy of Hegel*, (Dover Publications Inc, 1955), Part IV, pp. 374–438: this is one of the best and most readable accounts of Hegel's philosophy. In the section referred to his views of law are set out and explained.

9. FRIEDRICH, C.J. *The Philosophy of Law in Historical Perspective*, (University of Chicago Press, 1958), chap. 15: this, too, is one of the clearest short expositions of Hegel's views on law and government. Its main interest lies in the way it shows how the use of his philosophy to support a totalitarian regime is a perversion of what he said. There is a briefer account of the Historical School.

10. CAIRNS, H. *Legal Philosophy from Plato to Hegel*, (The John Hopkins Press, 1949), chap. 14: this contains an account of Hegel's philosophy, with particular

reference to his theory of law. It is not as easy reading as the rest of Cairn's book.

1. SABINE, G.H. *A History of Political Theory*, (3rd ed., Harrap & Co, Ltd, 1963), chaps. 30, 32 and 35: the first of these chapters contains a most readable exposition of Hegel's dialectic method and theory of society and concludes with a critical appraisal of it. The latter part of chapter 32 gives an account of the Spencerian philosophy. Chapter 35 concerns Fascism and National Socialism.

2. MAINE, H.J.S. *Ancient Law*, (ed. F. Pollock, John Murray, 1930), chap. 1: Maine's view is relevant here in so far as he made the famous generalisation about the movement of progressive societies hitherto being from status to contract.

3. DICEY, A.V. *Law and Public Opinion in England during the 19th Century*, (2nd ed., Macmillan & Co, Ltd, 1932), chaps. 7–8: Dicey draws attention in detail to tendencies since Maine wrote towards a return to status.

4. *Law and Opinion in England in the 20th Century*, (ed. M. Ginsberg, Stevens & Sons, Ltd, 1959), chap. 1: the hints thrown out by Dicey are pursued and the changes in society and social conditions in the 20th century are examined.

5. GRAVESON, R.H. *Status in the Common Law*, (The Athlone Press, 1953), chap. 3: it is pointed out that English law never did quite fit Maine's statement, for the movement away from status was not necessarily towards contract. The effects of state interference today and standard form contracts are considered.

6. DIETZE, G. *Two Concepts of the Rule of Law*, (Liberty Fund, Inc, 1973): action and reaction is a feature of historical development. In 19th century Germany the "Law State" evolved as a reaction to "State Law" (or police state), but the influence of the latter made the former merely a constitutional form for governmental action. Liberalism had to yield to nationalism, which glorified the state, and to socialism, which tended towards totalitarianism. The step from the "national-social" Weimar Republic to the "national-socialism" of Nazism was a short one.

7. On the Nazi and Fascist conceptions of law, see J.W. JONES: *The Nazi Conception of Law*, (Oxford Pamphlets on World Affairs, No. 21, 1939); J.W. JONES: *Historical Introduction to the Theory of Law*, (Oxford, 1940), pp. 278–300; G. DEL VECCHIO: "The Crisis in the State" (1935), 51 LAR, 615; J. STONE: "Theories of Law and Justice of Fascist Italy" (1937), 1 MLR, 177; H.A. STEINER: "The Fascist Conception of Law" (1936), 36 Col LR, 1267; A.H. CAMPBELL: "Fascism and Legality" (1946), 62 LQR, 141; N.S. MARSH: "Some Aspects of the German Legal System under National Socialism" (1946), 62 LQR, 366.

General Accounts of the Historical Approach

8. POUND, R. *Interpretations of Legal History*, (Cambridge University Press, 1923), chaps. 1 and 4: the first chapter reviews the historical approach. The points are made that Savigny's view was idealistic, that he based law on social pressure and that he assumed evolution as a datum. Chapter 4 deals with the ethnological and biological interpretations. (For a critical review, see F. POLLOCK: "Plea for Historical Interpretation" (1923), 39 LQR, 163).

1. ALLEN, C.K. *Law in the Making*, (7th ed., Oxford, 1964), pp. 87–129: the origins and general nature of the historical and biological approaches are first described. Later the views of Savigny's school are considered and criticised in detail.

2. LIGHTWOOD, J.M. *The Nature of Positive Law*, (Macmillan & Co, 1883), chap. 12: Savigny's theory of law is approached through a comparison of English and German views as to the relationship between law and morality. There is a very full account of Savigny's doctrine and the criticisms of it by Ihering.

3. PATTERSON, E.W. *Jurisprudence*, (The Foundation Press, Inc, 1953), pp. 403–35: this begins with an explanation of five uses that have been made of history. Savigny's views are explained and considered, followed by accounts of Maine, the American historical movement (including the Field-Carter controversy), Spencer and Hegel. The account of Hegel is particularly recommended.

4. STONE, J. *Social Dimensions of Law and Justice*, (Stevens & Sons, Ltd, 1966), chap. 2: the work of Savigny is set against the cultural background of his time, and due acknowledgment is made to the pioneer contribution he made to sociological jurisprudence. His main problem was reconciling his thesis of the *Volksgeist* with the reception of Roman Law into Germany. His later works, the *History* and *System*, are shown to represent the unfolding of the broad plan outlined in his original essay. The major objections to the *Volksgeist* theory are developed. For further objections, see pp. 160–3.

5. FRIEDMANN, W. *Legal Theory*, (5th ed., Stevens & Sons, Ltd, 1967), chaps. 16, pp. 174–78; and 18: Savigny and his followers are dealt with in outline, but Maine is given prominence and attention is drawn to some of the developments since his day. In chapter 18 the Nazi and Fascist theories are considered.

6. BODENHEIMER, E. *Jurisprudence*, (Harvard University Press, 1962), pp. 65–69; 70–79: the roots of the Historical School are briefly explored and an account is given of the work of Savigny, Puchta, and their English and American followers. The Biological School is also considered.

7. JONES, J.W. *Historical Introduction to the Theory of Law*, (Oxford, 1940), chap. 2: a good deal of information is provided as to the background to the debate between the German codifiers and their opponents. The teaching of Savigny is considered critically and the work of Beseler and Gierke is also set out.

8. VINOGRADOFF, P. *Outlines of Historical Jurisprudence*, (Oxford University Press, 1920), I, chaps. 6 and 7: in the first of these chapters is explained how reaction to reason and conquest produced the age of Romanticism. An account is also given of the struggle between the "Germanists" and "Romanists". In the latter chapter evolutionary theories are dealt with, especially those of Maine and the biologists.

9. KAUFMAN, A. and HASSEMER, W. "Enacted Law and Judicial Decision in German Jurisprudential Thought" (1969), 19 UTLJ, 461, 462–469: this gives a brief review of the function of judges according to Savigny and Puchta, and especially the relation between their approach and legal conceptualism.

10. HOLDSWORTH, W.S. *Some Makers of English Law*, (Cambridge University Press, 1938), chap. 12: the chapter begins with an account of the Historical School and

the movement in England. This is followed by sketches of Maine, Maitland and Pollock.

1. JOLOWICZ, H.F. *Lectures on Jurisprudence*, (ed. J.A. Jolowicz, The Athlone Press, 1963), chap. 8: this gives a brief and simplified account of the Historical School.

2. PATON, G.W. *A Text-Book of Jurisprudence*, (4th ed., G.W. Paton and D.P. Derham, Clarendon Press, Oxford, 1972), pp. 19–21: this gives a very brief, general account and some of the principal criticisms.

3. POUND, R. *Jurisprudence*, (West Publishing Co, 1959), I, pp. 81–87; II, pp. 169–83, 217 *et seq.*: in these pages will be found a general account of the teachings of the Historical School. Much the same was previously said by Pound in "The Scope and Purpose of Sociological Jurisprudence" (1910–11), 24 Harv LR, 591, at pp. 598–604, where he also points out that the Historical School proceeded too much on an *a priori* basis.

4. POUND, R. "The End of Law as Developed in Juristic Thought" (1916–17), 30 Harv LR, 201, at pp. 209 *et seq.*: the historical jurists were more concerned with the content of law than with its purpose. Maine's teaching is alleged to have been derived rather more from Roman law than from other systems.

5. RATTIGAN, W.H. *The Science of Jurisprudence*, (3rd ed., Wildy & Sons, 1909), ss. 10–11: as an answer to the Austinian conception of law as a command, a summary is given of the importance of customary and historical development of the law.

6. GOLUNSKII, S.A. and STROGOVICH, M.S. "The Theory of the State and Law" in *Soviet Legal Philosophy*, (trans. H.W. Babb, Harvard University Press, 1951), pp. 408–413: the doctrines of the Historical School and of Hegel are considered and criticised from a Marxist point of view.

7. De MONTMORENCY, J.E.G. "Savigny" in *Great Jurists of the World*, (edd. J. Macdonell and E. Manson, John Murray, 1913), 561: this gives an account of Savigny's life and work.

8. HALL, J. *Readings in Jurisprudence*, (The Bobbs-Merrill Co, 1938), chap. 2: extracts are given from the writings of Savigny, Puchta, Barker, Stammler, Pound, Korkunov, Maine, Campbell and Carter.

9. COHEN, M.R. and COHEN, F.S. *Readings in Jurisprudence and Legal Philosophy*, (Prentice-Hall, Inc, 1951), pp. 73–76, 110–13; 124–25; 386–94: these pages contain extracts from the writings of Hegel (on Property and Contract), Maine, Savigny and Carter.

10. MORRIS, C. *The Great Legal Philosophers*, (University of Pennsylvania Press, 1959), chaps. 12 and 13: the first of these chapters contains extracts from Savigny's *On the Vocation*; the second contains extracts from Hegel's *Philosophy of Right.*

11. LLOYD, D. *Introduction to Jurisprudence*, (3rd ed., Stevens & Sons, Ltd, 1972), chap. 9: the essentials of Savigny's doctrine are set out and there are also extracts from Savigny and Maine among modern writings on anthropology and custom.

12. LLOYD, D. *The Idea of Law*, (Penguin Books, Ltd, A 688, 1964), pp. 251–55: these

pages provide an outline of the views of Savigny and touch on the English
representatives of the Historical School. At pp. 202–4 Hegel's approach is touched
on.

1. HARRISON, F. *On Jurisprudence and the Conflict of Laws*, (Oxford, 1919), chap. 3:
   Annotations by A.H.F. LeFroy, pp. 173–79: the value of the historical method
   is considered with reference to the work of Savigny, Maine and others.

2. AMOS, M.S. "Some Reflections on the Philosophy of Law" (1927), 3 CLJ, 31, at
   pp. 32–33: this is interesting for the critical remarks that are made on the limited
   value and the dangers of too close an adherence to the Historical School.

3. POSNETT, H.M. *The Historical Method in Ethics, Jurisprudence, and Political
   Economy*, (Longmans, Green & Co, 1882): in this little work the place of the
   historical method in evolving a theory out of social experience is considered.
   The methods of Spencer, Austin, Bentham, and Maine, *inter alia*, are dealt with.

Law and Anthropology

4. MAINE, H.J.S. *Ancient Law*, (ed. F. Pollock, John Murray, 1930), chap. 1 and
   Note B: this is the classic exposition of how custom originated in judgments, and
   then became codified, the codified law being thereafter developed by "progressive"
   societies.

5. STONE, J. *Social Dimensions of Law and Justice*, (Stevens & Sons, Ltd, 1966),
   chap. 3: the general theme of finding correlations between social and legal
   development is introduced with an account of the work and contribution of
   Maine, and a less full account of the work of Vinogradoff. The latter part of the
   chapter pursues that theme into modern society and shows the increasing
   difficulties of finding simple correlations.

6. BURROW, J.W. *Evolution and Society. A Study in Victorian Social Theory*,
   (Cambridge University Press, 1966), chap. 5: Maine's sociological contribution
   is assessed in the light of what is known of his career and the influences on his
   thought.

7. HOCART, A.M. *Kings and Councillors*, (Cairo Printing Office, 1936): the social
   organisation for ritual and the evolution of this into government is traced out in
   detail and is supported by an abundance of evidence. This most important book
   is unfortunately difficult to obtain.

8. MALINOWSKI, B. *Crime and Custom in Savage Society*, (Kegan Paul, 1932),
   pp. 1–68: the idea of the savage who blindly follows custom is dispelled as a
   myth. Rules of law with a definite obligation to obey stand out from mere rules
   of custom. Law consists in the mutuality of service involved in complex social
   arrangements.

9. MALINOWSKI, B. "A New Instrument for the Interpretation of Law – especially
   Primitive" (1941–42), 51 Yale LJ, 1237: four meanings of "law" are
   distinguished, and which of them are applicable to primitive society is considered.
   The chief source of social constraint lies in the organisation of the group for the
   achievement of certain ends.

10. HOGBIN, H.I.P. *Law and Order in Polynesia*, (Christophers, 1934): note also

Malinowski's Introduction. The latter repeats his thesis that reciprocity is one of the elements in the dynamic mechanism of legal enforcement. Law needs to be defined with reference to function, not form. Hogbin, too, develops the reciprocal nature of legal obligations.

1. SCHAPERA, I. "Malinowski's Theories of Law" in *Man and Culture*, (ed. R.W. Firth, Routledge & Kegan Paul, Ltd, 1957), 139: Malinowski's views are critically discussed. His concept of primitive law is alleged to have changed in his writings.

2. HOBHOUSE, L.T., WHEELER, G.C., GINSBERG, M. *The Material Culture and Social Institutions of the Simpler Peoples*, (Chapman & Hall, 1930), especially chap. 2: a warning is given in the opening pages of how easy it is to form theories on the basis of preconceived ideas and to see only corroborative evidence. The authors are accordingly extremely modest in drawing conclusions. The main point is that the stage of economic culture is determined by the ways in which people obtain their food. On this basis a classification of primitive peoples is given. In chapter 2 there is an attempt to correlate social institutions with the stage of economic development. The tables on pp. 86–119 are well worth studying.

3. VINOGRADOFF, P. "The Teaching of Sir Henry Maine" in *Collected Papers*, (Oxford, 1928), chap. 8: in this appraisal of Maine's work the dividing line between his contribution and that of the Savigny school is indicated. The historical method as followed by the German school is said to have been inadequate.

4. ROBSON, W.A. "Sir Henry Maine Today" in *Modern Theories of Law*, (ed. W.I. Jennings, Oxford University Press, 1933), chap. 9: Maine's work is appraised in detail. His contributions to legal theory are evaluated and their shortcomings indicated in the light of more modern research.

5. ALLEN, C.K. "Maine's 'Ancient Law'" in *Legal Duties*, (Oxford, 1931), 139: this is a study of *Ancient Law*, which is described as a manifesto of Maine's work. The principal criticisms of his conclusions are recounted and considered.

6. LYALL, A.C., GLASSON, E., von HOLTZENDORFF, F., COGLIOLO, P.: "Sir Henry Maine" (1884), 4 LQR, 129: these are appreciations of Maine written by an Englishman, Frenchman, German and an Italian, and their respective estimates of his work.

7. DIAMOND, A.S. *Primitive Law, Past and Present*, (2nd ed., Longmans, Green & Co, 1971): Maine is severely criticised. Primitive societies are shown to have been more complex than Maine supposed. Also, primitive law is said to have had little connection with religion. He takes issue with Maine on several other points as well.

8. DIAMOND, A.S. *The Evolution of Law and Order*, (Watts & Co, 1951): the point is repeated that the association of law with religion is a comparatively late development. This work expands the theme of *Primitive Law, Past and Present* (*supra*).

9. HARDY, M.J.L. *Blood Feuds and the Payment of Blood Money in the Middle East*, (Beirut, 1963): this short account of the pre- and post-Mohammed methods of

settling disputes about injuries shows that there was a close connection between
religious and secular institutions.

1. GLUCKMAN, M. *The Judicial Process among the Barotse of Northern Rhodesia*,
   (2nd ed., Manchester University Press, 1967): this contains a record of the
   settlement of actual disputes that arose among the Lozi tribe. Their judicial
   process is basically similar to that of western countries. The functions and nature
   of law are considered and compared with the law of developed societies.

2. MARCH, J.G. "Sociological Jurisprudence Revisited, A Review (more or less) of
   Max Gluckman" (1955–56), 8 Stan LR, 499: a long critical review of Gluckman's
   The Judicial Process among the Barotse and the task which he tries to accomplish.

3. GLUCKMAN, M. *Politics, Law and Ritual in Tribal Society*, (Blackwell, Oxford,
   1965): this is a work of general interest on the growth and evolution of societies.
   Chaps. 3–5 are the most relevant to the development of law and administration,
   and presents a view developed from the author's earlier works.

4. MacCORMACK, G. "Professor Gluckman's Contribution to Legal Theory" (1976),
   Jur R, 229: Gluckman attempted to show that there is a basic similarity in the
   notion of "law" in the Lozi tribe and developed systems. He examines the
   contention and maintains that he fails to show this, and also that he was mistaken
   in using classifications and criteria for comparison drawn from his own society.

5. GULLIVER, P.H. *Social Control in an African Society. A Study of the Arusha:
   Agricultural Masai of Northern Tanganyika*, (Routledge & Kegan Paul, 1963): in
   societies which lack centrally organised courts and centrally appointed judges,
   disputes are settled by means of networks of relationships that exist within the
   society, or by a process of bargaining. Resort to supernatural settlement operates
   in the last resort. The illustrative cases are of particular interest.

6. HOCART, A.M. *Kingship*, (Oxford University Press, 1927): the significance of
   various ceremonial rites and doctrines relating to monarchy are traced back to
   their original sources.

7. DRIBERG, J.H. "The African Conception of Law" (1934), 16 JCL, (3rd Ser.),
   230: the nature of African tribal law is considered. Its overall object is to
   maintain social equilibrium.

8. HOEBEL, E.A. *The Law of Primitive Man*, (Harvard University Press, 1954):
   the "law-ways" of the Eskimos, Ifuago (Phillipines), Comanche, Kiowa and
   Cheyenne Indians, Tobriand Islanders and the Ashanti (West African) are
   investigated. Maine is criticised for having introduced the myth of the rigid
   nature of law, but is defended against Diamond's criticism of his association of
   primitive law and religion. The general conclusion is that all primitive societies
   have rules enforced by controlled sanctions.

9. CAIRNS, H. *Law and the Social Sciences*, (Routledge & Kegan Paul, Ltd, 1935),
   chap. 2: the functional approach has yielded fruit. The contributions of
   anthropology are enumerated and explained.

10. LOWIE, R.H. "Incorporeal Property in Primitive Society" (1927–28), 37 Yale LJ,
    551: the idea of primitive communism is inconsistent with the prevalence of
    individually owned forms of incorporeal property, such as spells and enchantments.

1. LLEWELLYN, K.N. and HOEBEL, E.A. *The Cheyenne Way*, (University of Oklahoma Press, 1941): three possible methods of approach are considered, namely a search for norms of conduct, a description of practice and an examination of trouble cases. The third is adopted since this tests the norms and combines with it the behaviour of society. A case study of the law of the Cheyenne Indians is conducted on this basis.

2. TWINING, W. *Karl Llewellyn and the Realist Movement*, (Weidenfeld and Nicolson, 1973), chap. 8: this chapter is devoted to a detailed examination of Llewellyn's anthropological contribution in conjunction with Hoebel. The significance of pioneering case-analysis as a tool of field-work in anthropology is discussed. See also TWINING, W. "Two works of Karl Llewellyn – II" (1968), 31 MLR, 165, which is an earlier version of chap. 8 of the larger work.

3. FULLER, L.L. "Irrigation and Tyranny" (1965), 17 Stan LR, 1021: this paper is a critical commentary of K.A. Wittfogel's thesis that communities depending upon large-scale irrigation systems usually tend towards tyranny. Professor Fuller is inclined to support the thesis, but for wholly different reasons. In the course of his analysis he considers the various sociological and other considerations that this kind of investigation is bound to bring in.

4. ROBERTS, S. "Law and the Study of Social Control in Small-scale Societies" (1976), 39 MLR, 663: in primitive societies though people talk in normative terms there is no distinct class of legal rules. Hence, law cannot provide a starting point for study. What is important is to get away from the notion of a legal system and towards the people who use social machinery. Why do they obey? In what circumstances do rules acquire, retain or lose social acceptance?

5. MAINE, H.J.S. *Dissertations on Early Law and Custom*, (John Murray, 1901); *Village Communities in the East and West*, (John Murray, 1895); *Lectures on the Early History of Institutions*, (John Murray, 1905): these three works are of general interest and might be consulted for Maine's own views.

6. BARKUN, M. *Law Without Sanctions. Order in Primitive Societies and the World Community*, (Yale University Press, 1968): primitive law does show how law can work without formal institutions and maintain order and also react to social needs. Mediation is crucial to peaceful arrangements. Lasting social integration can be produced by having shifting and overlapping interests. On this basis, it is contended that it becomes possible to work out a world order without a world government.

7. PATON, G.W. *A Text-Book of Jurisprudence*, (4th ed., G.W. Paton and D.P. Derham, Clarendon Press, Oxford, 1972), chap. 2: no single factor should be regarded as being characteristic or predominant. This is a convenient account of the development of law in the light of modern research.

8. SIMPSON, S.P. and STONE, J. *Cases and Readings on Law and Society*, (West Publishing Co, 1948), Part I: a large number of extracts are given from various legal historians and anthropologists on primitive law and social control.

9. LLOYD, D. *Introduction to Jurisprudence*, (3rd ed., Stevens & Sons, Ltd, 1972), pp. 566–571: primitive people do possess "law", distinguishable as such, and which is flexible and capable of developing. Extracts are given from Hoebel, Gluckman and Fuller.

1. JØRGENSEN, S. *Law and Society*, (Akademisk Boghandel, 1972), chap. 2: law is said to originate in religion and rite and is rooted in taboos. There is a connection between the evolution of law as an independent system of rules and the development of the technique of solving social conflicts. Nomadic and agrarian cultures give rise to a collectivist ideology (status), urbanisation brings in an individualist ideology (contract), while technology develops rules on objectivizing lines (reducing individualism).

2. BODENHEIMER, E. "Philosophical Anthropology and the Law" (1971), 59 Calif LR, 653: the problems of Man need to be related to all layers of human personality, and Man's biological, psychological etc. structure needs to be related to his culture (including law). Legal and social goals are seen to be linked to empirical traits in Man. Freedom, equality and security are deep-rooted tendencies which call for recognition and protection without ascribing priority to any one. It is the task of law to work out the adjustments.

3. LLOYD, D. *The Idea of Law*, (Penguin Books, Ltd, A 688, 1964), pp. 231–39: it is untrue to say that in primitive societies religious and secular rules cannot be distinguished, nor that primitive law is rigid, nor that sanctions are absent. The vital contrast between primitive law and modern law is that in the former there is no centralised agency for developing law. Development does, however, take place in other ways. Primitive law is also contrasted with modern International law.

4. SAWER, G. *Law in Society*, (Oxford, 1965), chaps. 3–4: the question whether primitive societies have "law" reflects a difference as to sociological theory and is not merely a dispute about the use of words. Primitive societies may, however, serve as models for social study. In chap. 4 the works of some of the leading authorities are commented on.

5. HALL, J. *Readings in Jurisprudence*, (The Bobbs-Merrill Co, 1938), chap. 19: extracts from Malinowski and Timasheff are given.

6. COHEN, M.R. and COHEN, F.S. *Readings in Jurisprudence and Legal Philosophy*, (Prentice Hall, Inc, 1951), chap. 12: extracts from various authors are given, including Malinowski and Hoebel.

7. For further general reading the following might be consulted: R.H. LOWIE: *Primitive Society*, (Routledge & Kegan Paul, Ltd, 1921), chaps. 14 and 15; W.I. THOMAS: *Primitive Behaviour*, (McGraw Hill Book Co, Inc, 1937), chap. 15: D. DAUBE: *Biblical Law*, (Cambridge University Press, 1941); H.F. JOLOWICZ: *Historical Introduction to Roman Law*, (3rd ed., Cambridge University Press, 1952); G.R. DRIVER and J.C. MILES: *The Assyrian Law*, (Oxford, 1935); G.R. DRIVER and J.C. MILES: *The Babylonian Laws*, (Oxford, 1952–55), 2 vols.; E.A. WESTERMARCK: *The Origin and Development of the Moral Ideas*, (Macmillan & Co, Ltd, 1906), 2 vols.

19. Economic Approach

1. MARX, K. and ENGELS, F. *Manifesto of the Communist Party*, (Foreign Languages Publishing House, Moscow, 1955): the essentials of the development of the class struggle, the establishment of the proletariat dictatorship and the allegedly inevitable triumph of communism are set out here.

2. SCHLESINGER, R.B. *Soviet Legal Theory*, (2nd ed., Routledge and Kegan Paul, Ltd, 1951): the legal theory underlying the Marxist approach to law and society is explained from its theoretical beginnings down to modern times.

3. PATON, G.W. "Soviet Legal Theory" (1946–47), 3 Res Judicata 58: this is a review article of the earlier version of Schlesinger's book. It rehearses the theory that the state is an engine of compulsion and surveys the early Soviet theory. There is no separation of powers, nor special sanctity of codes. The legal profession, courts, Peoples' courts, provincial courts, procedure, evidence and criminal law are touched on.

4. DAVID, R. and BRIERLEY, J.E.C. *Major Legal Systems in the World Today*, (Stevens & Sons, Ltd, 1968), part II: this gives a penetrating and highly readable account of the theoretical Marxist basis of socialist law and its principal practical manifestations. The Section includes also accounts of the positions in other Communist countries. Since the book is a work on comparative law, the treatment of each legal system proceeds on the basis of policy and function.

5. BOBER, M.M. *Karl Marx's Interpretation of History*, (2nd ed., Harvard University Press, 1948): this work provides a careful and detailed study of the factors underlying Marxist ideas. Its various aspects are critically examined and the weaknesses indicated.

6. GSOVSKI, V. *Soviet Civil Law*, (Ann Arbor, 1948), I and II, especially Part I, chap. 5: the first volume is an extended account of Soviet law, its theory and various branches of it; the second volume gives the texts of various codes. Part I ov Volume I deals generally with the nature and sources of Soviet law. In chapter 5 the concept of law is examined. Present-day developments and the attempts to reconcile these with Marx's teachings are also dealt with.

7. GRZYBOWSKI, K. *Soviet Legal Institutions*, (Ann Arbor, 1962): this is now a somewhat dated analysis of Soviet law. It is a comparative study. Of particular interest are chapters 4 and 5, the former showing how law aids in the training of the population, the latter showing the acceptance of law as a necessary institution.

8. HAZARD, J.N. *Law and Social Change in the U.S.S.R.*, (Stevens & Sons, Ltd, 1953): this is an important collection of studies of various aspects of Soviet law and of the ways in which traditional legal conceptions are moulded to serve governmental policy.

9. JOHNSON, E.L. *An Introduction to the Soviet Legal System*, (Methuen & Co, Ltd, 1969): this book, written primarily for non-lawyers, is nevertheless of great interest to lawyers. Not only does it deal with the theoretical and historical background, but it also deals with developments in various branches of law, constitutional, procedural and substantive.

10. ENGELS, F. *The Origin of the Family, Private Property and the State*, (Foreign

Languages Publishing House, Moscow, 1954): the historical evolution of society
from its primitive to its modern stage in terms of the class struggle is explained.
Law is linked with the state. The anthropology is suspect.

1. ENGELS, F. *Anti-Duhring*, (Foreign Languages Publishing House, Moscow, 1954):
   in this polemic against the contentions of Duhring a good many of the
   theoretical points of the Marx-Engels theory of social evolution can be found.

2. MARX, K. *Capital*, (Foreign Languages Publishing House, Moscow, 1954), I, II and
   III: the work was left unfinished, and it is not easy reading. In it the labour
   theory of value and the relation of capital to labour is examined minutely.

3. OAKESHOTT, M.J. *The Social and Political Doctrines of Contemporary Europe*,
   (2nd ed., Cambridge University Press, 1941), chap. 3: fairly extensive quotations
   are given from the writings of Marx, Engels and Lenin.

4. *Soviet Legal Philosophy*, *(20th Century Legal Philosophy Series)*, Vol. V, (trans.
   H.W. Babb, Harvard University Press, 1951): works and sections of works are
   given in such an order as to depict the successive stages of development in Soviet
   "interpretations" of Marx. The writers are V.I. Lenin, P.I. Stuchka, M.A. Reisner,
   E.B. Pashukanis, J.V. Stalin, A.Y. Vyshinsky, P. Yudin, S.A. Golunskii,
   M.S. Strogovitch and I.P. Trainin. The Introduction by J.N. Hazard should be
   read as an essential preliminary.

5. For general reference see also K. MARX and F. ENGELS: *Selected Correspondence*,
   (Foreign Languages Publishing House, Moscow, 1956); K. MARX and F. ENGELS:
   Selected Works, (Foreign Languages Publishing House, 1951), I and II.

6. SALTER, F.R. *Karl Marx and Modern Socialism*, (Macmillan & Co, Ltd, 1921):
   this is an early work bringing Marx as a man to life and discussing his principal
   contentions. It is of considerable interest as showing the extent to which his
   prophecies had already materialised as well as failed to do so even at that date.

7. LASKI, H.J. *Karl Marx*, (Allen & Unwin, Ltd, 1922): this is a short account of
   Marx's background, his life and career and an appreciation of his philosophy.

8. BUKHARINE, N.I. *Le Theorie du Materialisme Historique*, (Editions Sociales
   Internationales, 1925): this is of general interest. It gives an early picture of the
   application of Marxist theories in Russia, written shortly after the revolution but
   before many of the major problems arose. Bukharine's views were later officially
   repudiated.

9. *Marxism and Modern Thought*, (trans. R. Fox, Routledge & Sons, Ltd, 1935):
   lengthy extracts are given of the writings of Bukharine and six others. These are
   of general interest, especially Bukharine's contribution, as showing the attitude
   of early Soviet writers.

10. AVINERI, S. *The Social and Political Thought of Karl Marx*, (Cambridge University
    Press, 1970): this is of general interest. This book traces the development of
    Marx's thought in the light of his earlier writings as well as the later and, in
    particular, its intellectual origins in Hegel. It is pointed out that, while he
    criticised Hegel for failing to take account of alternative possibilities in historical
    development, Marx's own theory is open to precisely the same charge.

1. CHAMBLISS, W.J. and SEIDMAN, R.B. *Law, Order and Society*, (Addison-Wesley, 1971): Marx is not mentioned in this somewhat one-sided analysis. State machinery is not a neutral framework within which conflicts are resolved, but the prize of the conflict. In a divided society law is the weapon to seize; it is not an umpire. Most laws reflect attempts by groups in power to protect their economic interests. Courts are confined to minor change, which means that they in the main uphold the system. Criminal law is said to be weighted in favour of the rich.

2. VYSHINSKY, A.Y. *The Law of the Soviet State*, (trans. H.W. Babb, The Macmillan Co, New York, 1954), especially chap. 1: this is in a sense an official exposition of Soviet law and the Soviet view of law. It is marred by its derisive and violent language. An account is given of the organisation and structure of Soviet government, but its content of legal theory is evasive and self-contradictory.

3. FULLER, L.L. "Pashukanis and Vyshinsky: A Study in the Development of Marxian Legal Thinking" (1948–49), 47 Mich LR, 1157: Vyshinsky's book (*supra*) is critically reviewed and both his and Pashukanis's doctrines are compared, the latter being explained in some detail. Vyshinsky's book shows by implication that the Soviet conception of Marxism can alter in the face of facts.

4. DENISOV, A. and KIRICHENKO, M. *Soviet State Law*, (Foreign Languages Publishing House, Moscow, 1960): the nature and character of law are explained with reference to the social structure of the U.S.S.R. Particular attention is devoted to the rights of citizens. The Appendix gives the text of the Constitution (Fundamental Law) of the USSR. This Constitution was superseded in 1977.

5. *Government, Law and Courts in the Soviet Union and Eastern Europe*, (edd. V. Gsovski and K. Grzybowski, Stevens & Sons, Ltd, 1959), I and II: these volumes cover the law and governmental institutions of eleven countries (including Russia) in eastern Europe (East Germany is omitted). The object is to inquire into the extent to which individual rights are protected. The result is an extremely critical and somewhat one-sided account. In the Introductory chapter Gsovski deals with the doctrines of Marxism as they apply to law.

6. RENNER, K. *The Institutions of Private Law and their Social Functions*, (trans. A. Schwarzschild, ed. O. Kahn-Freund, Routledge & Kegan Paul, Ltd, 1949): Renner's thesis has previously been considered in the chapter on Ownership. It might usefully be considered here as a demonstration of the function of law from a Marxist point of view.

7. SAWER, G. *Law in Society*, (Oxford, 1965), pp. 177–82: this is a brief critique, primarily of K. Renner's work, but designed to bring out the interrelation between law and social behaviour.

8. SCHLESINGER, R.B. *Marx, His Time and Ours*, (Routledge & Kegan Paul, Ltd, 1950): this is a detailed study of the basis of Marx's thought and his analysis of society, together with its national and international implications. This calm and impersonal assessment of merits and demerits of Marxism is well worth study.

9. POPPER, K.R. *The Open Society and Its Enemies*, (5th ed., Routledge & Kegan Paul, Ltd, 1966): both volumes argue against the inevitability of evolution. Volume II begins with a critique of Hegel and proceeds to a detailed investigation of Marxism on this basis.

1. SABINE, G.H. *A History of Political Theory*, (3rd ed., Harrap & Co, Ltd, 1963), chaps. 33 and 34: the first of these chapters deals with the dialectic interpretation of Marx and Engels; the second with post-Marxist communism. The relation between Hegel and Marx is particularly stressed.

2. HAZARD, J.N. "Soviet Law: an Introduction" (1936), 36 Col LR, 1236: the origin of the capitalist state according to Marxist interpretation is explained. This is a most helpful simplification of Marx's own laboriously detailed exposition. The principles of law which derive from this view of history are also explained.

3. DOBRIN, S. "Soviet Jurisprudence and Socialism" (1936), 52 LQR, 402: this was written before the doctrines of Pashukanis were finally discredited. The difficulties in the way of evolving a theory of law in Russia are explained. With reference to Pashukanis's doctrine, the theories of such pre-1914 German writers, which accorded with Marxist dogma and which influenced Pashukanis, are examined.

4. BERMAN, H.J. *Justice in the U.S.S.R. An Interpretation of Soviet Law*, (Harvard University Press, 1963): in Part I the author demonstrates the mental feats performed by Soviet jurists to move away from Marxist doctrines but at the same time to preserve him as the official prophet. In Part II the roots of Soviet legal thinking are traced back over 1000 years. In Part III the "parental" nature of Soviet law is examined. This is the tutoring of the masses for membership in the communist society.

5. BERMAN, H.J. "The Educational Role of the Soviet Court" (1972), 21 ICLQ, 81: a Soviet court has to educate the parties and the public. In criminal law, the court has not only to decide guilt or innocence, but also the causes and conditions of the crime and offer suggestions to eliminate them. In civil law, the educational role makes itself evident in procedure as well. In both types of cases social organisations participate. In ideological crimes, the accused is made an object lesson.

6. SCHLESINGER, R.B. "Recent Developments in Soviet Legal Theory" (1942), 6 MLR, 21: Soviet jurists now realise the need for a theory of law. The various theories that have been proffered since the abandonment of Pashukanis's theory are considered, as well as the Soviet attitude towards international law.

7. GSOVSKI, V. "The Soviet Concept of Law" (1938), 7 FLR, 1: after examining the stages through which the attitude towards law has passed the conclusion is reached that traditional concepts have been reinstated.

8. BODENHEIMER, E. "The Impasse of Soviet Legal Philosophy" (1952–53), 38 Corn LQ, 51: based on the collection entitled *Soviet Legal Philosophy* (*supra*), this is an independent demonstration of the development of Soviet views about law and the difficulties into which they have been led. It is a very useful article.

9. RHYNE, C.S. "The Law: Russia's Greatest Weakness" (1959), 45 Am BAJ, 246, 309: after describing his personal experience the author lists his impressions: the pre-trials procedure behind the facade of legal form, Party domination and the difference in justice for Party and non-Party people, no opportunity for any activity which might endanger the system, tyranny through bureaucracy and the "parasite" laws, emergence of a new elite, and rule by law.

1. LAPENNA, I. *State and Law: Soviet and Yugoslav Theory*, (The Athlone Press, 1964): the development of Soviet and Yugoslav interpretations of Marxist doctrines relating to state and law are set out. This is a demonstration, with many quotations, of the inconsistencies, evasions and distortions that have been resorted to by Russian writers.

2. KIRALFY, A.K.R. "Characteristics of Soviet Law" (1952), 2 Os HLJ, 279: attention is drawn to the influential position of the Communist Party, though this at that date had no standing in law. Various other aspects of Soviet public and private law and procedure are also considered.

3. NOVE, A. "Some Aspects of Soviet Constitutional Theory" (1949), 12 MLR, 12: this article constitutes a summary of the main contentions of the Marxist attitude to law. The basic premise is that the Party represents the wishes of the people. Therefore, the law and the constitutional forms of government should express Party policy. The dangers in all this of the abuse of power are pointed out.

4. BERMAN, H.J. "Soviet Law and Government" (1958), 21 MLR, 19: the Russian revolution, it is observed, is still unfolding. The central feature of their system is the identity of politics and social control. A planned economy cannot function without a highly developed legal system, but the law does not bind the highest authority.

5. SAVITSKY, V. "The Public and the Law in the USSR" (1965), 51 Am BAJ, 143: public order is maintained, not only by official organs, but also by volunteer public order groups and comrades' courts, whose tasks and powers are statutorily regulated.

6. BERMAN, H.J. "The Challenge of Soviet Law" (1948–49), 62 Harv LR, 220, 449: to compare Soviet with American law is to accept the challenge of Soviet law. The article traces the development of socialist law from its Marxist theoretical basis down to the time of Stalin. The author traces socialist and capitalist features to be found in Soviet and American law, and the difference in the respective traditions of development. Russia plunged crudely into revolution. America is proceeding slowly towards similar ends. There are lessons to be learned.

7. FRIEDMANN, W. "Modern Trends in Soviet Law" (1953–54), 10 UTLJ, 87: this is a note reviewing the gradual movement away from the influence of Marx's formulae and the withering away of law, revolutionary legality and the subservience of law to politics. Then came the need to rehabilitate law and protect citizens, resulting in concepts and doctrines similar to those elsewhere.

8. HAMPSCH, G.H. "Marxist Jurisprudence in the Soviet Union: a Preliminary Survey" (1959–60), NDL, 525: the roots of Soviet jurisprudence lie in its antecedents. The author surveys the doctrinaire basis of approach. Whereas bourgeois moral codes are bound up with religious beliefs, Russian morality is subordinate to the class-struggle. Insofar as law is also an instrument of the class-struggle, law becomes part of morality after all.

9. RAZI, G.M. "Around the World Legal Systems (II). The Soviet System" (1960), 6 How LJ, 1: the author contrasts Western and Soviet approaches, and gives a detailed explanation of what is implied in regarding law an instrument of policy.

Law is also propaganda, which means that its excellence has to reflect the worth of communism. He then traces the evolution of these notions.

1. TALLON, V. "Law in the Soviet Union" (1971), 115 SJ, 167: the interests of government are paramount. Where these are not involved, the courts are concerned to do justice. The office of the Procurator General and the various courts and similar bodies are described.

2. VANNEMAN, P. "The Hierarchy of Laws in the Communist Party-state System in the Soviet Union" (1974), 8 Int Lawyer, 285: law is a matter of politics. The decline of terror required the promotion of law, but there are different groups of interest each wanting to promote law for its own ends. So although law needs to be fostered, what is not clear is who should control it. In this light the legitimacy of the Party State organs and the hierarchy of laws are examined from the Constitution or Basic Law down to the lowest levels.

3. CONQUEST, R. *Justice and the Legal System in the USSR*, (The Bodley Head, 1968): this booklet provides brief accounts of the development and present state of Soviet jurisprudence and outlines of some of its main branches. Each chapter has a valuable bibliography.

4. MORGAN, G.G. *Soviet Administrative Legality*, (Stanford University Press, 1962): the central figure in this book is the Public Prosecutor. The picture which emerges is that there is little in the way of protection for the rights of the individual against administrative acts. Even the Public Prosecutor cannot question the acts of higher officials.

5. HAZARD, J.N. "Socialism, Abuse of Power and Soviet Law" (1950), 50 Col LR, 448: nationalisation brings the citizen into direct contact with officialdom. Where there is no competition between those who provide public services there tends to be slackness and abuse. The various measures that have been adopted in Russia to deal with this problem are considered. Such measures cannot curb policy, but they do restrain officials.

6. KIRALFY, A.K.R. "The Campaign for Legality in the USSR" (1957), 6 ICLQ, 625: the problem of balancing security for the individual and unquestioning obedience to the government is considered with reference to various aspects of Soviet administration.

7. KIRALFY, A.K.R. "The Rule of Law in Communist Europe" (1959), 8 ICLQ, 465: this article sets out the extent to which the government is free from control and the extent to which individuals and bodies can find remedies.

8. NIKIFOROV, B.S. "Fundamental Principles of Soviet Criminal Law" (1960), 23 MLR, 31: this is of general interest. A Russian writer explains the enactment of 1958.

9. HAZARD, J.N. "Soviet Codifiers Release the First Drafts" (1959), 8 AJCL, 72: this is another comment on the new criminal code and criminal procedure.

10. HAZARD, J.N. "Cleansing Soviet International Law of anti-Marxist Theories" (1938), 32 AJIL, 244: the denunciation of Pashukanis called for a revision of international law theories. The theoretical aspects of Korovin's and Pashukanis's theories of international law are explained.

1. KOROVIN, E.A. "The Second World War and International Law" (1946), 40 AJIL,
   742: this represents a Russian and typically monocular view of the role of the
   USSR in international affairs since the end of the Second World War. It contains
   a plea for a new view of sovereignty.

2. SETON-WATSON, H. "Soviet Foreign Policy in 1961" (1961), 2 International
   Relations, 197: the trend of events and the policy of the USSR determine their
   attitude towards international law. In the light of these factors the position in
   1961 is reviewed.

3. HAZARD, J.N. "Renewed Emphasis Upon a Socialist International Law" (1971),
   65 AJIL, 142: this is a comment on a Soviet writer. Since 1950 a new socialist
   international law is said to be in the making. The theoretical difficulties of how
   Russia could share an international law with capitalist countries and how an
   instrument of domination could be encouraged began to disappear as more
   socialist countries emerged.

4. BUTLER, W.E. " 'Socialist International Law' or 'Socialist Principles of
   International Relations'? " (1971), 65 AJIL, 796: proletarian internationalism
   became a principle of domestic and foreign policy in international relations after
   1917. From this derive the rights and duties of socialist states *inter se* with
   regard to co-operation and mutual help. The 1968 intervention in Czechoslovakia
   was justified as the "people" requested help against their own government. From
   principles of international relations should be distinguished principles of
   international law, which still only form a basis for a new international law in the
   future.

5. TAMMELO, I. "Coexistence and Communication: Theory and Reality in Soviet
   Approaches to International Law" (1965), 5 Syd LR, 29: this is an important
   demonstration of the immense language communication problems that divide
   the Soviets and the West. Their attitude to international law is explained in the
   light of this problem.

6. HAZARD, J.N. and WEISBERG, M.L. *Cases and Materials on Soviet Law*,
   (Columbia University Press, 1950): the cases presented in this volume are most
   valuable in conveying an idea of the conditions of life and the contexts in which
   legal problems arise in Russia. It also reveals the extent to which the Soviet
   Supreme Court intervenes on behalf of the individual.

7. HAZARD, J.N., SHAPIRO, I., and MAGGS, P.B. *The Soviet Legal System.*
   Contemporary Documentation and Historical Commentary, (revised ed., Oceana
   Publications, Inc., Dobbs Ferry, New York, 1969): this is a very good and
   carefully selected collection of extracts from constitutions, statutes, regulations,
   orders, judicial decisions, writings, etc. on a range of topics including constitutional,
   administrative, procedural and substantive law. Each chapter is prefaced with a
   brief commentary on the development of the law and its present-day setting and
   problems.

8. BUTLER, W.E. "Sources of Soviet Law" (1975), 28 CLP, 223: this paper reviews
   the various law-making organs of the Soviet Union, the hierarchy of their
   authority, including the part played by treaties and agreements. It is of interest
   to be told that custom is now playing a more positive and expanding role.

9. SCHLESINGER, R.B. "A Glance at Soviet Law" (1949), 65 LQR, 504: this is a

comment on the collection of materials, which at the time of writing was in circulation in advance of publication (*supra*). Certain decisions of the Soviet courts are discussed in so far as these shed light on their general attitude.

1. FEIFER, G. *Justice in Moscow*, (The Bodley Head, Ltd, 1964): a journalist writes in detail of the working and spirit of ordinary tribunals in Moscow. It is note-worthy that development has been moving nearer to West European ideas and that it has come to be realised that legality is more effective in cultivating a loyal citizenry than arbitrariness. The chief feature of Soviet trials is that they try, not the crime, so much as the man; the emphasis is on safeguarding and improving society.

2. SIMPSON, S.P. and STONE, J. *Cases and Readings on Law and Society*, (West Publishing Co, 1948), I, Part IV, chap 1; III, Part VI, chaps. 1 s. 3 and 3: in Book I the economic background of law is given with extracts from Marx and the American writer Brooks Adams (*inter alia*). In Book III, chap. 1, extracts from Marx and Engels, Lenin, Stalin and other publications are given. Chapter 3 contains extracts from various Russian and non-Russian writers on the nature of law.

3. STRACHEY, E.J.St.L. *The Theory and Practice of Socialism*, (Victor Gollancz, 1936): this book might be consulted as a matter of general interest. It contains an analysis along socialist lines and indicates the differences between socialism and communism.

4. LASKI, H.J. *The State in Theory and Practice*, (Allen & Unwin Ltd, 1935): the ways in which owners of property and producers of goods used social institutions to accomplish their own ends are traced. A change is not possible without revolution. Capitalism and war are said to be related and armaments tend to increase under pressure from industrialists.

5. LASKI, H.J. *Law and Justice in Soviet Russia*, (Hogarth Press, 1935): this is a panegyric of Soviet administration of law, especially criminal law, and of its superiority over the common law. The idea of social service has led to emphasis on the rehabilitation of offenders. (See also H.J. LASKI: *Studies in Law and Politics*, Allen & Unwin, Ltd (1932), especially pp. 276 *et seq.*).

6. LASKI, H.J. "The Crisis in the Theory of the State" in *Law: A Century of Progress*, (New York University Press, 1937; reprinted in *A Grammar of Politics*, 4th ed., Allen & Unwin, Ltd, 1938): the Marxist conception of the state and law is defended and the doctrine of the withering away of law is foreshadowed even as late as 1937.

7. HOOK, S. *From Hegel to Marx*, (Victor Gollancz, Ltd, 1936): the development of Marx's views is traced in detail, as well as his reactions to the theories of various other writers since Hegel.

8. WEBB, S. and B. *Soviet Communism: A New Civilisation?* (Longmans Green & Co, Ltd, 1935), I and II: these volumes may be used for reference purposes. They contain a detailed estimate of developments in Russia, and although legal theory is not dealt with specifically they provide a useful background to most aspects of Soviet law.

9. DJILAS, M. *The New Class*, (Thames & Hudson, 1957): this is a frank appraisal of

communism by a disillusioned communist. It provides a good deal of information about the origins of Marx's ideas and about the result of their implementation in practice.

1. SCHMIDT, F. "The Four Elements of Law" (1974), 33 CLJ, 246: the author seeks to answer the Marxists' contention that law is only an expression of ruling class interests by pointing out that this is only one of four "elements": the law of survival of individuals and groups; the law of toleration, which recognises that those being tolerated have something to give in return; laws of the ruling classes; and laws based on agreements. Various aspects of these are illustrated with reference to English and Swedish law.

2. HARRINGTON, M. "Revolution" in *Is Law Dead?* (ed. E.V. Rostow, Simon and Schuster, New York, 1971), chap. 10: the author begins by pointing out that the Marxist idea of a violent revolution is now outdated. What is needed is a revolution in the law itself, and he discusses how this might come about.

3. RUSSELL, B. *Freedom and Organisation, 1814–1914,* (Allen & Unwin, Ltd, 1934), chaps. 15–20: the progress of socialism is traced from the first British socialist, Robert Owen, and the British trade union movement. There is an account of the life and work of Marx, the application of dialectic materialism in his political view is explained and its weaknesses indicated.

4. KELSEN, H. *The Communist Theory of Law,* (Stevens & Sons, Ltd, 1955): the views on law of the various writers whose works are included in *Soviet Legal Philosophy (supra)* are critically considered. Some of the contradictions in their theories are exposed. The book is on the whole nihilistic in its attitude.

5. KELSEN, H. *The Political Theory of Bolshevism,* (University of California Press, 1948): this is a short critique of the communist theory, and in particular the dangers of relying on Hegel's dialectics are pointed out. The various contradictions into which the Soviet theorists have been forced are also indicated.

6. OLIVECRONA, K. *Law as Fact,* (Einar Munksgaard, Copenhagen; Humphrey Milford, 1939; reprinted Wildy & Sons, 1962), pp. 181–92: it is pointed out that the Marxists emphasise the use of force in capitalist societies but try to conceal it in their own. Force is an instrument without which society cannot function. There can be, therefore, no foundation for the prediction that law and state will wither away. Moral standards, too, are dependent on the regular application of force.

7. BERMAN, H.J. "Principles of Soviet Criminal Law" (1946–47), 56 Yale LJ, 803: the early Revolutionary period introduced "crime by analogy" i.e., socially dangerous acts. After 1936 criminal law was viewed as necessary even under socialism.

8. KIRALFY, A.K.R. "The Juvenile Law-breaker in the USSR" (1952), 15 MLR, 472: when confronted with a familiar problem the Soviet authorities have had to resort to familiar methods of dealing with it. The need to put young offenders to useful work and to stress family responsibility is pointed out.

9. TAY, A.E-S. "The Foundation of Tort Liability in a Socialist Legal System: Fault versus Social Insurance in Soviet Law" (1969), 19 UTLJ, 1: the tendency towards strict liability and the economic function of tort tend to be strong when

social insurance is only beginning. Thereafter there is a tendency for fault to re-assert itself. The author traces the history of the Soviet return to fault liability.

1. TAY, A.E-S. "Principles of Liability and the 'Source of Increased Danger' in the Soviet Law of Tort" (1969), 18 ICLQ, 424: a major exception to the rule of strict liability has been carved in the area of "extra-hazardous" activities. This shows how the interpretation of the law has brought it more and more towards Western tort law.

2. RUDDEN, B. "Soviet Tort Law" (1967), 42 NYULR, 583: there is tension between Marxist philosophy and an effective system of recovery. In early Soviet law fault was rejected and causation was the sole criterion. But the interpretation of causation has re-introduced fault through contributory negligence, the requirement of unlawfulness, risk (fault presumed from "extra-hazardous" activities) and in the function of liability.

3. HAZARD, J.N. "Soviet Government Corporations" (1942–43), 41 Mich LR, 850: after a brief historical introduction to the topic, the creation and nature of these corporations are examined. They are independent legal persons which manage state-owned property.

4. BERMAN, H.J. "Commercial Contracts in Soviet Law" (1947), 35 Calif LR, 191: Soviet state business enterprises are described very fully from the highest directing authorities downwards. Of particular interest are the extension of the concept of legal person and the tasks of the special tribunals which deal with commercial contracts. The contracts are examined in detail, and some specimen decisions are included at the end.

5. COLLARD, D. "State Arbitration in the USSR" (1955), 18 MLR, 474: there has to be some speedy and efficient method of dealing with disputes between commercial concerns. This is accomplished by state arbitration. The nature and function of this institution are examined.

6. BERMAN, H.J. "Soviet Family Law in the Light of Russian History and Marxist Theory" (1946–47), 56 Yale LJ, 26: the pre-Revolutionary position in Russia and the Marxist theory of family relations are set out first. In the immediate post-Revolutionary period there was a tendency to preach the withering away of the family as well as law. Now, however, it is said that the task of law is to strengthen the socialist family. The various ways in which this end is sought are explained.

7. SVERDLOV, G.M. "Modern Soviet Divorce Practice" (trans. D. Collard, 1948), 11 MLR, 163: this article is of interest as showing the increasingly strict attitude taken by the Soviet government towards the sanctity of marriage.

8. STONE, O.L. "The New Fundamental Principles of Soviet Family Law and their Social Background" (1969), 18 ICLQ, 392: this paper is useful in presenting the constitutional, historical and social background of the law relating to marriage, parent and child, adoption, maintenance, guardianship, divorce and nullity.

9. JOHNSON, E.L. "Matrimonial Property in Soviet Law" (1967), 16 ICLQ, 1106: Soviet matrimonial property law recognises community of acquests by which

each party benefits from the work of the other. The chief problem is liability for debts.

1. WOLFF, M.M. "Some Aspects of Marriage and Divorce Laws in Soviet Russia" (1949), 12 MLR, 290: the position is contrasted with the pre- and immediate post-Revolution positions. The steps towards increased respect for the family tie are traced out.

2. COHEN, J.A. "The Chinese Communist Party and Judicial Independence: 1949–1959" (1969), 82 Harv LR, 967: the 1954 Chinese Constitution guaranteed judicial independence, but this appears to have been regretted soon after and courts were increasingly subordinated to Party control. The author examines in detail what "independence" means in this context and how the provision came to be included in the Constitution, and traces the subsequent relations between judges and the Party step by step. (See also S. LUBMAN: "Form and Function in the Chinese Criminal Process" (1969), 69 Col LR, 535).

3. KAMENKA, E. and TAY, A.E-S. "Beyond the French Revolution: Communist Socialism and the Concept of Law" (1971), 21 UTLJ, 109: the rise of socialist thought is traced from its various strands in the French Revolution and through the 19th century in Marxist and German thinking. The authors then turn to developments in China since 1949. They distinguish between four types of social regulation: emphasis on law and regulation, expressing the will of the organised community; emphasis on the individual, which is opposed to organised solidarity; emphasis on a non-human ruling interest, public policy or institution to which individuals are subordinate; and rule by force. All these strands are found in Russia and China.

4. TAY, A.E-S. "Law in Communist China" (1968–71), 6 Syd LR, 153, 335: (1973–76), 7 Syd LR, 400: the Chinese development should be considered in the light of four ideal types of social regulation: emphasis on law as expressing the will of the organised community, emphasis on the individual, emphasis on institutionalised administration, and emphasis on force. To grasp the Chinese situation one needs to know her history, Marxism, Soviet theory and development and contemporary sociology. Against this background the three articles deal with the position in Imperial China, in the Kuomintang, the harsh repression during 1949–1954, the Constitution and the new legality during 1954–57, and the destruction of all this during the Cultural Revolution.

5. FRIEDMANN, W. *Legal Theory*, (5th ed., Stevens & Sons, Ltd, 1967), chap. 29: Renner's doctrine is first summarised and is followed by an account of legal developments in the USSR and in Britain.

6. JONES, J.W. *Historical Introduction to the Theory of Law*, (Oxford, 1940), pp. 270–78: the teachings of Marx about the progress of the class struggle and the evolution of communism are explained with reference to developments in the USSR.

7. LLOYD, D. *Introduction to Jurisprudence*, (3rd ed., Stevens & Sons, Ltd, 1972), chap. 10: Hegel's doctrine is first explained and then Marx's adaptation of it. There is also a general outline of the position in Russia from the Revolution onwards, with assessments of recent developments. There are also brief accounts of the position in Yugoslavia and China.

1. LLOYD, D. *The Idea of Law*, (Penguin Books, Ltd, A 688, 1964), pp. 204–7, 220–22: the origin of Marx's doctrines in Hegelianism is explained briefly. In the latter pages the position in the Soviet Union and the principal contrasts between this and Western countries are set out.

2. PATTERSON, E.W. *Jurisprudence*, (The Foundation Press, Inc, 1953), pp. 435–38: the account of Marx follows that of Hegel. The main weaknesses of the Marxist theory are pointed out.

3. STONE, J. *Social Dimensions of Law and Justice*, (Stevens & Sons, Ltd, 1966), chapter 10, and pp. 579–88: the severity of law in the Stalin period is not a "deviation" from "pure Marxism", since the Marxist doctrine is ambivalent. The state, differing from the bourgeois state, can and should survive in socialism, which is but a transitional condition. At pp. 579–88 there is further discussion of the persistence of the economic determinist thesis.

4. BODENHEIMER, E. *Jurisprudence*, (Harvard University Press, 1962), pp. 79–81, 239–40: the first section contains a very brief account of three main principles underlying the Marxist theory; the second mentions the theory of Pashukanis in outline.

5. ROSS, A. *On Law and Justice*, (Stevens & Sons, Ltd, 1958), pp. 347–57: Marx is said to have confused determinism with predestination. Certain parallels between the approaches of the Historical School and Marxism are indicated, and the general attitudes of both are criticised.

6. TIMASHEFF, N.S. "The Crisis in the Marxian Theory of Law" (1939), 10 NYULQR, 519: the manner in which Soviet jurists, led by Vyshinsky, revised their original ideas about law so as to accommodate its indispensability in the socialist scene is demonstrated.

7. TIMASHEFF, N.S. *An Introduction to the Sociology of Law*, (Harvard University Committee on Research in the Social Sciences, 1939), pp. 371–74: there is a brief discussion of Marxist doctrine in the general context of theories which amount to a negation of law.

8. SOROKIN, P. *Contemporary Sociological Theories*, (Harper & Bros, New York, 1928), chap. 10: the economic interpretation of law goes much further back than Marx and Engels. The objections to the Marxist doctrines are set out in detail. The chapter also deals with relation between economic and other social phenomena.

9. CARLSTON, K.S. *Law and Structure of Social Action*, (Stevens & Sons, Ltd, 1956), pp. 74–84: the main difference in the position of the individual in the western world from that in the Communist world is said to be that in the former his choice of the roles that he plays in daily life is relatively free from governmental interference. The sphere of policy determination is more free from legal control in the communist world than in the west.

10. CAIRNS, H. *Law and the Social Sciences*, (Kegan Paul, Trench, Trubner & Co, Ltd, 1935), chap. 4: the inter-relation between law and economics is discussed. Various institutions of law are considered from this point of view and the weakness of an exclusively economic interpretation is pointed out.

1. JENKS, E. "Recent Theories of the State" (1927), 43 LQR, 186, at pp. 196–203: this article was written at an early stage in the history of the Revolution and is mainly based on the views of Bukharine, which have since been discredited in Russia. It points out the main objections to Marxism, but also notes that there is some connection between economic conditions and legal doctrines.

2. FRIEDRICH, C.J. *The Philosophy of Law in Historical Perspective*, (University of Chicago Press, 1958), chap. 16: the theory of Marx and Engels is explained with reference to its Hegelian basis. The point is made that the Marxist exposure of ideologies has revealed its own ideology of social justice.

3. FINCH, J.D. *Introduction to Legal Theory*, (2nd ed., Sweet & Maxwell, Ltd, 1974), chap. 9: this chapter gives a very general review of the basic doctrines of Marx and Engels and an outline of their application in Russia from the Revolution down to the present.

4. GINSBERG, M. *On Justice in Society*, (Heinemann, London, 1965), chap. 5: the ethical basis of economic justice is considered, chiefly in relation to property rights. The law fixes certain minima, but above that property differences need to be justified on a principle of proportionate equality, i.e., that differential treatment requires justification. What the relevant differences are is considered in detail. In the course of the chapter the shortcomings of the Marxist analysis are set out.

5. JØRGENSEN, S. "Ideology and Science" (1974), Scand SL, 89: metascience is the science of science. The author begins by considering the characteristics of science and the distinction between theory and ideology. Marxism is taken as an illustration of the relation between scientific theory and political ideology. The Marxist identity of politics and science and of law and politics is treated as unacceptable. The questionable nature of Marxist anthropology is also pointed out.

6. BRUNNER, E. *Justice and the Social Order*, (trans. M. Hottinger, Lutterworth Press, 1945), chap. 18, especially pp. 156–60: the question of social and economic justice is considered primarily from a Christian point of view. At pp. 156–60 justice in a capitalist and in a communist order are contrasted.

7. KANTOROWICZ, H.U. "Has Capitalism Failed in Law?" in *Law: A Century of Progress*, (New York University Press, 1937), II, p. 320: the author denies that capitalism has failed. The criticisms of capitalism are considered. Its failure has lain in not adapting law to changing conditions, but this has nothing to do with capitalism as such.

8. WILBERFORCE, R.O. "Law and Economics", *Presidential Address to the Holdsworth Club, 1966*: this is of general interest. Lord Wilberforce argues that lawyers have approached great changes in economic life with the aid of out-of-date or traditional concepts. These do not yield results which accord with the realities of the contemporary world. There is now a need for lawyer-economists and economist-lawyers.

9. ROBINSON, H.W. "Law and Economics" (1939), 2 MLR, 257: this is of general interest. It constitutes a plea for a greater correlation of law and economics and criticises economists for not having faced the problems revealed by Marxism.

1. REUSCHLEIN, H.G. *Jurisprudence – its American Prophets*, (The Bobbs-Merrill Co, Inc, 1951), pp. 91–94, 265–71: Brooks Adams, writing at the beginning of the century, was an exponent of the idea that the common law was determined by economic factors. In the later passage the views of Laski are considered.

2. BEARD, C.A. *An Economic Interpretation of the Constitution of the United States*, (The Macmillan Co, New York, 1935): the thesis is that the Constitution was drafted by a small group who stood to benefit financially and who were especially concerned with the protection of acquired property. He endorses the theme that economic factors do play some part in moulding the law, but emphasises the fact that they are not exclusive.

3. BURDICK, F.M. "Is Law the Expression of Class Selfishness?" (1911–12), 25 Harv LR, 349: after an examination of English and American decisions the author concludes that law is not the expression of class interests, but represents an honest attempt to do justice impartially.

4. COMMONS, J.R. "Value in Law and Economics" in *Law: A Century of Progress*, (New York University Press, 1937), II, 332: the varying criteria of value since Adam Smith are considered. Whereas the economists tended to base themselves on Bentham and the lawyers on Blackstone, it is said that neither side went to extremes.

5. PARRY, D.H. "Economic Theories in English Case-law" (1931), 47 LQR, 183: the various ways in which economic theories can influence law and the influence of particular economic theories are examined.

6. BOHLEN, F.H. *Studies in the Law of Torts*, (The Bobbs-Merrill Co, 1926), pp. 368–77: in the course of discussing the Rule in *Rylands* v. *Fletcher*, the effect of the different social and economic conditions in England and America are considered.

7. POUND, R. *Interpretations of Legal History*, (Cambridge University Press, 1923), chap. 5: the origins of the economic interpretation of law are set out. The attempt to discover an exclusively economic interpretation is viewed critically, especially in relation to the Rule in *Rylands* v. *Fletcher* and the doctrine of common employment (now obsolete). It is pointed out that those who attacked the injustice of the doctrine of common employment assumed the justice of the doctrine of vicarious responsibility. (See also R. POUND: "The Scope and Purpose of Sociological Jurisprudence" (1911–12), 25 Harv LR, pp. 162–68).

8. POUND, R. "The Economic Interpretation and the Law of Torts" (1939–40), 53 Harv LR, 365: this is a detailed examination of whether the economic factor is the sole or decisive factor. It is pointed out that many rules of tort are not and never were in accordance with the interests of the English landed gentry. The attack on the doctrine of common employment is further considered.

9. POUND, R. "Fifty Years of Jurisprudence" (1937–38), 51 Harv LR, pp. 777–85: the various tenets of the economic theory of law are reviewed with reference to developments in Russia.

10. POUND, R. *The Ideal Element in Law*, (University of Calcutta, 1958), chap. 9:

the economic interpretation can furnish only a partial explanation. Three of the main deficiencies are discussed.

1. POUND, R. *Jurisprudence*, (West Publishing Co, 1959), I, pp. 227–64: three types of economic interpretations are distinguished. At pp. 254–64 the Marxist doctrine of economic determinism is dealt with.

2. GOLD, J. "Common Employment" (1937), 1 MLR, at pp. 225–30: the doctrine of common employment is ascribed to class bias and contentions to the contrary by Bohlen, Burdick and Pound are criticised.

3. STEINER, J.M. "Economics, Morality and the Law of Torts" (1976), 26 UTLJ, 227: the author considers alternative economics theories of law concerning "interaction damage" and finds them wanting. The issues are ultimately political: who uses government and for what end?

4. HALL, J. *Theft, Law and Society*, (2nd ed., The Bobbs-Merrill Co, Inc, 1952), chap. 3: in this chapter the economic factors that have shaped the law of larceny are traced.

20. Sociological Approaches

Sociology of Law and Sociological Jurisprudence

1. POUND, R. "Sociology of Law and Sociological Jurisprudence" (1943–44),
   5 UTLJ, 1: the sociology of law is said to proceed from sociology towards law,
   sociological jurisprudence from history and philosophy to the utilisation of the
   social sciences. The work of some sociologists and anthropologists is considered.

2. LEPAULLE, P. "The Function of Comparative Law with a Critique of Sociological
   Jurisprudence" (1921–22), 35 Harv LR, 838: in the earlier part of the article
   the difference between sociological jurisprudence and sociology is discussed. The
   difference relates to the method and objective.

3. GURVITCH, G. *Sociology of Law*, (Routledge & Kegan Paul, Ltd, 1947): whenever
   men come together in society there is a common feeling out of which emerges
   rules of behaviour. The task of sociology is to enumerate and classify the main
   types of social life. The task of sociological jurisprudence is to study the types of
   law which these produce. The first part of the book concerns the work of others.
   In the latter part the thesis is that there are several layers of social organisation.
   At the eighth layer there is said to be the "collective mind", which interacts with
   spiritual values and sets standards. The function of law is to regulate behaviour
   so as to harmonise with the values of the collective mind.

4. TIMASHEFF, N.S. "What is 'Sociology of Law'?" (1937), 43 AJS, 225: human
   behaviour in society in its relation to law is the object of the sociology of law. It
   is a causal investigation whose chief methods are introspective observations of
   one's own consciousness in relation to law, the study of behaviour in relation to
   law and experimental tests.

5. TIMASHEFF, N.S. *An Introduction to the Sociology of Law*, (Harvard University
   Committee on Research in the Social Sciences, 1939): law is a combination of
   power and ethics. Ethics is the realisation of patterns of conduct by means of
   group conviction; power is the imposition of patterns of conduct by force. The
   two are independent, but they overlap, "ethical imperative co-ordination".
   "Law" covers rules emanating from the state, "upper state level of law", and
   rules emanating from social groups, e.g., clubs, "lower social level".

6. SAWER, G. *Law in Society*, (Oxford, 1965): the book does not develop any
   specific theory, but deals generally with such matters as the distinction between
   the sociology of law and sociological jurisprudence, aspects of primitive and
   archaic systems, courts, judges, lawyers and the development of an accepted social
   order (which becomes identified with "lawyers"Law") and social administration
   which introduces modifications. In time these, too, become absorbed into the
   accepted social order. In the course of all this there are many superficial accounts
   of well-known theories.

7. CAIRNS, H. *The Theory of Legal Science*, (University of North Carolina Press,
   1941): a pure science of law should study human behaviour as a function of
   disorder. Law consists of one set of patterns of conduct concretised in rules.
   Jurisprudence is not as yet in a position to formulate sociological principles;
   so its function is merely to describe. The field of study comprises six elements
   that are said to be present in all systems.

1. STONE, J. *Social Dimensions of Law and Justice,* (Stevens & Sons, Ltd), Chap. 1: the need for both overall theory and guidance in dealing with *ad hoc* problems is considered in detail. Attention is also paid to the best way in which lawyers might study the "external relations" of law, and there are reviews of the development of sociological study. The question whether there is a meaningful distinction between sociology of law and sociological jurisprudence is discussed. The views of Timasheff and Cairns are criticised.

2. RAZ, J. "On the Function of Law" in *Oxford Essays in Jurisprudence (Second Series),* (ed. A.W.B. Simpson, Oxford University Press, 1973), Chap. 11: the concept of the function of law is important in many kinds of discussions. The main distinction drawn is between normative and social functions of law. The object of the paper is to provide a comprehensive scheme of classifying the functions of law. For a short critique, see S.L. PAULSON, Review of *Oxford Essays in Jurisprudence (Second Series),* (1974), 87 Harv LR, 898, pp. 903–905.

3. HALL, J. *Foundations of Jurisprudence,* (The Bobbs-Merrill Co, Inc, 1973), pp. 44–47: post-Kantian social theory tried to envisage social reality as basic. Social action is the core of social reality, and this is substituted for the classical notion of "reality" and practical reason.

4. HALL, J. *Comparative Law and Social Theory,* (Louisiana State UP, 1963): the author surveys the development of comparative law and the sociology of law. The former is a study of historical development, culture and human relations, so it should be closely related to the sociology of law. Together the two should evolve a humanistic sociology of law, which would include a study of common legal concepts and institutions, the functioning of law in society and social studies of positive law. All social science should be legally oriented.

5. SOROKIN, P. *Contemporary Sociological Theories,* (Harper & Bros, 1928): the various forms which sociological theorising has assumed are examined in detail. The important feature of the book is its presentation of the factual material by which theories are to be evaluated.

6. GINSBERG, M. *Reason and Unreason in Society,* (Longman, Green & Co, 1947), Part I: this is of general interest only. The problems and methods of sociology, the development of the subject and the work of some leading figures in the field are dealt with.

7. SEAGLE, W. *The Quest for Law,* (Alfred A. Knopf, 1941): this is a historical study. The phenomena of social life are investigated in order to discover the regularities and connections between certain social phenomena as such, or between certain natural and social phenomena. As applied to law, the study involves a consideration of laws of all times and places.

8. CASTBERG, F. *Problems of Legal Philosophy,* (2nd ed., Oslo University Press; Allen & Unwin, Ltd, 1957), pp. 10–15: sociology aims at discovering the social rules which govern the legal relations of human beings. It is a causal science dealing with law as a psycho-physical phenomenon.

9. JØRGENSEN, S. *Law and Society,* (Akademisk Boghandel, 1972), chap. 1: legal and social science are compared. The general pattern of the latter is to proceed by observation, description, analysis, generalisation, theory, collection of data, verification and correction. Law is a social science empirically founded on real

phenomena. Understanding law requires a vertical (historical) and horizontal (sociological) perspective.

1. BLACK, D.J. "The Boundaries of Legal Sociology" (1971—72), 81 Yale LJ, 1086: there is too much confusion of science and policy in legal sociology. The social scientist may be influenced by values in his choice of problems and in his approach to them. But legal sociology should confine itself to legal life as a system of behaviour and not concern itself with policy. Law for this purpose consists of observable acts, not rules. Effectiveness is central, i.e., conformity of actual behaviour with rules.

2. TRUBEK, D.M. "Towards a Social Theory of Law: an Essay on the Study of Law and Development" (1972—73), 82 Yale LJ, 1: this paper is largely a commentary on social scientists who have striven to understand the function of law in the Third World. Scholars should keep aside values and see the phenomena of legal life; they should strive to construct universal conceptual categories. The relation between law and social life and the concept of law and development, and their various aspects, are reviewed at length.

3. SCHIFF, D.N. "Socio-legal Theory: Social Structure and Law" (1976), 39 MLR, 287: analysis of law is linked to analysis of the social situation, the part it plays in the creation, maintenance or change of that situation. The question should be: What is society? rather than, What is law? The discrepancies in the methods of writers who develop an analysis of law in society is necessary to the understanding and development of such studies. The work of various authorities, in particular Durkheim and Ehrlich, is dealt with.

4. SALMOND, J.W. *Jurisprudence*, (11th ed., G.L. Williams, Sweet & Maxwell, Ltd, 1957), pp. 14—17: the nature of legal sociology is considered very generally. Works on the sociology of law are approved as being useful, but those on sociological jurisprudence are treated as being of little value.

5. KOCOUREK, A. *An Introduction to the Science of Law*, (Little, Brown & Co, 1930), pp. 226—28: the aims and objects of the sociological school are briefly summarised.

6. SHKLAR, J.N. *Legalism*, (Harvard University Press, 1964): The entire plea in this book is that legal theorists should abandon "legalism" and pay heed to the social situation around them. "Legalism" is the attitude of mind that makes a morality of rule following; but this is only one morality in a pluralist society. Law, it is argued, is an instrument of politics and, as such, may appropriately be applied in certain situations, but not in others. The book is a criticism of Positivism and Natural Law theorising, but no constructive suggestion is offered to further its plea.

7. EHRLICH, E. "Montesquieu and Sociological Jurisprudence" (1915—16), 29 Harv LR, 582: Montesquieu's work is regarded as the pioneer attempt to found a sociology of law, and is considered from this angle.

8. ILBERT, C. "Montesquieu" in *Great Jurists of the World*, (edd. J. MacDonell and E. Manson, John Murray, 1913), 417: an account is given of the life and work of Montesquieu. His sociological approach is touched on in the course of the discussion of *The Spirit of Laws*.

1. HAZO, R.G. "Montesquieu and the Separation of Powers" (1968), 54 Am BAJ, 665: an account is given of his life and contributions. These were a new classification of governments, a pioneer insistence on the influence of climate and environment and the doctrine of the separation of powers.

2. HOLMES, O.W. "Montesquieu" in *Collected Legal Papers*, (Constable & Co, Ltd, 1920), 250: in this charmingly written account of Montesquieu's life an attempt is made to show how threads drawn from various aspects of his career and character united to produce *The Spirit of Laws.*

3. EMMET, D. *Rules, Roles and Relations*, (Macmillan, 1966): neither sociology nor ethics can be insulated from each other. Patterns of social behaviour are not just regularities of how people act, but are the result of ideas as to what is the right, useful or proper thing to do. People rely on expectations of mutual behaviour, derived from social roles. The nature of sociological explanation and moral judgment, and the influence of roles, are considered along these lines.

4. SEIDMAN, R.B. "The Judicial Process Reconsidered in the Light of the Role-theory" (1969), 32 MLR, 516: this article presents the difficulties and problems of deciding "clear" and "trouble" cases from the sociological angle of the role-theory.

5. OTTE, G. "Role Theory and the Judicial Process: a Critical Analysis" (1971–72), 16 St Louis ULJ, 420: in so far as law is the way judges behave, judicial behaviour becomes a key to understanding law. Role studies have yielded good results in other fields, and it is likely to do the same in the judicial field. But a role approach is only one explanation of judicial behaviour; it has its difficulties.

6. MARSHALL, G. "Political Science and the Judicial Process" (1957), PL, 139: the judicial process, interpretation of legislative language, the judicial function as a legislative one, policy and trends are viewed in the light of political science analysis.

7. MONTROSE, J.L. "Legal Theory for Politicians and Sociologists" (1974), 25 NILQ, 321: a comprehensive theory of law is a theory of the state. Philosophy should contribute logical analysis and teleological evaluation; sociology should contribute a statically conceived classification as well as a dynamically conceived causative science.

8. HONORÉ, A.M. "Groups, Laws and Obedience" in *Oxford Essays in Jurisprudence (Second Series)*, (ed. A.W.B. Simpson, Clarendon Press, Oxford, 1973), chap. 1: a theory of law is, *inter alia*, a theory about attitudes to obedience and disobedience. Analysing rule, command and norm is to start too far inside the phenomenon of "law". All laws are laws of a group and one should therefore begin by understanding what a "group" is. The examination includes "shared understandings" about the curtailment of liberty, "group prescriptions" and the institutionalization of these. For a short explanatory comment, see S.L. PAULSON, Review of *Oxford Essays in Jurisprudence (Second Series)*, (1974), 87 Harv LR, 898, at pp. 901–903.

R. von Ihering

9. von IHERING, R. *Law as a Means to an End*, (trans. I. Husik, The Boston Book

Co, 1913): this is Ihering's classic exposition of his view that law is designed to fulfil some purpose.

1. von IHERING, R. *Geist des römischen Rechts*, (Leipzig, 1898), II, pp. 309–89: this is a prior revelation of Ihering's conviction that law serves purpose. He perceived in his study of Roman law that it was based on interests and that the task of the law was the reconciliation of conflicting interests.

2. STONE, J. *Legal System and Lawyers' Reasonings*, (Stevens & Sons, Ltd, 1964), pp. 224–229: the Pandectists tried to bridge the gap between Roman law and the needs of the countries that had received it centuries later. But deduction from the *Corpus Juris* provided answers unsuited to contemporary needs. It is in this context that the work of Ihering is touched on.

3. STONE, J. *Human Law and Human Justice*, (Stevens & Sons, Ltd, 1965), pp. 147–159: the work of Ihering is discussed in relation to contemporary thought. He reacted against the individualist attitude of mind, including that of Bentham and Mill, however much he admired their work. It is pointed out that as a theory of justice his concept of social utility is unhelpful, since this is not something given or known, but what is sought to be discovered.

4. PATTERSON, E.W. *Jurisprudence*, (The Foundation Press, Inc, 1953), pp. 459–64: this contains a short account of the work of Ihering.

5. JENKINS, I. "Rudolph von Ihering" (1960–61), 14 Vand LR, 169: Ihering's work is appraised in an interesting way. The author contends that Ihering sought to inquire into the foundations of legal order and to relate law to the whole of man's cultural and spiritual setting. His followers, on the other hand, have limited themselves to tracing the relation between law and political and economic forces.

6. MORRIS, C. *The Great Legal Philosophers*, (University of Pennsylvania Press, 1959), chap. 16: extracts from Ihering's works are included and might be regarded as fairly representative of his main thesis.

7. FRIEDRICH, C.J. *The Philosophy of Law in Historical Perspective*, (University of Chicago Press, 1958), chap. 17: the earlier part of this chapter is devoted to an account and estimation of Ihering's contribution.

8. MACDONELL, J. "Rudolph von Ihering" in *Great Jurists of the World*, (edd. J. MacDonell and E. Manson, John Murray, 1913), 590: an account is given of the life, character and various works of Ihering. There are also short appraisals of the latter.

9. GOLUNSKII, S.A. and STROGOVICH, M.S. "The Theory of the State and Law" in *Soviet Legal Philosophy*, (trans. H.W. Babb, Harvard University Press, 1951), pp. 413–15: the views of Ihering are considered from a Marxist point of view and rejected. He is praised for having attempted to be more "realistic" than his predecessors, but is alleged to have failed to perceive the class character of the institutions with which he dealt.

10. *The Jurisprudence of Interests*, (trans. M.M. Schoch, Harvard University Press, 1948): it is convenient to append some reference to the Tübingen School here (although in the text it is dealt with immediately before the work of Pound).

This School more or less took up the task where Ihering left it and considers purpose in the practical interpretation of the law.

E. Ehrlich

1. EHRLICH, E. *Fundamental Principles of the Sociology of Law*, (trans. W.L. Moll, Harvard University Press, 1936), especially pp. 489–506: in this series of essays the author develops his central thesis that the development of law lies in society. There are also discussions of the methods of legal sociology, justice, custom and codification.

2. EHRLICH, E. "Sociology of Law" (trans. N. Isaacs, 1921–22), 36 Harv LR, 129: laws may differ from country to country, but in so far as there is a social order among civilised societies, there are elements in common. Society is older than law and must have had some kind of order before legal provisions came into being.

3. MORRIS, C. *The Great Legal Philosophers*, (University of Pennsylvania Press, 1959), chap. 18: extracts from the works of E. Ehrlich are given.

4. VINOGRADOFF, P. *Collected Papers*, (Oxford, 1928), II, chap. 11: the trend towards sociological jurisprudence is considered, principally with reference to the work of Ehrlich.

5. SAWER, G. *Law in Society*, (Oxford, 1965), pp. 174–7: this is a brief critique of Ehrlich's doctrine, pointing out its inconsistencies.

J. Bentham

6. BENTHAM, J. *An Introduction to the Principles of Morals and Legislation*, (edd. J.H. Burns and H.L.A. Hart, University of London, The Athlone Press, 1970), especially chaps. 1–6; and *A Fragment on Government* in *Works*, (ed. J. Bowring, William Tait, 1843), I: the principle of utility is set out at length. It runs through most of his work and frequent allusions to it are also found elsewhere (see also B. PAREKH, *Bentham's Political Thought*, (Croom-Helm, 1973).

7. BENTHAM, J. *The Theory of Legislation*, (trans. R. Hildreth, ed. C.K. Ogden, Routledge & Kegan Paul, Ltd, 1950): this is another of Bentham's important contributions. The editor's Introduction is especially deserving of study for he makes out a reasoned case for supposing that Bentham will prove to have been one of the greatest Europeans.

8. HOLDSWORTH, W.S. *A History of English Law*, XIII, (ed. A.L. Goodhart and H.G. Hanbury, Methuen & Co, Ltd, 1952), pp. 41–155: in this posthumously published volume of Holdsworth's *History* is to be found a full account of the background and the life and work of Bentham, and shorter accounts of James and J.S. Mill. At pp. 68–81 the principle of utility is discussed.

9. *Jeremy Bentham and the Law. A Symposium*, (edd. G.W. Keeton and G. Schwarzenberger, Stevens & Sons, Ltd, 1948), especially chaps. 12 and 13: Bentham's contribution to law is discussed from various angles. In chapter 8, G. Schwarzenberger, "Bentham's Contribution to International Law and Organisation", considers Bentham's contribution to international law, including his invention of the name, while in chapter 12, W. Friedmann, "Bentham and Modern Legal Thought", draws attention to the inter-related nature of Bentham's thought and considers his many contributions as a lawyer and social reformer. In chapter 13, A.J. Ayer, "The Principle of Utility", examines the principle of utility in detail. It might also be

noted that H.F. Jolowicz, "Was Bentham a Lawyer?", followed up his contribution about Bentham in this volume with a further article, entitled "Jeremy Bentham and the Law" (1948), 1 CLP, 1.

1. AUSTIN, J. *Lectures on Jurisprudence*, (5th ed., R. Campbell, John Murray, 1885), I, chaps. 2–4: Austin, as befits Bentham's pupil, endeavours to work the utility principle into his discussion of the nature of law. Utility is the test by which the tendency of action is evaluated. The principle is considered in relation to the laws of God, and is defended against certain objections.

2. HART, H.L.A. "Bentham, Lecture on a Master Mind" in *More Essays in Legal Philosophy. General Assessments of Legal Philosophies*, (ed. R.S. Summers, Oxford, 1971), 18 (reprinted from (1962), 48 Proc. of the British Academy, 297): novelties of method which Bentham introduced have raised new questions. His criticisms of existing institutions were intended to show that there was a middle course between conservatism and anarchy. His utilitarianism and his pleasure-pain calculus need to be re-interpreted. Particular attention is given to his contribution to linguistic philosophy, his view of "right" and the relevance of *mens rea*.

3. HART, H.L.A. "Bentham and Sovereignty" (1967), 2 Ir Jur (NS), 327: Bentham was a greater thinker than Austin. Austin's concept of sovereignty excluded legal limitations on sovereign power, any division of it and a plurality of sovereigns each with full power. Bentham did not commit himself to such extremes although his treatment of sovereignty is hesitant and sometimes obscure.

4. BURNS, J.H. "Bentham on Sovereignty: an Exploration" in *Bentham and Legal Theory*, (ed. M.H. James, reprint of articles in (1973), 24 NILQ), p. 133: the movement in Bentham's thinking is outlined. Some of the differences between him and Austin are touched on, but the main interest lies in the change of view as to the possibility and nature of limitations on sovereign power. Ultimately the distinction is alluded to between "operative power", which is vested in the legislature, administration and judiciary, and "constitutive power", which resides in the people and invests and divests supreme power in government.

5. PATTERSON, E.W. *Jurisprudence*, (The Foundation Press, Inc, 1953), pp. 439–59: this is a short but very good account of Bentham. A brief account of his life is given and is followed by a discussion of his principle of utility with reference to ethics and legislation in turn.

6. ROSS, A. *On Law and Justice*, (Stevens & Sons, Ltd, 1958), chap. 13: Bentham's utilitarianism is subjected to acute criticism. "Social welfare" is a mythical idea, since the community is not an independent unit.

7. DOWRICK, F.E. *Justice According to the English Common Lawyers*, (Butterworths, 1961), chap. 6: the idea of utility as a principle of justice is examined, primarily with reference to the work of Bentham. Mention is also made of his predecessors, and of his successors, who gave it much of its impetus.

8. STONE, J. *Human Law and Human Justice*, (Stevens & Sons, Ltd, 1965), chap. 4: the utilitarian philosophy of Bentham is developed at length. Its origins, background and influence are gone into in detail. The major criticisms of his pleasure-pain calculus are also discussed.

1. MILNE, A.J.M. "Bentham's Principle of Utility and Legal Philosophy" in *Bentham and Legal Theory*, (ed. M.H. James, reprint of articles in (1973), 24 NILQ), p. 9: what is valuable in Bentham's legal philosophy owes nothing to his principle of utility. His psychological hedonism is based on false assumptions and fails to distinguish between reasons and causes of action. He also failed to explain a "community".

2. LYONS, D.B. *In the Interests of the Governed. A Study in Bentham's Philosophy of Utility and Law*, (Clarendon Press, Oxford, 1973), chaps. 1–5: the author believes that Bentham has been misunderstood and that critics of his utilitarianism failed to perceive that Bentham embraced a dual standard – the community interest as the test in the public or political sphere, and self-interest in the private sphere. It is also pointed out that account has to be taken of change in Bentham's views.

3. JOLOWICZ, H.F. *Lectures on Jurisprudence*, (ed. J.A. Jolowicz, The Athlone Press, 1963), pp. 101–6: this contains a brief account of Bentham's work and influence.

4. BAUMGARDT, D. *Bentham and the Ethics of Today*, (Princeton University Press, 1952), especially pp. 165–320: in this important book the author considers Bentham's ethical theory and the evolution of his thought with reference to his writings. At pp. 165–320 the principle of utility is considered with reference to *An Introduction to the Principles of Morals and Legislation*.

5. COING, H. "Bentham's Influence on the Development of *Interessenjurisprudenz* and General Jurisprudence" (1967), 2 Ir Jur (NS), 336: the author begins by outlining Bentham's influence on Germanic thought through Beneke and Ihering. He then shows that German *Interessenjurisprudenz* did not get quite as far as Bentham's principle of the greatest happiness of the greatest number.

6. HOLDSWORTH, W.S. *Some Makers of English Law*, (Cambridge University Press, 1938), pp. 248–56: a somewhat short account is given of Bentham and his work and the reasons for its influence.

7. ATKINSON, C.M. *Jeremy Bentham. His Life and Work*, (Methuen & Co, 1903): a readable and detailed account is given of Bentham's life and work. The book is of general interest.

8. EVERETT, C.W. *The Education of Jeremy Bentham*, (Columbia University Press, 1931): Bentham's early career is recounted. Chapter 9 is of direct relevance in that it deals with the origins of his *An Introduction to the Principles of Morals and Legislation*.

9. ALLEN, C.K. *Legal Duties*, (Oxford, 1931), 119: in this paper, entitled "The Young Bentham", an account is given of his early career as providing a background to his later work.

10. HOLLOND, H.A. "Jeremy Bentham, 1748–1832" (1948), 10 CLJ, 3: this gives a most readable and convenient account of Bentham's life and work in historical perspective.

11. OGDEN, C.K. *Jeremy Bentham, 1832–2032*, (Kegan Paul, Trench, Trubner & Co, Ltd, 1932): this short booklet contains a lecture which assesses Bentham's work with reference to the past, present and future. A list of the reforms effected by him is given at pp. 19–20.

1. SMITH, J.C. "Law, Language, and Philosophy" (1968), 3 U Br Col LR, 59:
   Bentham was in his way an acute semanticist. In the course of reviewing the
   attitude to language of various legal philosophers, that of Bentham is explained
   and considered.

2. HERON, D.C. *An Introduction to the History of Jurisprudence*, (J.W. Parker & Son,
   1860), Part VI, chap. 3: an account is given of Bentham's work and influence.

3. RANDALL, H.J. "Jeremy Bentham" (1906), 22 LQR, 311: this contains a general
   appreciation of Bentham's contribution. See also J.L. STOCKS: *Jeremy Bentham,
   1748–1832*, (Manchester University Press, 1933).

4. NYS, E. "Notes Inedites de Bentham sur le Droit International" (1885), 1 LQR,
   225: this is a short account (in French) of certain notes left by Bentham on the
   formation of an international order. The Notes themselves are reproduced
   verbatim.

5. ZANE, J.M. "Bentham" in *Great Jurists of the World*, (edd. J. MacDonell and
   E. Manson, John Murray, 1913), 532: this is, on the whole, an uncomplimentary
   appraisal of Bentham's work. It is stated that his lack of historical sense, his
   contempt for case-law and his ignorance of Roman law disqualify him from the
   title to being a jurist. It is also alleged that he was out of touch with the times.

6. JENNINGS, W.I. "A Plea for Utilitarianism" (1938), 2 MLR, 22: the subject of
   "jurisprudence" begins with Bentham. Generality in it is not to be found in
   legal concepts so much as in social phenomena.

7. COHEN, F.S. *Ethical Systems and Legal Ideals*, (Falcon Press, 1933), chaps. 2 and 3:
   it is unquestionable that criticism and improvement of law has to stem from an
   ethical basis. The most appropriate basis is utilitarian. The law should be
   criticised according as it tends to produce happiness.

8. ECKHOFF, T. "Justice and Social Utility" in *Legal Essays. A Tribute to Frede
   Castberg*, (Universitetsforlaget, 1963), 74: the principles of justice and social
   utility are explained and compared and the parts they respectively play are
   demonstrated.

9. BAKER, E.C. "Utility and Rights: Two Justifications for State-action increasing
   Equality" (1974–75), 84 Yale LJ, 39: the utilitarian justification is compared
   with Professor Dworkin's. The former is the guaranteed minimum approach
   justifying some measure of state interference. Dworkin's is the guaranteed
   fulfilment approach. It is contended that there should be a combination of the
   two.

10. LUMB, R.D. "Natural Law and Legal Positivism" (1958–59), 11 JLE, pp. 503–8:
    the Utilitarian doctrine, as expounded by Bentham and Austin, is compared
    with natural law and criticised on various grounds.

11. MORRIS, C. *The Great Legal Philosophers*, (University of Pennsylvania Press, 1959),
    chapter 11: at pp. 262–76 there are extracts from *An Introduction to the
    Principles of Morals and Legislation*. The rest of the chapter contains passages
    from *The Limits of Jurisprudence Defined*. Chapter 15, which contains extracts
    from the writings of J.S. Mill, might also be consulted.

12. RUSSELL, B. *Freedom and Organisation: 1814–1914*, (Allen & Unwin, Ltd, 1934),

chaps. 9–12: chapter 9 deals with Bentham, and chapter 12 with the Benthamite doctrine. The two intervening chapters deal with Mill and Ricardo.

1. FRIEDRICH, C.J. *The Philosophy of Law in Historical Perspective*, (The University of Chicago Press, 1958), chap. 11: the influence of Hobbes is traced through Hume to the Utilitarians. Among the latter, the contributions of Bentham and of Austin are discussed.

2. MURRAY, R.H. *The History of Political Science from Plato to the Present*, (Heffer & Sons, Ltd, 1926), chap. 10: the utilitarian outlook is examined in detail from the time of Hume onwards. There are good accounts of the work of Bentham and of the two Mills.

3. SABINE, G.H. *A History of Political Theory*, (3rd ed., Harrap & Co, Ltd, 1963), chaps. 31 and 32: these two chapters are concerned with liberalism, in the course of which the greatest happiness principle of Bentham is considered at length as well as his views on law. In the first part of the second chapter Mill's contribution is dealt with.

R. Pound

4. POUND, R. "The Scope and Purpose of Sociological Jurisprudence" (1910–11), 24 Harv LR, 591, at pp. 611–19; (1911–12), 25 Harv LR, pp. 140–47, 489: the origins of the sociological movement are first traced out in the course of a general survey of jurisprudential schools. The work of Ihering is touched on and his insistence on interests. Sociological jurisprudence tries to ensure that law-making, interpretation and application take more account of social facts.

5. POUND, R. "A Survey of Social Interests" (1943–44), 57 Harv LR, 1, (being a rewriting of "A Study of Social Interests" (1921), 15 Papers and Proceedings of the American Sociological Society, 16): interests are divided into individual, public and social. For some purposes it is convenient to regard a given claim from the point of view of one category, for other purposes from another. When weighing interests they should be considered on the same plane. Generally, it is expedient to consider interests on a social plane. The scheme of interests is set out in detail.

6. POUND, R. "Interests of Personality" (1914–15), 28 Harv LR, 343, 445: after a general explanation of what "interests" are, individual interests are considered in detail. It is pointed out that the securing of individual interests is also a social interest: hence they should be considered on this plane. The ways in which individual interests might be classified are then considered.

7. POUND, R. "Individual Interests of Substance – Promised Advantages" (1945–46), 59 Harv LR, 1: the task of a legal order is to secure reasonable individual expectations so far as they may be harmonised with the least friction and waste. The history of the law shows a progressive recognition of the interest, both social and individual, in the fulfilment of promises.

8. POUND, R. "Mechanical Jurisprudence" (1908), 8 Col LR, 605: law is a means towards the administration of justice. It should be judged by its results. It should neither become too scientific for people to appreciate its working, nor petrified by technicality (mechanical). The institutions of law should be founded on policy and adapted to human needs.

1. POUND, R. "Law in Books and Law in Action" (1910), 44 Am LR, 12: attention is drawn to the growing divergence between legal principle and how it actually operates. Jurisprudence should proceed by taking account of social facts.

2. POUND, R. "The Administration of Justice in the Modern City" (1912–13), 26 Harv LR, 302: the problem that confronted administrators immediately after the American Revolution is contrasted with those confronting modern administrators. On this basis the need for a sociological approach is stressed.

3. POUND, R. "The End of Law as Developed in Legal Rules and Doctrines" (1913–14), 27 Harv LR, 195: this is a lengthy inquiry into the policies underlying successive periods of legal development, starting with archaic law and ending with modern law.

4. POUND, R. "The End of Law as Developed in Juristic Thought" (1913–14), 27 Harv LR, 605: (1916–17), 30 Harv LR, 201: this is an inquiry parallel to the last one, but viewed from the angle of legal theory.

5. POUND, R. "The Theory of Judicial Decision" (1922–23), 36 Harv LR, 640, 802, 940: judges are guided by the prevalent legal theory. In the 17th and 18th centuries this was the theory of Natural Law. A theory of judicial decision for today has to take account of two factors, to decide the particular dispute justly and to declare the law for the future. All this brings in the idea of social engineering.

6. POUND, R. "Fifty Years of Jurisprudence" (1936–37), 50 Harv, 557: (1937–38), 51 Harv LR, 444, 777: in the last decade of the 19th century the Historical and Analytical Schools were dominant. The 20th century has witnessed the rise of the Social-philosophical school. The various movements of the century are reviewed.

7. POUND, R. in *My Philosophy of Law*, (Boston Law Book Co, 1941), p. 249: law is a form of social control and the end of law is, therefore, social control, which is to adjust relations and order behaviour so as to satisfy as many demands as possible with the least friction and waste.

8. POUND, R. "Natural Natural Law and Positive Natural Law" (1952), 68 LQR, 330; (1960), 5 Nat LF, 70: the distinction is drawn and amplified in the second article. The function of natural law ideology is said to be both creative and critical.

9. POUND, R. "The Lawyer as a Social Engineer" (1954), 3 JPL, 292: a social engineer is one who makes a social process achieve its purpose with the minimum waste or friction. The lawyer's task is to satisfy as many demands as possible in this way. The ways in which this has to be accomplished are explained, and there is a plea for a Department of Justice.

10. POUND, R. *The Spirit of the Common Law*, (Marshall Jones Co, Boston, 1921), chap. 8: the preceding chapters deal with different stages of legal development. The present stage is that of the socialisation of law, which requires social engineering. The differences in the results that would be obtained by a social approach to law from those obtained by other approaches are illustrated.

11. POUND, R. *An Introduction to the Philosophy of Law*, (Yale University Press, 1922),

chap. 2, especially pp. 89–99: the question, "What is the end of law?" has had various answers given to it throughout the ages. At the present time the wants of man are prominent, and there is a need to balance the wants and desires of men. There is some discussion as to how interests are to be valued and balanced.

1. POUND, R. *Interpretations of Legal History*, (Cambridge University Press, 1923), chap. 7: in this chapter the "engineering interpretation" is explained and advocated. It is introduced by way of an explanation of Kohler's views.

2. POUND, R. *Contemporary Juristic Theory*, (Ward Ritchie Press, 1940), chap. 3: this contains a discussion of social engineering and the adjustment of interests so as to produce the minimum of waste and friction.

3. POUND, R. *Social Control Through Law*, (Yale University Press, 1942): law is a means of social control by controlling internal (i.e., human) nature. The function of law is social engineering, but in this task morals, religion and education also have a part to play.

4. POUND, R. *Jurisprudence*, (West Publishing Co, 1959), I, chap. 6; II, pp. 79 *et seq.*, 186 *et seq.*, 272 *et seq.*: in chapter 6 of the first volume there is a full historical survey of the different types of sociological jurisprudence. It puts Anglo-American and Continental thought in perspective. In the second volume theories of law from social-philosophical and sociological points of view are considered, including the views of Comte, Ehrlich and others. The sociological view of the relationship between law and morals is also explained.

5. MORRIS, H. "Dean Pound's Jurisprudence" in *More Essays in Legal Philosophy. General Assessments of Legal Philosophies*, (ed. R.S. Summers, Oxford, 1971; reprinted from (1960), 13 Stan LR, 185), 43: although primarily a critique of Pound's *Jurisprudence*, this is a survey of Pound's thinking generally. It draws attention to the serious gaps and inadequacies in some of the basic ideas that constitute his life-long theme, namely, the nature of jurisprudence, his approach to the nature of "law", his critique of analytical jurisprudence and his analysis of an "act".

6. PATTERSON, E.W. "Roscoe Pound on Jurisprudence" (1960), 60 Col LR, 1124, especially at pp. 1128–29: this is a review of Pound's *Jurisprudence (supra)*. Sociology is specifically touched on at p. 1128.

7. PATTERSON, E.W. "Pound's Theory of Social Interests" in *Interpretations of Modern Legal Philosophies*, (ed. P. Sayre, Oxford University Press, New York, 1947), chap. 26: the characteristics of a social interest are discussed, foremost among which is the fact that it should serve as a measuring device for individual interests. For legislative purposes, social interests are guides to what ought to become law; for judicial purposes, they are analogous to rules of law. "Weighing" interests means "making a choice".

8. PATTERSON, E.W. *Jurisprudence*, (The Foundation Press, Inc, 1953), pp. 509–27: an explanatory account is given of Pound's philosophy. This is a useful summary of his many writings.

9. PATON, G.W. "Pound and Contemporary Juristic Theory" (1944), 22 Can BR, 479: the relation of Pound's work to administrative law, modern Realism, sociology and sociological jurisprudence and legal philosophy is discussed in

turn. According to the analysis, Pound is regarded as a sociological jurist rather than as a sociologist. Pound's "social engineering" is said to be a relativist philosophy (i.e., relative to time and place) despite Pound's own criticism of relativist philosophies as "give it up philosophies".

1. STONE, J. "A Critique of Pound's Theory of Justice" (1934–35), 20 Iowa LR, 531: Pound's theory is examined with reference to its origins and the claims which Pound makes. The difficulties which it encounters are also indicated.

2. STONE, J. "The Golden Age of Pound" (1962), 4 Syd LR, 1: this is primarily a review of Pound's *Jurisprudence*. Its importance lies in the criticisms that are made of the theory of interests. Stone also questions Patterson's interpretation of Pound's meaning of "social interest" (*supra*).

3. STONE, J. "Roscoe Pound and Sociological Jurisprudence" (1964–65), 78 Harv LR, 1578: this tribute, written as a memorial to Roscoe Pound, estimates the present state of sociological jurisprudence in relation to Pound's work. (For other appreciations in the same volume, see T.C. CLARK: "Tribute to Roscoe Pound", p. 1; E.N. GRISWOLD: "Roscoe Pound – 1870–1964", p. 4; A.E. SUTHERLAND: "One Man in his Time", p. 7; A.L. GOODHART: "Roscoe Pound", p. 23; A.W. SCOTT: "Pound's Influence on Civil Procedure", p. 1568; A.T. von MEHREN: "Roscoe Pound and Comparative Law", p. 1585).

4. STONE, J. *Human Law and Human Justice*, (Stevens & Sons, Ltd, 1965), chap. 9: in this chapter the author collates all his previous accounts, critiques and defences of Pound's work. The ambiguities in Pound's position and the difficulties which his theory of interests encounters are set out in detail.

5. STONE, J. *Social Dimensions of Law and Justice*, (Stevens & Sons, Ltd, 1966), chap. 4: Pound's scheme of listing *de facto* interests, though criticised, is adopted as being the best model. Of particular interest is the author's rejection of Pound's category of "public interests". The nature of interests and public policy are explained at length.

6. HARDING, A.L. "Professor Pound makes History" in *Southern Methodist University Studies in Jurisprudence*, (ed. A.L. Harding, SMU Press, 1957), IV, p. 3: this is a discussion of Pound's address in 1906 and the impact which his thought, as expounded in it, has since made.

7. BOWKER, W.F. "Basic Rights and Freedoms: What are they?" (1959), 37 Can BR, 43: this may be read as a contrast to Pound's scheme. Individual interests are listed on a different plan altogether. (The other contributions to this volume are also useful).

8. LEPAULLE, P. "The Function of Comparative Law with a Critique of Sociological Jurisprudence" (1921–22), 35 Harv LR, 838: after explaining the difference between sociological jurisprudence and sociology (*supra*), Pound's theory is criticised on the ground that there are basic weaknesses in his idea of "interest" and "balancing".

9. FRIED, C. "Two Concepts of Interests: Some Reflections on the Supreme Court's Balancing Test" (1962–63), 76 Harv LR, 755: a distinction is drawn between "wants" and "interests". The balancing test is ambiguous, for it can be stated in different ways. In order to decide in which way the issue should be stated, the

court has to decide upon its own role. The issue should be stated in a way that does not pre-judge it.

1. ROSS, A. *On Law and Justice*, (Stevens & Sons, Ltd, 1958), chaps. 12 and 17: in the first of these chapters the point is made in the course of a general discussion of justice that one meaning of this word is the equal balancing of the interests to be affected by a decision. But the question remains as to how interests are to be "weighed". Chapter 17 is a powerful criticism of the whole idea of "interests". Interests are attitudes based on needs as distinct from those based on morals. All interests are experienced by individuals, but they may coincide, be connected or be shared. The division of them into individual and social categories is regarded as futile.

2. DICKINSON, J. "Social Order and Political Authority" (1929), 23 Am Pol Sc R, 293, at pp. 294–301: the author points out the futility of trying to catalogue interests and gives reasons why any such attempt is bound to fail.

3. LLEWELLYN, K.N. *Jurisprudence. Realism in Theory and Practice*, (University of Chicago Press, 1962), chap. 1: the doctrine of balancing of interests gives no indication of how to identify interests and how to balance them. In this paper the "realist" criticism of Pound's doctrine is formulated.

4. WILSON, B. "A Choice of Values" (1961), 4 Can BJ, 448: Pound's idea of social engineering is said to be particularly appropriate to modern social legislation. The balancing of interests is considered with reference to the law of nuisance.

5. PROSSER, W.L. *Handbook of the Law of Torts*, (2nd ed., West Publishing Co, 1955), chap. 1, pp. 12–20: social engineering is considered with reference to the law of torts, which is concerned with the adjustment of conflicting interests of individuals so as to achieve a desirable social result. The various factors that have to be taken into account are listed and explained.

6. GROSSMAN, W.L. "The Legal Philosophy of Roscoe Pound" (1934–35), 44 Yale LJ, 605: Pound's doctrine is explained with reference to the work of three of his predecessors, namely, Ihering, Kohler and James. The engineering theory itself is critically examined and its shortcomings indicated.

7. AMOS, M.S. "Roscoe Pound" in *Modern Theories of Law*, (ed. W.I. Jennings, Oxford University Press, 1933), 86: what people think about law affects the kind of law that they make. It is not possible for judges simply to apply the law. They need to think as legislators, i.e., to take account of the purpose of law.

8. DOWRICK, F.E. *Justice According to the English Common Lawyers*, (Butterworths, 1961), chap. 7: Pound's contribution towards the achievement of social justice is explained and is then compared with similar, though isolated, utterances and decisions that have been made by English judges.

9. SAWER, G. *Law in Society*, (Oxford, 1965), chap. 9: the main concern of this chapter is with Pound's interest theory. Attention is drawn to the inadequate treatment of the interests of institutions as such.

10. MORRIS, C. *The Great Legal Philosophers*, (University of Pennsylvania Press, 1959), chap. 22: this reproduces Pound's contribution to *My Philosophy of Law* (*supra*).

1. KOCOUREK, A. "Roscoe Pound as a Former Colleague Knew Him" in *Interpretations of Modern Legal Philosophies*, (ed. P. Sayre, Oxford University Press, New York, 1947), chap. 19: this provides an amusing and lively sketch of Pound as a man.

2. CLARK, T.C., GRISWOLD, E.N., SUTHERLAND, A.E., GOODHART, A.L.: "Roscoe Pound" (1964–65), 78 Harv LR, 1, 4, 7, 23: these four tributes to Pound's life and work provide assessments of his contribution.

3. WIGDOR, D. *Roscoe Pound. Philosopher of Law*, (Greenwood Press, Connecticut, 1974): this book gives a biographical account of Pound, both as a man and also the background to the development of his thought. It is of general interest.

L. Duguit

4. DUGUIT, L. *Law in the Modern State*, (trans. F. and H.J. Laski, Allen & Unwin, Ltd, 1921): the meaning of sovereignty and the collapse of traditional ideas about sovereignty and the state are set out in detail. The Introduction, pp. xvi–xxxiv, outlines the main points of Duguit's doctrine and the objections to it.

5. DUGUIT, L. in *Modern French Legal Philosophy*, (trans. F.W. Scott and J.P. Chamberlain, The Macmillan Co, New York, 1921), Part II, chaps. 8–11: Duguit sets out his theory in some detail and compares the theories of some other writers. Chapter 9 is the most important, as it contains the core of this theory. Also of interest is Part I, chap. 11, in which Charmont critically summarises Duguit's doctrine.

6. DUGUIT, L. "The Law and the State" (trans. F.J. de Sloovère, 1917), 31 Harv LR, 1: the state is not a person apart from the individuals in it; nor is there any will of the state apart from those of individuals. The whole idea of natural rights of Man is unsupported, since Man has always lived in society, i.e., has always been dependent.

7. DUGUIT, L. "Objective Law" (trans. M. Grandgent and R.W. Gifford, 1920), 20 Col LR, 817: (1921), 21 Col LR, 17, 126, 242: the distinction between "objective" and "subjective" law is explained. An inquiry into the latter is useless. Men are united in society; they have common as well as diverse needs. This produces a division of labour, i.e., organic solidarity. An economic or moral rule becomes a legal rule when it is penetrated by the consciousness of the mass of individuals composing a given group. (This serial article should only be used by way of comparison with Duguit's other writings).

8. LASKI, H.J. "M. Duguit's Conception of the State" in *Modern Theories of Law*, (ed. W.I. Jennings, Oxford University Press, 1933), chap. 4: Duguit's work is regarded as an outstanding contribution to legal and social philosophy. Nevertheless, certain radical criticisms are levelled at his conception of social solidarity and the inferences which he purported to draw from it.

9. ALLEN, C.K. *Legal Duties*, (Oxford, 1931), pp. 158–167: Duguit's idea that there are no rights, only duties, is considered in detail. In the course of the discussion his general doctrine is outlined.

10. ALLEN, C.K. *Law in the Making*, (6th ed., Oxford, 1958), pp. 574–90: Duguit's thesis is explained in order to show how he arrived at his idea of decentralisation. Criticism is directed at this idea from the angle of administrative law. (This section has been omitted from the 7th ed., 1964).

1. BROWN, W.J. "The Jurisprudence of M. Duguit" (1916), 32 LQR, 168: the main points of Duguit's thesis are outlined and their implications are considered. The author's criticism is that the law and the social sciences should be kept separate, for otherwise it would not be possible to construct a science of law.

2. GUPTA, A.C. "The Method of Jurisprudence" (1917), 33 LQR, 154: W.J. Brown's criticism of Duguit on the ground that the latter confuses law and the social sciences is objected to. No one has succeeded in delimiting either subject and there is, therefore, no reason why a science of law from a sociological point of view should not be attempted.

3. ELLIOTT, W.Y. "The Metaphysics of Duguit's Pragmatic Conception of Law" (1922), 37 Pol Sc Q, 639: criticism is directed at Duguit's central idea of social solidarity and his views on the function of the state. The article also exposes the idealism that underlies Duguit's theory.

4. BUCKLAND, W.W. *Some Reflections on Jurisprudence*, (Cambridge University Press, 1945), pp. 6–11: this is a short but incisive critique of Duguit's contentions concerning sovereignty and the validity of law.

5. JOLOWICZ, H.F. *Lectures on Jurisprudence*, (ed. J.A. Jolowicz, The Athlone Press, 1963), chap. 10: this is a simplified and short account of Duguit's doctrine.

6. GOLUNSKII, S.A. and STROGOVICH, M.S. "The Theory of the State and Law" in *Soviet Legal Philosophy*, (trans. H.W. Babb, Harvard University Press, 1951), pp. 422–25: this brief critique is interesting in that it comes from Soviet writers who are viewing law from a Marxist point of view.

7. JENNINGS, W.I. "The Institutional Theory" in *Modern Theories of Law*, (ed. W.I. Jennings, Oxford University Press, 1933), chap. 5: the author points out that the "institutional theory", which originated in the work of Hauriou and Renard, is a sociological theory. It seeks to explain why society is organised in a particular way.

8. STONE, J. "Two Theories of 'The Institution'" in *Essays in Jurisprudence in Honor of Roscoe Pound*, (ed. R.A. Newman, The Bobbs-Merrill Co., Inc., 1962), 296: this is a long and difficult article. Two different interpretations are contrasted and each is examined in detail.

9. HONORÉ, A.M. "Groups, Laws and Obedience" in *Oxford Essays in Jurisprudence (Second Series)*, (ed. A.W.B. Simpson, Clarendon Press, Oxford, 1973), chap. 1: the idea of law is approached through that of a group. A group has shared understandings, which require prescriptions limiting liberty. There are inter-locking prescriptions, initial and remedial, and these have to become institutionalised. For an explanatory comment, see S.L. PAULSON, Review of *Oxford Essays in Jurisprudence (Second Series)*, (1974), 87 Harv LR, 898, at pp. 901–903.

10. RAZ, J. "The Institutional Nature of Law" (1975), 38 MLR, 489: the distinctive feature of a legal system is to be found in the norm-applying institutions with power to make binding decisions, but which are themselves bound to apply norms guiding behaviour. A legal system differs from other systems in claiming to regulate any type of behaviour, in claiming supremacy and in being open. (For a critical note, see J. Reid and D. Schiff in (1976), 39 MLR, 118.)

11. MacCORMICK, D.N. "Law as Institutional Fact" (1974), 90 LQR, 102: there is a

distinction between an institution of law, e.g., contract, and an instance of it, e.g., a particular contract. An institution of law has to possess a set of institutive rules, which give presumptively sufficient criteria for determining the existence of an instance of it; a set of consequential rules, which specify the jural relations that follow; and a set of terminative rules.

General

1. BRODERICK, A. "Hauriou's Institutional Theory: an Invitation to Common Law Jurisprudence" (1965), 4 Sol Q, 281: the evolution of Hauriou's thought is traced through various stages. An institution is a social, not a juridical, phenomenon. In order to have juridical significance it is necessary to see whether an institution produces certain effects.

2. STONE, J. *Social Dimensions of Law and Justice*, (Stevens & Sons, Ltd, 1966), chap. 11 *et seq.*: these chapters stress the importance of institutions in the social functioning of law and the formation of socio-ethical convictions. Social control is exercised through adjustment of the inter-relation of institutions. The views of Hauriou, Renard and Romano are given prominence. Their relation to Duguit's work is considered, especially its misrepresentation at the hands of Hauriou.

3. STONE, J. *Social Dimensions of Law and Justice*, (Stevens & Sons, Ltd, 1966): this volume pursues in massive detail the combination of judicial technique, ideals of justice and social interests in the task of social control through law. In the first chapter the waste of labour resulting from the lack of co-ordination of the work of social scientists and lawyers is deplored. In the course of the book the author does attempt to throw bridges across the morass of knowledge between the various islands of systematised sciences.

4. BODENHEIMER, E. *Jurisprudence*, (Harvard University Press, 1962), chaps. 6 and 8: the first of these chapters deals with the utilitarianism of Bentham and Mill, whose doctrines are compared and contrasted; and also with the views of Ihering. The second chapter is concerned with sociological jurisprudence. The views of various jurists are considered, including Ehrlich and Pound. It is to be noted that the Realist approach is also subsumed under this chapter.

5. FRIEDMANN, W. *Legal Theory*, (5th ed., Stevens & Sons, Ltd, 1967), chaps. 26 and 27: in the first chapter, the utilitarianism of Bentham and Mill is dealt with. Ihering saw that the wisdom of Roman law lay, not in refining concepts, but in moulding them to serve practical ends. In the second chapter, the views of modern sociologists and the need for balancing interests are considered.

6. DICEY, A.V. *Law and Public Opinion in England during the 19th Century*, (2nd ed., Macmillan & Co, Ltd, 1932), chaps. 1, 2, 6, 7 and 8: this classic work depicts the background to law extremely well. It demonstrates the influence of public opinion on law and the nature of law-making opinion. Chapter 6 deals with Benthamite utilitarianism; chapters 7 and 8 deal with the growth of collectivism.

7. *Law and Opinion in England in the 20th Century*, (ed. M. Ginsberg, Stevens & Sons, Ltd, 1959), especially pp. 99–225: Ginsberg's introductory contribution is most useful in explaining the developments in the present century since Dicey's day. The pages referred to are concerned specifically with particular aspects of the law.

1. FRIEDMANN, W. *Law in a Changing Society*, (Stevens & Sons, Ltd, 1959): the first two chapters deal generally with the reaction of law to social pressure and with the use of law as an instrument of social engineering. Most of the remaining chapters deal with specific aspects of the law. (See also *Law and Social Change in Contemporary Britain*, Stevens & Sons, Ltd, 1951, which has been superseded to some extent by the other book).

2. *An Introduction to the History of Sociology*, (ed. H.E. Barnes, University of Chicago Press, 1948): this is a collection of essays on the individual personalities of various countries, starting with Comte. It is useful for reference.

3. HALL, J. *Living Law of Democratic Society*, (The Bobbs-Merrill Co, Inc, 1949), Part II: Savigny's postulate of a *Volksgeist* is considered as a criterion of valuation. This is followed by a consideration of the work of Bentham, Duguit and Pound.

4. ALLEN, C.K. *Law in the Making*, (7th ed., Oxford, 1964), pp. 20–39: in the course of a general survey of jurisprudential thought the functional outlook is explained. The contributions of Ehrlich and Pound are outlined and critically appraised.

5. PATON, G.W. *A Text-Book of Jurisprudence*, (4th ed., G.W. Paton and D.P. Derham, Clarendon Press, Oxford, 1972), pp. 22–36: distinction is drawn between sociological jurisprudence and legal sociology. The work of Ehrlich, Cairns, Pound and the general scope of functional study is discussed.

6. JONES, J.W. "Modern Discussions of the Aims and Methods of Legal Science" (1931), 47 LQR, 62, at pp. 65, 72–78: in the course of a general review of the writings of various legal philosophers the work of Ihering, Duguit and Ehrlich is touched on. The article as a whole is useful in helping to place their contributions, and those of others, in perspective.

7. JOLOWICZ, H.F. *Lectures on Jurisprudence*, (ed. J.A. Jolowicz, The Athlone Press, 1963), chap. 13: this gives a general account of sociology and deals briefly with the theories of Ihering, Ehrlich, Pound and some others.

8. CASTBERG, F. *Problems of Legal Philosophy*, (2nd ed., Oslo University Press, Allen & Unwin, Ltd, 1957), chap. 3: the solving of problems according to the social purposes and functions of the law is considered. This is not an account of sociological jurisprudence, but a critical evaluation of it as a technique of decision.

9. CARDOZO, B.N. *The Growth of the Law*, (Yale University Press, 1924), chaps. 4 and 5: there has to be a continuous re-adaptation of law so as to make it fulfil its purpose. When taking account of the ends of the law many factors have to be balanced.

10. CARDOZO, B.N. *The Nature of the Judicial Process*, (Yale University Press, 1921), chaps. 2 and 3: the method of sociology is to let the welfare of society fix the path, direction and distance to which rules are to be extended or restricted. The task of the judge in this connection is explained at length.

11. SETHNA, M.J. "The True Nature and Province of Jurisprudence from the Viewpoint of Indian Philosophy" in *Essays in Jurisprudence in Honor of Roscoe*

Pound, (ed. R.A. Newman, The Bobbs-Merrill Co, Inc, 1962), 99: jurisprudence should combine analytical, historical, philosophical, and, above all, sociological study. Sociological jurisprudence and the sociology of law are distinguished, and work of the chief supporters is outlined. Particular attention is paid to Pound's social engineering, and there is also mention of the American Realists.

1. HARVEY, C.P. "A Job for Jurisprudence" (1944), 7 MLR, 42: this is a plea that jurists should pay more attention to practical problems and the issues involved in them in the light of the social conditions of the day. W.B. KENNEDY: "Another Job for Jurisprudence" (1945), 8 MLR, 18: Harvey's proposals are criticised one by one; C.P. HARVEY: "A Job for Jurisprudence", *ibid.*, p. 236: a reply to Kennedy.

2. ROBINSON, H.W. "Law and Economics" (1938–39), 2 MLR, 257: an economist dwells on the importance of the legal framework for the functioning of an economic system. Changes in the foundations of the economic system can only come through law. Therefore, economic ends are one of the factors to be taken into account in framing law.

3. ROSTOW, E.V. *Planning for Freedom*, (Yale University Press, 1959): this work may be consulted as a work on sociology. It is an important contribution, written by one who is both a lawyer and an economist, but primarily from an economic point of view. It concerns the function of law as an instrument of social change, and the mechanism for accomplishing it. (See review by W. FRIEDMANN: "Planning for Freedom" (1961), 24 MLR, 209).

4. McDOUGAL, M.S. "The Comparative Study of Law for Policy Purposes: Value Classification as an Instrument of Democratic World Order" (1952), 61 Yale LJ, 915: this article is an example of an application of sociological jurisprudence. A useful comparative study should begin, it is said, with an idea of what is being compared, the purpose of comparison and adequate techniques.

5. LASSWELL, H.D. and McDOUGAL, M.S. "Legal Education and Public Policy: Professional Training in the Public Interest" (1942–43), 52 Yale LJ, 202: this article is another example of the application of sociological jurisprudence. There should be an integration of law and other social sciences in the training of lawyers. This should be organised with reference to influence principles, value principles and skill principles. On similar lines, see M.S. McDOUGAL: "The Law School of the Future: from Legal Realism to Policy Science in the World Community" (1946–47), 56 Yale LJ, 1345).

6. LASSWELL, H.D. "The Interplay of Economic, Political and Social Criteria in Legal Policy" (1960–61), 14 Vand LR, 451: this is a difficult article. It enters into complex questions as to the criteria to be adopted towards economic activities.

7. SCHWARZENBERGER, G. "The Three Types of Law" (1949), 2 CLP, 103: this is an inquiry into the different functions of law in three types of society.

8. WEBER, M. *On Law in Economy and Society*, (ed. M. Rheinstein, trans. E.A. Shils and M. Rheinstein, Harvard University Press, 1954), especially chap. 1: this may be used for reference. The book envisages an idealised type of society with which actual societies might be compared.

1. MORRIS, C. "Law, Reason and Sociology" (1958–59), 107 U Pa LR, 147: this article is based on M. Weber's analysis of the judicial process. A judge has to act on values when adapting the law. It is argued that some means should be found for discriminating between unjust rules, which should be remedied by legislation, and those which might be remedied by the courts.

2. CARSON, W.G. "Some Sociological Aspects of Strict Liability and the Enforcement of Factory Legislation" (1970), 33 MLR, 396: moral fault is not irrelevant in taking decisions about daily action. The point is discussed with reference to procedure under the Factory Act.

3. COHEN, J. "The Value of Value Symbols in Law" (1952), 52 Col LR, 893: the scientist starts with hypothetical symbols and hopes to translate them into fact judgments; the lawyer starts with facts and seeks normative judgments. Hence his symbols are value-charged. They are instruments, not of discovery, but of ordering society. In order to make them effective instruments, emphasis should shift from the search for the appropriate symbol to the actual fact-situations, the values involved and the probable effect of giving policy decisions.

4. COHEN, J., ROBSON, R.A.H., BATES, A. *Parental Authority: The Community and the Law*, (Rutgers U.P. 1958): this is an investigation into the moral sense of a community in a particular sphere. The kind of information obtained and significant facts are related to the law regarding the matter.

5. COWAN, T.A. "The Relation of Law to Experimental Science" (1948), 96 U Pa LR, 484: there are many ways in which legal theory can be usefully related to other social sciences. But for this purpose the existing divisions of jurisprudence are inadequate.

6. COSSIO, C.S. "Jurisprudence and the Sociology of Law" (trans. P.J. Eder and F. Uno, 1952), 52 Col LR, 356, 479: this is a long and difficult article, but might be referred to for a critique of the demarcation between "dogmatic jurisprudence" and the sociology of law.

7. CARLSTON, K.S. *Law and Structure of Social Action*, (Stevens & Sons, Ltd, 1956), especially chap. 1: this is of general interest. It deals with organisations, which have become a feature of modern society. Old categories of thinking, which were adapted to take account of the relations of individuals, have had to be re-adapted to organisations, and this has proved to be inadequate. What is required is a new approach based on social realities.

8. REUSCHLEIN, H.G. *Jurisprudence – Its American Prophets*, (The Bobbs-Merrill Co, Inc, 1951), pp. 63–71, 103–53; 299–306: in the first section the work of Livingston and Field, two utilitarians in the Benthamite tradition, is considered. Their main preoccupation was with legislation and codification. In the second section, as a prelude to Pound, the work of his forerunners, including Montesquieu, Ihering, Ehrlich and Duguit, is dealt with. Pound's own contribution is set out at length. In the final section the work of Seagle and Timasheff is dealt with.

9. SIMPSON, S.P. and STONE, J. *Cases and Readings on Law and Society*, (West Publishing Co., 1949), II, chap. 4: this chapter deals mainly with the limits on law as a means of social control. The material has been collected from various sources.

1. HALL, J. *Readings in Jurisprudence*, (The Bobbs-Merrill Co, 1938), chaps. 4, 5, 17, 18, 22 and 23: chapter 4 deals with utilitarianism and contains extracts from Bentham, Mill, Ihering and Lorrimer. Chapter 5 deals with the doctrine of Duguit, Part III, which includes the remaining chapters mentioned above, deals generally with the scientific approach to social questions.

2. COWAN, T.A. *The American Jurisprudence Reader*, (Oceana Publications, 1956), pp. 135–156: the nature of sociological jurisprudence is explained and is followed by extracts from Pound, Cardozo, Cairns and Patterson.

3. LLOYD, D. *Introduction to Jurisprudence*, (3rd ed., Stevens & Sons, Ltd, 1972), chap. 6: modern sociology is introduced via brief accounts of the work of Ihering, Weber, Ehrlich, Pound and writers since Pound. There are extracts from Ihering, Ehrlich, Pound, The American Restatement of Torts, de Jouvenal, J. Stone and other recent writers.

4. LLOYD, D. *The Idea of Law*, (Penguin Books, Ltd, A 688, 1964), chap. 9, especially pp. 207–13: natural law theory was individualist. During the 18th and 19th centuries it assumed an economic pattern in the doctrine of laissez faire. The utilitarians provided a philosophy for society as a whole. In this brief account the views of Ihering, Weber, Ehrlich and Pound are mentioned.

5. LASSWELL, H.D. *Power and Personality*, (Norton & Co, New York, 1948): the unifying factor in modern society is power. This conclusion is derived empirically from an observation of political Man.

6. *The Sociology of Law. Interdisciplinary Readings*, (ed. R.J. Simon, Chandler Publishing Co, 1968): this collection of papers is divided into the first and second stage of Sociological Jurisprudence, and the early and contemporary empirical research. Each part is prefaced by an explanation of its relationship to the whole and of the individual contributions in it.

7. *Towards a General Theory of Action*, (ed. T. Parsons and E.A. Shils, Harvard University Press, 1954), especially Part I: this might be used for reference. Part I concerns the approach to a general theory of social action and the reasoning processes that are required in working one out. The various essays are not written from a legal point of view, but they open up possibilities of a theory of law which might fit in with a general theory of society.

8. SPROTT, W.J.H. *Science and Social Action*, (Watts & Co, 1954): in this book, which is of general interest, various problems of modern society are raised and discussed.

9. SPROTT, W.J.H. *Sociology*, (Hutchinson University Library, London, 1966): this book provides an introduction to sociology. It is useful for the lawyer in so far as the different types of study, pursuits and concerns of sociology are explained so that the lawyer might discern where his interests can be fitted in.

10. JOHNSON, H.M. *Sociology: A Systematic Introduction*, (Routledge & Kegan Paul, Ltd, 1961): this is a more detailed study of general sociology than that of W.J.H. Sprott. It is not a legal work, but it may usefully be consulted for the methods and aims of sociology.

1. *Sociological Theory*, (ed. L.A. Coser and B. Rosenberg, The Macmillan Co, New York, 1957): this is a book of readings, which might be used for general reference.

21. Modern Realism

American Realism

1. RUMBLE, W.E. *American Legal Realism. Skepticism, Reform and the Judicial Process*, (Cornell University Press, 1968): this lucid and easily-read book provides the first comprehensive review of the Realist movement. It covers the intellectual background from which it sprang, philosophical and especially sociological, and considers the views of all the leading Realists and their relationship to one another. Various criticisms are considered at different points and misunderstandings of the Realist position indicated.

2. HOLMES, O.W. "The Path of the Law" in *Collected Legal Papers*, (Constable & Co, Ltd, 1920), 167: in this paper Holmes pioneers the view that law consists of prophecies of what courts will do and considers some of the implications of such a view. He also introduces his famous "bad man's" outlook on law.

3. LLEWELLYN, K.N. *The Bramble Bush*, (Tentative Printing and 2nd ed., Columbia University School of Law, 1930): Llewellyn's earlier and more robust "rule skepticism" is put forward. The principal point is that law is what officials do.

4. LLEWELLYN, K.N. *Jurisprudence: Realism in Theory and Practice*, (University of Chicago Press, 1962), chaps. 1–3, 5, 7, 8: various articles are reprinted in this volume. In chapter 1 the point is made that words are the centre of thinking about law and tend to obscure clear thought. Rules are not without importance, but they are less important than are traditionally supposed. In the course of a reply to Pound, the nine points of the Realist programme are set out. Chapter 3 lays emphasis on what officials do. The need for a temporary divorce of the "is" and the "ought" is explained and the point is repeated that ideas are of value. Chapter 7 amplifies that. The method of the new jurisprudence is to check doctrine against results and to take account of all crafts, traditions and ideas. To exclude the last would be to omit a vital factor. The judges' personalities are only one factor.

5. FRANK, J.N. *Law and the Modern Mind*, (English ed., Stevens & Sons, Ltd, 1949): the Preface is especially interesting in that Frank modifies certain views which are found in the text (written in 1930). This work might be regarded as one of the classic expositions of "fact skepticism".

6. LLEWELLYN, K.N. "The Normative, the Legal, and the Law-jobs: the Problem of Juristic Method" (1939–40), 49 Yale LJ, 1355: ethical considerations are only a part of what makes up "legal". Beneath all doctrines lie problems. Five "law-jobs" are considered. There has to be machinery for dealing with actual situations. The problem of juristic method is to make the machinery cope suitably with law-jobs and the upkeep and improvement of method and machinery.

7. LLEWELLYN, K.N. "Law and the Social Sciences – especially Sociology" (1948–49), 62 Harv LR, 1286: law has moved away from other social disciplines because lawyers are obsessed with rules. The case is presented for re-establishing useful contacts by taking account of the function of legal institutions, which brings in the individual who applies the law to a given situation.

8. LLEWELLYN, K.N. *The Common Law Tradition. Deciding Appeals*, (Little, Brown & Co, 1960), and Appendix B on "Realism": rules alone will not provide a basis

319

for predicting decisions. But rules should be, and are to a large extent, applied according to the judge's "situation-sense", and this is the product of a number of far-reaching factors which do provide a workable basis for prediction. This book seeks to restore the lost confidence of the Bar in the predictability of judicial decisions by showing the way in which they can be predicted. In Appendix B the author explains that this thesis is in fact a development of that originally propounded in *The Bramble Bush*.

1. TWINING, W. *Karl Llewellyn and the Realist Movement*, (Weidenfeld and Nicolson, 1973): this biographical assessment of Llewellyn's contribution is valuable as an account of American Realism (chapters 1–5 and 15) as well as of the part he played (chapters 6–14). The book provides an insight into Llewellyn's thought and through it into realism. His works are discussed *seriatim* and his contribution assessed.

2. TWINING, W. "Two Works of Karl Llewellyn" (1967), 30 MLR, 514; (1968), 31 MLR, 165: these deal with two of his major works, and their substance has been incorporated into the author's biography.

3. SEIDMAN, R.B. "The Judicial Process Reconsidered in the Light of the Role-theory" (1969), 32 MLR, 516: this article is a presentation of the difficulties and problems of deciding "clear" and "trouble" cases from the sociological angle of the role-theory.

4. OTTE, G. "Role Theory and the Judicial Process: a Critical Analysis" (1971–72), 16 St Louis ULJ, 420: if law is the way judges behave, then their behaviour is a key to understanding law. After an explanation of what role-study involves, it is applied to certain judges. While appreciating the limits and difficulties of such a study, it is believed to be promising.

5. CLARK, C.E. and TRUBEK, D.M. "The Creative Role of the Judge: Restraint and Freedom in the Common Law Tradition" (1961–62), 71 Yale LJ, 255: K.N. Llewellyn's thesis in *The Common Law Tradition* is criticised on the ground that it does not take adequate account of the subjective element. It is pointed out that no guidance is offered as to how judges are to exercise their "situation-sense" that will lead them to the "immanent law" in each situation. The omission of the subjective element removes one of the most important factors that should be taken into account in achieving what Llewellyn seeks to achieve, viz., "reckonability".

6. FRANK, J.N. *If Men were Angels*: *Some Aspects of Government in a Democracy*, (Harper & Bros., New York, 1942), especially chaps. 6–8: this book marks a change in Frank's thought. The emphasis shifts away from his anti-rule polemic to the uncertainties in the fact-finding process. The charges of Pound against the Realists are alleged to be misdirected in respect of even one Realist.

7. FRANK, J.N. "Words and Music: Some Remarks on Statute Interpretation" (1947), 47 Col LR, 1259: the legislature composes the piece, but the judges play it, each according to his own interpretation in the light of the evidence before him.

8. FRANK, J.N. "Say it with Music" (1947–48), 61 Harv LR, 921: judicial reactions to oral evidence in trial-courts and the various influences at work there are examined. Suggestions are made for minimising the personal factor.

1. FRANK, J.N. "Short of Sickness and Death: a Study of Moral Responsibility in Legal Criticism" (1951), 26 NYULR, 545: this is a further lengthy investigation into the fallibilities of the fact-finding process.

2. FRANK, J.N. *Courts on Trial, Myth and Reality in American Justice*, (Princeton University Press, 1949): it is senseless to speak of rules creating rights or that rights can be known before they are tested in the courts. The chief concern of the book is with the fact-finding process and the factors that influence judges and juries.

3. FRANK, J.N. "What Courts do in Fact" (1932), 26 Ill LR, 645: this represents Frank's earlier view. Specific decisions are the essence of the law; all else is subsidiary. Rules are only "hunch producers". All such factors operate through the judge's personality. Facts are what the court thinks happened. A judge often arrives at his decision before trying to explain it.

4. FRANK, J.N. "Are Judges Human?" (1932), 80 U Pa LR, 17, 233: Frank continues his campaign against the belief that law consists of rules. The personal element in the judicial process is stressed and examined with a view to improving the process.

5. FRANK, J.N. "Cardozo and the Upper-Court Myth" (1948), 13 LCP, 369: this is a review of the *Selected Writings of Benjamin Nathan Cardozo*, (ed. M.E. Hall, Fallon Publications, 1947). He accuses Cardozo of having by-passed what goes on in trial courts. Much space is devoted to an explanation of the distinction between "rule-skepticism" and "fact-skepticism".

6. RUTTER, I.C. "The Trial Judge and the Judicial Process" (1962–63), 15 JLE, 245: the author agrees with Judge Frank that far too little attention has been paid to what goes on in trial courts. Much of the scepticism has resulted from too much preoccupation with appellate courts. It is in trial courts that the great importance of rules can be seen.

7. *THE HOLMES READER*, (ed. J.J. Marke, Oceana Publications, 1955): selections from Holmes's writings and judgments are given. The concluding chapter appraises his contribution. For further tributes to Holmes's work the following might be consulted: (1930–31), 44 Harv LR, 677, (which includes a full list of his judicial opinions); W.H. HAMILTON: "On Dating Mr. Justice Holmes" (1941–42), 9 UCLR, 1; M. de W. HOWE: "The Positivism of Mr. Justice Holmes" (1950–51), 64 Harv LR, 529; H.M. HART: "Holmes's Positivism – an Addendum", *ibid*, 929; M. de W. HOWE: "Holmes's Positivism – a brief Rejoinder", *ibid*, 937; J.C.H. WU: "Justice Holmes and the Common Law Tradition" (1960–61), 14 Vand LR, 221; *Mr. Justice Holmes*, (ed. F. Frankfurter, Coward McCann, Inc., 1931); M. de W. HOWE: *Justice Oliver Wendell Holmes. The Shaping Years*, (Harvard University Press, 1951); *Justice Holmes. The Proving Years* (1963).

8. LLEWELLYN, K.N., ADLER, M.J., COOK, W.W. "Law and the Modern Mind: a Symposium" (1931), 31 Col LR, 83: these represent three views on Frank's book. Llewellyn is adulatory, though he adheres to his view as to the importance of rules. Adler is critical; the book is, in his opinion, simply dogmatic and not an argument. Cook defends Frank against Adler's criticisms.

9. PAUL, J. *The Legal Realism of Jerome N. Frank*, (Matinus Nijhoff, The Hague,

1959), especially chaps. 2, 4 and 5: Frank's place in the Realist movement and his impact are considered in detail. A good deal about Realism in general can be gathered from the book, especially from chapter 6.

1. VERDUN-JONES, S.N. "The Jurisprudence of Jerome N. Frank. A Study in American Legal Realism" (1973–76), 7 Syd LR, 180: this is a severely critical assessment of Frank's contribution. His concept of science (ability to predict) was too narrow. It did not occur to him that the requirement of accuracy is relative to the material being studied. He ignored the theoretical underpinnings of psychology and chose only bits that suited him. He adopted an observational standpoint, but was a polemical reformer all the time. His focus of inquiry on fact-finding was a major distortion since he lost sight of the overall process of decision-making. He only succeeded in largely undermining the authority of the judicial process, and ignored law and social sciences.

2. OLIPHANT, H. "A Return to *Stare decisis*" (1928), 14 Am BAJ, 71, 107, 159: the proposal is that attention should be paid to the non-vocal behaviour of judges, i.e., what they actually do. This attitude having now been lost, in order to recapture it there should be a study of the social structure and *stare decisis* can then be used effectively.

3. COHEN, F.S. "Transcendental Nonsense and the Functional Approach" (1935), 35 Col LR, 809: the traditional language of the law is a device for formulating decisions reached on other grounds. The methods that would be employed in a functional approach are explained. The point is made, however, that the judicial "hunch" is in part the product of the study of rules.

4. COHEN, F.S. "The Problems of a Functional Jurisprudence" (1937), 1 MLR, 5: the Realists are functional in their approach. This can be seen in what they set out to achieve and the types of results that are to be expected.

5. COHEN, F.S. "Field Theory and Judicial Logic" (1949–50), 59 Yale LJ, 238: a dependable approach to the prediction of decisions can be worked out by observing the judge's use of precedents, which will reveal his value patterns. Even though the opinions of individual judges vary, certain lines of precedents are to be discovered.

6. YNTEMA, H.E. "The Rational Basis of Legal Science" (1931), 31 Col LR, 924: thinking about law is referable to experience. The case for Realism is argued and defended.

7. YNTEMA, H.E. "American Legal Realism in Retrospect" (1960–61), 14 Vand LR, 317: law, being a means to certain ends, should be correlated with other social and natural sciences. Legal research should be conducted on scientific lines and with factual data, such as statistics. A distinction is drawn between legal science, which should be descriptive, and the art of the judge, which is normative.

8. YNTEMA, H.E. "The Hornbook Method and the Conflict of Laws" (1927–28), 37 Yale LJ, 468, especially at p. 480: in the course of this review of a treatise on conflict of laws, the point is made that it is not symbols but habits of thought that control decisions. Decision is reached after an emotional experience by the judge in which logic and principles play a subsidiary part.

9. BINGHAM, J.W. "What is the Law?" (1912), 11 Mich LR, 1, 109: the lawyer studies external sequences with a view to forecasting sequences of the same sort.

Rules and principles are not the law; law is what happens in a state, i.e., what courts do. The real field of study should include many factors other than rules, for it is such factors which provide the motives for decisions. See also "The Nature of Legal Rights and Duties" (1913), 12 Mich LR, 1.

1. KOCOUREK, A. Review of Bingham's two articles in (1913) 8 Ill LR, 138: Bingham's thesis is criticised on a number of points. See J.W. BINGHAM: "Legal Philosophy and the Law" (1914), 9 Ill LR, 98, for his reply to Kocourek's criticisms *seriatim*.

2. SCHROEDER, T. "The Psychological Study of Judicial Opinions" (1918), 6 Calif LR, 89: Judicial conduct is determined by a chain of causation running back to infancy. Every choice, conclusion, etc. is determined by some dominant personal motive.

3. HAINES, C.G. "General Observations on the Effects of Personal, Political and Economic Influences on the Decisions of Judges" (1922), 17 Ill LR, 96: this is a most interesting investigation into the factors mentioned.

4. COOK, W.W. "The Logical and Legal Bases of the Conflict of Laws" (1923–24), 33 Yale LJ, 457: the decision lies in the construction of the premises of the legal syllogism. Rules are useful tools, but they are not the premises. This point is developed with reference to the conflict of laws.

5. ULMAN, J.N. *A Judge Takes the Stand*, (Alfred A. Knopf, 1933): a judge writes on various aspects of the judicial process. Of the greatest interest is his treatment of the emotional factors that play on judges. He asserts emphatically that rules and precedents do exercise a decisive influence sometimes, even against the judge's own feelings.

6. HUTCHESON, J.C. "The Judgement Intuitive: the Function of the 'Hunch' in Judicial Decisions" (1929), 14 Corn LQ, 274: this develops the theme that the judicial decision is the product of innumerable factors.

7. HUTCHESON, J.C. "Lawyer's Law, and the Little, Small Dice" (1932–33), 7 Tul LR, 1: this stresses the point that, whatever principles there may be, the judge has on occasions to make up his mind which way he wants to decide.

8. RADIN, M. "Legal Realism" (1931), 31 Col LR, 824: "Realism" signifies opposition to "Conceptualism" as an ideal itself. But conceptualism has its place. Moreover not all judges are "realists" and, therefore, the Realists should take account of how non-Realist judges behave.

9. RADIN, M. *Law as Logic and Experience*, (Yale University Press, 1940): lawyers are realists in what they do, but conceptualists in what they say. This book considers the interrelationship between these two poles. Logic is necessary. Law needs to be applied to facts, but the facts that reach the courts are past and "dead". The attempt to resurrect them is fraught with difficulties. Therefore, a new approach is suggested, namely, that the courts should work out the best solution for the future out of the situation that has arisen (cf. arbitral award).

10. GRAY, J.C. *The Nature and Sources of the Law*, (2nd ed., R. Gray, The Macmillan Co, New York, 1921), especially chap. 4: Gray's cardinal thesis is that law is what the courts do and that all else, including statutes, are only sources of law.

1. POUND, R. "Law in Books and Law in Action" (1910), 44 Am LR, 12: the divergence between legal principles and what actually occurs is illustrated. Particular attention is drawn to the fact that judicial thinking is out of touch with contemporary social and economic thinking.

2. MOORE, W.U. and HOPE, T.S. "An Institutional Approach to the Law of Commercial Banking" (1929), 38 Yale LJ, 703: the problem of predicting official decisions is developed along Realist lines. The thesis is that prediction will be aided if attention is paid, not only to judicial reactions to the individual cases, but also the reactions to "institutional" (repeated, usual) behaviour.

3. KALES, A.M. "'Due Process'. The Inarticulate Major Premise and the Adamson Act" (1916–17), 26 Yale LJ, 519: the "inarticulate major premise" behind the "due process" formula is examined in the light of social factors.

4. NELLES, W. "The First American Labor Case" (1931–32), 41 Yale LJ, 165: this is of general interest as showing the influences that were at work behind the decision in an industrial dispute *primae impressionis.*

5. NELLES, W. "Towards Legal Understanding" (1934), 34 Col LR, 862, 1041: the factors underlying decisions that bring about changes and development in the law are subjected to detailed examination. Law is not independent of personal wills.

6. KEYSER, C.J. "On the Study of Legal Science" (1928–29), 38 Yale LJ, 413: the subject-matter of such a study is the conduct of the officials who answer questions as to what is just. The science of law consists of propositions concerning such conduct, the circumstances and stimuli behind it.

7. LERNER, M. "The Supreme Court and American Capitalism" (1932-33), 42 Yale LJ, 668: the Supreme Court has to work within the framework of a constitution and rules, but attention is also drawn to the social and cultural environment and the personalities of the judges.

8. SCHMIDHAUSER, J.R. "*Stare Decisis,* and the Background of the Justice of the Supreme Court of the United States" (1962), 14 UTLJ, 194: this is a statistical study of the personal background of various judges of the Supreme Court. The tentative conclusion is drawn that such factors do affect judicial behaviour.

9. ARNOLD, T.W. *Symbols of Government,* (Yale University Press, 1935), especially pp. 1–104, 199–288: the scientific approach is advocated, (but the differences between the subject-matter of social and physical sciences are not stressed). Lawyers use symbols which will give the result desired by the individual rather than by society. That is why legal science fails to adapt itself to society.

10. ROBINSON, E.S. *Law and Lawyers,* (The Macmillan Co, New Yor, 1935), especially pp. 1–19, 46–121, 284–323: law is unscientific. It can only be made "naturalistic" (i.e., realistic) with the aid of psychology, which all lawyers should study. What is required is a psychology that takes account of legal doctrines while not interpreting them literally. What a judge says is a sound starting point in the study of judicial deliberation, because this adds to the arguments that were present in arriving at the original conclusion. They serve to persuade himself as well as others. The discrepancy between legal values and

those of common sense is brought about by rules. This is due to the need for consistency and rules are important.

1. ABRAHAM, H.J. *The Judicial Process*, (3rd ed., New York and Oxford University Press, 1976): this is not a "realist" book, but it gives useful insights into the sort of thing that goes on "behind the scenes" in the American administration of justice.

2. WEYRAUCH, W.O. *The Personality of Lawyers*, (Yale University Press, 1964): interviews with 130 German lawyers, representing judges, attorneys, students etc., are analysed and evaluated. The results are set out in the form of generalisations about the prejudices and predilections peculiar to lawyers. The conclusions are admittedly unverified hypotheses as yet, and are the result of an original line of research along the lines of realist doctrine.

3. CECIL, H. (LEON, H.C.). *The English Judge*, (Hamlyn Lectures, Stevens & Sons, Ltd, 1970): this is an amusing, light account of the background, training, public image, virtues and vices of judges, quoting opinions of members of the public. Judges are not as out of touch with the realities of modern life as is generally alleged. Suggestions are made for improvement in appointment and in other ways.

4. SHETREET, S. *Judges on Trial*, (ed. G.J. Borrie, North Holland Publishing Co, 1976): judicial independence, appointment and promotion, removal, checks short of removal of various kinds are discussed. Sources include interviews and journalistic data in addition to academic material.

5. ARNOLD, T.W. "The Jurisprudence of Edward S. Robinson" (1936–37), 46 Yale LJ, 1282: in this appraisal of Robinson's work particular emphasis is laid on the psychological approach to law, which Robinson viewed as a study in modern anthropology.

Mechanical Aids to Prediction

6. LOEVINGER, L. "Jurimetrics: the Next Step Forward" (1949), 33 Minn LR, 455: this article is of interest as introducing the term "Jurimetrics" for a growing new discipline, which applies the methods of mathematical and scientific investigation to legal problems.

7. BEUTEL, F.K. "Some Implications of Experimental Jurisprudence" (1934–35), 48 Harv LR, 169: the requirements of an experimental science are explained, and the possibility of their adaptation to legal science is discussed.

8. BEUTEL, F.K. *Some Potentialities of Experimental Jurisprudence as a New Branch of Social Science*, (University of Nebraska Press, 1957): this contains the results in detail, statistical and other data, which were obtained by putting the approach outlined above into operation.

9. NUSSBAUM, A. "Fact Research in Law" (1940), 40 Col LR, 189: the revolt against conceptualism on the Continent and in America is the background to the use of fact research and statistics in law. An account is given of fact research, followed by a discussion of the value of statistics. The latter, it is said, are of little value.

10. MOORE, W.U. and CALLAHAN, C.C. "Law and Learning Theory: A Study in

Legal Control" (1943–44), 53 Yale LJ, 1: the authors set out factual evidence of the effect on human behaviour of enactments and administrative procedure on a matter of parking vehicles. The statistics are then analysed with a view to deriving a psychological and objective theory of behaviour. C.L. HULL: *ibid*, p. 331, reviews the results as a psychologist. H.E. YNTEMA, *ibid*, p.338, in his review raises several objections.

1. KRISLOV, S. "Theoretical Attempts at Predicting Judicial Behaviour" (1965–66), 79 Harv LR, 1573: scientists value predictability because it tests theory. What is sought is understanding. There is a distinction between predicting and forecasting. The social scientist can do no more than forecast. Four techniques of achieving this are discussed.

2. SNYDER, E. "The Supreme Court as a Small Group" (1958), 36 Social Forces, 232: over a period of 32 years the voting patterns in the Supreme Court revealed a liberal, conservative and an uncommitted group. Judges often moved from the last to either of the former; no judge moved from the liberal to the conservative group; and rarely did a judge move from the conservative to the liberal group without some pause in the uncommitted group. New judges tended to join the uncommitted group.

3. MURPHY, W.F. "Courts as Small Groups" (1965–66), 79 Harv LR, 1565: how useful are theories and data about human behaviour in small groups? Voting records are not enough; we need to consider interpersonal interaction. There is the role of "task leadership" in solving the problem efficiently, and "social leadership" in providing the atmosphere that facilitates co-operation. Some of the limitations of this kind of inquiry are indicated.

4. TANENHAUS, J. "The Cumulative Scaling of Judicial Decisions" (1965–66), 79 Harv LR, 1583: the object is to determine whether, e.g., votes cast by members of a court in a group of cases can be arranged in an ordinal scale. Cumulative scaling tries to determine whether persons who respond affirmatively to a weak stimulus do in fact respond affirmatively to stronger stimuli; and whether persons who respond negatively to a strong stimulus will respond similarly to all weaker ones. This approach is said to be useful in showing that a set ot attitudes is shared by members of a court so that their probable behaviour in future cases might be predicted.

5. KORT, F. "Quantitative Analysis of Fact-patterns in Cases and their Impact on Judicial Decisions" (1965–66), 79 Harv LR, 1595: the relation between facts and decisions should be explored by statistical methods. In this connection the acceptance or rejection of facts by appellate courts from lower court records as well as the dependence by appellate court decisions on the accepted facts have to be considered.

6. *Comparative Judicial Behaviour*, (edd. G. Schubert and D. Danielski, Oxford University Press, 1970): this is of general interest, some of its chapters being of greater relevance than others. These concern attempts to relate the personal backgrounds of judges and their decisions with reference to American, Japanese, Phillipino and Hawaiian courts. Scalogram analysis is applied to Indian and Canadian judges and their decisions.

7. SLAYTON, P. "Quantitative Methods and Supreme Court Cases" (1972), 10 Os HLJ 429: methods fall into three kinds: subject-centred (variations of responses

to stimuli), judgment approach (variations in stimuli themselves), response approach (combination of both). Scalogram analysis is the last. This is gathering strength under the influences of realism and psychology.

1. ALITO, S.A. "The 'Released Time' Cases Revisited: a Study of Group Decision-making by the Supreme Court" (1973–74), 83 Yale LJ, 1202: the decisions analysed reveal the influence of the pattern of interaction among the judges on those who have to interpret their decisions. It is argued that lower courts and commentators were misled and confused because they did not know of the true nature of the interactions.

2. LAWLOR, R.C. "What Computers Can Do: Analysis and Prediction of Judicial Decisions" (1963), 49 Am BAJ, 337: computers could find and analyse the law and predict decisions. Predictability is possible not only in so far as there is "legal" *stare decisis* but also an element of personal *stare decisis* (consistency of attitude).

3. WIENER, F.B. "Decision Prediction by Computers: Nonsense Cubed – and Worse" (1962), 48 Am BAJ, 1023: the claim that computers could be used to predict decisions rests on untenable assumptions. If one knows which rule a judge will apply and which way the facts will be found, then a computer is unnecessary; if these are not known a computer is useless. Even in the matter of information storage and retrieval, there might always be human error in programming. There is also the problem of classification and indexing.

4. ROHNER, R.J. "Jurimetrics, No!" (1968), 54 Am BAJ, 896: this gives a dream of the future in which judges, lawyers and law-books will have been replaced by machines.

5. BROWN, J.R. "Electronic Brains and the Legal Mind: Computing the Data Computer's Collision with Law" (1961–62), 71 Yale LJ, 239: computers are making an impact on the law. But the administration of the law involves an indispensable human element. Computers should be able to help in making good law, which no machine can do. It is not enough to sort out the bad.

6. TAPPER, C.F.H. *Computers and the Law*, (Weidenfeld and Nicolson, 1973), chaps. 6–9: in these chapters the application of computer techniques to case-law is carefully investigated, including retrieval, trial and prediction of judicial decisions. In connection with the last, there is a detailed description of the various researches that have been conducted. On the whole, the author's own conclusion is on the negative side.

7. KAYTON, I. "Can Jurimetrics be of Value to Jurisprudence?" (1964–65), 33 Geo Wash LR, 287: "jurimetrics" is the scientific investigation of legal problems. Its tools are symbolic logic and digital computers. After a detailed demonstration of their use the conclusion is that jurimetrics can be of limited value.

8. MEYER, P. "Jurimetrics: the Scientific Method in Legal Research" (1966), 44 Can BR, 1: this considers the value of jurimetrics in saving drudgery, analysing evidence, predicting judgments, drafting and law reform. Of special interest is the portion dealing with the use of behavioural models to predict the behaviour of members of a group, such as a court, and the use of models in *stare decisis*.

9. FULLER, L.L. "An Afterword: Science and the Judicial Process" (1965–66),

79 Harv LR, 1604: science works with simplified, hence abstracted, models. In the social sciences the difficulty is to know what to abstract and what correction to make when applying the model to life. The process of abstraction is governed by a personal element. Hence the results of such models are built into them from the outset. Predictive theories offer no guidance to discovery. We have to decide on the end and then find the best means for achieving it. Science can help with means, not with ends.

1. STONE, J. *Legal System and Lawyers' Reasonings*, (Stevens & Sons, Ltd, 1964), pp. 37–41; *Social Dimensions of Law and Justice*, (Stevens & Sons, Ltd, 1966), pp. 687–96: the value of computer techniques in the judicial process is considered in the first book, and in providing quantitative analyses of judicial behaviour in the second. While computers are useful for information retrieval, they cannot supplant the need to make creative decisions.

2. Symposium on "Jurimetrics" (1963), 28 LCP, 1–270: this collection of papers might be used for further reference. Various writers enlarge upon the new methods, possibilities and limitations of their use.

3. *Modern Uses of Logic in Law* (MULL) 1959–1966: this journal is devoted to jurimetrics. Its contributions tend to be extremely technical, but may be consulted as to the sort of problems that are being tackled and methods of dealing with them.

General Accounts and Critiques of Realism

4. POUND, R. *Jurisprudence*, (West Publishing Co, Inc, 1959), I, pp. 247–54, 264–81: the place of the American Realists in the history of juristic thought is discussed and the forms which it has assumed are distinguished, explained and criticised.

5. PATTERSON, E.W. *Jurisprudence*, (The Foundation Press, Inc, 1953), chap. 17 and pp. 537–58: this provides a most valuable account of the background to the Realist movement, including the pragmatism of C.S. Peirce and William James. There is also a very good appraisal of the work of Holmes and of the Realists generally.

6. BURRUS, B.R. "American Legal Realism" (1962), 8 How LJ, 36: this is a general account of realism, which traces its influences in Gray, Holmes, and Pound's sociology, and the pragmatism and instrumental logic of William James and John Dewey. Realism is not a "school"; there are a number of people who share a common ferment and methods of attack. The work of Llewellyn and Frank is mentioned. Realism emphasises law in fact rather than law in books, judicial discretion and the limits of predictability. Methods of attack include interview statistics, sociological statistics and psychology.

7. ANONYMOUS. "Holmes, Peirce and Pragmatism" (1974–75), 84 Yale LJ, 1123: this is a note explaining the relationship of Holmes's work to that of Charles Peirce.

8. GOODHART, A.L. "Some American Interpretations of Law" in *Modern Theories of Law*, (ed. W.I. Jennings, Oxford University Press, 1933), chap. 1: the reasons for the growth of this movement in America are considered. The main points of the Realist case and its weaknesses are indicated.

1. LLOYD, D. *Introduction to Jurisprudence*, (3rd ed., Stevens & Sons, Ltd, 1972), chap. 7: Realism arose as part of the movement towards increased empiricism. There is a brief account of "fact-skeptics" and "rule-skeptics" and an appraisal of the work of Holmes and of the Realists generally, together with an assessment of jurimetrics and behaviourism.

2. LLOYD, D. *The Idea of Law*, (Penguin Books, Ltd, A 688, 1964), pp. 213–17: American Realism developed out of the reliance on science and technology as a key to solving problems as well as the rise of pragmatism.

3. GILMORE, G. "Legal Realism: its Cause and Cure" (1960–61), 70 Yale LJ, 1037: realism is one response to the crisis in America produced by the growing multiplicity of cases and the changing role of legislation.

4. FRIEDMANN, W. *Legal Theory*, (5th ed., Stevens & Sons, Ltd, 1967), pp. 292–304: this is a valuable assessment of the work of the American Realists in the sociological field.

5. JONES, J.W. *Historical Introduction to the Theory of Law*, (Oxford, 1940), pp. 191–202: the American Realist movement is considered in the context of the psychological interpretation of law. The views of Frank are considered. It is pointed out that the Realists have not done more than stress the importance of intuition. The psychological approach as a whole is appraised.

6. BODENHEIMER, E. *Jurisprudence*, (Harvard University Press, 1962), pp. 116–20: the work of the American Realists is set out briefly.

7. PATON, G.W. *A Text-Book of Jurisprudence*, (4th ed., G.W. Paton and D.P. Derham, Clarendon Press, Oxford, 1972), pp. 22–28: the American Realists are regarded as being the left-wing of the sociological approach, and their contributions are assessed.

8. STONE, J. *Social Dimensions of Law and Justice*, (Stevens & Sons, Ltd, 1966), pp. 62–71; 680–87; 734–42: the contribution of American Realism is set in the context of a broad survey of sociological jurisprudence. The account centres on the work of Llewellyn, and it is said that the changes in his thought show how realism, shorn of its initial excesses, has come to reinforce a number of sociological insights. Much of the debate over realism in the 1930's was at cross purposes. The problems of fact-finding and law-finding are also dealt with, and Frank's programme is critically examined.

9. KEETON, G.W. *The Elementary Principles of Jurisprudence*, (2nd ed., Pitman & Sons, Ltd, 1949), pp. 21–24: this is a brief, general summary of the functional and Realist approaches.

10. JOLOWICZ, H.F. *Lectures on Jurisprudence*, (ed. J.A. Jolowicz, The Athlone Press, 1963), chap. 9: a simplified account is given of the main contentions of the movement and a criticism of these.

11. GARLAN, E.N. *Legal Realism and Justice*, (Columbia University Press, 1941): in the course of this important study it is shown that the Realists cannot avoid talking about law as it ought to be. It examines critically the implications of their contentions. The bibliography at the end is most comprehensive.

1. MECHEM, P. "The Jurisprudence of Despair" (1935–36), 21 Iowa LR, 669: this is a critique of the views of Arnold and Robinson. The Realists wish to escape from the hampering restriction of law; hence the movement might be called "Lazy Jurisprudence".

2. FULLER, L.L. "American Legal Realism" (1934), 82 U Pa LR, 429: W.U. Moore's behaviourism (*supra*) is criticised on the ground that mere observation of conduct without taking account of the ends that are being sought is inadequate. A judge's reaction is always to the situation as a whole, which includes many factors ignored by the Realists.

3. FULLER, L.L. *Law in Quest of Itself*, (The Foundation Press, Inc, 1940): throughout the book positivism from Hobbes onwards, and especially the Realist movement, is subjected to strong criticism. It is maintained that the "is" and the "ought" cannot be separated.

4. McDOUGAL, M.S. "Fuller vs. The American Realists: an Intervention" (1940–41), 50 Yale LJ, 827: this is principally a criticism of Fuller's advocacy of natural law on the ground of vagueness.

5. DICKINSON, J. "Legal Rules and their Function in the Process of Decision" (1931), 79 U Pa LR, 833, 1052: rules do have influence, for in many cases they do govern the decision. It is important to appreciate how the rule-element and the discretion-element interact. The study of judicial psychology alone is not enough, for this can only operate within a given rule.

6. KANTOROWICZ, H.U. "Some Rationalism about Realism" (1934), 43 Yale LJ, 1240: the Realists are criticised for confusing natural and cultural sciences; in the latter the question is not whether people do this or that, but whether they ought to have done what they did. The Realists also confuse explanation and justification and law and ethics. On the other hand, they fail to distinguish between realities and their meaning. Lawyers are concerned with meaning.

7. COHEN, M.R. "On Absolutisms in Legal Thought" (1936), 84 U Pa LR, 681: in rejecting the mechanical function of rules one should not reject rules altogether. The argument that law does not correspond with fact loses some of its force when it is remembered that there always has to be some discrepancy between theory and practice.

8. COHEN, M.R. "Positivism and the Limits of Idealism in the Law" (1927), 27 Col LR, 237, especially pp. 249–30: positivism is itself an ideal. As soon as it is realised that law is not a closed system, ideals as to what ought to be come in. Yet the ideal and the actual are never completely identical. The need for abstract general rules is pointed out at pp. 249–50.

9. COHEN, M.R. *Law and the Social Order*, (Harcourt, Brace & Co, 1933), pp. 184–197, 198–267, 352–69: principles are needed in the development of the law. The law cannot abandon the striving towards consistency. It consists of norms regulating conduct, rather than describing it. The contentions of the Realists are examined from a theoretical point of view. The work of Holmes, Gray and Frank is assessed.

10. CARDOZO, B.N. *The Nature of the Judicial Process*, (Yale University Press, 1921), pp. 124–30: the extreme Realist position is disavowed as containing the seeds of

fallacy and error. The significance of law before it reaches the courts is pointed out.

1. CARDOZO, B.N. *The Growth of the Law,* (Yale University Press, 1924), pp. 31–55: varying views as to the nature and origin of law can lead to varying decisions on the merits of a lawsuit. Law stands at some point behind actual adjudication. It is more than a collection of isolated judgments; it is a stock of rules and principles which will be enforced by courts.

2. KELSEN, H. *General Theory of Law and State,* (trans. A. Wedberg, Harvard University Press, 1949), pp. 165–78: it is said by some jurists that the task of legal science is to predict the behaviour of judges. But there is a difference between normative rules and rules deducible from observation. A sociological interpretation of law presupposes a normative interpretation.

3. POUND, R. "The Call for a Realist Jurisprudence" (1930–31), 44 Harv LR, 697: a faithful portrayal of what courts do is not the whole task of a science of law. The aims and contentions of the Realists are critically appraised.

4. POUND, R. *The Ideal Element in Law,* (University of Calcutta, 1958), chap. 10: the various brands of realism are classified and surveyed critically.

5. HART, H.L.A. *The Concept of Law,* (Oxford, Clarendon Press, 1961, reprinted 1975), pp. 132–44: the denial of rules is inconsistent with the authoritative character of a judicial decision, for it is authoritative by virtue of rules. The inadequacy of regarding law as simply predictions of what courts do is indicated.

6. TAYLOR, E.H. "H.L.A. Hart's Concept of Law in the Perspective of American Legal Realism" (1972), 35 MLR, 606: a close comparison is not possible. On the separation of law and morality, Hart and Realists would agree on the "penumbral" areas, but differ on its scope. Hart overlooks competing legal premises, alternative precedents reaching identical conclusions. Realism thus offers more scope for morality. Both Hart and Realists would agree that the logical form alone is insufficient. Hart thinks that Realists deny rules, which is not the case; they deny that certainty can be achieved through rules. Holmes's prediction theory was not a definition of law, but a matter of focus.

7. ALLEN, C.K. *Law in the Making,* (7th ed., Oxford, 1964), pp. 41–48: this is a somewhat denigratory account of the Realist movement in which its rise is attributed to the complex situation obtaining in America.

8. PATTERSON, E.W. "Can Law be Scientific?" (1930), 25 Ill LR, 121: the advantages of mathematical symbols to make new hypotheses explicit is not available in law. The ways in which law might be made explicit and scientific are discussed. Legal rules are not myths; they mark the boundaries of judicial thought.

9. COOK, W.W. "Scientific Method and the Law" (1927), 13 Am BAJ, 303: the task confronting the judge is considered. Past judicial behaviour can be generalised into rules, which are then used to forecast future decisions.

10. WADE, H.W.R. "The Concept of Legal Certainty. A Preliminary Skirmish" (1941), 4 MLR, 183, especially pp. 191–99: Frank's attack on certainty in law is critically considered.

1. BROWN, R.A. "Police-power – Legislation for Health and Personal Safety" (1928–29), 42 Harv LR, 866: this is an examination of judicial decisions on the "due process" clause by investigating the judges who made them. Personal prejudice is not the only factor; various others come in (p. 872). See also R.A. BROWN: "Due Process of Law, Police Power and the Supreme Court" (1926–27), 40 Harv LR, 943.

2. HARVEY, C.P. "A Job for Jurisprudence" (1944), 7 MLR, 42: jurisprudence has failed to cope with practical problems. The mistake has lain in elevating it into a science.

3. KENNEDY, W.B. "Another Job for Jurisprudence" (1945), 8 MLR, 18: this is a reply to Harvey and arguing against a purely factual approach. For C.P. HARVEY's reply, see "A Job for Jurisprudence" (1945), 8 MLR, 236.

4. KENNEDY, W.B. "A Review of Legal Realism" (1940), 9 FLR, 362: Realism has failed to catch hold because of (a) a consistent adherence to the scientific technique in its approach to the criticism of traditional law; (b) submersion of rules by over-emphasis on fact-finding; (c) absence of skepticism regarding the hypothetical theories of the social sciences; (d) the creation of a new form of word-magic and verbal gymnastics.

5. CAVERS, D.F. "In Advocacy of the Problem Method" (1943), 43 Col LR, 449, at pp. 453–54: it is alleged that the Realists secretly like legal concepts; they dissect them whereas "traditionalists" put them together. Their approach is unsuited to legal education.

6. HARRIS, R.C. "Idealism Emergent in Jurisprudence" (1935–36), 10 Tul LR, 169: with reference to the rise of idealism in America, it is maintained that resort to the subjective psychological processes is itself a form of idealism.

7. WRIGHT, J.S. "Professor Bickel, the Scholarly Tradition, and the Supreme Court" (1970–71), 84 Harv LR, 769: a judge defends the Warren Court against the attack by Professor Bickel on its objectives. He points out that in an era of challenge and assertions of human rights, a value-neutral "scholarly tradition", such as that advocated by Bickel, is inappropriate, if not impossible. Further, Bickel's own approach is rooted in certain values which need to be exposed.

8. LINDE, H.A. "Judges, Critics, and the Realist Tradition" (1972–73), 82 Yale LJ, 227: the Constitution of a country is addressed primarily to governments and to courts only as a consequence. Realist analyses of court decisions simply record judicial reactions. Realism in judicial action is a demand for certain ideologies to be adopted by the judges.

9. JONES, H.W. "Law and Morality in the Perspective of Legal Realism" (1961), 61 Col LR, 799: there are greater affinities between realism and natural law tradition than between analytical and natural law tradition. Positive law only authorises alternative choices, the final choice being made on the basis of what ought to be. The ethical theory to be drawn from realism is that the moral dimension of the law is not to be found in rules and principles, but in the process of decision. Choice and decision are inevitable in the life of the law. This is guided by moral considerations.

10. KESSLER, F. "Theoretic Bases of Law" (1941–42), 9 UCLR, 98, at pp. 109–12:

the early Realists represented an early form of positivism, later they developed the functional approach. The Realist approach is said to achieve a synthesis between natural law philosophy and positivism.

1. HALL, J. "American Tendencies in Legal Philosophy and the Definition of 'Law'", (1956), 3 Comparative Law Review of Japan, 1: the chief contributions of the Realist movement are set out. Among other criticisms levelled at them it is pointed out that they resort to law in the traditional sense in order to discover who the officials are, and that separation of the "is" and the "ought" is not possible.

2. TAYLOR, R. "Law and Morality" (1968), 43 NYULR, 611: the realists are criticised for not going far enough. They focus attention too much on the judge. Commands as binding as those issued by judges emanate from other sources. These are all "laws".

3. DEWEY, J. "Logical Method and Law" (1924), 10 Corn LQ, 17: this deals generally with the instrumental nature of legal logic as distinct from syllogistic logic. He is, therefore, in a sense a spiritual father of the Realist movement. See also J. DEWEY: *The Quest for Certainty*, (G.P. Putnam's Sons, 1929).

4. *My Philosophy of Law*, (Boston Law Book Co, 1941): this contains views of J.W. Bingham, M.R. Cohen, W.W. Cook, J. Dewey, J. Dickinson, W.B. Kennedy, K.N. Llewellyn, U. Moore and E.W. Patterson (and others).

5. REUSCHLEIN, H.G. *Jurisprudence – its American Prophets*, (The Bobbs-Merrill Co, Inc, 1951), pp. 183–275: this work may usefully be consulted for studies of most of the American Realists and the principal features of their work.

Scandinavian Realism

6. HÄGERSTRÖM, A. *Inquiries into the Nature of Law and Morals*, (ed. K. Olivecrona, trans. C.D. Broad, Almqvist & Wiksell, Stockholm, 1953): the substance of Hägerström's teachings are contained in this volume. Many legal concepts, e.g., rights, duties, are dismissed as myths, and everything which cannot be expressed either as fact or emotion is condemned as metaphysical.

7. OLIVECRONA, K. *Law as Fact*, (Einar Munksgaard, Copenhagen; Humphrey Milford, London, 1939; reprinted Wildy & Sons, 1962; 2nd ed., Stevens & Sons, Ltd, 1971): law is a set of social facts, and its "binding force" is a myth. Obedience is due to people's psychological reactions to certain procedures and forms of expression. These propositions are developed with exemplary clarity. At pp. 213–15 there is a short critique of American Realism.

8. MacCORMACK, G. "Hägerström on Rights and Duties" (1971), Jur R, 59: Hägerström's views on rights and duties derive from his inquiry into Roman law, which he thought was magic-based. An explanation of rights and duties involves an inquiry into the social conditions giving rise to a belief in rights and duties and how they are preserved. Membership of groups generates feelings which give rise to ideas of right and duty. The author criticises various aspects of Hägerström's views.

9. SIMMONDS, N.E. "The Legal Philosophy of Axel Hägerström" (1976), Jur R, 210: Hägerström anticipated the significance of language from a functional point of

view. The author traces the origins of his views from its Kantian basis to his
attack on idealism and objective values. Utterances about duty have social and
psychological backgrounds; there are feelings of duties. It is the regular operation
of command and coercion that establishes a system of conduct which is seen as
being obligatory.

1. ROSS, A. *On Law and Justice*, (Stevens & Sons, Ltd, 1958), especially chaps. 1–9:
   legal norms are addressed to judges and are operative because they are felt to be
   binding by them. Prescriptions of conduct by citizens are only "derivative and
   figurative". Validity is regarded from a descriptive point of view, viz., that norms
   are acted on by judges. Hence, the criterion of validity is predictability of
   decisions. There may thus be degrees of validity depending on the degree of
   predictability. The last eight chapters deal with the criteria for evaluating the law.

2. ROSS, A. *Directives and Norms*, (Routledge & Kegan Paul, Ltd, 1968): he modifies
   his previous view slightly. Instead of saying that prescriptions of conduct are
   only derivatives from norms directed to judges, he now concedes that there are
   two sets of norms: logically, there are only the norms directed to judges, but
   psychologically, there are also those directed to citizens.

3. LUNDSTEDT, A.V. *Legal Thinking Revised*, (Almqvist & Wiksell, Stockholm,
   1956): this is the most extreme rejection of everything metaphysical amongst
   the Scandinavian school. Nothing is valid, which cannot be proved as fact. The
   main distinction is between the science of law, which should have nothing to do
   with values, and valuations, which are necessary but individualistic. Instead, the
   method of law is that of "social welfare".

4. OLIVECRONA, K. "Law as Fact", in *Interpretations of Modern Legal Philosophies*,
   (ed. P. Sayre, Oxford University Press, New York, 1947), chap. 25: the "binding
   force" of law is examined with the aid of the concept of duty. The connection
   between the idea of a rule and the feeling of being bound is a psychological one.

5. MERRILLS, J.G. "Law, Morals and the Psychological Nexus" (1969), 19 UTLJ,
   46: the author considers critically and takes issue with Olivecrona's thesis that
   morality is shaped by legal enforcement. He thinks that Olivecrona fails to
   distinguish between acceptance of a rule as binding and the morality of it. He
   also criticises Olivecrona for grossly underestimating the influence of morals on
   law.

6. OLIVECRONA, K. "Legal Language and Reality" in *Essays in Jurisprudence in
   Honor of Roscoe Pound*, (ed. R.A. Newman, The Bobbs-Merrill Co, Inc, 1962),
   p. 151: the views of various groups of thinkers to find some realistic basis for
   rights are considered and rejected. There are also critical comments on the views
   of the American Realists, Hägerström and Lundstedt. The discussion then
   proceeds with the function of legal language.

7. OLIVECRONA, K. "The Legal Theories of Axel Hägerström and Vilhelm Lundstedt"
   (1959), 3 Scand SL, 125: the views of Hägerström and Lundstedt are explained.
   The illusory nature of a right is further discussed. Right has a behaviourist
   function.

8. ARNHOLM, C.J. "Olivecrona on Legal Rights. Reflections on the Concept of
   Rights" (1962), 6 Scand SL, 11: Olivecrona's views are explained. The difference

between his views and those of the American Realists is said to be the difference between a juristic and a sociological concept.

1. STONE, J. *Legal System and Lawyers' Reasonings*, (Stevens & Sons, Ltd, 1964), pp. 92–93: in the course of a discussion of the imperative theory of law there is a passing reference to Olivecrona's idea of "independent imperative". It is said that there are many situations in which there are actual commands addressed to individuals, and for these the idea of "independent imperative" is inappropriate.

2. ROSS, A. *Towards a Realistic Jurisprudence*, (trans. A.I. Fausbøll, Einar Munksgaard, Copenhagen, 1946): the normative and factual aspects of law are inescapable. The former are alleged to be rationalisations of emotional experiences.

3. HART, H.L.A. "Scandinavian Realism" (1959), CLJ, 233: this is a critical review of A. Ross's *On Law and Justice*.

4. CHRISTIE, G.C. "The Notion of Validity in Modern Jurisprudence" (1963–64), 48 Minn LR, 1049: the views of Kelsen and Ross as to the criterion of validity are compared with reference to concrete situations, and the former is preferred.

5. ARNHOLM, C.J. "Some Basic Problems of Jurisprudence" (1957), I Scand SL, 9: Ross's contention that the validity of a norm depends on whether a judge will act on it is criticised. Other interpretations of validity are also considered and rejected.

6. JØRGENSEN, S. "Argumentation and Decision" in *Liber Amicorum in Honour of Professor Alf Ross*, (Copenhagen, 1969), 261: after pointing out that Ross does not deal with the problem which faces the judge, the author discusses the approaches of natural law theory, argumentation theory and decision theory. The first proceeds a priori; the second makes it possible to discuss values and the question is one of good and bad argumentation; while the last takes account of values themselves.

7. LUNDSTEDT, A.V. *Superstition or Rationality in Action for Peace?* (Longmans, Green & Co, 1925): this is a strongly expressed polemic against traditional views about legal concepts and an uncompromising rejection of everything metaphysical.

8. LUNDSTEDT, A.V. "Law and Justice: A Criticism of the Method of Justice" in *Interpretations of Modern Legal Philosophies*, (ed. P. Sayre, Oxford University Press, New York, 1947), chap. 21: the idea that justice underlies law and determines its content is attacked with illustrations drawn from criminal law and torts. Judgments of justice are expressions of feeling. Such evaluations should be made with reference to public welfare.

9. CASTBERG, F. *Problems of Legal Philosophy*, (2nd ed., Oslo University Press; Allen & Unwin, Ltd, 1957), especially pp. 27–37: a Norwegian writer takes issue with the Realists. The importance and indispensability of norms and values are the underlying theme.

10. MARSHALL, G. "Law in a Cold Climate. The Scandinavian Realism" (1956), I Jur R (NS), 259: this is a discussion in dialogue form of what the Scandinavians mean by positivism and some of their other doctrines.

1. MacCORMACK, G. "Scandinavian Realism" (1970), Jur R, 33: this refers to the group of writers who seem to explain law in terms of fact. "Fact" includes external experience and ideas, beliefs and feelings. The works of Hägerström, Lundstedt, Olivecrona and Ross are discussed. Both Olivecrona and Ross, it is said, explain validity in terms of psychological reactions. This view is criticised.

2. LEWIS, J.U. "Karl Olivecrona: 'Factual Realism' and Reasons for Obeying a Law" (1970), 5 U Br Col LR, 281: this article gives a very good account of the theory of Olivecrona and the basis on which it was formed. It also contains an assessment of the weakness and the relevance of his views in contemporary jurisprudence.

3. REDMOUNT, R.S. "Psychological Views in Jurisprudential Theories" (1958–59), 107 U Pa LR, 472: the psychological bases of the theories of the Scandinavian Realists and of Bentham and Petrazhitsky are examined. The dependance of human beings on their environment is stressed.

4. SMITH, J.C. "Law, Language, and Philosophy" (1968), 3 U Br Col LR, 59: in the course of reviewing the attitude to language of various legal philosophers, the attitudes of Hägerström and Olivecrona, among others, are explained and considered.

5. LLOYD, D. *Introduction to Jurisprudence*, (3rd ed., Stevens & Sons, Ltd, 1972), chap. 8: the work of Hägerström, Olivecrona, Lundstedt and Ross is briefly reviewed. See also D. LLOYD, *The Idea of Law*, (Penguin Books, Ltd, A 688, 1964), pp. 217–19.

6. FRIEDMANN, W. *Legal Theory*, (5th ed., Stevens & Sons, Ltd, 1967), pp. 304–311: this is a brief account of the work and contribution of the Scandinavian Realist School.

7. BODENHEIMER, E. *Jurisprudence*, (Harvard University Press, 1962), pp. 120–25: this is another brief account of the work of the Scandinavian Realists.

8. FINCH, J.D. *Introduction to Legal Theory*, (2nd ed., Sweet & Maxwell, Ltd, 1974), pp. 130–135 and chap. 8: the first few pages contain a brief discussion of the view of Olivecrona in relation to Kelsen. Chapter 8 deals with Scandinavian and American realism. After noting their similarities, the view of Ross (mainly derived from *On Law and Justice*) is dealt with, followed by brief accounts of Gray, Holmes, Llewellyn and Frank.

9. HALL, J. *Foundations of Jurisprudence*, (The Bobbs-Merrill Co, Inc, 1973), pp. 54–62: American Realists use "law" in the sense of legal sociology to signify factual patterns of official behaviour. Ross's rejection of "validity" as being only rationalisations deduced from certain feelings is considered and criticised.

22. Natural Law

General

1. d'ENTREVES, A.P. *Natural Law*, (Hutchinson's University Library, 1951): this is the best and most convenient survey of the contributions of natural law doctrine to thought. The principal issues connected with naturalist philosophy are examined.

2. ROMMEN, H.A. *The Natural Law*, (trans. T.R. Hanley, B. Herder Book Co, 1947): the movement away from natural law is deplored. Natural law is said to be essential to a philosophy of social order and justice. Part I traces the history of natural law thought from Greek times down to the present. In Part II the content of natural law is examined.

3. HAINES, C.G. *The Revival of Natural Law Concepts*, (Harvard University Press, 1930): natural lawyers are said to fall into three groups. In the light of this division the doctrines of natural lawyers are examined from Greek times onwards. The modern revival of natural law theory and the reasons for it are considered in detail. Much of the book is concerned with natural law thinking in America.

4. SABINE, G.H. *A History of Political Theory*, (3rd ed., Harrap & Co, Ltd, 1963), chaps. 2–6, 8–9, 13, 21–23, 26–29: this book provides one of the best surveys of the history of thought from Greek times to the present.

5. POUND, R. *The Ideal Element in Law*, (University of Calcutta, 1958), chaps. 2–6: there is always an ideal element underlying the law; even analytical positivism is founded on an ideal. A survey of natural law doctrine and its contributions is followed by discussions of the relation between law and morals and the end of law.

6. PATTERSON, E.W. *Jurisprudence*, (The Foundation Press, Inc, 1953), chaps. 13–14: six meanings of the expression "natural law" are distinguished. There are good accounts of the work of Aristotle, Cicero and Aquinas. Human nature as assumed in naturalist theory is critically appraised. In chapter 14 the work of Kant is dealt with at some length and there are slighter accounts of Stammler and some others.

7. STONE, J. *Human Law and Human Justice*, (Stevens & Sons, Ltd, 1965), chaps. 1–3: the first two of these chapters give an introduction to the natural law theory of the Greeks and Roman down to the evolution of international law and natural law as a criterion of the validity of positive law. In the last chapter the work of Kant is dealt with and the part played by individual rights on English and American law is considered.

8. JOLOWICZ, H.F. *Lectures on Jurisprudence*, (ed. J.A. Jolowicz, The Athlone Press, 1963), chaps. 2–5: these chapters survey natural law theory from Greek times until the 18th century. It provides a perspective of the various movements in thought.

9. HOLLAND, T.E. *The Elements of Jurisprudence*, (13th ed., Oxford, 1924), pp. 31–40: natural law is said to be based on morality, and the interpretations of the Stoics, Cicero, Aquinas and Hobbes, *inter alia*, are also mentioned. The effects and implications of naturalist doctrine are enumerated.

1. PATON, G.W. *A Text-Book of Jurisprudence*, (4th ed., G.W. Paton and D.P. Derham, Clarendon Press, Oxford, 1972), chap. 4: natural law theory concerns law in relation to purpose, the basis of law and the relation between law and justice. There is a brief survey of the views of the Greeks, Romans, Christian Fathers, 17th century and modern writers. Particular mention is made of the attitude of the common law.

2. VINOGRADOFF, P. *Collected Papers*, (Oxford, 1928), II, chap. 18: the need to satisfy the desire for justice was met by appeal to natural law. The various stages in the development of this idea are developed.

3. SALMOND, J.W. "The Law of Nature" (1895), 11 LQR, 121: the lack of interest on the part of common lawyers in legal philosophy is attributed to the separation of ideas of law and moral questions as preserved by the different words "right" and "law", whereas Continental jurists have one word to connote the two ideas. Both are said to go too far in their respective attitudes. There is a clear historical account of speculation about natural law and natural rights from Greek times down to the 19th century.

4. SALMOND, J.W. *Jurisprudence*, (7th ed., Sweet & Maxwell, Ltd, 1924), pp. 26–30; (12th ed., P.J. Fitzgerald, 1966), pp. 15–25: it is significant that whereas Salmond's own treatment of natural law was cursory and "illustrated sufficiently" by a few sample quotations from very ancient writers, his latest editor sees fit to develop much more fully a theme which has sprung to life in recent years.

5. SEAGLE, W. *The Quest for Law*, (Alfred A. Knopf, 1941), chap. 14: natural law is more than a matter of individual preference. It can be a dangerous and shattering force. In this chapter the uses to which natural law theory have been put are traced down to the 18th century.

6. CHLOROS, A.G. "What is Natural Law?" (1958), 21 MLR, 609: the question What is natural law? is still a fruitful one for considering the different types of order that will result from the application of natural law theory. It is said that there is little or no difference between natural law thinking and the sociological approach. A framework for jurisprudential study based on a broad classification of natural law theory is outlined.

7. CHROUST, A.H. "On the Nature of Natural Law" in *Interpretations of Modern Legal Philosophies*, (ed. P. Sayre, Oxford University Press, New York, 1947), chap. 5: natural law is opposed to positive law and to empiricism. It proceeds deductively from presuppositions and represents a quest for the absolute and ultimate meaning of law and justice.

8. POUND, R. "The Scope and Purpose of Sociological Jurisprudence" (1910–11), 24 Harv LR, 591, at pp. 604–11; (1911–12), 25 Harv LR, 140, at pp. 147–62: the philosophical approach is surveyed broadly. Among the 19th century doctrines there is special mention of Stammler.

9. POUND, R. "Fifty Years of Jurisprudence" (1937–38), 51 Harv LR, 444, at pp. 463–72: the modern revival of natural law is dealt with.

10. POUND, R. "The End of Law as Developed in Juristic Thought" (1913–14), 27 Harv LR, 195, at p. 605; (1916–17), 30 Harv LR, 201: this surveys thinking about law from Greek times down to the 19th century. The theme which is

stressed is the way in which legal theory has been used to satisfy the paramount social need of the age. The investigation is pursued into the 20th century in "Twentieth-century Ideas as to the End of Law" in *Harvard Legal Essays*, (Harvard University Press, 1934), 357.

1. POUND, R. *Interpretations of Legal History*, (Cambridge University Press, 1923), chap. 2: the ethical interpretation of legal history is considered historically with reference to the part played by ideals.

2. POUND, R. *Jurisprudence*, (West Publishing Co, 1959), I, chaps. 2–4, 7–8; II, chap. 11: the above are collated and re-stated generally.

3. WINDOLPH, F.L. *Leviathan and Natural Law*, (Princeton University Press, 1951): an attempt is made to construct a natural law theory on a positivist basis principally by separating politics from morality. But the upshot of the argument is that it is not necessary to introduce a moral element into the idea of the validity of law.

4. MAINE, H.J.S. *Ancient Law*, (ed. F. Pollock, John Murray, 1906), chaps. 3–4 and Notes F–G: in chapter 3 equity in Roman law, the origin of the *jus gentium* and the influence of Greek philosophy on the Romans is considered. In chapter 4 the modern history of natural law is dealt with. Its influence in giving rise to international law is stressed. In the Notes Pollock comments on and questions some of Maine's contentions.

5. POUND, R. "Natural Natural Law and Positive Natural Law" (1952), 68 LQR, 330; (1960), 5 Nat LF, 70: the contrast is between a rationally conceived ideal relation between men, on the one hand, and universal precepts that are logically derived from actual experience, on the other. The functions of "natural natural law" are explained.

6. SILVING, H. *Sources of Law*, (Wm. S. Hein & Co, Inc, New York, 1968), "'Positive' or 'Natural Law'?", p. 251: in these pages will be found a general discussion of the relation between positive and natural law. An interesting contention is that positivism has provided a new type of natural law, which is said to occur when courts decide, not according to what was understood by the legislators at the time the law was laid down, but according to contemporary legal science. Also of interest is the naturalist call for positivism in law as a guarantee of certainty and hence of justice, and the assertion that positivism is grounded in a basic assumption that the law and those who make it shall behave rationally. When this assumption breaks down, e.g., in Nazi Germany, the limit of the bindingness of law is reached.

7. HARPER, F.V. "The Forces Behind and Beyond Juristic Pragmatism in America" in *Receuil d'Etudes sur les Sources du Droit en l'Honneur de F. Geny*, (Librairie du Receuil Sirey, 1934), II, 243: philosophy has followed physical science, but it has led social science by giving direction to it.

8. GOODHART, A.L. *English Law and the Moral Law*, (Stevens & Sons, Ltd, 1955), pp. 28–37: there is an "objective morality" which jurists should not ignore. This constitutes the "revived natural law". It has its basis in a sense of obligation: why do people regard moral law as obligatory? The reasons are considered at length.

1. THAYER, A.S. "Natural Law" (1905), 21 LQR, 60: moral ideas are described as
   ghosts of habit. They have become idealised and hence are thought to be perfect.

2. JØRGENSEN, S. *Law and Society*, (Akademisk Boghandel, 1972), chap. 3: natural
   law theory was shaped by legal science. It may defend the established order, or
   it may favour change. The development of ideas requires an environment of
   trained jurists.

3. BRUNNER, E. *Justice and the Social Order*, (trans. M. Hottinger, Lutterworth
   Press, 1945), chap. 12: the author's aim is to evolve a Protestant version of
   natural law. Three meanings of natural law are contrasted, the objective interpretation of pre-Christian times, the subjective individualist interpretation and
   the Christian interpretation. The chapter is mainly concerned with showing how
   Christian theology came to appropriate natural law theory.

4. WU, J.C.H. *Fountain of Justice. A Study in Natural Law*, (Sheed & Ward, 1955):
   this book is written from a devoutly Christian (Thomist) point of view. The
   common law of England and America is the material on which the argument is
   constructed.

5. BROWN, B.F. "Natural Law: Dynamic Basis of Law and Morals in the Twentieth
   Century" (1957), 31 Tul LR, 491: this is a vigorous re-statement of an essentially
   Thomist position. Natural law is the common basis of law and morals. Law
   bears an immutable relationship to Natural law; it has the character of law only
   so far as it has this relation. The separation of law and morals will undermine the
   common law.

6. *Southern Methodist University Studies in Jurisprudence*, (ed. A.L. Harding, S.M.U.
   Press), II, (1955), chaps. 3–4: these are respectively a critical appraisal of the
   value of the natural law theory for the problems of today, and the revived
   natural law of today. III, (1956), chap. 4: natural law is discussed from a
   Christian point of view.

7. ELLUL, J. *The Theological Foundation of Law*, (trans. M. Wieser, S.C.M. Press,
   Ltd, 1946, first British ed., 1961): divine law is opposed to natural law. The
   latter became corrupt after the Fall of Man and therefore no profitable theory
   can be built on it. The true law is that revealed by God through Christ.

8. NORTHROP, F.S.C. *The Complexity of Legal and Ethical Experience*, (Little,
   Brown & Co, 1959): it is contended that judgments of goodness and badness are
   scientifically verifiable. If so, a normative discipline like law assumes the
   character of a science. Law has three levels: positive law, living law and natural
   law. The last is derived from a true and, as far as possible, complete knowledge
   of Man. Such knowledge comes from experimentally verified findings of physics,
   biology and other natural science. Nature, as thus interpreted by science, is the
   source of verification for law. For an application of this approach to international
   law, see F.S.C. NORTHROP: "Naturalistic and Cultural Foundations for a More
   Effective International Law" (1949–50), 59 Yale LJ, 1430; "Contemporary
   Jurisprudence and International Law" (1952), 61 Yale LJ, 623.

9. WILD, J.D. *Plato's Modern Enemies and the Theory of Natural Law*, (University of
   Chicago Press, 1953): "value" and "existence" are intertwined. Fulfilment of
   existence is "good", and its frustration is "evil". Existence has a tendential

character, and such tendency is fact on which certain norms are grounded. On this basis it becomes possible to construct a theory of natural law.

1. KELSEN, H. "A 'Dynamic' Theory of Natural Law", in *What is Justice?* (University of California Press, 1957), 174: J.D. Wild's theory is subjected to criticism. Modern natural law takes a monistic view of "ought" and "is"; but this is mistaken. To show factual grounds for the content of the rules of natural law does not show why natural laws ought to be binding.

2. STONE, J. *Human Law and Human Justice*, (Stevens & Sons, Ltd, 1965), pp. 196–202: these pages contain an account of J.D. Wild's theory of natural law and criticism of it. The main comment is that the fact that people have a sense of obligation does not explain why they ought to obey this sense. Other criticisms are the vagueness of his terminology, and there are so many different opinions as to what constitutes "fulfilment" of "tendency" that it ceases to be objective fact.

3. LASERSON, M.M. "'Positive' and 'Natural' Law and their Correlation" in *Interpretations of Modern Legal Philosophies*, (ed. P. Sayre, Oxford University Press, New York, 1947), chap. 20: positive law keeps up with ideas of what ought to be in a series of periodic jumps. Intuitive law is individually variable and socially adaptable. This is natural law.

4. HALL, J. *Studies in Jurisprudence and Criminal Theory*, (Oceana Publications Inc, 1958), chap. 2: current theories of natural law fail to take account of facts. Realism has paid too much attention to facts and too little to values. Positivism is too concerned with pure ideas. The author pleads for an "integrative jurisprudence" which will combine values, facts and ideals.

5. HALL, J. *Living Law of Democratic Society*, (The Bobbs-Merrill Co, Inc, 1949), chap. 2: various trends of thought throughout history are reviewed in the light of the need for values. The Stoic theory is praised as having contained an integrative view of law, i.e., made ideals part of the essence of positive law.

6. HALL, J. *Foundations of Jurisprudence*, (The Bobbs-Merrill Co, Inc, 1973), chaps. II, III, V: the salient features of classical natural law are discussed (Plato, Aristotle, Ockham, Aquinas and Kant). The author points out the difficulty of classifying writers as "naturalist" or "positivist" and concludes that it is important to concentrate on basic issues with reference to their underlying philosophies and not on labels such as "Natural Law" and "Positivism". He stresses the need to include a moral value in any definition of positive law. Positivist "neutrality" is exposed as a myth since valuation is implicit in all theories. The distinctiveness of positive law is said to depend on six criteria. The distinction between law and other norms lies in the fact that only law exhibits all these criteria.

7. DEWEY, J. *Philosophy and Civilisation*, (G.P. Putnam's Sons, 1931), 166: "nature" and "reason" are ambiguous terms. Their use as synonyms of "morality" has given rise to different interpretations.

8. LLOYD, D. "Legal and Ideal Justice" in *Legal Essays. A Tribute to Frede Castberg*, (Universitetsforlaget, 1963), III: this begins by contrasting the kind of natural law that one gets by deriving it from nature as it is and from ideals of what ought

to be. Instead of searching for absolute values it is thought to be more fruitful to explore how the values of a developing society may best be realised in the conditions of today.

1. *Law and Philosophy. A Symposium*, (ed. S. Hook, New York University Press, 1964), Part II: various versions of natural law theory are outlined by different authors, while others offer criticisms. The whole is of general interest.

2. COWEN, D.V. *The Foundations of Freedom*, (Cape Town, OUP, 1961), chap. 10: in the course of a general appraisal of a naturalist approach there is a brief review of the Greek and Roman periods, the Middle Ages and Renaissance.

Critical Appraisals

3. BENTHAM, J. *The Theory of Legislation*, (trans. R. Hildreth, ed. C.K. Ogden, Routledge & Kegan Paul Ltd, 1950): chap. 13, s. 10: Bentham was a redoubtable opponent of natural law theory. His attacks are to be found in many other places in his writings.

4. AUSTIN, J. *Lectures on Jurisprudence*, (5th ed., R. Campbell, John Murray, 1885), II, pp. 567–75, chaps. 31–32: jurisprudence, as the science of positive law, should be kept distinct from what law ought to be. The different senses in which the term "natural law" is used are explained, and there is also a discussion of *jus naturale* in relation to *jus gentium*.

5. KELSEN, H. "The Metamorphoses of the Idea of Justice" in *Interpretations of Modern Legal Philosophies*, (ed. P. Sayre, Oxford University Press, New York, 1947), chap. 18, especially pp. 395–97: the idea of justice is considered in relation to natural law. The assumption that what is just is natural assumes that a just regulation of human nature proceeds from nature. Natural law theories have so far failed to define the content of this just order. The article contains discussions of Aristotle's and Plato's views on justice.

6. KELSEN, H. *What is Justice?* (University of California Press, 1957), pp. 137–97; 209: various criticisms of the traditional naturalist doctrine are developed in detail. Its vitality derives from the fact that it serves as justification. Natural law doctrine is said to stand or fall with the assumption that value is inherent in reality. Values of law determine whether conduct is lawful or unlawful; this is decided according to the validity of the norm. Values of justice determine whether the law is just or unjust. These cannot be objectively verified and a science of law has no place for them.

7. ROSS, A. *On Law and Justice*, (Stevens & Sons, Ltd, 1958), chaps. 10–11: natural law philosophy is the product of an infantile fear of life's inconsistencies. Its history is traced from Homeric times to the present. Chapter 11 subjects natural law doctrine to incisive criticism. The ideology does not exist that cannot be defended by appeal to natural law.

8. ROSS, A. *Towards a Realistic Jurisprudence*, (trans. A.I. Fausbøll, Einar Munksgaard, 1946), 21–32: the concept of natural law is considered in the course of a general survey of theories of law and is rejected.

9. KORKUNOV, N.M. *General Theory of Law*, (trans. W.G. Hastings, The Boston Book Co, 1909), chap. 3: there are elements common to various systems of law

which are imposed by necessity. This has given rise to a belief in natural law which exists without human agency. Natural law in Roman law and in the 17th century, as well as the attacks upon it by the Historical School, are set out.

1. SHKLAR, J.N. *Legalism*, (Harvard University Press, 1964): "legalism" is the attitude of mind which makes a morality of rule following. Naturalist, no less than Positivist, legal theorists are tainted with it. But this morality is only one among many in a pluralist society. Hence the efforts of Naturalists, including their polemics against Positivism, are narrow and out of touch with social realities. Natural Law theory is said to be an ideology of agreement.

2. GOLUNSKII, S.A. and STROGOVICH, M.S. "The Theory of the State and Law" in *Soviet Legal Philosophy*, (trans. H.W. Babb, Harvard University Press, 1951), pp. 402–6: this gives a general explanation of what natural law and the Roman *jus gentium* are. The developments, which are commonly ascribed to natural law theory, are explained on Marxist lines.

3. BUCKLAND, W.W. *Some Reflections on Jurisprudence*, (Cambridge University Press, 1945), chap. 3: the old conception of natural law made the rightness and wrongness of law the criterion of its validity. There is a brief account of the use which has been made of naturalist theory.

4. HOLMES, O.W. "Natural Law" in *Collected Legal Papers*, (Constable & Co, Ltd, 1920), 310: there is a human tendency to demand the superlative in all things, which might account for the search for criteria of universal validity. The naturalist attitude of mind is dealt with.

5. LLEWELLYN, K.N. *Jurisprudence. Realism in Theory and Practice*, (The University of Chicago Press, 1962), chap. 5: the lawyer's natural law is an effort to harness the philosopher's natural law to the solution of specific problems. Guidance for a particular society should be rooted in it. Viewed in this way, there need not be any irreconcileable antinomy between natural law and realism.

6. KESSLER, F. "Theoretic Bases of Law" (1941–42), 9 UCLR, 98, especially pp. 99–108: natural law philosophy believes in certain fundamental principles inherent in all ordered society. While giving credit to the achievements of natural law, the author criticises its claim to eternal validity. Positivism is also criticised. It is contended that realism enables the best in both to be combined.

7. KESSLER, F. "Natural Law, Justice and Democracy – Some Reflections on Three Types of Thinking about Law and Justice" (1944–45), 19 Tul LR, 32: the contributions of natural and positive law theory to the relationship between law, justice and democracy are assessed. Natural law philosophy is contrasted with the objective idealism of Plato on the one hand, and positive law on the other.

8. AQUINAS, St. T. *Summa Theologica*, (trans. Fathers of the English Dominican Province, R. & T. Washbourne, Ltd, 1915), I, 2, eq. 90–97: distinctions between different kinds of law are drawn and explained. The importance of promulgation is stressed.

9. DAVITT, T.E. "Law as a Means to an End – Thomas Aquinas", (1960–61), 14 Vand LR, 65: various features of God-made and Man-made law are explained and their interrelation considered. This is a clear summary of Aquinas's views.

1. SLESSER, H. *The Judicial Office and Other Matters*, (Hutchinson & Co, Ltd), chap. 5: the place which Aquinas occupies in relation to prior and subsequent thought is discussed at length.

2. COPLESTON, F.C. *Aquinas*, (Penguin Books, Ltd, 1955): the relationship between Aquinas's thought and that of the Greek philosophers is considered. The value of his scheme is assessed at length, and there is also some account of modern Thomism.

3. NIELSEN, K. "An Examination of the Thomist Theory of Natural Law" (1959), 4 Nat LF, 44: the doctrines of Aquinas are considered with reference to the interpretations of Copleston (*supra*) and Maritain. The essence of the doctrine is outlined at pp. 52–56. The thesis of the article is to take issue with the conception of a natural moral law. For a critical commentary on Nielsen, see V.J. BOURKE: "Natural Law, Thomism – and Professor Nielsen" (1960), 5 Nat LF, 112.

4. NIELSEN, K. "The Myth of Natural Law" in *Law and Philosophy. A Symposium*, (ed. S. Hook, New York University Press, 1964), p. 122: the fact that human life is purposive is no evidence of the mind of God. "Purpose" may signify "function" or "aim". Men have aims, but these are no indication of Man's function.

5. HARDING, R.W. "The Evolution of Roman Catholic Views of Private Property as a Natural Right" (1963), 2 Sol Q, 124: Aquinas's views about property are examined in order to show that for him the natural right of property was common ownership. The idea that private ownership is a natural right is said to be a later development and a departure from Aquinas's teachings.

6. BRODERICK, A. "The Radical Middle: The Natural Right of Property in Aquinas and the Popes" (1964), 3 Sol Q, 127: Aquinas's doctrine of property is explained so as to remove what is alleged to be R.W. Harding's misconception. The last section on the jurisprudential value of natural rights deals with value as guides to just enactments.

7. STONE, J. *Human Law and Human Justice*, (Stevens & Sons, Ltd, 1965), pp. 51–55: in these pages there is a brief and very general account of Aquinas's thought in relation to the development of Greek and Christian thinking.

8. *Southern Methodist University Studies in Jurisprudence*, (ed. A.L. Harding, SMU Press), I, (1954), chaps. 1–2: these deal respectively with Cicero's and Aquinas's concepts of law.

9. ULLMANN, W. "Baldus's Conception of Law" (1942), 58 LQR, 386: this is of general interest as giving the views of a 14th century scholar of natural law.

10. MONTROSE, J.L. "Edmund Burke and the Natural Law" in *Precedent in English Law and Other Essays*, (ed. H.G. Hanbury, Irish, U.P., Shannon, 1968), chap. 3: Burke, it is pointed out, was not an opponent of natural law. There is a distinction between the "classical" natural law (as taught by Aristotle and Aquinas) and "ideal" natural law, which is rationalism attempting to set up detailed norms deduced from reason and remain valid for all men and all times. Burke opposed the latter, but supported the former.

11. BLACKSTONE, W. *Commentaries on the Laws of England*, (16th ed., J.T. Coleridge,

T. Cadell and J. Butterworth & Son, 1825), I, pp. 38–43: the law of nature is the will of the Maker. There is also the revealed or divine law as found in the Scriptures. Human law should not contradict these. But Blackstone admitted that he knew of nothing that could invalidate an Act of Parliament (p. 91).

1. KANT, I. *The Philosophy of Law*, (trans. W. Hastie, T. & T. Clark, 1887): some of Kant's views, but not the full range of his thought on the subject, is to be found in this work.

2. COHEN, M.R. *Reason and Law*, (The Free Press, Glencoe, 1950), chap. 4: Kant's philosophy of law is explained. Kant accepts God, freedom and immortality. Law is a part of morality.

3. STONE, J. *Human Law and Human Justice*, (Stevens & Sons, Ltd, 1965), pp. 82–88: this gives a clear and convenient account of Kant's doctrines and the incorporation of his concept of justice in his concept of Law. The rest of the Chapter (chap. 3) discusses the development and weaknesses of the Kantian position.

4. HUME, D. *A Treatise on Human Nature*, in *The Philosophical Works of David Hume*, (edd. T.H. Green and J.H. Grose, Longmans, Green & Co, 1874): the idea of "reason" is considered with unrelenting logic and its ambiguities are exposed. He launched a devastating attack on the prevailing doctrines of natural law.

5. MORRIS, C. "Four 18th Century Theories of Jurisprudence" (1960–61), 14 Vand LR, 101: The views of Hume, Montesquieu, Rousseau and Kant are primarily dealt with, and there is mention of Bentham. See also *The Justification of the Law*, (University of Pennsylvania Press, 1971), esp. chap. 5, pp. 111–121.

6. GIERKE, O. *Natural Law and the Theory of Society, 1500–1800*, (trans. E. Barker, Cambridge University Press, 1950), especially chap. 1, Sect. V, s. 14; chap. 2, Sect II, s. 17: not only is the natural law theory of associations important for its own sake, but so are the introduction by Barker and Appendix 1 by Troeltsch. The former gives a very good account of the part played by natural law throughout the ages. The latter discusses the differences between German and Western European thought.

7. GIERKE, O. *Political Theories of the Middle Age*, (trans. F.W. Maitland, Cambridge University Press, 1900), especially chap. 9: the medieval theory is said to be dominated by the principle of unity and the supremacy of law.

8. POLLOCK, F. *Essays in the Law*, (Macmillan & Co, Ltd, 1922), chap. 2: the law of nature is an ultimate principle of fitness with regard to the nature of Man as a rational and social being, which is, or ought to be, the justification for every form of positive law. The doctrines of Aristotle, the Stoics, the Romans and medieval writers are outlined.

9. STAMMLER, R. *The Theory of Justice*, (trans. I. Husik, The Macmillan Co, New York, 1925): as a neo-Kantian Stammler seeks to find a universally valid method of just law. This enables him to evolve a "natural law with a changing content".

10. GINSBERG, M. "Stammler's Philosophy of Law" in *Modern Theories of Law*, (ed. W.I. Jennings, Oxford University Press, 1933), chap. 3: this is a convenient summary of Stammler's doctrine and an evaluation of it.

1. ALLEN, C.K. "Justice and Expediency" in *Interpretations of Modern Legal Philosophies*, (ed. P. Sayre, Oxford University Press, New York, 1947), chap. 1: there has to be a compromise between extremes of intellectual abstraction and realism. The views of Stammler, together with those of Geny and Pound, are considered.

2. ALLEN, C.K. *Law in the Making*, (7th ed., Oxford, 1964), pp. 8–27: the modern law of nature is relativistic. In the light of this, Stammler's "natural law with a variable content" is explained. There is mention also of J. Kohler, L. Duguit and the French Natural Law School.

3. STONE, J. *Human Law and Human Justice*, (Stevens & Sons, Ltd, 1965); pp. 167– 181: this gives a clear account of Stammler's difficult doctrine and of its relation to Kant's philosophy. The critique brings out the unpractical character of Stammler's thought, but also stresses its importance in 20th century thought.

4. STONE, J. *Human Law and Human Justice*, (Stevens & Sons, Ltd, 1965): chap. 7. This is a difficult but useful account of the versions of naturalist thinking since World War II. Of particular interest are the accounts of certain modern attempts to base some sort of natural law on existential tendencies. Such tendencies are the "facts" on which values can be grounded.

5. *Legal Philosophies of Lask, Radbruch and Dabin*, (trans. K. Wilk, Harvard University Press, 1950), Parts I and II: J. Dabin presents the modern Catholic doctrine of natural law. The view of G. Radbruch as contained here is not his final view. Since 1945 he has leaned towards a naturalist interpretation of law.

6. STONE, J. *Human Law and Human Justice*, (Stevens & Sons, Ltd, 1965), pp. 235–262: in these pages is to be found a full and sympathetic account of Radbruch's thought and its development. The earlier part of the chapter (chap. 8) serves as a prologue to modern relativist thinking, for which Radbruch is noted. Despite the possibility that in certain respects his post-1945 position is reconcileable with his earlier position, it is pointed out that there remain fundamental shifts.

7. FRIEDMANN, W. "Gustav Radbruch" (1960–61), 14 Vand LR, 191: this is a penetrating and understanding account of the life of Radbruch and the development of his thought.

8. DEL VECCHIO, G. *Formal Bases of Law*, (trans. J. Lisle, The Boston Book Co, 1914): this is a forceful attempt to rehabilitate natural law. The question whether and under what conditions a universal definition of law is possible is discussed at length.

9. DEL VECCHIO, G. *Philosophy of Law*, (trans. T.O. Martin, The Catholic University of America Press, 1953): from pp. 23–243: various theories from Greek times to the present are reviewed. In the second part the concept of law is examined. It is maintained that there is an unchangeable element in it.

10. COWAN, T.A. *The American Jurisprudence Reader*, (Oceana Publications, 1956), pp. 70–91: extracts are given from case-law and writings. The latter include those of Haines, Pound, Brown and Chroust.

Practical Contributions of Natural Law Theory

1. POUND, R. *The Spirit of the Common Law*, (Marshall Jones Co, 1921), chap. 4: the rights of Man are considered with reference to the needs of successive ages. In England there was a tendency to identify common law rights with natural rights.

2. RADCLIFFE, C.J. *The Law and its Compass*, (Faber & Faber, Ltd, 1961): Christianity has been abandoned as the source of common law ideology, but there has to be some compass by which the law guides its course. Contact with natural law theory should not be lost.

3. DOWRICK, F.E. *Justice According to the English Common Lawyers*, (Butterworths, 1961), chap. 4: the theological interpretation of natural law is explained first, and then its influence on English law. St. German's ideas follow Aquinas closely.

4. VINOGRADOFF, P. *Collected Papers*, (Oxford, 1928), II, chap. 9: the first part deals with reason as discussed by St. German; the second part deals with conscience and equity.

5. KEETON, G.W. "Natural Justice in English Law" (1955), 8 CLP, 24: the influence of ideas about natural justice is illustrated with reference to case-law.

6. AMES, J.B. *Lectures on Legal History and Miscellaneous Legal Essays*, (Harvard University Press, 1913), 435: the old principle of strict responsibility is said to be "unmoral" (*quaere*, whether it seemed so at the time). The development towards the fault principle is regarded as following a moral principle.

7. ST. GERMAN, C. *The Doctor and Student: Dialogue between a Doctor of Divinity and a Student in the Laws of England*, (17th ed., W. Muchall, 1787), Dialogue I, chaps. 1, 2, 4, 5 and 16: there is an initial account of the Thomist system. This is followed in chap. 5 by an explanation of the way in which reason operates in English law.

8. SLESSER, H. *The Judicial Office and Other Matters*, (Hutchinson & Co, Ltd, 1943), chap. 3: where there is no rule a judge applies a sociological and a transcendental method. He is influenced by Christianity and natural law. (See also H. SLESSER: *The Administration of Law*, (Hutchinson's University Library, 1949), chap. 4, for a shorter version).

9. O'SULLIVAN, R. "The Philosophy of the Common Law" (1949), 2 CLP, 116: this purports to show that the common law has been nourished by Christian philosophy and theology.

10. Le FROY, A.H.F. "The Basis of Case-Law" (1906), 22 LQR, 293, 416: the considerations underlying case-law are examined in detail. Among these are naturalist concepts, such as justice and reason.

11. HOLDSWORTH, W.S. *A History of English Law*, (Methuen & Co, Ltd), II, 602: in this short Appendix the law of nature is discussed in relation to the common law.

12. STRAUSS, L. *Natural Right and History*, (University of Chicago Press, 1953): natural rights are classified as Socratic, Platonic, Aristotelian and Thomist. The

history of natural rights is traced from the Stoic idea to the 19th century. The views of Hobbes, Locke, Rousseau and Burke are considered in the latter part of the book.

1. JONES, J.W. "Acquired and Guaranteed Rights" in *Cambridge Legal Essays*, (edd. P.H. Winfield and A.D. McNair, Heffer & Sons, Ltd, 1926), 223: the basis and origins of natural right are considered historically.

2. RITCHIE, D.G. *Natural Rights*, (Allen & Unwin, Ltd, 1894): various systems of natural rights are discussed in detail. Part I deals with the theory behind them; Part II with individual rights. The author warns that abstract theories are always open to divergent interpretations.

3. O'SULLIVAN, R. "The Bond of Freedom" (1943), 6 MLR, 177: this is a plea for a return to natural law theory. The great creative effort of the common law is said to have been the achievement of freedom – the creation of the *liber homo*.

4. O'MEARA, J. "Natural Law and Everyday Law" (1960), 5 Nat LF, 83: Natural Law is not an arbiter of legal validity, but it can provide ethical guidance in the day by day application of law. Judges should resort to fundamental ethical considerations in applying their discretion.

5. CORWIN, E.S. "The 'Higher Law' Background of American Constitutional Law" (1928–29), 42 Harv LR, 149, 365: the supremacy of the Constitution is partly due to the belief that it embodies certain principles of right and justice, which are entitled to prevail *ex proprio vigore*. The origin of these is examined at length with reference to the Greeks, Cicero, their development in the Middle Ages and in the common law. The work of Locke and Coke, in particular, is dealt with at length.

6. HUMPHREYS, R.A. "The Rule of Law and the American Revolution" (1937), 53 LQR, 80: the claim to omnipotence by the British Parliament was met by the argument that Parliament itself was subject to the rule of law, i.e., natural law.

7. GRANT, J.A.C. "The Natural Law Background of Due Process" (1931), 31 Col LR, 56: the theme of this article is similar to the above, but it is concerned more specifically with judicial interpretation of "due process".

8. HOGAN, H.J. "The Supreme Court and Natural Law" (1968), 54 Am BAJ, 570: the old ideas of natural law are now discredited. This is the era of state power and there is now more than ever a need for the expression of social conscience. It is argued that the Supreme Court is the body best fitted to do this.

9. REUSCHLEIN, H.G. *Jurisprudence – its American Prophets*, (The Bobbs-Merrill Co, Inc, 1951), pp. 5–28; 342–404: the Puritans brought to America the view that the true laws are God's laws, and this gave rise to the rights of Man as embodied in the Constitution. In the latter section the modern idea of a "higher" law is considered.

10. WRIGHT, B.F. *American Interpretations of Natural Law*, (Harvard University Press, 1931): the views of different American writers since the 17th century are surveyed. A distinction is drawn between natural law as a description of existing order and as a prescription for what ought to be.

1. WRIGHT, R.A. "Natural Law and International Law" in *Interpretations of Modern Legal Philosophies*, (ed. P. Sayre, Oxford University Press, New York, 1947), chap. 33: this article stresses the importance of viewing international law, not as positive law, but as based on fundamental principles.

The Validity of Unjust Law

2. HART, H.L.A. "Positivism and the Separation of Law and Morals" (1957–58), 71 Harv LR, 593: the positivist case is clarified and certain misconceptions about it removed. The arguments of the naturalists are considered and rejected.

3. HART, H.L.A. *The Concept of Law*, (Oxford, Clarendon Press, 1961, reprinted 1975), chap. 9: the relationship between law and morality is considered point by point, and the positivist position is defended.

4. FULLER, L.L. "Positivism and Fidelity to Law – a Reply to Professor Hart" (1957–58), 71 Harv LR, 630: Fuller takes issue with Hart. In this detailed and spirited reply the points made by Hart are answered. It is one of the best expositions of the naturalist position.

5. FULLER, L.L. *The Morality of Law*, (revised ed., Yale University Press, 1969): "Law is the enterprise of subjecting human conduct to the governance of rules". On this basis eight conditions are laid down without which no system can continue as a system. These eight comprise the "inner" morality of law. The "external" morality concerns policies and ideals which guide the development of law, but there can be no "law" in the sense indicated unless the desiderata of its "inner" morality are present. This "inner" morality is largely indifferent to "external" morality, except where the aims tend to impair the "inner" morality.

6. SUMMERS, R.S. "Professor Fuller on Morality and Law" in *More Essays in Legal Philosophy. General Assessments of Legal Philosophies*, (ed. R.S. Summers, Oxford, 1971; reprinted from (1966), 18 JLE, 1), 101: this is a highly critical review of Fuller's *The Morality of Law*. The author points out the inadequacies of the distinction between moral duties and moral aspirations and of a theory of law in terms of purpose alone. Such a one neglects how legal institutions come to be, structure and the role of force. The eight ways of making law fail overlook other crucial ways in which failure may occur.

7. JENKINS, I. "The Matchmaker, or Towards a Synthesis of Legal Idealism and Positivism" (1959–60), 12 JLE, 1: positivists and idealists are participants in a common enterprise and they differ only in the contributions which they respectively make. Positivists assert the distinctness of law, not its isolation or self-sufficiency. Idealists stress the mutual relevance of the "is" and the "ought" because law is a means to an end.

8. RUBEN, D-H. "Positive and Natural Law Revisited" (1972), 49 The Modern Schoolman 295: there is a normative use of "obligation" – if a man has an obligation this constitutes a reason for obeying (moral obligation); and a descriptive use – a man's case falls under a social rule (legal obligation). If "obligation" is understood in the normative sense, as Blackstone and Fuller do, it is necessary to build moral criteria into the definition of law; if it is understood in the descriptive sense, it is not necessary to do this. On grounds of linguistic usage the author prefers the latter usage.

1. PAPPE, H.O. "On the Validity of the Judicial Decisions in the Nazi Era" (1960), 23 MLR, 260: this is primarily a demonstration of a misapprehension that underlies the Hart-Fuller controversy (*supra*). It is shown that they both proceed on a misreport of a decision by a German court: the court did not hold a certain enactment of the Nazi government to be void.

2. BODENHEIMER, E. "Significant Developments in German Legal Philosophy since 1945" (1954), 3 AJCL, 379: since the collapse of the Nazi regime with its extremely positivist attitude, there has been a revival of a value philosophy. In this connection the alteration in Radbruch's views is discussed.

3. von HIPPEL, E. Note in (1959), 4 Nat LF, 106: the attitude of German courts both before and after 1945 is commented on. Radbruch is alleged to have turned "about face" since 1945. The rejection of positivism and the growth of naturalist principles is illustrated. See also Note by J. MESSNER, *ibid*, p. 101.

4. KAUFMANN, A. and HASSEMER, W. "Criteria of Justice" (1971), 4 Ottawa LR, 403: there is an important distinction between legal theory and legal philosophy. For the former the criteria of rightness are proper principles of interpreting and applying existing law; it assumes, however, that the law is binding. Legal philosophy makes no such assumption, since the existing law is itself judged. The criteria for this are those of justice.

5. VAN NIEKERK, B. "The Warning Voice from Heidelberg – the Life and Thought of Gustav Radbruch" (1973), 90 SALJ, 234: certain rights merit absolute respect. The end never justifies abhorrent means, nor is every law deserving of obedience merely because it is law. Radbruch favoured the classical approach to natural law and called on judges and lawyers to deny to statutes conflicting with natural law efficacy and if necessary the quality of "law". The paper reviews the influence of his thought on some post-War German cases.

6. HOWE, M. de W. "The Positivism of Mr Justice Holmes" (1950–51), 64 Harv LR, 529: Holmes is defended against the charge that it is his type of positivism that enables regimes like Nazism to arise. Holmes, it is said, never did make a rigid separation of "is" and "ought". To him the ultimate source of law lay in the moral sentiments of the community.

7. CARPENTER, R.V. "The Problem of Value Judgments as Norms of Law" (1954–55), 7 JLE, 163: the thesis is that positivism gives rise to regimes like that of Nazi Germany. For a vigorous answer to this charge, see G.O.W. MUELLER: "The Problem of Value Judgments as Norms of the Law: the Answer of a Positivist", *ibid*, 567.

8. FULLER, L.L. *Law in Quest of Itself*, (The Foundation Press, Inc, 1940): the positivist separation of the "is" from the "ought" is not possible, for the moral "ought" enters into every legal activity. This is the underlying theme of the book.

9. FULLER, L.L. "American Legal Philosophy at Mid-century" (1953–54), 6 JLE, 457, at pp. 467 *et seq*.: purpose is a fact and a standard for judging facts. Therefore, the separation of the "is" and the "ought" and the idea that one cannot derive a statement about what ought to be from a statement of what exists are both said to be false assumptions. If a thing is to achieve a certain end, it has to function in a certain way. Therefore, ends and means are closely connected.

1. MARITAIN, J. *The Rights of Man and Natural Law*, (Geoffrey Bles, The Centenary Press, 1944): this short essay reviews the position of the individual in society. One of its characteristics is its intrinsic morality and an unjust law is not "law".

2. COHEN, M.R. "Positivism and the Limits of Idealism in the Law" (1927), 27 Col LR, 237: the law cannot be divorced from what it ought to be. The ideal and the actual are inseparable, but never completely identifiable. The limits of idealism are considered.

3. COHEN, M.R. *Reason and Nature*, (Kegan Paul, Trench & Trubner & Co, Ltd, 1931), Part III, chap. 4: the above theme is developed in greater detail.

4. MacGUIGAN, M.R. "Law, Morals, and Positivism" (1961), 14 UTLJ, 1: the separation between law and morals is examined historically. It is not morals, but the law, that suffers from such a separation, for it removes the moral support behind law.

5. LUMB, R.D. "Natural Law and Legal Positivism" (1958–59), 11 JLE, 503, 508–12: the relation between the legal and moral "ought" is considered. It is suggested that the theorist should rightly be concerned with the impact of morals on law and vice versa, but that he should concern himself, first, with law as it is and then with values.

6. CHLOROS, A.G. "Some Aspects of the Social and Ethical Element in Analytical Jurisprudence" (1955), 67 Jur R, 79: the purpose of this article is to expose some of the arbitrary assumptions, which it is asserted, underlie Austin's analytical jurisprudence. There is an ethical principle beneath it in the form of an "intellectual natural law". A parallel is drawn between Platonic theory of Forms and certain aspects of Analytical Jurisprudence.

7. BRECHT, A. "The Myth of *Is* and *Ought*" (1940–41), 54 Harv LR, 811: the history of the separation between the "is" and the "ought" is first considered. But it is maintained that by examining one's own inner processes it is possible to discover some natural or biological "is" which directs one towards an ethical "ought". In this way it would be possible to establish a factual link between the "is" and the "ought". Phenomenology is the method of doing this. Feeling something as an "ought" is part of human equipment. This "ought" is a datum of the word "is".

8. STUMPF, S.E. "Austin's Theory of the Separation of Law and Morals" (1960–61), 14 Vand LR, 117: the article begins by explaining the positivist case and that Austin did not deny the influence of morals. But the very concept of law is meaningless until the nature of man is brought into consideration. It is alleged that Austin himself contemplated implicitly the moral characteristics of law and sovereignty.

9. SMITH, J.C. "Law, Language, and Philosophy" (1968), 3 U Br Col LR, 59: after reviewing the attitude to language of various legal philosophers, the linguistic background of the positivist-naturalist controversy is set out in its different aspects. The paper is explanatory rather than conclusive.

10. SAMEK, R.S. *The Legal Point of View*, (Philosophical Library, New York, 1974): chapters 10–12: positivists are right in saying that moral standards are not directly relevant to the solution of legal problems, but they are wrong in rejecting

them. If morality does help to shape law, there is need for a permanent relation between law and morality. The views of Professors Hart and Fuller are considered, and in particular the former's "minimum morality" is severely criticised.

1. LLOYD, D. *The Idea of Law*, (Penguin Books, Ltd, A 688, 1964), pp. 102–105, 111–15: the question of the validity of law is discussed briefly in the context of a general discussion of positivism. Positivism is defended against the charge that it has fostered the growth of dictatorships, and the assertion that absolute moral values do exist is also considered.

2. MEYER, P. "Justice in Politics" in *Legal Essays. A Tribute to Frede Castberg*, (Universitetsforlaget, 1963), 125: there is a middle way between positivism and natural law, depending upon the way in which values can be important in social administration.

3. CRABB, J.H. "Airing a Couple of Myths about Natural Law" (1964), 39 NDL, 137: two misconceptions are considered. One is that natural law is a peculiarly Roman Catholic conception; the other is that natural law "exists" as some kind of law superior to statute and case-law.

4. TAYLOR, R. "Law and Morality" (1968), 43 NYULR, 611: in answering the question "what is a law?" the author insists on the separation between laws and morality. They can be re-united if one considers law as an activity, for then the end in view becomes relevant.

Bibliographical index

Note:- References are to page numbers. Figures in brackets indicate the paragraph number on a particular page. Thus "24(3)" indicates paragraph (3) on page 24.

353

BENAS, B.B. "Problems for the Conveyancer. The Construction of Statutes" (1952) 102 LJ 269 ... 132(11)

BENNION, F.A.R. "Copyright and the Statute of Westminster" (1961) 24 MLR 355 ... 56(6)

BENTHAM, J. *A Comment on the Commentaries* (ed. C.W. Everett) 120(6), 135(10)

BENTHAM, J. *A Fragment on Government* in *Works* (ed. J. Bowring) ... 46(9), 302(6)

BENTHAM, J. *An Introduction to the Principles of Morals and Legislation* (edd. J.H. Burns and H.L.A. Hart) ... 2(3), 176(1), 302(6), 304(4)(8), 305(11)

BENTHAM, J. "Nomography, or the Art of Inditing Laws" in *Works* (ed. J. Bowring) ... 235(1)

BENTHAM, J. *Of Laws in General* (ed. H.L.A. Hart) ... 20(4), 120(7), 136(1), 172(3), 206(8), 243(7)

BENTHAM, J. *The Limits of Jurisprudence Defined* (ed. C.W. Everett) ... 2(4), 172(3), 206(8), 243(7), 246(3), 305(11)

BENTHAM, J. *Theory of Fictions* (2nd ed. C.K. Ogden) ... 12(3)

BENTHAM, J. *The Theory of Legislation* (trans. R. Hildreth) ... 302(7), 342(3)

BENTHAM, J. *Works* (ed. J. Bowring) ... 30(6), 46(9), 172(4), 207(1), 212(11), 235(1), 302(6)

Bentham and Legal Theory (ed. M.H. James) ... 244(5)(6), 303(4), 304(1)

BENTIL, K.J. "The Court of Appeal's Adherence to its Jurisprudence" (1974), 124 LJ, 733 ... 85(9)

BENTWICH, N. "The Jurisdiction of the Privy Council" (1964) 114 LJ 67 ... 88(7)

BERGER, R. *"Doctor Bonham's Case:* Statutory Construction or Constitutional Theory?" (1969) 117 U Pa LR 521 ... 47(9)

BERLE, A.A. "The Theory of Enterprise Entity" (1947) 47 Col LR 343 ... 201(3)

BERLE, A.A. and MEANS, G.C. *The Modern Corporation and Private Property* ... 189(8), 216(7)

BERLIN, I. *Two Concepts of Liberty* ... 68(5)

BERMAN, H.J. "Commercial Contracts in Soviet Law" (1947) 35 Calif. LR 191 ... 291(4)

BERMAN, H.J. *Justice in the U.S.S.R. An Interpretation of Soviet Law* ... 285(4)

BERMAN, H.J. "Principles of Soviet Criminal Law" (1946–47) 56 Yale LJ 803 ... 290(7)

BERMAN, H.J. "Soviet Family Law in the Light of Russian History and Marxist Theory" (1946–47) 56 Yale LJ 26 ... 291(6)

BERMAN, H.J. "Soviet Law and Government" (1958) 21 MLR 19 ... 286(4)

BERMAN, H.J. "The Challenge of Soviet Law" (1948–49) 62 Harv LR 220, 449 ... 286(6)

BERMAN, H.J. "The Educational Role of the Soviet Court" (1972) 21 ICLQ 81 ... 285(5)

BERMAN, H.T. *The Nature and Functions of Law* ... 93(9)

BEST, W.M. "Codification of the Laws of England" (1856) Trans. Jur. S. 209 ... 237(12)

BEUTEL, F.K. "Some Implications of Experimental Jurisprudence" (1934–35) 48 Harv. LR 169 ... 325(7)

BEUTEL, F.K. *Some Potentialities of Experimental Jurisprudence as a New Branch of Social Science* ... 325(8)

BEUTEL, F.K. "The Necessity of a New Technique of Interpreting the N.I.L. (Uniform Negotiable Instruments Law) - the Civil Law Analogy" (1931–32) 6 Tul LR 1 ... 125(9)

BIENENFELD, F.R. *Rediscovery of Justice* ... 37(5)

BIGELOW, M.M. *The Law of Torts* (3rd ed.) ... 23(2), 184(8)

BIGGS, J.M. *The Concept of Matrimonial Cruelty* ... 183(9)

BINGHAM, J.W. "Legal Philosophy and the Law" (1914) 9 Ill LR 98 ... 323(1)

BINGHAM, J.W. "Some Suggestions Concerning 'Legal Cause' at Common Law" (1909) 9 Col LR 16, 136 ... 153(3), 180(12)

BINGHAM, J.W. "The Nature and Importance of Legal Possession" (1915) 13 Mich LR 534, 623 . . . 205(2)

BINGHAM, J.W. "The Nature of Legal Rights and Duties" (1913) 12 Mich LR 1 . . . 322(9)

BINGHAM, J.W. "What is the Law?" (1912) 11 Mich. LR 1, 109 . . . 322(9)

BIRNBAUM, H.F. "*Stare Decisis* vs. Judicial Activism. Nothing Succeeds like Success" (1968) 54 Am BAJ 482 . . . 87(3)

BISHOP, W.W. "The International Rule of Law" (1960–61) 59 Mich LR 553 . . . 157(6)

BLACK, D.J. "The Boundaries of Legal Sociology" (1971–72) 81 Yale LJ 1086 . . . 299(1)

BLACK, M. *Language and Philosophy* . . . 16(6)

BLACKSHIELD, A.R. "Five Types of Judicial Decision" (1974), 12 Os HLJ, 539 . . . 95(7)

BLACKSTONE, W. *Commentaries on the Laws of England* (16th ed.) . . . 46(4), 79(4), 120(5), 135(8), 188(5), 344(11)

BLOM-COOPER, L.J. and DREWRY, G.R. *Final Appeal – a Study of the House of Lords in its Judicial Capacity* . . . 86(2)

BLOM-COOPER, L.J. and DREWRY, G.R. "The House of Lords: Reflections on the Social Utility of Final Appellate Courts" (1969) 32 MLR 262 . . . 86(1)

BLOOM, H. "Law Commission: Interpretation of Statutes" (1970), 33 MLR, 197 . . . 115(2)

BOBER, M.M. *Karl Marx's Interpretation of History* (2nd ed.) . . . 282(5)

BOBERG, P.Q.R. "Reflection on the *Novus Actus Interveniens* Concept" (1959) 76 SALJ 280 . . . 181(12)

BODENHEIMER, E. *Jurisprudence* . . . 7(2), 17(7), 35(3), 42(2), 120(2), 137(7), 242(8), 248(8), 265(4), 275(6), 293(4), 313(4), 329(6), 336(7)

BODENHEIMER, E. "Law as Order and Justice" (1957) 6 JPL 194 . . . 35(6)

BODENHEIMER, E. "Modern Analytical Jurisprudence and the Limits of its Usefulness" (1955–56) 104 U Pa LR 1080 . . . 13(2)

BODENHEIMER, E. "Philosophical Anthropology and the Law" (1971) 59 Calif LR, 653 . . . 281(2)

BODENHEIMER, E. "Power and Law: a Study of the Concept of Law" (1939–40) 50 Ethics, 127 . . . 265(5)

BODENHEIMER, E. "Significant Developments in German Legal Philosophy since 1945" (1954) 3 AJCL 379 . . . 350(2)

BODENHEIMER, E. "The Impasse of Soviet Legal Philosophy" (1952–53) 38 Corn LQ 51 . . . 285(8)

BODENHEIMER, E. "The Province of Jurisprudence" (1960–61) 46 Corn LQ 1 . . . 36(9)

BOGGS, A.A. "Proximate Cause in the Law of Tort" (1910) 44 Am LR 88 . . . 180(11)

BOHLEN, F.H. "Fifty Years of Torts" (1936–37) 50 Harv LR 725, 1225 . . . 157(10)

BOHLEN, F.H. "Incomplete Privilege to Inflict Intentional Invasions of Interests of Property and Personality" (1925–26) 39 Harv LR 307 . . . 23(3)

BOHLEN, F.H. "Mixed Questions of Law and Fact" (1924) 72 U Pa LR 111 . . . 157(9)

BOHLEN, F.H. *Studies in the Law of Torts* . . . 158(1), 180(1), 185(8), 295(6)

BOND, H. "Possession in the Roman Law" (1890) 6 LQR 259 . . . 205(6)

BONDY, O. "Hans Kelsen's Relativistic Approach to Ethics" in *Law, State and International Legal Order. Essays in Honor of Hans Kelsen* (edd. S. Engel and R.A. Métall), p. 51 . . . 264(3)

BONNECASE, J. "The Problem of Legal Interpretation in France" (1930) 12 JCL (ser. 3) 79 . . . 126(5)

BONNER, G.A. "Statute Law – a Proposal for Reform" (1976) 73 LS Gaz 747 . . . 236(3)

BORCHARD, E.M. "Governmental Responsibility in Tort" (1926–27) 36 Yale LJ at pp. 774–780 . . . 189(3)

BORCHARD, E.M. "Some Lessons from the Civil Law" (1916) 64 U Pa LR 570 . . . 111(1)

BORRIE, G. "Judicial Conflicts of Interest in Britain" (1970), 18 AJCL, 697 . . . 162(4)

BOURKE, J.P. "Damages: Culpability and Causation" (1956) 30 Aust LJ 283 . . . 182(6)

BOURKE, V.J. "Natural Law, Thomism – and Professor Nielsen" (1960) 5 Nat LF 112 . . . 344(3)

BOWKER, W.F. "Basic Rights and Freedoms: What are they?" (1959) 37 Can BR 43 . . . 309(7)

BOWLE, J. *Western Political Thought* . . . 42(7)

BOYNTON, P.A. "The Season of Fiction is Over: a Study of the 'Original Position' in John Rawls' *A Theory of Justice*" (1977) 15 Os HLJ 215 . . . 34(4)

BRADLEY, F.E. "Modern Legislation in the United Kingdom" (1894) 10 LQR 32 . . . 116(4)

BRANDEN, N. "Free Will, Moral Responsibility and the Law" (1969) 42 Southern Calif LR 264 . . . 175(9)

BRAY, J.J. "Law, Liberty and Morality" (1971), 45 Aust LJ, 452 . . . 73(9), 227(5)

BRAY, J.J. "The Juristic Basis of the Law Relating to Offences against Public Morality and Decency" (1972), 46 Aust LJ, 100 . . . 73(10)

BRAYBROOKE, E.K. "Custom as Source of English Law" (1951) 50 Mich LR 71 . . . 135(2)

BRAZIER, M. "Judicial Immunity and the Independence of the Judiciary" (1976) PL 397 . . . 48(7)

BRAZIER, R. "Overruling House of Lords Criminal Cases" (1973), Crim LR, 98 . . . 87(9)

BRECHT, A. "The Myth of *Is* and *Ought*" (1940–41) 54 Harv LR 811 . . . 241(5), 351(7)

BRETT, P. *An Essay on a Contemporary Jurisprudence* . . . 4(3), 105(8), 176(8)

BRETT, P. "The Implications of Science for the Law" (1972), 18 McGill LJ, 170 . . . 145(6)

BRIDGE, J.W. "The Academic Lawyer: mere Working Mason or Architect?" (1975), 91 LQR 488 . . . 7(6)

BRIERLEY, J.E.C., DAVID, R. and *Major Legal Systems in the World Today* . . . 282(4)

BRINTON, H. "Morals and Law" (1972), 136 JPJ, 251 . . . 71(6)

British Philosophy in Mid-Century (ed. C.A. Mace) . . . 15(6), 16(6)

BROADHURST, S. "Is Copyright a Chose in Action?" (1895) 11 LQR 64 . . . 214(1)

BRODERICK, A. "Hauriou's Institutional Theory: an Invitation to Common Law Jurisprudence" (1965) 4 Sol Q 281 . . . 201(2), 313(1)

BRODERICK, A. "The Radical Middle: The Natural Right of Property in Aquinas and the Popes" (1964) 3 Sol Q 127 . . . 216(6), 344(6)

BROOKFIELD, F.M. "The Courts, Kelsen and the Rhodesian Revolution" (1969), 19 UTLJ, 326 . . . 62(3), 266(3)

BROTHWOOD, M. "Parliamentary Sovereignty and U.K. Entry" (1968) 118 New LJ 415 . . . 63(8)

BROWN, B.F. "Natural Law: Dynamic Basis of Law and Morals in the Twentieth Century" (1957) 31 Tul LR 491 . . . 340(5)

BROWN, J.M. "A Note on Professor Oakeshott's Introduction to the Leviathan" (1953) 1 Pol S 53 . . . 41(1)

BROWN, J.R. "Electronic Brains and the Legal Mind: Computing the Data Computer's Collision with Law" (1961–62) 71 Yale LJ 239 . . . 327(5)

BROWN, L.N. "Cruelty without Culpability or Divorce without Fault" (1963) 26 MLR 625 . . . 184(4)

BROWN, L.N. "The Offence of Wilful Neglect to Maintain a Wife" (1960) 23 MLR 1 . . . 184(3)

BROWN, L.N. "The Sources of Spanish Civil Law" (1956) 5 ICLQ 364 . . . 113(11)

BROWN, R. "A Comment on L.J. Mac-Farlane's 'Justifying Rebellion: Black and White Nationalism in Rhodesia'" [1968] 6 J Comm PS 155 . . . 61(10)

COHEN, M.R. *Reason and Nature* . . .
15(4), 351(3)

COHEN, M.R. "The Place of Logic in
the Law" (1916–17) 29 Harv LR
622 . . . 94(8)

COHEN, M.R. "The Process of Judicial
Legislation" (1914) 48 Am LR 161
. . . 102(11), 117(7), 121(8)

COHEN, M.R. and COHEN, F.S.
*Readings in Jurisprudence and Legal
Philosophy* . . . 43(10), 121(8), 217(1),
276(9), 281(6)

COHN, E.J. "Precedents in Continental
Law" (1935) 5 CLJ 366 . . . 112(6)

COHN, E.J. and SIMITIS, C. "'Lifting
the Veil' in the Company Law of the
European Continent" (1963) 12
ICLQ 189 . . . 193(7)

COHN, H. "Praelegomena to the Theory
and History of Jewish Law" in *Essays
in Jurisprudence in Honor of Roscoe
Pound* (ed. R.A. Newman) 44 . . .
38(5)

COING, H. "Bentham's Influence on
the Development of *Interessenjurisprudenz* and General Jurisprudence" (1967) 2 Ir Jur (NS) 336 . . .
304(5)

COLE, R.H. "Windfall and Probability:
a Study of 'Cause' in Negligence Law"
(1964) 52 Calif LR 459 . . . 179(8)

COLE, W.G. "Private Morality and
Public Law" (1968) 54 Am BAJ
158 . . . 227(3)

COLLARD, D. "State Arbitration in
the U.S.S.R." (1955) 18 MLR 474
. . . 291(5)

COMMONS, J.R. *Legal Foundations of
Capitalism* . . . 24(7)

COMMONS, J.R. "Value in Law and
Economics" in *Law: A Century of
Progress* II, 332 . . . 295(4)

Comparative Judicial Behaviour (edd.
G. Schubert and D. Danielski) . . .
326(6)

Computers and Privacy, Cmnd, 6353,
6354 . . . 222(6)

COMTE, A. *The Positive Philosophy*
(trans. H. Martineau) . . . 243(4)

CONANT, M. "Systems Analysis in the
Appellate Decision-making Process"
(1970), 24 Rutgers LR, 293 . . .
149(6)

CONARD, A.F. "New Ways to Write
Laws" (1947) 56 Yale LJ 458 . . .
235(6)

Congenital Disabilities (Civil Liability)
Act, 1976 . . . 187(9)

CONQUEST, R. *Justice and the Legal
System in the U.S.S.R.* . . . 287(3)

COOK, W.W. "Act, Intention and Motive
in the Criminal Law" (1916–17)
26 Yale LJ 645 . . . 176(6), 183(8)

COOK, W.W. "'Facts' and 'Statements
of Facts'" (1936–37) 4 UCLR 233
. . . 11(8)

COOK, W.W. "Hohfeld's Contribution
to the Science of Law" in W.N.
Hohfeld, *Fundamental Legal Conceptions as Applied in Judicial Reasoning*
(ed. W.W. Cook) . . . 20(2), 25(8),
26(1), 211(4)

COOK, W.W. *Lectures on Legal Topics*
. . . 8(2), 24(1), 211(5)

COOK, W.W. "Note on the Associated
Press Case" (1918–19) 28 Yale LJ
387 . . . 24(3)

COOK, W.W. "Privileges of Labor
Unions in the Struggle for Life"
(1917–18) 27 Yale LJ 779 . . . 24(2)

COOK, W.W. "Scientific Method and
the Law" (1927) 13 Am BAJ 303 . . .
7(1), 331(9)

COOK, W.W. "Statements of Facts in
Pleading under the Codes" (1921)
21 Col LR 416 . . . 11(8)

COOK, W.W. "The Alienability of
Choses in Action" (1916) 29 Harv
LR 816 . . . 24(4)

COOK, W.W. "The Alienability of
Choses in Action: a Reply to
Professor Williston" (1917) 30 Harv
LR 449 . . . 24(4)

COOK, W.W. "The Logical and Legal
Bases of the Conflict of Laws"
(1923–24) 33 Yale LJ 457 . . . 15(9),
99(1), 323(4)

COOK, W.W. "The Utility of Jurisprudence
in the Solution of Legal Problems" in
Lectures on Legal Topics 338 . . . 8(2),
24(1), 211(5)

COOK, W.W., LLEWELLYN, K.N.,
ADLER, M.J., – –, "Law and the
Modern Mind: a Symposium" (1931)
31 Col LR 83 . . . 321(8)

DENMAN, D.R. *Origins of Ownership* . . . 212(7)

DENNING, A.T. "Giving Life to the Law" (1976) 1 Malaya LR ciii . . . 147(7)

DENNING, A.T. "Law in a Developing Community" (1955) 33 PA 1 . . . 158(5)

DENNING, A.T. *The Changing Law* . . . 76(4), 144(8)

DENNING, A.T. "The Independence and Impartiality of the Judges" (1954) 71 SALJ 345 . . . 162(2)

DENNING, A.T. "The Independence of the Judges" *Presidential Address to the Holdsworth Club* (1950) . . . 162(1)

DENNING, A.T. "The Need for a New Equity" (1952) 5 CLP 1 . . . 230(2)

DENNING, A.T. *The Road to Justice* . . . 78(6), 161(1), 162(2), 172(1)

DENNING, A.T. "The Way of an Iconoclast" (1959) 5 JSPTL (NS) 77 . . . 147(6), 230(3)

d'ENTREVES, A.P. *Natural Law* . . . 337(1)

de PINNA, L.A. "Marginal Notes and Statutes" (1964) 114 LJ 3 . . . 129(10)

de PINNA, L.A. "Schedules to Statutes" (1964) 114 LJ 519 . . . 129(10)

DERHAM, D.P. "Precedent and the Decision of Particular Questions" (1963) 79 LQR 49 . . . 91(1)

de SLOOVÈRE, F.J. "Extrinsic Aids in the Interpretation of Statutes" (1940) 88 U Pa LR 527 . . . 132(4)

de SLOOVÈRE, F.J. "The Functions of Judge and Jury in the Interpretation of Statutes" (1932–33) 46 Harv LR 1086 . . . 120(1)

de SMITH, S.A. *Judicial Review and Administrative Action* . . . 125(6)

de SMITH, S.A. Note in (1956) 19 MLR 541 . . . 129(3)

de SMITH, S.A. "Statutory Restriction of Judicial Review" (1955) 18 MLR 575 . . . 125(5)

de SMITH, S.A. "The Constitution and the Common Market: a Tentative Appraisal" (1971) 34 MLR 597 . . . 64(9)

de SMITH, S.A. "The Limits of Judicial Review: Statutory Discretions and the Doctrine of Ultra Vires" (1948) 11 MLR 306 . . . 125(4)

DEUTSCH, J.G. "Precedent and Adjudication" (1973–74) 83 Yale LJ 1553 . . . 98(4)

DEVLIN, P. "Judges and Lawmakers" (1976) 39 MLR 1 . . . 104(8), 122(3)

DEVLIN, P. "Law and Morals" *Presidential Address to the Holdsworth Club* (1961) . . . 71(8)

DEVLIN, P. "Law, Democracy and Morals" (1962) 110 U Pa LR 635 . . . 71(8)

DEVLIN, P. "Mill on Liberty in Morals" in *The Enforcement of Morals* chap. 6 . . . 68(3)

DEVLIN, P. *Samples of Law Making* . . . 130(3), 140(2), 156(7)

DEVLIN, P. "The Common Law, Public Policy and the Executive" in *Samples of Law Making* chap. 6 . . . 156(7)

DEVLIN, P. *The Enforcement of Morals* . . . 68(3), 71(9)

DEVLIN, P. "The Enforcement of Morals", *Maccabaean Lecture in Jurisprudence of the British Academy* . . . 71(7), 72(1)

DEVLIN, P. "The Process of Law Reform" (1966) 63 LS Gaz 453 . . . 232(8)

de VRIES, H.P., DAVID, R. and *The French Legal System* . . . 111(9)

de WAAL, C.H. Note in [1959] CLJ 173 . . . 130(6)

DEWEY, J. "Austin's Theory of Sovereignty" (1894) 9 Pol Sc Q 31 . . . 256(5)

DEWEY, J. *How we Think* . . . 11(4), 96(3)

DEWEY, J. "Logical Method and Law" (1924) 10 Corn LQ 17 . . . 96(4), 333(3)

DEWEY, J. *Philosophy and Civilisation* . . . 200(7), 341(7)

DEWEY, J. "The Historical Background of Corporate Personality" (1925–26) 35 Yale LJ 655 . . . 200(6)

DEWEY, J. *The Quest for Certainty* . . . 333(3)

DIAMOND, A.L. "Codification of the Law of Contract" (1968) 31 MLR 361 . . . 116(8), 239(3)

DIAMOND, A.L. "Repeal and Desuetude of Statutes" (1975) 28 CLP 107 . . . 131(10)

ESTEP, S.D. "The Legislative Process and the Rule of Law: Attempts to Legislate Taste in Moral and Political Beliefs" (1960–61) 59 Mich LR 575 . . . 157(6)

EVANS, F. "Law Reporting: a Reporter's View" (1904) 20 LQR 88 . . . 81(12)

EVERETT, C.W. *The Education of Jeremy Bentham* . . . 304(8)

EVERSHED, F.R. *The Court of Appeal in England* . . . 84(9)

EVERSHED, F.R. "The Judicial Process in Twentieth Century England" (1961) 61 Col LR 761 . . . 104(4), 121(9)

EVERSHED, F.R. "The Work of Appellate Courts" (1962) 36 Aust LJ 42 . . . 84(9)

FARMER, J.A. "Natural Justice and Licensing Applications: Hohfeld and the Writ of Certiorari" [1967] 2 NZULR 282 . . . 22(8)

FARNSWORTH, E.A. " 'Meaning' in the Law of Contracts" (1966–67) 76 Yale LJ 939 . . . 11(2)

FARRAN, C.D'O "An Unusual Claim to British Nationality" (1956) 19 MLR 289 . . . 51(7)

FARRAR, J.H. *Law Reform and the Law Commission* . . . 114(7), 147(1), 233(7), 239(7)

FARRAR, J.H. "Law Reform Now – a Comparative View" (1976) 25 ICLQ 214 . . . 232(1)

FEIFER, G. *Justice in Moscow* . . . 289(1)

FEINBERG, J. "Rawls on Intuitionism" in *Reading Rawls. Critical Studies on Rawls' A Theory of Justice* (ed. N. Daniels), chap. 5 . . . 33(2)

FELLMAN, D. "Religion in American Public Law" (1964) 44 BLR 287 . . . 76(10)

FENWICK, C.G. "When is there a Threat to Peace? – Rhodesia" (1967) 61 AJIL 753 . . . 63(4)

FERNANDO, T.S. "Are the Maintenance of the Rule of Law and the Ensuring of Human Rights possible in a developing Society?" (1968) 2 Malayan LJ iii . . . 49(3)

Festschrift für Oscar Adolf Germann . . . 28(8)

FIELD, D.D. "Codification" (1886) 20 Am LR 1 . . . 237(1)

FIELD, D.D. "Codification – Mr Field's Answer to Mr Carter" (1890) 24 Am LR 255 . . . 237(2)

FIFOOT, C.H.S. *Judge and Jurist in the Reign of Queen Victoria* . . . 190(6), 208(10)

FINCH, J.D. *Introduction to Legal Theory* (2nd ed.) . . . 43(4), 243(5), 252(8), 258(6), 267(10), 294(3), 336(8)

FINKELSTEIN, M. "Further Notes on Judicial Self-limitation" (1925–26) 39 Harv LR 221 . . . 53(1)

FINKELSTEIN, M. "Judicial Self-limitation" (1923–24) 37 Harv LR 338 . . . 53(1)

FINNIS, J.M. "Revolutions and the Continuity of Law" in *Oxford Essays in Jurisprudence (Second Series)*, (ed. A.W.B. Simpson) chap. 3 . . . 19(7), 62(9), 266(7)

FINNIS, J.M. "Scepticism, Self-refutation, and the Good of Truth" in *Law, Morality, and Society. Essays in Honour of H.L.A. Hart* (edd. P.M.S. Hacker and J. Raz) chap. 14 . . . 253(5)

FISK, M. "History and Reason in Rawls' Moral Theory" in *Reading Rawls. Critical Studies on Rawls' A Theory of Justice* (ed. N. Daniels) chap. 3 . . . 33(2)

FITZGERALD, P.J. "Are Statutes Fit for Academic Treatment?" (1971) 11 JSPTL (NS) 142 . . . 9(1)

FITZGERALD, P.J. "Law and Logic" (1964) 39 NDL 570 . . . 15(1)

FITZGERALD, P.J. "Voluntary and Involuntary Acts" in *Oxford Essays in Jurisprudence* (ed. A. G. Guest) chap. 1 . . . 174(1)

FITZGERALD, P.J. and WILLIAMS, G.L. "Carelessness, Indifference and Recklessness: Two Replies" (1962) 25 MLR 49 . . . 185(5)

FLATHMAN, R.E. *The Practice of Rights* . . . 24(8), 31(2)

FLETCHER, A.K. "The Legal Regulation of Morality" (1975) 125 New LJ 1027 . . . 74(9)

FRIDMAN, G.F.L. "The 'Right' to
Strike" (1964) 114 LJ 647, 667 . . .
77(6)

FRIED, C. *An Anatomy of Values:
Problems of Personal and Social
Choice* . . . 34(6), 146(3)

FRIED, C. "Moral Causation" (1963–
64) 77 Harv LR 1258 . . . 172(8)

FRIED, C. "Two Concepts of Interests:
Some Reflections on the Supreme
Court's Balancing Test" (1962–63)
76 Harv LR 755 . . . 309(9)

FRIEDLAND, M.L. "Prospective and
Retrospective Judicial Lawmaking"
(1974) 24 UTLJ 170 . . . 107(5)

FRIEDMANN, W. "Bentham and Modern
Legal Thought" in *Jeremy Bentham
and the Law. A Symposium* (edd.
G.W. Keeton and G. Schwarzenberger)
chap. 12 . . . 302(9)

FRIEDMANN, W. "Gustav Radbruch"
(1960–61) 14 Vand LR 191 . . .
346(7)

FRIEDMANN, W. "Judges, Politics
and the Law" (1951) 29 Can BR
811 . . . 119(10), 149(8)

FRIEDMANN, W. *Law and Social Change
in Contemporary Britain* . . . 121(5),
195(12), 196(11), 216(9), 219(2),
314(1)

FRIEDMANN, W. *Law in a Changing
Society* . . . 119(9), 144(3), 197(1)
216(9), 219(2), 314(1)

FRIEDMANN, W. "Legal Philosophy
and Judicial Lawmaking" (1961) 61
Col LR 821 . . . 105(4), 144(6)

FRIEDMANN, W. *Legal Theory* (5th
ed.) . . . 41(11), 91(13), 105(3),
112(5), 119(8), 144(4), 204(5),
217(3), 242(9), 248(9), 265(1),
275(5), 292(5), 313(5), 329(4),
336(6)

FRIEDMANN, W. "Legal Theory and
the Practical Lawyer" (1941) 5 MLR
103 . . . 144(5)

FRIEDMANN, W. "Limits of Judicial
Lawmaking and Prospective Overruling" (1966) 29 MLR 593 . . .
106(9)

FRIEDMANN, W. "Modern Trends in
Soviet Law" (1953–54) 10 UTLJ 87
. . . 286(7)

FRIEDMANN, W. "Modern Trends in
the Law of Torts" (1937) 1 MLR 39
. . . 159(3)

FRIEDMANN, W. Note in (1941–43)
6 MLR 235 . . . 134(1)

FRIEDMANN, W. "Planning for Freedom" (1961) 24 MLR 209 . . . 315(3)

FRIEDMANN, W. "*Stare Decisis* at
Common Law and Under the Civil
Law of Quebec" (1953) 31 Can BR
723 . . . 92(1), 113(3)

FRIEDMANN, W. "The New Public
Corporations and the Law" (1947)
10 MLR 233, 377 . . . 195(11)

FRIEDMANN, W. "*Trethowan's* Case,
Parliamentary Sovereignty, and the
Limits of Legal Change" (1950–51)
24 Aust LJ 103 . . . 55(9)

FRIEDRICH, C.J. *The Philosophy of
Law in Historical Perspective* . . .
40(5), 258(2), 267(4), 273(9),
294(2), 301(7), 306(1)

FRIENDLY, H.J. "Reactions of a
Lawyer – Newly Made Judge"
(1961–62) 71 Yale LJ 218 . . . 96(10)

FRIENDLY, H.J. "The Gap in Law-
making – Judge who Can't and
Legislators who Won't" (1963) 63
Col LR 787 . . . 123(1)

FULLER, L.L. "American Legal Philosophy at Mid-Century" (1953–54)
6 JLE 457 . . . 250(4), 350(9)

FULLER, L.L. "American Legal
Realism" (1934) 82 U Pa LR 429 . . .
109(5), 237(11), 330(2)

FULLER, L.L. "An Afterword: Science
and the Judicial Process" (1965–66)
79 Harv LR 1604 . . . 327(9)

FULLER, L.L. "Freedom – a Suggested
Analysis" (1954–55) 68 Harv LR
1305 . . . 68(4)

FULLER, L.L. "Irrigation and Tyranny"
(1965) 17 Stan LR 1021 . . . 280(3)

FULLER, L.L. *Law in Quest of Itself*
. . . 240(9), 330(3), 350(8)

FULLER, L.L. *Legal Fictions* . . . 229(3)

FULLER, L.L. "Pashukanis and
Vyshinsky: a Study in the Development of Marxian Legal Thinking"
(1948–49) 47 Mich LR 1157 . . .
284(3)

FULLER, L.L. "Positivism and Fidelity
to Law – a Reply to Professor Hart"
(1957–58) 71 Harv LR 630 . . . 133(6),
240(3), 251(5), 349(4)

FULLER, L.L. "Reason and Fiat in Case
Law" (1945–46) 59 Harv LR 376 . . .
150(5)

HAMSON, C.J. "Moot Case on Defamation" (1948) 10 CLJ 46 . . . 25(1)

HAMSON, C.J. Note on *Bell* v. *Lever Bros.* (1937) 53 LQR 118 . . . 94(4)

HAMSON, C.J. Note on *Rookes* v. *Barnard* [1961] CLJ 189; [1964] CLJ 159 . . . 77(6)

HANBURY, H.G. *Modern Equity* (8th ed.) . . . 215(2)

HANBURY, H.G. "The Field of Modern Equity" (1929) 45 LQR 196 . . . 215(2)

HANCOCK, W.K. *Survey of British Commonwealth Affairs* . . . 55(2), 260(9)

HAND, L. "How Far is a Judge Free in Rendering a Decision?" in *The Spirit of Liberty* 103 . . . 147(4)

HAND, L. *The Bill of Rights. The Oliver Wendell Holmes Lectures 1958* . . . 151(4)

HAND, L. "The Speech of Justice" in *The Spirit of Liberty* 13 . . . 147(4)

HAND, L. *The Spirit of Liberty* . . . 147(4)

HANKS, P.J. "Re-defining the Sovereign: Current Attitudes to Section 4 of the Statute of Westminster" (1968) 42 ALJ 286 . . . 56(8)

HANNIGAN, A. St. J.J. "Native Custom, its Similarity to English Conventional Custom and its Mode of Proof" (1958) 2 JAL 101 . . . 141(3)

HANSON, A.H. *Parliament and Public Ownership* . . . 218(3)

HARARI, A. *The Place of Negligence in the Law of Torts* . . . 90(10)

HARDING, A.L. "Professor Pound Makes History" in *Southern Methodist University Studies in Jurisprudence* IV, p. 3 . . . 309(6)

HARDING, C.S.P. "European Community Law in the United Kingdom" (1976) 140 JPJ 456, 470 . . . 66(6)

HARDING, R.W. "Lord Atkin's Judicial Attitudes and their Illustration in Commercial Law and Contract" (1964) 27 MLR 434 . . . 148(6)

HARDING, R.W. "The Evolution of Roman Catholic Views of Private Property as a Natural Right" (1963) 2 Sol Q 124 . . . 216(5)(6), 344(5)

HARDY, M.J.L. *Blood Feuds and the Payment of Blood Money in the Middle East* . . . 273(2), 278(9)

HARE, R.M. "Rawls' Theory of Justice" in *Reading Rawls. Critical Studies on Rawls' A Theory of Justice* (ed. N. Daniels) chap. 4 . . . 33(2)

HARGREAVES, A.D. *An Introduction to the Principles of Land Law* (4th ed., G.A. Grove and J.F. Garner) . . . 211(9)

HARGREAVES, A.D. "Modern Real Property" (1956) 19 MLR 14 . . . 212(3)

HARGREAVES, A.D. "Terminology and Title in Ejectment" (1940) 56 LQR 376 . . . 212(3)

HARNO, A.J. "Privileges and Powers of a Corporation and the Doctrine of *Ultra Vires*" (1925–26) 35 Yale LJ 13 . . . 193(10)

HARPER, F.V. "The Forces Behind and Beyond Juristic Pragmatism in America" in *Recueil d'Etudies sur les Sources du Droit en l'Honneur de F. Gény* II, 243 . . . 144(2), 339(7)

HARPER, T. "Indecency and Other Things" (1975) 125 New LJ 71 . . . 75(1)

HARRIMAN, E.A. "*Ultra Vires* Corporations Leases" (1900–1) 14 Harv LR 332 . . . 194(5)

HARRINGTON, M. "Revolution" in *Is Law Dead?* (ed. E.V. Rostow), chap. 10 . . . 219(6), 290(2)

HARRIS, D.R. "Comment" (1964) 4 Melb ULR 498 . . . 207(10)

HARRIS, D.R. "The Concept of Possession in English Law" in *Oxford Essays in Jurisprudence* (ed. A.G. Guest) chap. 4 . . . 206(7)

HARRIS, D.R. "The Constitutional Crisis in South Africa" (1959) 103 SJ 995 . . . 59(8)

HARRIS, D.R. "The Right to Strike" (1964) 108 SJ 451, 472, 493 . . . 77(8)

HARRIS, D.R. "Trade Disputes and the Law" (1964) 108 SJ 795 . . . 77(8)

HARRIS, J.W. "Kelsen's Concept of Authority" (1977) 36 CLJ 353 . . . 263(4)

HARRIS, J.W. "Trust, Power and Duty" (1971) 87 LQR 31 . . . 22(9), 168(10)

HARRIS, J.W. "When and Why does the *Grundnorm* Change? (1971) 29 CLJ 103 . . . 62(8), 263(5)

HARVEY, C.P. "A Job for Jurisprudence" (1944) 7 MLR 42; (1945) 8 MLR 236 ... 9(7), 315(1), 332(2)(3)

HARVEY, W.B. "A Value Analysis of Ghanaian Legal Development since Independence" (1964) 1 UGLJ 4 ... 146(4)

HARVEY, W.B. "The Challenge of the Rule of Law" (1960–61) 59 Mich LR 603 ... 157(6)

HARVEY, W.B. "The Rule of Law in Historical Perspective" (1960–61) 59 Mich LR 487 ... 157(6)

HASSEMER, W., KAUFMANN, A. and "Criteria of Justice" (1971) 4 Ottawa LR 403 ... 350(4)

HASSEMER, W., KAUFMANN, A. and "Enacted Law and Judicial Decision in German Jurisprudential Thought" (1969) 19 UTLJ 461 ... 126(8), 266(9), 275(9)

HASTIE, W. "Introduction" to G.F. Puchta and Others, *Outlines of the Science of Jurisprudence* (trans. W. Hastie) ... 250(6)

HAVARD, J.D.J., CAMPS, F.E. and "Causation in Homicide – a Medical View" (1957) Crim LR 576 ... 181(8)

HAVIGHURST, A.F. "James II and the Twelve Men in Scarlet" (1953) 69 LQR 522 ... 48(4)

HAVIGHURST, A.F. "The Judiciary and Politics in the Reign of Charles II" (1950) 66 LQR 62, 229 ... 48(4)

HAWKINS, F.V. "On the Principles of Interpretation with Reference especially to the Interpretation of Wills" (1858–63) 2 Trans. Jur S 298 ... 123(3)

HAYEK, F.A. *Law, Legislation and Liberty* ... 37(4), 70(1)

HAZARD, J.N. "Cleansing Soviet International Law of anti-Marxist Theories" (1938) 32 AJIL 244 ... 287(10)

HAZARD, J.N. *Law and Social Change in the U.S.S.R.* ... 217(6), 282(8)

HAZARD, J.N. "Renewed Emphasis Upon a Socialist International Law" (1971) 65 AJIL 142 ... 288(3)

HAZARD, J.N. "Socialism, Abuse of Power and Soviet Law" (1950) 50 Col LR 448 ... 287(5)

HAZARD, J.N. "Soviet Codifiers Release the First Drafts" (1959) 8 AJCL 72 ... 287(9)

HAZARD, J.N. "Soviet Government Corporations" (1942–43) 41 Mich LR 850 ... 291(3)

HAZARD, J.N. "Soviet Law: an Introduction" (1936) 36 Col LR 1236 ... 285(2)

HAZARD, J.N., SHAPIRO, I., and MAGGS, P.B. *The Soviet Legal System. Contemporary Documentation and Historical Commentary* (revised ed.) ... 288(7)

HAZARD, J.N. and WEISBERG, M.L. *Cases and Materials on Soviet Law* ... 288(6)

HAZO, R.G. "Montesquieu and the Separation of Powers" (1968) 54 Am BAJ 665 ... 300(1)

HEARN, W.E. *The Theory of Legal Duties and Rights* ... 21(2), 30(5), 167(3), 213(8), 249(2), 257(5)

HEARNSHAW, F.J.C. *The Social and Political Ideas of some Representative Thinkers of the Age of Reaction and Reconstruction* (ed. F.J.C. Hearnshaw) ... 246(6)

HEATH, P.L., PASSMORE, J.A. and "Intentions" (1955) Aristotelian Society Supp. Vol. 29, 131 ... 182(11)

HEGEL, G.W.F. *Philosophy of Right* (trans. T.M. Knox) ... 273(7), 276(10)

HEILBRONER, R.L. "The Roots of Social Neglect in the United States" in *Is Law Dead?* (ed. E.V. Rostow) chap. 8 ... 219(6)

HEMMING, G.W. "The Law Reports" (1885) 1 LQR 317 ... 81(10)

HENKIN, L. "Morals and the Constitution: the Sin of Obscenity" (1963) 63 Col LR 393 ... 73(3)

HENKIN, L. "Some Reflections on Current Constitutional Controversy" (1960–61) 109 U Pa LR 637 ... 151(8)

HENRY, R.L. "*Jurisprudence Constante* and *Stare Decisis* Contrasted" (1929) 15 Am BAJ 11 ... 112(8)

HEPPLE, B.A., O'HIGGINS, P. and TURPIN, C.C. "Rhodesian Crisis: Criminal Liabilities" [1966] Crim LR 5 ... 61(2)

HERON, D.C. *An Introduction to the History of Jurisprudence* ... 42(11), 305(2)

JENNINGS, J. "The Growth and Development of Automatism as a Defence in Criminal Law" (1961–62) 2 Os HLJ 370 . . . 177(5)

JENNINGS, W.I. "A Plea for Utilitarianism" (1938) 2 MLR 22 . . . 305(6)

JENNINGS, W.I. *Constitutional Laws of the Commonwealth* (3rd ed.) . . . 55(1)

JENNINGS, W.I. "Courts and Administrative Law – the Experience of English Housing Legislation" (1935–36) 49 Harv LR 426 . . . 124(9)

JENNINGS, W.I. "Judicial Process at its Worst" (1937–39) 1 MLR 111 . . . 124(10)

JENNINGS, W.I. *Parliament* (2nd ed.) . . . 46(10)

JENNINGS, W.I. "The Institutional Theory" in *Modern Theories of Law* (ed. W.I. Jennings) chap. 5 . . . 312(7)

JENNINGS, W.I. *The Law and the Constitution* (5th ed.) . . . 50(3), 171(9)

JENNINGS, W.I. "The Statute of Westminster and Appeals to the Privy Council" (1936) 52 LQR 173 . . . 55(6)

JENSEN, O.C. *The Nature of Legal Argument* . . . 94(12)

Jeremy Bentham and the Law. A Symposium, (edd. G.W. Keeton and G. Schwarzenberger) . . . 230(5), 302(9)

JEWELL, R.E.C. "Education and Deprived Children: statute and prerogative" (1962) 125 JPJ 320, 356 . . . 189(6)

JEWKES, J. "The Nationalisation of Industry" (1953) 20 UCLR 615 . . . 218(2)

JOHNSON, E.L. *An Introduction to the Soviet Legal System* . . . 282(9)

JOHNSON, E.L. "Matrimonial Property in Soviet Law" (1967) 16 ICLQ 1106 . . . 291(9)

JOHNSON, H.M. *Sociology: A Systematic Introduction* . . . 317(10)

JOHNSTON, W.J. "The English Legislature and the Irish Courts" (1924) 40 LQR 91 . . . 54(10)

JOINT COMMITTEE OF THE YOUNG BARRISTERS COMMITTEE OF THE BAR COUNCIL AND THE YOUNG SOLICITORS GROUP OF THE LAW SOCIETY "Codification of the Law" (1970) 58 Law Guardian 11 . . . 239(5)

JOLLY, A. "The *Jus Tertii* and the Third Man" (1955) 18 MLR 371 . . . 215(6)

JOLOWICZ, H.F. *Historical Introduction to Roman Law* (3rd ed.) . . . 40(3), 140(7), 281(7)

JOLOWICZ, H.F. "Jeremy Bentham and the Law" (1948) 1 CLP 1 . . . 302(9)

JOLOWICZ, H.F. *Lectures on Jurisprudence* (ed. J.A. Jolowicz) . . . 4(5), 249(9), 265(7), 276(1), 304(3), 312(5), 314(7), 329(10), 337(8)

JOLOWICZ, H.F. "Was Bentham a Lawyer?" in *Jeremy Bentham and the Law. A Symposium* (edd. G.W. Keeton and G. Schwarzenberger) chap. 1 . . . 302(9)

JOLOWICZ, J.A. "Fact Based Classification of Law" in *The Division and Classification of the Law* (ed. J.A. Jolowicz) . . . 231(4)

JOLOWICZ, J.A., WINFIELD, P.H. and *A Textbook of the Law of Tort* (10th ed., W.H.V. Rogers) . . . 195(3)

JONES, E.M., MAYO, L.H. and "Legal Policy Decision Process: Alternative Thinking and the Predictive Function" (1964–65) 33 Geo Wash LR 318 . . . 101(6)

JONES, H.W. "Extrinsic Aids in the Federal Courts" (1939–40) 25 Iowa LR 737 . . . 132(12)

JONES, H.W. "Law and Morality in the Perspective of Legal Realism" (1961) 61 Col LR 799 . . . 70(5), 332(9)

JONES, H.W. "Statutory Doubts and Legislative Intention" (1940) 40 Col LR 957 . . . 117(6)

JONES, H.W. "The Rule of Law and the Welfare State" (1958) 58 Col LR 143 . . . 157(2)

JONES, J. MERVYN "Claims on Behalf of Nationals who are Shareholders in Foreign Companies" (1949) 26 BYIL 225 . . . 192(3)

JONES, J.W. "Acquired and Guaranteed Rights" in *Cambridge Legal Essays* (edd. P.H. Winfield and A.D. McNair) 223 . . . 348(1)

JONES, J.W. "Forms of Ownership" (1947–48) 22 Tul LR 82 . . . 216(8)

JONES, J.W. *Historical Introduction to the Theory of Law* . . . 42(1), 203(2), 248(7), 265(2), 274(7), 275(7), 292(6), 329(5)

KANTOROWICZ, H.U. "Some Rationalism about Realism" (1934) 43 Yale LJ 1240 . . . 330(6)

KANTOROWICZ, H.U. *The Definition of Law* (ed. A.H. Campbell) . . . 12(2), 75(6), 168(5)

KANTOROWICZ, H.U. and PATTERSON, E.W. "Legal Science – a Summary of its Methodology" (1928) 28 Col LR 679 . . . 1(4), 145(4)

KANYEIHAMBA, G.W. and KANTENDE, J.W. "The Supranational Adjudicatory Bodies and the Municipal Governments, Legislatures and Courts: a Confrontation" (1972) PL 107 . . . 67(1)

KARST, K.L. and HOROWITZ, H.W. "Affirmative Action and Equal Protection" (1974) 60 Vir LR 955 . . . 38(1)

KAUFMANN, A. and HASSEMER, W. "Criteria of Justice" (1971) 4 Ottawa LR 403 . . . 350(4)

KAUFMANN, A. and HASSEMER, W. "Enacted Law and Judicial Decision in German Jurisprudential Thought" (1969) 19 UTLJ 461 . . . 126(8), 266(9), 275(9)

KAUPER, P.G. "The Supreme Court and the Rule of Law" (1960–61) 59 Mich LR 531 . . . 157(6)

KAVANAGH, P.B. "Judging as an Act of Will" (1970) 120 New LJ 529 . . . 103(6)

KAVANAGH, P.B. "*Stare Decisis* in the House of Lords" (1972–73) 5 NZULR 323 . . . 87(7)

KAYTON, I. "Can Jurimetrics be of Value to Jurisprudence?" (1964–65) 33 Geo Wash LR 287 . . . 327(7)

KE CHIN WANG, H. "The Corporate Entity Concept (or Fiction Theory) in the Year Book Period" (1942) 58 LQR 498; (1943) 59 LQR 72 . . . 189(12)

KEELER, J.F. "Contractual Action for Damages against Unincorporated Bodies" (1971) 34 MLR 615 . . . 198(4)

KEETON, G.W. "Judge Jeffreys as Chief Justice of Chester, 1680–83" (1961) 77 LQR 36 . . . 48(5)

KEETON, G.W. "Natural Justice in English Law" (1955) 8 CLP 24 . . . 347(5)

KEETON, G.W. "The Constitutional Crisis in South Africa" (1953) 6 CLP 22 . . . 58(4)

KEETON, G.W. *The Elementary Principles of Jurisprudence* (2nd ed.) . . . 4(9), 18(2), 21(8), 127(10), 138(4), 171(2), 177(3), 186(3), 188(4), 208(3), 213(3), 249(4), 329(9)

KEETON, G.W. "The Judiciary and the Constitutional Struggle, 1660–1688" (1962) 7 JSPTL (NS) 56 . . . 48(5)

KEETON, G.W. and LLOYD, D. (edd.) *The British Commonwealth. The Development of its Laws and Constitutions* . . . 99(8), 105(7), 110(8), 237(8)

KEETON, G.W., EASTWOOD, R.A. and *The Austinian Theories of Law and Sovereignty* . . . 2(5), 246(4)

KEETON, R.E. "Creative Continuity in the Law of Torts" (1961–62) 75 Harv LR 463 . . . 106(8), 157(7)

KEETON, R.E. *Legal Cause in the Law of Torts* . . . 179(7)

KEETON, R.E. *Venturing to do Justice. Reforming Private Law* . . . 230(4)

KEIR, D.L. and LAWSON, F.H. *Cases in Constitutional Law* (4th ed.) . . . 47(4)

KEITH, A.B. "Notes on Imperial Constitutional Law" (1923) 5 JCL (3rd ser.) 274 . . . 57(5)

KEITH, A.B. *The Dominions as Sovereign States* . . . 58(9)

KEITH, A.B. *The Government of the British Empire* . . . 55(3)

KELLY, D. St. L. "Legal Concepts, Logical Functions and Statements of Facts" (1968) 3 Tasm LR 43 . . . 8(8)

KELSEN, H. "A 'Dynamic' Theory of Natural Law" in *What is Justice?* 174 . . . 341(1)

KELSEN, H. *Allgemeine Staatslehre* . . . 261(1)

KELSEN, H. "Centralisation and Decentralisation" in *Authority and the Individual* 210 . . . 260(2)

KELSEN, H. "Derogation" in *Essays in Jurisprudence in Honor of Roscoe Pound* (ed. R.A. Newman) 339 . . . 260(3)

KELSEN, H. *Essays in Legal and Moral Philosophy* (trans. P. Heath, ed. O. Weinberger) . . . 263(6)

KORT, F. "Quantitative Analysis of Fact –
patterns in Cases and their Impact on
Judicial Decisions" (1965–66) 79
Harv LR 1595 . . . 326(5)

KORZYBSKI, A. *Science and Sanity*
(2nd ed.) . . . 16(6)

KOTZÈ, J.G. "Judicial Precedent" (1917)
34 SALJ 280; (1918) 144 LT 349 . . .
112(13)

KOVEN, H., KOCOUREK, A. and
"Renovation of the Common Law
through *Stare Decisis*" (1934–35)
29 Ill LR 971 . . . 107(4)

KRISLOV, S. "Theoretical Attempts at
Predicting Judicial Behaviour" (1965–
66) 79 Harv LR 1573 . . . 326(1)

KRUSE, L.F. VINDING *The Foundations
of Human Thought* (trans. A. Fausbøll
and I. Lund) . . . 16(6)

KRUSE, L.F. VINDING *The Right of
Property* (trans. P.T. Federspiel) . . .
213(10)

KUIPERS, S.A., MITCHELL, J.D.B. - - -
and GALL, B. "Constitutional Aspects
of the Treaty and Legislation relating
to British Membership" (1972) 9 CMLR
134 . . . 65(3)

KUNZ, J.L. "On the Theoretical Basis
of the Law of Nations" (1925) 10
Trans Gro S 115 . . . 268(3)

KUNZ, J.L. "The Vienna School of Law
and International Law" (1936)
11 NYULQ 370 . . . 268(3)

KUTSCHER, H. "Community Law and
the National Judge" (1973) 89 LQR
487 . . . 65(6)

LAIRD, D.H. "The Doctrine of *Stare
Decisis*" (1935) 13 Can BR 1 . . . 83(8)

LAMBERT, E. "Codified Law and Case
Law: their Part in Shaping the Policies
of Justice" in *Science of Legal Method:
Select Essays by Various Authors*
(trans. E. Bruncken and L.B. Register)
. . . 104(3)

LAMBERT, E. and WASSERMAN, M.J.
"The Case Method in Canada and the
Possibilities of its Adaptation to the
Civil Law" (1929) 39 Yale LJ 1 . . .
112(2)

LAMONT, W.D. *The Principles of Moral
Judgment* . . . 11(9), 35(7), 170(1)

LAMONT, W.D. *The Value Judgment*
. . . 146(5)

LANDIS, J.M. "A Note on 'Statutory
Interpretation'" (1929–30) 43 Harv
LR 886 . . . 118(5)

LANDIS, J.M. "Statutes and Sources of
Law" in *Harvard Legal Essays* 213 . . .
116(2)

LANDON, P.A. Note on *Bell* v.
Lever Bros (1935) 51 LQR 650 . . .
94(4)

LANG, A.G. "Is there a *Ratio Decidendi?*"
(1974) 48 Aust LJ 146 . . . 92(3)

LANG, A.J.G. "Madzimbamuto and
Baron's Case at First Instance" [1965]
Rhod LJ 65 . . . 60(8)

LANGDELL, C.C. *A Brief Survey of
Equity Jurisdiction* (2nd ed.) . . .
214(11)

LAPENNA, I. *State and Law: Soviet and
Yugoslav Theory* . . . 286(1)

LASERSON, M.M. "'Positive' and
'Natural Law' and their Correlation"
in *Interpretations of Modern Legal
Philosophies* (ed. P. Sayre) chap. 20
. . . 241(3), 341(3)

LASKI, H.J. *A Grammar of Politics* (4th
ed.) . . . 47(2), 257(2), 289(6)

LASKI, H.J. "Judicial Review of Social
Policy in England" (1925–26) 39 Harv
LR 832 . . . 156(9)

LASKI, H.J. *Karl Marx* . . . 283(7)

LASKI, H.J. *Law and Justice in Soviet
Russia* . . . 289(5)

LASKI, H.J. "M. Duguit's Conception of
the State" in *Modern Theories of
Law* (ed. W.I. Jennings) chap. 4 . . .
311(8)

LASKI, H.J. Note on the Judicial Interpretation of Statutes in Annexe V
to the *Report of the Committee on
Ministers' Powers* . . . 123(7)

LASKI, H.J. *Studies in Law and
Politics* . . . 289(5)

LASKI, H.J. "The Crisis in the Theory
of the State" in *Law: A Century of
Progress* . . . 289(6)

LASKI, H.J. "The Personality of
Associations" (1915–16) 29 Harv LR
404 . . . 190(5), 196(9)

LASKI, H.J. *The State in Theory and
Practice* . . . 289(4)

LASSWELL, H.D. *Power and Personality*
. . . 317(5)

LEIGHTON, G.C.K., McDOUGAL, M.S. and "The Rights of Man in the World Community: Constitutional Illusions versus Rational Action" (1949–50) 59 Yale LJ 60 . . . 145(8)

LEITCH, W.A. "A Canadian Contrast on 'Computers and the Law'" (1969), 20 NILQ 274 . . . 221(3)

Le MAY, G.H.L. "Parliament, the Constitution and the 'Doctrine of the Mandate'" (1957) 74 SALJ 33 . . . 59(9)

LEON, H.C. See CECIL, H.

LEONHARD, R. "Methods Followed in Germany by the Historical School of Law" (1907) 7 Col LR 573 . . . 271(4)

LEPAULLE, P. "The Function of Comparative Law with a Critique of Sociological Jurisprudence" (1921–22) 35 Harv LR 838 . . . 297(2), 309(8)

LERNER, M. "The Supreme Court and American Capitalism" (1932–33) 42 Yale LJ 668 . . . 151(1), 324(7)

LEVI, E.H. An Introduction to Legal Reasoning . . . 97(5), 118(1), 133(7)

LEVY, B.H. Cardozo and Frontiers of Legal Thinking . . . 99(6), 102(5), 153(10)

LEVY, B.H. "Realist Jurisprudence and Prospective Overruling" (1960–1) 109 U Pa LR 1 . . . 106(6)

LEWIS, C. "The Truth about Precedent" (1976) 73 LS Gaz 957 . . . 80(4)

LEWIS, C.S. Studies in Words . . . 16(6)

LEWIS, J.R. "Using the Veil for Improper Purposes" (1966) 4 Legal Exec 72 . . . 193(4)

LEWIS, J.U. "Annual Survey of Canadian Law: Part 2. Jurisprudence" (1976) 8 Ottawa LR 427 . . . 6(2)

LEWIS, J.U. "Blackstone's Definition of Law and Doctrine of Legal Obligation as a Link between Early Modern and Contemporary Theories of Law" (1968) 3 Ir Jur (NS) 337 . . . 172(2), 243(6)

LEWIS, J.U. "Jean Bodin's 'Logic of Sovereignty'" (1968) 16 Pol S 206 . . . 256(1)

LEWIS, J.U. "John Austin's Concept of 'Having a Legal Obligation': a Defence and Reassessment in the Face of Some Recent Analytical Jurisprudence" (1975) 14 W Ont LR 51 . . . 172(6)

LEWIS, J.U. "Karl Olivecrona: 'Factual Realism' and Reasons for Obeying a Law" (1970) 5 U Br Col LR 281 . . . 173(2), 336(2)

LEWIS, J.U. "Obligation and the Law" (1971) 5 Ottawa LR 84 . . . 227(7)

LEWIS, J.U. "Sir Edward Coke (1552–1633): His Theory of 'Artificial Reason' as a Context for Modern Basic Legal Theory" (1968) 84 LQR 330 . . . 47(8)

LEWIS, N. "Trade Unions and Public Policy" (1965) 4 Sol Q 12 . . . 78(4)

LEWIS, W.A. "Monopoly and the Law" (1943) 6 MLR 97 . . . 160(11)

LEWIS, W.A. "Spare-time Activities of Employees" (1946) 9 MLR 280 . . . 160(10)

Liber Amicorum in Honour of Professor Alf Ross . . . 100(7), 335(6)

LIGHTWOOD, J.M. A Treatise on Possession of Land . . . 206(4), 212(2)

LIGHTWOOD, J.M. "Possession in Roman Law" (1887) 3 LQR 32 . . . 205(5)

LIGHTWOOD, J.M. The Nature of Positive Law . . . 2(8), 248(10), 275(2)

LINDE, H.A. "Judges, Critics and the Realist Tradition" (1972–73) 82 Yale LJ 227 . . . 332(8)

LINDLEY, N. "The History of the Law Reports" (1885) 1 LQR 137 . . . 81(9)

LINDSAY, A.D. The Modern Democratic State . . . 257(3)

LINDSELL, W.H.B., CLERK, J.F. and Torts (14th ed.) . . . 158(10), 185(6), 195(2)

Lionel Cohen Lectures . . . 156(6)

LIPSTEIN, K. "Protected Interests in the Law of Torts" (1963) CLJ 85 . . . 157(8)

LIPSTEIN, K. "The Doctrine of Precedent in Continental Law with Special Reference to French and German Law" (1946) 28 JCL (3rd ser., Pt. III), 34 . . . 111(7)

LIPSTEIN, K. "The Reception of Western Law in a Country of a Different Social and Economic Background: India" (1957–58) 8–9 Revista del Instituto de Derecho Comparado, 69, 213 . . . 272(7)

LIPSTEIN, K. "The Reception of Western Law in Turkey" (1956) 6 Annales de la Faculté de Droit d'Istanbul, 10, 225 ... 272(6)

LLEWELLYN, K.N. *Cases and Materials on the Law of Sales* ... 24(9)

LLEWELLYN, K.N. "Impressions of the Conference on Precedent" in *Jurisprudence: Realism in Theory and Practice* 116 ... 150(4)

LLEWELLYN, K.N. *Jurisprudence: Realism in Theory and Practice* ... 26(10), 99(9), 118(2), 123(9), 150(4), 172(7), 310(3), 319(4), 343(5)

LLEWELLYN, K.N. "Law and the Social Sciences – especially Sociology" (1948–49) 62 Harv LR 1286 ... 319(7)

LLEWELLYN, K.N. *The Bramble Bush* ... 22(3), 90(4), 101(4), 169(6), 319(3)(8)

LLEWELLYN, K.N. *The Common Law Tradition. Deciding Appeals* ... 97(2)(3), 103(11), 127(4), 142(2), 319(8), 320(5)

LLEWELLYN, K.N. "The Normative, the Legal and the Law-jobs: the Problem of Juristic Method" (1939–40) 49 Yale LJ 1355 ... 97(1), 319(6)

LLEWELLYN, K.N. "What Price Contract? – an Essay in Perspective" (1930–31) 40 Yale LJ 704 ... 159(8)

LLEWELLYN, K.N., ADLER, M.J. and COOK, W.W. "Law and the Modern Mind: a Symposium" (1931) 31 Col LR 83 ... 321(8)

LLEWELLYN, K.N. and HOEBEL, E.A. *The Cheyenne Way* ... 280(1)

LLOYD, D. "Actions Instituted By or Against Unincorporated Bodies" (1949) 12 MLR 409 ... 197(10)

LLOYD, D. "Codifying English Law" (1949) 2 CLP 155 ... 237(7)

LLOYD, D. "Damages for Wrongful Expulsion from a Trade Union" (1956) 19 MLR 121 ... 77(3), 199(2)

LLOYD, D. "Do we Need a Bill of Rights?" (1976) 39 MLR 1 ... 53(4)

LLOYD, D. *Introduction to Jurisprudence* (3rd. ed.) ... 14(9), 43(9), 57(2), 73(8), 91(10), 100(5), 105(6), 112(12), 121(5), 138(8), 249(8), 264(5), 276(11), 280(9), 292(7), 317(3), 329(1), 336(5)

LLOYD, D. "Judicial Review of Expulsion by a Domestic Tribunal" (1952) 15 MLR 413 ... 77(3)

LLOYD, D. "Law and Public Policy" (1958) 8 CLP 42 ... 155(7)

LLOYD, D. "Legal and Ideal Justice" in *Legal Essays. A Tribute to Frede Castberg* 111 ... 341(8)

LLOYD, D. "Ministers' Powers and the Courts" (1948) 1 CLP 89 ... 156(8)

LLOYD, D. Note in (1953) 16 MLR 359 ... 198(3)

LLOYD, D. *Public Policy* ... 155(6)

LLOYD, D. "Reason and Logic in the Common Law" (1948) 64 LQR 468 ... 94(11)

LLOYD, D. "The Disciplinary Powers of Professional Bodies" (1950) 13 MLR 281 ... 77(3), 197(11)

LLOYD, D. *The Idea of Law* ... 8(3), 23(8), 36(6), 38(9), 43(2), 69(8), 75(3), 105(5), 138(9), 193(3), 215(12), 226(3), 242(10), 258(5), 268(8), 276(12), 281(3), 293(1), 317(4), 329(2), 336(5), 352(1)

LLOYD, D. *The Law Relating to Unincorporated Associations* ... 196(8)

LLOYD, D. "The Right to Work" (1957) 10 CLP 36 ... 77(3)

LLOYD, D., KEETON, G.W. and (edd.) *The British Commonwealth. The Development of its Laws and Constitutions* ... 99(8), 105(7), 110(8), 237(8)

LLOYD, W.H. "Pylkington's Case and its Successors" (1921) 69 U Pa LR 20 ... 50(4)

LOBINGIER, C.S. "Customary Law" in *Encyclopaedia of the Social Sciences* (ed. E.R.A. Seligman) IV, 662 ... 136(5)

LOCKE, J. *An Essay on Human Understanding* (33rd ed.) ... 243(1)

LOCKE, J. *Two Treatises of Government* (ed. P. Laslett) ... 41(5)(7)

LOEVINGER, L. "Jurimetrics: the Next Step Forward" (1949) 33 Minn LR 455 ... 325(6)

Logic and Language (ed. A.G.N. Flew) ... 16(6), 150(3), 174(7)

LOVELL, C.R. "The Growth of Judicial Review in the United States" (1955) BSALR 107 ... 52(3)

398 Bibliographical Index

MAITLAND, F.W. "The Corporation Sole" in *Selected Essays* (edd. H.D. Hazeltine, G. Lapsley, P.H. Winfield) chap. 1 . . . 188(3)

MAITLAND, F.W. "The Crown as a Corporation" in *Selected Essays* (edd. H.D. Hazeltine, G. Lapsley, P.H. Winfield) chap. 2 . . . 188(3)

MAITLAND, F.W. "The Unincorporate Body" in *Selected Essays* (edd. H.D. Hazeltine, G. Lapsley, P.H. Winfield) chap. 3 . . . 196(5)

MAITLAND, F.W. "Trust and Corporation" in *Selected Essays* (edd. H.D. Hazeltine, G. Lapsley, P.H. Winfield) chap. 4 . . . 196(6)

MAITLAND, F.W., POLLOCK, F. and *The History of English Law before the Time of Edward I* (2nd ed.) . . . 188(7), 189(11), 209(1), 211(10)

MALBURN, W.P. "The Violation of Law Limiting Speed as Negligence" (1911) 45 Am LR 214 . . . 158(11)

MALINOWSKI, B. "A New Instrument for the Interpretation of Law – especially Primitive" (1941–42) 51 Yale LJ 1237 . . . 277(9)

MALINOWSKI, B. *Crime and Custom in Savage Society* . . . 215(10), 277(8)

Man and Culture (ed. R.W. Firth) . . . 278(1)

MANN, F.A. "The Interpretation of Uniform Statutes" (1946) 62 LQR 278 . . . 131(1)

MANNING, C.A.W. "Austin Today: or 'The Province of Jurisprudence' Re-examined" in *Modern Theories of Law* (ed. W.I. Jennings) chap. 10 . . . 246(7)

MANSON, E. "One Man Companies" (1895) 11 LQR 185 . . . 191(2)

MANSON, E. "The Evolution of the Private Company" (1910) 26 LQR 11 . . . 191(3)

MARCH, J.G. "Sociological Jurisprudence Revisited. A Review (more or less) of Max Gluckman" (1955–56) 8 Stan LR 499 . . . 279(2)

MARITAIN, J. *The Rights of Man and Natural Law* . . . 351(1)

MARKBY, W. *Elements of Law* (6th ed.) . . . 29(2), 140(5), 170(5), 177(1), 186(8), 207(12), 213(7), 248(11)

MARSH, N.S. "Civil Liberties in Europe" (1959) 75 LQR 530 . . . 146(2)

MARSH, N.S. "Deduction and Induction in the Law of Torts: a Comparative Approach" (1950–51) 33 JCL (3rd ser. Pt. III) 59 . . . 112(9)

MARSH, N.S. "Principle and Discretion in the Judicial Process" (1952) 68 LQR 226 . . . 109(6), 158(2)

MARSH, N.S. "Some Aspects of the German Legal System under National Socialism" (1946) 62 LQR 366 . . . 274(7)

MARSH, N.S. "The Interpretation of Statutes" (1967) 9 JSPTL (NS) 416 . . . 114(6)

MARSHALL, G. "Law in a Cold Climate: the Scandinavian Realism" (1956) 1 Jur R (NS) 259 . . . 335(10)

MARSHALL, G. *Parliamentary Sovereignty and the Commonwealth* . . . 45(2), 46(8), 54(11)

MARSHALL, G. "Parliamentary Supremacy and the Language of Constitutional Limitation" (1955) 67 Jur R 62 . . . 54(2)

MARSHALL, G. "Political Science and the Judicial Process" (1957) PL 139 . . . 300(6)

MARSHALL, G. "Positivism, Adjudication, and Democracy" in *Law, Morality, and Society. Essays in Honour of H.L.A. Hart* (edd. P.M.S. Hacker and J. Raz), chap. 7 . . . 255(8)

MARSHALL, G. "Rights, Options and Entitlements" in *Oxford Essays in Jurisprudence (Second Series)* (ed. A.W.B. Simpson) . . . 31(1)

MARSHALL, G. "What is Parliament? The Changing Concept of Parliamentary Sovereignty" (1954) 2 Pol S 193 . . . 54(1)

MARSHALL, H.H. "The Binding Effect of Decisions of the Judicial Committee of the Privy Council" (1968) 17 ICLQ 743 . . . 88(9)

MARSHALL, H.H. "The Judicial Committee of the Privy Council: a Waning Jurisdiction" (1964) 13 ICLQ 697 . . . 88(7)

MARSHALL, H.H. "The Legal Effects of U.D.I." (1968) 17 ICLQ 1022 . . . 62(1)

MARSHALL, O.R. "The Problem of Finding" (1949) 2 CLP 68 . . . 209(9)

PAREKH, Bhikhu, *Bentham's Political Thought* ... 245(1), 302(6)

PARKER, C.F. "Law Reporting and the Revision of Judgments" (1955) 18 MLR 496 ... 82(7)

PARKER, H.L. "Recent Developments in the Supervisory Powers of the Courts over Inferior Tribunals" *Lionel Cohen Lectures*, V ... 156(6)

PARKER, H.L. "The Criminal Division of the Court of Appeal" (1969) 46 Law Guardian 11 ... 84(7)

PARKER, H.L. "The Role of the Judge in the Preservation of Liberty" (1961) 35 Aust LJ 63 ... 68(8)

PARKER, R. "The Pure Theory of Law" (1960–61) 14 Vand LR 211 ... 261(2)

PARRY, C. "Further Considerations upon the Prince of Hanover's Case" (1956) 5 ICLQ 61 ... 51(8)

PARRY, C. Note in [1955] CLJ 142 ... 51(5)

PARRY, C. Note in [1957] CLJ 1 ... 51(12)

PARRY, D.H. "Economic Theories in English Case-law" (1931) 47 LQR 183 ... 295(5)

PARSONAGE, M. "Epilepsy and Driving" (1969) 133 JPJ 290 ... 178(4)

PARSONS, O.H. "Should All Laws Always be Obeyed?" (1972) 122 New LJ 908 ... 227(8)

PARSONS, O.H. "The Meaning of *Rookes v. Barnard*" LRD (1964) ... 77(6)

PARTINGTON, M., O'HIGGINS, P. and "Industrial Conflict: Judicial Attitudes" (1969) 32 MLR 53 ... 160(8)

PASSMORE, J.A. and HEATH, P.L. "Intentions" (1955) Aristotelian Society Supp. Vol. 29, 131 ... 182(11)

PATON, G.W. *A Text-book of Jurisprudence* (4th ed., G.W. Paton and D.P. Derham) ... 14(8), 17(5), 21(7), 83(6), 91(9), 101(3), 127(9), 138(5), 171(1), 176(5), 186(1), 188(9), 206(3), 213(4), 232(5), 238(5), 249(5), 265(11), 276(2), 280(7), 314(5), 329(7), 338(1)

PATON, G.W. "Negligence" (1949–50) 23 Aust LJ 158 ... 158(8)

PATON, G.W. "Possession" (1935) 1 *Res Judicata* 187 ... 206(2)

PATON, G.W. "Pound and Contemporary Juristic Theory" (1944) 22 Can BR 479 ... 308(9)

PATON, G.W. "Soviet Legal Theory" (1946–47) 3 *Res Judicata* 58 ... 282(3)

PATON, G.W. (ed.) *The Commonwealth of Australia* ... 56(2)

PATON, G.W. and SAWER, G. "*Ratio* and *Obiter Dictum* in Appellate Courts" (1947) 63 LQR 461 ... 93(1)

PATTERSON, E.W. "Can Law be Scientific?" (1930) 25 Ill LR 121 ... 331(8)

PATTERSON, E.W. "Cardozo's Philosophy of Law" (1940) 88 U Pa LR 71 ... 153(11)

PATTERSON, E.W. "Hans Kelsen and His Pure Theory of Law" (1952–53) 40 Calif LR 5 ... 261(4)

PATTERSON, E.W. "Judicial Freedom of Implying Conditions in Contract" in *Recueil d'Etudes sur les Sources du Droit en l'Honneur de F. Gény*, II, 379 ... 159(9)

PATTERSON, E.W. *Jurisprudence* ... 1(3), 137(8), 168(1), 249(6), 250(4), 264(4), 275(3), 293(2), 301(4), 303(5), 308(8), 328(5), 337(6)

PATTERSON, E.W. "Pound's Theory of Social Interests" in *Interpretations of Modern Legal Philosophies* (ed. P. Sayre) chap. 26 ... 308(7)

PATTERSON, E.W. "Roscoe Pound on Jurisprudence" (1960) 60 Col LR 1124 ... 308(6)

PATTERSON, E.W., KANTOROWICZ, H.U. and "Legal Science – a Summary of its Methodology" (1928) 28 Col LR 679 ... 1(4), 145(4)

PAUL, J. *The Legal Realism of Jerome N. Frank* ... 321(9)

PAULSEN, M.G. "*De Funis*: the Road not Taken" (1974) 60 Vir LR 917 ... 38(1)

PAULSON, S.L. "Classical Legal Positivism at Nuremburg" (1975) 4 Philosophy and Public Affairs 132 ... 169(2), 247(6)

PAULSON, S.L. "Constraints on Legal Norms: Kelsen's View in the Essays" (1975) 42 UCLR 768 ... 263(6)

PAULSON, S.L. "*Jus Non Scriptum* and the Reliance Principle" (1976) 75 Mich LR 68 ... 139(4)

POUND, R. "A Study of Social Interests" (1921) 15 Papers and Proceedings of the American Sociological Society, 16 . . . 306(5)

POUND, R. "A Survey of Social Interests" (1943–44) 57 Harv LR 1 . . . 154(9), 306(5)

POUND, R. *An Introduction to the Philosophy of Law* . . . 42(4), 102(9), 307(11)

POUND, R. "Causation" (1957–58) 67 Yale LJ 1 . . . 181(1)

POUND, R. "Classification of Law" (1923–24) 37 Harv LR 933 . . . 242(4)

POUND, R. "Common Law and Legislation" (1907–8) 21 Harv LR 383 . . . 119(3)

POUND, R. "Comparative Law and History as Bases for Chinese Law" (1947–48) 61 Harv LR 749 . . . 273(3)

POUND, R. *Contemporary Juristic Theory* . . . 308(2)

POUND, R. "Courts and Legislation" (1915) 7 Am Pol Sc R 361: *Science of Legal Method: Select Essays by Various Authors* (trans. E. Bruncken and L.B. Register) chap. 7 . . . 119(6)

POUND, R. "Do We Need a Philosophy of Law?" (1905) 5 Col LR 339; *Jurisprudence in Action* 389 . . . 7(5), 154(8)

POUND, R. "Fifty Years of Jurisprudence" (1936–37) 50 Harv LR 557; (1937–38) 51 Harv LR 444, 777 . . . 25(7), 26(1), 242(3), 295(9), 307(6), 338(9)

POUND, R. "Individual Interests of Substance – Promised Advantages" (1945–46) 59 Harv LR 1 . . . 306(7)

POUND, R. "Interests of Personality" (1914–15) 28 Harv LR 343, 445 . . . 306(6)

POUND, R. *Interpretations of Legal History* . . . 271(7), 274(8), 295(7), 308(1), 339(1)

POUND, R. *Jurisprudence* . . . 2(1), 25(9), 30(4), 75(5), 102(10), 119(7), 138(6), 143(1), 154(9), 171(5), 186(4), 207(8), 213(5), 237(3), 248(5), 276(3), 296(1), 308(4)(5)(6), 309(2), 328(4), 339(2)

POUND, R. "Juristic Science and Law" (1917–18) 31 Harv LR 1047 . . . 154(7)

POUND, R. "Justice According to Law" (1913) 13 Col LR 696; (1914) 14 Col LR 1, 103 . . . 143(1)

POUND, R. *Justice According to Law* . . . 143(1)

POUND, R. *Law and Morals* . . . 143(2)

POUND, R. "Law and State – Jurisprudence and Politics" (1943–44) 57 Harv LR 1193 . . . 257(10)

POUND, R. "Law and the Science of Law in Recent Theories" (1933–34) 43 Yale LJ 525 . . . 13(9)

POUND, R. "Law in Books and Law in Action" (1910) 44 Am LR 12 . . . 307(1), 324(1)

POUND, R. "Legal Rights" (1915–16) 26 IJE 92 . . . 25(8), 30(3)

POUND, R. "Mechanical Jurisprudence" (1908) 8 Col LR 605 . . . 143(5), 306(8)

POUND, R. *My Philosophy of Law* 249 . . . 307(7), 310(10)

POUND, R. "Natural Natural Law and Positive Natural Law" (1952) 68 LQR 330; (1960) 5 Nat LF 70 . . . 307(8), 339(5)

POUND, R. *Readings on the History and System of the Common Law* (2nd ed.) . . . 30(9)

POUND, R. *Social Control Through Law* . . . 308(3)

POUND, R. "Sociology of Law and Sociological Jurisprudence" (1943–44) 5 UTLJ 1 . . . 297(1)

POUND, R. "Spurious Interpretation" (1907) 7 Col LR 379 . . . 121(1)

POUND, R. "The Administration of Justice in the Modern City" (1912–13) 26 Harv LR 302 . . . 307(2)

POUND, R. "The Call for a Realist Jurisprudence" (1930–31) 44 Harv LR 697 . . . 331(3)

POUND, R. "The Economic Interpretation and the Law of Torts" (1939–40) 53 Harv LR 365 . . . 295(8)

POUND, R. "The End of Law as Developed in Juristic Thought" (1913–14) 27 Harv LR 605; (1916–17) 30 Harv LR 201 . . . 276(4), 307(4), 338(10)

POUND, R. "The End of Law as Developed in Legal Rules and Doctrines" (1913–14) 27 Harv LR 195 . . . 307(3)

RHYNE, C.S. "The Law' Russia's
Greatest Weakness" (1959) 45 Am BAJ
246, 309 . . . 285(9)

RICHARDS, D.A.J. "Equal Opportunity
and School Financing: Towards a
Moral Theory of Constitutional
Adjudication" (1973–74) 41 UCLR
32 . . . 37(7)

RICHARDS, I.A., OGDEN, C.K. and
The Meaning of Meaning (10th ed.)
. . . 16(6)

RIDEOUT, R.W. "Protection of the
Right to Work" (1962) 25 MLR 137
. . . 78(1)

RIDEOUT, R.W. "*Rookes* v. *Barnard*"
(1964) 3 Sol Q 193 . . . 78(2)

RIESMAN, D. "Possession and the Law
of Finders" (1939) 52 Harv LR 1105
. . . 209(8)

RIKER, W.H. "Public Safety as a
Public Good" in *Is Law Dead?* (ed.
E.V. Rostow), chap. 11 . . . 219(6)

RITCHIE, D.G. *Natural Rights* . . .
348(2)

ROBERTS, S. "Law and the Study of
Social Control in Small-scale Societies"
(1976) 39 MLR 663 . . . 280(4)

ROBERTSON, L.J. "The Judicial
Recognition of Custom in India"
(1922) 4 JCL (ser. 3) 218 . . . 141(1)

ROBINSON, E.S. *Law and Lawyers* . . .
99(3), 324(10)

ROBINSON, H.W. "Law and Economics"
(1939) 2 MLR 257 . . . 294(9), 315(2)

ROBINSON, M.J. "'Social Legislation
and the Judges': a Note by Way of
Rejoinder" (1976) 39 MLR 43 . . .
125(1)

ROBINSON, R. *Definition* . . . 12(1)

ROBSON, P. "Reason and Revolution"
(1972) SLT 137 . . . 85(8)

ROBSON, R.A.H., COHEN, J., - - -,
BATES, A. *Parental Authority: the
Community and the Law* . . . 316(4)

ROBSON, W.A. *Justice and Administrative Law* (3rd ed.) . . . 153(4)

ROBSON, W.A. "Sir Henry Maine Today"
in *Modern Theories of Law* (ed. W.I.
Jennings) chap. 9 . . . 278(4)

ROBSON, W.A. "The Public Corpora-
tion in Britain Today" in *Problems of
Nationalised Industry* (ed. W.A.
Robson) chap. 1 . . . 195(7)

ROGERS, J.G. "A Scientific Approach
to Free Judicial Decision" in *Recueil
d'Etudes sur les Sources du Droit en
l'Honneur de F. Gény* II, 552 . . .
145(1)

ROGERS, S. "On the Study of Law
Reports" (1897) 13 LQR 250 . . .
82(8)

ROHNER, R.J. "Jurimetrics, No!"
(1968) 54 Am BAJ 896 . . . 327(4)

ROMMEN, H.A. *The Natural Law* (trans.
T.R. Hanley) . . . 337(2)

ROSEN, L. "Legal Cruelty and Cruelty"
(1964) 108 SJ 887 . . . 184(4)

ROSS, A. *Directives and Norms* . . .
16(3), 169(8), 334(2)

ROSS, A. *On Guilt, Responsibility and
Punishment* . . . 175(3)

ROSS, A. *On Law and Justice* . . .
16(2), 18(7), 27(5), 51(3), 111(12),
119(4), 137(6), 169(7), 261(8), 271(8),
293(5), 303(6), 310(1), 334(1), 335(3),
336(8), 342(7)

ROSS, A. Review of Kelsen's *What is
Justice?* (1957) 45 Calif LR 564 . . .
261(7)

ROSS, A. *Towards a Realistic Jurisprudence* (trans. A.I. Fausbøll) . . . 335(2),
342(8)

ROSS, A. "Tu-tu" (1956–57) 70
Harv LR 812 . . . 211(7)

ROSTOW, E.V. *Planning for Freedom*
. . . 315(3)

ROSTOW, E.V. "The Democratic
Character of Judicial Review" (1952–
53) 66 Harv LR 193 . . . 50(1)

ROSTOW, E.V. "The Enforcement of
Morals" (1960) CLJ 174 . . . 72(3)

ROSTOW, E.V. "The Rightful Limits of
Freedom in a Liberal Democratic
State: of Civil Disobedience" in *Is
Law Dead?* (ed. E.V. Rostow) chap. 2
. . . 228(3)

"Round Table Discussion: 'What should
be the Relation of Morals to Law?' "
(1952) 1 JPL 259 . . . 70(6)

ROUSSEAU, J-J. *Contrat Social* . . .
41(9)

RUBEN, D-H. "Positive and Natural
Law Revisited" (1972) 49 The Modern
Schoolman 295 . . . 252(7), 349(8)

RUDDEN, B. "Soviet Tort Law" (1967)
42 NYULR 583 . . . 291(2)

SEIDMAN, R.B., CHAMBLISS, W.J. and *Law, Order and Society* . . . 284(1)
Selected Writings of B.N. Cardozo (ed. M.E. Hall) . . . 106(5), 321(5)
SEN, A.K. "Rawls versus Bentham: an Axiomatic Examination of the Pure Distribution Problem" in *Reading Rawls. Critical Studies on Rawls' A Theory of Justice* (ed. N. Daniels) chap. 12 . . . 33(2)
SETHNA, M.J. "The True Nature and Province of Jurisprudence from the Viewpoint of Indian Philosophy" in *Essays in Jurisprudence in Honor of Roscoe Pound* (ed. R.A. Newman) 99 . . . 5(4), 314(11)
SETON-WATSON, H. "Soviet Foreign Policy in 1961" (1961) 2 International Relations 197 . . . 288(2)
SHAND, J., STEIN, P.G. and *Legal Values in Western Society* . . . 155(3), 217(4), 226(4)
SHANKS, C.M., DOUGLAS, W.O. and "Insulation from Liability through Subsidiary Corporations" (1929–30) 39 Yale LJ 193 . . . 190(8), 201(3)
SHAPIRO, I., HAZARD, J.N., - - -, and MAGGS, P.B. *The Soviet Legal System. Contemporary Documentation and Historical Commentary* (revised ed.) . . . 288(7)
SHAPIRO, M. "The Supreme Court and Constitutional Adjudication: of Politics and Neutral Principles" (1962–63) 31 Geo Wash LR 587 . . . 164(4)
SHARTEL, B. "Meanings of Possession" (1932) 16 Minn LR 611 . . . 205(1)
SHATTUCK, C.E. "The True Meaning of the Term 'Liberty' in those Clauses in the Federal and State Constitutions which Protect 'Life, Liberty and Property'" (1890–91) 4 Harv LR 365 . . . 23(1)
SHATWELL, K.O. "Some Reflections on the Problems of Law Reform" (1957–58) 31 Aust LJ 325 . . . 230(8)
SHELDRAKE, P. "Jurisprudence in the Law Course" (1975) 13 JSPTL (NS) 343 . . . 10(8)
SHELLENS, M.S. "Aristotle on Natural Law" (1959) 4 Nat LF 72 . . . 39(8)
SHERIDAN, L.A. "Law Teachers and Law Reform" (1976) 10 JALT 89 . . . 232(4)

SHETREET, S. *Judges on Trial* . . . 325(4)
SHIRBANIUK, D.J. "Actions By and Against Trade Unions in Contract and Tort" (1957–58) 12 Tor LJ 151 . . . 198(11)
SHKLAR, J.N. *Legalism* . . . 146(6), 169(4), 241(8), 299(6), 343(1)
SHUMAN, S.I. "Justification of Judicial Decisions" (1971) 59 Calif LR 715 . . . 98(1), 255(2)
SIDGWICK, H. *Elements of Politics* (2nd ed.) . . . 47(1), 256(7)
SIDHU, G.T.S. "Independence of the Judiciary" (1976) 1 Malaya LR ix . . . 162(6)
SILK, J. "One Man Corporations – Scope and Limitations" (1952) 100 U Pa LR 853 . . . 191(5)
SILKIN, S.C. "The Rights of Man and the Rule of Law" (1977) 28 NILQ 3 . . . 53(6), 219(5)
SILVING, H. "Analytical Limits of the Pure Theory of Law" (1942–43) 28 Iowa LR 1 . . . 267(1)
SILVING, H. "Customary Law" in *Sources of Law*, 125 . . . 136(7)
SILVING, H. "Law and Fact in the Light of the Pure Theory of Law" in *Interpretations of Modern Legal Philosophies*, (ed. P. Sayre), chap. 31 . . . 267(2)
SILVING, H. "'Positive' or 'Natural Law'? " in *Sources of Law*, 251 . . . 339(6)
SILVING, H. *Sources of Law* . . . 38(2), 111(10), 128(3), 136(7), 339(6)
SILVING, H. "'Stare Decisis' in the Civil and in the Common Law" in *Sources of Law*, 83 . . . 111(10)
SILVING, H. "Statutes" in *Sources of Law*, 9 . . . 128(3)
SILVING, H. "The Jurisprudence of the Old Testament" (1953) 28 NYULR 1129 . . . 38(2)
SILVING, H. "The Lasting Value of Kelsenism" in *Law, State and International Legal Order. Essays in Honor of Hans Kelsen* (edd. S. Engel and R.A. Métall), p. 297 . . . 264(3)
SILVING, H. "The Origins of the 'Rule of Law'" in *Sources of Law*, 233 . . . 38(2)
SIMITIS, C., COHN, E.J. and "'Lifting the Veil' in the Company Law of the European Continent" (1963) 12 ICLQ 189 . . . 193(7)

STOUT, R. "Is the Privy Council a Legislative Body?" (1905) 21 LQR 9 . . . 129(6)

STRACHAN, D.M.A. "Variations on an Enigma: the Scope and Application of the 'But For' Causal Test" (1970) 33 MLR 386 . . . 182(1)

STRACHEN, B. "The Mystery of a Man's Mind – his Intention" (1966) 130 JP 447 . . . 183(3)

STRACHEY, E.J.St.L. The Theory and Practice of Socialism . . . 289(3)

STRAUSS, L. Natural Right and History . . . 347(12)

STREET, H. "Law and Administration: Implications for University Legal Education" (1953) 1 Pcl S 97 . . . 9(8)

STREET, H. The Foundations of Legal Liability . . . 184(9)

STREET, H. The Law of Torts (6th ed.) . . . 195(5)

STREET, H., GRIFFITHS, J.A.G. and Principles of Administrative Law (4th ed.) . . . 195(8)

STREET, J.H.A. A Treatise on the Doctrine of Ultra Vires . . . 193(11)

STROGOVICH, M.S., GOLUNSKII, S.A. and "The Theory of the State and Law" in Soviet Legal Philosophy (trans. H.W. Babb) 351 . . . 267(6), 276(6), 301(9), 312(6), 343(2)

STUMPF, S.E. "Austin's Theory of the Separation of Law and Morals" (1960–61) 14 Vand LR 117 . . . 241(1), 351(8)

STURGES, W.A. "Unincorporated Associations as Parties to Actions" (1923–24) 33 Yale LJ 383 . . . 198(2)

SUMMERS, R.S. "Evaluating and Improving Legal Process – a Plea for 'Process Values'" (1974–75) 60 Corn LQ 1 . . . 156(3)

SUMMERS, R.S. "Legal Philosophy Today – an Introduction" in Essays in Legal Philosophy (ed. R.S. Summers) 1 . . . 6(1)

SUMMERS, R.S. "Naive Instrumentalism and the Law" in Law, Morality, and Society. Essays in Honour of H.L.A. Hart (edd. P.M.S. Hacker and J. Raz) chap. 6 . . . 144(1)

SUMMERS. R.S. "Notes on Criticism in Legal Philosophy" in More Essays in Legal Philosophy (ed. R.S. Summers) 1 . . . 10(5)

SUMMERS, R.S. "Professor Fuller on Morality and Law" in More Essays in Legal Philosophy. General Assessments of Legal Philosophies (ed. R.S. Summers) 101 . . . 349(6)

SUMMERS, R.S. "Professor H.L.A. Hart's Concept of Law" (1963) DLJ 629 . . . 251(8)

SUMMERS, R.S. Review of H.L.A. Hart's Law, Liberty and Morality (1963) 38 NYULR 1201 . . . 72(2)

SUMMERS, R.S. "The New Analytical Jurists" (1966) 41 NYULR 861 . . . 172(5), 242(5)

SUMMERS, R.S. "The Technique Element in Law" (1971) 59 Calif LR 733 . . . 263(8)

SUMNER, W.G. Folkways. A Study of the Sociological Importance of Usages, Manners, Customs, Mores and Morals . . . 271(5)

SUSSMAN, G., MOORE, W.U. and "The Lawyer's Law" (1931–32) 41 Yale LJ 566 . . . 163(8)

SUTHERLAND, A.E. "Judicial Reticence and Public Policy" (1958) 3 Jur R 1 . . . 147(5)

SUTHERLAND, A.E. "One Man in His Time" (1964–65) 78 Harv LR 7 . . . 309(3), 311(2)

SUTTON, R.J. "The English Law Commission: a New Philosophy of Law Reform" (1966–67) 20 Vand LR 1009 . . . 234(2)

SVERDLOV, G.M. "Modern Soviet Divorce Practice" (trans. D. Collard, 1948) 11 MLR 163 . . . 291(7)

SWAN, K.R. "Patent Rights in an Employee's Invention" (1959) 75 LQR 77 . . . 215(3)

SWEET, C. "Choses in Action" (1894) 10 LQR 303 . . . 214(1)

SWEET, C. "Choses in Action" (1895) 11 LQR 238 . . . 214(1)

SWINTON, K. "Challenging the Validity of an Act of Parliament: the Effect of Enrollment and Parliamentary Privilege" (1976) 14 Os HLJ 345 . . . 50(8)

WALZER, M. *Obligations: Essays on Disobedience, War and Citizenship* ... 228(2)

WAMBAUGH, E. *The Study of Cases* (2nd ed.) ... 81(6), 82(9), 91(4), 107(9)

WARREN, E.H. "Collateral Attack on Incorporation. A. De Facto Corporations" (1906–7) 20 Harv LR 456; (1907–8) 21 Harv LR 305 ... 197(3) (4)(5)

WARREN, E.H. *Corporate Advantages without Incorporation* ... 196(10)

WARREN, E.H. "Executed *Ultra Vires* Transactions" (1909–10) 23 Harv LR 496 ... 194(4)

WARREN, E.H. "Executory *Ultra Vires* Transactions" (1910–11) 24 Harv LR 534 ... 194(4)

WARREN, E.H. "Torts by Corporations in *Ultra Vires* Undertakings" (1925) 2 CLJ 180 ... 194(13), 195(1)

WASSERMAN, M.J., LAMBERT, E. and "The Case Method in Canada and the Possibilities of its Adaptation to the Civil Law" (1929) 39 Yale LJ 1 ... 112(2)

WASSERSTROM, R.A. *The Judicial Decision* ... 97(7), 108(9), 147(8)

WASSERSTROM, R.A. "The Obligation to Obey the Law" in *Essays in Legal Philosophy* (ed. R.S. Summers) 274 ... 227(2)

WATSON, A. *Legal Transplants* ... 231(8), 272(9)

WATSON, A. "Legal Transplants and Law Reform" (1976) 92 LQR 79 ... 231(8), 273(1)

WATSON, K.T. "The Meaning of Recklessness" (1961) 111 LJ 166 ... 183(4)

WEBB, J.V.D., SIMON, J.E.S. and "Consolidation and Statute Law Revision" (1975) PL 285 ... 234(4)

WEBB, S. and B. *Soviet Communism: A New Civilisation?* ... 289(8)

WEBER, M. *On Law in Economy and Society* (ed. M. Rheinstein, trans. E.A. Shils and M. Rheinstein) ... 315(8)

WECHSLER, H. "Toward Neutral Principles of Constitutional Law" (1959–60) 73 Harv LR 1 ... 151(5)

WEDDERBURN, K.W. "Corporate Personality and Social Policy: the Problem of the Quasi-corporation" (1965) 28 MLR 62 ... 197(8), 199(8)

WEDDERBURN, K.W. Note in (1965) 28 MLR 205 ... 77(6)

WEDDERBURN, K.W. "The *Bonsor* Affair: a Post-script" (1957) 20 MLR 105 ... 199(6)

WEDDERBURN, K.W. "The Right to Threaten Strikes" (1961) 24 MLR 572; (1962) 25 MLR 513; (1964) 27 MLR 257 ... 77(6), 199(7)

WEDDERBURN, K.W. *The Worker and the Law* (2nd ed.) ... 77(1)

WEERAMANTRY, C.G. *The Law in Crisis. Bridges of Understanding* ... 219(3)

WEILER, P.C. "Legal Values and Judicial Decision-making" (1970) 48 Can BR 1 ... 103(9), 107(3), 152(3)

WEILER, P.C. "The 'Slippery Slope' of Judicial Intervention. The Supreme Court and Canadian Labour Relations 1950–1970" (1971) 9 Os HLJ 1 ... 78(7)

WEILER, P.C. "Two Models of Judicial Decision-making" (1968) 46 Can BR 406 ... 152(2)

WEINBERG, J.R. *An Examination of Logical Positivism* ... 16(6)

WEIR, J.A. "Chaos or Cosmos? *Rookes, Stratford* and the Economic Torts" [1964] CLJ 225 ... 77(6)

WEISBERG, M.L., HAZARD, J.N. and *Cases and Materials on Soviet Law* ... 288(6)

WELSH, R.S. "The Constitutional Case in Southern Rhodesia" (1967) 83 LQR 64 ... 60(5)

WELSH, R.S. "The Criminal Liability of Corporations" (1946) 62 LQR 345 ... 194(9)

WELSH, R.S. "The Function of the Judiciary in a Coup d'Etat" (1970) 87 SALJ 168 ... 62(6)

WESTEN, P.K. "Introduction" to "Symposium: Drugs and the Law" (1968) 56 Calif LR 1 ... 75(9)

WESTERMARCK, E.A. *The Origin and Development of the Moral Ideas* ... 281(7)

Case Index

General Index

Abortion, 187
Abstract jurisprudence, 3
Acceptance (recognition), 17, 50,
    137–138, 248, 249, 334
Accident, 179
    liability, 159
Act, 174–177, 182, 308
    "basic" and "non-basic", 176
    involuntary, 174, 177–178, 179
    voluntary, 174–179
Act of Parliament (see also "Legislation",
    "Statute"), 45–47, 56, 64–65
    of Union, 54
Active force theory, 180
Activist lawmaking, 104
Actus reus, 176, 177–178
Adaptation to change, 219–239
Administrative (official) activities,
    156–157
    discretion, 49
    law (legality), 114, 124, 125,
        287, 312
Advantages, 20–31
Aims of legal education, 7–10
Allegiance, 61
Ambiguity, 27, 28, 30, 114, 116, 118,
    119, 121, 122
Ambit of the common law, 109, 144
American Constitution, 43, 52, 256
    Realism, 22, 70, 99, 106, 109,
        118, 163, 166, 172, 237, 253,
        308, 310, 313, 319–333, 343
    Supreme Court, 150–151, 152,
        157, 163–164, 324, 326–327,
        332, 348
Analogy, 94, 96, 99–101, 105, 119,
    121, 133, 153, 290
Analysis, 21, 26, 27, 29, 30
    quantitative, 326, 328
Analytical School, 1–6, 12, 102, 172,
    240–269, 307–308, 337
Animal, 186
Animism, 259
Animus and *corpus* theory, 205,
    207–208
Anthropology, 276, 277–281, 297,
    325
Anti-trust legislation, 160
Applied jurisprudence, 2
Approaches to interpretation, 119–125
Argumentation theory, 100, 101, 335

Artificial reasoning, 47
Associations, 190, 196–199, 345
Assyrian law, 281
Authority, 69, 241, 263
    of deciding tribunal, 82–89
Automation, 220–223, 327–328
Automatism, 177–178
Axiology, 35

Babylonian laws, 281
Bad man, 319
Bailment, 210
Balancing interests, 76, 154–155, 301,
    306, 308–310, 313
Bargaining power, 159
Behaviour (see also "Conduct"), 137,
    168, 171, 174–178, 280, 284, 297,
    300, 326
    group, 326–327
    of lawyers, 14, 321–323, 324,
        326, 330, 336
Behavioural model, 326–327
Beneficiary, 214–215
BGB, 239
Biblical law, 38, 281
Bill of Rights, 53, 151, 219
Binding force, 173, 333–334
Biological interpretation, 274, 275
Birth, 186–187
Blood-feuds, 273, 278
    -money, 273, 278
Bolshevism (see "Marxism")
Boroughs, 190
Bourgeois thought, 267, 293
Bracket theory, 203
British nationality, 51

Canons of interpretation, 119, 122, 126,
    127–134, 235
Capitalism, 151, 190, 217, 283–284,
    289, 290, 294, 324
Caput, 199
Case-law (see also "Precedent"), 104,
    110, 150, 220, 221, 237, 347, 352
    and interpretation, 125
Case *primae impressionis*, 103, 324
Categories of illusory reference, 95
Causation (cause), 143, 153, 178–182
    "but for" test of, 178, 179,
        181–182
    concurrent, 178, 179
    factual, 179, 181
    "insulation" theory of, 180
    legal, 178–180

437